DEBATING ORGANIZATION

DEBATING ORGANIZATION

Point–Counterpoint in Organization Studies

Edited by

Robert Westwood and Stewart Clegg

Blackwell Publishing

350 Main Street, Malden, MA 02148-5018, USA
108 Cowley Road, Oxford OX4 1JF, UK
550 Swanston Street, Carlton South, Melbourne, Victoria 3053, Australia
Kurfürstendamm 57, 10707 Berlin, Germany

First published 2003 by Blackwell Publishing Ltd

Library of Congress Cataloging-in-Publication Data

Debating organization : point–counterpoint in organization studies /
edited by Robert Westwood and Stewart Clegg.
        p. cm.
Includes bibliographical references and index.
    ISBN 0–631–21692–8 (hbk : alk. paper) — ISBN 0–631–21693–6 (pbk : alk. paper)
  1. Organizational sociology. 2. Industrial sociology. I. Westwood,
Robert Ian. II. Clegg, Stewart.

HM786 .D425 2003
302.3′5—dc21

                                                                            2002013551

A catalogue record for this title is available from the British Library.

Set in 10/12pt Ehrhardt
by Graphicraft Limited, Hong Kong
Printed and bound in the United Kingdom
by MPG Books Ltd, Bodmin, Cornwall

For further information on
Blackwell Publishing, visit our website:
http://www.blackwellpublishing.com

Contents

List of Figures

Notes on the Contributors

Neal Ashkanasy is a Professor of Management in the UQ Business School, University of Queensland. He has a Ph.D. in Social and Organizational Psychology from the University of Queensland, and has research interests in leadership, organizational culture, business ethics, and, more recently, emotions in organizational life. He is on the editorial board of the *Academy of Management Journal* and the *Journal of Management*, and has published in journals such as *Accounting, Organizations and Society*, the *Journal of Management*, the *Journal of Organizational Behavior*, the *Journal of Personality and Social Psychology*, and *Organizational Behavior and Human Decision Processes*. He is co-editor of *The Handbook of Organizational Culture and Climate* (2000), *Emotions in the Workplace* (2000) and *Managing Emotions in the Workplace* (2002). In addition he administers two e-mail discussion lists: Orgcult, the Organizational Culture Caucus list, and Emonet, the Emotions in the Workplace list. He is the 2001–2 Chair of the Managerial and Organizational Cognition Division of the Academy of Management.

Kimberly (Kim) B. Boal, Ph.D. University of Wisconsin–Madison, is Professor of Organizational Studies and Strategic Management and Area Coordinator of Management at Texas Tech University, Lubbock. He is Co-editor-in-chief (with Paul Hirsch, Northwestern University) of the *Journal of Management Inquiry*. His research interests include the philosophy of science, mergers and acquisitions, the resource-based view of the firm, strategic change, and strategic leadership.

Peter Case, Reader in Organizational Studies at Oxford Brookes University, holds higher degrees from the University of Massachusetts and the University of Bath. A sociologist by training, he is interested in challenging the various strategies of self-defeat pursued by humans in the organizations they co-create and exploring more compassionate alternatives. His work has been published in such journals as *Organization*, the *Journal of Management Studies*, *Management Learning* and *Studies in Cultures, Organizations and Societies*. He is a board member of the Standing Conference on Organizational Symbolism.

Andrew Chan teaches in the Department of Management at the City University of Hong Kong. After a number of years in vocational education he gained a Ph.D. in Organization Studies from the University of Lancaster Management School. He is the author of *Critically Constituting Organization* (2000). His research is around questions concerning the technology of the internet from the perspectives of Heidegger and McLuhan.

Robert Chia is Professor of Strategy and Organization at the School of Business and Economics, University of Exeter. He is the author of three books and a number of journal articles on organization theory and management. Prior to entering academia he worked for sixteen years in aircraft maintenance engineering, manufacturing management, and human resource management. Since entering academia he has remained actively engaged with the practitioner world, particularly through consultancy work and executive training and education. His main research interests revolve around the centrality of a processual world view and its implications for: strategic vision, foresight and decision making; complexity and creativity; East–West differences in managerial attitudes; comparative cultural studies, and the modernism/postmodernism debate.

Stewart Clegg is Professor of Management at the University of Technology, Sydney. He is well known for his research in organization studies, and especially for his role as co-editor, with Cynthia Hardy and Walter Nord, of the *Handbook of Organization Studies* (1996), which won the George R. Terry Book Award of the American Academy of Management in 1997 for the "most outstanding contribution to management knowledge." He has published extensively in the journals and in books, on topics ranging from East Asia and Japan, to power, to postmodernism and social theory.

Barbara Czarniawska holds a Skandia Chair in Management Studies at Gothenburg Research Institute, School of Economics and Commercial Law, Göteborg University. Her research focuses on control processes in complex organizations, most recently in the field of big-city management. In terms of methodological approach she combines institutional theory with the narrative approach. She has published in the field of business and public administration in Polish, her native language, as well as in Swedish, Italian, and English, the most recent positions being *Narrating the Organization* (1997), *A Narrative Approach to Organization Studies* (1998), *Writing Management* (1999), and *A City Reframed* (2000). She has been a member of the Royal Swedish Academy of Sciences since 2000 and a member of the Royal Swedish Academy of Engineering Sciences since 2001.

Lex Donaldson, B.Sc. (Aston), Ph.D. (London), is a professor in the Australian Graduate School of Management of the Universities of New South Wales and Sydney. He was previously a Senior Research Officer at London Business School. He has published a series of books defending and developing functionalist and positivist organizational theory: *In Defence of Organization Theory* (1985), *American anti-Management Theories of Organization* (1995), *For Positivist Organization Theory* (1996), *Performance-driven Organizational Change* (1999), and *The Contingency Theory of Organizations* (2001). He has published articles in journals such as *Administrative Science Quarterly*, the *Academy of Management Journal*, the *Academy of Management Review*, *Human Relations*, the *Journal of Management Studies*, *Organization Science*, *Organization Studies* and *Sociology*.

Silvia Gherardi is Professor of the Sociology of Organization at the University of Trento, Italy, where she is responsible for the Research Unit on Cognition Organizational Learning and Aesthetics (RUCOLA). Her research activity focuses on workplace learning and knowing. Her theoretical background is in qualitative sociology and organizational symbolism. She has also conducted research studies and training programs for the development of women's competences and participation in organizations.

Royston Greenwood is Telus Professor of Strategic Management and Associate Dean (Research) in the School of Business, University of Alberta. His primary research interests are threefold: understanding the dynamics of change in highly institutionalized sectors, the social construction of markets for services, and the managerial practices of professional service firms. He is working on the impact of governance structures (especially the competitive advantage and limitations of the professional partnership), the nature of "theorization" processes within organizational fields (especially health and professional services), and the processes by which ideas and services become legitimized. His work has appeared in the

Administrative Science Quarterly, the *Academy of Management Journal*, the *Academy of Management Review*, *Organization Studies*, *Organization Science*, and the *Journal of Management Studies*. He serves on three editorial boards and is Associate Editor of the newly launched *Strategic Organization*.

John Hassard is Professor of Organizational Analysis at the University of Manchester Institute of Science and Technology (UMIST) and Senior Research Associate in Organizational Analysis at the Judge Institute of Management Studies, University of Cambridge. He worked previously at the London Business School and the University of Keele. His research interests lie mainly in organization theory and empirical studies of enterprise reform (with special reference to manufacturing in transitional economies). He chairs the editorial board of the *Sociological Review*.

Bob Hinings is Professor Emeritus and Senior Research Fellow in the Center for Professional Service Firm Management and Health Organization Studies in the School of Business at the University of Alberta. His research interests are in organizational design, organizational change, and institutional theory, with particular reference to professionally based organizations. He is a Fellow of the Royal Society of Canada and a Fellow of the Academy of Management.

James G. (Jerry) Hunt, Ph.D. University of Illinois at Urbana–Champaign, is Paul Whitfield Horn Professor of Management, Trinity Company Professor in Leadership, and Director of the Institute for Leadership Research at Texas Tech, Lubbock. He is Senior Editor of *Leadership Quarterly* and a former editor of the *Journal of Management*. His research interests include the philosophy of the science of management, leadership, macro-organizational aspects, and the temporal aspects of leadership and organizational studies.

Stephen J. Jaros, Ph.D. University of South Florida, Tampa, is Associate Professor of Organizational Behavior at Southern University, Baton Rouge, LA. His research interests include the philosophy of science, human resource management, and organizational and managerial behavior.

P. Devereaux Jennings is a tenured Associate Professor in the Faculty of Commerce at the University of British Columbia, Vancouver. Dev is an "Action Editor" for the *Academy of Management Review*. His areas of research interest are organizations and the natural environment, organizational geography, and comparative human resource management systems – primarily from an institutional and political approach. He has taught sessions on organizations as well as natural and human resource management for executives and managers, courses in methodology and organization theory for Ph.Ds., the integrated M.B.A. core in 1998 and 1999, and both organizational analysis and organizational behavior for undergraduates. Professor Jennings received his Ph.D. and M.A. at Stanford University and his B.A. from Dartmouth College.

Marc T. Jones received his Ph.D. in strategy from the University of California, Irvine. He has published numerous research articles across a range of disciplines, including organization studies, strategic management, international political economy, cultural studies, and business and society. His research interests focus on the distributional effects of globalization, corporate restructuring, and new organizational forms.

Mihaela Kelemen is Senior Lecturer in the Department of Management at the University of Keele. Her research covering topics such as critical approaches to quality management, postmodern theories of organizations, and economies in transition has been published in numerous journals and books. Her book on critical quality management is due for publication in 2002, while a collection *Eastern European Management* (co-edited with Monika Kostera) is to follow.

Roderick M. Kramer is William R. Kimball Professor of Organizational Behavior at the Graduate School of Business, Stanford University. His research interests are trust and distrust in organizations, organizational paranoia, cooperation, and organizational creativity. He is the author or co-author of over seventy-five scholarly articles. His research has appeared in numerous academic journals and books, including *Administrative Science Quarterly*, the *Annual*

Review of Psychology, the *Journal of Personality and Social Psychology*, the *Journal of Experimental Social Psychology*, and *Organizational Behavior and Human Decision Processes*. He is also co-editor of a number of books, most recently *Trust in Organizations*, with Tom Tyler (1996), *The Psychology of the Social Self*, with Tom Tyler and Oliver John (1999), and *Power and Influence in Organizations*, with Margaret Neale (1998). He has been an associate editor of *Administrative Science Quarterly* and has served on the editorial boards of *Organization Science* and *Organizational Behavior and Human Decision Processes*. He earned his Ph.D. in social psychology from the University of California Los Angeles in 1985.

Stephen Linstead is Professor of Management at Essex Management Centre, University of Essex. He holds degrees from the Universities of Keele and Leeds and the CNAA, and has previously taught at universities including Lancaster, and the University of Wollongong. His recent publications include *Sex, Work and Sex Work* (2000) with Jo Brewis, *The Aesthetics of Organization* (2000) with Heather Höpfl and *The Language of Organization* (2001) with Robert Westwood. Forthcoming are *Post-modern Organization Theory*, *The Underside of Organization* and *Text/Work*. He co-edits the journal *Culture and Organization*.

Michael Lounsbury is an assistant professor in the School of Industrial and Labor Relations and the Department of Sociology at Cornell University. His research focuses on the relation between organizational and social change, entrepreneurship, and the rise of new industries and practices. He has been working on projects that investigate the emergence of the recycling industry and the dynamics of product characterization in the mutual fund industry. Professor Lounsbury's work has been published in journals such as *Administrative Science Quarterly*, the *Academy of Management Journal*, the *Academy of Management Review*, and the *Strategic Management Journal*. In addition he is co-editor of *Social Structure and Organizations Revisited*, volume 19 in the series of books Research in the Sociology of Organizations.

Judi Marshall is a Professor of Organizational Behaviour in the School of Management, University of Bath. Her early research was on managerial job stress. Since joining Bath in 1978 her main research interests have been women in management (publishing *Women Managers* in 1984 and *Women Managers Moving On* in 1995), organizational cultures and career development. She has especially developed self-reflective sense-making approaches and action-oriented inquiry practices. She teaches on a range of academic courses, and is Director of Studies for the M.Sc. in Responsibility and Business Practice.

Bill McKelvey received his Ph.D. from the Sloan School of Management at MIT and is Professor of Strategic Organizing at the Anderson Graduate School of Management, UCLA. Early articles focus on organization and sociotechnical systems design. His book *Organizational Systematics* (1982) remains the definitive treatment of organizational taxonomy and evolutionary theory. In 1997 he became Director of the Center for Rescuing Strategy and Organization Science (SOS). From the Center he initiated activities leading to the founding of the UCLA Center for Computational Social Science. Recently he co-edited *Variations in Organization Science* (with Joel Baum, 1999) and a special issue of a journal (with Steve Maguire, 1999). Recent publications: "Model-centered organizational epistemology," in J. A. C. Baum (ed.), *Companion to Organizations* (2002); "Emergent order in firms: complexity science vs the entanglement trap," in E. Mitleton-Kelly (ed.), *Organizations are Complex Social Systems* (2002); "Microstrategy from macroleadership: distributed intelligence via new science," in A. Y. Lewin and H. Volberda (eds), *Mobilizing the Self-renewing Organization* (2002).

William McKinley received his Ph.D. in organizational sociology from Columbia University, and is a professor of management at Southern Illinois University, Carbondale. His research interests are organizational restructuring and downsizing, organizational change, organizational decline, epistemological issues in organizational research, and the sociology and philosophy of organization science. His publications have appeared in *Administrative Science Quarterly*, the *Academy of Management Journal*, the *Academy of Management Review*, the *Academy of Management Executive*, the *Journal of Management Inquiry, Organization, Organization Science, Accounting, Organizations and Society, Advances in Strategic Management*, and other outlets. Professor McKinley has served on the editorial board of the *Academy of Management Review*, as well as guest editing a special issue of *Organization Science* on organizational decline and adaptation.

Albert J. Mills is Professor of Management at St Mary's University in Halifax, Nova Scotia. His research activities center on the impact of organized settings upon people, focusing on organizational change and human liberation. His early images of organization – of frustration, of power disparities, of conflict, and of sexually segregated work – were experienced through a series of unskilled jobs and given broader meaning through campaigns for peace and social change. University provided him not only with an "education" but an opportunity and a base from which to research the problems of discrimination at work. He has published in a number of journals, and his more recent books include *Managing the Organizational Melting Pot* (co-edited with Pushkala Prasad et al., 1997); *Reading Organization Theory* (with Tony Simmons, 1999) and *Gender, Identity and the Culture of Organizations* (co-edited with Iiris Aaltio, 2002).

Rolland Munro is Professor of Organisation Theory and Director of the Centre for Social Theory and Technology at the University of Keele, having previously lectured at the University of Edinburgh. Moving between the different tropes of culture and knowledge, he has published articles on belonging, identity, information, and power, mainly in leading sociological and organizational journals. Edited books include *The Consumption of Mass* and *Ideas of Differences*; he is writing a book on our cultural and social entanglement with technology provisionally called *The Demanding Relation*, linking up his ideas of motility, disposal, and punctualizing.

Barbara Parker is professor in the Albers School of Business and Economics, University of Seattle. Her research interests include globalization, strategic approaches to managing diversity, expatriate adjustment, international joint venture management, and cause-based business/non-profit partnerships. As holder of the Robert O'Brien Chair in the Albers School of Business and Economics she has played a leadership role in establishing the Joint Center for Nonprofit and Social Enterprise Management, and introduced an M.B.A. concentrating on social enterprise management. Her book *Globalization and Business Practice* was published in 1999. Her articles appear in many journals, including the *Journal of International Management, Human Relations*, the *Journal of Business Research, International Executive*, and the *Journal of Intercultural Relations*.

Nelson Phillips is Beckwith Professor of Management Studies at the Judge Institute of Management, University of Cambridge. Prior to joining the Institute he was an Associate Professor in the Faculty of Management of McGill University, where he was also the Director of McGill's executive M.B.A. program the International Masters of Practicing Management. His research interests include knowledge management, multinationals and international development, interorganizational collaboration, and a general interest in management in cultural industries. He has published a number of books and articles, including articles in the *Academy of Management Journal*, the *Journal of Management Studies*, the *Journal of Management Inquiry, Business and Society*, the *Journal of Business Ethics, Business Ethics Quarterly, Organization Science, Organization*, and *Organization Studies*. Professor Phillips obtained a Ph.D. in organizational analysis from the University of Alberta in 1995.

Burkard Sievers is Professor of Organization Development in the Department of Economics and Social Sciences at Bergische Universität Wuppertal, where he teaches and writes on management and organization theory from a psychoanalytical perspective. He received his Dr.Soz.Wiss. from the University of Bielefeld in 1972. He has held visiting appointments at the Institute of Social Research at the University of Michigan and at other universities in Australia, Brazil, Canada, and the United Kingdom. He is co-editor of *Freie Assoziation–Psychoanalyse–Kultur–Organisation–Supervsion*. He is a board member of the International Society for the Psychoanalytical Study of Organizations. Dr Sievers was awarded the 1995 International Award for Participation from the HBK-Spaarbank in Antwerp for his book *Work, Death, and Life Itself* (1994).

Karl E. Weick is the Rensis Likert Distinguished University Professor of Organizational Behavior and Psychology and Professor of Psychology at the University of Michigan. He is a former editor of *Administrative Science Quarterly*. He is studying hand-offs as a source of med-ical errors, distributed sense making in public health diagnoses, and organizational design.

Robert Westwood is a Reader in the School of Business, University of Queensland. He was educated in the United Kingdom in psychology, philosophy, and organization studies but has worked in Asia and Australasia since 1983. His research interests include cross-cultural management issues, gender and organization, the meaning of work, power–language issuesin organizations, and critical approaches in organization studies. Bob has published extensively in these areas. His most recent book is *The Language of Organization* (co-edited with Steve Linstead, 2001). He is an Associate Editor of *Culture and Organisation* and on the editorial board of *Organization Studies*.

Acknowledgments

The editor and publishers gratefully acknowledge the following for permission to reproduce copyright material:

Bob Dylan, "Love minus Zero – No Limit," copyright © 1965 by Warner Bros Inc. Copyright renewed 1993 by Special Rider Music. All rights reserved. International copyright secured. Reprinted by permission. Recorded on the Warner Bros album *Bringing it all back Home*, 1965.

The publishers apologize for any errors or omissions in the above list and would be grateful to be notified of any corrections that should be incorporated in the next edition or reprint of this book.

1

The Discourse of Organization Studies: Dissensus, Politics, and Paradigms

Robert Westwood and Stewart Clegg

INTRODUCTION: THE POWER AND POLITICS OF ORGANIZATION STUDIES AS A DISCOURSE

To publish a book called *Debating Organizations* is a political intervention. It is political in two related senses. First, it participates in the mundane politics that frame the "organization studies" field. It is political also in the sense that it participates in that discourse captured under the rubric of "organization studies," a discourse constituted by a matrix of texts, theories, concepts, practices, and institutional forms and arrangements. We conceive of organization studies (OS) as a discourse comprising an agglomeration of texts – in the broad sense – demarcating a discursive space linked to the signifier of organizations and instantiating an institutional context. As a discourse, OS is a knowledge–power nexus. It lays claim to a capacity to talk about organizations and related phenomena intelligibly and authoritatively. As all discourses it works through practices of inclusion–exclusion. That is, some texts and some claims to knowledge are deemed legitimate, right, proper, and are allowed incorporation; others are deemed illegitimate, improper, wrong – or even bad and mad – and are excluded. Of course, different authorities may see the world in different terms.

Organization studies cannot be represented by some notion of a coherent, homogeneous and all-encompassing discourse, as our suggestion of competing authorities is meant to suggest. Normally, all discourses tend to be partial, incomplete and inconsistent. Discourses are also dynamically interdependent, displaying layers of embeddedness. As a discourse OS refers to other major discourses: for example, it clearly has a proximate general relation to discourses of psychology and sociology while it has little relationship to discourses of Catholicism – although specific areas such as "business ethics" may draw on general Catholic notions of "social justice," for instance – so that it must also be allowed that discourses contain "subdiscourses."

Discourses vary in terms of their longevity, coherence, and power effects. Some attain an apparent coherence and centrality for members who define themselves, or may be defined as, a given language community. Membership of such a community allows members to constitute positions of intelligibility from whence that which they claim to speak may be made meaningful and/or truthful-seeming. It also constructs an institutional frame constituting a material context of power and control, through which those authoritative interests vested in discourses are disseminated, protected, and policed. Boundaries will be marked, staked out, and preserved. From within these boundaries, other discourses may appear more fragile, containing more obvious fractures and inconsistencies, with knowledge claims that are more tenuous and localized. The positions of intelligibility they construct will often be seen as more ambiguous, uncertain and weakly delineated. Such discourses, constituted as outside the authoritative boundaries, will typically instantiate only insubstantial institutional frameworks or none at all. All discourses are in a constant state of change as the interactional and textual work that sustains them ebbs and flows. They broaden, develop, and strengthen, but they also wither, decay, and die and are reconstituted as they synthesize, bifurcate, coalesce, and fragment. Authority, in the discursive world, may be a more fragile thing than it presumes, when viewed politically.

The political nature of OS discourses, like all discursive spaces, trades in a knowledge–power nexus. Whilst they may lack coherence and consensus, all elements in these discourses claim to make knowledgeable representations about organizations. Any such knowledge claim is, immediately, an exercise of power. Knowledge representations are a claim to a discursive space, a carving out of a position that simultaneously excludes other possible representations. We will consider this aspect of discourse by exploring OS as a contested topographical terrain marked, throughout its history, by fragmentation and diversity. The discourse of OS is also political in the more mundane sense in which it is characterized by institutional structures and arrangements, hierarchies, instruments of control, and the paraphernalia of power and command systems. We will deal with this aspect of the discourse in the second half of the chapter.

A Topography of the Discourse of Organization Studies

From birth: the post-Weberian divide and other fissures in the discourse

While OS has a relatively short history, characterized by diversity and a degree of fragmentation, and its texts are multitudinous and various not only with respect to content but also with respect to the theoretical and methodological stances adopted, it can be seen to comprise many partially overlapping discourses the overall frame of which we will refer to as the discourse of OS. The discourse has also constituted a significant institutional frame, but that too is somewhat *ad hoc* and disjointed in places. We see OS as a contested discursive terrain, within which there has always been (and continues to be) a variety of voices engaged in a political process of claims for recognition, acceptance, and dominance. That OS is a "contested terrain" has been attested to by numerous authors over the years (e.g., Burrell and Morgan, 1979; Perrow, 1973; Clegg and Hardy, 1999). We would argue that it has always been thus. Koontz (1961) referred to the "management theory jungle," a view he did not revise when he revisited the theme nearly twenty years later (Koontz, 1980). In the interim, Perrow (1973) reported on the state of the field in similar terms. A decade later Astley and Van de Ven (1983) pointed to disparate logics and vocabularies fragmenting a dispersed field. Pfeffer (1982: 1) lamented that "The domain of organisation theory is coming to resemble more of a weed patch than a well tended garden" and, extending the metaphor, suggested that a "good deal of pruning and weeding is needed" (ibid.: 2). He also questioned whether a sense of progress was discernible and whether the domain's constituents – managerial and administrative practitioners – were served by this proliferation and lack of selective breeding. After surveying the field and critically dissecting various perspectives, he set out a pro-legomenon for a redirected and revitalized discipline. Pfeffer attributes the diversity and fragmentation of the field, in large part, to its relative immaturity and its inter-disciplinary nature, which negates the productivity of research and the speed and efficiency of clinical diagnosis of organization conditions.

What is the genesis of the discourse of OS? The field awaits a Foucauldian genealogy and we do not intend to attempt that daunting task here. Pfeffer (1982) offers his own prosaically historical account. Unlike many others, including contributors to this volume, he does not trace the field to the work of Weber, Saint-Simon or Comte; indeed, Weber is referred to only twice and then only in passing and in relation to more recent theories of rationality and size–structure relationships. Pfeffer's concern is with the institutional development of the field in its location in the academic sanctums of US universities and journals. From this purview, Freeman (1982) notes that there is no entry for "organization" in the index of the *American Journal of Sociology* for the period from its foundation in 1895 to 1947. Pfeffer acknowledges that the roots of industrial psychology go back to the early 1900s but notes the distinction between organizational psychology – with a distinct focus on organizations – and industrial psychology as more recent. Locating psychology as the central element in the early core of OS studies is, perhaps, a reflection of the more individualistic and micro-level concerns that have driven much US-based theorizing. Continuing his institutional historicizing, Pfeffer points to the establishment of the *Administrative Science Quarterly* in 1956 as the first journal dedicated to the "emerging field of organisational behaviour and administration" (Pfeffer, 1982: 28). The emergence of the *Academy of Management Journal* in 1958 is seen to indicate the coalescence of a recognizable contextual field for OS. He appears to concur with Scott (1981) in identifying the late 1940s to early 1950s as the period in which OS emerges. Pfeffer does, usefully, tie the development of the discourse to the wider social context, arguing that this context has an implicit relation to developments within the field. He acknowledges that "much additional work remains to be done in understanding the sociology and ideology of organisation theory" (Pfeffer, 1982: vii). This remains true, although there have been significant contributions from, among others, Burrell and Morgan (1979), Clegg and Hardy (1999), Hassard (1993), and Reed (1992).

Pfeffer's historical location, apart from ignoring Weber, also neglects the foundational work of Fayol (1916), Mayo (1933), Gauss (1936), Gulick and Urwick (1937), Barnard (1938), Mooney and Reiley (1939),[1] Roethlisberger and Dickson (1939), Merton (1940), and Urwick (1943). This is not to mention the "classics" – Taylor, Pareto, Babbage, Adam Smith, Machiavelli and Sun Tzu! Orthodox histories tracing these early influences can be found in Perrow (1973), Scott (1981), and Wren (1972). The point we want to make, however, is that diversity and contestation are apparent right from the outset. Mayo's concerns are clearly different from those of Gauss or Barnard; Weber's analysis, interpretation, and intention were very different from those of Fayol, a matter that was recognized early on – for instance, in his overview, Koontz (1961) identified six differentiated approaches to the study of organizations and management, which he expanded to eleven in 1980.

Other writers, such as Burrell (1999) and Clegg and Hardy (1999) do position Weber as central to the emergence of OS as a field. Indeed, Burrell points out that alternative read-ings of the Weberian project produce an almost immediate fragmentation. On the one hand there is an interpretation that sustains the integrity of *verstehen* and Weber's deeply critical analysis of the march of rationalism, the impersonalism of modernity's modes of organizing, and the antidemocratic and exclusive practices of the emerging order. On the other hand is Parsons' appropriation of Weber for the purposes of promoting a structural functionalist interpretation of social systems and organizing. From this perspective, rationality is merely a tool, one that can be applied to the effective structuring of organizations. Weber's dark concerns with the irrationality of what passes for rationality within the "iron cage" are ignored in favor of an interpretation that focuses on matters of efficiency, effectiveness, and stability in organized systems. The epistemological differentiation between understanding and explanation/prediction that Weber articulated is a demarcation still sustained within contemporary discourse; in this volume Case and McKinley (chapter 5) bear witness to the continuing importance of the divide. For Burrell (1999), at its very inception OS is a contested discourse. The bifurcation of readings of Weber as, on the one hand, contributing to a structural-functionalist project for locating the sources of order, and on the other as a critical analysis in which the modernist rationalist trajectory is seen as dehumanizing, undemocratic and damagingly centripetal, is a fissure that continues to slice through the discourse. In more substantive terms, much of the early debate in OS from the 1940s to the early 1960s, following Weber, was concerned with the properties, functions and dysfunctions of bureaucracy. This includes classic debates about inherent tendencies to order versus inherent tendencies to conflict within organized systems.

Returning to a textual history of the discourse, Selznick's (1948) "Foundations for a Theory of Organization" represented an explicit crystalization of a theoretical stance that, in many respects, became the core of a dominant orthodoxy in OS, that of structural-functionalism. As an overarching ontological and epistemological position it was promulgated in authoritatively influential works by Merton (1940, 1949) and Parsons (1956, 1964), and carried through into, amongst other areas, theories of formal structure (e.g., Blau and Scott, 1962), varieties of systems perspectives (e.g., Katz and Kahn, 1966; Kast and Rosenzweig, 1985), structural contingency theory (e.g., Blau and Schoenherr, 1971; Pugh et al., 1969), and certain environment–organization relationship theories (e.g., Aldrich, 1979; Lawrence and Lorsch, 1967). In this volume Donaldson (Chapter 4a) clearly states that contemporary contingency theory is underpinned by structural-functionalism and acknowledges the debt to Merton. As he says, "organisations become structured so as to provide effective functioning."

There are those who argue that the OS field once had coherence and consensus. Donaldson (1985), for example, maintains that organization theory has a solid core of normal science centered on contingency theory and its structural-functionalist underpinnings. Atkinson (1971) had earlier proclaimed this as a general sociological interpretation of an apparent consensus. Almost three decades later, Reed (1999) was also to see structural-functionalist interpretations of systems theory as the dominant approach throughout the 1950s to the 1970s. However, the apparent coherence of the field around structural-functionalist informed contingency theory was, according to Burrell (1999), an illusion. There were always alternative and dissenting voices. Even during the 1960s, when the structural-functionalist perspective apparently occupied center stage, there coexisted major alternative approaches. Still central, for example, remain Weick's conceptualization of organization as a process, not a structure – a verb, not a noun (Weick, 1969) – an important and sustained ontological differentiation (see Weick, chapter 6a). Cyert, March and Simon also emphasized process and de-emphasized structure as well as making rationality problematic and proposing an embryonically political model of organization (e.g., March and Simon, 1958; Cyert and March, 1963). Meanwhile, in a totally different intellectual space Goffman (1961) applied his poetic, dramaturgical skills to deliver vivid insights into organizations, while Bittner (1965) developed an ethnomethodological perspective which focused on organization as, above all, a socially managed accomplishment. The core debates identified by Astley and Van de Ven (1983) in their overview of OS centered on issues of the organization–environment relationship and strategic choice, posing challenges to the overall contingency determinism of the Aston school of theorists: these were the high visibility debates of the early 1970s (Child, 1972), around which subsequent polemics were to circle (Donaldson, 1985). Of note here is that in this 1983 summary of the field all the perspectives considered were broadly within the structural-functionalist orthodoxy.

It is evident that Child's (1972) advocacy of "strategic choice" against structural determination drew much of its insight from the impact of the sustained attack on structural-functionalist and systems perspectives on organizations heralded by the publication of Silverman's *The Theory of Organisation: A Sociological Framework* (1970). Referred to as an "Action Frame of Reference," Silverman's perspective drew on Weberian *verstehen*, as well as the phenomenology of Schutz (1964) and particularly, the social constructionism of Berger (Berger, 1966; Berger and Luckmann, 1965). Meanings become the point of focus, and, as Silverman says (1970: 127), "actions arise out of meanings which define social reality." In some respects this represented a turn in the discourse, not that Silverman was the only theorist pursuing a phenomenologically inspired or social constructivist epistemology (we have already noted Bittner and Goffman) – but Silverman produces an open engagement with and critique of the orthodox position. He expressly denounces the kind of structural determinism and objectification he sees prevailing in the orthodoxy and declares positivistic explanations as "inadmissible." Following developments within sociology around symbolic interactionism, social constructivism, and ethnomethodology through the 1960s and 1970s, an alternative perspective on organizations came increasingly to the fore. It took a number of forms, including ethnomethodological (Silverman and Jones, 1976; Zimmerman, 1970) and dramaturgical approaches (Mangham and Overington, 1987). It is best captured under the general rubric of interpretivism (Burrell and Morgan, 1979). It is an approach that entered more into the mainstream following the emergence of organizational culture as a focus of interest for both practitioners and scholars in the early 1980s.

Burrell and Morgan (1979) provided a significant exploration of the fissures within the discourse through their delineation of the field into four "paradigmatic" positions. They again position the "functionalist paradigm" as the orthodoxy within the field, particularly the systems perspective. Interestingly they also see Silverman's Action Frame as residing just within the functionalist paradigm. The "radical humanist paradigm" was at that time the least developed. Its roots were in Lukacs, Gramsci and the Critical Theorists. Burrell and Morgan recognized the lack of development of this paradigm in OS but they do cite, for example, Beynon (1973) and Clegg (1975). It is an approach that has been reinvigorated since the 1980s (Alvesson and Willmott, 1992; Fischer, 1990; Forester, 1985). We noted in the preceding paragraph the emergence of an alternative to the dominant functionalist orthodoxy in OS from the "interpretive paradigm," and this too has expanded latterly with ethnomethodological (Richards, 2001) and social constructivist approaches continuing to have an impact – the latter being represented in this volume by Czarniawska (chapter 4b). The fourth paradigm, that of "radical structuralism" is perhaps the one that declined most through the 1980s and 1990s. It draws upon either a Marxist or a neo-Marxist analysis, or a radical interpretation of Weber. Under the former we have the work of Braverman (1974) and labor process theory, and the work of Allen (1975) and researchers such as Hyman

(1975), who offered a radical interpretation of industrial relations. Under the latter were writers such as Eldridge and Crombie (1974), Miliband (1973), Mouzelis (1975), and Clegg and Dunkerley (1980).

These four "paradigms" are framed within the matrix constituted by a subjective–objective dimension and radical change–regulation dimension. These fissures are still apparent to a large extent, although there have been shifts in and around the frame. The frame is perhaps inadequate in as much as it cannot provide for the incursion of postmodern perspectives into the discourse. Burrell and Morgan saw the second dimension – radical change versus regulation – as a means of resurrecting the older debate between conflict and order that had dominated sociology and early organizational analysis until the 1960s. They saw the supposed demise or resolution of that debate as false and reinstated it as the core differentiating problematic in OS. This debate resurfaces in an interesting context in this volume with the discussion about institutional theory. In the Lounsbury–Phillips debate (chapter 7) we see a sophisticated attempt to move institutional theory towards a more processual position, one that can account for change (something also taken up by Jennings and Greenwood (chapter 6b). More in line with Burrell and Morgan's original concerns, contrast Donaldson's (chapter 4a) and Hinings's (chapter 9a) structural-functionalist conception of organizations as systems of order with Phillips's (chapter 7b) or Munro's (chapter 9b) concerns with power, modes of domination, and change.

Burrell and Morgan discussed four debates precipitated by the essential subjective–objective fissure. These debates were over: (1) ontology – nominalism versus realism; (2) epistemology – positivism versus antipositivism; (3) methodology – ideographic versus nomothetic; (4) human nature – voluntarism versus determinism. The first three of these obviously correspond to three key debates that occupy Part I of this book. They are clearly fissures that continue to be inscribed within the OS discourse. We will turn to those debates as represented here shortly. Before that we will examine further fragmentations in the discourse marking the contemporary scene.

A contemporary configuration of a fecund field

The OS discourse became even more pluralistic after the 1980s with the emergence and consolidation of a number of different perspectives, some of which were prefigured in Burrell and Morgan's (1979) analysis, while others were not. One of these was organizational economics, a market-based approach. The relationship between economics and organization theory has been, for the most part, awkward and tenuous. Much of the disjuncture circulates around differences in levels of analysis, with economics only fitfully engaging with organizational-level phenomena, mostly via theories of the firm, the most significant contribution in this respect being Coase (1937). The past twenty years have seen a somewhat tighter coupling of economics and organization theory, to a large extent precipitated by Oliver Williamson's (1975, 1990) transaction cost economics and, to a lesser degree, agency theory. More latterly, aspects of strategic management theory, resource-based theories and the so-called structure–conduct–performance perspective have incorporated economic theories to explain the constitution of organizations, their interactions with the market and each other, their competitive position, and the requisite forms and strategies they need to adopt. Transaction cost analyses suggest that the very formation of organizations rests on the economic imperatives of minimizing or reducing the costs of economic exchange, given the realities of market uncertainties and imperfections, and the dangers of opportunistic behavior. It rests firmly on assumptions of determinedly rational economic behavior, albeit of a bounded nature. Such economic imperatives drive not only the constitution of organizations, but also the nature of interorganizational relationships, strategic positioning and organizational design. Organizations, their forms and relationships, are a function of rationally economic responses to markets. This has been a powerful paradigm within OS studies since the early 1980s. Reed (1999: 33) situates population ecology models (Hannan and Freeman, 1989) in the same intellectual space as transaction cost theory. While acknowledging differences, he argues that they share assumptions "that unify internal administrative forms and external market conditions by means of an evolutionary logic which subordinates collective and individual action to efficiency and survival imperatives largely beyond human influence."

The perceived exclusivity of economic rationalism, overreliance on the market as the level of analysis, and the universalizing tendencies of organizational economic perspectives has led to criticisms that an "undersocialized" conception of economic action is engendered. Granovetter (1985) has argued for a more radically "embedded" account of the social organization of economic action. The essence of the critique is that economic theories decontextualize both economic action and the organizational forms thereby derived, by underplaying the significance of the social and cultural forces within which economic action is constituted. Making the "economic" an autonomous sphere for analysis can be achieved only by suppressing everything that, in fact, does not make it so – such as social relations, ties, and networks. Granovetter argues that economic exchanges are embedded in complex, ongoing social relationships with attendant values and patterns that extend beyond mere economic utility. Economic exchanges are differentially framed by the specificities of institutional, social, and cultural contexts and the relationships and values that inhere within them. Economic action is both embedded in and emergent out of ongoing, socially constructed relationships that are not confined to matters of simple economic efficiency. The structuring of economic behavior, then, reflects this social embeddedness and the values that circulate within the cultural, social, and institutional context.

Another critique, made forcefully by Perrow (1986), suggests that organizational economic approaches lack a theory of power and a full consideration of human agency. Whilst the issue of power has been central to OS since Weber, it has been oddly neglected theoretically, except at the more micro-level of interpersonal or inter-unit influence. Significant exceptions have been Clegg (1975, 1979, 1989; Clegg and Dunkerley, 1980) and, in a different key, Pfeffer's (Pfeffer and Salancik, 1978) resource dependence model. An interest and focus on power has re-emerged more latterly under the influence of Foucault.

The second approach to have taken a key position in the OS discourse since the 1980s is institutional theory. The foundation for this was Meyer and Rowan's (1977) analysis of the symbolic properties of organizational forms. In the 1980s the approach focused heavily on how new institutions take form, and particularly on issues of symbolic legitimation and isomorphism (DiMaggio and Powell, 1983; DiMaggio, 1988). The essence of the approach is that organizational forms/structures have symbolic as well as functional resonances. The symbolic properties of organizations draw upon and speak to the institutional context in which a particular organization is situated. The symbolic properties must resonate with and draw support from the institutional environment and the values and interests represented therein. Thus, organization forms are determined by expectations of what types of structures and practices are likely to meet with institutional support, disregarding the utility of those structural choices for matters of internal functionality and efficiency. The approach is imbued with a functionalist purview, although there is some sophistication in current renditions and their focus on the processes of institutionalization. Indeed, by the late 1980s the approach began to respond to criticisms – both internally and externally generated – that it also had neglected the role of agency and the effect of power relations (DiMaggio, 1988; Hirsch and Lounsbury, 1997). It was also increasingly recognized that the theory had become a theory more of stasis than of change (Powell, 1991). The approach has undergone important shifts and reorientations, leading some to refer to a new institutionalism (Powell and DiMaggio, 1991; Hirsch and Lounsbury, 1997) characterized most profoundly by an interest in the *processes* of institutionalization and a greater preparedness to address the issues of power and agency. Lounsbury (chapter 7a) provides an account of these developments and is challenged from the viewpoint of critical discourse analysis by Phillips (chapter 7b). Jennings and Greenwood (chapter 6b) also utilize developments in new institutionalism to attempt a synthesis of enactment theory and institutional theory to explain processes of change in institutionalized areas of organizational life. Once again, not only do we see contestation within the wider OS discourse as these approaches enter and struggle to carve out a place, but we also see fairly intense debate within approaches.

The most recent fissure in the OS discourse has emerged from the "postmodern turn" in the analysis of sociocultural phenomena.[2] As we have indicated, Burrell and Morgan's (1979) schema cannot easily accommodate the approach. Perhaps a new category to add to their scheme (if one were needed) is that of radical poststructuralism. However, it is misleading to pretend that postmodernism is a coherent discourse; indeed, most of the key protagonists we have annotated above disavow the label. There are major differences, for example, between Foucault and Derrida (there are even major shifts within Foucault's corpus from his "archeology" through his "genealogy" to his concern with "care for the self "). However (permitting ourselves a huge gloss), there are some points of commonality relative to other approaches in social and organizational analysis.

It is important to distinguish between postmodernity – as an historicized delineation that posits a new *Zeitgeist* contrasted with that of modernity – and postmodernism as an intellectual practice that problematizes philosophy and all matters of ontology and epistemology. Postmodernity suggests that modernity, initiated by the Enlightenment project of progressive development through rationalism, has come to an end and that a new set of social-cultural, technological, and semiotic conditions have come into play. For some the postmodern signals radical disjuncture in the formation and operation of capital and/or in sociocultural forms in a postindustrial world (e.g., Jameson, 1991). This, and related changes in work and technology, have prompted talk about postmodern organizations (e.g., Clegg, 1990). Lyotard (1984) argues more profoundly that the change has more to do with the state of knowledge and with shifting problematics of legitimacy under conditions of radically altered technology. Postmodernism represents a radical challenge to the traditions of Western philosophy. It challenges, subverts, or reverses many of the sacred shibboleths of that tradition. It rejects both idealism and realism. Postmodernism is a reaction against the presumed certainties delivered by reason (the promise of modernism) and by the grand, totalizing narratives through which they were represented. It seeks to move beyond the illusions of structuralism's base–superstructure relations and concern with origins, centers, and fixities. It derides what Derrida (1976) refers to as logocentrism in Western thought, which involves a strong orientation towards "an order of meaning – thought, truth, reason, logic, the Word – conceived of as existing in itself, as foundation" (Culler, 1983: 92). Postmodernism rejects any metaphysics of presence in which a knowing consciousness guarantees the meaning of any experience, utterance or text. It subverts and challenges existent hierarchizations and privileging of knowledge: speech–writing, centre–periphery, subject–object, self–other. Correspondence and representational theories of language and knowledge are called into question. The "linguistic turn" in postmodernism sees meaning circulate in an endless, deferred, play of difference constituted by relations of signifier to signifier, without the anchor of a signified representing an external "real world." There is no point of external entry into this "seamless web" of signifying relations, no outside, or metaposition of objectivity from which a disinterested, innocent, or neutral analysis or commentary can be constructed. There is, however, a practice of closure by which to construct discourses that pretend to truth, fixity, and finality. There are claims to speak with knowledge and certainty, which offer representations of the real. However, these claims can be made only through an exercise of power within which a given discourse espouses an area of knowledge as its own and, in so doing, excludes alternative knowledge claims. This reflects Foucault's well known knowledge–power nexus (Foucault, 1980; Rouse, 1994). Indeed, every act of signification is an exercise of power in which social life and meaning can be seen only as an endless play of textual strategies, as meanings are constructed and deconstructed in ongoing interactional activity.

Postmodernism or poststructuralism applied to OS first began to appear in the mid to late 1980s (Burrell, 1988; Cooper, 1986; Cooper and Burrell, 1988; Martin, 1990; Travers, 1989; Westwood, 1987). Important anthologies and/or summaries appeared in Hassard and Parker (1993), Hassard and Pym (1990), and Reed and Hughs (1992), with precursors in Morgan's *Beyond Method* (1983) and Reed's *Redirections in Organizational Analysis* (1985). Much of this early work was primarily an exploration of the feasibility of the application of the postmodern perspective to OS. It was only later that more detailed analysis was forthcoming and the approach was applied to more specific organizational issues. These have included postmodern or deconstructive reinterpretations of organization (Burrell, 1997; Chia, 1998, 1996, also this volume, chapter 3b; Cooper, 1986; Kilduff, 1993), reinterpretations of organizational culture (Calas and Smircich, 1991; Chan, 2000, also this volume, chapter 10b; Linstead and Grafton-Small, 1992), viewing human resource management from a power–knowledge viewpoint (Townley, 1993, 1994), reassessing leadership (Calas and Smircich, 1991), identity, gender and the body (Brewis, 1999, 2000; Brewis et al., 1997; Brewis and Linstead, 2000; Hassard et al., 2000; Kerfoot and Knights, 1993), reconceptualizing power (Clegg, 1987, 1989; Dandeker, 1990; Jermier et al., 1994), communication, technology, and organization (Cooper, 1987, 1993; Kallinicos, 1995).

It is important to recognize that the fissure introduced by the postmodern perspective is a deep and radical one, given that it represents such a divergent appreciation of the ontological basis of organization. As Chia (chapter 3b) argues, organization is a process, not an entity. It is a world-making process: an elemental process of becoming in which flux is fixed through the structuring effects of language. Conceiving organization as process immediately has radical implications for epistemology and for methodology. Postmodernism is antithetical to the epistemology of positivism, neopositivism and all forms of naive realism.

Burrell and Morgan's (1979) "interpretive paradigm" continues to be much in evidence in the current OS discourse. Whilst there are those who still pursue OS via an ethnomethodological (see Richards, 2001), dramaturgical (e.g., Kärreman, 2001), and even a symbolic interactionist perspective, a broad social constructivist approach tends to be more dominant (see Czarniawska, 1992, 1998, this volume, chapter 4b). We have already made reference to the roots and some of the elemental features of social constructivism. It should be noted that, while a distinction is often drawn between interpretivist and constructivist approaches, there is much commonality (Schwandt, 1994). The essence of social constructionism is a concern for the lived experience and meaning making of people in their localized and specific contexts. The "object" of study is the life world and meanings constructed by people in and through their social interactions. Reality, in this sense, is not external and pre-given, but is the meaningful social outcome of coacting partners attempting to make sense of what is going on and, usually, to construct mutually accommodating lines of action (although they may understand each other all too well but wish to signal conflict and hostility. It is important not to let a functionalist overemphasis on order swamp the constructionist analysis). Organizational ontology reflects such constructivist concerns through stressing that there is no external and material organization beyond the mutually constituting activity of members' interactional work. Organization is an accomplishment: its status and being are dependent upon the ongoing interactional efforts and sense making of involved members. Methodologically, there is no objective world to be observed and recorded in a direct sense, rather the researcher needs to *interpret* the socially constructed world, the meanings and meaning-making processes of those involved in creating and sustaining their particular life world. This naturally makes language, especially language-in-use, a prime investigatory and interpretive focus. It is here that social constructionism abuts discourse analysis, which has also witnessed an increased level of activity (Grant et al., 1998; Mumby, 1993). In a related intellectual and discursive space we also find varieties of narrative and storytelling analysis (Boje, 1991, 1995, 2001; Gabriel, 1991, 1995, 1997; Phillips, 1995). In this volume we see Phillips (chapter 7b) outline a version of discourse analysis informed by critical theory. Also in this volume Czarniawska (chapter 4b) again positions Berger and Luckmann (1965) as the "main manual of the constructionists-to-be" and insists on examining the "how" of social constructions, not the outcomes in forms of representations. In other words, the interest is in the *processes* by which social meanings and social representations are constructed. This includes the processes that construct institutions – and their deconstruction – and the very processes by which things become objectified and reified. Like other constructivists, Czarniawska's concerns are with epistemology and, one might say, with the mundane epistemological processes of everyday social action. Neither ontology nor methodology is to be decided *a priori*. The ontological statuses of phenomena are part of what is researched and the methods are determined by the phenomena under investigation, the particular context, and the types of questions being asked.

A perspective with a long heritage – for example, in versions of labor process theory – but one that has re-emerged latterly with its application to OS, is critical theory. We have already noted some key ontological and epistemological aspects of a critical theory approach to organizations. This tradition draws upon Habermas, Adorno, Horkheimer, and other adherents of the Frankfurt school of critical theorists. A key thesis in this approach is that management and organization occupy such a central and defining position in contemporary social structures, processes, and discourses that they warrant critical scrutiny. The supposed rationality, neutral efficiency, and positive contribution of management/organization should not be taken for granted. Critical theory seeks to reveal the ideological underpinning of structures, practices and discourses that masquerade as innocent and commonsensical. It seeks to expose power systems and relationships that are repressive and exploitative. To quote two of the major proponents of the critical perspective, critical management seeks to challenge:

the myth of objectivity and argues for a very different, critical conception of management in which research is self-consciously motivated by an effort to discredit, and ideally eliminate, forms of management and organization that have institutionalised the opposition between the purposefulness of individuals and the seeming givenness and narrow instrumentality of work–process relationships. (Alvesson and Willmott, 1992: 4)

Of chief importance with respect to this diverse topography within OS is the recognition that almost all of these diverse perspectives (or, if you will, approaches or paradigms) remain in play. This is an indication of the potential inapplicability of the notion of "paradigm" to the field. There has been no discernible point in the history of the field where a paradigm has attained sufficient dominance that it has a status approximating that of a "normal" science. Nor has there been a revolutionary period in which an opposing and previously marginal paradigm has supplanted the functions of a normal science. The contemporary topography of the OS discourse has no more consensus or coherence than it ever had: if anything it is more polyphonous. As Donaldson (1985, chapter 4a), Hinings (chapter 9a) and Ashkanasy (chapter 10a) make abundantly clear, a positivistic, structural-functionalist approach is alive and well in the discourse – although not as dominant as it once was or as Donaldson (1988, 1995) would like it. Environmental determinist and evolutionary models are also still evident, as are decontextualized and deterministic organizational economic models within a rationalist, functionalist perspective, and they continue to thrive. Despite the disavowal of positivism and a nuanced discussion of social realist ontology, McKelvey (chapter 2a), McKinley (chapter 5a) and Boal, Hunt and Jaros (chapter 3a) all occupy positions within the trajectory of the traditional orthodoxy in OS. Whilst they would reject the label and the dichotomising,[3] they reside on the "normal organization science" side of Marsden and Townley's (1999) bifurcation of the field into "normal organization science" and "contra-organization science." If it is meaningful, this distinction delineates the deepest fissure in the OS discourse today. On the contra side we find the interpretivists, social constructivists, the "posties" (poststructuralists and postmodernists), and the critical theorists. Although not a perfect alignment, in some respects the point–counterpoint positions in this volume are aligned across this divide.

It also needs to be noted that the contestation is not just across paradigm positions or approaches because much debate occurs within paradigms and within the frame of particular orientations. For example, Pfeffer (1993) is not only antithetical to social constructivist positions he is also highly critical of rational choice theory. Similarly, Donaldson (1985, 1990, 1995) elevates contingency theory above other "orthodox" approaches such as population ecology, organizational economics and institutional theory. It would seem that there is struggle within the orthodoxy as well as against the opposition outside the boundaries of what is considered to be "normal." Similarly there are debates between, say, critical theorists and postmodernists, or social constructionists and deconstructionists. Even within so-called postmodern purviews there is much diversity and contestation.

Responding to Diversity: The Politics, Ethics, and Pragmatics of the Discourse

Introduction: closure, openness, and straw persons

What are the responses to the contested nature of the field from the various discursive arenas? Some appear to be alarmed by the diversity, lack of coherence, and contestation. We have already noted Pfeffer's (1982) consternation at the "weed patch" that is the field and his suggestion for some prudent pruning. A decade later he made a more programmatic call for paradigm closure (Pfeffer, 1993). He argued that progress in the field can be made only if there is consensus around a paradigm – and for him this should be around the orthodoxy of structural functionalism. He further suggested some institutional means for ensuring paradigm purity and an effective policing of the boundary of this politically constituted and more limited discourse, one which critics have jokingly referred to as the "Pfefferdigm" – because it promotes a Pfefferian paradigm as its view of the world. The rest of us are urged to stop making sense in other terms and knuckle down to the serious business of forging common sense making around the Pfefferdigm.

Others have shown similar alarm at the fragmentation of the field and urged consensus and paradigm closure, although they have not been as willing as Pfeffer to introduce institutional politics to achieve this (Donaldson, 1985, 1995). Donaldson prefers to allow what is defined within the framework of positivist theory as reasoned argument and the testament of empirical findings to achieve the desired result. McKinley has been equally disturbed by the state of the field, its divisions and lack of progress, and argued that greater construct objectification based upon definitional consensus over core constructs is the way forward (McKinley and Mone, 1998; McKinley and Scherer, 2000, and this volume, chapter 5a). Definitional consensus would also lead to convergence over measurement. Like Pfeffer, there is advocacy of a politically informed institutional device to facilitate the consensus in the form of a "democratically produced" construct dictionary (McKinley and Mone, 1998). The nature of the democratic process is a moot point and obviously further deepens the politicization of the field. McKelvey is even more pessimistic, declaring OS to be prescientific, the antidote to which, it is suggested, is a strategy based upon Campbellian realist ontology by which it can best move forward to scientific status (McKelvey, 1997, 1999, and chapter 2a). He sees the resolution not in terms of paradigm closure or diversity but in terms of "models" that deliver desired results to external constituents (McKinley, 2001). In effect, he sees the field as a market, where the pragmatics of delivering useful outcomes should decide which approaches survive and which do not. In McKinley, as in Pfeffer, we see an overt pragmatic politics promulgated as the means to redirect and give impetus to the field. Even Reed (1999: 26) referred to the field as "a cacophony of querulous voices totally lacking in general moral force and analytic coherence." Reed's solution is not a retreat behind a more narrowly construed paradigm delineation, but a careful exposition of core problematics and the search for synthesis.

Within the field, others are more prepared to tolerate or even celebrate the polyphony. Clegg et al. (1996) say that they value conversation, discourse, and open, cooperative inquiry across boundaries. This requires, they suggest, a certain agnosticism (Nord and Connell, 1993) wherein they eschew belief in any ultimate form of knowledge. There is a long tradition that puts value in the engagement of alternative or opposing positions. In the literature on creativity there is a strong belief that diversity, and even conflict, is conducive to creativity. The notion of creative abrasion reflects this dynamic. Hardy (1994) has also argued that a state of fragmentation means that the discourse retains an open texture and that means there are spaces in which weaker, emergent or less dominant and orthodox positions can find a place. This is important with respect to the politics of the discourse. Burrell (1999) has argued that the proponents of paradigm incommensurability in OS have put their case with this political dynamic in mind. We shall return to the issue of incommensurability shortly.

In putting this book together we signal our recognition of the diversity in the field, but we do not share the alarm exhibited by some of its practitioners. We see the field as healthily fecund – a ripe arena with much creative and productive energy. We contend that it has always been so, and is likely to continue thus. In constituting a book in this format our intention and aspiration was not necessarily to precipitate synthesis and resolution in the hope of "progressing" the field. Not that synthesis and rapprochement are necessarily a bad thing. Rather, we see value in having varied positions available to the reader in the same space, so that the diversity can be appreciated and the differences better understood. It is apparent that much of the opposition and antagonism in the field is often based on mis-understanding. There is much attacking of straw-persons in evidence in this volume too. One such straw person implicitly or explicitly identified among the contributions is a simplistic view of positivism as the guiding philosophy of orthodox OS. At best, positivism is shorthand for a certain, often unexplicated, set of assumptions guiding the scientific OS enterprise. Equally, we are alarmed by the various postmodern straw persons that have come under attack, particularly in terms of a presumed relativism, amorality, and rampant subjectivity. It is clear that many opponents (including some of those in this volume) have not taken the trouble to familiarize themselves fully with postmodernism but prefer to rail at what they would want it to be, as Quixotic "windmills" at which their barbs and lances might tilt. Part of the function of the book is to help to diminish such lacunae. We are not supportive of attempts to artificially achieve closure in the discourse through institutional politics. Such politics already exist and we have no wish to see them further rigidified and strengthened.

Institutional politics in organization studies

Organization studies is a field of practice. It has not reached the stage of professional practice and institutional framing that, say, medicine has, but it is a bounded field of practice and the bounds are policed by those institutional parameters instantiated within its discourse. The paraphernalia of professional academic practice inevitably constitutes a power field. There are mechanisms of control in place that police boundaries – that deter-mine what is included and taken as legitimate and proper and what is excluded and deemed to be improper and illegitimate. OS is an unstable field in some respects, but there are some deeply entrenched professional practices that are extremely robust. Chief among these are the rules of entry into the profession, the rules of research, and the rules of publication. Clearly these exhibit interdependence. To practise in the field there is a clear and distinct trajectory of professional development and qualification attainment. To get published, par-ticipants need to meet certain epistemological, methodological, and stylistic requirements. An obvious manifestation of this resides in the politics of publication, particularly journal publication. As one of the chief outcomes of practice in professional knowledge fields, publication is of acute significance to the construction and maintenance of the field. Journals not only represent the prime mode of dissemination of knowledge, they are also part of the technology by which any field constitutes and sustains a professional status and through which membership of the field/profession is policed. The openness of a field is at issue in and through the practice of publication.

Keepers of the dominant and orthodox position within OS tend to be institutionally able to sustain and perpetuate their foundations, almost as holders of the citadels of publishing power, to the extent that they have control and manipulation of key journal publication processes. In the citadels that are thus maintained, work that does not fit dominant perspectives tends to be delegitimized and struggles to find its way into published form. One strategic response is for the less powerful and nonorthodox approaches to try and establish their own institutional frame and publications. An example of this is the Standing Conference on Organizational Symbolism (SCOS), which began as an offshoot of EGOS and had an early focus on the symbolic processes of organizations, particularly with respect to organizational cultures. It is now "home" to an eclectic set of researchers who seek to pursue nonorthodox, postmodernist, and/or critical perspectives. It has its own association, annual conference, and journal. However, the politics of the field maintain SCOS and similar offshoots somewhat at the margin, and participation in SCOS and output related to it does not provide an entrée into the dominant institutional orthodoxy. Being pragmatically blunt: a presentation at a SCOS conference does not count for as much, in professional terms, as a presentation at an Academy of Management conference if one were seeking a post at a top US business school!

We want to consider further some aspects of the politics of the discourse by examining two events that struck us as having resonance with the concerns of this book and by exploring, reflexively, aspects of the process by which the book came into being.

The first event was a private one and relates to the involvement by one of us in a research meeting, one that we suspect was not at all atypical of the micropolitics of research. The meeting involved four researchers who met to discuss a research opportunity that had presented itself. Without going into detail, the discussion focused on possible lines of research and their potential outcomes. Three of the researchers present were from orthodox, micro-psychological traditions within OS. Although the research issues were potentially socially important and complex, the direction of the discussion was led by considerations of methodological conventionality, the availability of measurements, and the publishability of the variables addressed. The story has resonance not only with the methodology of OS but also with the politics of research and scholarly practice as well as the wider issue of the point, meaning, and value of research conducted under the rubric of OS.

Practitioners in the field are usually acutely aware of the politics of research and publication. Professional training, development, and socialization already inscribe practitioners with sharply delineated ideas about research practice, methodology, modes of writing and accompanying stylistics, and a broad ethos with which to approach the research task and generally conduct themselves as professionals within their field. We are not suggesting that there is complete homogeneity in this regard, but there are some dominant orthodoxies that many practitioners imbibe as they work themselves into the practice – as they practise. The point is not to bemoan such rather obvious politics but to note that, as our example suggests, the orthodox frame not only polices the boundary through the mechanics of publication but also actually works to shape proactively the way research questions are addressed and the types of issues that are deemed worthy of investigation. We are reminded of Burrell's (1993) attempt to have a video presentation he made at a conference institutionally legitimated as a properly productive academic outcome, as well as a controversy concerning an Afro-American academic at Harvard University, from the School of Afro-American Studies, who made a rap record, for which he was severely reprimanded by the university authorities. As Taylor and Saarenen (1994) suggest, "If you publish an article in the leading journal in your discipline, your arguments and conclusions can be challenged but your seriousness cannot be doubted. A media product, by contrast, appears frivolous and would never be characterised as 'the public use of reason'."

It is not just the media in which output should be produced that is prescribed by the orthodoxy in OS but also the writing style. As part of the rhetoric of objectivity within the orthodoxy, the writing style should, ideally, be cleansed of anything intimating the subjectivity of the author(s). The language should be impersonal, neutral, and devoid of feeling. The rigors and confinements of academic style have been ably summed up by Richardson (1992):

> Nearly every time [social scientists] broke into prose, they tried to suppress [their own] life: passive voice; absent narrator; long, inelegant, repetitive authorial statements and quotations; "cleaned up" quotations, each sounding like the author; hoards of references; sonorous prose rhythms; dead or dying metaphors; lack of concreteness or overly detailed accounts; tone deafness; and, most disheartening, the suppression of narrativity (plot, character, event).[4]

It is these stylistic expectations that we largely conform to here, it should be acknowledged. We want to be seen as serious! There exists a conceit that the mode and style of representation in academic writing can be separated from the meanings that the representation pretends to convey. This is a conceit not shared by some. Richardson (1994) documents the conventions of academic writing practice and reveals the inherent metaphoricality of scientific writing and the implication of stylistics for research practice, a point also made by Rhodes (2001) in *Writing Organizations*. In this volume both Case (chapter 5b) and Gherardi (chapter 11) make use of or make reference to the use of irony within academic writing practice.

Another aspect of the micropolitics of scholarly practice is the use of the reference and the citation. These are, at one level, indicators to fellow practitioners that the author shows mastery of the discourse, at another level they are a recirculation of accepted texts that have attained legitimacy in the discourse. The deployment of particular citations and references from within the extant discourse to bolster and justify a new entrant reflexively reaffirms the efficacy of the discourse. At the same time, the ability to cite and reference properly reaffirms the author's status as a *bona fide* member of the scholarly community (see Bjorkegren, 1993). As Taylor and Saarenen (1994) again note, "On the assembly line of knowledge, the intellectual produces print, which, in turn, produces the intellectual." As Westwood (1999) has noted, there is an odd dynamic of supplementarity in the use of references in relation to the presented text. "The reference list performs a peculiar supplementarity to the body of the text, signaling by its presence an absence in the text. The text presents as a coherent, complete account, but, without references, is incomplete. The references mark out a discourse beyond the text: indexing the intertext." By similar logic, there is an odd supplementarity in this introduction to this text.

There is one other matter we should note: this is a book. By which we mean more than to state the self-evident. Obviously this is a book. But in being a book it is not being a journal. And in the hierarchies of knowledge that shape the OS field, increasingly the US norm that a journal is better than a book, that, indeed, books are some inferior form of scientific life compared with the rigorously refereed journal article, is a widely held article of faith. Don't write books – produce articles, is an exhortation that we have heard many an academy cohort of graduate students receive. Now, in the United States, where graduate classes are many and the thesis is less in the overall weight of things, this may be sage advice. A small thesis – in terms of weight and length – probably would not translate into a good book. Indeed, one of us has had occasion to advise publishers to reject a number of US theses for publication simply on the grounds that they were insufficiently substantial to conform to the norms of the book. Yet the US norm is not the universal norm – in most other academic cultures with which we are familiar the thesis is the sole product of the apprenticeship and the norm is that a substantial piece of work that narrates a significant research journey should be produced. Such work, particularly if it has an integrated narrative flow throughout its chapters – it tells an unfolding story – may be less easily rendered in the discrete charms of the journal article formula.

We could go on and explore this type of institutional politics *ad nauseam*, but the point is perhaps made. It is important to recognize this volume as a participant in those processes and to reflect on what that means. To pursue that reflexively we want to detail a second recent event.

Terms of engagement: the politics of debate

The second event that resonated with the concerns of this book was the occurrence of an Australian general election, one that was concluding as we set about writing. We shall first make the general point before linking it with the specifics of this volume.

As has become *de rigueur* in this age of the media spectacle and the sound bite, the leaders of the two major parties[5] were invited to conduct a televised "debate." The leaders of the two parties went head-to-head, being dramaturgically framed in the typical manner. At issue – and this is the point of resonance – is the politics of exclusion that typifies such debates. Only the two major parties were invited to debate in this ultimate of modern forums. None of the lesser parties was given the opportunity to participate – something that vexed, and was the cause of public complaint by, the leader of the third most powerful party – the Democrats. This fact echoes Burrell's (1999) observation that debating is a practice engaged in by the powerful and privileged. This raises the question of who and what are excluded from debate. Demonstrators against and detractors of globalization have claimed that at key forums, such as the World Trade Forum in Seattle and in Milan, they and certain key oppositional positions are excluded from the debate taking place among the official representatives of the global economy. However, even those demonstrators occupy relatively privileged positions of access compared with some of the more marginalized recipients of the effects of globalization and they are, through the use of spectacle, able to garner some attention. The general point is that orchestrating a debate will always exclude somewhat more than it includes. And editors are orchestrators *par excellence*.

The issue of exclusion causes us to reflect on the role of editors in general, and in projects such as this in particular. Editors clearly occupy a position of power – in the way a text is defined and framed, in the processes of selection, and in the act of editing itself. This is particularly trenchant with respect to journal editorship, a power we have wielded elsewhere and on other occasions, but is no less evident here. We have exercised such power. While some of its effects are apparent materially in the form this text has taken there are other, less visible, effects of the process. Who was excluded from these "debates" through the editorial process? While that is hard to answer, because, in principle, so many are excluded, we can approach the issue by reflecting a little on the process of inclusion. We presume that, like many academic edited texts, the volume you are now reading results from a process that includes both careful designs mixed with happenstance and serendipity. The issues addressed in the book are our selection – and we are fully aware of how partial that selection is – but guided by sets of presumed relevances in the extant discourse. How were authors chosen? Naturally, we identified people who had written on the issues under consideration, but in so doing we were in part driven by criteria such as reputation, academic standing, and quality of published output. Publishers enter the political process too; they indicated their desire to see "known" people, with reputations, included in the project. These strategies were not uniformly applied; we have made a conscious effort to also include authors who we felt had written cogently or interestingly on the issues but whose reputations are perhaps not yet fully established. Again, we circle back into the politics and the issue of what "reputation" signifies as we play our part in this political game of brokerage.

The point is not to flatter, or demean, our contributors; rather it is to reflect on the politicized nature of the production of texts – in general, but in this instance particularly in OS. As we have noted, this politicization is not confined to the production of monographs. Who and what were excluded? There is no debate on organizational aesthetics, for example, or on sexuality and organizations, or on humor – all things we find fascinating. It is apparent that we were operating with some notion of what was more central and what more peripheral to the field, and also with some notion of what was contested and what was not. We were also, presumably, led to our selections in part by reflections of appeal and marketability. These are clearly political notions concerned with the power effects of inclusion and exclusion. Marshall, Mills, and Gherardi too reflect on the politics of exclusion in chapter 11.

We were conscious that the book's format, in terms of point–counterpoint, is deliberately provocative, but we had not anticipated the antipathy that the form fomented among some of our contributors. It was salutary, for example, to be reminded of the masculinist nature of the form (Gherardi et al., chapter 11). The word "debate" derives from the old French meaning "to strike down," so the combative element is etymologically imbued. There are obvious dangers inherent to the point–counterpoint structure, some of which have already been intimated. There is the danger that it is a privileged form that simply reproduces existing power structures – including gendered ones. There is also the danger, as Peter Case notes (chapter 5b), that the adversarial nature of the form will not lead to active and fruitful engagement, but rather will result in defensiveness and obscurantism, hostility, or even studied avoidance.

Perhaps naively, we hoped that a point–counterpoint, debate format would allow a more active and productive engagement between positions in OS that typically would not be engaged – indeed, would not even inhabit the same textual space. The whole project is clearly premised on the view that the field of OS is characterized by diversity and heterogeneity. There are perspectival differences not only with respect to methodology and theoretical stance but also more radically in terms of ontological concerns of what problems should be addressed and upon whose behalf. The book is informed by the value that heterogeneity is worth while in itself as a celebration of intellectual curiosity. We believe that the field develops best through the tensions generated by the active engagement of varying positions and paradigms. It struck us that too often debate is not met and opportunities for the productivity of thesis meeting antithesis, or the mere juxtaposition of radically opposing perspectives, are lost. Regrettably, certain institutional orthodoxies often collude with this isolationism and paradigm exclusionism. In other respects there is simple inertia, ego–defensiveness, or lack of opportunity. Against these currents of torpor of one kind or another we have sought to provide a vehicle through which the rich topography of the field can be more fully explored within the same space. Topographies of clashing tectonics, robust monoliths, volcanic irruptions and ghostly implosions were our desire. We wanted to set before the reader as full an array as possible of the areas of critical contestation around core issues. We sought an expressly polyvocal, multipositional text constructed around dyads of point and counterpoint, thesis to antithesis, paradigm against paradigm. That was the aspiration.

In order to facilitate this aspiration we adopted a unique process. Once authors had been identified and their cooperation assured each was asked to provide a brief position statement of two or three pages in length. These position statements were passed over to their respective counterpoint contributors anonymously. Contributors were then invited to construct drafts of a full text. These were also exchanged anonymously. At the same time the editors provided some feedback and commentary. In the last stage, authors construct a second draft in light of feedback and commentary and submit a final version. The process had some complexity and, it must be admitted, proved difficult to adhere to absolutely.

The somewhat convoluted process was adopted in order to facilitate active engagement between positions, rather than a mere passive juxtaposition. The effectiveness of the strategy and process was, frankly, mixed – as readers will become aware. In some cases counterparts have actively engaged; there are even instances of suggested rapprochement. At the other extreme are situations where the authors elected not to engage and were happy to state their case and let it stand beside that of the counterpoint in splendid isolation. For Czarniawska (chapter 4b) this was an express strategy, following Rorty, to "argue for the attractiveness of one's position and not against the position of others." There is value for the reader in having counterpoint positions juxtaposed in the same textual space.

Another organizing effect of the book is the alignment and sequencing of contributions. The point, obviously, is to construct positions of difference. After identifying issues we sought to locate positions of difference with respect to them. The tacit reasoning appears to have to been to seek out maximal differentiation. Broadly, although this is not uniform,[6] the point position has been sourced from the more orthodox or mainstream positions on the issues. The counterpoint is typically representative of an oppositional, critical, or radical position on the issue and/or in relation to the espoused orthodoxy. We are aware that this framing is not innocent; in a sense it reflects certain viewpoints about what is orthodox and what is not. Such viewpoints are clearly ideologically informed and eminently debatable. What, then, do we mean by orthodox and mainstream? What we have not done, as appears to have been inferred by some of our contributors, is to expressly juxtapose paradigmatic forms of neopositivism with varieties of postmodern critique – although in some instances that is the result. However, it will become apparent to the reader that this is not the only point of differentiation in the alignment of debating positions. Our notion of orthodoxy had several nodes of identification, nodes that were rarely present collectively in any one case. These nodes would include what we, however problematically, would characterize as a broadly neopositivist epistemology but also included more mundane indicators, such as appearance in mainstream journals, managerialist value orientations, and august institutional location. In one sense it is a comment on the nature of the contemporary field of OS that the distinction between orthodoxy and nonorthodoxy is extremely problematic. This is partly why we did not adopt a systematic strategy in framing the debates – it was often a more prosaic matter of identifying people who had something to say that was different from a counterpart on the issue at hand.

An interesting by-product of this process of selection and alignment is that proportionally there are more US-based scholars in the point position and more Europeans and others in the counterpoint position. This may reflect a certain geopolitics within the field, but it may also be an artifact of our own backgrounds and location. Nonetheless, there is a geopolitical material reality that underlies the experience of which there is further evidence in a cross-citation study comparing the *Administrative Science Quarterly* (US-based) and *Organization Studies* (Europe-based). This revealed that articles in the *ASQ* mainly cited US scholars in US journals whereas in *Organization Studies* the citations were more expansive and inclusive (Üsdiken and Pasadeos, 1995). For instance, Weber and Foucault don't rate in the *ASQ* although they make the top ten in *Organization Studies*.

The ethics of the discourse

One major issue in the discourse of OS is the question of ethics. Reed (1996: 25–6) argues that, at its inception with Saint-Simon, OS was concerned with the moral capacity of organizations to resolve the growing conflicts in society between collective needs and individual wants. Organization was a method of imparting required order. Today, Reed continues, OS lacks a moral force. It is an issue touched on implicitly or explicitly by a number of the contributors and one that impinges on or is an effect of the discourse at a number of levels. At a very broad level there is the matter of whether science in general, and OS in particular, is, or should be, value-free. From a positivist, neopositivist, or "strong" realist perspective, ontological practice aims to provide knowledge of things "as they really are" and epistemological practice seeks to provide an objective account of that reality. A presumed distance between the object to be investigated and the investigating subject accompanies the objectivism. Any researcher influence on the object of study is deemed to be contaminative and a threat to validity, with steps taken to eliminate or reduce such influence. Values are considered to be confounding variables, thus the aspiration, at least, is to a value-free science. The science of explanation is differentiated from any application that may be derived from the explanation. McKinley (chapter 5a) makes a somewhat extreme statement in this regard when asserting his belief that "organizational scholars are relatively isolated from the 'real world'. I am not overly concerned about the unanticipated destructive effects their construct objectification might have on that world." However, the explanatory aim is supposed to deliver possibilities for prediction and control (Hesse, 1980). This clearly raises the question, although it is infrequently addressed, of who is to predict and control, for whom, or for what purpose? For constructivism an ontological practice is entailed in which organization's and people's socially constructed, localized and contextualized realities (and they may be multiple) are apprehended from the perspective of those engaged in such constructions of reality. In epistemological terms the distance between object and subject is dissolved. The constructivists recognize their impact on the research "object" and the act of interpretation, and seek a reflexive strategy to take that into account. The understandings evolved from the research practice are a co-enactment between researchers and researched. In this case, the values of the researcher cannot be bracketed out, and the values of the "object" of the research are very much of interest. Whilst not uniformly so, often there is an aspiration that an understanding of constructions will lead to more sensitized policies and treatments of those whose life world is examined. Alternatively, it may be the intention that the researched gain insight into their own constructive processes and become aware of alternative and improved constructive realities that they can participate in. From the perspective of critical theory the ontology can be described as historical realism and the concern is with the political, social, and discursive structures that are responsible for maintaining a particular power order. Once again the values of the researcher and of the researched are present in the research context, the interpretation, and the effect. The motivating value is emancipatory. The aim of research practice is to critique and ultimately transform the power structures that are seen as repressive and exploitative in some form. Indeed, from this perspective, avoidance of values would be considered as unethical. (The contributor most sympathetic to this perspective is Phillips, chapter 7b.)

The above is not meant to imply that a positivist or realist position is unethical or displays no interest in ethics. Rather, ethical matters are, in a sense, external to the research practice. Ethical standards are applied and enforced that legalistically frame the research practice. These standards, which on the one hand guide the researcher and protect the research object, are also there to ensure that the researcher does not contaminate the "object" of study. However, this tends to mean at the micro-levels of research practice – the *effects* of research, *in their application*, are another matter. Some researchers within the positivist/realist position, including contributors such as Donaldson, would argue that the highest ethical standard is the pursuit of "truth" and the revelation of the objective contours of reality. Others would argue from an ethics of pragmatics. In the simplest form the argument would be that the research practice is ethical if it results in the improvement of organizational practice. There is surface plausibility here. Given the centrality of organizations to all we do, who would challenge the notion that producing more effective organizations was not a worthy enterprise? Of relevance to these concerns is the debate on globalization in this volume. Whilst both authors give a nuanced account, Jones (chapter 8b) has a more critical stance and analyses more the power effects on the marginalized and disadvantaged. Parker (chapter 8a) tends somewhat more to see the positive transformative effects of improved transnational corporations and global financial and trade systems. Despite the plausible aim of improving organizations, questions still remain about who has access to the knowledge of the researcher, who deploys it and to what ends. In some more radical forms of constructivism the researcher ensures that ownership of the research, the data, the results, and the effects either rest with or are shared with the researched (Cancian and Armstead, 1992; Elden and Chisholm, 1993; Hall et al., 1982; Reason, 1988; Reason and Rowan, 1981). In much orthodox research in OS the question of "for whom is the research" undertaken is either not addressed or glossed as being a nonquestion (since the research is purely objective and neutral and the applications are someone else's business), or there is acceptance – explicit or taken for granted – that the research is for managers and/or policy formulators. This can mean that OS takes on a distinctly managerialist hue. This position is apparent, for example, in Pfeffer (1982). In this volume McKinley (chapter 5a) seems to concur when, citing Beyer and Trice (1982), he argues that the inability to objectify constructs means that the field is unable to generate "objective, believable knowledge that is utilizable . . . by managers." Specific notions of audience and usage imply a value position and are implicitly used to invoke an ethic.

Postmodernism has often been castigated for being amoral and/or promoting an ethical relativism. This is a misreading; for instance, the moral purpose of Foucault is abundantly clear (e.g., see Simons, 1995) and Derrida has been at pains to reject accusations of amorality (see Bernstein, 1991). Similarly, in this volume, Case (chapter 5b) is keen to avoid being positioned as a nihilist and supporter of moral relativism. He clearly asserts that there is a "political and moral dimension to the choices made by social scientific researchers." He sees the language of research and theory as ineluctably inhabited by ideology and by practices of power. Indeed, he considers the struggle between subjective and objective forms of knowledge as a moral struggle. Along with others, Case sees a moral hazard in the expressly manipulative, predictive and controlling aspects of the positivistic enterprise. In similar vein

Czarniawska (chapter 4b) defends constructionism against the charge of amorality. This emanates, falsely in her opinion, from either interpreting constructivism as relativistic and incapable of taking a moral stance, or from regarding it as being merely descriptive and thus not taking a moral but merely an ethnographic position. Czarniawska counters by pointing out that constructivism supports neither deterministic nor absolute voluntaristic postures. She is, however, clear about the moral imperative in research practice, maintaining that any question about the purpose of research activity should be answered from an ethicopolitical position and not a methodological-ontological one. Hassard and Kelemen (chapter 2b) also take on the moral imperative, asserting that we live in times of moral ambiguity and that researchers' own ethical positions should guide their research practice. They also advocate the postmodernist ethic of trying to ensure that the repressed, marginalized and the silenced in society are given a voice through research practice. We would argue that whilst this might be desirable in an abstract sense, glib adherence to the doctrine could be misleading. Merely "giving a voice" does not guarantee a resolution of the conditions that construct a group's marginality or repression; indeed, it can exacerbate the situation by providing a clearer target to aim at.

Ethics within the OS discourse was not formally included in this volume – perhaps it should have been – but, significantly, the issue emerged variously among the contributors such that we felt it worth while to raise some of the issues here.

Debating Organization: Fissures in the Topography

Introduction: critical fracture lines

We have already indicated fracture lines constituted by very different approaches within OS, both historically and contemporaneously. There is a multiplicity of more specific fissures and points of contention around issues and themes, and we do not intend to pay attention to all of them here. Furthermore, the volume itself represents our contributors' attempt to identify and explore some of the key debates and so it would be redundant to elaborate overly upon them here. However, we want to provide some indication and some context for those debates. In line with our earlier argument, the points of fracture apparent in the discourse today have, in many respects, remained present since the discourse came into being. We have, for example, already noted the early divergent interpretations of Weber that constituted a fracture – or rather a set of fractures – persisting down to today.

We have also noted that for Pfeffer (1982) the discourse disperses around a twin problematic of levels of analysis and approaches to action. The former is, for him, a matter of whether organization theory takes organizations themselves as the appropriate unit of analysis or a suborganizational unit such as individuals or groups. The latter problematic is concerned with the determination of action and is partly a question of causality. His first category of action is a form of voluntarism in which action is a function of rational, purposive, goal-seeking behavior. The second is a form of determinism under which action is shaped by the external context. The third (although misrepresented by Pfeffer) is a form of social constructionism wherein action emerges as people interact and locate and constitute meaning. Clearly these cleavages are also still apparent within the discourse: for instance, contrast the positions of Donaldson and Czarniawska (chapter 4). Indeed, Reed's (1999) more recent survey of the field, which identifies four key areas of debate, reproduces most of Pfeffer's problematic as essential contested domains. One of these, which he terms individualism versus collectivism, resonates with Pfeffer's problematic of units of analysis. A second theme, where Reed contrasts agency and structure, approximates Pfeffer's concerns with action, where structure resonates with notions of external determinism, and agency deals with the bringing into being of structures, and other meaningful forms, through human action and interaction. Reed's third theme is a straightforward epistemological dissensus between a broadly conceived constructivism and an equally broadly conceived positivism. A point of fragmentation not attended to by Pfeffer is a local–global problematic. At one level this looks like a unit of analysis argument but on closer inspection actually refers to the postmodern concerns for metanarratives and totalizing theories. The issue is whether it is sensible to attempt the construction of universalizing, decontextualized, and grand explanatory systems. The alternative is to see this as representing a logocentric fallacy, an imposition of fictive order and homogeneity on flux and diversity, and a gross knowledge–power ploy reactionary in scope and serving only to bolster existing center–periphery relations. Instead of global explanation what would instead be legitimized would be localized investigations that seek to understand the politics of meaning making within immediate and specific contexts.

Some of these core fractures are tackled by contributions to this volume either directly or indirectly. Most occur in Part I, dealing with the foundational issues of the status of the field/discipline, its ontology, epistemology, and methodology. The other debates occur around more focused issues or themes, although even here these foundational debates resurface frequently. Before moving to the debates around the three related issues of ontology, epistemology, and methodology we want to consider the nature and status of OS as a field, discipline, or, as we would say, a discourse. We have already argued that this discourse is relatively new and, as such, does not have the coherence or power effects of some more established discourses. We constituted this debate for our contributors in terms of whether the notions of field or discipline are applicable and whether the discourse had constituted an institutional frame and, if so, its nature. We also invited consideration of the proper and legitimate scope, content, and boundaries of the field/discipline. In particular we wanted to address the issue of whether or not the field/discipline has, should have, or could have, coherence and consensus with respect to matters of scope, content, and boundary.

Politics revisited: paradigm incommensurability

The nature and status of the field and/or its perceived status as a discipline are clearly of some interest but are perhaps less at issue than are conceptions about the coherence of the field and the desirability of its being so. This has been a concern for some time, but has perhaps intensified in the last couple of decades. This more recent engagement with the issue has revolved around the incommensurability debate and the articulation of various programmatic agendas for the discipline/field that aim to reconstitute OS as a consensual, coherent framework within which more effective development might flourish – often thought of in terms of a gathering of resources against competitors. Such activity entails attempts to delineate carefully the field/discipline, to give specificity to scope and content, and to police the boundaries of the discourse. It reflects the "weeding and pruning" that Pfeffer (1982) referred to. The counterpoint is the view that such an exercise is both untenable and undesirable. Whether as field or discipline (and the inclinations from the counterpoint are towards the former), OS has been, is, and should remain, an open discourse characterized by inherent indeterminacy with respect to the questions of scope, content, and boundary.

Let us deal directly with the vexed issue of paradigm plurality and incommensurability. Some concerned with the status and strength of the field maintain that diversity and paradigm plurality is *the* problem that hampers the legitimate – or legitimizing – progress of the field. The argument is that OS is characterized by the existence of different paradigms and that it is this, in particular, that is responsible for the fragmentation of the field and for its lack of cohesion and progress. This was the line taken by Pfeffer in 1982 and one that he has pursued more radically since, particularly in his 1993 *AMR* piece. Pfeffer sees OS as a failed field, as a failed science. Its scientific status and sense of progress are hampered by a lack of consensus about key issues in the scientific enterprise: what problems to address, what level of analysis, what epistemology, what methodology? Pfeffer's solution is overtly political: to maneuver one central paradigm into a position of dominance, require compliance with it, and institutionally police the boundaries of the orthodoxy. Donaldson (1985) makes a similar plea for paradigm consensus but without the authoritarian accompaniment. McKelvey (chapter 2a) shares Pfeffer's analysis of the state of the field but rejects the solution, as we have discussed. Calls for defense of the orthodox faith have not been met without rebuttal. Van Maanen (1995), for instance, mounted a spirited attack on Pfeffer, making a plea for intellectual openness.

The debate surrounding paradigms and their incommensurability in OS was most intense following the publication of Burrell and Morgan's (1979) work, since they cast the whole argument in terms of paradigm and made much of the incommensurability thesis. Initial critique of their work objected to the reduction of the field to a simple and static 2×2 matrix. However, the argument took a different turn and became more heated following Donaldson's (1985) defense of the structural-functionalist orthodoxy in OS. This was followed by a special issue of *Organization Studies* (1988) devoted to debate of the issues raised by Donaldson's contribution, marked by Aldrich's broad support for Donaldson (Aldrich, 1988). Reed (1985) also considered the state of the field and the issue of paradigm plurality. He argued that there were four types of response: integrationism, isolationism, imperialism, and plurality – responses still in play today. Reed's preference then was for tolerant and productive pluralism but by 1999 he seemed to have shifted slightly, rejecting the retreat to certainty represented by Donaldson and Pfeffer *and* the "distortions of relativism" represented by advocates of paradigm isolationism as well as some proponents of a postmodern perspective (Reed, 1999: 45).

The proponents of paradigm incommensurability have sometimes come not from within orthodoxy but from the more critical edges of discourse, where asserting incommensurability is seen to preserve OS as an open text in which multiple voices can find expression. Incommensurability provides the disengagement and hence protected environment that the weaker, less established, or more marginal paradigm positions need so that they can continue to develop (see Jackson and Carter, 1991). Burrell (1999) is in sympathy with this idea and supportive of the multiple metaphorical lens approach advocated by Morgan (1988). Willmott (1993) and Hassard (1988, 1991) both reject the paradigm incommensurability thesis, but on different grounds. Hassard promotes a multiple paradigm research practice, repeated in this volume (chapter 2b), which states that paradigms are not fully incommensurable because there are points of contact or transition zones. He sees not only paradigm diversity in OS but increasing levels of methodological diversity, seen as a healthy antidote to the failed dominance of positivistic epistemology. The multi-paradigm position represents an alternative to either paradigm imperialism or paradigm isolationism.

We would argue that there are no paradigms in OS. Less dramatically we suggest that the use of the concept of paradigm has been misplaced and has misled the field into a time-consuming and redundant debate. It is widely acknowledged that the original Kuhnian conceptualization (Kuhn, 1962) was flawed in that the notion of paradigm was loosely and variously defined. Even Kuhn subsequently revised his views on paradigms significantly (Kuhn, 1970a, 1971). But more important in our view is that the notion of paradigm was developed in relation to the natural sciences – and physics in particular. It is significant to note that in his preface Kuhn tells us that it was the disparity between the fractious debates in the social science community over the legitimacy of research problems and methods and the relative quietude apparent in the natural science communities that was the motive for his investigation of paradigms. Given that the idea of a paradigm was developed in relation to a careful historico-philosophical investigation of the development of theories in the natural sciences, why should we expect such an investigation to have a bearing on developments in the social sciences? This can be the case only if we assume absolute equivalence between scientific endeavors, if we affirm the "unity of science" banner under which Kuhn's book was (ironically) published, regardless of the phenomena under investigation, if we assume a superordinate, single, unified, and monolithic conception of *all* science.

In his 1969 (Kuhn, 1970b) postscript to the original, Kuhn engages in some remedial repair following critiques of his work. He admits to the definitional confusion, suggesting that "paradigm" has been used both to delineate what unites a community of scientists and as a set of puzzle solutions that act as exemplars to a group of scientists. On reflection he finds the former inappropriate and replaces paradigm with "disciplinary matrix." The matrix is multifaceted but centrally includes "symbolic generalizations," beliefs in particular models, and shared values. The argument by McKelvey (chapter 2a) that if paradigms were truly incommensurable one would not be able to talk about them simultaneously is undercut by Kuhn's reinterpretation of disciplinary matrices. One can clearly talk about different "paradigms"; there is no inherent limitation in terms of available language or real problems of translation (as Kuhn makes clear in the postscript). Incommensurability, if there is any, rests on differential values and beliefs. This would be more akin to Castenada's struggle to understand the shaman's world view (Castenada, 1970) than it would be a problem of language. Paradigm, in Kuhn's revision, refers to the tacit knowledge that scientists acquire through solving problems and through the exemplars they draw upon to do so. This enables them to perceive phenomena and puzzles in terms of similarities with past situations and to apply routines provided by exemplars. It is not clear to us that this situation prevails in OS, or in most of the social sciences. Incommensurability may be manifest in different vocabularies but such difficulty is, in principle, translatable and thus surmountable, as long as the translation is two-way and contextually acute. More importantly, incommensurability is a function of tacitness and of variable values, which lead scientists to have different world views and perceptions of problems.

One might argue, as McKelvey (chapter 2a) does, that OS is not a science: that it is in a prescientific, preparadigmatic state. But this presumes too much and practises "physics envy" to a heightened degree. Not waiting for Godot, but waiting for Newton. We would prefer to argue that OS is not a science in the mold of a natural science, nor should it be; that the label of "science" must allow different forms of science to exist and not apply the canons of a presumedly uniform (itself contestable) conception of a natural science to all types of research and theorizing activity. Geology, evolutionary biology, and cosmology, for instance, are not generalizing sciences such as physics aspires to be for the simple reason that their data is already there, elapsed, fragmentary, and not subject to experimentation. McKelvey wants to push OS towards a particular type of scientific status informed by Campbellian realism, which he depicts as a viable postpositivist epistemology. He undercuts Hassard's and others' attack on positivist epistemology in OS by arguing that positivism was "epitaphed" by Suppe (1977). This is an argument repeated by Boal, Hunt, and Jaros (chapter 3a). In fact McKelvey would write the epitaph of most current OS researchers by arguing that they are, for the most part, classical positivists, flawed logical empiricists, or relativists, and that each of these epistemologies has no legitimate philosophical basis, and thus should be terminated with prejudice. He claims scientific realism, *à la* Suppe and Campbell, to be the epistemology that has informed the natural sciences for some time and regards it as the only viable epistemology if OS is to progress. However, whilst pronouncing on the delegitimation of positivism he suggests the "shibboleth" still lingers in OS – and cites Pfeffer and Donaldson as exemplars (see also McKelvey, 1999). Whilst undoubtedly Suppe's arguments have been influential, it is incorrect to suggest that his is the only contemporary epistemology of (natural) science that has coinage today or that it has not been contested (see, for example, Leplin, 1984; Papineau, 1996; Putnam, 1981). Among the alternatives that have wider acceptance than McKelvey gives credit are van Frassens' antirealist constructive empiricism (van Frassen, 1980), or other varieties of constructivism (e.g., Fosnot, 1996; Galison and Stump, 1996).

Point–counterpoint: constituting debates in OS

Foundational debates: ontology, epistemology, and methodology
These three issues represent the most elemental, persistent, and incisive of fractures in the OS discourse. They represent fundamental issues on which there continue to be radically different perspectives that have implications for the whole conduct of OS.

Whilst it is probably fair to say that for the vast majority of researchers in OS the *ontological* status of organizations and other organizational phenomena is nonproblematic and taken for granted, the ontological question is elemental to how the study of OS phenomena is conceived of and constituted. We have already signaled the importance of the issue at numerous points, indirectly, for example, with respect to the question of levels of analysis. That issue can reflect levels of comfort with notions of the ontology of individual persons as opposed to the existence of organizations as entities. Following from the discussion in the previous section, Boal, Hunt, and Jaros (chapter 3a) cite the philosophy of Russell and Moore to posit realist ontology in the classic sense of entities existing independently of our perception of them. They contrast this with subjectivism, symbolic or interpretive interactionism, social constructionism, and postmodernism. Like McKinley, they seek to distinguish between scientific realism and positivism – claiming that this allows them to include unobservable phenomena as real. The reality of scientific phenomena can be inferred from their effects even if the putative phenomena in question are not directly observable. A basis for the realist position is objectivity, which they assert against what they depict as postmodern objections based on the determination of reality by language/culture, as well as incommensurability arguments, the idea that certainty and truth are unattainable, and the view that observations are themselves already theory-laden.

In contrast to Boal, Hunt, and Jarros, Chia (chapter 3b) pursues a "becoming ontology" as opposed to the long tradition of a "being ontology" that posits reality as atomistic, thing-like, unchanging, and preformed. He shows how the particularity of Western thinking and ontology has been shaped by language, and particularly by the effects of the alphabet and typography. He sees organization as a process and definitely not as an entity – not even a socially constructed one. Organization is a process through which order is realized, and more fundamentally as a process for "real-izing the real" – or, as his title suggests, as a world-making process.

Ontological issues recur in several of the other contributions. As becomes apparent, it is virtually impossible to talk about *epistemology* and methodology without giving some consideration to ontology. We constituted this debate in terms of what remains perhaps the most central epistemic division in the discourse, that between what we would still term a positivistically informed position and one that is social constructivist. We hold to the view that the dominant orthodoxy in organization theory is informed by an approach that emerged from a positivistic philosophy of science coupled with neostructural functionalism. Some areas of empirical OS have made little movement away from the classical hypothetico-deductive model. This is the position maintained by Donaldson, and he provides a succinct reprise of that here. He rejects the formal strictures of logical positivism but sustains a positivist and, at times, almost Popperian view of epistemology in OS. He is firm in his belief that such an approach offers the best prospect for delivering viable generalizations and for establishing causal relations beyond commonsense apprehension. Social constructionism, as far as Donaldson is concerned, will always fail to deliver this because it remains tied to mere description anchored to the historically specific and to accounts of individual intentions. He positions his type of positivism within a normal science paradigm of structural functionalism that is primarily manifest in OS in the form of contingency theory.

In disciplines/fields other than OS (for example, anthropology) the intellectual *Zeitgeist* has precipitated a challenge to the positivistic orthodoxy, one informed by questions posed by a deeper appreciation of the reflexive nature of knowledge and knowledge construction. As we have noted earlier there are various forms of constructivism opposed to positivism. In this volume Czarniawska (chapter 4b) outlines and defends social constructionism. Donaldson accuses social constructionism of only delivering at the level of common sense, which Czarniawska counters by suggesting that it is actually the study of common sense. Social constructionism is the attempt to examine how people construct a sense of social reality through their interactions. It also seeks to surface that which is taken-for-granted and studies how people construct their own ontologies. She maintains that social constructionism is not anti-realist in any naive sense, but that it is against essentialism.

The discussion of *methodology* (chapter 5) also dwells considerably on the terrain of ontology and epistemology. Orthodox OS aspires to the status of a "hard" science and has deployed methodologies that treat organizational phenomena as objectified entities, the properties of which can be captured as data and subjected to analysis. Aspirations to objectivity, replicability, validity, and reliability, and to practice that permits the unproblematic representation of underlying reality, have led to a strong preference for methodologies that enable the quantification of properties of a phenomenon and statistical manipulation of data that are taken to represent it. Empirical investigation is preceded by theory building, which identifies variables and anticipates their causal relationships, through the hypothetico-deductive method. Statistical manipulation seeks to reveal the nature and extent of the relationship between measured variables. Such revealed relationships, where they are in the predicted direction, support the theory, thus bolstering its claim to represent the reality of the area of the phenomenal world under investigation. Adherence to this methodological practice secures objective representations of organizational realities, even if periods of accumulation are required, and even if the current version of reality is tenuously subject to the possibility of future falsifiability. The practice and the representations offered are held to be value-free and uncontaminated by the presence of the researcher.

This has proven to be a highly robust orthodoxy and one that, essentially, remains dominant in OS studies. It has, however, come under progressive and increasing challenge, particularly from, to use a catchall, "interpretativist" epistemologies (including symbolic interactionist, ethnomethodological, and social constructivist perspectives). More recently, poststructuralist and postmodern perspectives have radically challenged the epistemological ground of organization studies and thus the methodologies by which it is presumed "knowledge" is constructed and represented. Two issues are at the heart of these more radical critiques. The first concerns representational issues, especially the capacity of orthodox methods adequately to represent phenomena. Not surprisingly, methodological practice is predicated in turn on ontology and epistemology. Once the entitative nature of organizations is questioned, making organizations into social constructions or texts, and once knowledge about organizations is problematized and decentered, the notion of appropriate methodological practice must also shift.

The second critical issue is the burgeoning awareness of reflexive practice, challenging the objectivity and value-free assumptions of orthodox positions. That objects of knowledge are socially constructed and that the researcher's subjectivity cannot be divorced from that process entails negation of the security of the sense that there is an objective reality that can be transparently represented. It is through research practice that the researcher reflexively makes available or constitutes the "objects" of and for investigation. Case (chapter 5b) cites Cicourel's (1964) warnings about how language, cultural meanings, and the properties of measurement all construct a frame through which the researcher observes, selects, and filters phenomena. There are no pre-existing phenomena outside of this "grid." In this sense scientific theories and explanations are themselves social constructions, as admitted by Donaldson (chapter 4a). Consequently, debate about methodology is actually a language game in which participants move in a Foucauldian power–knowledge nexus. Case wants to join Feyerabend (1975) in a celebration of methodological diversity, seeing orthodox empiricism as only one pathway to representation and knowledge. But he does not propose methodological anarchy without ethical responsibility, hence his notion of *subjective authenticity*, and, as we have seen, he sees neopositivism, as both epistemology and method, as "morally dubious" in its deterministic, reductive, and manipulative effects.

In somewhat similar vein, Linstead (1993) proposed a deconstructive ethnography for which the practices by which representations of the "real" are mounted within mundane (organizational) contexts become the "object" of study. In other words, this proposes research that does not offer up a representation of organizational phenomena so much as interrogate the means by which organization members produce such representations, and seek to have them accepted and legitimized, and thus deconstruct such practice. Ethnography, while not new to OS, can be seen as a more viable methodology than the representational number fetishism of orthodoxy. Ethnography does not impose *a priori* structures and categories on to the phenomena under investigation; it does not objectify and seek transparently to represent, and it is capable of attending to issues of reflexivity. The challenge is not to make reality problematic through practices that aim to reveal pluralities but rather to question the means by which any such representation is accomplished.

McKinley's (chapter 5a) counterposition also focuses on the objective–subjective dichotomy and accepts that the abstractions that social scientists deal with in their theorizing are social constructions. The issue is the nature and quality of such constructions. Objectivity, from his perspective, is gained via the achievement of a construct consensus that overrides subjective idiosyncrasies. There is a need for consensus over construct definition, argues McKinley, and he has gone so far as to suggest a "democratically produced construct dictionary" to achieve this (McKinley and Mone, 1998). (It sounds a little bit like Godard's *Alphaville*: a place where words – and their associated concepts – can easily disappear.) He argues that OS is in a weak state because of its limited construct consensus and that postmodern approaches, whilst providing operational creativity, inhibit the emergence of such consensus through a surfeit of creative imagination. Abstracted, constructed, consensually agreed constructs should be the phenomena that OS deals with. This would resolve the ontological dilemma, since the objectification that a definitional consensus process brings about would provide/produce object-like phenomena for investigation.

Framing debates: environment, institution, globe

The three debates featured in Part II are all concerned, in very different ways, with the wider context in which organizations are constituted and function.

The relationship between organizations and their *environments* has been an ever-present central concern within OS, and various formulations have addressed the relationship. As with other issues, there are paradigmatic matters of ontology and epistemology that underpin the different perspectives taken. There have been disparities with regard to the various degrees of determinism that the external environment exerts with respect to organizational form and functioning. There have also, as a corollary, been discussions about the nature and permeability of any boundary between organizations and their environments. Some perspectives argue from a more determinist position, suggesting that elements in the environment are responsible for the determination of organizational form and function. A variant on this is population ecology, which offers a Darwinian-type explanation of the capacity of an environment to support a given population of organizations (Hannan and Freeman, 1977, 1989), with implications for how organizations are structured to ensure "fit" with the environment in order to ensure their survival. Even aspects of institutional theory have determinist elements, albeit in a different form from those of population ecology. The alternative is to give greater credence to the interpretive and determining power of organizational actors. This debate was rehearsed early on in organization theory (e.g., debates between John Child, Howard Aldrich, and the Aston school) but continues to be a current theme. The debates also abut with the question of the limits and form of rational decision making within organizations.

The population ecology and organizational evolutionary perspectives continue to be a vital subfield within OS (Baum and Singh, 1994; Hannan and Carroll, 1992; Hannan and Freeman, 1989; Singh, 1990). We could have constituted a debate from within, or in juxtaposition to, that project. (For a recent overview, including internal contestations, see Baum, 1999.) Instead we elected for a more subtle debate around Weick's notion of enactment. We originally anticipated an engagement between contemporary interpretations of environmental determinism and the notions of sense making and enactment championed by Weick. However, Jennings and Greenwood's account (chapter 6b) is appreciative of Weick's position and actually seeks some rapprochement between enactment and institutional theory. They attempt this in view of their interpretation that the conundrum for an enactment perspective is explaining exogenous sources of change in institutional arrangements whilst the conundrum for enactment "theory" is explaining endogenous sources. Weick (chapter 6a) clarifies some of the misunderstandings that have arisen around enactment.

Jennings and Greenwood's contribution provides a very fruitful segue into the next debate around *power and institution*. We have noted earlier that, although in some respects power is fundamental to the very constitution of organization, it has languished in a relatively neglected or impoverished state for much of OS's history. This is partly a result of attempts to delegitimate power in theories of bureaucracy which stressed the formal and impersonal rule of authority. Subsequently, however, power has emerged conceptually as both an inherent structural feature of organizations and as a resource that organization parties can marshal to exert influence. The dominant theoretical underpinning has focused on some form of dependence model, following Dahl's classic formulation, which has been extended into organizational theory through strategic contingency theory. More recently, following Clegg's (1989) work, a conception of power/institutions, influenced by Foucauldian theory, has developed. The debate here was not constituted directly in terms of power, but rather in terms of the power–institution relationship. We have already outlined the core orientation of institutional theory (IT) in terms of organizational forms/structures having symbolic as well as functional resonances. The symbolic properties of organizations draw upon and refer to the institutional context in which a particular organization is situated. The symbolic properties must resonate with and draw support from the institutional environment and the values and interests represented therein. Thus, organization forms are determined by expectations of what types of structures and practices are likely to meet with institutional support, disregarding the utility of those structural choices for matters of internal functionality and efficiency. It is an approach imbued with a functionalist purview, although, as noted, there is some sophistication in current renditions and their focus on the processes of institutionalization. Lounsbury (chapter 7a) provides a very cogent account of institutional theory, particularly in terms of the concerns of new institutionalism and other developments in the area. He is particularly keen to demonstrate how institutional theory is moving to counter criticisms that it has failed to address issues of agency, power, and change.

The debate with Phillips occurs around issues of power, agency, and the processes of institutionalization. Phillips is critical of institutional theory's focus on the constraining effects of institutions to the neglect of their enabling effects. He is further at odds with what he sees to be a neglect of micro-level issues and processes and of the textual or discursive constitution of institutional theory. Indeed, he mounts his attack from the position of critical discourse theory. He wants to see institutions as socially constructed in and through discourse – and argues that institutional theory neglects the *processes* of institutionalization, claiming that it focuses on effects, not construction processes. Critical discourse theory draws upon a social constructivist epistemology to analyze *how* institutions are brought into being as discursive accomplishments. Their textual nature means that they are tenuous and in a state of flux, thus conditions of change are brought more into the foreground. Since discourses are also processes of knowledge–power, critical discourse theory is better able to address power issues in the institutionalization process.

We now turn to *globalization*, which, to be frank, we elected to pursue rather less for its extant theoretical contribution to OS than for the imperative that OS come to terms with its implications.

In setting up the debate we conceived of the issue broadly, recognizing the reality of globalization processes, but also recognizing that the exact nature of globalization remains problematic and contested. In particular we wanted to have the issues of globalization addressed in terms of its manifestation and impact, not only on international business and finance, but also in all other cultural spheres. The arguments typically produced in the international business literature suggest that globalization has distinct implications for business strategies, structures, and practices, and that as these become clearer their adoption is essential for business success and competitive advantage. Others extend the argument, suggesting that globalization will bring benefits beyond those accruing to corporations. Variously it is argued that globalization can encourage national economic and social development, aid international understanding and reduce conflict, facilitate the spread of democracy, and so on. Others suggest that this kind of argument serves as a rhetorical device driven by the aspirations of political-business elites, while it masks a less positive reality. Critics argue that the sociocultural aspects of globalization are neglected in the rationalist economic/business rendering. The accusation is that it has more than a taint of postcolonial imperialism about it. The benefits may accrue to the First World (although even that is contested by some), but the Third World will be further marginalized and impoverished in the process. Some nations, communities, and groups may not only fail to benefit materially and economically from the process, but damage may be done to sociocultural systems, and even to the range of distinctive or perhaps unique cultural identities valorized within these systems. The perspective adopted by international business advocates is really only an extension of the kind of orientalist mindset that has characterized Western discourse and its relations with the "other" from the beginnings of colonial expansion onwards.

Whilst both contributors provide a nuanced and detailed analysis, Jones's (chapter 8b) purview is the more gloomy and critical. He focuses more on the fragmenting and marginalizing structural effects of the globalization project of advanced capitalism. He sees the socioeconomic formation being reconfigured into a privileged "techno" economy and a disadvantaged and disenfranchised "grunge" and informal economy. The transnational corporation (TNC) is, in his view, central to and constitutive of this structural formation and is effects. Parker (chapter 8a) tries to locate and analyze a balance of effects of globalization – some negative and destructive, admittedly, but some also positive and developmental. She argues that globalization has inclusionary effects as well as exclusionary. A key feature of her position is that TNCs are but one player, and that it is meaningless to caricature them as purveyors of evil. The reality is that TNCs are just part of a complex network of relationships between local and global organizations involving commercial enterprises, state bodies, communities and NGOs as well as other players in the not-for-profit and voluntary sectors. In that complex network the effects of globalization are materialized and debated over – such effects are neither uniformly bad nor uniformly good.

Debating structure and culture: entity versus process

The debates in Part III deal with two aspects of organization that have generated among the most voluminous empirical and theoretical output: organizational structure and organizational culture. The former has been the subject of intense and central scrutiny since OS came into being. The latter is more recent, but has generated intense interest both practically and theoretically since the 1980s. In the debates constituted here we have two of the most sharply delineated sets of positions in the whole volume.

Within the functionalist paradigm, *structural* contingency theory has occupied a position at the heart of organization design/structure orthodoxy. It addresses the complexities associated with determining organizational effectiveness in the light of the obvious realization that no single structural form is optimally effective as a vehicle for the attainment of organizational goals. Optimal structures are contingent upon a range of variables impinging on organizations such as size, technology, task uncertainty, and strategy. These are characteristics of the organization but are themselves dependent upon the environment in which the organization functions in terms, for example, of its turbulence and complexity. Organization effectiveness is a function of the capacity to develop/design organization structures that "fit" these contingent conditions. The theory, at its core, is one of environmental adaptation. It is a view of organization structure and design that has been championed by Donaldson and Pfeffer and continues to be the theoretic rational for much of the research and explanation in OS. Üsdiken and Pasadeos (1993) have shown in their analysis of citations that positivist approaches in general, and contingency theory in particular, are still central to US-based organization theorists. Hinings (chapter 9a) regards the emergence of organization theory as a distinct subject separate from the sociology of organizations as an effect of its promulgation of structural contingency theory. Indeed, he sees the question of structure as having been the root question in OS since its foundations in Weber. Structure also remains central to what Hinings sees as a second key strand of contemporary organization theorizing, namely approaches that seek to explain organizational variation through identifying configurations and constructing typologies. The significance of establishing a thorough and complex taxonomy for the development of OS has also been emphasized by McKelvey (2001). Hinings admits that the value of taxonomizing is that it can reduce complexity. He goes on to discuss the centrality and criticality of structure, albeit from a different viewpoint, for both population ecology and institutional theory. Structure, he argues, is also at the center of more recent debates about new organizational forms and organizational transformations.

Structural contingency theory has been critiqued from a variety of perspectives. Social constructivist arguments suggest that it represents an abstract, determinist view of organization structure devoid of human agency and blind to the emergent, socialized generation of structures. It has also been challenged on the basis of an unwarranted continuing adherence to functionalism and/or a form of systems adaptation theorizing with roots in organicist and evolutionary rhetoric. A more radical challenge is provided by postmodernist or deconstructive approaches in which the notion of organization is itself made problematic. Cooper (1986), for example, in deconstructing the notion of organization, shows how organization is inscribed out of dis-organization, which, through reversal, becomes the prior state. He also destabilizes the notion of organization structure by working with notions of margin and supplementarity, which disassemble the boundary of organization.

Munro (chapter 9b) maintains that structural contingency theory has failed to respond to the challenge of social interactionism, the turn to culture, and the sociology of organizations' earlier concerns with the more generic question of "social order" and the varied responses to that problematic than contingency theory chooses to acknowledge. More damagingly, he argues that, pragmatically, there is a turn away by enterprises from the concern for structure as organizations practically seek out flexibility and a multitude of mutations and variations of organizational forms and relationships have proliferated. He argues that contingency theory has imploded, since a rationale for structure is now virtually incidental to the defining forces of markets. There is no single, simple form of order – indeed, order is a process constantly at play with disorder. (There are echoes of Chia – chapter 3b – here.)

Structure is a rather irrelevant supplementarity to the real task of responding to markets and their dynamics. In opposition to the structural determinism of Hinings and Donaldson, Munro sees structure as an effect of interactional processes, or as a legitimating device or "rhetoric of motives." For him the rhetoric of structures and authority is dying, weakened by the struggle against market rhetoric, a rhetoric that actually seeks the dissolution of structures. Managers struggle in this newly constituted discursive clash. Their very role and function are disturbed and are under renegotiation. Managers must make themselves visible and in a sense construct their identities within the miasma of uncertain and shifting organizational and market forces. Organizing is actually a matter of shifting relationships in which managers seek to find a location and a presence. It is a politicized process in which structure is found and then dismantled in an ongoing double process.

The *corporate culture* literature has shown explosive growth since the early 1980s, on both the academic and the popular fronts. An industry has grown up on the promise of achieving a type of organizational unitarianism, displaying coherence and unidirection-ality to enhance organizational performance without having to rely upon strategies of coercion or the expensive bureaucratic monitoring and control systems of the past. Apart from the skeptics who contest the value of the culture metaphor at all, and the very existence of corporate cultures, the most intense debates have been around three core issues. First, there has been contestation about the meaning, content, and operation of culture and the appropriateness of its extension from anthropology into organization studies. For some culture is merely metaphorical, if not rhetorical – a kind of managerialist textual strategy – whilst for others it is a complex of shared social values, symbolic representations and organizational practices that are concretely determining of individual and group motivation and behavior. Second, there is criticism of the presumption that there could be a unitary cultural form that embraces all organizational members and brings the desired motivational impetus: the type of unitarian ideal of which organizational practitioners have long dreamed. A value consensus has developed, it is argued, such that the "invisible hand" of culture has been seen to guide people's actions in appropriate directions, irrespective of what "really" happens. The critique is that organizations are inherently plural and that any presumed coherence is either a fiction or a politically accomplished outcome. Either way, if the notion of culture is to be retained, the notion of a unifying, monolithic single culture is increasingly seen to be untenable; instead, organizations need to be thought of as composed of multiple cultures, some of which may be antithetical to the "official culture." Third, there is the question of whether a culture can be "engineered" through managerial intervention and constructed in a determined, controllable, and controlled manner. Manipulations of values, of symbols, and of structures and practices have been variously advocated as ways to construct or alter the cultures of organizations. That this is a feasible project is strongly contested by those for whom these interventions are in violation of the very concept of "culture."

In this volume Ashkanasy (chapter 10a) presents an orthodox case for culture as an authentic phenomenon that has an impact on organizations and is measurable. He argues this from a structuralist realist perspective, in contrast to what he terms social interactionist and "linguistic convenience" ontologies. His conception of cultures is orthodox: he sees them as comprised of shared values, with universal values, that can be effectively measured. He accepts that cultures can be multilayered within an organization, but that there is still a determinable effect upon behavior and, albeit complex, also on performance. He is at pains to differentiate corporate culture from organizational climate. In contrast, Chan argues that culture is a process – it is a verb, an activity – not an entity. This parallels Chia's (chapter 3b) treatment of "organization" in general. For Chan culture is an accomplishment in which meaning is instantiated through words and deeds. It is an achievement of order in an ethnomethodological sense, always in flux and in need of renewal. Any determinable pattern is a *post facto* abstraction imposed on this process. Chan invokes a Weickian sense of enactment to depict the culture forming process.

Debating identity and relationships

Gender issues in organization studies have had a short but vigorous history. Informed originally by the pragmatics of discrimination and segmentation, and by the concerns of feminist critique, the issues have increased dramatically in complexity and sophistication. A critical point in contemporary debates centers on the conception of gender and its place and relevance in organizations and organization theory. On the one hand are those who have argued for notions of the gendered structuring of organizations from a position that sees this structural disadvantage as the main problematic to address. Those who support the articulation of gender differences and explore the implications of that difference for individuals and organizations are in a similar vein. In contrast to positions that take categories of gender as useful and tenable, either as given or as nonproblematical, are those who adopt a more radical, postmodern feminism. The issue here is to make categories of gender problematic by focusing on the processes by which gendered subjectivities and identities are constructed. This would entail an analysis of the location of gendered selves in the knowledge–power nexus. It is to these latter issues that Gherardi, Marshall, and Mills attend in chapter 11. They first question the debate structure proposed for the volume, and use that as a vehicle to launch into a discussion of the gendered nature of debate, inquiry, and explanation. There is much concern with the problem of a degendered epistemology. Part of this involves a discussion of the impossibility of getting outside a male-constructed language game and epistemic hegemony. Possible responses from within that prison house are to engage in the subversive and "eccentric" practices of hypocrisy, transgression, and irony.

The issue of *trust* has long been crucial in OS, given its centrality in all manner of coordinated human interaction and exchange. Whilst explicit in the early sociological deliberations of Weber, Simmel, and Parsons, trust has remained something of a subtext, perhaps apart from the important work of Alan Fox (1974), until its recent re-emergence center-stage during the 1990s. It is not easy to determine the motivating spirit behind the flurry of interest in the issue of trust. One view is to see it as an expected and belated return to a core aspect of human interaction. Another view would see it as a reaction to the partial dissolution of tight structures and the emergence of the more loosely coupled, contingent, temporary, and networked structure of many contemporary organizational forms and relationships. Still others would see it as partial offshoot of corporate culture perspectives where explicit controls are traded off against more tacit and implicit systems of control and coordination. Whatever the precipitating cause, the issue of trust has grabbed the attention of the academy.

As with corporate culture, trust has rapidly become seen as a strategic issue. Managers' attention has been drawn to the issue by consultants' offers to intervene and repair situations of distrust or to design contexts in which trust can be built into organizational practice and so enhance performance. Trust is fast becoming the new social cement (after culture) which will reintroduce coherence and stable order to organizations and relations between organizations. Such maneuvers are met with critical skepticism in some quarters, including

Sievers (chapter 12b). There is a dissenting view of trust, however: the regeneration of interest in trust may be a desperate response to the conditions of postmodernity. On this view, the turbulence, uncertainties, fragmentations, implosions, and dedifferentiations precipitated by postmodern conditions engender a search for fresh grounds for certainty and solidity in relationships and institutions, and trust is invoked to fill the void. Some see a kind of romantic nostalgia in this for the surety that bonds of interpersonal trust were presumed to provide in earlier times. From this perspective, nostalgia – the sickness of late modernity – may be seen as hopeless romanticism, at best; at worst it is a cynical rhetorical exercise designed to paper over the harsh realities of a sociality ineluctably inscribed by fragmentation, dissolution, turbulence, and *ennui*. The disbelief in the power of grand narratives, the end of history and its teleology, the loss of attachment to various certainties postulated through representations of a world of simulacra, the dissolution of identity, these are all features of the postmodern that seem to auger a systemic climate of distrust. This is an age of anxiety, one that would more likely see neurosis in play – for which nostalgia is a symptom – rather than trust.

Kramer (chapter 12a) provides an admirably balanced account of trust. He argues for the "virtues of trust," and supports his account with a careful analysis of the evidence to date, but he is wary of any naivety and urges that the virtues be pursued with prudence. He is suspicious of the blandishments of the abundant populist claims for the achievement and benefits of trust that have been so current in recent years. He outlines the benefits of trust for organizations in terms of its role in reducing transaction costs, generating spontaneous sociability, and facilitating "appropriate forms of deference to authority." He also discusses alternatives to trust, as various "proxies" for personalized knowledge, such as role-based and rule-based trust.

Sievers (chapter 12b) is "distrustful of popularism and supposed attempts at engineering trust. This is unsurprising, given that he generally interprets modern organizations as characterized by "psychotic and perverse dynamics." Organizations are characterized by an absence of trust that is masked and repressed. The current concern with trust is, for him, an indication that something is wrong – that trust is absent from relationships. He traces the etymology of trust to "faith," as well as to risk, but claims this too is repressed. As in his previous work on motivation (Sievers 1986), he sees trust as a pale substitute for the lack of meaning that the world of work presents to most people. He argues that the discourse on trust currently lacks depth in that it does not question assumptions about the nature of people or organizations, or even the concept of trust itself. It also lacks a macro-perspective in terms of wider context: there is too much emphasis on the individual or social psychological level. The emphasis is on a managerial engineering of trust that neglects broader organizational and societal factors that shape and frame it. Finally, he suggests that the methods advocated emphasize rational and behavioral aspects but neglect unconscious dynamics of trust.

Conclusion: Debatable Evaluation

The book is a success, not only because of the quality of the contributions but also because we draw together diverse perspectives that create a polyphonous and energetically charged space within the covers of one book. In this respect, we have produced – orchestrated – the book we wanted. But we also received more than we assumed we had wanted and we are thankful for that. We received notice that the book is partly flawed because of the format of debate within which we conceived it. As some of our contributors make quite clear, debate such as is constructed within its covers can be seen to reproduce power relations, particularly those that are gendered, and the debate format fails to engender engagement that is always fruitful. But against such criticisms, which may lead ultimately to abdication and silence, or, in what may be the same effect, to "disengenderment" and disengagement, we are appreciative of the fact that we have produced some engagement that otherwise might not have happened. In fact a number of points of proposed or hinted rapprochement do emerge.

One source of disquiet, which is, perhaps, characteristic of a prolix, complex, and polyphonic field, is the extent of Don Quixotism that has been revealed on almost all sides, with conceptual windmills repeatedly set up for easy – and pyrrhic – victory because the analytic lances, as they pierce, glance back on to the protagonist, revealing mutual ignorance. The critique of positions that are less than wholly comprehended in anything like their own terms seems to be a common characteristic of what passes for engagement in our field. Clearly, there is a continued need for the development of OS as a field of plurality, where, with careful cultivation, not only a thousand flowers might bloom, but also the skills of good husbandry that enable those who tend some crops to see value and worth in other crops, perhaps enriching the quality of their own product through selective cross-pollination.

Whether the type of pragmatic intercourse that we trust the book will engender will be a consequence of its use by students, colleagues, and researchers – and we hope that it will – we think that one fruitful outcome is to have taken us even further away from nostalgia for OS's fall from some earlier state of theoretical grace, a theoretical Eden, where the Tower of Babel was yet to be built. It is a fact that some colleagues, some texts, and some courses, regularly regale those held captive in their thrall to such Creation myths. With such views we would urge our readers to have no truck. We believe that one positive impact the book is likely to make is in its use as a practical resource for exploration and debate of various positions within the actual disposition of the field – rather than being reinforcements for those already arming the barricades of various theoretical dogmas.

Finally, our verdict is that the book achieves much of what we sought: it is open but structured, querulous but designed, and finished but not complete. For that we require you, dear reader.

NOTES

1 Originally published in 1931 as *Onward Industry*.
2 There is no space here for an elaboration of the roots of postmodernism (and readers will no doubt be aware of the foundational impact of various Continental philosophers and social analysts such as Foucault, Derrida, Baudrillard, Jameson, Deleuze, and Lyotard). We could play the game of spotting the genesis of postmodernism – what was the role of Nietzsche or de Sade, the impact of Dadaism, situationism and surrealism, the platform construction of Saussure and Wittgenstein? But these intellectual pursuits – fascinating as the detective work is – do not really help us here. An anthology (Cahoone, 1996) attributes the first use of the term "postmodern" to the German philosopher Pannwitz in 1917. We would refer the reader to that anthology for an extensive orientation to postmodernism – others can be found in Best and Kellner (1991), Harvey (1989), Seidman and Wagner (1992), and Turner (1990).

3 We are not entirely comfortable with this mode of categorization either.
4 Interesting that this quotation is an example of itself!
5 The Australian Labor Party (ALP) and the Liberal Party (the latter being, in coalition, the incumbent party in power).
6 For example, it would be difficult to locate Weick in mainstream orthodoxy. The radicalness of the Weickean stance is, however, itself debatable.

REFERENCES

Aldrich, H. E. (1979) *Organizations and Environments*. Englewood Cliffs, NJ: Prentice Hall.
——(1988) Paradigm warriors: Donaldson versus the critics of organization theory. *Organization Studies*, 9 (1): 19–25.
Allen, V. L. (1974) *Social Analysis: A Marxist Critique and Alternative*. London and New York: Longman.
Alvesson, M., and Willmott, H., eds (1992) *Critical Management Studies*. London: Sage.
Astley, W. G., and Van de Ven, A. H. (1983) "Central perspectives and debates in organization theory," *Administrative Science Quarterly*, 28: 245–70.
Atkinson, M. (1971) *Orthodox Consensus and Radical Alternative: A Study in Sociological Theory*. London: Heinemann.
Barnard, C. I. (1938) *The Functions of the Executive*. Cambridge, MA: Harvard University Press.
Baum, J. A. C. (1999) "Organizational ecology," in S. R. Clegg and C. Hardy (eds) *Studying Organization: Theory and Method*, pp. 71–108. London: Sage.
Baum, J. A. C., and Singh, J., eds (1994) *Evolutionary Dynamics of Organizations*. New York: Oxford University Press.
Berger, P. L. (1966) *Invitation to Sociology*. Harmondsworth: Penguin.
Berger, P. L., and Luckmann, T. (1965) *The Social Construction of Reality*. New York: Doubleday.
Bernstein, R. J. (1991) *The New Constellation: The Ethical–Political Horizons of Modernity/Postmodernity*. Cambridge: Polity Press.
Best, S., and Kellner, D. (1991) *Postmodern Theory: Critical Interrogations*. London: Macmillan.
Beyer, J. M., and Trice, H. M. (1982) "The utilization process: a conceptual framework and synthesis of empirical findings," *Administrative Science Quarterly*, 27: 591–622.
Beynon, H. (1973) *Working for Ford*. Harmondsworth: Penguin/Allen Lane.
Bittner, E. (1965) "The concept of organization," *Social Research*, 32 (3): 239–55.
Bjorkegren, D. (1993) "What can organization and management learn from art?" in John Hassard and Martin Parker (eds) *Postmodernism and Organizations*. London: Sage.
Blau, P. M., and Schoenherr, R. (1971) *The Structure of Organizations*. New York: Basic Books.
Blau, P. M., and Scott, W. R. (1962) *Formal Organizations*. San Francisco: Chandler.
Boje, D. (1991) "Organizations as storytelling networks: a study of story performance in an office supply firm," *Administrative Science Quarterly*, 36: 106–26.
——(1995) "Stories of the storytelling organization: a postmodern analysis of Disney as 'Tamara-land'," *Academy of Management Journal*, 38 (4): 997–1035.
Boje, D., Alvarez, R. C., and Schooling, B. (2001) "Reclaiming story in organization: narratologies and action sciences," in R. I. Westwood and S. Linstead (eds) *The Language of Organization*, pp. 132–75. London: Sage.
Braverman, H. (1974) *Labor and Monopoly Capital*. New York: Monthly Review Press.
Brewis, J. (1999) "How does it feel? Women managers, embodiment and changing public sector culture," in S. Whitehead and R. Moodley (eds) *Transforming Managers: Gendering Change in the Public Sector*, pp. 84–106. London: Taylor & Francis.

——(2000) "Sex, work and sex at work: using Foucault to understand organizational relations," in J. Barry, J. Chandler, H. Clark, R. Johnston, and D. Needle (eds) *Organization and Management: A Critical Text*, pp. 70–96. London: Thompson.

Brewis, J., and Linstead, S. (2000) *Sex, Work, and Sex Work: Eroticising Organisation*. London: Sage.

Brewis, J., Hampton, M. P., and Linstead, S. (1997) "Unpacking Priscilla: subjectivity and identity in the organization of gendered appearance," *Human Relations*, 50 (10): 1275–304.

Burrell, G. (1988) "Modernism, postmodernism and organizational analysis" II, "The contribution of Michel Foucault," *Organization Studies*, 9 (2): 221–35.

——(1993) "Eco and the bunnymen," in John Hassard and Martin Parker (eds) *Postmodernism and Organizations*. London: Sage.

——(1997) *Pandemonium: Towards a Retro-organization Theory*. London: Sage.

——(1999) "Normal science, paradigms, metaphors, discourses and genealogies of analysis," in S. R Clegg and C. Hardy (eds) *Studying Organization: Theory and Method*, pp. 388–404. London: Sage.

Burrell, G., and Morgan, G. (1979) *Sociological Paradigms and Organizational Analysis*. London: Heinemann.

Cahoone, L., compiler (1996) *From Modernism to Postmodernism: An Anthology*. Oxford: Blackwell.

Calas, M., and Smircich, L. (1991) "Voicing seduction to silence leadership," *Organization Studies*, 12 (4): 567–601.

Cancian, F. M., and Armstead, C. (1992) "Participatory research," in E. F. Borgatta and M. Borgatta (eds) *Encyclopedia of Sociology* III. New York: Macmillan.

Castenada, C. (1970) *The Teachings of Don Juan: A Yacqui Way to Knowledge*. Harmondsworth: Penguin.

Chan, A. (2000) *Critically Constituting Organization*. Amsterdam and Philadelphia: Benjamins.

Chia, R. (1996) *Organizational Analysis: A Deconstructive Approach*. Berlin and New York: de Gruyter.

——(1998) *In the Realm of Organization: Essays for Robert Cooper*. London: Routledge.

Child, J. (1972) "Organisational structure, environment and performance: the role of strategic choice," *Sociology*, 6 (1): 1–22.

Cicourel, A. (1964) *Method and Measurement in Sociology*. New York: Free Press.

Clegg, S. R. (1975) *Power, Rule, and Domination*. London: Routledge.

——(1979) *The Theory of Power and Organization*. London: Routledge.

——(1987) "The language of power and the power of language," *Organization Studies*, 8: 61–70.

——(1989) *Frameworks of Power*. London: Sage.

——(1990) *Modern Organizations: Organization Studies in a Postmodern World*. London: Sage.

Clegg, S. R., and Dunkerley, D. (1980) *Organization, Class and Control*. London: Routledge.

Clegg, S. R., and Hardy, C. (1999a) *Studying Organization: Theory and Method*. London: Sage.

——(1999b) "Introduction," in S. R. Clegg and C. Hardy (eds) *Studying Organization: Theory and Method*, pp. 1–22. London: Sage.

Clegg, S. R., Hardy, C., and Nord, W., eds (1996) *Handbook of Organization Studies*. London and Thousand Oaks, CA: Sage.

Coase, R. (1937) "The nature of the firm," *Economica*, 4: 386–405.

Cooper, R. (1986) "Organization/disorganization," *Social Science Information*, 25 (2): 299–335.

——(1987) "Information, communication and organization: a poststructural revision," *Journal of Mind and Behaviour*, 8 (3): 395–416.

——(1989) "Modernism, postmodernism and organization analysis: the contribution of Jacques Derrida," *Organization Studies*, 10 (4): 479–502.

——(1993) "Technologies of representation," in P. Ahonen (ed.) *Tracing the Semiotic Boundaries of Politics*, pp. 279–312. Berlin: Mouton de Gruyter.

Cooper, R., and Burrell, G. (1988) "Modernism, postmodernism and organizational analysis: an introduction," *Organization Studies* 9 (1): 91–112.

Culler, J. (1983) *On Deconstruction: Theory and Criticism after Structuralism*. London: Routledge.

Cyert, R. M., and March, J. M. (1963) *A Behavioral Theory of the Firm*. Englewood Cliffs, NJ: Prentice Hall.

Czarniawska, Barbara (1992) *Exploring Complex Organizations: A Cultural Perspective*. Newbury Park, CA: Sage.

——(1998) *A Narrative Approach to Organization Studies*. Thousand Oaks, CA: Sage.

Dandeker, C. (1990) *Surveillance: Power and Modernity*. Cambridge: Polity Press.

Derrida, J. (1976) *Of Grammatology*. Baltimore, MD: Johns Hopkins University Press.

DiMaggio, P. J. (1988) "Interest and agency in institutional theory," in L. G. Zucker (ed.) *Institutional Patterns and Organizations: Culture and Environment*, pp. 3–22. Cambridge, MA: Ballinger.

DiMaggio, P. J., and Powell, W. W. (1983) "The iron cage revisited: institutional isomorphism and collective rationality in organizational fields," *American Sociological Review*, 48: 147–60.

——eds (1991) *The New Institutionalism in Organizational Analysis*. Chicago: University of Chicago Press.

Donaldson, L. (1985) *In Defence of Organization Theory: A Reply to the Critics*. Cambridge: Cambridge University Press.

——(1988) "In successful defence of organization theory: a routing of the critics," *Organization Studies*, 9 (1): 28–32.

——(1990) "The ethereal hand: organizational economics and management theory," *Academy of Management Review*, 15: 369–81.

——(1995) *American Anti-management Theories of Organization: A Critique of Paradigm Proliferation*. Cambridge and New York: Cambridge University Press, 1995.

Elden, M., and Chisholm, R., eds (1993) *Varieties of Action Research*, special issue of *Human Relations* 46 (2).

Eldridge, J. E. T., and Crombie, A. D. (1974) *A Sociology of Organizations*. London: Allen & Unwin.

Fals-Borda, O., and Rahman, M. A. (1991) *Action and Knowledge: Breaking the Monopoly with Participatory Action Research*. New York: Intermediate Technology/Apex.

Fayol, H. (1916/1949) *General and Industrial Management*. London: Pitman.

Feyerabend, P. (1975) *Against Method*. London: New Left Books.

Fischer, F. (1990) *Technocracy and the Politics of Expertise*. Newbury Park, CA: Sage.

Forester, J., ed. (1985) *Critical Theory and Public Life*. Cambridge, MA: MIT Press.

Fosnot, C., ed. (1996) *Constructivism: Theory, Perspectives, and Practice*. New York: Teachers' College Press.

Foster, H. (1983) *Postmodern Culture*. London: Pluto Press.

Foucault, M. (1980) *Power/Knowledge: Selected Interviews and other Writings, 1972–1977*, ed. C. Gordon. Brighton: Harvester Press.

Fox, Alan (1974) *Beyond: Contract: Work, Power and Trust Relations*. London: Faber.

Freeman, J. (1982) Organizational life cycles and natural selection processes, in B. M. Staw and L. L. Cummings (eds) *Research in Organizational Behaviour* IV, pp. 1–32. Greenwich, CT: JAI Press.

Gabriel, Y. (1991) "On organizational stories and myths: why is it easier to slay a dragon than to kill a myth?" *International Sociology*, 6 (4): 427–42.

——(1995) "The unmanaged organization: stories, fantasies and subjectivity," *Organization Studies*, 16 (3): 477–501.

——(1997) "Meeting God: when organizational members come face to face with the supreme leader," *Human Relations*, 50 (4): 315–42.

Galison, P., and Stump, D., eds (1996) *The Disunity of Science: Boundaries, Contexts, and Power*, Stanford, CA: Stanford University Press.

Gaus, J. M. (1936) "A theory of organizations in public administration," in *The Frontiers of Public Administration*. Chicago: University of Chicago Press.

Goffman, E. (1961) *Asylums: Essays on the Social Situation of Mental Patients and other Inmates*. Garden City, NY: Anchor Books.

Granovetter, M. (1985) "Economic action and social structure: the problem of embeddedness," *American Journal of Sociology*, 91: 481–510.

Grant, D., Kinnoy, T., and Oswick, C., eds (1998) *Discourse and Organization*. London: Sage.

Gulick, L., and Urwick, L. (1937) *Papers on the Science of Administration*. New York: Institute of Public Administration, Columbia University.

Hall, B., Gillette, A., and Tandon, R., eds (1982) *Creating Knowledge: A Monopoly?* Participatory Research in Development. New Delhi: Society for Participatory Research in Asia.

Hannan, M., and Carroll, G. R. (1992) *Dynamics of Organizational Populations: Density, Competition and Legitimation*. New York: Oxford University Press.

Hannan, M., and Freeman, J. (1977) "The population ecology of organizations," *American Journal of Sociology*, 82: 929–64.

——(1989) *Organizational Ecology*. Cambridge, MA: Harvard University Press.

Hardy, C. (1994) "Understanding interorganizational domains: the case of refugee systems," *Journal of Applied Behavioral Science*, 30 (3): 278–96.

Harvey, D. (1989) *The Condition of Postmodernity*. Oxford and Cambridge, MA: Blackwell.

Hassard, J. (1988) "Overcoming hermeticism in organization theory: an alternative to paradigm incommensurability," *Human Relations*, 41 (3): 247–59.

——(1991) "Multiple paradigms and organizational analysis: a case study," *Organization Studies*, 12 (2): 275–99.

——(1993) *Sociology and Organization Theory: Positivism, Paradigms and Postmodernity*. London: Sage.

Hassard, J., and Parker, M., eds (1993) *Postmodernism and Organizations*. London: Sage.

Hassard, J., and Pym, D., eds (1990) *The Theory and Philosophy of Organizations: Critical Issues and New Perspectives*. London: Routledge.

Hassard, J., Holliday, R., and Willmott, H., eds (2000) *Body and Organization*. London: Sage.

Hesse, E. (1980) *Revolutions and Reconstructions in the Philosophy of Science*. Bloomington, IN: Indiana University Press.

Hirsch, P. M., and Lounsbury, M. (1997) "Ending the family quarrel: toward a reconciliation of 'old' and 'new' institutionalisms," *American Behavioral Scientist*, 40: 406–18.

Hyman, R. (1975) *Industrial Relations: A Marxist Introduction*. London: Macmillan.

Jackson, N., and Carter, P. (1991) "In defence of paradigm incommensurability," *Organization Studies*, 12 (1): 109–207.

Jameson, F. (1991) *Postmodernism, or, The Cultural Logic of Late Capitalism*. Durham NC: Duke University Press.

Jermier, John M., Knights, David, and Nord, Walter R., eds (1994) *Resistance and Power in Organizations*. New York: Routledge.

Kallinicos, J. (1995) "The architecture of the invisible: technology as representation," *Organization*, 2 (1): 117–40.

Karreman, D. (2001) "The scripted organization: dramaturgy from Burke to Baudrillard," in R. Westwood and S. Linstead (eds) *The Language of Organization*, pp. 89–111. London: Sage.

Kast, F. E., and Rosenzweig, J. E. (1985) *Organization and Management: A Systems and Contingency Approach*, fourth edition. New York: McGraw-Hill.

Katz, D., and Kahn, R. L. (1966) *The Social Psychology of Organizations*. New York: Wiley.

Kerfoot, D., and Knights, D. (1993) "Management, masculinity and manipulation: from paternalism to corporate strategy in financial services," *Journal of Management Studies*, 30 (4): 659–77.

Kilduff, M. (1993) "Deconstructing organizations," *Academy of Management Review*, 18 (1): 13–31.

Koontz, H. (1961) "The management theory jungle," *Academy of Management Journal*, 4: 174–88.

——(1980) "The management theory jungle revisited," *Academy of Management Review*, 5: 175–187.

Kuhn, T. S. (1962) *The Structure of Scientific Revolutions*. Chicago: University of Chicago Press.

——(1970a) "Reflection on my critics," in I. Lakatos and A. Musgrave (eds) *Criticism and the Growth of Knowledge*. Cambridge: Cambridge University Press.

——(1970b) *The Structure of Scientific Revolutions*, second edition. Chicago: University of Chicago Press.

——(1971) "Second thoughts on paradigms," in F. Suppe (ed.) *The Structure of Scientific Theories*. Urbana, IL: University of Illinois Press.

Lawrence, P. R., and Lorsch, J. W. (1967) *Organizations and Environment*. Boston, MA: Harvard University, Graduate School of Business Administration.

Leplin, J., ed. (1984) *Scientific Realism*. Berkeley, CA: University of California Press.

Linstead, S. A. (1993) "From postmodern anthropology to deconstructive ethnography," *Human Relations*, 46 (1): 97–120.

Linstead, S., and Grafton-Small, R. (1992) "On reading organizational culture," *Organization Studies*, 13: 331–55.

Lyotard, J-F. (1979/1984) *The Postmodern Condition: A Report on Knowledge*. Manchester: Manchester University Press.

Mangham, I., and Overington, M. (1987) *Organizations as Theatre*. Chichester: Wiley.

March, J. G., and Simon, H. A. (1958) *Organizations*. New York: Wiley.

Marsden, R., and Townley, B. (1999) "The owl of Minerva: reflections on theory in practice," in S. R. Clegg and C. Hardy (eds) *Studying Organizations: Theory and Method*, pp. 405–21. London: Sage.

Martin, J. (1990) "Deconstructing organizational taboos: the suppression of gender conflict in organizations," *Organization Science*, 1 (4): 339–59.

Mayo, E. (1933) *The Human Problems of an Industrial Civilization*. New York: Macmillan.

McKelvey, B. (1997) "Quasi-natural organization science," *Organization Science*, 8: 351–80.

——(1999) "Toward a Campbellian realist organization science", in J. A. C. Baum and B. McKelvey (eds) *Variations in Organization Science: In Honor of Donald T. Campbell*, pp. 383–411. Thousand Oaks, CA: Sage.

——(2001) "Model-centered organization science epistemology," in J. A. C. Baum (ed.) *Companion to Organizations*, Thousand Oaks, CA: Sage.

McKinley, W., and Mone, M. A. (1998) "The re-construction of organization studies: wrestling with incommensurability," *Organization*, 5: 169–89.

McKinley, W., and Scherer, A. G. (2000) "Some unanticipated consequences of organizational restructuring," *Academy of Management Review*, 25: 735–52.

Merton, R. K. (1940) "Bureaucratic structure and personality," *Social Forces*, 18: 560–8.

——(1949) *Social Theory and Social Structure*. Glencoe, IL: Free Press.

Meyer, J., and Rowan, B. (1977) "Institutionalized organizations: formal structure as myth and ceremony," *American Journal of Sociology*, 83: 340–63.

Miliband, R. (1973) *The State in Capitalist Society*. London: Quartet.

Mintzberg, H. (1983) *Structuring in Fives: Designing Effective Organizations*. Englewood Cliffs, NJ: Prentice-Hall.

Mooney, J. D., and Reiley, A. C. (1939) *The Principles of Organization*. New York: Harper.

Morgan, G., ed. (1983) *Beyond Method*. London: Sage.

——(1988) *Images of Organization*. London: Sage.

Mouzelis, N. (1975) *Organization and Bureaucracy*, second edition. London: Routledge.

Mumby, Dennis K., ed. (1993) *Narrative and Social Control: Critical Perspectives*. Newbury Park, CA: Sage.

Nord, W. R., and Connell, A. F. (1993) From quicksand to crossroads: an agnostic perspective on conversation. *Organization Science*, 4 (1): 108–20.

Organization Studies (1988) Special issue *Offence and Defence*, 9 (1).

Papineau, D., ed. (1996) *The Philosophy of Science*. Oxford: Oxford University Press.

Parsons, T. (1956) "Suggestions for a sociological approach to the theory of organizations," *Administrative Science Quarterly*, 1: 63–85.

——(1964) "A sociological approach to the theory of organizations," in *Structure and Process in Modern Societies*. Glencoe, IL: Free Press.

Perrow, C. (1973) "The short and glorious history of organizational theory," *Organizational Dynamics*, 2: 2–15.

——(1986) "Economic theories of organization," *Theory and Society*, 15 (1) 11–45.

Pfeffer, J. (1982) *Organizations and Organization Theory*. Boston, MA: Pitman.

——(1993) "Barriers to the advance of organizational science: paradigm development as a dependent variable," *Academy of Management Review*, 18 (4): 599–620.

Pfeffer, J., and Salancik, G. (1978) *External Control of Organizations*. New York: Harper & Row.

Phillips, N. (1995) "Telling organizational tales: on the role of narrative fiction in the study of organizations," *Organization Studies*, 16 (4): 625–49.

Powell, W. W. (1991) "Expanding the scope of institutional analysis," in W. W. Powell and P. J. DiMaggio, *The New Institutionalism in Organizational Analysis*, pp. 183–203. Chicago: University of Chicago Press.

Powell, W. W., and DiMaggio, P. J. (1991) *The New Institutionalism in Organizational Analysis*. Chicago: University of Chicago Press.

Pugh, D. S., Hickson, D., and Hinings, R. (1969) "The context of organizational structures," *Administrative Science Quarterly*, 14: 91–114.

Putnam, H. (1981) *Reason, Truth and History*. Cambridge: Cambridge University Press.

Reason, P., ed. (1988) *Human Inquiry in Action*. London: Sage.

Reason, P., and Rowan, J., eds (1981) *Human Inquiry: A Sourcebook for New Paradigm Research*. Chichester: Wiley.

Reed, M. (1985) *Redirections in Organization Analysis*. London: Tavistock.

——(1992) *The Sociology of Organizations*. London: Harvester.

——(1996) chapter 1.1 of *Handbook of Organization Studies*. London: Sage.

——(1999) "Organization theorizing: a historically contested terrain," in S. R. Clegg and C. Hardy (eds) *Studying Organization: Theory and Method*, pp. 25–50. London: Sage.

Reed, M., and Hughes, M. D., eds (1992) *Rethinking Organization: New Directions in Organizational Research and Analysis*. London: Sage.

Rhodes, C. (2001) *Writing Organizations*. Amsterdam: Benjamins.

Richards, D. S. (2001) "Talking sense: ethnomethodology, postmodernism and practical action," in R. Westwood and S. Linstead (eds) *The Language of Organization*, pp. 20–46. London: Sage.

Richardson, L. (1992) "The consequences of poetic representation: writing the other, writing the self," in Carolyn Ellis and Michael G. Flaherty (eds) *Investigating Subjectivity: Research on Lived Experience*, pp. 125–37. Newbury Park, CA: Sage.

——(1994) "Writing: a method of inquiry," in N. K. Denzin and Y. S. Lincoln (eds) *Handbook of Qualitative Research*, pp. 516–29. Thousand Oaks, CA: Sage.

Roethlisberger, F. J., and Dickson, W. J. (1939) *Management and the Worker*. Cambridge, MA: Harvard University Press.

Rouse, J. (1994) "Power/knowledge," in G. Gutting (ed.) *The Cambridge Companion to Foucault*, pp. 92–114. Cambridge: Cambridge University Press.

Schutz, A. (1964) *Collected Papers*, ed. M. Natanson. The Hague: Nijhoff.

Schwandt, T. A. (1994) "Constructivist, interpretivist approaches to human inquiry," in N. K. Denzin and Y. S. Lincoln (eds) *Handbook of Qualitative Research*, pp. 118–37. Thousand Oaks, CA: Sage.

Scott, W. R. (1981) *Organizations: Rational, Natural, and Open Systems*. Englewood Cliffs, NJ: Prentice Hall.

Seidman, S., and Wagner, D. G., eds (1992) *Postmodernism and Social Theory*. Oxford: Blackwell.

Selznick, P. (1948) "Foundations of the theory of organization," *American Sociological Review*, 13: 25–35.

Sievers, Burkard (1986), "Beyond the surrogate of motivation," *Organization Studies* 7: 335–51.

Silverman, D. (1970) *The Theory of Organizations: A Sociological Framework*. London: English Language Book Society/Heinemann.

Silverman, D., and Jones, J. (1976) *Organizational Work: The Language of Grading/ The Grading of Language*. London and New York: Collier-Macmillan.

Simons, R. (1995) *Foucault and the Political*. London: Routledge.

Singh, J., ed. (1990) *Organizational Evolution: New Directions*. Newbury Park, CA: Sage.

Suppe, F. (1977) *The Structure of Scientific Theories*, second edition. Chicago: University of Chicago Press.

Taylor, M. C., and Saarinen, E. (1994) *Imagologies: Media Philosophy*. London: Routledge.

Townley, B. (1993) "Foucault, power/knowledge, and its relevance for human resource management," *Academy of Management Review*, 18: 518–45.

——(1994) *Reframing Human Resource Management: Power, Ethics and the Subject at Work*. London: Sage.

Travers, A. (1989) "Symbolic life and organizational research in a postmodern frame," in B. Turner (ed.) *Organizational Symbolism*, pp. 271–90. Berlin: de Gruyter.

Turner, B. S., ed. (1943) *Theories of Modernity and Postmodernity*. London: Sage.

Urwick, L. (1943) *The Elements of Administration*. New York: Harper.

Üsdiken, B., and Pasadeos, Y. (1995) "Organizational analysis in North America and Europe: a comparison of co-citation networks," *Organization Studies*, 16 (3): 503–26.

van Fraassen, Bas C. (1980) *The Scientific Image*. Oxford: Clarendon Press.

Van Maanen, J. (1995) "Fear and loathing in organizations," *Organization Studies*, 6 (6): 687–92.

Weick, K. E. (1969) *The Social Psychology of Organizing*. Reading, MA: Addison-Wesley.

Westwood, R. I. (1987) "Social criticism: a social critical practice applied to a discourse on participation," in I. L. Mangham (ed.) *Organization Analysis and Development*. London: Wiley.

——(1999) "A 'sampled' account of organization. Being a de-authored, reflexive parody of organization/ writing," *Studies in Cultures, Organizations and Societies*, 5: 195–233.

Williamson, O. E. (1975) *Markets and Hierarchies: Analysis and Antitrust Implications*. New York: Free Press.

——(1990) *Organization Theory: From Chester Barnard to the Present and Beyond*. New York: Oxford University Press.

Wilmott, H. (1993) "Breaking the paradigm mentality," *Organization Studies*, 14 (5): 681–719.

Wren, D. A. (1972) *The Evolution of Management Thought*. New York: Ronald Press.

Zimmerman, D. H. (1970) "Record keeping and the intake process in a public welfare organization," in S. Wheeler (ed.) *On Record*, pp. 319–54. New York: Russell Sage.

PART I

Foundations

2

Organization Studies: Discipline or Field?

COMMENTARY: WHAT KIND OF SCIENCE SHOULD ORGANIZATION STUDIES STRIVE TO BE?

"Can organization studies become a science?" It is this question that drives McKelvey's narrative. The appropriate answer, of course, as anyone who has had an education in philosophy would realise, is "It all depends on what you mean by a 'science'." McKelvey does not mean by a science something that would describe itself as positivist. Indeed, he argues that much of the critique of positivism within organization studies has been utterly misguided. It has critiqued a caricature rather than a contemporary practice. So, first, he slays a few Viennese sacred cows that still metaphorically hang around positivism from its inception as logical positivism. Clearing away the detritus that this leaves, he moves to a contemporary statement of what it is that scientists do when they do science, according to Suppe's philosophy of science. Nine tenets define this practice, none of which would be acceptable to logical positivism, all of which might readily be taken to describe some of what it is that scientists do when they do research. To be taken seriously, a critique of positivism would have to address these ten axioms rather than the old warhorse of logical positivism. Thus McKelvey rejects postmodernism because it does not take these seriously and because what it does take seriously is a critique of logical positivism. It also takes Kuhnian relativism seriously as well, according to McKelvey.

McKelvey identifies three kinds of relativism: ontological, epistemological and semantic, with a position of ontological relativism being seen as the strongly relativist position while the other two are weaker forms of relativism. The strong position claims that observation and facts are both theory-laden, a position that the author rejects as a feasible description of any observable practice in science. In fact, he finds organization studies in a parlous state; they can claim no feasible philosophy of science grounds for their practice and they suffer from low levels of institutional legitimacy.

Where organization studies seek legitimacy is in forms of postpositivism. There are two types: first, those that are labeled contra-science, usually seen as deriving from some irrationalist further expression of German romanticism/idealism. Second, there is post-Kuhnian philosophy of science, of one or other of three subtypes – scientific realism, evolutionary epistemology, and the Semantic Conception of Theories – the first two terms of which are subsequently collapsed to *Campbellian realism*. Few organization studies practitioners seem aware of the latter subtypes, according to McKelvey, and are mostly influenced by the former.

Campbell defines an adequate epistemology as one where the goal of objectivity in science is maintained in tandem with the possibility of using metaphysical terms and entities, such as causality, and which uses evolutionary epistemology to winnow out less probable theories, terms, and beliefs, allowing only the strong to survive, while avoiding the danger of systematically replacing metaphysical with operational terms. What will be winnowed out will be more fallible, individual interpretations and social constructions of the meanings of theory terms in favor of greater coherence. It replaces a correspondence theory of truth with one that is a coherence theory, elaborated at length in terms of the Semantic Conception of Theories.

After a detailed exegesis of the philosophies of science espoused, McKelvey turns his attention again to the field of organization studies, using the term "field" advisedly. It is a term deriving from Kuhn's vocabulary for describing a prescientific intellectual endeavor. Organization studies fit the term. So how will they advance from a field to a science? When they offer unquestionably convincing concrete solutions to central problems defined by the community of scientists, and ultimately users, and when they conclusively resolve fundamental issues of appropriate research problems and their solutions, elements to be studied, methods of observation, experimentation, and theorizing to establish reliable predictive success. What he sees as being crucial to scientific status is having concrete problem solutions on offer to powerful user groups. In descending order, these are owners, CEOs and managers, employees, constituencies worrying about externalities, customers, and consulting firms. While these may well be the powerful constituencies, it is not clear that all of them would have an interest in coherence. Certainly, highly remunerated owners, CEOs, and managers have a material interest in demonstrating the incoherence of other strategies than those that bring them success, and it would be a rare consultant that would want coherence across time in terms of solutions – where would be the revenue stream or value proposition in that? What should be clear is that some at least of the powerful users exist in highly dynamic and competitive markets that place a premium on discontinuity, or incoherence. In addition to user value, McKelvey argues that the evolution of the tribal fields that comprise organization studies into an organization science will also be predicated on the production of scientific quality defined in terms of natural science simulacra, and dynamic explanations that can account for order.

McKelvey anticipates organization studies having to make a formidable ascent up the evolutionary scale to paradigm closure if they are to be taken seriously; Kelemen and Hassard argue by contrast that their strength should be seen in the plurality of paradigms, in a loose Kuhnian sense, which they have to offer. Kelemen and Hassard's driving question may be represented as "Why should organization studies not be a science?"

There are four reasons why the field of organization studies will be both unlikely to secure the closure required for it to become a coherent science as well as it being unwise for it to do so. First, positivist epistemology has severe shortcomings in explaining what is happening in organizations. On this point, at least, McKelvey and Kelemen and Hassard agree, although their diagnosis of the relation of organization studies to positivism differs. Second, they suggest that organizational realities are becoming more complex and diverse, to such an extent that one-dimensional representation is no longer appropriate. Third, contemporary society faces an apparent moral crisis as the old technically rational criteria for decision choice recede in their efficacy and usefulness and, fourth, organization studies academics seek unique contributions for faster career advancement in academia.

The lack of wisdom would reside in the truncated opportunities for engaging more effectively in conversation with other colleagues and with practitioners from the viewpoint of literacy in multiple paradigms. Multiple paradigms can better serve multiple purposes: creating theories that control and predict the social world; understanding how meaning is constructed, negotiated, and enacted; emancipating various groups of people, or providing practical solutions to short-term organizational problems. Multiparadigm research that sought to address all these objectives might be better research, suggest Kelemen and Hassard, as well as be research that might better articulate repressed or marginalized interests. But it has legitimacy costs, which they outline. However, on balance the pursuit of multiparadigmatic studies within the field is seen as advantageous, feasible and increasing in frequency.

Paradigms should be seen as linguistic communities, they suggest: "as a heterogeneous collection of language conventions embedded in the practice of a particular context." Rather than promoting overarching grand narratives derived from the authority of science they suggest that researchers should be more accepting of small narratives, and seek to engage research subjects in and around these stories in a morally aware and acute practice. Each narrative strategy – grand and small – has a distinct discursive politics: grand narrative discursive positions will seek consensus by reinforcing a prevailing technical language, while small narrative positions will attempt to destabilize and challenge the *status quo* that this supports. From the latter perspective, the field becomes more socially responsible: by fostering multiple perspectives that undercut grand narratives, researchers articulate unheard, liminal, and marginalized voices, to aid in constructing a more democratic reality.

In conclusion, it would be difficult to imagine two more polarized contributions, in terms of style, lucidity, and content. McKelvey's complexity is modeled in his mode of theorizing while he strives for coherence; Kelemen and Hassard's complexity is much less contextualized within the wider terrain of professional philosophy of science and is more embedded in the actual practices of organization studies. Eschewing these as hopelessly flawed, McKelvey can only seek enlightenment elsewhere. Before his organization studies personnel can become organization scientists they must first become philosophers. The philosophy that Kelemen and Hassard espouse, as with that of their mentor's, the later Wittgenstein, seeks to get the philosophical fly out of the philosophical fly bottle, to dissolve the technical sense of the problems embedded in professional philosophers' language games and return analysis to the language games of everyday organizational life.

2a From Fields to Science: Can Organization Studies make the Transition?

Bill McKelvey

It is no secret that the body of research about organizations is multiparadigmatic (Pfeffer, 1993; Donaldson, 1995). Kuhn (1962) charac- terizes such a body of research as prescientific. Two questions arise. First, does it matter if a discipline is a multiparadigmatic collection of what Kuhn calls "fields"? It is clear from Pfeffer's (1993) analysis that multiparadigmatic disciplines are held in low status by members of other sciences in universities when it comes to funding and salaries (proxies for external legitimacy) – as I will detail later on.

The answer to the first raises the second. How does a multifield community of scholars become a science? A debate now rages in organization studies, as it has in the philosophy of science for decades, as scholars search for an answer. At its heart, the debate is about epistemology – the rules used to determine whether statements about real-world phenomena are to be believed as true or not. This, in turn, raises questions such as "Do real-world phenomena really exist?" "What are the important research questions?" "What is truth?" "When do we recognize one statement as more truthful than another?" "Who decides what the rules are?" "Is there just one agreed-upon body of rules or can/does each scholar simply adhere to his/her own personal rules?"

On one side are so-called *normal science* philosophers (Suppe, 1977; Putnam, 1981; Nola, 1988; Holton, 1993, Koertge, 1989; Sokal and Bricmont, 1998), along with Pfeffer (1982), Sutton and Staw (1995), and Donaldson (1996) in organization studies – and most authors in journals such as *Administrative Science Quarterly*, *Academy of Management Journal*, *Organization Science*, *Management Science*, and *Strategic Management Journal*. This side believes that it is desirable and possible to have one body of rules – one epistemology – that guides scholars toward a more or less truthful set of statements about real-world phenomena. Normal science epistemology now rests in the hands of scientific realists who believe in a probabilistic truth (de Regt, 1994; Aronson et al., 1994; Hooker, 1995; Azevedo, 1997; McKelvey, 1999b). Putnam sees realism as a search for " 'intrinsic' property, a property something has 'in itself', apart from any contribution made by language or the mind" (1987: 8). Chia views normal science as "a search for transcendental truths" (1996: 15), as does Bhaskar (1975).[1]

Speaking of the opposite side, Chia says, *"the purpose of inquiry is not so much an attempt to converge at a single point called Truth, but that the process of enquiry is a matter of continually reweaving webs of beliefs to produce new and novel insights into the human condition"* (1996: 15, my italics). This side is populated by the so-called historical relativists (Hanson, 1958; Kuhn, 1962; Feyerabend, 1975), and poststructuralists, deconstructionists/postmodernists (Saussure, 1974; Derrida, 1978; Baudrillard, 1983; Culler, 1983; Lyotard, 1984; Latour, 1987; Sarup, 1988 along with Smircich and Calás, 1987; Cooper and Burrell, 1988; Hassard, 1993, 1995; Alvesson and Deetz, 1996; Chia, 1996; Clegg and Hardy, 1996, and Burrell, 1997) in organization studies.[2] Besides its emphasis on the production of "novel insights," this side worries about the seeming impossibility of ever being able to accurately represent any aspect of real-world phenomena in the text of a language when the meanings of the terms used to represent phenomena are so dependent upon the idiosyncratic subjective interpretations of word meanings by individual scholars. Relativists also hold that, given the elements of subjectivity inherent in the research process, views of truth about various phenomena are also always moderated by the subjective individual interpretations of individual scholars – a view most strongly advocated by Feyerabend (1975), who is interpreted as saying, "Anything [any epistemology] goes."

Consider two points in the quotation from Chia: (1) "converge at a single point called Truth" and (2) "produce new and novel insights." This parallels Reichenbach's (1938) classic distinction between "justification logic" (in search of Truth) and "discovery logic." Kuhn's 1977 book, *The Essential Tension*, also is about the priority of one or the other "logic." It is true that logical positivists (Ayer, 1959; Hanfling, 1981) did attempt to search for a universal and unequivocal "Truth." But this epistemology has been discredited, as I will briefly demonstrate below. It has been replaced with a combination of three postpositivist programs: evolutionary epistemology, scientific realism, and the Semantic Conception of Theories, which I will also describe later.

No one to date claims to have found any discovery *logic* – novel insights and new theories are profligate without any logic being agreed upon. What worries normal scientists most is not a dearth of new insights but rather the possibility that the insights result from individual bias rather than careful study and reporting of real world phenomena and, therefore, have questionable truth value. Thus, with respect to searching for more truthful (novel) statements, the "anything goes" relativism of Feyerabend – upon which rests the entire postmodernist edifice – has also been discredited along with other key elements of historical relativism, as I will briefly recount below.

I will argue that those who take the antiscience view – presumably the "counterpoint" view in this volume – are off the track. The question is not whether organization studies need more novel insights – these abound. It is, rather, can organization studies become a science? I focus on "becoming" rather than the "either–or" debate because the latter is really a false dichotomy. Actually, it exists only because organization studies scholars are quite misguided as to old *and* modern epistemology. My "point" view will not argue the case for an organization science by attempting to solidify the existing positivist rhetoric nor by totally rejecting the postmodernist view of social phenomena. Instead I will focus my argument on how organization studies might become a science, given recent developments in philosophy, agent modeling trends in other sciences, and current postmodernist ontological assumptions about social phenomena.

Why Positivism and Historical Relativism were Rejected

Much of the rhetoric in support of postmodernism in organization studies is founded upon inaccurate critiques of positivism (for example, see Silverman, 1970; Mitroff, 1972; Burrell and Morgan, 1979; Whitley, 1984; Astley, 1985; Knights, 1992; Guba and Lincoln, 1994; Wicks and Freeman, 1998; Girod-Séville and Perret, 2001). As Hunt (1994) argues, these critiques typically are based on a caricature of positivism (1) that may have been a dream of some early positivists that no scientist ever followed; and/or (2) presumes aspects of positivism that philosophers rejected long ago. While it is important to understand why philosophers rejected many aspects of positivism, it is also important to recognize that a positivist legacy still remains.

The pre-Campbellian legacy

Putnam (1981: 114) states that both logical positivism and the main thesis of relativism – incommensurability – are self-refuting. For example, a self-refuting statement is "All generalizations are false." Logical positivists define the components of science to be either analytic statements (primarily mathematics and formal logic) or synthetic statements (empirical findings) that unequivocally define the meaning of theoretical statements, with all other statements being meaningless. This fundamental definition is self-refuting, since it is neither analytic nor synthetic. The incommensurability thesis is self-refuting, as follows. If we know enough about the terms of one paradigm to say that they are incommensurable with the terms of another paradigm then we know enough about the terms to render their incommensurability false. For example, the availability of many cross-paradigm terms is illustrated in the *Handbook of Organization Studies* (Clegg et al., 1996). It contains chapters falling into the positivist, interpretist, and postmodernist paradigms. Yet the obvious presumption of the editors is that the terms used in each chapter share meaning across paradigms – otherwise the editors are in the awkward position of having "edited" a book much of which they do not understand. Self-refuting aside, Suppe (1977) devotes 187 pages to more detailed arguments refuting the received view and historical relativism. Even so, there is a constructive legacy that I bring forward below along with a further brief comment on *The Received View* (Putnam's 1962 inclusion of logical positivism and logical empiricism under one label). Though the idea of incommensurable paradigms and paradigm shifts has been refuted, positive aspects of relativism remain, which emerge as semantic relativism in Campbellian realism (elaborated in McKelvey, 1999b).

Rejection of the received view

Pragmatism and instrumentalism are outside the mainstream of current philosophy of science. In the mature sciences most philosophers and scientists worry primarily about the truth of their theory, and especially the truth of someone else's. How should organizational scholars deal with the fundamental dilemma of science: how to conduct truth tests of theories, given that many of their constituent terms are unobservable and unmeasurable – seemingly unreal Realm 3 terms,[3] and thus beyond the direct first-hand sensory access of investigators?

Given a goal of truth-testing, consider the following hypothesis, for example:

Firms with configurations of competence enhancing HR system attributes that are unique, causally ambiguous, and synergistic will have sustained competitive advantage over firms that have HR system configurations that are typical, causally determinate, and nonsynergistic. (Lado and Wilson, 1994: 718, my emphasis)

Though some might consider "firms" a Realm 1 term, most probably would define a firm as a Realm 2 or Realm 3 entity – especially as economists might define it. (Friedman says firms behave "*as if* they were seeking rationally to maximize their expected returns," 1953: 22, his italics.) I have single-underlined what probably are Realm 2 terms and dotted underlined possible Realm 3 terms in this hypothesis. I do not think this hypothesis is any better or worse than most. I picked it because it spread across human resource, organizational, and strategic levels of analysis. To narrow the hypothesis for illustration, if a researcher says some sample of firms is nonsynergistic and therefore will not show a sustained competitive advantage, how is one to know for sure that "nonsynergistic" and "sustained competitive advantage" are terms having real properties that exist, since we cannot experience them directly with our human senses? If the terms do not exist, how does one know whether the statement is true or not? How may one conduct truth-testing research about unreal terms and entities? And how to know for sure whether "nonsynergistic" is really the causal agent? Avoiding metaphysical terms was the prime directive for the logical positivists.

Comte, Friedman, and Pfeffer insist that the only way to truth-test is to focus exclusively on Realm 1 terms. This is called *naive realism* or *classical positivism*. But even in organizational demographics, which Pfeffer championed in his 1982 book, Realm 2 and Realm 3 terms have crept in, as Lawrence (1997) demonstrates.

Despite efforts by Comte, Friedman, Pfeffer, and others, sociology, psychology, economics, and organization science bristle with metaphysical terms.

Logical positivism. The Vienna Circle physicists, mathematicians, and philosophers who created logical positivism – ca. 1907 – faced a similar problem. They began wondering how to deal with Hegelian idealism (nothing is real), German mechanistic materialism (things that can't be seen can't be truthfully researched), quantum, and relativity theories (can't be seen and are probabilistic or relativistic at best). Their quandary produced the logical positivist epistemology. It rigorously avoided metaphysical terms, and emphasized an objective external physical world, clear separation of unreal theory terms and real observation terms, axiomatic/syntactic language, formal logic, empirical verification, theory terms defined by reference to observation terms, and reductionism down to basic physical entities.[4] It developed an intricate solution to the problem of how to conduct truth tests of explanatory theories, given the circle's self-imposed conditions of (1) empirical tests based only on terms and entities amenable to direct knowing, (2) definition of theory terms as unreal and referring to physical entities that cannot be seen or touched and hence without any experienced indication that they are real, (3) abhorrence of causality as metaphysical, (4) directly experienced verification of truth and falsity, and (5) a required axiomatic/syntactic logically precise formal scientific language. Its notorious "correspondence rules" were meant to be the means whereby the direct knowing attached to directly sensed observation terms transferred to unreal theory terms in a method so logically rigorous that if a "real" observation term was verified as true, it logically followed that the related "unreal" theory term was also true. And, given that scientists had discovered that the basic law of force, in formal syntactic form, was the root axiom applying to motion, heat, energy, electromagnetism, and economics, it was a small step for positivists to conclude that all "true" sciences sprang from the same set of self-evidently true axioms – the Unity of Science movement.

Since "causality" is metaphysical and, thus, not allowed, positivists necessarily took an instrumentalist approach. This left them with the problem of having to defend the *theoretician's dilemma* and the *structural symmetry thesis* (Hempel, 1965). The theoretician's dilemma is: (1) if theory terms can be defined by observation terms, then theory terms are unnecessary; (b) if theory terms cannot be defined by observation terms, then surely they are unnecessary. If theory terms are not necessary, positivists are in the position of being operationalists. This is untenable, because they knew that a theory or explanation did not change each and every time an instrument was improved or operational measure redefined. The structural symmetry thesis is: (1) every adequate explanation is potentially a prediction; (2) every adequate prediction is potentially an explanation. Given their abhorrence of causality as metaphysical and their belief in instrumentalism, they could not avoid connecting explanation with prediction. The problem here was that 2 is frequently false. Thus "The sun rises because it circles the earth" is an explanation that follows from a prediction we all make every morning. But we now know it to be totally false.

Logical empiricism. The more extreme logically indefensible views of logical positivism were slowly softened by Reichenbach (1938), Braithwaite (1953), Nagel (1961), Kaplan (1964), and Hempel (1965). They continued the logical positivists' abhorrence of metaphysical terms and entities, eschewed causality because it was metaphysical, elevated the importance of laws and counterfactual conditionals (if A were x then B would be y), introduced the covering law model of explanation, weakened the verifiability requirement to a testability criterion, accepted probability and incremental confirmation, and allowed meaning to seep up from real observation terms to unreal theory terms – that is, allowed theory terms to have meanings only approximately tied to observation terms. To oversimplify, besides knocking off the extremes of logical positivism, logical empiricists zeroed in on the role of theories and laws in producing truthful explanations while protecting against attempts to inadvertently base explanations on "accidental regularities." Most of the "findings"

in Peters and Waterman (1982) classify as accidental regularities. Why? A law is defined to consist of a counterfactual conditional and a theory must include at least some laws or lawlike statements (Hunt, 1991). A finding not anticipated by a theoretical, lawlike statement risks being an accidental regularity. Strategy studies are particularly prone to accidental regularities thought to be observed in cases or emerging from atheoretical econometric analyses.

Theories have to "refer" to underlying structures and processes that explain why A might lead to B. The counterfactual conditional motivates the need for experiments. What we see may be an accidental regularity. But if we use a theory about an underlying process to predict that, if an effect A were created in an experiment we would produce B, and then with an experiment we, in fact, show that "If A then B," we have increased our right to believe that we have identified an underlying generative process where A leads to B. This requirement is given the label *nomic necessity*. The identification of a theory about an underlying structure or process, containing some counterfactual conditional laws, is absolutely necessary to protect against building explanations around accidental regularities. This is at the heart of Hempel's deductive-nomological model of explanation. Mainly through the efforts of Reichenbach (1938, 1949) probability relations were accepted in addition to exact predictions. Hempel responded to this with his deductive-statistical model, though he still insisted on "high probability." This protected the logical empiricists' view of an effective science as one producing findings having high "instrumental reliability" – meaning that highly reliable predictions were still considered a necessity.

What remains from positivism
The classic arguments rejecting the Received View are detailed by Suppe (1977: 62–115), based on the 1969 Illinois symposium and his own additional analyses. He concludes that "the vast majority of working philosophers of science seem to fall on that portion of the spectrum which holds the Received View fundamentally inadequate and untenable, but with considerable disagreement why it is untenable" (1977: 116). Suppe identifies nine principles

held by positivists that philosophers have subsequently modified to be acceptable. They avoid the pitfalls while at the same time formalize the important contribution the Received View still makes to modern epistemology. The principles act as the foundation upon which evolutionary epistemology, scientific realism, and the Semantic Conception are built.

1 *The truth or falsity of a principle or law cannot be determined solely by a formalized (mathematical) statement or empirical (experimental) finding* (Putnam, 1962). The Vienna Circle's Carnap (1966) held that any statement that was not either formally or empirically true was "cognitively meaningless." Philosophers now agree that many scientific statements are neither formal nor empirical (Putnam, 1962) or are both (Suppe, 1977).

2 *Accepting that the strict separation between formal and empirical statements cannot be substantiated, it is also true that theoretical and observation terms also may be inseparable.* Thus, for organization studies, which of the following are theoretical, as opposed to observational, terms: new, *r*-type, overcapacity, environment, gross revenues, age, old, U-form, communication channels, interdependences, social network, graphs, stories, culture? A term may be theoretical, observational, or both.

3 *Given that the strict separation between theoretical and observation languages does not hold, it becomes important to realize that theoretical terms have "antecedent meanings" that are neither totally unconnected nor perfectly synonymous with the meanings of observation terms* – otherwise they would be unrelated or inseparable from operational (observation) terms. Positivists tried to have strict separation followed by a "rigorous" connecting (via correspondence rules) between theory terms and observation terms. But this led to Hempel's theoretician's dilemma. Consequently, one of the constant agendas of a science, then, is working on the connection between theory and observation terms.

4 *The meaning of theoretical terms may be based on formal (mathematical) or iconic (as in the billiard ball model of atoms or Burns and Stalker's, 1961, machine model of organizations) models.* Note, however, that "meaning" lies as much with the semantic interpretation of the syntax of models as with the syntax itself. Furthermore, model syntax does more than simply represent meanings. An analysis of models in physics and economics reported by Morgan and Morrison (2000) details just how much models alter the course of a scientific body of knowledge and, as they put it, act as "autonomous agents."

5 *Auxiliary hypotheses and theories outside a theory in question are always necessary for theoretical language to be appropriately connected to observation language.* No empirical study or mathematical analysis can incorporate all aspects of all theories about some phenomena, or all theories of data, sampling, analytical method. In any single study, some auxiliary effects are randomized, assumed away, ignored, or simply missed. Consequently, no single study can ever refute a set of existing beliefs. To think so is called "dogmatic falsificationism" (Hunt, 1991).

6 *Appropriately connecting theories to phenomena also requires that all procedural details pertaining to empirical and/or experimental causal sequences be described.* Causal effects, patterns of correlation, experimental and regression or econometric time-series methods supporting causal analysis must be clearly delineated.

7 *The idea that the entire content of theories may be axiomatizable or formalizable does not hold.* After World War II positivists came to believe that, given that analytical mechanics (classical physics), electromagnetism, thermodynamics, and economics could all be reduced to the basic axiomatic syntax of $F = ma$, reduction to foundational axioms should be a universal defining element. This became the aforementioned Unity of Science movement, holding that any discipline that could not be so axiomatized was not a science. This ruled out biology as a science, though Williams (1970, 1973) and Ruse (1973) attempted an axiomatic basis for it.

8 *Axiomatization, which is formalization without semantic interpretation, is meaningless.* This statement becomes the basis of the Semantic Conception of Theories, which I briefly discuss later.

9 *Formalization is a necessary component of acceptable epistemology, but is not sufficient, given the dynamic nature of scientific inquiry.* This stems from the rejection of historical relativism

and becomes the basis of evolutionary epistemology and Campbellian realism, which I also mention later.

If it occurs to you that these principles outline the normal course of research practice in science in general and in much of organization studies you are essentially correct. But remember, positivists held all these statements to be false. Perhaps now you can begin to see why the Received View was a dream about how science should be practiced that no scientist ever carried out. For postmodernists to base their rhetoric on the negative of these statements, which are key beliefs of the Received View, doesn't make much sense because they were never actually followed. Having denounced the Received View, to then imply, as postmodernists do, that current "normal" science – which essentially *does* follow the foregoing principles – is misguided, is poor logic. This puts postmodernists in the position of arguing that, since not-A is false, therefore A must be false, surely a falsity in itself.

Rejection of historical relativism

Historical relativism
The Received View's focus on justification logic created a static view of science. Other philosophers began to study science in motion and as an artifact of the intersubjective social constructions of meanings within scientific subcommunities. According to Suppe (1977), the founding contributors are Toulmin (1953), Bohm (1957), Hanson (1958), Feyerabend (1962, 1975), and Kuhn (1962, 1977). Suppe's review of these author's contributions, along with his critique, amounts to over seventy pages.

Kuhn's views dominate. *Weltanschauung* (world view) dynamics consist of long periods of relative stability, termed *normal science*, broken intermittently by *paradigm shifts*. In Kuhn's view, science evolves through long periods of convergent "normal puzzle solving" activities punctuated infrequently by dramatic paradigm shifts – caused by accumulated anomalies. While the anomalies cannot be accounted for within the dominant paradigm of a scientific

discipline, they increasingly appear to be explicable in the terms of other, often newer, less dominant paradigms. These less dominant paradigms slowly accrue followers as their ability to explain the anomalies becomes increasingly evident to the several subcommunities of scientists. These scientific subcommunities within a discipline, each with different exemplars and different conceptual perspectives, see the world and conduct their research differently. The puzzles set by one paradigm may not be seen as significant within other paradigms; the anomalies of one paradigm may be inexplicable within another paradigm. Consequently there is no "neutral" comparative language, and, so, incommensurability results, preventing scientists in different *Weltanschauungen* from being able to conduct cross-paradigm theory tests.

Complaints against Kuhn's framework are legion. (1) Masterman (1970) identifies twenty-one definitions of the term "paradigm." (2) Putnam (1981) notes that relativism is self-refuting – any approach is allowed except antirelativism. (3) Others complain that under Kuhn's framework science becomes irrational and subjective, leaving it with no objective or independent basis of resolving disputes – "an anti-empirical idealism" (Suppe, 1977: 151) that is no different than Hegelian idealism (Scheffler, 1967). (4) Many disagree that a correct reading of scientific history offers any indication of disjunctive shifts between normal puzzle solving and revolution (Suppe, 1977). (5) Meanings may not in fact change just because paradigms shift.

Many scholars interpret historical relativism as antithetical to positivism. Thus historical relativism "made scientific knowledge a social phenomenon in which science became a subjective and, to varying degrees, an irrational enterprise" (Suppe, 1977: 705). However, there are strong and weak forms of relativism. Nola (1988) separates relativism into three kinds:

1 *Ontological relativism* "is the view that what exists, whether it be ordinary objects, facts, the entities postulated in science, etc., exists only relative to some relativizer, whether that be a person, a theory or whatever" (p. 11).
2 *Epistemological relativisms* may allege that (a) what is known or believed is relativized to

individuals, cultures, or frameworks; (b) what is perceived is relative to some incommensurable paradigm; (c) there is no general theory of scientific method, form of inquiry, rules of reasoning or evidence that has privileged status. Instead they are variable with respect to times, persons, cultures, and frameworks (pp. 16–18). 3 *Semantic relativism* holds that truth and falsity are "relativizable to a host of items from individuals to cultures and frameworks. What is relativized are variously sentences, statements, judgements or beliefs" (p. 14).

Nola observes that Hanson, Kuhn, and Feyerabend espouse both semantic and epistemological relativism (moderate relativism), but not ontological relativism (the strongest form). In short, Kuhn is not a Hegelian idealist, accepts individual interpretations of the meanings of terms, and sees epistemologies as social constructions within scientific subcommunities that evolve over time. With Nola's clarification in mind, we can now turn to Suppe's critique of relativism:

Objectivity
The strong form of historical relativism holds that observation and facts are both theory-laden – there is no such thing as neutral observation or neutral facts. This would be ontological nihilism where real-world phenomena simply do not exist as criterion variables against which to truth-test theories. This thesis – that objects, facts, and properties are colored by the nature of the theory held by an observer – is rejected by Scheffler (1967) as being no different than Hegelian idealism in which all objects in the world are perceptions and "in the mind." If this is true, one of the basic tenets of science fails, namely objectivity. However, Suppe (1977) says that neither Toulmin, Bohm, Hanson, Feyerabend, nor Kuhn ever pin their claims on the strong form. They all accept a weaker form – that objects, facts, and properties, as they exist, are independent of an observer – that is, neutral – but that the nature of objects, facts, and properties thought to be observed by an individual might indeed be determined by the influence of the *Weltanschauung*. The facts of nature, as represented by language terms, are colored, if not camouflaged, by individual interpretations of semantic meanings and

social constructions of meanings within scientific subcommunities that impinge on individual scholars. Suppe accepts this as a tenable outlook, but only if *Weltanschauungen* exist. He then attacks their existence, as follows.

Historical accuracy
Hunt (1991: 326) observes that the complaint about an inaccurate reading of scientific history is particularly telling, since the basis of Kuhn's attack on the positivists is that they misread history. Hunt continues his analysis by quoting Hull (1975: 397) as saying, "The periods which he [Kuhn] had previously described as pre-paradigm contained paradigms not that different from those of normal science. [N]or does normal science alternate with revolutionary science; both are taking place all the time. Sometimes a revolution occurs without any preceding state of crisis." Laudan (1977: 74, 151) concludes:

[V]irtually every major period in the history of science is characterized both by the coexistence of numerous competing paradigms, with none exerting hegemony over the field, and by the persistent and continuous manner in which the foundational assumptions of every paradigm are debated within the scientific community. . . . Kuhn can point to no major science in which paradigm monopoly has been the rule, nor in which foundational debate has been absent. (Quoted in Hunt, 1991: 326).[5]

Meaning variance
Relativists claim that as a field shifts from one *Weltanschauung* to another the meanings of all of the underlying theory terms also change – the basis of incommensurability. Suppe (1977: 199–208) argues that the strong form preferred by Feyerabend and Bohm – that "any change in theory alters the meanings of all the terms in the theory" – is untenable. No historical relativist has established that *any* change in a theory changes all the terms. He then offers several arguments why a weaker form preferred by Toulmin, Kuhn, and Hanson – that "meanings of terms in theories are determined partially by the principles of the theory" – is also untenable. (1) Theories are constantly reformulated to generate propositions fitting particular empirical circumstances for deductive tests. (2) Once it is agreed that only "some" terms might change meaning, the opposite is

true, which is that some terms do not change in meaning.[6] (3) Theories are not simply "linguistic formulations" in the sense that a theory changes just because terms, as linguistic entities, change. Theories are not thought to change if translated from English to Japanese. Thus the linguistic terms are amenable to translation just as happens when English terms are translated into Japanese.

Agreement

A *Weltanschauung* is typically a complex framework supposedly emerging from the collective beliefs of a scientific community. These beliefs are the result of years of training, exemplars such as textbooks, apprenticeships, research programs, and journal articles. Beliefs are also composed of all the relevant theory language of principle and terms, various theory formulations, experimental methods, and so on – truly a multifaceted belief system. How likely is the community of individual scientists to agree on all of these items? More likely each individual is somewhat different by virtue of being trained at different places, apprenticed to different mentors, and studying different books and articles. If the individuals are diverse, the strong form of *Weltanschauung* is illusory – the diversity of training and experience greatly reduces the likelihood that the interpreted meanings of one subcommunity will be incommensurable to members of other subcommunities. If we accept the weak form, however, then the level of incommensurability is not high enough to support Kuhn's argument that incommensurability does not allow cross-paradigm truth tests. Again, Einstein's change of *t* in the Lorentz equations is a classic case in point. And, again, in the Clegg et al. *Handbook* (1996), while various chapters come from authors in different "weak form" subcommunities, with considerable diversity of backgrounds and interpretations of textual meanings, the editors clearly thought that most readers would understand most textual meanings throughout the book.

Suppe (1977: 217–21), reflecting the Illinois symposium and his own analysis, concludes: (1) historical relativists deserve credit for alerting us to the dynamics of how science progresses; (2) the idea is false that scientific communities are possessed of such strongly incommensurable

Weltanschauungen that any means of cross-paradigm truth testing is impossible.

Organization studies was never positivist anyway

Sutton and Staw, in their *Administrative Science Quarterly* forum on "What theory is *not*" (1995) say, "We agree with scholars like Kaplan (1964) and Merton (1967) who assert that theory is the answer to queries of *why*" (1995: 378, their italics). This leads to causality. Sutton and Staw say that "explicating . . . causal logic" is critical (p. 372) to proper theorizing. A researcher "must develop causal arguments to explain *why* persistent findings have been observed" (pp. 374–5), "a predicted relationship must be explained to provide theory" (p. 375), a theory must be "abstract enough to be generalized to other settings" (p. 375). They summarize: "Theory emphasizes the nature of causal relationships, identifying what comes first as well as the timing of such events. Strong theory . . . delves into underlying processes so as to understand the systematic reasons for a particular occurrence or non–occurrence" (p. 378). In their view, theories that predict the effects of underlying causal processes on outcome variables are more fruitful.[7]

The definition of "what theory *is*" in the Sutton and Staw (1995) article about "what theory is *not*" is not a wholly correct account of logical empiricism. But they are half right. Yes, logical empiricism emphasizes laws, predictive relationships among variables, generalization, and explanation based on underlying processes. But Sutton and Staw also focus on "explicating . . . causal logic" and "causal arguments," citing Kaplan (1964) for philosophical support – Kaplan's book being one of the last important logical empiricist statements. If Kaplan (1964) uses the term "causal" once in his entire book I have not found it! In listing his "types of laws" (pp. 104–15), nowhere does he include "causal law." For Kaplan, laws are associations of properties, as in "'For all *x*'s, if *x* has the property *f* then it has the property *g*,' or more colloquially, 'all *f*'s are *g*'s'" (p. 94) – no causal arrow is apparent! The wonderfully informative article by Bacharach (1989), the cornerstone of the *AMR* forum, is not wholly correct logical empiricism either – though he cites Nagel (1961), Kaplan (1964), and Hempel (1965), all exemplars of logical empiricism. For him, "explanatory potential" depends on "necessary and sufficient" antecedents, "causal linkages," and "recursive causal logic." He defines research as "ideal" when "the theory constructionist is seeking to find and explain causal relations . . . ." None of this fits the logical positivist program. Causality is a metaphysical term they avoided like the plague.

To label organizational researchers as either classical positivists (Comte, Pfeffer) or flawed logical empiricists (Kaplan, Sutton and Staw, Bacharach), or relativists (Kuhn, Perrow, Chia, Burrell) is to suggest they have no current legitimate philosophical basis:

1 *Classical positivism* (which accepts research based only on real terms) is rejected because most causal and/or explanatory terms are metaphysical (Bhaskar, 1975; Suppe, 1977; Aronson et al., 1994).

2 *Logical empiricism* is rejected for reasons noted above (see also Suppe, 1977, 1989; Papineau, 1996).

3 *Relativism* now receives virtually no support by modern philosophers, as also noted previously (see also Suppe, 1977; Putnam, 1981; Nola, 1988; Azevedo, 1997).

Or, if you think all of the theories in the *Handbook* (Clegg et al., 1996) fall within the foregoing three categories, you are then disconnecting them – in legitimacy terms – from current mainstream philosophy of science – which I will briefly describe shortly.

Pragmatists could argue that legitimacy comes more from a theory being useful and valued by external constituencies than from positivist or relativist legitimacy, as does Van de Ven (1989). Unfortunately external constituencies, such as those studied by Pfeffer (1993), also do not ascribe much legitimacy to organization studies. From Pfeffer's list of seventeen ways in which multiparadigm disciplines suffer low status, I list those affecting funding and salaries as proxies of judgments by external constituencies.

1 Paradigm consensus → much better funding.

2 Paradigm consensus → greater dispersion of funding across high and low-status departments.

3 Paradigm consensus → higher connectivity between productivity and salary.

4 Paradigm consensus → less dissatisfaction associated with salary dispersion within departments.

5 Paradigm consensus → less bias by institutional affiliation by those charged with allocating grants.

6 Paradigm consensus → more autonomy from central university administration.

Inasmuch as "institutional legitimacy" is a central pillar of modern organization science (Powell and DiMaggio, 1991; Scott, 1995), surely low legitimacy from both philosophy of science and external user communities leaves organization studies in a dismal state. The legitimacy of organization studies is undercut by one of its own theories!

On becoming a Science

Relativist rhetoric in organization studies, critiquing positivism as the springboard for an alternative epistemology, flogs a dead horse. We need to get past this. Yes, organization studies needs to become a science – with an epistemology I will briefly define below. But relativist-based postmodernism is misguided in its epistemology, since it offers little by way of justification logic. Still, *its ontology is correct.* I begin by "marrying" normal science epistemology with postmodernist ontology. Next I touch on three post-Kuhnian normal science postpositivisms. Finally I suggest a process by which organization studies might become a science.

Creating one macro-paradigm

There are two broad classes of "postpositivisms." First, there are the contra-science postpositivisms most familiar to organizational researchers, such as: social constructionism (Bloor, 1976; Brannigan, 1981), phenomenology, interpretism, and hermeneutics (Natanson, 1958; Heidegger, 1962; Schutz, 1962; Goldstein, 1963), radical humanism and radical structuralism (Burrell and Morgan, 1979), critical theory and postmodernism (Burrell and Morgan, 1979; Smircich and

Calás, 1987; Cooper and Burrell, 1988). Recently the pull toward the subjectivist postpositivisms in organization science has increased substantially (Reed and Hughes, 1992; Hassard and Parker, 1993; Hassard, 1995; Chia, 1996; Clegg et al., 1996; Marsden and Townley, 1996; Burrell, 1997; Bentz and Shapiro, 1998; McKinlay and Starkey, 1998). These postpositivisms undermine the idea that there is indeed a universal scientific method that falteringly, but inexorably, winnows out more incorrect theories.

Second, post-Kuhnian normal science. Current philosophy of science divides into three primary postpositivisms, all of which have strong adherents among the leading philosophers: scientific realism, evolutionary epistemology, and the Semantic Conception of Theories. These seem relatively unknown to organizational researchers.[8] None is in evidence in the theory forums. By undermining the rhetoric of the relativists and by producing a reconstructed logic better fitting the reality of the strong sciences and the logic-in-use (Kaplan, 1964) of organizational research, these postpositivisms offer a more effective means of incorporating the constructive elements of relativism, particularly social constructionism, phenomenology, semantic relativism (Nola, 1988), and poststructuralism (Sarup, 1988; Cilliers, 1998) while at the same uncovering a path toward a more effective organization science (Henrickson and McKelvey, 2002).

I focus on whether one can apply the justification logic (Reichenbach, 1938) of normal science realist epistemology to the organizational ontology recognized by contra-science proponents. Suppose each side is *half* correct. Organization scientists make ontological assumptions about the nature of organizations as existing entities having attributes, a nature, an essence. They also follow a set of epistemological rules governing scientific method. Briefly put, contra-science holds that organizations are ontological entities not fruitfully studied via normal science because they consist of behaviors *unique* or *idiosyncratic* to each individual and subunit of an organization.[9] Therefore they call for a new epistemology. Normal scientists see contra-science epistemology as fraught with subjective bias and with no means of self-correction. Wishing to follow the epistemology of "good" science, normal science organizational researchers adopt an ontology calling for levels of uniformity among organizational behavioral decisions, activities, or events that do not exist – a clearly false ontology according to contra-science adherents. While the foundation of the argument is more complicated, in simple terms we have four combinations, shown in figure 2.1. The paradigm war (Pfeffer, 1993, 1995; Perrow, 1994; Van Maanen, 1995a, b) pits 1 against 4. This debate is stalled. No one advocates 2. *Only 3 is left.*

The other post-Kuhnian normal science postpositivisms

Campbellian realism offers a way of integrating objectivist and subjectivist methods. The Semantic Conception puts models at the center of science. Agent-based models integrate postmodern ontology with model-centered normal science. Based on elements of these normal science postpositivisms, I wrap up with a Guttman scale of effective science.

Campbellian realism

Though Suppe (1977) wrote the epitaph on positivism and relativism, a strong positivist legacy remains – outlined earlier. From this legacy a *model-centered*, *realist*, *evolutionary epistemology* has emerged. I argue that model-centered *realism* accounts to the legacy of positivism, while evolutionary realism accounts to the dynamics of science highlighted by relativism, all of which I place under the label *Campbellian realism* (McKelvey, 1999b). Below

		Epistemology: Normal science	Epistemology: Contra-science
Ontology	Normal science	1	2
Ontology	Contra-science	3	4

Figure 2.1 Epistemology/ontology combinations

I briefly reprise key points of Campbellian realism and then turn to the model-centered science of the Semantic Conception.

Campbell's view may be summarized into a tripartite framework that replaces the dynamics of Kuhn's historical relativism with a dynamic realist epistemology. First, much of the literature has focused on the selectionist evolution of the human brain, our cognitive capabilities, and our visual senses (Campbell, 1974, 1988), concluding that these capabilities do indeed give us accurate enough information to survive in the world we live in (reviewed by Azevedo, 1997). Second, Campbell (1991, 1995) draws on the hermeneuticists' coherence theory in a selectionist fashion to argue that, over time, members of a scientific community (as a tribe) attach increased scientific validity to an entity as the meanings given to that entity increasingly cohere across members. This process is based on hermeneuticists' use of coherence theory to attach meaning to terms (elaborated in Hendrickx, 1999).[10] Third, Bhaskar (1975) and Campbell (1988, 1991) combine scientific realism with semantic relativism (Nola, 1988), thereby producing an ontologically strong relativist dynamic epistemology. In this view, the coherence process within a scientific community continually develops in the context of selectionist testing for ontological validity. The socially constructed, coherence-enhanced theories of a scientific community are tested against an objective reality, with a winnowing out of the less ontologically correct theoretical entities. This process, consistent with the strong version of scientific realism proposed by de Regt (1994), does not guarantee error-free "Truth" (as Laudan, 1981, observes) but it does move science in the direction of increased truthlikeness (Popper's, 1968, *verisimilitude*) as the least predictive and/or least satisfactory explanations are successively abandoned.[11]

Campbellian realism is crucial to organizational researchers because elements of positivism and relativism remain in organization studies, as noted previously. Campbell folds into one epistemology (1) the use of metaphysical terms, (2) objectivist empirical investigation, (3) individual subjective interpretations of meanings and a recognition of socially constructed meanings of terms, and (4) a dynamic process

by which a multiparadigm discipline might reduce to fewer but more significant theories and/or *Weltanschauungen*. It does not deny objectivity via the search for a probabilistic truth over time by many researchers connecting to real-world phenomena, nor does it deny individual subjectivity, idiosyncratic interpretation of textual meanings, and social construction processes within scientific subcommunities.

Campbell defines a *critical, hypothetical, corrigible, scientific realist, selectionist evolutionary* epistemology as follows (McKelvey, 1999b: 403):

1 A scientific realist postpositivist epistemology that maintains the goal of objectivity in science without excluding metaphysical terms and entities.

2 A selectionist evolutionary epistemology governing the winnowing out of less probable theories, terms, and beliefs in the search for increased verisimilitude that may do so without the danger of systematically replacing metaphysical terms with operational terms.

3 A postpositivist epistemology that incorporates the dynamics of science without abandoning the goal of objectivity.

4 An objectivist, selectionist, evolutionary epistemology that includes as part of its path toward increased verisimilitude the inclusion of, but also the winnowing out of, the more fallible, individual interpretations and social constructions of the meanings of theory terms comprising theories purporting to explain an objective external reality.

The epistemological directions of Campbellian realism have strong foundations in the scientific realist and evolutionary epistemology communities (see Hahlweg and Hooker, 1989; Hooker, 1995; Azevedo, 1997; McKelvey, 1999b). While philosophers never seem to agree exactly on anything, nevertheless, broad consensus does exist that these statements reflect what is best about current philosophy of science.

The Semantic Conception
Starting with Beth's seminal work dating back to World War II (Beth, 1961), we see the emergence of the Semantic Conception of Theories.[12]

From axioms to phase spaces. After Beth, three early contributors emerge: Suppes (1961, 1967),

Suppe (1967, 1977, 1989), and van Fraassen (1970, 1980). A phase space is defined as a space enveloping the full range of each dimension used to describe an entity. The task of a theory is to represent the full dynamics of the variables defining the space, as opposed to the positivists' axiomatic approach where the theory builds from foundational axioms. The statements of the theory are not defined by how well they link to the axioms but rather by how well they define the many variables characterizing a phase space – and phase transitions as well.

Isolated idealized structures. The current reading of the history of science by philosophers shows that no theory ever attempted to represent or explain the full complexity of phenomena. Classic examples given are the use of point masses, ideal gasses, pure elements and vacuums, frictionless slopes, and assumed uniform behavior of atoms, molecules, genes, and rational actors. Scientific laboratory experiments are always carried out in the context of closed systems whereby many of the complexities of natural phenomena are set aside. Suppe (1977: 223–4) defines these as "isolated idealized systems." Using her mapping metaphor, Azevedo (1997), a realist, explains that no map ever attempts to depict the full complexity of the target area – it might focus only on rivers, roads, geographic contours, arable land, or minerals, and so forth – seeking instead to satisfy the specific interests of the map maker and potential users. Similarly for a theory – it predicts the progression of an idealized state space over time, predicting shifts from one abstraction to another under the assumed ideal conditions.[13] A theory (1) "does not attempt to describe all aspects of the phenomena in its intended scope; rather it abstracts certain parameters from the phenomena and attempts to describe the phenomena in terms of just these abstracted parameters" (Suppe, 1977: 223), (2) assumes that the phenomena behave according to the selected parameters included in the theory, and (3) that the phenomena are typically specified in terms of their several parameters with the full knowledge that no empirical study or experiment could successfully and completely control all the complexities that might affect the designated parameters.

Suppe says, "If the theory is adequate it will provide an accurate characterization of what the phenomenon *would have been* had it been an isolated system . . ." (p. 224).

Model-centered science. The central feature of the Semantic Conception is the central role given to models. In organizational studies models are typically off to the side. (1) A theory is induced after an investigator has gained an appreciation of some aspect of organizational behavior. (2) A "box and arrow" iconic model is often added to give a pictorial view of the interrelation of the variables, show hypothesized path coefficients, or possibly a regression model is estimated. (3) The model develops in parallel with the theory as the latter is tested by seeing whether effects predicted by the theory can be discovered in some sampling of real-world phenomena. In contrast, the Semantic Conception views theory, model, and phenomena as independent entities. Science is bifurcated into two independent but not unrelated activities:

1 *Analytical adequacy* is tested by seeing whether outcomes predicted by the theory, stated as counterfactual conditionals in which *p* is the result of transcendental generative processes *g*, materialize as expected in the simulated world of the model – which is an isolated idealized depiction of the real world moved into a laboratory. This is the theory–model link.
2 *Ontological adequacy* is tested by comparing the behavior of the model's idealized substructures against parallel subsystems in that portion of real-world phenomena defined as within the scope of the theory. This is the model–phenomena link.

"Theory" is always hooked to and tested via a model. It does not attempt to use its "if *g*, then *q*" epistemology to explain "real world" behavior. It attempts only to explain "model" behavior. It does its testing in the isolated idealized world structured into the model. Developing ontological adequacy runs parallel with improving the theory–model relationship. How well does the model *represent* real-world phenomena? Thus, how well does a drug shown to work on "idealized" lab. rats work on people of different ages, weights, and physiologies? The centrality of models as autonomous mediators between theory and phenomena reaches fullest expression in Morgan and Morrison (2000) as they extend the Semantic Conception. I tease out the coevolution of analytical and ontological adequacy tests in McKelvey (2002).

Families of models. One of the primary difficulties encountered with the axiomatic conception is the idea that only one fully adequate model should unfold from the underlying axioms. Since the Semantic Conception does not require axiomatic reduction, it tolerates multiple models. Thus "truth" is not defined in terms of reduction to a single model or root axioms. In evolutionary theory there is no single axiomatic theory of evolution. There are in fact subordinate families of theories (multiple models) within the main families about natural selection, heredity, variation, and taxonomic grouping. Organization studies also consists of various families of theories, each having families of competing models within it – evident in Clegg et al. (1996).

Agent-based models
Most sciences are not reductionist; they are molecular reductionist (Schwab, 1960). This leads to the hierarchy of sciences: physics, chemistry, biology, psychology, sociology/economics, for example.[14] At the lower bound of a discipline – where it stops trying to explain increasingly smaller entities – it makes an assumption about the microstate phenomena below the lower bound. Thus, at some level, psychologists leave explanation to biologists, and they to chemists, and they to physicists. Traditionally scientists have assumed uniform microstates. For example, Brownian motion (discovered in 1829) was assumed uniform in physics models until well into the twentieth century. Most sciences eventually abandon the uniformity assumption in favor of stochastic idiosyncrasy as they mature. In recent times, as normal sciences have made this transition, they have put more effort into agent-based models.

There are many kinds of agent-based (adaptive learning) models. Some are very simple, some quite complicated.[15] Agents can be at any level of analysis: atomic particles, molecules,

genes, species, people, firms, and so on. The distinguishing feature is that the agents are not uniform. Instead they are probabilistically idiosyncratic. Therefore, at the level of human behavior, they fit the postmodernists' ontological assumption. Using agent-based models is the best way to marry postmodernist ontology with the Semantic Conception's model-centered science and the current assumptions of effective modern sciences.[16] Specifically:

1   Behavioral activities of human agents are discrete, random, and idiosyncratic.
2   Agents have some minimal adaptive learning capability.
3   Agents have no ambition other than to incrementally improve their own "fitness," however they define it.
4   Organizations having greater agent fitness improvements will have a survival advantage over those that do not.

There is no uniform rationality or constrained maximization assumption. But agents may incrementally improve the level of their rationality along with other kinds of learning.

Guttman scale of effective science
If the Semantic Conception of science is defined as focusing on the *formalization of families of models*, the *theory–model experimental test*, and the *model–phenomena ontological test*, organizational research generally misses the mark. Its empirical tests are typically defined in terms of a direct "theory–phenomena" corroboration, with the result that (1) it does not have the bifurcation of theory–model experimental and model–phenomena ontological tests, (2) the strong counterfactual type of confirmation of theories is seldom achieved because the attempt is to predict real-world behavior rather than model behavior, (3) model substructures are considered invalid because their inherent idealizations usually fail to represent real-world complexity – instrumental reliability is low – and (4) models are not formalized (this may be optional).

   To summarize the most important elements of the realist/Semantic Conception, and show how well organizational research measures up, I list the criteria of effective science as follows:

7 Verisimilitude and/or instrumental
reliability   Highest scientific standard
6 Verisimilitude via
selection
5 Separation of
experimental and
ontological tests
4 Experiments
3 Model-centeredness
2 Nomic necessity
(focus on underlying
generative mechanisms)
1 Avoidance of
metaphysical terms   Minimal scientific standard

The list appears as a Guttman scale. I posit that it goes from easiest to most difficult. To become a legitimate and effective science from the philosophical perspective, realist/Semantic Conception epistemology holds that theories in organizational research must be accountable to these criteria. Existing strong sciences such as physics, chemistry, and biology meet all of them. I detail the logic of this scale elsewhere (McKelvey, 2002). If a science is not based on nomic necessity and centered around (preferably) formalized computational or mathematical models it has no chance of meeting the top five of the seven criteria. Such is the message of late twentieth-century (postpositivist) philosophy of science.

From fields to science

Organization studies as prescience
Kuhn's 1962 classic is surely one of the best known philosophical works of the twentieth century. Most follow-on reviews, critiques, or developments skip quickly past the second chapter, digging into his views about paradigm shifts, incommensurability, and relativism. Specifically, attention invariably focuses on the dynamics, over time, of those sciences having already reached paradigm status – Kuhn's indication being that the "fields" and/or "schools" (1970: chapter 2) have coalesced into a single paradigm. In the sciences most philosophers pay attention to, this happened decades, if not centuries, ago. But, as Pfeffer's review (1993) shows, "science" – as Kuhn defines it – has not happened in management and/or organization studies – the wishful labeling of the journal *Organization Science* notwithstanding.

For hopeful organization scientists, a more detailed study of the prescience-to-science transition everyone else ignores is required. None of the foregoing lessons about the nonpostmodernist postpositivisms has value if organization studies cannot get from the multiparadigm or multifield *prescience* stage to the dominant paradigm *science* stage. But to worry about this we need to understand how Kuhn defines prescience and science.

Random fact gathering.

In the absence of a paradigm or some candidate for paradigm, all of the facts that could possibly pertain to the development of a given science are likely to seem equally relevant. As a result, early fact-gathering is a far more nearly random activity than the one that subsequent scientific development makes familiar. Furthermore, in the absence of a reason for seeking some particular form of more recondite information, early fact-gathering is usually restricted to the wealth of data that lie ready to hand. . . . Only very occasionally, as in the cases of ancient statics, dynamics, and geometrical optics, do facts collected with so little guidance from pre-established theory speak with sufficient clarity to permit the emergence of a first paradigm. . . . What is surprising, and perhaps also unique in its degree to the fields we call science, is that such initial divergences should ever largely disappear. . . . For they do disappear to a very considerable extent and then apparently once and for all. (Kuhn 1970: 15, 16, 17)

How to characterize the prescience stage?[17] Kuhn identifies various attributes of the prescience stage (Hoyningen-Huene 1993: 190):

1   Universal consensus about the choice of problems is missing.
2   Speculative theories are more frequent.
3   Journals have to contend with competing approaches. Pfeffer (1993) presents data showing high journal rejection rates also characterize multiparadigm, prescience fields.
4   Books often are the preferred medium, as opposed to short, technical journal articles.
5   In the preparadigm stage schools are forced to constantly explicate and legitimize their foundations.
6   Schools take the low-hanging-fruit approach, settling for the more readily available facts.
7   Fields and schools are less separated from the rest of society – for example, seemingly

anyone (freelance authors and consultants) can write about complexity-theory-applied-to-firms but this would not be true of quantum theory. 8 Fields and schools are more apt to be influenced by factors from outside.

Kuhn ignores most of this continuum to focus only on the "clash of schools" that, as a rule, immediately precedes the paradigm stage. Following Kuhn and Hoyningen-Huene (1993), in studying the transition from fields to science, my treatment emphasizes (1) a subcommunity's epistemology-based legitimacy as well as its own choices about which research problems to emphasize, and (2) Pfeffer's (1993) emphasis on legitimacy from external users – who also have a say in what problems become important to a discipline.[18]

When do clashing schools disappear to leave a single dominant paradigm? Kuhn (1977: chapter 13) recognizes five values held by strong scientific communities: accuracy, consistency, scope, simplicity, and fruitfulness. In the context of these values, Hoyningen-Huene (1993: 192–3) suggests three criteria by which one school wins out over the others:

1 It offers convincing solutions to problems whose centrality to the community of scientists (and ultimately users, as becomes clear below) is unquestioned.
2 It conclusively resolves issues regarded as fundamental. These issues bear on the articulation of research problems and their solutions, questions regarding which elements of the real world are to be studied, what methods of observation, experimentation, and theorizing are accepted, and reliable predictive success.
3 It offers novel "concrete problem solutions" (CPSs). These lie at the core of Kuhn's argument; I define them below.

Following C. S. Pierce, Hacking (1981: 131) joins with Van Fraassen (1980) in the latter's "constructive empiricism" as a way of substituting good methodology for the realist's search for "truth." In this view, a school wins out by methodological domination. As Hacking also observes, as does McGuire (1992), this also characterizes Lakatos's development of "scientific programs." Lakatos may be interpreted as saying that a winning school must do relatively better in keeping theoretical growth ahead of empirical growth – that is, *theory must lead to fact finding*, not the reverse.

Concrete problem solutions. Kuhn's claim is that CPSs "constitute a particularly important element of the research-governing consensus of a scientific community" (Hoyningen-Huene, 1993: 135). They take precedence over other criteria for achieving the status of becoming a science. Specifically, the other criteria are: "explicit definitions of concepts" (compare economics with organization studies), "laws or general theories conceived in abstraction . . . from individual cases," and "explicit unequivocal methodological concepts" (p. 137). These comprise the core elements of a successful truth-testing epistemology – Reichenbach's justification logic. Hoyningen-Huene's analysis shows that, for Kuhn, agreement about CPSs dominates agreement about specific epistemological "rules" as the means of identifying scientific status (1993: 137–40). Laudan (1981) also emphasizes the "problem-solving model" as the core feature of becoming a science and of scientific progress.

Concrete problem solutions are defined as "exemplary models for scientific practice" (Hoyningen-Huene, 1993: 136). Training is key. The best test is to ask whether textbooks used to train entering scientists show consensus on their "selection of problems and solutions" (p. 186). The positive side of this is that the students are quickly and efficiently trained. Oppositely, this process also produces the dogmatism of normal science disciplines (pp. 187–8). How are research problems identified in the first place? First, a research problem – in a paradigmatic science – isn't important unless there is a well accepted theory or conceptual system that can *lead* fact finding (p. 161) – since this is a critical element in scientific progress, as noted above. Thus, while "method" is critical – as also noted above – it is still *theory that must lead fact-finding!* Second, a research problem needs a *contextual background* (p. 161). The "*drive to understand and explain nature is an essential condition. . . .* Accepted canons of explanation are part of what tells [us] which problems are still to be resolved, which phenomena remain unexplained" (Kuhn, 1977:

29). I have emphasized the ontological context, though Hoyningen-Huene (1993: 161) also mentions "instrumentation, theorems, theories, ontological and methodological convictions" as well, that are often taken for granted. "Context" could reflect external phenomena and the explaining of it but it could also be comprised of other disciplines and their paradigm rules.

It may come as a surprise to relativists and postmodernists to discover that Kuhn appears to be emphasizing the deductive criterion that "theory must lead" as well as "context" for defining research problems. His *theory first* dictum anticipates the Semantic Conception's emphasis of theory → formal theory → model-centered science. His *context is essential* dictum anticipates scientific realism's view that the "drive to understand and explain nature" – meaning real-world phenomena – is fundamental to effective science. No Hegelian idealism or ontological nihilism here! One can only wonder how these two dictums have become buried in the post-Kuhnian rush toward relativism and postmodernism – a mad rush nicely detailed in Hunt (1991: chapter 10).

A typology of effectiveness criteria
With this typology I am proposing to outline a path by which organization *studies* might more quickly become organization *science*. Being in a business school, I am prone to normative tendencies and the engineering of things, including science, in this instance. This is a dangerous business, as Pfeffer has found out (Perrow, 1994; Van Maanen, 1995a, b). In fact, Kuhn had already outlawed Pfeffer's "power elites" approach twenty years before Pfeffer tried it. "[T]he transition to normal science can by no means be forced by social measures alone. . . . If the paradigmatic achievements are lacking, they can't be created by decree, nor can the real attraction of alternatives be stifled by social pressure. . . . Kuhn's philosophy of science offers no recipes for determining how a given branch of pre-normal science can attain or accelerate the transition to normal science" (a statement by Hoyningen-Huene, 1993: 193, based on several cites to the basic Kuhnian material, including especially Kuhn, 1970).

Fields/disciplines as sources of answers. It is clear from the foregoing that CPSs cannot be defined solely from ontological context – scientific disciplines get involved as well. All phenomena are hierarchically ordered and, as I have noted earlier, sciences, given molecular reductionism, are also arranged hierarchically. Still, there is an orderly approach to defining CPSs across levels within a specific science, and even when sciences are joined (as with biochemistry) – paradigm clashes do not usually surface. Not so with organizations. With these, analytical levels usually have one or more disciplines attached – psychology, social psychology, sociology, anthropology, economics, among others – each vying for top-school status. Further, social science disciplines tend to have additional school clashes within them. Multiparadigmaticism in organization studies resulting from the several levels of organizational analysis is ever present. Possibly one of the disciplines will successfully extend its paradigm to all levels. Economics is making halting progress in this direction, as it moves down inside firms with agency and game theories. Ironically, the relevance of several social science disciplines at each organizational level of analysis – even if each discipline were itself strongly monoparadigmatic – has made organization studies multiparadigmatic and, thus, prescientific. In fact the more monoparadigmatic (and more scientific) disciplines become, the more prescientific organization studies becomes!

It is clear from Kuhn's and Hoyningen-Huene's analyses that CPSs are defined in the contexts of both disciplines and real-world phenomena to be explained – with roughly equal balance. The additional ideas added by Lakatos, Hacking, and Laudan focus on the significance of method, but methods also are equally driven by discipline and reality. Pfeffer (1993) does offer a way out that I do accept: paradigms as dependent variables – with dependence defined in terms of external user communities. Dependence could be defined in terms of disciplines, but then we would be right back to square one. Only attention to what solves concrete problems as defined by user communities might allow organization studies to rise above multiparadigmaticism.[19]

Targets of solutions: external user communities.
Pfeffer (1993) notes that successful sciences
bring strong and reliable messages to their
external *user* constituencies. He also gives strong
evidence to the effect that organization studies
has minuscule legitimacy at this time. Kepler
wrote some 800 astrological reports. His improvements to the science of orbital mechanics,
even with primitive instruments (he did not
have a telescope) vastly improved the accuracy
of astrological predictions. Skipping seventy
years, Newton refined the laws of motion.
Skipping another 150 years, the invention and
use of the steam engine led Carnot to discover
the second law of thermodynamics. Skipping
another century, as the genetic engineering
discipline contributes more and more toward
improving health it is gaining in status, size,
usefulness, and resources. While the continued
search for novelty across all organizational
phenomena remains important – emphasized
to the exclusion of most everything else by
postmodernists (Golinski, 1998)[20] – the success
of organization studies depends on bringing
more findings to constituents that have the
"reliability of use" value people are accustomed
to receive from effective sciences. Thus, if
organization studies were to produce findings
of *epistemological quality* for the following
external constituencies, its legitimacy would be
greatly enhanced:

1 *Owners, CEOs, managers.* CPSs aimed at
economic rents (above industry-average profits);
or service-related outcome variables for managers heading up public-sector organizations
and government agencies.
2 *Employees.* CPSs aimed at employment,
careers, livelihood.
3 *Constituencies worrying about externalities.*
CPSs dealing with broader societal policy and
environmental issues.
4 *Customers.* CPSs that improve the quality
and price of outputs.
5 *Consulting firms.* CPSs they can take to
clients.

There is a zero-sum game among the aims of
the first four groups – as each benefits the others
are apt to suffer. As each user community is
more clearly served, however, more globally
optimal CPSs become more salient and possible.

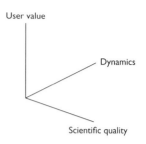

Figure 2.2   Typology of effective science

Typology.   I have highlighted *user value* as one
dimension of effective science (see figure 2.2).
The message of Campbellian realism is that
would-be social scientists are held to a much
higher standard of reliability and quality knowledge for users than are consultants and tradebook authors. The simplest indicator of the
scientific quality dimension is the Guttman scale
I mentioned earlier. This second dimension
focuses on lessons from the reconstructed logic
of realist, evolutionary epistemology coupled
with lessons from the Semantic Conception.
A third dimension reflects an additional
characteristic of successful sciences. On the
grounds that organizational research users are
little different from the users of successful
sciences, it is clear from a broad reading of
all successful sciences that *dynamics* is the
third critical dimension. Here, dynamics
includes the following. (1) Phenomena that
are covered by the first law of thermodynamics
– that is, the *equation* of energy (or its equivalents) from one kind of order to another,
with mathematics acting as the logical and/
or accounting system. This is really the
efficiency dimension – obviously of great interest to organization studies users. (2) *Rates*
at which energy of one kind is converted into
other kinds. In biology this is the metabolic
rate. In a rapidly changing world the rate
at which events progress in organizations is
increasingly important. Users have been very
poorly served on this aspect to date. (3) More
fundamentally, dynamics focuses on *order
creation* – the more telling message from complexity science. For example, in Mainzer's book
Thinking in Complexity (1997) every chapter
starts with the question "How to explain emergent order . . . ?"[21]

Disciplines reduced to clashing schools

On university campuses, inside their respective buildings, the social science disciplines follow internally validated effectiveness criteria. Often these criteria are good for maintaining "discipline," but they do not measure up very well on the three dimensions of my typology. Space precludes detailed ratings of each discipline, but compared with the "real" sciences they fare quite poorly. In the territory occupied by organization studies, disciplines-as-paradigms are reduced to the status of clashing schools in Kuhn's framework. My analysis indicates that organization studies will remain a prescience until discipline-based quality controls are subordinated to the three dimensions of the typology. The elements of the several disciplines that best measure up with respect to these dimensions stand to fuse into the core paradigm of a nascent organization science.

Kuhn (1977) collects many of his papers into an anthology titled *The Essential Tension* – between scientific legitimacy and novelty. Most of the philosophical community (Lakatos, Shapere, Scheffler, McMullin, Laudan, Fuller, etc.) has joined him in exploring the dynamics of science as one dominant paradigm seems to be replaced by another in a continuing cycle of tradition and change in the mature, successful sciences. All of this discussion is in the context of "What is scientific progress?" Since organization studies is a prescience, this discussion is largely irrelevant. Instead of progress by so-called paradigm revolution, we get novelty more from the proliferation of schools, with older schools ever more vigorously defending their shrinking membership. The advantage of attending to the dimensions of the typology is that this provides a supraschool means of evaluating the contribution of each.

The choice is not between paradigm closure versus paradigm diversity. Rather, I see it as drawing enough closure around some well established models – as in model-centered science – whatever school they come from, that serve to offer (1) findings of scientific quality about (2) organizational dynamics to the main (3) external user constituencies of organization studies. Whether the models come from dominant schools or marginal schools is irrelevant. Schools supplying the most models offering

value to the user constituencies will win out. Right now we have lots of possibly "scientific" findings seen as irrelevant by users and lots of trade book and consulting bromides possibly useful but of unreliable quality. No wonder organization studies has low legitimacy in the eyes of both users and the broader scientific community.

The several schools or underlying disciplines do bring some strengths of strong theory and method to organization studies. However, they also bring parochial allegiances and discipline ideologies that, for the most part, are not doing well on any of the typological dimensions. It is clear that organization studies will never become a science in its own right as long as it is held hostage by parochial discipline perspectives – for example, authors publishing in economics or sociology journals just because it looks good at tenure review time! For example, genetic engineering benefits from many relevant disciplines, but it also has become a scientific discipline in its own right, and has a strong user constituency – people benefiting from cancer cures. The same thing needs to happen in organization studies. We need the equivalent of patients who get better as a result of using our findings.

As organization studies moves toward becoming a science it needs to pick off constructive elements from the underlying disciplines but it needs to drop the dysfunctional ideologies and other parochial perspectives. An author producing a study and findings attractive to an underlying discipline is not very likely to produce scientific value useful to the more relevant external user constituencies. This is not to say such studies should not be done. But eventually good value has to arrive at the doorstep of the user constituencies.

Conclusion

There is more to my "counterpoint" than simply reprising the myth of positivism – a horse thirty years dead. I do begin by outlining key failures leading to the abandonment of the Received View (logical positivism and logical empiricism) – for which Suppe (1977) writes the epitaph. This is truly an academic exercise, however, because organization studies never followed positivism anyway. Furthermore, the more serious elements of postmodernism rest on Kuhnian (1962) relativism, a perspective also buried three decades ago by most respectable philosophers. Given these developments, I highlight several "other" post-Kuhnian postpositivisms: scientific realism, evolutionary epistemology, Campbellian realism, the Semantic Conception's model-centered science, and agent-based models. These can be reduced to a Guttman scale of scientific quality. But this is not enough for organization studies *fields* to resolve into an effective *science*. I agree with Pfeffer's (1993) delineation of why organization studies is an ignored, low-status field. But, eschewing a committee of elites, I suggest a three-dimensional typology of research objectives that, together – and defined as I do so here – stand a good chance of sending organizational studies on its way toward becoming a science: *user value, scientific quality*, and *dynamics*.

Notes

1   Philosophical terms can sometimes be intimidating to readers not well versed in the subject, but space precludes offering as many definitions here as one might like. However, McKelvey (2002) offers a glossary of over sixty relevant definitions.

2   As my discussion unfolds you will see that it focuses on *tension* between justification and discovery logic. This list of citations is headed by the historical relativists. This literature forms the base of postmodernism. Because the latter is very diffuse in its subject matter and often pointedly obscure in its use of language (see Foucault, 1977, 1980, for example), as Alvesson and Deetz (1996) admit, I focus my critique on the relativist foundation. The organization studies part of the list is all postmodernism. In general, the latter consists of a responsible core made up of poststructuralists (Saussure to Lyotard in the list) and a more antiscience element. Drawing on Cilliers (1998), Henrickson and McKelvey (2002) show that poststructuralist ontology fits very well with complexity science and agent-based modeling – the modern interpretations of normal science. The

antiscience group is prone to make accusations such as Burrell's (1996: 656) assertion that modernist science (epitomized by Einstein the Zionist who was invited to be the President of Israel) caused the holocaust of 6 million Jews, or Latour's (1988) attack against Pasteur's modernism that ignores the countless millions of lives Pasteur saved as a result of his modernist scientific and political organizing efforts. There is also considerable evidence that postmodernism was a convenient, self-indulgent philosophy promulgated by godfathers who were closet Nazis (Weiss, 2000).

3   Harré (1989) decomposes the world of observation into three "realms": (1) entities that are currently observable (directly accessible to the human senses) (number of employees in a firm); (2) entities currently unobservable but potentially detectable (process event networks in a firm); (3) metaphysical entities beyond any possibility of observation by any conception of current science (psychological need, environmental uncertainty, underlying cause). Pols (1992) terms Realm 1 observations "direct knowing" and Realm 3 observations "indirect knowing."

4   A reading of Suppe (1977) and Hunt (1991) would confirm the centrality of these tenets of logical positivism. Key publications explicating positivism are Carnap (1923, 1966), Neurath et al. (1929), Schlick (1991), Ayer (1959), Neurath and Cohen (1973), and Hanfling (1981).

5   Geneticists and paleontologists have debated the cause of evolution ever since R. A. Fisher's classic book in 1930. Is it ecology or selfish genes (Eldredge, 1995)? These groups each understand the others' terms. Physicists have debated whether physics was an exact or probabilistic science ever since Brown discovered Brownian motion in 1829. Regarding quanta, this led to Einstein's famous phrase "God doesn't play dice," his introduction of "hidden variables" to explain the emergence of wave packets even though a detector wasn't present at the second slit in the double-slit experiment, the Born–Einstein debate (about whether quanta were real, absent a detector) that went on for years (Mermin, 1991), and Murray Gell-Mann's

(1994: 150) implied "The more exact the measure the more probabilistic the law" (my paraphrase) – they also all understood the terms and eventually came up with relevant experiments that satisfied most everyone except Einstein (Omnès, 1999). The debate between exact and probabilistic physics paradigms continued some 100 years.

6   To pick an example, consider the most famous so-called paradigm shift, that from Newton to Einstein. In his 1905 paper Einstein drew mainly on the work of Faraday seventy years earlier. The reason he cited Faraday was that he (Einstein) defined the problem as how to specify a theory of relative motion for the electrodynamics of moving bodies parallel to the already existing theory of relative motion in Newtonian mechanics. By 1895 both Poincaré and Lorentz had announced principles of relativity but to balance the equation governing the relative motion of two inertial systems they retained the concept, ether. In contrast, since the speed of light was discovered to remain constant (Einstein, unaware of the discovery, assumed it as a principle), Einstein accommodated relativity by allowing time to change. Thus, in the Lorentz transformation equations, $t' = t$ became $t' = (t - vx/c^2) / (1 - v^2/c^2)^{1/2}$. Note that none of the terms on the right side of the equation changed meaning, only the term t' changed. What is important to note is that there would have been no reason for Einstein to do what he did if the other terms *had not remained unchanged* – a clear violation of incommensurability. *The fundamental significance of relativity theory is in fact that none of the terms changed meaning except time.* In addition, the new idea appeared as a journal article in an unknown Einstein's first year of publication after his doctorate. How on earth could referees in the old paradigm accept for publication an article by an unknown author in a different, supposedly incommensurable paradigm? This makes sense only if relativity was in fact *not* incommensurable with existing "Newtonian" thinking. See Holton (1988) for the full range of views on whether or not relativity theory was incommensurable with Maxwell, Poincaré, and Lorentz.

7   One of the editors correctly points out that "queries of why" (in the quotation from Sutton and Staw, 1995) could focus on explanations without having clear evidence of transcendental causal processes. Thus we can explain "the weather" perfectly, though totally accurate prediction is still not possible. In fact the editor is pointing to one of the reasons why the Received View failed – there are all sorts of logical problems in trying to equate explanation with prediction (the classic being that farmers predicted the sun rising to great accuracy with the explanation that the Sun goes around the Earth) – as noted elsewhere in the chapter.

8   An early exception is a critique of phenomenology and formal organization from a realist perspective by Clegg (1983).

9   Chia (1996) centers much of his discussion of epistemology on the reflexivity issue. I do not disagree that reflexivity is present in organizations; I am just not sure it counts for very much. If our "science" is so reflexive – meaning that scientific findings feed back to managers to affect their behavior and organizational functioning in ways that alter the phenomena we study – why do we need all those consultants to put academic ideas into practice? Managers would read our journals, put the ideas into practice, and save billions. OD would be history!

10   It is not unlike the conversational approach to representation discussed by Clegg and Hardy (1996). See note 13.

11   This line of reasoning is elaborated in McKelvey (1999b).

12   More fully developed views on the Semantic Conception are Suppe (1989), Thompson (1989), Morgan and Morrison (2000), and McKelvey (2002).

13   Clegg and Hardy (1996) also use a "map" metaphor when writing about the "representation" process. Their depiction helps us understand how a conversational integration of intersubjective meanings helps people see what is *not* in the map's representation of some reality. Their postmodernist perspective is clearly different from Azevedo's but serves to illustrate how, if the map maker were also conversing, a social construction of meanings could lead to a more accurate

mapping or, in Azevedo's terms, a more accurate theory. Clegg and Hardy say at one point, "No objective grounds exist from which to criticize any one genre of representation [a map; a theory] from another" (p. 676). Here is where postmodernists part company from realists. Realists such as Azevedo would say that real-world phenomena act as criterion variables against which a representation may be tested for accuracy. To continue the Clegg–Hardy story, as soon as the people in the room viewing the map walk out into the landscape they are in a position to test and then improve the map's representation – over time and with lengthy conversation, and perhaps even coupled with epistemologically correct research findings.

14 This hierarchy rests on two ideas. First, the phenomena studied increase in size, from the invisible particles studied by physicists to societies and economies. Second, the hierarchy is implicitly *reductionist*. "Extreme" reductionists believe, for example, that chemical bonding processes are ultimately best explained by resorting to the laws of physics; or that the behavior of biomolecules is best explained by chemical processes – though now both physics and chemistry are used to explain biomolecule functioning. I say "extreme" because, for example, no sensible physicist is going to try to explain the behavior of a cat or a society by reaching down to theories about how collapsing wave functions lead to the creation of physical particles – even Schrödinger didn't try that.

15 Basic sources in agent-based modeling are: Weisbuch (1991) and Gaylord and Nishidate (1996) on cellular automata, Mitchell (1996) on genetic algorithms, Wasserman (1989) on neural networks, Prietula et al. (1998) on agent modeling in organization studies, and McKelvey (1999a) on Kauffman's (1993) *NK* model applied to organizations. For a broader view of agent modeling in organization studies see the journal *Computational and Mathematical Organization Theory*.

16 I elaborate on Mainzer's (1997) view of the order-creation side of complexity science more fully in McKelvey (2001). And, building on Cilliers's (1998) work, Henrickson and McKelvey (2002) show how well the

poststructuralist core of postmodernism integrates with complexity science and agent-based models.

17 Masterman (1970) distinguishes between the "non-paradigm" stage and the "multiple paradigm" (field or school) stage. Kuhn (1970: postscript) also came to view the paradigm concept as applying to schools at about the same time as Masterman's identification of the multiparadigm stage.

18 Kuhn's view in No. 8 above *appears* at odds with Pfeffer's view of the role of external legitimacy and my "user value" criterion below, but I don't think so. External legitimacy based on research findings offering value to users is different from low-status fields (not offering much value) at the mercy of random, outside agenda setting. In the former the causal arrow is *discipline-supplied value → external legitimacy*; in the latter the causal arrow is *external agendas → discipline agendas*, with actual discipline-supplied value not yet in the equation.

19 But in trying to solve CPSs it is also important to recognize that both Hassard (1995) and Azevedo (1997) observe that multiple paradigms offer the advantage of multiple lenses, just as optical, infrared, ultraviolet, and x-ray instruments, or earth-based, orbital, and space probes offer astronomers different views of astronomical phenomena.

20 Golinski proposes "that the uncoupling of historical and sociological inquiry from issues of truth, or realism, or objectivity opened the way to a remarkably productive [novel] period in the understanding of science. . . ." (1998: x). No doubt! Imagine how much creativity there could be in the discovery of drugs if researchers didn't have to worry about whether patients' health improved! We see this every day in the dietary supplement industry – no one worries about efficacy until people start dying. "Medicine," whether surgery or ethical drugs, is not perfect but surely no one would say that its track record is not one of steady improvement as the troublesome practices and drugs are selected out over time.

21 I have developed the idea of rates in organizational function in McKelvey (1997). For further development of the order-creation

side of complexity science see McKelvey (2001).

References

Alvesson, M., and Deetz, S. (1996) "Critical theory and postmodernism approaches to organizational studies," in S. R. Clegg, C. Hardy, and W. R. Nord (eds) *Handbook of Organization Studies*, pp. 191–217. Thousand Oaks, CA: Sage.

Aronson, J. L., Harré, R., and Way, E. C. (1994) *Realism Rescued*. London: Duckworth.

Astley, W. G. (1985), "Administrative science as socially constructed truth," *Administrative Science Quarterly*, 30: 497–513.

Ayer, A. J. (1959) *Logical Positivism*. Glencoe, IL: Free Press.

Azevedo, J. (1997) *Mapping Reality: An Evolutionary Realist Methodology for the Natural and Social Sciences*. Albany, NY: State University of New York Press.

Bacharach, S. B. (1989) "Organizational theories: some criteria for evaluation," *Academy of Management Review*, 14: 496–515.

Baudrillard, J. (1983) *Simulations*. New York: Semiotext.

Bentz, V. M., and Shapiro, J. J. (1998) *Mindful Inquiry in Social Research*. Thousand Oaks, CA: Sage.

Beth, E. (1961) "Semantics of physical theories," in H. Freudenthal (ed.) *The Concept and the Role of the Model in Mathematics and Natural and Social Sciences*, pp. 48–51. Dordrecht: Reidel.

Bhaskar, R. (1975) *A Realist Theory of Science*. Leeds: Leeds Books. Second edition, London: Verso, 1997.

Bloor, D. (1976) *Knowledge and Social Imagery*. London: Routledge.

Bohm, D. (1957) *Causality and Chance in Modern Physics*. London: Routledge.

Braithwaite, R. B. (1953) *Scientific Explanation*. Cambridge: Cambridge University Press.

Brannigan, A. (1981) *The Social Basis of Scientific Discoveries*. Cambridge: Cambridge University Press.

Burns, T., and Stalker, G. M. (1961) *The Management of Innovation*. London: Tavistock.

Burrell, G. (1996) "Normal science, paradigms, metaphors, discourses, and genealogies of analysis," in S. R. Clegg, C. Hardy, and W. R. Nord (eds) *Handbook of Organization Studies*, pp. 642–58. Thousand Oaks, CA: Sage.

——(1997) *Pandemonium: Toward a Retro-organization Theory*. Thousand Oaks, CA: Sage.

Burrell, G., and Morgan, G. (1979) *Sociological Paradigms and Organizational Analysis*. London: Heinemann.

Campbell, D. T. (1974) "Evolutionary epistemology," in P. A. Schilpp (ed.) *The Philosophy of Karl Popper* XIV, 1–2, Library of Living Philosophers. La Salle, IL: Open Court. Reprinted in G. Radnitzky and W. W. Bartley III (eds) *Evolutionary Epistemology, Rationality, and the Sociology of Knowledge*, pp. 47–89. La Salle, IL: Open Court.

——(1988) "Descriptive epistemology: psychological, sociological, and evolutionary," in D. T. Campbell, *Methodology and Epistemology for Social Science: Selected Papers*, ed. E. S. Overman, pp. 435–86. Chicago: University of Chicago Press.

——(1991) "Coherentist empiricism, hermeneutics, and the commensurability of paradigms," *International Journal of Educational Research*, 15: 587–97.

——(1995) "The postpositivist, non-foundational, hermeneutic epistemology exemplified in the works of Donald W. Fiske," in P. E. Shrout and S. T. Fiske (eds), *Personality Research, Methods and Theory: A Festschrift honoring Donald W. Fiske*, pp. 13–27. Hillsdale, NJ: Erlbaum.

Carnap, R. (1923) "Über die Aufgabe der Physik und die Andwendung des Grundsätze der Einfachheit," *Kant-Studien*, 28: 90–107.

——(1966) *Philosophical Foundations of Physics*. New YorK: Basic Books.

Chia, R. (1996) *Organizational Analysis as Deconstructive Practice*. Berlin: de Gruyter.

Cilliers, P. (1998) *Complexity and Postmodernism: Understanding Complex Systems*. London: Routledge.

Clegg, S. R. (1983) "Phenomenology and formal organizations: a realist critique," in S. B. Bachrach (ed.) *Perspective in Organizational Sociology: Theory and Research*, pp. 109–52. Greenwich, CT: JAI Press.

Clegg, S. R., and Hardy, C. (1996) "Conclusion representations," in S. R. Clegg, C. Hardy, and W. R. Nord (eds) *Handbook of Organization*

Studies, pp. 676–708. Thousand Oaks, CA: Sage.

Clegg, S. R., Hardy, C., and Nord, W. R., eds (1996) *Handbook of Organization Studies*. Thousand Oaks, CA: Sage.

Cooper, R., and Burrell, G. (1988) "Modernism, postmodernism and organizational analysis: an introduction," *Organization Studies*, 9: 91–112.

Culler, J. (1983) *On Deconstruction: Theory and Criticism after Structuralism*. London: Routledge.

De Regt, C. D. G. (1994) *Representing the World by Scientific Theories: The Case for Scientific Realism*. Tilburg: Tilburg University Press.

Derrida, J. (1978) *Writing and Difference*. London: Routledge.

Donaldson, L. (1995) *American Anti-management Theories of Organization: A Critique of Paradigm Proliferation*. Cambridge: Cambridge University Press.

——(1996) *For Positivist Organization Theory*. Thousand Oaks, CA: Sage.

Einstein, A. (1905) "Zur Elektrodynamik bewegter Körper" (On the electrodynamics of moving bodies), *Annalen der Physik*, 17: 891–921.

Eldredge, N. (1995) *Reinventing Darwin*. New York: Wiley.

Feyerabend, P. K. (1962) "Explanation, reduction, and empiricism," in H. Feigl and G. Maxwell (eds) *Current Issues in the Philosophy of Science*, pp. 28–97. New York: Holt Rinehart & Winston.

——(1975) *Against Method*. London: New Left Books.

Fisher, R. A. (1930) *The Genetical Theory of Natural Selection*. London: Oxford University Press.

Foucault, M. (1977) *Discipline and Punish: The Birth of the Prison*, trans. A. S. Smith. New York: Random House.

——(1980) *Power/Knowledge: Selected Interviews and Writings*, ed. C. Gordon. New York: Pantheon.

Friedman, M. (1953) *Essays in Positive Economics*. Chicago: University of Chicago Press.

Gaylord, R. J., and Nishidate, K. (1996) *Modeling Nature: Cellular Automata Simulations with Mathematica.*® New York: Springer.

Gell-Mann, M. (1994) *The Quark and the Jaguar*. New York: Freeman.

Girod-Séville, M., and Perret, V. (2001) "Epistemological foundations," in R-A. Thiétart et al. (eds) *Doing Management Research*, trans. S. Wauchope, pp. 13–30. London: Sage.

Goldstein, L. J. (1963) "The phenomenological and naturalistic approach to the social," in M. Natanson (ed.) *Philosophy of the Social Sciences*, pp. 286–301. New York: Random House.

Golinski, J. (1998) *Making Natural Knowledge*. Cambridge: Cambridge University Press.

Guba, E., and Lincoln, Y. S. (1994) "Competing Paradigms in Qualitative Research," in N. K. Denzin and Y. S. Lincoln (eds) *Handbook of Qualitative Research*, pp. 105–17. Thousand Oaks, CA: Sage.

Hacking, I. (1981) "Lakatos's philosophy of science," in I. Hacking (ed.) *Scientific Revolutions*, pp. 128–43. Oxford: Oxford University Press.

Hahlweg, K., and Hooker, C. A. (1989) "Historical and theoretical context," in K. Hahlweg and C. A. Hooker (eds) *Issues in Evolutionary Epistemology*, pp. 23–44. Albany, NY: State University of New York Press.

Hanfling, O. (1981) *Logical Positivism*. Oxford: Blackwell.

Hanson, N. R. (1958) *Patterns of Discovery*. Cambridge: Cambridge University Press.

Harré, R. (1989) "Realism, reference and theory," in A. P. Griffiths (ed.) *Key Themes in Philosophy*, pp. 53–68. Cambridge: Cambridge University Press.

Hassard, J. (1993) "Postmodernism and organizational analysis: an overview," in J. Hassard and M. Parker (eds) *Postmodernism and Organizations*, pp. 1–23. London: Sage.

——(1995) *Sociology and Organization Theory: Positivism, Paradigms and Postmodernity*. Cambridge: Cambridge University Press.

Hassard, J., and Parker, M. (1993) *Postmodernism and Organizations*. Thousand Oaks, CA: Sage.

Heidegger, M. (1962) *Being and Time*, trans. J. Macquarrie and E. Robinson. New York: Harper & Row.

Hempel, C. G. (1965) *Aspects of Scientific Explanation*. New York: Free Press.

Hendrickx, M. (1999) "What can management researchers learn from Donald Campbell, the philosopher?" in J. A. C. Baum and B. McKelvey (eds) *Variations in Organization Science: In Honor of Donald T. Campbell*, pp. 339–82. Thousand Oaks, CA: Sage.

Henrickson, L., and McKelvey, B. (2002) "Foundations of 'new' social science: institutional legitimacy from philosophy, complexity science, postmodernism, and agent-based modeling," *Proceedings of the National Academy of Sciences.*

Holton, G. (1988) *Thematic Origins of Scientific Thought: Kepler to Einstein*, revised edition. Cambridge, MA: Harvard University Press.

——(1993) *Science and Anti-science.* Cambridge, MA: Harvard University Press.

Hooker, C. A. (1995) *Reason, Regulation, and Realism.* Albany, NY: State University of New York Press.

Hoyningen-Huene, P. (1993) *Reconstructing Scientific Revolutions*, trans. A. T. Levine. Chicago: University of Chicago Press.

Hull, D. (1975) Review of Hempel, Kuhn, and Shapere, *Systematic Zoology*, 24: 395–401.

Hunt, S. D. (1991) *Modern Marketing Theory: Critical Issues in the Philosophy of Marketing Science.* Cincinnati, OH: Southwestern.

——(1994) "On the rhetoric of qualitative methods: toward historically informed argumentation in management inquiry," *Journal of Management Inquiry*, 23: 221–34.

Kaplan, A. (1964) *The Conduct of Inquiry.* New York: Chandler.

Kauffman, S. A. (1993) *The Origins of Order: Self-organization and Selection in Evolution.* New York: Oxford University Press.

Knights, D. (1992) "Changing spaces: the disruptive impact of a new epistemological location for the study of management," *Academy of Management Review*, 17: 514–36.

Koertge, N. (1989) *A House Built on Sand: Exposing Postmodernist Myths about Science.* New York: Oxford University Press.

Kuhn, T. S. (1962) *The Structure of Scientific Revolutions.* Chicago: University of Chicago Press.

——(1970) *The Structure of Scientific Revolutions*, second edition. Chicago: University of Chicago Press.

——(1977) *The Essential Tension.* Chicago: University of Chicago Press.

Lado, A. A., and Wilson, M. C. (1994) "Human resource systems and sustained competitive advantage: a competency-based perspective," *Academy of Management Review*, 19: 699–727.

Latour, B. (1987) *Science in Action.* Milton Keynes: Open University Press.

——(1988) *The Pasteurization of France*, trans. A. Sheridan and J. Law. Cambridge, MA: Harvard University Press.

Laudan, L. (1977) *Progress and its Problems.* Berkeley, CA: University of California Press.

——(1981) "A confutation of convergent realism," *Philosophy of Science*, 48: 19–48.

Lawrence, B. L. (1997) "The black box of organizational demography," *Organization Science*, 8: 1–22.

Lyotard, J-F. (1984) *The Postmodern Condition: A Report on Knowledge.* Manchester: Manchester University Press.

Mainzer, K. (1997) *Thinking in Complexity: The Complex Dynamics of Matter, Mind, and Mankind.* New York: Springer.

Marsden, R., and Townley, B. (1996) "The owl of Minerva: reflections on theory in practice," in S. R. Clegg, C. Hardy, and W. R. Nord (eds) *Handbook of Organization Studies*, pp. 659–75. Thousand Oaks, CA: Sage.

Masterman, M. (1970) "The nature of a paradigm," in I. Lakatos and A. Musgrave (eds) *Criticism and the Growth of Knowledge*, pp. 59–90. Cambridge: Cambridge University Press.

McGuire, J. E. (1992) "Scientific change: perspectives and proposals," in M. H. Salmon et al. (eds) *Introduction to the Philosophy of Science*, pp. 132–78. Englewood Cliffs, NJ: Prentice-Hall.

McKelvey, B. (1997) "Quasi-natural organization science," *Organization Science*, 8: 351–80.

——(1999a) "Avoiding complexity catastrophe in coevolutionary pockets: strategies for rugged landscapes," *Organization Science*, 10: 294–321.

——(1999b) "Toward a Campbellian realist organization science," in J. A. C. Baum and B. McKelvey (eds) *Variations in Organization Science: In Honor of Donald T. Campbell*, pp. 383–411. Thousand Oaks, CA: Sage.

——(2001) "Social Order–Creation Instability Dynamics: Heterogeneous Agents and Fast-motion Science – on the Hundredth Anniversary of Bénard's Paper," presented at the Workshop on Thermodynamics and Complexity Applied to Organizations, pp. 28–9. Brussels: EIASM.

——(2002) "Model-centered organization science epistemology," plus "Glossary of epistemology terms," in J. A. C. Baum (ed.) *Companion to Organizations*, pp. 752–89 and 889–98. Thousand Oaks, CA: Sage.

McKinlay, A., and Starkey, K. (1998) *Foucault, Management, and Organization Theory*. Thousand Oaks, CA: Sage.

Mermin, D. N. (1991) "Is the moon there when nobody looks? Reality and the quantum theory," in R. Boyd, P. Gasper, and J. D. Trout (eds) *The Philosophy of Science*, pp. 501–16. Cambridge, MA: Bradford/MIT Press.

Merton, R. K. (1967) *On Theoretical Sociology*. New York: Free Press.

Mitchell, M. (1996) *An Introduction to Genetic Algorithms*. Cambridge, MA: MIT Press.

Mitroff, I. (1972) "The myth of objectivity, or, Why science needs a new psychology of science," *Management Science*, 18: B613–18.

Morgan, M. S., and Morrison, M., eds (2000) *Models as Mediators: Perspectives on Natural and Social Science*. Cambridge: Cambridge University Press.

Nagel, E. (1961) *The Structure of Science*. New York: Harcourt Brace.

Natanson, M. (1958) "A study in philosophy and the social sciences," *Social Research*, 25: 158–72.

Neurath, O., and Cohen, R. S., eds (1973) *Empiricism and Sociology*. Dordrecht: Reidel.

Neurath, O., with H. Hahn and R. Carnap (1929) "Wissenschaftliche Weltauffassung. Der Wiener Kreis." Vienna: Wolf. Reprinted as "The scientific conception of the world: the Vienna circle," in M. Neurath and R. S. Cohen (eds) *Empiricism and Sociology*, pp. 301–18. Dordrecht: Reidel, 1973.

Nola, R. (1988) *Relativism and Realism in Science*. Dordrecht: Kluwer.

Omnès, R. (1999) *Understanding Quantum Mechanics*. Princeton, NJ: Princeton University Press.

Papineau, D., ed. (1996) *The Philosophy of Science*. New York: Oxford University Press.

Perrow, C. (1994) "Pfeffer slips," *Academy of Management Review*, 19: 191–4.

Peters, T. J., and Waterman, R. H., Jr (1982) *In Search of Excellence: Lessons from America's best-run Companies*. New York: Harper & Row.

Pfeffer, J. (1982) *Organizations and Organization Theory*. Boston, MA: Pitman.

——(1993) "Barriers to the advancement of organizational science: paradigm development as a dependent variable," *Academy of Management Review*, 18: 599–620.

——(1995) "Mortality, reproducibility, and the persistence of styles of theory," *Organization Science*, 6: 681–6.

Pols, E. (1992) *Radical Realism: Direct Knowing in Science and Philosophy*. Ithaca, NY: Cornell University Press.

Popper, K. R. (1968) *Logic of Scientific Discovery*, second edition. New York: Harper & Row.

Powell, W. W., and DiMaggio, P. J. (1991) *The New Institutionalism in Organizational Analysis*. Chicago: University of Chicago Press.

Prietula, M. J., Carley, K. M., and Gasser, L., eds (1998) *Simulating Organizations: Computational Models of Institutions and Groups*. Boston, MA: MIT Press.

Putnam, H. (1962) "What theories are not," in E. Nagel, P. Suppes, and A. Tarski (eds) *Logic, Methodology, and Philosophy of Science: Proceedings of the 1960 International Congress*, pp. 240–51. Stanford, CA: Stanford University Press.

——(1981) *Reason, Truth, and History*. Cambridge: Cambridge University Press.

——(1987) *The Many Faces of Realism*. La Salle, IL: Open Court.

Reed, M., and Hughes, M., eds (1992) *Rethinking Organization: New Directions in Organization Theory and Analysis*. London: Sage.

Reichenbach, H. (1938) *Experience and Prediction*. Chicago: University of Chicago Press.

——(1949) *The Theory of Probability*. Berkeley, CA: University of California Press.

Ruse, M. (1973) *The Philosophy of Biology*. London: Hutchinson.

Sarup, M. (1988) *An Introductory Guide to Post-structuralism and Postmodernism*, second edition. Athens, GA: University of Georgia Press.

Saussure, F. de (1974) *Course in General Linguistics*. London: Fontana/Collins.

Scheffler, I. (1967) *Science and Subjectivity*. Indianapolis, IN: Bobbs-Merrill.

Schlick, M. (1991) "Positivism and realism," trans. P. Heath, in R. Boyd, P. Gasper, and J. D. Trout (eds) *The Philosophy of Science*, pp. 23–55. Cambridge, MA: Bradford/MIT Press. Originally in *Erkenntnis* III (1932/3).

Schutz, A. (1962) "Concept and theory formation in the social sciences," in *Collected Papers*, ed. M. Natanson, I, *The Problem of Social Reality*, pp. 48–66. The Hague: Nijhoff.

Schwab, J. J. (1960) "What do scientists do?" *Behavioral Science*, 5: 1–27.

Scott, W. R. (1995) *Institutions and Organizations*. Thousand Oaks, CA: Sage.

Silverman, D. (1970) *The Theory of Organizations: A Sociological Framework*. London: Heinemann.

Smircich, L., and Calás, M. (1987) "Organizational culture: a critical assessment," in F. Jablin, L. Putnam, K. Roberts, and L. Porter (eds) *Handbook of Organizational Communication*, pp. 228–63. Newbury Park, CA: Sage.

Sokal, A., and Bricmont, J. (1998) *Fashionable Nonsense: Postmodern Intellectuals' Abuse of Science*. New York: Picador.

Suppe, F. (1967) "The Meaning and Use of Models in Mathematics and the Exact Sciences," unpublished doctoral dissertation, Ann Arbor, MI: University of Michigan.

——(1977) *The Structure of Scientific Theories*, second edition. Chicago: University of Chicago Press.

——(1989) *The Semantic Conception of Theories and Scientific Realism*. Urbana, IL: University of Illinois Press.

Suppes, P. (1961) "A comparison of the meaning and use of models in mathematics and the empirical sciences," in H. Freudenthal (ed.) *The Concept and the Role of the Model in Mathematics and Natural and Social Sciences*, pp. 163–77. Dordrecht: Reidel.

——(1967) "What is scientific theory?" in S. Morgenbesser (ed.) *Philosophy of Science Today*, pp. 55–67. New York: Meridian.

Sutton, R. I., and Staw, B. M. (1995) "What theory is *not*," *Administrative Science Quarterly*, 40: 371–84.

Thompson, P. (1989) *The Structure of Biological Theories*. Albany, NY: State University of New York Press.

Toulmin, S. (1953) *The Philosophy of Science: An Introduction*. London: Hutchinson.

Van de Ven, A. (1989) "Nothing is quite so practical as a good theory," *Academy of Management Review*, 14: 486–9.

van Fraassen, B. C. (1970) "On the extension of Beth's semantics of physical theories," *Philosophy of Science*, 37: 325–39.

——(1980) *The Scientific Image*. Oxford: Clarendon Press.

Van Maanen, J. (1995a) "Style as theory," *Organization Science*, 6: 133–43.

——(1995b) "Fear and loathing in organization studies," *Organization Science*, 6: 687–92.

Wasserman, P. D. (1989) *Neural Computing: Theory and Practice*. New York: Van Nostrand Reinhold.

Weisbuch, G. (1991) *Complex Systems Dynamics: An Introduction to Automata Networks*, trans. S. Ryckebusch, Lecture Notes II, Santa Fe Institute. Reading MA: Addison-Wesley.

Weiss, R. (2000) "Taking science out of organization science: how would postmodernism reconstruct the analysis of organizations?" *Organization Science*, 11: 709–31.

Whitley, R. (1984) "The scientific status of management research as a practically-oriented social science," *Journal of Management Studies*, 21: 369–90.

Wicks, A. C., and Freeman, R. E. (1998) "Organization studies and the new pragmatism: positivism, antipositivism, and the search for ethics," *Organization Science*, 9: 123–40.

Williams, M. B. (1970) "Deducing the consequences of evolution: a mathematical model," *Journal of Theoretical Biology*, 29: 343–85.

——(1973) "The logical status of natural selection and other evolutionary controversies," in M. Bunge (ed.) *The Methodological Unity of Science*, pp. 84–102. Dordrecht: Reidel.

2b Paradigm Plurality: Exploring Past, Present, and Future Trends

Mihaela Kelemen and John Hassard

Chapter 2b maps out the development of paradigm plurality in a number of organizational disciplines such as organization theory, strategic management, international business, operational research, and technology studies. In so doing, it argues that the benefits of paradigm plurality outweigh its shortcomings and that it is important that researchers preserve and encourage theories emerging from multiple paradigmatic viewpoints. Not only is this scenario possible from a substantive and theoretical point of view, but it is also highly desirable in light of the changes taking place in contemporary organizational realities and epistemologies.

Despite its controversial meanings, the concept of paradigm has increased in significance for the contemporary analysis of organizational phenomena, continuing to shape in a direct or indirect way the thinking and approach of most organizational researchers. The most common understanding of the concept of "paradigm" derives from Kuhn's work (1962, 1970): a paradigm is considered to be a set of shared beliefs and assumptions about the world. Consensus around such beliefs within a particular scientific community is regarded as a mark of maturity, while the existence of multiple paradigms bears the mantra of pre- or nonscience. For the purpose of this chapter we define paradigm in a rather loose manner as a shared set of views, values, and writing conventions around which research communities are being formed.

Despite arguments that paradigm purity is a sign of scientific maturity within a particular field of study (Pfeffer, 1993, 1997), we seem to be witnessing a shift towards paradigm plurality in numerous organizational disciplines, among them organization studies (Hassard, 1993; Schultz and Hatch, 1996), international business (Parkhe, 1993; Earley and Singh, 1995), strategic management (McKinley, 1995; Scherer, 1998), operational research (Mingers, 1992, 1997) and technology (Lewis and Grimes, 1999). In what follows we explore the conditions under which plural paradigms have emerged in the fields mentioned above. We then highlight the advantages and disadvantages of the approach, present specific strategies of multiparadigm research within the field of organization theory and finally conclude with a plea for a postmodern discursive approach to paradigm plurality.

Paradigm Plurality: a Rationale

The emergence of paradigm plurality within the fields mentioned above can be explained in a number ways. First, the positivist epistemology has severe shortcomings in explaining what is happening in organizations. Second, organizational realities are becoming more complex and diverse than ever before, such that representation in one dimension is no longer appropriate. Third, there is an apparent moral crisis facing contemporary society, and, fourth, one has to consider the quest for uniqueness and faster career advancement in academia.

Shortcomings of positivist epistemology

At the outset, positivism provided the theoretical foundations and the language for studying organizational phenomena. Chief among positivist assumptions are the belief that organizational reality is objective and scientifically apprehensible as well as an abiding commitment to the methods and aims of "natural" science, perceived to be superior to all other approaches for acquiring knowledge. This is not to say that positivist social science is monolithic: those who adhere to positivism's mission of applying social science to improve social conditions differ widely in their values and approaches as much as they share a commitment to disseminating knowledge that will facilitate action. Despite positivism's "positive" agenda, positivist explanations, particularly in management, seem to have reached their most refined forms, making it difficult to offer any new insights into the management of organizations (Jackson and Carter, 1992: 12).

Organization studies is not the only organizational discipline in which new paradigms have emerged. A significant number of other disciplines have grown dissatisfied with the prevailing positivist orthodoxy and turned towards exploring other alternatives. For example, a number of authors (Scherer and Dowling, 1995; McKinley, 1995; Scherer, 1998) discuss the emergence of alternative approaches in strategic management in response to the inability of positivist methods of research to capture and account for the social and contingent nature of strategy. While most scholars in strategic management still hold on to the explanatory power of positivism and its underlying research methodologies (cf. Shrivastava, 1987), one can witness "a growing 'mess' of models, approaches and schools of strategy-making" (Scherer and Dowling, 1995: 201). Scherer and Dowling advocate the need to bracket such schools, models, or paradigms with the view of arriving at a more comprehensive understanding of the processes through which strategy is enacted and the consequences it may have upon stakeholders and the overall environment. International business, a discipline whose roots are deeply embedded in positivist science, has more recently witnessed the emergence of more interpretive approaches which are argued to complement well the deductive stances (Parkhe, 1993; Earley and Singh, 1995). Technology studies have also benefited from research from plural paradigms (Grint, 1991). Lewis and Grimes (1999) have proposed a metatriangulation method for building theory from plural paradigms within the area of advanced manufacturing technology (AMT). In operational research, the acceptance of paradigm purity and the dominance of positivism began to break down over the 1990s, the debate turning to various forms of pluralism in both methodological and philosophical terms (Mingers, 1997). Currently, three paradigms seem to coexist in operational research, namely the so-called "hard" paradigm whose roots lie in positivism, the so-called "soft" paradigm, which bears close similarities with social constructivism, and a critical paradigm which emphasizes the oppressing and inequitable nature of the social world (Mingers, 1992). Again, a multiparadigm understanding of operational research is being advocated on the grounds of achieving deeper, more complex insights into organizational realities.

Shifts in organizational realities

People and organizations populate a universe vastly different from that of the past, a universe which is not all closed and settled, which is in many respects indeterminate and in the making. In such a plural, restless universe no single point of view can ever account for the multifaceted, contentious, and continuously changing organizational realities. Reed (1997) suggests that it is this stratified, multidimensional ontology that calls for multiple epistemological and methodological lenses to explore the plurality of organizational realities from alternative perspectives. Indeed, as researchers have attempted to keep pace with and comprehend organizational changes they have called upon varied epistemologies,

producing an explosion of diverse, often contentious perspectives (Lewis and Grimes, 1999). Organizations are now seen to inhabit a so-called postindustrial (White and Jaques, 1995) space where new forms of production and distribution have come into being. For example, the network, the process-driven, and the virtual organization coexist alongside bureaucratic organizations. Fordist technologies of mass production and distribution coexist alongside post-Fordist technologies that allow flexible specialization and niche distribution (Piore and Sabel, 1984). These dramatic transformations are seen to have called for new ways of theorizing (Burrell, 1996).

The moral crisis

It is now widely recognized that we live in uncertain times defined in terms of constant change and inability to secure final meanings located in an "objective" reality (Parker, 1998; MacIntyre, 1985). The challenge of theorizing such uncertainty has given rise to numerous debates as to how to best account for the problematic nature of the individual, the organization, and society at large. According to Bauman (1993, 1995), one of the most important goals of modernity was to construct a world free of moral ambiguity by transferring individual responsibilities to impersonal, scientific methods and procedures. While such transfer took place via the rise of bureaucracy, the inherent morality of scientific procedures became itself questionable as it led to numerous human disasters rather than improved the social condition of humanity. With no prescriptive frameworks to guide our actions, it becomes more and more difficult to justify our research position simply on ontological or epistemological grounds. It follows that our personal ethical stance should guide our engagement with the social world and more specifically our research of organizational practices (Parker, 1999). Given the existence of a plurality of personal moral values it is inevitable that we will end up with a proliferation of theories, models, and paradigms reflecting individuals' ideological positions.

The quest for uniqueness and career advancement in academia

The quest for uniqueness and career advancement in the academic world has led to a situation where social scientists are keener than ever to "come up" with new models, theories, and approaches in order to carve a space for themselves which will ensure immediate recognition and faster career advancement (McKinley and Mone, 1998). This has led to the proliferation of disciplines and analytical perspectives, such as entrepreneurship, e-commerce, knowledge management, and actor network theory. There is nothing inherently wrong in the apparent fragmentation of organizational analysis: what is worrying, however, is the various wars fought between such disciplines and schools of thought, each trying to secure legitimacy in the eyes of the scientific community and recruit followers at the expense of the rest. Such wars are fought around the view that various schools, models, paradigms are incommensurable – in other words, they share no ontological, epistemological, and methodological grounds, and therefore communication between them is impossible. Such a state of affairs is seen to be attractive to some theorists because of the reputational advantages associated with safeguarding the distinctiveness and survival of their own theory (McKinley and Mone, 1998), which may have emancipatory value in that the overarching positivist paradigm can be challenged by other voices (Jackson and Carter, 1991) or may lead to the stagnation of the entire field (Gioia and Pitre, 1990, Willmott, 1993).

Paradigm Plurality

A map of advantages

The advantages of paradigm plurality have been widely acknowledged in the literature. For example, it is argued that the use of a single paradigm produces too narrow a view to reflect the multifaceted nature of organizational reality (Gioia and Pitre, 1990). Consequently the use of multiple paradigms is "a better way of fostering more comprehensive portraits of complex organizational phenomena" (ibid.: 587).

Furthermore, knowledge about more than one paradigm raises awareness of alternative research styles and agendas and, in so doing, fosters innovation and creativity in research (Brocklesby, 1997; Morgan, 1983). Knowledge of other paradigms allows a researcher to become detached from a "preferred" view of the world and engage in exploring new avenues. While some of these avenues may lead to contradictory findings, researchers could build upon such contradictions to produce accounts which are richer and more illuminating and question the interests reflected by and re-enacted in such accounts. Paradox and contradiction are in fact the driving engine of scientific innovation (Lewis, 2000).

By becoming literate in multiple paradigms, researchers can engage more effectively in conversation with other colleagues and with practitioners. Only through an open and democratic dialogue, involving all stakeholders, can organizational disciplines decide what is important to study, the appropriate methodologies and the effects emerging theories will have upon the surrounding social realities. Cooperation rather than competition could prove much more valuable in the enterprise of knowledge production.

Paradigm plurality allows reconciliation between the various agendas pursued by researchers. We have identified four different agendas. (1) Some researchers aim to create theories that control and predict the social world. (2) Others are driven by an interest in understanding how meaning is constructed, negotiated, and enacted, (3) Others pursue some form of critical science which aims to emancipate various groups of people (Alvesson and Willmott, 1996). (4) Finally, there are researchers whose main agenda consists of providing practical solutions to short-term organizational practices. While there are substantial tensions between these agendas, some research would benefit if it were pursued at their crossroads. It is widely accepted that most organizational researchers embrace the first two positions without necessarily considering the effects their work has upon the objects of inquiry. Gaining understanding is what drives their research; what happens afterwards is no longer the concern of the theorist. However, such findings could be put to the service of improving organizational efficiency or emancipating organizational members (agendas 3 and 4).

Finally, the pursuit of multiparadigm research ensures the preservation and legitimization of points of view that might otherwise be perceived as marginal or indeed be suppressed by the dominant orthodoxy. Thus those theories that speak in the name of "the silent" and "the unheard" (see, for example, labor process theory, critical theory, feminism, poststructuralism) construct a place from which to voice their concerns. If management and organization studies are to be indeed "ethical" they have to encourage a plurality of diverse voices, some of which will stand in total opposition to the interests promulgated by positivist social science.

A map of disadvantages

There are indeed numerous hurdles and disadvantages to doing multiparadigm research. One's socialization in one particular paradigm and its reinforcement through existing institutions make it difficult for researchers to question their preconceived ideas about the world, binding them to a particular vision of the world. Furthermore, researchers' acceptance and engagement with plural paradigms does not come in an easy way. It requires much more training and effort than a single perspective. It is more common for positivists to explore alternative paradigms than for interpretivist/critical researchers to go "back to basics" and study positivism. Committing oneself to more than one paradigm comes with cognitive and emotional personal costs: leaving behind or pushing away (temporarily) a particular paradigm in order to engage with a new one can be a painful operation. Indeed, for some individuals it may be impossible to move across paradigms, either because they believe their moral duty to be allegiance to one particular set of interests or because they do not possess the emotional repertoire needed to venture into new paradigms.

Knowing and acting effectively in a new paradigm makes substantial demands upon the individual, demands which can be satisfied only through active bodily involvement, experience, and practice (Brocklesby, 1997). Assuming that the researcher becomes socialized within the language and practice of a new paradigm, problems arise if there are conflicts between the world views promulgated by these. The researcher must search for strategies to reconcile these conflicts, a process that requires a great deal of cognitive resources, determination, and courage.

Operating across paradigms makes it more difficult to engage in acts of "scientific certification." Researchers pursue certification of their knowledge as much as they pursue knowledge itself, because knowledge without an audience is useless (McCloskey, 1994). In so doing, they rely on multiple rhetorical devices as instruments of persuasion. Thus a positivist account would make use of statistical data in order to convey a particular point of view, while a social constructivist analysis would ground the argument in rich ethnographic data. A multiparadigm study would have recourse to both types of evidence, but in so doing, one could end up upsetting both camps for not taking seriously the conventions and rigors embraced by the respective scientific camp.

Career choices may also be more limited as pluralist research is not a legitimate enterprise. Finally, the use of multiple lenses comes also with a theoretical caveat. Scherer and Steinmann (1999) warn that mixing several positions does not necessarily lead to more comprehensive and better explanations of the organizational world. When each of them has deficiencies, a combination would be even worse.

The Pursuit of Multi-paradigm Research: the Case of Organizational Studies

An increasing number of organization theorists have advocated the need to engage in multiparadigm research. This is not only theoretically feasible but crucial if researchers want to better comprehend the complex nature of contemporary organizations.

Gioia and Pitre (1990) argue for the theoretical feasibility of multiparadigm research. They suggest that one must accept that paradigms share certain common concepts, entities or "transition zones," otherwise new theories would have no basis by which to refute or amend previous theories. With reference to

Kuhn's (1970) later works, they suggest that, in order for a paradigm to gain credibility and achieve a position of dominance, it would have to question continually an existing paradigm and its favorite assumptions and procedures. In order to question old paradigms, the new paradigm has to understand and speak in terms that can be understood by its prospective audience. According to Gioia and Pitre's interpretation, Kuhn's later works suggest that even though there might not be a common language in which the contents of rival theory can be fully expressed or evaluated, there is a degree of commensurability, for otherwise new theory would never develop and could never be evaluated.

In support of the theoretical feasibility of multiparadigm research, Weaver and Gioia (1994) build on Giddens's theory of structuration. They do so to argue that the typical divides between determinism and voluntarism, object and subject, description and prescription, and holism and individualism, can be resolved via a dialogue between paradigms. They argue that various paradigms reflect various facets of one social phenomenon, and the denial of this principle would mean that we have different phenomena rather than multi-faceted ones. According to Weaver and Gioia, the use of any single research paradigm would produce a view which is too narrow to reflect the multifaceted nature of organizational reality. Thus each paradigm constitutes a legitimate part of a larger scheme and it is important to pursue multiparadigm research from the position that paradigms are distinctive but at the same time permeable.

Schultz and Hatch (1996: 55) also advocate the need for multiparadigm research: "multiparadigm thinking is both likely and desirable, in light of predictions about diversity in postindustrial society." They propose a strategy of paradigm crossing, named "interplay," which is defined as the simultaneous recognition of both contrasts and connections between paradigms. In interplay, the researcher is seen to move back and forth between paradigms, allowing multiple views to be held in tension. Lewis and Grimes (1999) have provided a step-by-step guide to building theory from multiple paradigms, a process they label metatriangulation.

In the United Kingdom multiparadigm thinking and research have been advocated by Hassard (1988, 1991, 1993). His work is concerned not only with the theoretical underpinnings of paradigm commensurability (1988) but also with producing empirical accounts of a multiparadigmatic nature (1991, 1993). Hassard argues that although the late Kuhn talks about tentative communication between paradigms, this position is still not satisfactory: "for the goal of paradigm mediation, Kuhn fails to go far enough toward a form of analysis which would retain paradigm identity while offering an alternative to hermeticism" (1988: 253). He suggests we turn to the later works of Wittgenstein, which provide a more acceptable solution to overcoming theoretical hermeticism in organization theory. Wittgenstein (1953) considers that our metalanguage, or everyday language game (our basic language, the first language that we accommodate), underlies all technical and special language games. As a result, the rules and conventions of our metalanguage in use "allow us to deal not only with a present language game but also with a new language game into which we may be trained" (Hassard, 1988: 257). Since the metalanguage in use is the basis for training into other technical languages, it appears clear that understanding and using two or more technical language games at the same time is achievable. Hassard's (1991, 1993) fourfold account of work behavior in the fire service is an illustration of how researchers could muster more than one language game and write multifaceted accounts of the same organizational phenomenon.

While the above authors attempt to preserve the identity of each paradigm, others suggest that boundaries might need to dissolve at least on a temporary basis in order to ensure the creation of common reference systems, or dictionaries which are democratically accepted by all. McKinley (1995), for example, suggests that the adoption of a "reasonable realism" may be the key to overcoming hermeticism. Reasonable realism, in its quest for a truth that can be known only with uncertainty, could help to create a common reference system by which paradigms can be reconciled and evaluated. The aim is to disconfirm all paradigms that do not conform to that reality as defined by standard constructs. This argument is refined further by McKinley and Mone (1998). Here the ambiguity of the key constructs that form the building blocks of organization studies is identified as the major reason for persistent interschool incommensurability. The authors recommend the creation of a dictionary that would include democratically produced definitions of key organization studies constructs.

Contrary to this idea, Scherer and Dowling (1995) suggest that there is little point in searching for the "right" criteria to evaluate systems of orientation from an observer's perspective. Instead, researchers should seek methods for how to interact and communicate with each other in order to improve practice. Instead of acting as passive observers, researchers should engage in the resolution of the paradigm debate as active participants. Given that the ultimate goal of science is to improve practice, a dialogue among the participants will have a significant impact on improving managerial and organizational practice.

Wicks and Freeman (1998) have also discussed this appeal to pragmatism. They urge researchers to move beyond epistemological distinctions between paradigms by making room for ethics and thus increasing the relevance of research. Pragmatism is highlighted as a useful tool in that it sheds light on the moral dimension of organizing. Wicks and Freeman (1998) do not think it is possible to simply combine various paradigms or split the difference between them in order to create a compelling alternative to the current situation. They advocate instead a different approach to organization studies termed "pragmatic experimentation." Building on Richard Rorty's (1985) work, the authors construct an alternative vision of organization theory, one that subscribes to usefulness as a central organizational value. The pragmatic value of usefulness requires those engaged in research to scrutinize the practical relevance of a set of ideas as defined by their purposes and those shared by the community. Researchers doing this type of work would see organization studies as a vehicle to help people lead "better" lives and would promote novel and innovative approaches aimed at precisely the same aim.

The Discursive Approach in Multiparadigm Research

Organizational analysis is a discursive domain. Researchers rely on language to convey, construct, and enact meaning as well as to persuade their audience of a particular argument. Thus, when researchers adhere to certain paradigmatic assumptions, they embrace the language of a particular "scientific" community which, in their view, is superior to others. The language conventions, techniques, and representational practices that are recognized as legitimate, and are mustered by the members of a particular scientific community, establish their so-called "paradigm" (Kaghan and Phillips, 1998). A "paradigm," then, can be seen as a heterogeneous collection of language conventions embedded in the practice of a particular context.

It has been argued that the dominant positivist language game of organizational analysis no longer offers robust explanations of the increasingly complex and elusive structures and processes of organizational phenomena and that more localized "technical" language games may offer more realistic alternatives and insights. Various writers talk of a "postmodern condition" having emerged in philosophy, social science, and the humanities (see Harvey, 1990). For many, this represents an "alternative" explanatory medium for social theory and affairs, one founded on the recognition and importance of "local" rather than "grand" genres of intellectual discourse. One of the main exponents of this form of analysis has been Jean-François Lyotard, especially in his book *The Postmodern Condition* (1997). In a key passage, Lyotard (p. 27) discusses the role of *petit recit* (or small narratives) as the "quintessential form of imaginative invention, particularly in science" (1997: 60). For Lyotard *petit recit*, like Wittgenstein's (1953) "technical language games" (see Phillips, 1977), thrive in linguistic life worlds that are altogether different from those of "grand narratives," whose habitats, it is claimed, are now under threat.

As each "small narrative" possesses its own specific way of representing the world, conflicts between them are bound to arise. The notion of *differand* is advocated to account for the existence of a state of "continuous differ- ence" between small narratives and the diffi- culty in making judgments about linguistic conflicts. Consequently the researcher has to be an "active" player in the conversation of research by taking on the job of the "philo- sopher." In so doing, the researcher will, among others, attempt to seek out new idioms which can "speak for the silent" and, by and large, write about the world "in the service of the unknown" (Lyotard, 1997). Writing from this position locates the moral responsibility of the researcher who cannot claim innocence from the representational force that he or she brings to the theory (Calas and Smircich, 1999).

Deetz (1996) was among the first theorists to advocate this line of thought in organization studies. This position views research differ- ences arising not from the ontological and epis- temological assumptions of the individual researcher, and the procedures or methodo- logies used, but from the relation of research practices to the language games prevailing in the society at large and the ways in which re- search concepts emerge. Consequently, certain discursive positions embraced by researchers will seek consensus by reinforcing prevailing language; other positions will attempt to destab- ilize and challenge the *status quo*.

Consensus research is delineated by its search for hegemonic order, integration, and harmony. Such research focuses on representing organ- izational reality through a "neutral" language that is seen to be able to capture objectively what is going on in the social world. Research validity is a major concern and is often ensured via some form of triangulation. Organizational science is viewed as neutral and organizational theories as abstractions of researchers. On the other hand, dissensus research presents order as historicized and politicized and attempts to deconstruct its pil- lars in as much as they suppress conflict and struggle. Language is seen to be not a neutral instrument at the disposal of researchers but a means of reconstructing reality, a means of active engagement with the world. The ability to challenge assumptions and social practices is valued more highly than the representational validity of the research. Researchers engage in the exercise of science, seen as "political," for

they are also deemed part of networks that are not value-free.

In this chapter we advocate the importance of reflecting upon our discursive position and the sort of consequences it might have upon prevailing social order. Only by fostering mul- tiple perspectives that seek to address the limita- tions of consensual positions can researchers speak in the name of the unheard, of the liminal, and of the marginalized. Such multilensical research ensures that the boundaries between the core and the periphery are constantly chal- lenged and that organization studies plays a more significant role in constructing a more democratic reality. Adopting such a position has the disadvantages we have already dis- cussed, and more crucially it places a great deal of moral strain on the researcher, who must ensure that his/her intentions and the consequences of his/her efforts are seriously reflected upon.

Conclusion

Chapter 2b maps out the development of para- digm plurality in a number of organizational disciplines such as organization theory, strat- egic management, international business, opera- tional research, and technology studies. In so doing, it reviews some of the advantages and disadvantages of multiparadigm research, arguing that the overall benefits of paradigm plurality outweigh its shortcomings. The posi- tion adopted here is that it is crucial that researchers preserve and encourage theories emerging from multiple paradigms, a scenario that is not only possible from a substantive and theoretical point of view, but is also highly desirable in light of the changes taking place in contemporary organizational realities and epistemologies. The discursive turn that organizational analysis has taken infuses the researcher with moral responsibility for his/ her representations and theories.

Thus it is important to ask ourselves why certain voices and positions are absent from the conversation of research and what values and interests are being suppressed as a result of our theorizing. These are questions which organizational theorists can no longer avoid asking (Calas and Smircich, 1999). Our moral responsibility is to challenge and change some of the deeply entrenched research practices that continue to be hailed as "best practice" by the research community by making room for local voices and ensuring that a multitude of small stories are being told and heard. The proliferation of multiple local discourses will ensure that one dominant paradigm cannot replace all others and that there "will, thank goodness, always be the voices of dissent and the clamour of alternatives vying for aural space" (Burrell, 1996: 645).

References

Alvesson, M., and Wilmott, H. (1996) *Making Sense of Management: A Critical Introduction.* London: Sage.

Bauman, Z. (1993) *Postmodernist Ethics.* Oxford: Blackwell.

——(1995) *Life in Fragments: Essays in Postmodern Morality.* Oxford: Blackwell.

Brocklesby, J. (1997) "Becoming multimethodology-literate: an assessment of the cognitive difficulties of working across paradigms," in J. Mingers and A. Gill (eds) *Multimethodology: the Theory and Practice of combining Management Science Methodologies,* pp. 189–216. Chichester: Wiley.

Burrell, G. (1996) "Normal science, paradigms, metaphors, discourses and genealogies of analysis," in S. R. Clegg, C. Hardy, and W. R. Nord (eds) *Handbook of Organization Studies,* pp. 31–56. London: Sage.

Burrell, G., and Morgan, G. (1979) *Sociological Paradigms and Organizational Analysis.* London: Heinemann.

Calas, M. B., and Smircich, L. (1999) "Past postmodernism? Reflections and tentative directions," *Academy of Management Review,* 24 (4): 649–71.

Deetz, S. (1996) "Describing differences in approaches to organization science: rethinking Burrell and Morgan and their legacy," *Organization Science,* 7 (2): 191–207.

Earley, P. C., and Singh, H. (1995) "International and intercultural management research: what's next?" *Academy of Management Review,* 38 (2): 327–40.

Gioia, D., and Pitre, E. (1989) "Multiparadigm perspectives on theory building," *Academy of Management Review,* 5 (4): 584–602.

Grint, K. (1991) *The Sociology of Work: an Introduction.* London: Polity Press.

Harvey, D. (1990) *The Condition of Postmodernity.* Oxford: Blackwell.

Hassard, J. (1988) "Overcoming hermeticism in organization theory: an alternative to paradigm incommensurability," *Human Relations* 41 (3): 247–59.

——(1991) "Multiple paradigms and organizational analysis: a case study," *Organization Studies,* 12 (2): 279–99.

——(1993) *Sociology and Organization Theory: Positivism, Paradigms and Postmodernity.* Cambridge: Cambridge University Press.

Jackson, N., and Carter, P. (1991) "In defence of paradigm commensurability," *Organization Studies,* 12 (1): 109–27.

Kaghan, W., and Phillips, N. (1998) "Building the Tower of Babel: communities of practice and paradigmatic pluralism in organization studies," *Organization,* 5 (2): 191–215.

Kuhn, T. S. (1962, 1970) *The Structure of Scientific Revolutions.* Chicago: University of Chicago Press.

Lewis, M. (2000) "Exploring paradox: towards a more comprehensive guide," *Academy of Management Review,* 25 (4): 760–77.

Lewis, M., and Grimes, A. (1999) "Metatriangulation: building theory from multiple paradigms," *Academy of Management Review,* 24 (4): 672–90.

Lyotard, J-F. (1997) *The Postmodern Condition: A Report on Knowledge.* Manchester: Manchester University Press. First published in French 1979.

MacIntyre, A. (1985) *After Virtue: A Study in Moral Theory.* London: Duckworth.

McCloskey, D. N. (1994) *Knowledge and Persuasion in Economics.* Cambridge: Cambridge University Press.

McKinley, W. (1995) "Commentary: 'Towards a reconciliation of the theory of pluralism in strategic management: incommensurability and the constructivist approach of the Erlangen school'," *Advances in Strategic Management,* 12A: 249–60.

McKinley, W., and Mone, M. A. (1998) "The reconstruction of organization studies: wrestling with incommensurability," *Organization,* 5 (2): 169–89.

Mingers, J. (1992) "Theoretical, practical and critical or past, present and future?" in M. Alvesson and H. Willmott (eds) *Critical Management Studies*, pp. 90–112. London: Sage.

——(1997) "Multiparadigm multimethodology," in J. Mingers and A. Gill (eds) *Multimethodology: the Theory and Practice of combining Management Science Methodologies*, pp. 1–19. Chichester: Wiley.

Morgan, G., ed. (1983) *Beyond Method*. Newbury Park, CA: Sage.

Parker, M., ed. (1998) *Ethics and Organizations*. London: Sage.

——(1999) "Capitalism, subjectivity and ethics: debating labour process analysis," *Organization Studies*, 20 (1): 25–45.

Parkhe, A. (1993) "Messy research, methodological predisposition and theory development in international joint ventures," *Academy of Management Review*, 18 (2): 227–68.

Pfeffer, J. (1993) "Barriers to the advance of organizational science: paradigm development as a dependent variable," *Academy of Management Review*, 18 (4): 599–620.

——(1997) "Mortality, reproducibility, and the persistence of styles of theory," *Organization Science*, 6: 681–6.

Phillips, D. (1977) *Wittgenstein and Scientific Knowledge*. London: Macmillan.

Piore, M. J., and Sabel, C. F. (1984) *The Second Industrial Divide: Possibilities for Prosperity*. New York: Basic Books.

Reed, M. (1997) "In praise of duality and dualism: rethinking agency and structure in organizational analysis," *Organization Studies*, 18: 21–42.

Rorty, R. (1985) "Texts and lumps," *New Literary History*, 17: 1–15.

Scherer, A. G. (1998) "Pluralism and incommensurability in strategic management and organization theory: a problem in search of a solution," *Organization*, 5 (2): 147–69.

Scherer, A. G., and Dowling, M. J. (1995) "Towards a reconciliation of the theory of pluralism in strategic management: incommensurability and the constructivist approach of the Erlangen school," *Advances in Strategic Management*, 12A: 195–247

Scherer, A. G., and Steinmann, H. (1999) "Some remarks on the problem of incommensurability in organization studies", *Organization Studies*, 20 (3): 519–44.

Schultz, M., and Hatch, M. J. (1996) "Living with multiple paradigms: the case of paradigm interplay in organization culture studies," *Academy of Management Review*, 1 (2): 529–57.

Shrivastava, P. (1987) "Rigor and practical usefulness of research in strategic management," *Strategic Management Journal*, 8: 77–92.

Weaver, G. R., and Gioia, D. A. (1994) "Paradigms lost: incommensurability vs structurationist inquiry," *Organization Studies*, 15 (4): 565–90.

White, R. F., and Jaques, R. (1995) "Operationalizing the postmodernity construct for efficient organizational change management," *Journal of Organizational Change Management*, 8 (2): 45–71.

Wicks, A. C., and Freeman, R. E. (1998) "Organization studies and the new pragmatism: positivism, anti-positivism and the search for ethics," *Organization Science*, 9 (2): 123–40.

Willmott, H. (1993) "Breaking the paradigm mentality," *Organization Studies*, 14 (5): 681–719.

Wittgenstein, L. (1953) *Philosophical Investigations*. Oxford: Blackwell.

3

Ontology

The issue of the appropriate ontological status that organizations occupy has been around for a long time: it was a principal axis of David Silverman's (1970) trenchant critique of functionalist organization theory, that it more often than not conflated the goals of powerful organization actors with the goals of the organization, that, in practice, it was reified. Equally, there has long been an argument, sometimes labeled "structuralist" (erroneously, because there was little or no thematic continuity with notable structuralists such as Lévi-Strauss, Saussure, and others), which argues for the irreducible reality of features such as hierarchy, levels of control, and degree of centralization. In chapter 3(a), "Order is free: on the ontological status of organizations," by Boal, Hunt, and Jaros, we see the defense of structural properties (of organizations, of human personality and motivation, etc.) allied to an espousal of realist philosophy – a defense of the real existence of things that are not necessarily empirically immediately available in a fallible, probabilistic manner. Realist contingency, one might call this: the conviction that those things that one takes as real right now in whatever scientific (or other) language game one is engaged in may not be at some time in the future subject to other unknown moves in the game, accumulation of data, or change of interpretation. After some time spent attacking a diffuse "postmodernist/poststructuralist" set of targets, the chapter outlines the authors' "critical pluralist" position, based on a fashionable "edge of chaos" position, concluding with some knowledge standards that can be used in doing any research, in order to assign ontological security. Credibility means having respondents agree with the interpretation made of the research setting under review. Transferability refers to the ability to translate the knowledge made credible from one context to another. The knowledge in question is more dependable if more than one person is concerned with its construction and more confirmable if it is supported by the data gathered by the investigator. Despite the hostility shown by the authors to an emphasis on language and discourse, it is evident that they rely a great deal on the achievement of intersubjective agreement in language and discourse for the knowledge claims they make.

Chia's contribution on "Ontology: organizations as 'world-making'" begins with an example of a highly complex and significant process of organizational meaning making. The case in point was the 1884 Prime Meridian Conference, held in the US capital of Washington, DC. Fixing and stabilizing time universally was no mean thing and serves to represent, for Chia, that organization is a technology for producing what is taken to be real. Organization is not so much a solid, stable entity – a thing we experience – so much as an ongoing "world-making" activity. Chia proceeds historically through significant examples, such as the emergence of the alphabet and the Gutenberg typography. The significance of these as instrumental means for making the world real becomes apparent in the discussion of rationality. "Modern Western rationality . . . [is] . . . part of a more generic cognitive strategy for converting the otherwise intractable and mutable masses, material or otherwise, into usable resources by breaking them down and converting them into repeatable part elements." A second element in the emergence of modern rationality was the normalization of "systematic empiricism" as a way of (scientifically) seeing the world. Closely associated with this is an instrumental view of representation in which what is depicted is linguistically mirrored in words in a more or less accurate reflection. Over time, the presumption is that we progress in the metaphorical mirrors we make – hence there is a narrative of progress. All of this is premised on an ontology of "being," says Chia: against this he wishes to juxtapose one of "becoming." In the latter, "things" are merely stabilized patterns produced by language and imputed to phenomena in consequence rather than being an effect of the thinglike properties of phenomena that we take to be real. The process of ontology is elaborated in its particulars and then the implications for organizations are spelt out. The upshot of these is that the organizational world acquires its apparent externality, objectivity, and seemingly stable structure from routine practices which are regulated, at least in part, by discursive instrumentality. It only needs to be added that there other forms of instrumentalization as well: technological devices, machines, and stable patterns of relations.

The contrast is clear: language is either a handmaiden of science, capable of patient correction in the interests of "truth" as it reaches closer to the being of things, or science is one of the language games we are able to play – with huge material effects – as we transform the world, making it happen, attending to its becoming, a process in which organizations – as themselves patterned moments of becoming – play a central role.

3a Order is Free: On the Ontological Status of Organizations

Kimberly B. Boal, James G. (Jerry) Hunt, and Stephen J. Jaros

There is an old story about a young man, who on visiting England was told he must "see" Oxford University. On returning from his visit, he was asked what he thought of Oxford University. He reported that he had seen trees, rocks, people, and buildings, but he did not "see" Oxford University. Is Oxford University not real? Are only things that one can see and touch real? What about quarks, black holes, and gravity? What about organizations? On what basis can we conclude that they are real? We argue that organizations, like trees, rocks, and gravity, are real: all are real in their consequences. Thus we defend a realistic view of organizations against those who deny that reality.

Let us illustrate with a thought experiment. It is becoming increasingly popular to speak of competence-based competition (e.g., Hamel and Heene, 1994). The business press often, in fact, speaks of an organization's competences.

Postmodern critics might argue that organizations don't have competences. People have competences. Therefore, organizational competences exist only to the extent that people have competences. To argue otherwise, they might say, is to engage in the process of anthropomorphizing and reifying the concept of organizational competences.

However, let us imagine that we conducted a study of the effects of organizational competences on product quality. Now imagine that we collected information from every individual in every organization in the study with respect to their perceptions and beliefs as well as information on each of the organizations. Further imagine that we entered both the data from every individual and separate data on each organization's competences into a giant regression analysis. After accounting for all of the variance attributable to individual perceptions and beliefs, would there still be variance attributable to our categorization of *organizational* competences? We argue yes – yes, because competences are defined as complex, interconnected combinations of tangible basic resources (e.g., specific machinery) and intangible basic resources (e.g., specific organizational policies and procedures and the skills and knowledge-specific employees) that fit coherently together in a synergistic manner (Hunt, 2000: 144).[1]

Thus, because organizational competences are more than the sum of their parts, they are real. Therefore organizations are real. This reality can be inferred by its consequences, much in the same way as a physicist infers the existence of a black hole by the effect it has on surrounding gas clouds, stars, and so forth. This argument is consistent with the fundamental tenet of realism: all versions of realism hold that the world exists independently of its being perceived (Moore, 1903; Russell, 1929). We contrast this realist perspective against those who take a subjectivist (e.g., Kuhn, 1962, 1970; Lincoln and Guba, 1985), symbolic, or interpretive interactionist (e.g., Blumer, 1962), social constructionist (e.g., Berger and Luckmann, 1965), and especially what Weiss (2000), among others, labels "postmodernist" or "postpositivist" perspective (e.g., Alvesson and Deetz, 1996; Burrell, 1997; Clegg, 1990; Deetz, 2000).

While most subjectivists are to some degree realists because they seek to transcend "mere" opinion and ultimately reveal some deeper social reality assumed to represent the "truth" or "truths" (Jacobson and Jacques, 1997), at the extreme, postmodernists/poststructuralists hold that attempts to discover the genuine order of things are naive and mistaken and that the language produced by the empirical process does not equate with an increasingly accurate correspondence with reality (Hassard, 1993). Rather, collections of interrelated discourses and the associated practices of textual production make the world meaningful. That is, discourses, rather than revealing some preconstituted reality, create the world (Lawrence and Phillips, 1998).

Such perspectives reject the notion that searches for true theories by objective methods can exist. Objectivity is impossible (Mick, 1986) because observations are theory-laden (Kuhn, 1962). Often, these schools of thought juxtapose their position against both a mistaken view of "positivism" and contemporary social science (see Hunt, 1994b; McKelvey, 1997; Phillips, 1987). As Baum and Dobbin (2000) point out, "the paradigm war" in OMT is based upon an antiquated understanding of the philosophy of science. . . . OMT's 'positivists' are not positivists" (p. 400). Also, we would add, neither is contemporary social science positivist.

Let us be clear: the positivist and logical positivist tradition that began in 1907 at the University of Vienna (often referred to as the Vienna circle) in an attempt to deal with quantum mechanics' challenge to Newtonian physics, as well as the logical empiricism that followed (e.g., Carnap, 1950; Hempel, 1965), is not the "received" wisdom of today's contemporary social science (Hunt, 1990, 1993, 1994b; McKelvey, 1997). Indeed, Popper's (1968) falsificationist philosophy and the burgeoning literature in postmodernist and postmodernist-inflected feminist and "critical" organization studies belies the claims of positive/realist hegemony (Hunt, 1994b). (For example, see a special issue of the *Academy of Management Review* in 1992.) If anything, realistic perspectives are derided today as "received ignorance," not received wisdom, within the field of organization studies.

While it is true, as McKelvey points out, "most researchers . . . go blissfully about their empirical work without worrying about all that philosophical stuff" – pick a theory, propose an hypothesis, find some results at $p < 0.05$, get published, get tenure, get promoted . . ." (1999b: 402–3), there is a distinction to be made between the research practices of the field as a whole (as reflected by the kinds of journals publishing the above work) and the prevailing beliefs within that area of organization studies that explicitly addresses issues of organizational ontology and espistemology.

In the above area of inquiry, postmodernist views are ascendant and realist ideas are under attack. (This book is an example.) Lyotard (1984) argues, "to the extent that science does not restrict itself to stating useful regularities and seeks the truth, it is obliged to legitimate the rules of its own game . . ." (p. xxiii). Thus one goal of this chapter is to rehabilitate realism as an approach to studying the nature of organization and processes of organizing.

First, we describe the tenets of scientific realism along the fundamental philosophy-of-science dimensions of determinism, causality, ontology, and objectivity, and contrast differences between realism and positivism. Second, we compare and contrast how scientific realism differs from postmodernism and argue why we believe the scientific realism perspective is superior. Third, we extend the previous discussion by looking at our scientific realism perspective within the context of chaos, complexity, and dynamic systems perspectives. Finally, we revisit some of our earlier notions by arguing for a critical pluralist approach to directly compare realist and alternative perspectives. It also is important to note that, in order to make sure we cite all positions accurately, we rely more heavily than usual on direct quotations. These direct quotations are absolutely critical in position papers such as this one.

Scientific Realism

McKelvey (1997) notes that organizational scientists have always been "much more realist than positivist." Despite this, one might conclude that contemporary science is based on the philosophical movement that originated in Vienna at the turn of the twentieth century. This philosophical movement, "logical positivism," and its successor, "logical empiricism," are often treated as the "received view" and "normal science" (Kuhn, 1962/1970). But, while positivism and scientific realism do share some common themes – they differ in important ways as well. In order to clarify, here we describe what we mean by "scientific realism" in terms of determinism, causality, ontology, and objectivity. We also highlight differences between realism and positivism.

First let us be clear, the term "normal science" is a term that Kuhn used, and is not to be confused with contemporary science that is realist in its orientation. That notwithstanding, given that many postmodernists (e.g., Putnam, 1993 et al.) juxtapose their views against "positivism," it is useful to be clear about what positivism held in contrast to contemporary science. We draw upon Hunt's (1994b) historical analysis to address seven (mis)characterizations of positivism.

Tenets of scientific realism

Quantum mechanics destroyed the deterministic certainty of Newtonian physics. Logical positivists embraced "instrumentalism." For positivists, the purpose of theory was to predict, not explain (Bynum et al., 1985). Furthermore, in keeping with quantum mechanics, the best that could be accomplished was "probabilistic" prediction. As Einstein (1923) said, "As far as the laws of mathematics refer to reality, they are not certain; and as far as they are certain, they do not refer to reality" (p. 28). Hunt (1994b: 227) concludes, "to be positivist is not to be determinist."

Do realists seek causal explanations? Contrary to positivism, which has its roots in Humean skepticism that rejects many forms of causality as an unobservable metaphysical concept, the answer is yes. However, scientific realism recognizes that most organizational phenomena are complex, in the sense of having multiple, interacting causes and that sometimes causation is difficult to determine. Here, the crucial distinction between realists and positivists lies in the third dimension of our analysis, ontology – the researcher's belief about whether anything exists other than directly observable entities (e.g., trees, rocks).

According to Manicas (1987), positivists adopted a minimal realism (i.e., tangible objects like trees and rocks exist independently of our perception and labeling). But, drawing on Hume, positivists insist that theories contain only observables. In contrast, realism holds that unobservables (e.g., motivation, job attitudes, culture, cognitions – phenomena not directly apprehendable by human senses) can exist and are appropriate for theory construction. Thus, unlike positivists, realists can fall victim to reification – the error of wrongly treating unobservables as if they are observables.

Were positivists "functionalists"? Functionalism (e.g., Parsons, 1937; Radcliffe-Brown, 1952) generally seeks to understand a behavior pattern or a sociocultural institution by determining the role it plays in keeping a given system in proper working order or maintaining it as a going concern. Burrel and Morgan (1979) argue that functionalism is characterized by a concern for providing explanations of the *status quo*, social order, consensus, social integration, and solidarity.

However, positivists were strongly critical of drawing parallels between biological and social systems, and of functionalism and functional explanations. Hempel (1959: 297) claimed that functional explanations are mere "covert tautologies," and "devoid of objective empirical content" (p. 330). Functionalism is not positivistic. Therefore, if contemporary science or management theory is functionalist, it is not positivist.

Does positivism predispose the use of quantitative methods? Many of the members of the Vienna circle were physicists and mathematicians (e.g., Phillipp Frank, Moritz Schlick, Herbert Feigl, and Hans Hahn, Friedrich Waismann, Karl Menger, Kurt Odel and Rudolph Carnap, respectively). Thus they were sympathetic to quantification in science. However, as Hunt (1994b) notes, "equating positivism with quantitative methods is ahistorical" (p. 226). According to Phillips (1987), "There is nothing in the doctrine of positivism that necessitates a love of statistics or a distaste for case studies" (p. 96). Likewise, Broadbeck (1968) states, "quantification . . . is neither

necessary nor a sufficient condition for science" (p. 574). Hunt (1994b) calls for a rhetorical cease-fire on the qualitative–quantitative wars. As he notes, "most qualitative research is neither distinctively nonpositivist nor positivist. And much quantitative research is realist and not positivist" (p. 227).

According to Suppe (1977: 649), "it is a central aim of science to come to knowledge of how the world really is . . ." Thus, for the scientific realist, the products of science are theories that seek to explain and predict. The arbiter of the adequacy of our explanations and predictions is truth ("genuine knowledge") or "truthlikeness" (Popper's, 1972, verisimilitude), and the degrees or probabilities of truthlikeness (De Regt, 1994). Any empirical test involves two high-level theories: an *interpretive* theory to provide the facts and an *explanatory* theory to explain them (Boal and Willis, 1983; Lakatos, 1968). Inconsistencies between these two theories constitute the problem-fever of science.

Growth in science occurs in our attempts to repair these inconsistencies, first by replacing one theory, then the other, then possibly both, and opting for a new set-up which represents the most progressive problem shift, with the biggest increase in corroborated content. Growth in science can occur without refutations, and need not be either evolutionary or linear. What is required is that sufficiently many and sufficiently different theories are offered. According to McMullin (1984), scientific realism claims that "the long-run success of a scientific theory gives reason to believe that something like the entities postulated by the theory actually exist" (p. 26). We now elaborate on these statements lest they be misunderstood.

Are realists objectivists? Yes. Realism holds that science should pursue objectivity in that its statements should be capable of public tests with results that do not vary essentially with the tester (Hempel, 1970). However, this is not to be confused with a caricature of objectivism that implies that science has access to a "god's eye view" or a "unique privileged position" to reach an absolute truth. Realists recognize that any observations we make, and any evidence we claim to accumulate, are inevitably filtered through and limited by the characteristics of our senses, our methods of measurement, and the social-cultural context in which our research is conducted. The purpose of the scientific method is to attempt to enable us to arrive at a defensible knowledge claim. However, such claims are based on the recognition that they are contingent – subject to future refutation or revision.

Scientific realism strives for objectivity. As Hunt (1976) states, "Scientific knowledge, in which theories, laws, and explanations are primal, must be objective in the sense that its truth content must be intersubjectively certifiable." This notion of objectivity is not to be confused with those positions that offer a characterization of *objectivism* as the claim that there is an objective reality, about which we can say things that are objectively, absolutely, and unconditionally true or false.

But, as Beach (1984: 159) notes, objectivism is:

the thesis that there exists a systematic method of reasoning and a coordinate set of beliefs embodying its principles. . . . These principles may contain errors or half-truths, and yet may never attain a fixed and final form. Yet insofar as (a) their consistency is publicly verifiable, (b) their development is rational, and (c) their truth-content is demonstrably greater than that of rival contenders, they do constitute reliable criteria by which to evaluate subsidiary beliefs and hypothesis.

The above thesis is consistent with Popper's (1959) notion that science is revolution in permanence. He suggested that the ontological status of a theory is better than its rival "(a) if it has more empirical content, that is, if it forbids more 'observable' states of affairs, and (b) if some of this excess content is corroborated, that is, if the theory produces novel facts" (p. 163).

Scientific realism versus its critics

Scientific realism acknowledges fallibilism and probabilism in its knowledge claims (De Regt, 1994; Hunt, 1990, 1993). It rejects, however, arguments put forth by relativists (e.g., Feyerabend, 1975; Kuhn, 1962) that objectivity is impossible because: (a) language and culture determine reality (e.g., Sapir, 1949; Whorf, 1956); (b) paradigms that researchers hold are incommensurable (Feyerabend, 1975; Kuhn,

1962); facts undermine theories (Feyerabend, 1975; Kuhn, 1962); and (d) espistemically significant observations are theory-laden (Kuhn, 1962, 1970).

In terms of the first argument, linguistic relativism maintains that the language of culture determines the reality that its members see. As Hunt (1993) notes, "if the thesis of linguistic relativism were true, objective inquiry across cultures (languages) would indeed be problematic" (p. 81). However, Steinfatt's (1989: 63) extensive review of the literature on linguistic relativism leads him to conclude, "the differences between languages are not to be found in what *can* be said, but what it is relatively easy to *say*" (italics in original).

Postmodernists (e.g., Gergen and Whitney, 1996), and our counterpoint, argue that word meaning depends primarily on its contextual embedding or its social use within a material context. Meanings are determined through the historical development of specific language games (Mauws and Phillips, 1995). Only through the rules and conventions established through social interaction is it possible to speak of the things that are in the world.

Postmodernists (and our counterpoint) argue that since languages are representational they cannot perfectly capture the nature of that reality. However, we argue, a language's ability to represent can itself be improved even though it may not be perfected. This is the goal of construct validity. Furthermore, it is one thing to point out that our medium(s) of communication influence our perception of reality, and another to claim (as does our counterpoint) that the "medium is the message," implying there is little if any correspondence between language and reality.

We accept that specific letters and words used to label reality are arbitrary (e.g., that the English language uses the letters *t*, *r*, *e*, *e*, to identify a particular type of plant). This arbitrariness does not mean that there is not an object that exists in the world – an object with some kind of nondiscursive existence – that humans understand discursively to be a "tree." If all humans were suddenly to vanish, a *tree*, as we understand it by any language, would cease to exist (i.e., the concept of "tree" that is a product of the imperfections of a language's system of representation would cease to exist). However, does anyone think that "trees" as objects would cease to exist? Could squirrels no longer run up and down them?

To avoid the trap of solipsism, our counterpoint would seem to argue that there is a fundamental ontological difference between physical objects, such as trees, which are "directly observable," and what the counterpointers call "social objects," such as "organizations," which are not. The former being real, while the latter are merely reifications created by language. But this line of argument is incoherent, because the concept of "direct observability" seems to imply that perceptions of physical objects are not filtered by language. Thus physical objects can be perceived in an unmediated (nondiscursive) way. But this view would be contrary to that held by many postmodernists (e.g., Lennon and Whitford, 1994) who argue that "all our interactions with reality are mediated by conceptual frameworks or discourses which themselves are historically and socially situated" (p. 4).

Thus on what basis can a distinction be made between the effects of discourse and language on our perception of physical objects (i.e., objects with "thinglike" properties) and what our counterpointers call social objects? If our perception of everything is discursively constructed, how can they even know that a tree is "thinglike" and an organization is not? If language constructs the social world, it would seem to construct the physical world as well. If all reality is a "forest of signs," how can we apprehend "thinglike" objects without the mediation of language any more than what they call "social objects"? What is the ontological basis for claiming trees are thinglike and organizations are not?

Based on the incommensurability argument, we ask, "Do Copernicus and Ptolemy see the same thing when the sun rises?" According to the view that objectivity is impossible because all knowledge claims are embedded in paradigms that are incommensurable, the answer is: no! However, McKelvey (1999a) observed that if paradigms such as positivist, interpretivist, and postmodernist were incommensurable, then the editors of the *Handbook of Organization Studies* (Clegg et al., 1996) were

put in the awkward position of editing a book much of which they did not understand. Further, Hunt (1993) points out, the very claim that two paradigms are incommensurable must imply that one can compare them. "For incommensurability to pose a threat to objectivity, one would have to put forth a rival 'paradigm' that not only resulted in a conflicting conclusion, but a situation where the choice could not be made on objective evidence" (p. 82).

In terms of the facts undermining theory contention, despite the fact that scientific realism accepts fallibilism and probabilism, critiques of objectivism continue to succumb to Humean skepticism and the "problem of induction." According to this critique, since no conceivable number of facts conclusively proves a theory's truth, any process that reasons to the truth of a theory is improperly inductive. Note, the claim is that only deductive, and not inductive, logic is permissible (Watkins, 1984), because "to know" is to know with the *certainty* of the deductive logic of mathematics.

Many (e.g., Gomez and Jones, 2000) continue to uncritically accept such a position, as did Popper (1968). Postmodernists also make this claim when they discuss the impossibility of knowing for sure whether our knowledge claims are free of cultural or linguistic or ideological bias. However, restricting "knowing" to "knowing with certainty" amounts to nothing less than nihilism. Scientific realism, in contrast, embraces fallibilism. As such, all knowledge claims are tentative, subject to revision on the basis of new evidence. The concept of "certainty" does not belong to science (Hunt, 1993).

The final critique of the impossibility of objectivity is premised on the contention that all epistemically significant observations are theory-laden. The claim is that all observation is "interpreted" by theory, thus objectivity is impossible. However, Shalpere (1982) and Greenwood (1990) note that advocates of the theory-laden argument fail to distinguish between the two very different kinds of theories that are involved in empirical testing. On the one hand are the explanatory theories that we test empirically, and on the other hand are the interpretative theories that inform the data.

In addition, Boal and Willis (1983) note that there is an implicit "theory of testing" manifested in how we choose to analyze the data. Therefore, unquestionably, epistemically significant observations are not theory-free – nor should they be. Indeed, the real question is whether they are theory-neutral; that is, neutral with respect to the explanatory theory under investigation (Hunt, 1994a). What is required is that our measurement theories and our theories of testing must not presume the truth of our explanatory theory, that is, they must not beg the question.

Postmodernist critiques of realism typically juxtapose themselves against a form of "naive realism" that assumes the ontological status of organizations as real, that posits deterministic and totalizing accounts of the causes of that reality, and that identifies such reality as some kind of essential (usually functionalist) social process. Yes, scientific realism proposes that organizations are real; but real in a fallible, probabilistic way – one that acknowledges that knowledge claims about their reality are contingent, and part of a never-ending, subject-to-revision process of discovery. Scientific realism also makes no claims about whether the ontological status of organizations should buttress existing social relations. Clearly, many forms of organizations have served both reactionary and progressive ends.

When compared to scientific realism, postmodernist claims that organizations are "invoked texts" or "linguistic creations" fall short on the very criteria (determinism, totalization, and existentialism) that are invoked to attack such realism. Postmodernists tend to ascribe determinism to "hegemonic" social processes that inevitably result in functionalist, disciplinary organizational forms. At the same time, postmodernists tend to ascribe totalizing claims to the power of discourse and language. They also often argue that organizations are, in their essence, products of a functionalist, procapitalist society.

But how do the postmodern theorists escape discourse and culture to know all of this? What "god's eye" power enables these theorists to see what the realist cannot? As Eagleton (1983) remarked, poststructuralism "allows you to drive a coach and horses through everybody else's beliefs while not saddling you with the inconvenience of having to adopt any yourself"

(p. 144). And is not the claim that organizations are not real – that they are reified artifacts of language – itself, essentially, a "truth claim"?

The point of this piece is not to counter the straw man of naive realism with a straw man of naive postmodernism. Postmodernist-inspired scholars of organizations have analyzed the problems of determinism, existentialism, truth claims, and totalization in their own work (see Calas and Smircich, 2000; Jermier et al., 1994; Knights and Willmott, 1999). Yet none of these authors could claim to have solved these problems. Crucially, whereas scientific realism argues for theory testing subject to verification (or what we later term "critical pluralism"), that has proven fruitful in numerous areas of knowledge creation (medicine, physics, chemistry, mathematics), postmodernists, with few exceptions, have established no such standards for judging their knowledge claims other than the "trust" we have in those making them. Thus we would argue that, as of now, scientific realism holds the best prospects for knowledge claims and acquisition within the organization sciences.[2]

We agree with the authors of chapter 3(b) that "the organization" does not have a "straightforward and unproblematic existence independent of our discursively shaped understandings". But we do hold that the best available evidence suggests that organizations do have a problematic, nonstraightforward existence – an existence that can better be understood within a scientific-realist ontology and epistemology. Consistent with our argument, we draw on advances in the natural sciences and that are gaining momentum in the social sciences. These advances focus on complexity and dynamic systems perspectives to describe recent evidence produced on the nature of that reality (cf. Anderson et al., 1999; Hunt and Ropo, forthcoming; Ilgen and Hulin, 2000; Marion, 1999).

Complexity, Chaos, Dynamic Systems, and Order

Earlier, we presented arguments of those attacking scientific reality in terms of determinism. Frequently, these arguments have been virtually a caricature. Of course, we do not subscribe to this deterministic caricature. Rather, following a modification of J. Hunt (1991: 45–6) and Morgan and Smircich (1980), we conceive of scientific realism along a six-position realist/social constructionist philosophy of science continuum. On the extreme left is the reality as a concrete structure position with a machine metaphor and predictable, deterministic underlying laws. On the extreme right is the most radical social constructionist, reality as a projection of human imagination, position, where the "transcendental" metaphor is used and described in the following way:

knowledge here rests within subjective experience. The appreciation of world phenomena is seen as being dependent on the ability to understand the way in which human beings shape the world from inside themselves. . . . In each case [Husserl's, 1965, phenomenological tradition, studying experiential learning phenomenologically, and drawing on non-Western modes of philosophy], the grounds for knowledge demand that human beings transcend conventional scientific modes of understanding and begin to appreciate the world in revelatory, but as yet largely uncharted, ways. (Morgan and Smircich, 1980: 497)

Returning to the left side of the continuum, McKelvey (1997) captures its essence in the first part of his quotation:

Organization scientists have a truly archaic eighteenth-century view of science, a worst-case scenario, really, in that it is a linear deterministic Newtonian mechanics [view] without the power of mathematics: this is the "normal science straitjacket" alluded to by Daft and Lewin (1990). Now, twentieth-century natural science is dramatically different from the eighteenth-century version. (Favre et al., 1995; Mainzer, 1994; Prigogine and Stengers, 1984: 357)

Thus McKelvey's organization scientists tend, as would those earlier mentioned, to see scientific realism as the machine metaphor position. However, our own realism position would put us close to the middle of the six positions on the realist–social constructionist continuum. This position conceives of reality as a "contextual field of information." "This ontological position calls for epistemologies based on cybernetic metaphors, which emphasize the importance of understanding contexts in a holistic fashion" (Morgan and Smircich, 1980:

496). Here there is an emphasis on how organizations and environment evolve together. Causality is not a concern because it is impossible to find a point at which causal forces begin. Relationships change together and cannot be reduced to a set of determinate laws and propositions. The whole is stored in all the parts (see J. Hunt, 1991: 46–7; Morgan and Smircich, 1980: 495–6).

As scientific realists, we focus our realist position on what McKelvey (1997: 357, 1999a: 297–8) calls "stochastic idiosyncracy," where idiosyncratic process event occurrences in firms fit some probabilistic distribution, as opposed to uniformity assumptions about organizational phenomena. He argues that social constructionists such as Guba (1985) and Weick (1985), among others, express ideas consistent with stochastastic idiosyncracy assumptions. These assumptions deal with such complexity notions as: multiple causality, nonlinearity, self-organization, and adaptive learning (see, e.g., Cramer, 1993; Nicholis and Prigogine, 1989).

McKelvey goes on to point out that physicists, chemists, and biologists have used the above assumptions to develop a modernized twentieth-century natural science that still upholds: objective measurement, replication, prediction, generalization, falsifiability, and, finally, self-correction – all traditional hallmarks of "good" science (e.g., Favre et al., 1995; Nicholis and Prigogine, 1989).

We elaborate our position, first, by reiterating crucial concepts suggested by Newton's work (cf. Marion, 1999: 16–17) and we then juxtapose our position against that summary:

1 All physical events can ultimately be understood.
2 Every event has a predictable cause or causes.
3 Causal relationships are linear (proportional) and one-way.
4 All stable motion is based on periodic attractors – trajectories to which motion gravitates. A periodic attractor is stable; if perturbed it will return to its original motion. A pendulum is a good example and exhibits two stable attractors – back-and-forth motion, and no motion, as represented by a point on what is termed a "phase space plot." This point is

termed a "point attractor." An attractor also is finite with bounded behavior (its phase space is restricted to a confined area). Attractors here are periodic or quasiperiodic and provide predictable motion.

The essence of our contrasting position is captured with an extended description of complex systems by Levy (1992: 7–8):

A complex system is one whose component parts interact with sufficient intricacy that they cannot be predicted by standard linear equations; so many variables are at work in the system that its overall behavior can only be understood as an emergent consequence of the holistic sum of the myriad behaviors embedded within. Reductionism does not work with complex systems, and it is now clear that a purely reductionist approach cannot be applied; . . . in living systems the whole is more than the sum of its parts. This is the result of . . . complexity which allows certain behaviors and characteristics to emerge unbidden.

Or, as Marion and Uhl-Bien (2001: 397) state, "In contradiction to Einstein, God does play dice with the universe."

Be that as it may, we now examine the previous description in more detail. The system emerges from *interactions* (among components) and *resonances* (the release of potential energy through interactions) of individual units, where the behaviors of the components tend to *correlate* (share resonances, i.e., individual behaviors) with each other because of the interactions and to catalyze (speed up a process or make things happen that otherwise would not) interactions (a process termed *autocatalysis)* because of the energy contained in the resonance. These forces create the system order previously mentioned; that is, they are self-organizing. Marion (1999) uses a husband-and-wife example, where the two gravitate together in their attitudinal structure because they discuss and live their beliefs together. Autocatalysis begins when the behaviors mutually stimulate each other and these mutual stimulations lead to another cycle.

Unpredictability is a key part of this process. Correlation and autocatalysis build, but unpredictability is what inspires creation and renewal (Marion, 1999: xiii). Unlike the periodic attractor, above, involved in linear and periodic relations, the predictor here is labeled "strange" (Ruelle and Takens, 1971; Sanders,

1998). It is not periodic or even quasiperiodic. The behavior of the systems it represents never repeats itself. However, the attractor is patterned, that is, it has a geometric structure in finite phase space and it also is stable. This strange attractor is the product of nonlinearity and interactivity. Its lack of predictability is not only a function of interaction, resonance, correlation, and autocatalytic forces but also a function of sensitive dependence on initial conditions (path dependence). This dependence is known as the "butterfly effect" – a butterfly flapping its wings in one location can have an effect on a system far removed (cf. the discussion by Marion, 1999: 17).

We essentially have described some key aspects of complexity theory above. It is considered to lie in a transition zone between stable systems and chaotic systems – this location is typically referred to as "the edge of chaos." Neither stability nor chaos is capable of exhibiting the characteristics of complex systems – such behavior can exist only at the edge of chaos. Edge of chaos attractors, mentioned above, are stable enough to maintain information about themselves and their environment while being sufficiently vibrant to process that information. They map their environments by resonating or correlating with their environments and by interacting with and becoming a part of their environment. Different attractors within a system resonate with each other and augment the capabilities of the broader organization. In turn, they influence the "self-organizing" capabilities mentioned previously (cf. Marion, 1999).

Unlike complex systems, chaotic systems have no memory. Thus they are incapable of adapting (cf. Marion, 1999: 72–4). Clearly, the ideal organizational state is, indeed, complex, somewhere between stability and chaos, and Marion considers complexity theory to be a branch of chaos theory. He summarizes complexity and chaos theories quite comprehensively in the context of organization theory. He also demonstrates how one might empirically examine the growth in organizational populations using a chaotic model based on a general logistics equation (see Marion, 1999: 273–307). At the same time, he shows empirically how to test social systems for chaos.

Finally, he demonstrates procedures for identifying complex social structures.

John Holland's book *Hidden Order* (1995) provides an extended example that helps pull together our previous points, especially, those emphasizing order and consequences, and is especially relevant for the social sciences. Holland observes that in any given city there is a vast interdependent network of grocery stores, clothing stores, banks, service stations, schools, restaurants, malls, factories, transport systems, and the like. All these are focused on supporting the city's inhabitants. Consistent with our previous arguments, these very complex networks and their very high levels of efficiency and effectiveness emerge naturally.

Note that there are no committees coordinating the process, determining services, submitting bids for various roles, and the like, and in general making sure everything fits together. As we pointed out previously, all this order comes from the bottom up and helps reinforce Kauffman's (1995) argument that "order is free," since it is a bottom-up phenomenon with no overriding centralized ordering force from above (see Marion, 1999: 245–6). The key point is that human agency is sufficient but not necessary to obtain order, although, of course, it may be operative, along with numerous other agents, such as size, technology, leadership, belief systems, and the like. Thus social constructionism is not required for such order. Additionally, as we have argued throughout, all of these events and activities are consequential – all are real in their consequences, as are the organizations that bracket and are bracketed by them.

Finally, it also is important to recognize that this means of obtaining order is in sharp contrast to that in our counterpoint piece. There it is argued, essentially, that order is carved out of disorder, primarily by language.

Two important points about the nature of change are important to reiterate from our discussion of chaos, complexity, and dynamic systems perspectives. First, small changes at the beginning of a process of evolution can have very large effects downstream. Second, the outcome of a process is dependent upon the path it took to get there. Therefore small, almost random, changes accumulate over time to make the developmental path of every system in nature unique, if only slightly. Thus, on every tree, the leaves are similar but not identical.

Closely related to complexity and chaos theory in terms of its assumptions about nonlinearity, predictability, causality, attractors, and order, is dynamic systems theory (Hunt and Ropo, forthcoming). One of numerous approaches to dynamic systems theory is that of computational modeling (see Ilgen and Hulin, 2000). Without going into detail, we argue that computational modeling illustrates well our "reality as a contextual field of information" position on the previously mentioned continuum and reflects previous arguments concerning stochastic idiosyncracy, and related notions, while allowing for the kinds of "good" science arguments mentioned earlier by McKelvey (1997). Computational modeling, as well as other related dynamic systems approaches, is receiving increasing emphasis in the social sciences. (For more details see Hunt and Ropo, forthcoming, and Ilgen and Hulin, 2000.)

Revisiting Organizations as Reality

A crucial point, raised by McKelvey and discussed earlier, is that complexity, chaos, and dynamic systems perspectives are realist ways of dealing with stochastic idiosyncrasy and that they are not unlike the idea set forth by numerous social constructionists and postmodernists. It also was argued, following McKelvey, that a major virtue here was that the complexity manifestation of scientific reality upholds the tenets of "good" science, especially self-correction.

For those social constructionists and postmodernists who disagree with our previous arguments, let us make it clear that we do not believe in incommensurability, as suggested by such as Burrell and Morgan (1979) and others briefly treated earlier. Rather, we put forth the challenge of rapprochement, based on extensions of J. Hunt's (1991: 52–4) treatment of "critical pluralism." This term was originated by Siegel (1988) as a way of characterizing how scholars should view their and others' ways of knowing. The "critical" part of the label argues that nonevaluational, noncritical or mindless pluralism (considering rival candidate approaches as thwarting comparison and evaluation) is as bad as dogmatism. Here, all knowledge claims not only can, but must be, subjected to critical scrutiny (see S. Hunt, 1991). In other words, all knowledge claims must have appraisal standards.

Hirschman (1986) and Wallendorf and Belk (1989), marketing scholars, have been working toward such standards in the marketing field, which, like the management and organization field, has had a history of debates such as those in this book. We briefly touch on Hirschman's (1986: 244–7) approach to convey the flavor of such assessment, recognizing that she would be in the "social constructionist" mode, using our previous terminology. She argues that the criteria appropriate to her mode of inquiry consist of credibility, transferability, dependability, and confirmability.

1   *Credibility*. For social constructionists, traditional realist internal validity is inoperative. Multiple constructed realities operate, rather than one true reality composed of discrete causal processes. To determine the credibility of a particular interpretation, one should submit it to those upon whom it is based and seek their responses concerning authenticity. Of course, the social constructionist researcher must understand and probe the respondents' answers for truthfulness.

2   *Transferability*. This criterion is analogous to assessing external validity in realist research. Here, however, one is concerned with the *transferability* of a phenomenon to a second manifestation, recognizing implicitly that no two social contexts are ever identical. The transferability must be compared with interpretations constructed in other contexts. It can be knowable only on a *post hoc* basis.

3   *Dependability*. This criterion is roughly analogous to reliability in realist research. The researchers themselves are the instruments and must demonstrate reliability. Having multiple human investigators enhances dependability.

4   *Confirmability*. Confirmability for social constructionists is functionally analogous to neutrality and objectivity for realists. However,

the interpretation generated by researchers is not assumed to be value-free (as with realist research) but is expected to be *supportable* from the data as gathered by the inquirer.

Hirschman (1986: 248) goes on to argue essentially, as we have, for a form of critical pluralism "designed to reach as many different knowledges as possible."

Wallendorf and Belk (1989: 69) argue that "trustworthiness" is the bottom line. Consistent with Hirschman, they advocate "triangulation of sources, methods, and researchers" (p. 70) to evaluate the criteria she discusses.

Conclusion

Connell and Nord (1996a, b) have argued that debates between realists and postmodernists have proven to be as much as, if not more than, about competing interests and values as about "genuine" philosophical differences. They characterize these disagreements as saturated with emotions and ego efforts (the threat we experience and the defensiveness engendered when our life's work is fundamentally challenged) and politics (whether we see ourselves as questing for the truth for its own sake or seeking knowledge to improve the world, and debates over what an improved world should look like in terms of political and economic structures and institutions). But they also argue that the influence of emotions, interests, and values has had a substantive impact on the technical aspect of the debate, primarily as a source of attribution error – the mischaracterizations of realism, positivism, and postmodernism (as "anything-goes relativism") identified in this chapter and in some of the others in this book, and by others as well (see S. Hunt, 1994b).

Thus Connell and Nord imply that the intellectual atmosphere surrounding this debate has to an extent become polluted. They advocate a rhetorical "cease-fire." But does this mean that too many raw nerves have been exposed and picked at for fruitful discourse to occur? We think not, as long as researchers on both sides recognize their fallibility. We advocate a realist perspective and have attempted to explain why we believe that it is more constructive than postmodernism as an approach to studying organizations. But scientific realism and our argument for critical pluralism demand that we recognize that we could be wrong about this. We welcome further exchanges between researchers advocating differing perspectives on organizational reality as a means of learning more about it.

Acknowledgment

We gratefully acknowledge the help of Shelby D. Hunt on this chapter.

Notes

1 Not related to the present coauthor.
2 As our title indicates, our charge was to focus on the ontological aspects of reality. However, in so doing, our treatment sometimes unavoidably shades over into epistemological (knowledge claims) concerns and even touches on method. We have tried to minimize this epistemological emphasis, so as not to detract from the authors who were assigned to emphasize epistemology.

References

Academy of Management Review (1992) "Theory development forum," 17: 404–611.

Alvesson, M., and Deetz, S. (1996) "Critical theory and postmodernism approaches to organizational studies," in S. R. Clegg, C. Hardy, and W. R. Nord (eds) *Handbook of Organization Studies*, pp. 191–217. London: Sage.

Anderson, P., Meyer, A., Eisenhardt, K., Carley, K., and Pettigrew, A., eds (1999) *Organization Science*, 10 (3): 215–379.

Baum, J. A. C., and Dobbin, F. (2000) "Doing interdisciplinary research in strategic management – without a paradigm war," in J. A. C. Baum and F. Dobbin (eds) *Economics meets Sociology in Strategic Management*, pp. 389–410. Stamford, CN: JAI Press.

Beach, E. (1984) "The paradox of cognitive relativism revisited: a reply to Jack W. Meiland," *Metaphilosophy*, 15: 1–15.

Berger, P. L., and Luckmann, T. (1965) *The Social Construction of Reality*. New York: Doubleday.

Blumer, H. (1962) "Society as social interaction," in A. M. Rose (ed.) *Human Behavior and Social Processes: An Interactionist Approach*, pp. 179–92. Boston, MA: Houghton Mifflin.

Boal, K. B., and Willis, R. E. (1983) "A note on the Armstrong–Mitroff debate," *Journal of Management*, 9: 203–11.

Broadbeck, M., ed. (1968) *Readings in the Philosophy of the Social Sciences*. New York: Macmillan.

Burrell, G. (1997) *Pandemonium*. London: Sage.

Burrell, G., and Morgan, G. (1979) *Sociological Paradigms and Organizational Analysis*. London: Heinemann.

Bynum, W. F., Browne, E. J., and Porter, R. (1985) *Dictionary of the History of Science*. Princeton, NJ: Princeton University Press.

Calas, M. B., and Smircich, L. (2000) "Ignored for good reason: Beauvoir's philosophy as a revision of social identity approaches," *Journal of Management Inquiry*, 9: 193–9.

Carnap, R. (1950) *Logical Foundations of Probability*. Chicago: University of Chicago Press.

Clegg, S. 1990. *Modern Organizations: Organization Studies in the Postmodern Era*. London: Sage.

Clegg, S. R., Hardy, C., and Nord, W. (1996) *Handbook of Organization Studies*. London: Sage.

Connell, A., and Nord, W. (1996a) "The bloodless *coup:* the infiltration of organization science by uncertainty and values," *Journal of Applied Behavioral Science*, 32: 407–27.

——(1996b) "Uncertainty and values to the rescue," *Journal of Applied Behavioral Science*, 32: 445–54.

Cramer, F. (1993) *Chaos and Order: The Complex Structure of Living Things*, trans. D. L. Loewus. New York: VCH.

Daft, R. L., and Lewin, A. Y. (1990) "Can organization studies begin to break out of the normal science straitjacket? An editorial essay," *Organization Science*, 1: 1–9.

Deetz, S. (2000) "Putting the community into organizational science: exploring the construction of knowledge claims," *Organization Science*, 11: 732–8.

De Regt, C. D. G. (1994) *Representing the World by Scientific Theories: The Case for Scientific Realism*. Tilburg, Netherlands: Tilburg University Press.

Eagleton, T. (1983) *Literary Theory: An Introduction.* Minneapolis, MN: University of Minnesota Press.

Einstein, A. (1923) *Sidelights on Relativity.* New York: Dutton.

Favre, A., Guitton, H., Guitton, J., Lichnerowicz, A., and Wolfe, E. (1995) *Chaos and Determinism: Turbulence as a Paradigm for Complex Systems converging toward Final States,* trans. B. E. Schwarzback. Baltimore, MD: Johns Hopkins University Press.

Feyerabend, P. K. (1975) *Against Method.* London: Verso.

Gergen, K. J., and Whitney, D. (1996) "Technologies of representation in the global corporation: power and polyphony," in D. M. Boje, R. P. Gephart Jr, and T. J. Thatchenkery (eds) *Postmodern Management and Organization Theory,* pp. 331–57. Thousand Oaks, CA: Sage.

Gomez, P-Y., and Jones, B. C. (2000) "Conventions: an interpretation of deep structure in organizations," *Organization Science,* 11: 696–708.

Greenwood, J. D. (1990) "Two dogmas of neo-empiricism: the 'theory-informity' of observation and the Quinne–Duhem thesis," *Philosophy of Science,* 57: 553–74.

Guba, E. G. (1985) "The context of emergent paradigm research," in Y. S. Lincoln (ed.) *Organizational Theory and Inquiry,* pp. 79–104. Newbury Park, CA: Sage.

Hamel, G., and Heene, A. (1994) *Competence-based Competition.* Chicester: Wiley.

Hassard, J. (1993) "Postmoderism and organizational analysis: an overview," in J. Hassard and M. Parker (eds) *Postmoderism and Organizations,* pp. 1–23. London: Sage.

Hempel, C. G. (1959) "The logic of functional analysis." in L. Gross (ed.) *Symposium on Sociological Theory,* pp. 271–307. New York: Harper & Row.

——(1965) "Aspects of scientific explanation," in C. Hempel (ed.) *Aspects of Scientific Explanation and other Essays in the Philosophy of Science,* pp. 331–497. New York: Free Press.

——(1970) "Fundamentals of concept formation in empirical science," in O. Neurath (ed.), *Foundations of the Unity of Science* II, pp. 651–745. Chicago: University of Chicago Press.

Hirschman, E. C. (1986) "Humanistic inquiry in marketing research: philosophy, method, and criteria," *Journal of Marketing Research,* 23: 237–49.

Holland, J. (1995) *Hidden Order.* Reading, MA: Addison-Wesley.

Hunt, J. G. (1991) *Leadership: A New Synthesis.* Newbury Park, CA: Sage.

Hunt, J. G., and Ropo, A. (forthcoming) "Longitudinal organizational research and the third scientific discipline," *Group and Organization Management.*

Hunt, S. D. (1976) *Modern Marketing Theory: Critical Issues in the Philosophy of Marketing Science.* Cincinnati, OH: Southwestern.

——(1990) "Truth in marketing theory and research," *Journal of Marketing,* 54: 1–15.

——(1991a) *Modern Marketing theory: Critical Issues in the Philosophy of Marketing Science.* Cincinnati, OH: Southwestern.

——(1991b) "Positivism and paradigm dominance in consumer research: toward critical pluralism and rapprochement," *Journal of Consumer Research,* 18: 32–44.

——(1993) "Objectivity in marketing theory and research," *Journal of Marketing,* 57: 76–91.

——(1994a) "A realist theory of empirical testing resolving the theory-ladenness/objectivity debate," *Philosophy of the Social Sciences,* 24: 133–58.

——(1994b) "On the rhetoric of qualitative methods: toward historically informed argumentation in management inquiry," *Journal of Management Inquiry,* 3: 221–34.

——(2000) *A General Theory of Competition: Resources, Competences, Productivity, Economic Growth.* Thousand Oaks, CA: Sage.

Husserl, E. (1965) *Phenomenology and the Crisis of Philosophy.* New York: Harper Torchbooks.

Ilgen, D. R., and Hulin, C. D., eds (2000) *Computational Modeling of Behavior in Organizations: The Third Scientific Discipline.* Washington, DC: American Psychological Association.

Jacobson, S. W., and Jacques, R. (1997) "Destabilizing the field: poststructuralist knowledge-making strategies in a postindustrial era," *Journal of Management Inquiry,* 6: 42–59.

Jermier, J., Knights, D., and Nord, W. (1994) *Resistance and Power in Organizations.* London: Routledge.

Kauffman, S. A. (1995) *At Home in the Universe: The Search for the Laws of Self-organization and Complexity*. New York: Oxford University Press.

Knights, D., and Willmott, H. (1999) *Power and Identity in Work Organizations*. London: Sage.

Kuhn, T. S. (1962) *The Structure of Scientific Revolutions*. Chicago: University of Chicago Press.

——(1970) *The Structure of Scientific Revolutions*, second edition. Chicago: University of Chicago Press.

Lakatos, I. 1968. "Criticism and the methodology of scientific research programmers," *Proceedings of the Aristotelian Society*, 69: 149–86.

Lawrence, T. B., and Phillips, N. (1998) "Commentary. Separating play and critique: postmodern and critical perspectives on TQM/BPR," *Journal of Management Inquiry*, 7: 154–60.

Lennon, K., and Whitford, M., eds (1994) *Knowing the Difference: Feminist Perspectives in Epistemology*. New York: Routledge.

Levy, S. (1992) *Artificial Life: The Quest for New Creation*. New York: Random House.

Lincoln, Y. S., and Guba, E. G. (1985) *Naturalistic Inquiry*. Beverly Hills, CA: Sage.

Lyotard, J. F. (1984) *The Postmodern Condition: A Report on Knowledge*. Minneapolis, MN: University of Minnesota Press.

Mainzer, K. (1994) *Thinking in Complexity: The Complex Dynamics of Matter, Mind, and Mankind*. New York: Springer.

Manicas, P. T. (1987) *A History of Philosophy of the Social Sciences*. New York: Blackwell.

Marion, R. (1999) *The Edge of Organization: Chaos and Complexity: Theories of Formal Social Systems*. Thousand Oaks, CA: Sage.

Marion, R., and Uhl-Bien, M. (2001) "Leadership in complex organizations," *Leadership Quarterly*, 12 (4): 389–418.

Mauws, M. K., and Phillips, N. (1995) "Understanding language games," *Organization Science*, 6: 322–34.

McKelvey, B. (1997) "Quasi-natural organizational science," *Organization Science*, 8: 351–80.

——(1999a) "Avoiding complexity catastrophe in coevolutionary pockets: strategies for rugged landscapes," *Organization Science*, 10 (3): 294–321.

——(1999b) "Toward a Campbellian realist organization science," in J. A. C. Baum and B. McKelvey (eds) *Variations in Organization Science: In Honor of Donald T. Campbell*, pp. 383–411. Thousand Oaks, CA: Sage.

McMullin, E. (1984) "A case for scientific realism," in J. Leplin (ed.) *Scientific Realism*, pp. 8–40. Berkeley, CA: University of California Press.

Mick, D. G. (1986) "Consumer research and semiotics: exploring the morphology of signs, symbols, and significance," *Journal of Consumer Research*, 13: 196–213.

Moore, G. E. (1903) "The refutation of idealism," reprinted in *Philosophical Studies*, ed. G. E. Moore, pp. 1–30. London: Trench Trubner, 1922.

Morgan, G., and Smircich, L. (1980) "The case for qualitative research," *Academy of Management Review*, 5: 491–500.

Nicholis, G. I., and Prigogine, I. (1989) *Exploring Complexity: An Introduction*. New York: Freeman.

Parsons, T. (1937) *The Structure of Social Action*. New York: McGraw-Hill.

Phillips, D. C. (1987) *Philosophy, Science, and Social Inquiry*. Oxford: Pergamon.

Popper, K. R. (1959) *The Logic of Scientific Discovery*. New York: Harper & Row, 1968.

——(1972) *Objective Knowledge: An Evolutionary Approach*. London: Oxford University Press.

Prigogine, I., and Stengers, I. (1984) *Order out of Chaos*. New York: Bantam Books.

Putnam, L. L. Bantz, C., Deetz, S., Mumby, D., and Van Maanen, J. (1993) "Ethonography versus critical theory: debating organizational research," *Journal of Management Inquiry*, 2: 221–35.

Radcliffe-Brown, A. R. (1952) *Structure and Function in Primitive Society*. New York: Free Press.

Ruelle, D., and Takens, F. (1971) "On the nature of turbulence," *Communications in Mathematical Physics*, 20: 167–92.

Russell, B. (1929) *Our Knowledge of the External World*. New York: New American Library.

Sanders, T. I. (1998) *Strategic Thinking and the New Science*. New York: Free Press.

Sapir, E. (1929) "The status of linguistics as a science," *Language*, 5: 207–14. Reprinted in D. G. Mandelbaum (ed.) *Selected Writings of Edward Sapir in Language, Culture, and Personality*, pp. 34–41. Berkeley, CA: University of California Press, 1949.

Shapere, D. (1982) "The concept of observation in science and philosophy," *Philosophy of Science*, 49: 485–525.

Siegel, Harvey (1988) "Relativism for consumer research? Comments on Anderson," *Journal of Consumer Research*, 10: 157–68.

Steinfatt, T. M. (1989) "Linguistic relativity: toward a broader view," in S. Ting-Toomey and F. Korzenny (eds) *Language, Communications, and Culture*, pp. 35–78. Newbury Park, CA: Sage.

Suppe, F. (1977) *The Structure of Scientific Theories*, second edition. Chicago: University of Chicago Press.

Wallendorf, M., and Belk, R. W. (1989) "Assessing trustworthiness in naturalistic consumer research," in E. Hirschman (ed.) *Interpretive Consumer Research*. Provo, UT: Association for Consumer Research.

Watkins, J. (1984) *Science and Skepticism*. Princeton, NJ: Princeton University Press.

Weick, K. E. (1985) "Sources of order in underorganized systems: themes in recent organization theory," in Y. S. Lincoln (ed.) *Organizational Theory and Inquiry: The Paradigm Revolution*, pp. 106–36. Newbury Park, CA: Sage.

Weiss, R. M. (2000) "Taking science out of organization science: how would postmodernism reconstruct the analysis of organizations?" *Organization Science*, 11: 709–31.

Whorf, B. L. (1956) *Language, Thought, and Reality*. Cambridge, MA: MIT Press.

3b Ontology: Organization as "World-making"

Robert Chia

The purpose of chapter 3b is to trace the foundational roots of modern attitudes towards organization and management and to relocate their origins in the broader civilizational processes that have taken place especially in the last three millennia. Its central argument is that organization must not be understood as a concrete social entity (whether socially constructed or otherwise) with durable characteristics and tendencies. Instead, organization is better understood as the aggregative, unintended outcome of local efforts at ordering and regularizing our otherwise intractable and amorphous life world in order to make it more predictable and livable. Organization is more a tedious and interminable process of *faction*-ing out the real than a solid, static thing. This suggests that we ought to think about Organization Studies (OS) not as the study of "organizations," but as a sustained analysis of the generic organizational impulses shaping contemporary modes of analysis, codes of behavior, social mannerisms, dress, gestures, postures, the rules of law, disciplines of knowledge, and so on. These micro-ordering processes collectively serve to shape our identities and aspirations and to orient us towards ourselves and

our environment. This has profound consequences for what we take as the legitimate objects of analysis, our modes of theorizing and the imperatives we draw to inform managerial action. It is this broader dimension of organizing as "world making" which offers a richer alternative to the study of organization and its consequences for the world of affairs.

Introduction

In each period there is a general form of the forms of thought; and, like the air we breath, such a form is so translucent, and so pervading, and so seemingly necessary, that only by extreme effort can we become aware of it. (Whitehead, 1933: 20)

In 1884, more than 100 years ago, representatives from twenty-five major countries convened at the Prime Meridian Conference in Washington and came to an agreement on the exact length of the universal day. They proceeded to divide the earth into twenty-four time zones, each one hour apart, with Greenwich as the zero meridian. Prior to this momentous event a traveler from Washington to San Francisco would have had to reset his watch more than 200 times as he passed through each of the towns on the way to his destination. The pressure for adopting standard time zones came initially from the railroad companies but was gradually taken up across the world so that by the early twentieth century most countries had aligned themselves with Greenwich time. Crucially, it was the invention of first the telephone and then the wireless telegraph which made it possible for simultaneous events taking place in various parts of the world to be registered, coordinated and synchronized according to this universal standard time. The ability to experience distant events simultaneously, made possible by the wireless and dramatized by the sinking of the *Titanic* on the night of April 14, 1912, was a part of the major cultural shift taking place during that period. This expanding experience of simultaneity and presence was further reinforced by concerted attempts to standardize the previously agreed time zones across the world. The globalization of time occurred on July 1, 1913. At ten o'clock that morning the Eiffel Tower in Paris transmitted the first time signals around the world, thereby registering the advent of a universal framework for temporal coordination and control. Whatever sentiment and charm local time might have once had, the world was henceforth fated to wake up with buzzers and bells triggered by impulses that traveled around the world with the speed of light. This representation of private lived time and its systematic conversion into public "spatialized" domains marked a crucial moment in the shaping of the modern world order. In one single stroke it became possible to coordinate actions, intentions, and aspirations across space in an unprecedented way and to achieve a level of predictability and productivity in social interactions never before envisaged. This is a triumph of modern organization. It provides an important illustration of how an otherwise dispersed and heterogeneous concatenation of atomic event-occurrences spread out across a vast geographical space can be regularized and made to fit within a singular coordinated framework with highly productive consequences. Such is the scope and power of the phenomenon of organization.

The establishment of the World Standard Time over a century ago epitomizes a form of relentless social ordering that has had an incalculable impact on our everyday life and on our understanding of social reality. Like the invention of the alphabet and the printing press, several centuries before, it represents yet another momentous attempt to forge a universal system of communication and organization out of an otherwise inchoate and amorphous mass of local orderings and tacit understandings in the conduct of daily life. Organization is the quintessential technology for *real-izing* the *real*: for making what appears initially irrelevant and unconnected part of a universal order that gives sense and consequence to our everyday action and experience. Oxford University, quarks, black holes and gravity are real to us in our commonsense understanding, not because we can see or experience them, but because we are able to attribute *causal consequence* to their purported existence. The construction of identities, their simple location, and their causal attribution, however, are precisely modern *strategies of organization*: central features of our modern will-to-order. They reflect our capacity for "world making": for drawing together the seemingly dispersed and the unrelated into a coherent and plausible system of explanation.

Such forms of social ordering inevitably influence, amongst other things, how the flux and flow of our life worlds are structured and conceptualized into events, things, and situations; how identity is established and social entities are created; how taxonomies and systems of classification are produced, and with what effects; how reification takes place and causal relations are imputed, and with what consequences; and how symbols and representations are used to substitute for reality and with what outcomes, particularly in terms of organizational priorities and practices. *It is this second-order concern with the organization of our forms of social life, our ways of seeing, our modes of understanding and explanation, and our methods of knowledge creation that constitutes an alternative way of conceptualizing the role of organization studies.* One that invariably emphasizes the reality-constituting or ontological character of organization. What is significantly overlooked in much of conventional OS, therefore, is a rigorous and critical reflection on the underlying social, cultural, and historical forces shaping the way we see, think, and act within the institutionalized and organized structures of the modern world. Against the restricted and restrictive view of OS as an economic-administrative discipline, an expanded *social theory of organization* seeks to critically examine the generic organizing logic underpinning the societal and institutional strategies of rationalization that both Max Weber and Michel Foucault, among others, identified as the defining feature of modernity.

This chapter begins by examining the structuring effects of language on our perception and conception of reality. It attempts to show how language, and in particular the alphabetic system of writing, has substantially inspired an atomistic, entitative, and causal view of reality. This view of reality was reinforced by the arrival of a typographic system of thinking some 500 years ago following the invention of the printing press. It is argued here that the introduction of such a typographic mind set led to the modern obsession with collecting, classifying, and typologizing natural and social phenomena, precipitating the kind of *systematic empiricism* that we now associate with scientific realism. We then move on to briefly examine an alternative *becoming* ontology as the basis for reconceptualizing organization as an *emergent* process rather than as a stable phenomenon. From this alternative metaphysical orientation, it will be shown that organization involves the relentless arresting, fixing, and stabilizing of an intrinsically wild, fluxing, and changeable reality. "Organizations" are, in fact, islands of relatively stabilized patterns of interactional order selectively abstracted from a sea of chaos. They do not possess "thinglike" characteristics. We do not directly experience "an organization," even if we are admittedly affected by the complex of social relationships we find ourselves in at various points in our lives. Such organizing relationships are nothing more than the dynamic network of implicit assumptions, expectations, social obligations, rules, conventions, and protocols which shape how our individual identities are constructed and how as fundamentally social creatures we are expected to behave and act within a specific community at a given point in time. Organization, as such, is not so much a solid, stable entity as an ongoing "world-making" activity. This activity of

constructing and reinforcing our all-too-familiar organized world is intrinsic to the process of modern civilization. It goes far back to the invention of writing and, in particular, the invention of the alphabet.

The Alphabetization of the Western World

If today we are so often tempted to speak of the "European mind" or the "Western mind," vague as these determinations are, they have a factual basis in so far as we mean those cultures which have continued to employ the Greek invention. (Havelock, 1982: 346)

Any understanding of Western cultural evolution and change is impossible without a prior appreciation of the fundamental changes in *sense ratios*, and hence attitudes of *observational discrimination*, brought about by the invention of the alphabet. Introduced some 3,000 years ago by the Phoenicians, and appropriated and modified by the Greeks some three centuries later, alphabetic writing paved the way for the detribalizing of ancient Greece and its subsequent rise into prominence in the first millennium BC. Through the newly systematized alphabetic script, the Greeks created, from the fifth and fourth centuries BC, one of the richest literatures of all times, including poetry, drama, epics, history, and philosophy. The advantage of the alphabetic system over previous forms of scribal writing lay in its startling economy and flexibility of use in communication: as an achievement it has often been compared to the invention of the wheel and the domestication of the horse (McArthur, 1986). As a number of influential studies show (Gelb, 1952; Diringer, 1962; Ong, 1967, 1977, 1982; Havelock, 1982), the alphabetic system of writing dramatically altered the character of the preliterate Greek culture that had existed up to that period. Ong (1982), for instance, argues that the shift from oral to literate alphabetic culture did more than change patterns of art, politics, and commerce. It facilitated a profound shift in human consciousness, bringing about the linear, abstract form of Western logic that we take very much for granted today. This "ABCDE mindedness" brought about by the introduction of the alphabet creates a kind of chirographic bias that subtly ranks sight above sound and the eye above the ear. Knowing became inextricably linked to vision and it led Aristotle to subsequently write in the very first few lines of his *Metaphysics*, "Of all the senses, sight best brings about knowledge of things and reveals many distinctions" (Treddenick, 1933: 1). Moreover, thinking came to be intimately associated with visual metaphors: "observation" privileges visual data; "phenomenon" owes its origin in Greek to the notion of "exposure to sight"; "definition" comes from *definire*, to draw a line around; and sight is internalized into our vocabulary of knowledge – insight, idea, illuminate, enlighten, reflect, survey, perspective, point of view, show, overview, etc.

This shift in the balance of the senses away from the aural to the visual also favoured "a new kind of personality structure" (Ong, 1967: 8) because, as McLuhan and McLuhan (1988) convincingly argued, prolonged mimesis of the alphabet produced a dominant mode of perception which elevated the individual, the abstract, and the static as the basis of analysis. The phonetic alphabet first translates images into arbitrary consonants and sound syllables which, by themselves, are meaningless. These are then mentally reassembled back into the form of words from which meaning is then extracted. Meaning, therefore, becomes possible only at the operative level of words and not at the level of the individual alphabet. Literacy training systematically develops the ability to construct meaningful frames out of otherwise meaningless consonants and sound syllables. As McLuhan astutely observed, it is through "the meaningless sign linked to the meaningless sound [that] we have built the shape and meaning of Western man" (McLuhan, 1967: 50). Hence the Greeks did not just invent an alphabet, "they invented literacy and the literate basis of modern thought" (Havelock, 1982: 82). The alphabetic culture puts a premium on sharp outlines and clear-cut sequences and therefore promotes "literal meaning . . . as something altogether wholesome and altogether desirable" whilst at the same time regarding "other . . . more profoundly symbolic meaning with disfavor" (Ong, 1967: 47). The introduction of the alphabetic system made available a permanent visualized record in place of an acoustic one, thereby displacing the need for memory, repetition, and copiousness in speech performance.

However, not all systems of writing invented have had this effect. Ong maintains that, unlike Chinese writing, which does not at root work from words as sound, the alphabetic system works by "atomizing" linguistic sound, and in particular the syllable, into its acoustic components and then assigning a specific alphabetic shape to each of these sound elements. This breakthrough in streamlining an otherwise cumbersome assortment of signs and symbols gave language an overall orderly shape and made it much more manageable than ever before. Instead of having to deal with the hundreds of distinct pictograms (picture signs), ideograms (idea signs), and logograms (word signs) that are to be found in cuneiform, hieroglyphics, or Chinese writing, between twenty and thirty quasiphonetic symbols can now be used to portray an infinity of words and hence afford a much wider variety of expressions. Moreover, it enabled literacy to spread faster because this method of atomizing linguistic sound "placed the skill for reading theoretically within the reach of children at the stage where they are still learning the sounds of their own vocabulary" (Havelock, 1982: 83).

One unexpected consequence of the introduction of the alphabetic system was the popularizing of the method of *atomization* – the breaking up of sound into component elements and then reassembling them in space to form meaningful words. This brought with it an overwhelming sense of order and control that had never been before experienced. Thus "When the alphabet commits the verbal and conceptual worlds . . . to the quiescent and obedient order of space, it imputes to language and thought an additional consistency of which preliterate persons have no inkling" (Ong, 1967: 45). Ong therefore concludes that it is no accident that "formal logic was invented in an alphabetic culture" (1967: 45). It was this formal logic of analysis associated with alphabetization which eventually led to the almost obsessive fixing, naming, classifying, and thematizing of material and social phenomena as a way of creating order and predictability in an otherwise fluxing and amorphous life world.

Writing in general, and alphabetic writing in particular, is inextricably linked to the systematic ordering and organization of society. Thus "Communities developed ranks, castes and guilds, armies their divisions, priesthoods their hierarchies, merchants their inventories and farmers their fields and boundaries" (McArthur, 1986: 32). As Goody (1986) perceptively points out, modern nations are highly dependent on writing for their legislation and for their systems of governance. For Goody "the desk and the bureau" (p. 90) are critical to Weber's concept of bureaucracy. Likewise Green (1981) argues that the emergence of large-scale, centralized bureaucratic institutions is a consequence of the rise of writing, which "enabled the administration to grow and, through written liability, to maintain direct authority over even the lowest levels of personnel and clientele" (Green, 1981: 367).

In sum, the alphabet is, as McLuhan (1967) puts it, "an aggressive and militant absorber and transformer of cultures" (p. 48). It precipitated the abstraction, simple-location,[1] and objectification of phenomena for the purpose of analysis, and, by reducing all our senses into visual and pictorial or enclosed space, precipitated the rise of the Euclidean sensibility which has dominated our thought processes for over 2,000 years. The alphabetization of the Western world, and the method of atomization it introduced, constitute the most successful and widespread approach to organizing, structuring, and representing the aural–oral world of lived experience in a way that readily lends itself to cognitive manipulation. In this most fundamental sense the alphabetization of the Western world is a prime example of organization as a "world-making" activity. With its introduction came an entirely new emphasis on visual control and organization and the reliance on atomization as a generic method of analysis.

The Gutenberg Galaxy: the Rise of Typographic Thinking

Print gave the drive to collect and classify . . . Getting together an assemblage of snippets on classified subjects culled from any and every writer now paid a thousandfold. (Ong, 1967: 85)

Nearly two and a half millennia after the invention of the alphabet, around the year 1447, Johannes Gutenberg of Mainz became the first in the West to mechanize printing. Initially, printing appeared to complement manuscript writing, which was much in demand by the upper and middle classes, a demand which the monastic scribes became increasingly unable to cope with. Soon, however, like the cottage industries of more recent times, the slow and laborious process of producing the written word gave way to printing. This marked another significant moment in the modification of the visual/tactile/aural *sense ratios* that had been first rendered apart by the introduction of the alphabet. For whilst manuscript culture is effectively conversational in that "the writer and his audience are physically related by the form of publication" (McLuhan, 1967: 84), since each manuscript was commissioned by the instructions of a specific individual, the print culture created the distinction between authors and the consuming public. Henceforth, multiple copies of a manuscript could be made and distributed widely, so much so that it was very likely the readership might never have met the author of a particular piece of work. Conversational exchange gave way to the *commodification* of output. The invention of typography "extended the new visual stress of applied knowledge, providing the first uniformly repeatable commodity, the first assembly line, and the first mass-production" (McLuhan, 1967: 124). Typography, as the first mechanized handicraft, radically shaped not only private sense ratios but also the prevailing "patterns of communal interdependence" (McLuhan, 1967: 164). Uniform quantification, assembly, measurability, individualism, and centralized control became important priorities in the management of economic and social life.

Uniform quantification because print made it possible to produce almost identical copies in increasingly larger quantities. And this, in turn, generated a larger appetite for more of the same. For the first time ever, assembly and mass production, as we understand them today, became possible. Print, in facilitating the translation of the vernacular into a mass media, initiated the demand for uniformity and standardization and hence inspired the homogenizing forces of modernity. But it also promoted a widespread typesetting mode of thought through its emphasis on combining and recombining the otherwise discrete and infinitely manipulable individual characters of the alphabet. As Ong (1967) writes:

What was crucial for the ultimate locking of sound in space was the invention of the movable alphabetic type cast from matrices which had been made with punches . . . Some twelve to sixteen steps . . . intervened here between the written word (already one remove from the spoken) and the printed sheet . . . To perform them, knowledge of the language concerned is not necessary . . . The commitment of spoken words to space here in typography has a depth and intensity continuous with but far exceeding that achieved by alphabetic chirography . . . What happened with the emergence of alphabetic typography was not that man discovered the use of his eyes but that he began to link visual perception to verbalization to a degree previously unknown. (Ong, 1967: 48–50)

The idea that any phenomenon, material or social, can be captured and represented by first breaking it up into individual component pieces and then reassembling it as needs be, first initiated by the invention of the alphabet, but enormously magnified by the advent of typography, became the dominant metaphor for analysis. It is this typographic metaphor which serves as the *Leitmotiv* for modernist thought.

Centralized control and a linear, hierarchical order were also accentuated through the print culture because the latter provided possibly the first truly economical means significantly to overcome the hitherto troublesome limitations of space and time in terms of communication and influence. For print made it possible to achieve widespread communication at a distance and across time for the masses to be reached directly, thereby influencing their attitudes, cultural habits, and lifestyles. It was this principle of extension and intensification of communicational channels which made possible the kind of large-scale, centralized, and bureaucratic institutions that Green (1981) referred to in his perceptive analysis of the organization of society. Without the written word, communication would have had to be passed on by "word of mouth," thereby incurring inevitable

distortions. Without the alphabetic system the range of abstract meanings, perspectives, concepts, and ideas would have remained very limited or else evolved at a much slower pace than that achieved through the advent of literacy. Without the printed word, communication would have been restricted only to the privileged few and not to the critical masses required to produce revolutionary changes in the priorities and mind sets that paved the way for the Enlightenment to take place. The dramatic transformations and breakthroughs achieved in the West over the last 500 years especially would not have been possible.

Key Axioms of Modern Rationality

Industrial society rests on order. Order means everything in its place . . . a society bent on order should put the body into order by putting order into the body; society gains order by "training." (Schoenwald, 1973: 674)

The Enlightenment was a historical watershed because of the emphasis it gave to four key ideational imperatives that were inspired by the advent of literacy and rediscovered by the invention of the printing press. These continue to underpin many of the assumptions made in contemporary organizational theorizing. Firstly, there is the unquestioned commitment to a Parmenidean-inspired *being* ontology whereby reality is conceived as atomistic, thinglike, already formed, and essentially unchanging. It does not take much to see that the spread of the use of the alphabetic system in Greece coincided with the rise of this form of atomistic thinking, beginning especially with Parmenides in the fifth century BC and subsequently modified by his successors Leucippus and Democritus. As Aristotle wrote of Democritus:

Democritus gives to space the name "void," "nothing," and "the infinite." To each of his substances he gives the name "thing," and "the compact," and "being." He supposes them to be so small that they elude our senses; but they have forms of all sorts and shapes of all sorts and differ in size. So that already he is able to create from these, as elements, by aggregation, the masses that are perceptible to sight. (Aristotle, *On Democritus*, in Mansley Robinson, 1968: 197)

Reality, according to Democritus, consisted fundamentally of atomistic elements which when aggregated produced the visible masses that we find all around us. Thus, just like written words are aggregates of individual letters, so also the world is an aggregate of irreducible atomic elements.

This way of thinking about reality was significantly revived by the invention of the printing press, because it promoted a heightened awareness of the aggregative nature of words and hence of the thought processes associated with them. Such an intellectual orientation gave rise to a form of "atomistic rationalism" whereby individual agents were construed as the ultimate unit of social reality and hence the most appropriate unit of analysis. Moreover, causal attribution became a prominent preoccupation of rational analysis because, if reality is discrete and reducible to its aggregate components, it becomes possible to separate cause from effect and action from outcome. Thus individual agents are held to be relatively autonomous units capable of exercising deliberate choice and intentional action in any given set of circumstance. The result is that it is the individual's identity, cognition, actions, intentions, and capabilities that form the primary basis for description, classification, and analysis as well as causal attribution in social theorizing. This practice is also widespread in OS, for, although it is sometimes conceded that organizations are indeed reifications and hence cannot "have" competences, it is nevertheless taken that "individuals" are unquestionably real and hence can "have competences." Attributing properties, capabilities, and intentions to circumscribed individual actors presupposes an atomistic view of social reality; a culturally specified way of construing agency and action. For only when this view is upheld can social phenomena be isolated, analysed, and causally linked within a spatio-temporal framework of explanation.

Modern Western rationality, therefore, is better understood as part of a more generic cognitive strategy for converting the otherwise intractable and mutable masses, material or otherwise, into usable resources by breaking them down and converting them into repeatable part elements. The development of this approach was much inspired by the invention of the alphabet and the advent of typography, as we have tried to show. Whitehead (1926/1985: 60–4) maintains that, without the development of this method of analysis, scientific development, as exemplified by the achievements of Galileo and Newton, would have been impossible.

Secondly, with the Enlightenment came the revived emphasis on the observation of both natural and social phenomena and their subsequent location and classification into typological schemas. Vision and systematic observation became central to our forms of knowing. Berger (1972) convincingly argues that the Enlightenment systematically transformed our way of seeing from involved engagement to passive objectification. A "logic of the gaze" began to dominate thought. Bryson (1982) in a fascinating analysis of Western thought maintains that the modern "look" plays a functional and placating role in empirical investigations. It is fixing, prolonged, and contemplative. Its aim is to arrest and extract form from fleeting process. It is a vision disembodied, a vision decarnalized. Thus, in the gaze the observer: "arrests the flux of the phenomena, contemplates the visual field from a vantage-point outside the mobility of duration, in an eternal moment of disclosed presence" (Bryson, 1982: 94). The gaze is penetrating, piercing, fixing, objectifying. It is a violent act of forcibly and permanently "present-ing" that which otherwise would be a fluxing, moving reality.

With the Enlightenment and the rise to ascendance of a logic of the gaze came the overpowering need to scan, document, collect, classify, and sort out objects of interest, and to attribute causal powers to these artificially isolated objects of analysis. A culture of "collecting and classifying" (Elsner and Cardinal, 1994) emerged that was to produce hobbies and occupations such as the collection of stones, shells, butterflies, and plants, and modern institutions such as the museums and art galleries that make up an essential part of our contemporary cultural landscape. Through such careful observation and painstaking differentiation and classification of phenomena, it was believed, our knowledge of the universe could be systematically documented and the underlying natural order revealed. Classification tables of all sorts emerged during this period. Linnaeus's *Systema Naturae*, written in the early eighteenth century, provides one of the clearest examples of this revived obsession with observing, collecting, listing, and classifying empirical data. It precipitated the emphasis on what we now call "systematic empiricism": the second ideational imperative associate with the advent of the Enlightenment.

Initiated by Aristotle's call for grounding our knowledge in observation, and inspired by Descartes's rigorously logical method of doubting, systematic empiricism surfaced most prominently in the kind of logical positivism which held sway in intellectual circles for the best part of the earlier half of the twentieth century. It is within this theoretical soil, as Gergen and Thatchenkery (1998: 19) put it, that contemporary management and organizational thinking took root.

Thirdly, the triumph of Enlightenment knowledge brought with it the idea that language was primarily a medium designed to enable us to accurately represent linguistically our perceived reality. This representationalist view of language derives from the Cartesian split between mind and matter. The purpose of the Cartesian mind is to mirror accurately the nature of matter existing external to itself. Thus cognition, in this Cartesian sense, involves the ability to accurately "map" phenomena and events in the external world and to thereby establish their causal relationships in a rationalist system of explanation. In Rorty's (1980) terms the picture used to ideologically captivate the Western world for over three centuries is the image of the mind as a mirror, containing various linguistic representations of the world. For Rorty, it is this representationalist world view which has provided the fundamental premise for the legitimation of modern knowledge. Knowledge is deemed true and acceptable only if it is able to accurately represent external reality as it is in itself. Such a view implies that language is seen as merely a medium of communication and that it does not play an active and constitutive role in the production of social reality. Moreover, linguistic terms are believed to have an essential one-to-one relationship with observed phenomena, so

much so that only literal meanings provide a reliable basis for theory building. This belief about the transparency of language has led to the commonplace insistence on precision, accuracy, and parsimony in the organizational theory-building process (Pfeffer, 1993).

Finally, the grand narratives of progress and truth are key ideational imperatives of modernity (Gergen and Thatchenkery, 1998). For, if reason and observation were to work in harmony, and language gave us transparent and unmediated access to an objective reality, it would be possible to objectively validate and assess the status of any truth claims. This would, in turn, mean that an inexorable march towards a complete and ultimate truth was, in principle, possible. The result would be the systematic application of this established knowledge to produce absolute predictability and the total elimination of any surprises in all facets of our lives. Our world would then be increasingly subjected to our absolute control, and this, in turn, would be a utopian outcome for mankind. It is the inherent attractions of the narrative of progress that justifies the current "human genome" project and the still unabated search for a "theory of everything."

These four ideational imperatives provide the intellectual cornerstones for modern thought in general and OS in particular. Together, they serve as the recursive epistemological strategy underpinning the apparent diversity of ideas, concepts, and theories generated over the past four decades or so since the inception of organization studies as a legitimate academic field of study.

Summary: The Organizational Evolution of Western Thought

To summarize, our current modes of thought are inextricably shaped by basic organizational impulses deeply embedded within the Western civilizational process which have led us from the concrete material practices of dividing up carcases when hunting was the major preoccupation to our modern habit of dissecting experienced phenomena for the purpose of rational analysis. The invention of the phonetically based alphabet, with its clear emphasis on delineating one sound syllable from another, and on treating each as a distinct entity to be manipulated and dealt with, gave rise to the objectifying and reifying mentality we find so pervasive and compelling in the modern method of analysis in the West. Atomistic rationalism, best exemplified in Descartes's *Discourse on Method*, has had far-reaching consequences for our ways of understanding and comprehending both the social and the material world.

Moreover, the invention of the printing press precipitated a complementary "typesetting" mentality for dealing not just with the material world but with our amorphous life world of fleeting events and experiences. This practice, as we have shown, is best exemplified by Linnaeus's monumental attempt to observe, collect, name, and classify the many species of flora and fauna found in the natural world. In the social realm we find equivalents in the works of Wilkins and Spratt, founding members of the Royal Society in the seventeenth century (Kenner, 1987) and in Jeremy Bentham's "methodization" (Chia, 1998) as a prescribed approach for taming the urban masses that congregated into the cities as a result of the industrial revolution. It is this generic organizational strategy of observing, naming, listing, classifying, categorizing, and tabulating which constitutes the central thrust of systematic empiricism.

These two basic techniques of organization (i.e., atomistic rationalism and systematic empiricism) are, in turn, predicated upon the assumption that language and hence signifiers such as names, labels, classes, and categories are able to accurately capture the essence of the phenomenon being investigated. Clearly, since literal meaning involves the fixing of a relationship between a specific symbol and a referent, it carries with it an implicit assumption that reality itself must be also stable and relatively unchanging. For only then would it be possible for a static symbol to capture reality in full. This assumption is what gives rise to the representationalist epistemology underpinning modernist thought. Such a representationalist epistemology, in turn, fuels the belief in the idea of an almost inexorable progress towards complete, certain, and universal knowledge, thereby making the idea of the "accumulation" of knowledge through the

process of "theory building" a central pursuit in academic endeavors. The metaphor of "collection" and "accumulation" again becomes a dominant feature of this mode of thought. These key organizing axioms mark the epistemological limits of modernist thought and hence our current conceptualization of organization.

However, it is possible to reconceptualize organization and, hence, OS in a way which opens up new avenues for investigation. For this an alternative *becoming* ontology must be introduced.

A Becoming Ontology

Upon those who step into the same rivers flow other and yet other waters. (Heraclitus, *Fragments*, in Mansley Robinson, 1968: 91)

The pervasive intuition that "all things flow" and are in a continuous process of *becoming* and *changing* remains a vague and enduring but relatively untheorized aspect of Western consciousness. In the East it is readily accepted as a given. In the West, it first appeared as one of the key propositions of the Presocratic Greek philosopher Heraclitus. Since then, however, it has been the Parmenidean-inspired system of thought, with its emphasis on *being*, permanence, stability, and equilibrium which has held sway within the intellectual circles in academia. This remains the case despite the fact that a number of more recent thinkers, especially Henri Bergson (1911, 1913, 1946/1992), and Alfred North Whitehead (1926/1985, 1929, 1933), as well as other more contemporary "process physicists" (Bohm, 1980; Prigogine, 1996) have unequivocally upheld the "flux of things" (Whitehead, 1929: 240) as the ultimate basis of reality. As Bohm writes:

Not only is everything changing, but all *is* flux. That is to say, *what is* is the process of becoming itself . . . all objects, events, entities, conditions, structures, etc., are forms that can be abstracted from this process. (Bohm, 1980: 48, emphasis original)

It is this resurrecting of the primacy of movement and change (what Bohm calls the "implicate") over that of atomistic entities and end states which provides a radically alternative ontology for understanding organization as a world-making activity. For it is only when ultimate reality is taken to be ceaselessly changing and in process that the apparent *stability* and *solidity* of entities become an issue in intellectual analysis. From the point of view of a process ontology, organizations are "islands" of relatively stabilized order in a sea of chaos and flux: that is, relative to the temporal flow of our own consciousness, what we call organizations exhibit a degree of endurance through time. Such a *becoming* ontology greatly simplifies matters. As Rescher (1996) notes:

Instead of a two-tier reality that combines *things* together with their inevitable coordinated *processes*, it settles for a one-tier ontology of process alone. For it sees things . . . as the *manifestations* of processes. It replaces the troublesome ontological dualism of *thing* and *activity* with a monism of activities of different and differently organized sorts. (Rescher, 1996: 49, emphasis original)

In other words, an ontology of *becoming* can well absorb and explain more coherently, the problems and contradictions induced by the unquestioned commitment to a *being* ontology which may concede that change does occur but remains unable to explain *why* change does in fact take place if stability and equilibrium are the natural order of things. For process ontologists, what we call things are merely stabilized patterns that we impute to phenomena via the influence of language. This metaphysical "reversal" has radical consequences for our understanding of the meaning of organization, change, and the creative impulses underlying the processes of evolution.

Four axioms and imperatives are detectable in this processual approach to analysis. Firstly, in place of the modernist emphasis on the ontological primacy of substance, stability, order, regularity, and form, an ontology of *becoming* seeks to emphasize the Heraclitan primacy accorded to process, indeterminacy, flux, formlessness, and incessant change. This process orientation must not be equated with the commonsensical idea of the process that a system is deemed to undergo in transition. Rather it is a metaphysical orientation which emphasizes an ontological primacy in the processual nature of things; that sees things as always already momentary outcomes or effects of historical processes. It rejects what Rescher (1996) calls the *process reducibility thesis* whereby

processes are often assumed to be processes *of* primary "things." Instead, it insists that "things" are no more than "stability waves in a sea of process." (Rescher, 1996: 53). What this means is that "things" appear solid, stable, and clearly circumscribed, precisely because language is an ordering structure which inspires the carving up of the flux of our experiences into meaningful fragments. By so doing, the fragments themselves come to exhibit patterns of regularity over time. A process ontology, therefore, elevates a more intuitive, decentered, dynamic, and dispersive view of reality that actively resists linguistic capture and representation. Language can only "point to" or allude to an ultimate reality beyond the symbolic realm (Bohm, 1980: 16–17). What we call concepts and theories are therefore merely intuitive "*insights*, i.e. a way of looking at the world, and not a form of *knowledge* of how the world is" (Bohm, 1980: 4). Theories, as the Greek root *theoria* implies, are ways of viewing and not bodies of knowledge, as we generally assume them to be.

Secondly, from this commitment to a process ontology it follows that language, and in particular the activities of *naming* and *symbolic representation*, provide the first ordering impulse for the systematic structuring of our human life worlds. It maintains that the structured nature of language is what creates the impression that reality itself is stable, preorganized and lawlike in character. Without the acts of naming, classifying, and the creation of a subject–predicate structure through language, lived reality is but a "shapeless and indistinct mass" (Saussure, 1966: 111). Through the process of naming pre-established symbols are used to substitute for our tacit lived experiences. Thus, from this aboriginal flux of pure experience, our attention first carves out, and then conception names: "in the sky 'constellation,' on the earth 'beach,' 'sea,' 'cliff,' 'bushes,' 'grass.' Out of time we cut 'days' and 'nights,' 'summers' and 'winters.' We say what each part of the sensible continuum is, and all these abstract *whats* are concepts" (James, 1911/1996: 50). Names, symbols, concepts, and categories help objectify our experiences to ourselves and in so doing help make a more stable and predictable and hence livable world. Yet, in this process of operationalizing thought, many of our intuited forms of knowing are marginalized and subsequently forgotten. A *becoming* ontology, therefore, promotes a heightened appreciation of the limitations of language in understanding our experiences of reality and hence a deeper awareness of what lies behind symbols and language. As Bohm (1980) convincingly illustrates:

For example, consider the sentence "It is raining." Where is the "It" that would, according to the sentence, be "the rainer that is doing the raining"? Clearly, it is more accurate to say: "Rain is going on." Similarly, we customarily say, "One elementary particle acts on another," but . . . each particle is only an abstraction of a relatively invariant form of movement in the whole field of the universe. So it would be more appropriate to say, "Elementary particles are ongoing movements that are mutually dependent." (Bohm, 1980: 29)

Language promotes a certain style of thinking, and it is this very style of thinking which needs addressing in order to truly begin to think in processual terms. Moreover, this realization of the impact of linguistic structure on our sense of reality reminds us that social reality, as we know it, is very much an arbitrarily constructed artifact. Hence alternative social realities with radically different modes of thought, codes of behavior, and disciplines of knowledge are, in principle, possible, as many historical and anthropological studies have shown.

Thirdly, commitment to a *becoming* ontology entails modifying the conceptual asymmetry created between conscious action and *unconscious* forces, between the explicit and the tacit, between the visible and the invisible, and between presence and absence. The elevation of visual knowledge, instrumental rationality, intentionality, and choice in the modernist explanatory schema surreptitiously overlooks the role of the unconscious, hidden, and nomadic forces shaping rational choice and deliberate, planned action. A *becoming* ontology thus emphasizes the heterogeneous, multiple, and *alinear* character of real-world happenings. Events in the real world, as we experience it, do not unfold in a conscious, homogeneous, linear, and predictable manner. Instead they "leak in insensibly" (James, 1909/1996: 399). As such, human actions and motives must be

understood not simply in terms of actors' intentions but also in terms of unconscious metaphysics, embedded contextual experiences, accumulated memories, and cultural traditions that create and define the very possibilities for interpretation and action. Against the grand narratives of linear universal progress, timeless truths, total control, and predictability the *becoming* approach advocates a more tentative and modest attitude towards the status of our current forms of knowledge and towards the realization that intentions and outcomes are always a product of the creative "tension" between human will and the oftentimes unspecifiable set of circumstances surrounding individual action.

Finally, instead of thinking in terms of tightly-coupled causal explanations commitment to a processual approach to analysis privileges the ideas of resonance, recursion and resemblance as preferred expressions for describing nonlocal relationships between events and occurrences in space-time. Nonlocal descriptions imply that the dynamics of movement and change cannot now be explained in terms of simply-located origins and end points as well as linear trajectories; that is, in terms of the identity and location of cause and effect. This is because the initial condition for change can no longer be specified as a point in space but as some probabilistic region. Trajectories or causal relations are mere *idealizations* because of the inherent transience and instability of phenomena. Instead we now need to think in terms of "resonances" in a manner analogous to the coupling of sounds. "Resonances are not local events, inasmuch as they do not occur at a given point or instant. They imply a nonlocal description and therefore cannot be included in the trajectory description associated with Newtonian dynamics . . . they lead to *diffused* motion" (Prigogine, 1996: 42). Prigogine goes on to conclude that with this new understanding of reality, "Becoming is the *sine qua non* of science, and indeed, of knowledge itself" (1996: 153). This, in turn implies that the future is no more a deterministic given. Rather it becomes a "construction" (1996: 107).

It is argued that thinking in this more open-ended, allusive, and elliptical manner enables us to better appreciate how social phenomena, such as "individuals" and "organizations," can be viewed as temporarily stabilized event clusters loosely held together by relational networks of meaning rather than as concrete systems and entities simply located and with distinct and definable boundaries. What dominates the modernist view of the world is the idea of discrete and isolatable *systems* existing within the context of an external environment. Such a view helps pave the way for the privileging of a "tightly coupled" form of causal analysis. For if phenomena are indeed stable, systemic, and clearly bounded they then become much more amenable to causal explanations because it is possible to separate antecedent causes from consequent effects. It is this stubbornly held idea that reality is invariably "systemic" and hence isolatable in character that processual analyses seek to disabuse us of. These four theoretical emphases in a *becoming* ontology provide a fertile base for reconceptualizing organization and the function of OS.

Organization as "World-making"

Durkheim's (1933) interpretation of the division of labour stressed the *locatability* of people and objects in the social grid of society. . . . The division of labour thus becomes a set of strategies for translating the mute, mutable, and motile . . . into a locatable and speakable space. (Cooper, 1998: 124)

"Organizations" are culturally defined patterns of social abstraction. They do not exist externally to the mind. They cannot be immediately experienced. Rather, they are products of sense making in which regularities have been imputed to an arbitrarily delineated aspect of phenomenal experience. Organizing actions, on the other hand, are the real and observable material acts which make up our numerous microinterventions into the realm of lived experience in order to extract sense and to construct a pattern of order, meaning, control, and predictability from what would otherwise have been a "blooming, buzzing confusion." Organizing actions are, therefore, essentially effort-saving routines. Conservation of energy and the preservation of existence are what drive our will to organize. This is part of the survival instinct we inherit, and it is also what accounts for the civilizing process. As Marshall Sahlins writes

in *Evolution and Culture*, all living things have an inherent tendency to increase their "thermodynamic accomplishment," that is, the rate at which they are able to conserve energy and put it to use in the maintenance and upgrading of their organic structure. Hence "It is the amount [of energy] so trapped . . . and the degree to which it is raised to a higher state that would seem to be the way that a crab is superior to an amoeba, a goldfish to a crab, a mouse to a goldfish, a man to a mouse" (1960: 21). Thermodynamic accomplishment is therefore fundamental to the progress of all living systems. More specifically, the evolution of the human race, as a whole "*is* characterised by a *net* increase in the rate at which energy is harnessed and used" for self-preservation and to extend control over our environment (Ingold, 1986: 19). All efforts at organizing, therefore, contain a principle of economy that is directed at overcoming, if somewhat temporarily, time and space and to achieving a desired level of control and predictability in affairs of the world.

Language and symbolic representations provide perhaps the most basic of these organizational impulses. What language and symbols achieve is a form of *substitution* whereby a material utterance or inscription is made to stand for an absent image, idea, or concept. Thus the word "tree" stands for the isolated material phenomenon we repeatedly apprehend in the forest. This process of substitution is an essentially *economic* operation. The word "tree" *stands for* the intractable piece of materiality existing in the forest. By uttering the word we are able to evoke the necessary image without ever needing to physically bring the material piece of tree to whomsoever we are communicating with. Yet it must be noted that the alphabetic term does not in any significant way resemble the image it evokes. The connection between the word "tree" and the image of a tree is purely a product of *convention* (Saussure, 1966). This is what is meant when we say that the alphabet is an abstract language. Unlike Chinese ideograms, for example, there is no trace of resemblance between the word and the thing. Despite the arbitrary nature of this process of substitution, and in many cases reified construction, by learning the alphabetic system we come to quickly recognize what the word "tree" stands for. Meaning is less about having a specific image in mind than about how a term differentiates itself from other terms. This is also how more abstract concepts such as love and prosperity are grasped in the Western mind. Whereas the Chinese word for "prosperity," for instance, contains images of clothing, shelter, and paddy fields (i.e., the symbols of food) the word "prosperity" in the alphabetic system is defined by other words such as "success" or "wealth," each of which is itself abstract in its definition. Meaning, then, within the alphabetic system, relies on a network of other qualifiers and not on a specific referent. Such is the abstractive power of the alphabetic system, which has made it the dominant linguistic form in a technology-driven modern world. Moreover, once this substitution process has become habituated, as discussed previously, we begin to talk and think in more and more abstract and reified terms. So words like "the weather," the "market," the "strategy," or even "intention" and "choice" increasingly become common currency, even if their meanings and what they exactly refer to are not entirely clear. This is the reified (and rarified) realm within which much of modern organizational theorizing operates (Sandelands and Drazin, 1989; Chia, 1996).

Other languages such as the Sumerian pictograms, the Egyptian hieroglyphs, and the Chinese ideographs are far more concrete languages relying more on *resemblance* than on conventionally established practices of association. For this reason, Chinese and associated languages such as Japanese have developed a different form of logic from that of the alphabetic system. Needham (1962) calls this different logic "correlative thinking" whereby the real world is perceived as "an organism made of an infinity of organisms, a rhythm harmonising an infinity of lesser rhythms" (Needham, 1962, II: 292). This is a world view which resonates deeply with process thought. Shimizu (1987) has used the fundamental distinction between formal logic and correlative logic to explore different approaches to complexity in the biological sciences. He notes that, whilst it has often been popularly believed that analytical and holistic approaches are what characterize Western and Eastern ways of thinking, a deeper

and more valuable differentiation is to see the West as tending towards "serial information processing" whilst the Eastern tendency might be called "parallel information processing." In the latter instance the dominant emphasis is not so much the search for causal relations as the discovery of relationships between different pieces of information which on the surface appear to be totally unrelated to each other. Shimizu points out that this latter mode of thought is eminently suited to dealing with complex and disparate phenomena which do not initially appear connectable or to possess any apparent commonalities.

Such contrasting predispositions have led to a number of characteristically different emphases. King (1982) notes that in place of the one-on-one external causal sequences emphasized by the West there is an emphasis on contextual–causal interpretations. In place of a straight-line "progress" of events leading to a climax of some sort in a limited time-span, there is a historical process in which time is "cyclical." Moreover:

Individual entities, including man, will not be seen as so substantially separable from other entities as in Western thought, but rather as a single flowing event in which the interdependent relationships are as real, or even more real than the related entities themselves . . . In Eastern thought he is part and parcel of the universe in which his existence is set, one little wavelet in a vast ocean of being/non-being . . . his visceral values, existential concerns, and intuitional awareness will be fully as important in relating to and understanding the universe as his sheerly rational knowledge – if not more so. (King, 1982: xii)

Correlative thinking is emphatically dynamic, nondiscrete, and urges the "harmonizing of internal wills" through concrete existential engagement rather than abstract thinking. It is intimately linked to the ideographic character of its writing. Ideography, and calligraphy in particular, is a kinetic art consisting of the choreography of human gestures or "conversation of gestures" which is not reducible to human physiology. Language, thus, takes on the semblance of performance rather than static representation.

What this simple comparison between Eastern and Western logic tells us is that the form of language adopted immeasurably affects the way we apprehend our phenomenal worlds and how they come to be organized. Social reality, as we understand it, and as we often take so much for granted, is the product of a series of historically embedded decision-making processes so that a particular ontological outlook – that which views the world as comprising patterned regularities – comes to be taken as eminently natural. Thus, as Whitehead (1926/1985: 69) noted, the natural world is perceived "as with qualities which in reality do not belong to it, qualities which in fact are purely the offspring of the mind." In truth nature is "a dull affair, soundless, scentless, colourless; merely the hurrying of material endlessly, meaninglessly." Social reality is an *abstracted* version of the phenomenal real; the real that we existentially experience is inherently undifferentiated and perpetually in flux and ceaseless becoming. What is real is our concrete existential experience, not pseudo-objects created by our conceptualized understanding. The latter comes by way of subtraction and not by way of addition to these initial existential encounters. The issue of language and social convention, and the manner in which they shape our epistemology, our understanding of organization, and hence our management priorities, are, therefore, central to an expanded realm of OS. It is one which begins with the recognition that the modern world we live in and the social artifacts we rely upon to successfully negotiate our way through life are always already institutionalized *effects* of primary organizational impulses. Taken-for-granted social objects of analysis such as "the organization," "the economy," "the market," or even "stakeholders," or "the weather," are part of our discursively shaped understandings that derive from a particular set of ontological commitments. They are not natural phenomena existing in the realm of the real. Instead, like the idea of stellar "constellations," they are a product of our own unconscious "will to order." Order and organization, therefore, do not exist *a priori* to our human intervention. Instead, they have to be forcibly carved out of the undifferentiated flux of raw experience and conceptually fixed and labeled so that they can then become common currency for

communicational exchanges and for concerted social action.

Modern social reality, with its all-too-familiar features, has to be continually reconstructed and sustained through such aggregative discursive acts of reality construction. The idea that reality, as we know it, is socially constructed has become a commonly accepted claim. What is less commonly understood is *how* this reality gets constructed and from *what* it is constructed out of in the first place, and what sustains it. For the philosopher William James, as we have seen, our social reality is always already an abstraction from the brute reality of our pure empirical experience. Moreover, such abstractions always produce relative knowledge, since they necessarily exclude or marginalize some aspect of brute reality. It is precisely for this reason that we are able to find an infinite number of competing perspectives, since each such perspective is informed by a particular set of ideological imperatives. But what remains absolute is the immediacy of our unthought lived experience. Our prethought life world is an undifferentiated flux of fleeting sense impressions, and it is through acts of differentiating, fixing, naming, labeling, classifying, and relating – all intrinsic processes of organization – that social reality is systematically constructed, sustained and modified.

Conclusion

Language and discourse are multitudinal and heterogeneous forms of material *inscriptions* or verbal *utterances* occurring in space-time. They act at a far more constitutive level to form social objects such as "individuals" and "organizations." And, by circumscribing selected parts of the flux of phenomenal experiences, and fixing their identities, it becomes possible to talk about them as if they were naturally existing objective entities. This "entitative" form of thinking, which is overwhelmingly widespread in organizational theorizing, conveniently forgets the fact that organizational action is first and foremost an *ontological* activity. Viewed from this perspective, the apparent solidity of social phenomena such as "the organization" derives from the stabilizing *effects* of generic discursive processes rather than from the presence of independently existing concrete entities. In other words, phrases such as "the organization" do not refer to an extralinguistic reality. Instead they are conceptualized abstractions which it has become habitual for us to refer to as independently existing "things." Through the regularizing and routinization of social exchanges, the formation and institutionalization of codes of behavior, rules, procedures and practices, and so on, the organizational world that we have come to inhabit acquires its apparent externality, objectivity, and seemingly stable structure.

Moreover, organization itself should not be thought of as something performed by preexisting individual "agents." Instead the agents themselves, as legitimized objects of knowledge, must be understood as organizational *effects* too. The identity of the individual agent is constructed in the very act of organizing. The tendency to construe individuals as somehow prior to or free from organizational forces overlooks the ontological role of acts of organizing. From the point of view emphasized by this chapter, we ourselves are organized as we engage in acts of organizing. My identity is established in the very act of differentiating and detaching myself (i.e., the process of individuation) from my surroundings through material inscriptions and verbal utterances. The idea that primary reality is an undifferentiated flux and ceaselessly changing is central to a revised understanding of organization. Such a view does not dispense with an extralinguistic reality. What it does maintain, however, is that this reality does not initially possess "thinglike" characteristics. The apparent solidity, stability, and regularity of social reality are a human accomplishment. It is one forged out from a cacophony of lived experiences through recursive acts of organization. Thus how we come to acquire particular modes of thought, codes of behavior, social mannerisms, and so on becomes very much a concern of OS. Such a revised understanding is grounded on an alternative ontology of *becoming* in which "organizations" are viewed as islands of achieved regularity in a sea of chaos. It is this alternative set of metaphysical principles – becoming, process, language as abstraction and ordering, and organization as world-making –

which will open up new possibilities for rethinking the scope and function of OS.

Note

1   The term "simple-location" is used here to reflect the widespread rational belief that our phenomenal experiences, including our physical sensations, can be *fixed* spatially and hence systematically differentiated from other phenomenal experiences. In this way it becomes possible to locate the symptom felt and thus deal with it in a manner reminiscent of the way a doctor diagnoses ailments by establishing the part of the anatomy associated with the symptom and then dealing with it accordingly.

References

Berger, J. (1972) *Ways of Seeing*. London: Penguin.

Bergson, H. (1911) *Creative Evolution*. London: Macmillan.

——(1913) *An Introduction to Metaphysics*. London: Macmillan.

——(1946/1992) *The Creative Mind*. New York: Citadel Press.

Bohm, D. (1980) *Wholeness and the Implicate Order*. London: Routledge.

Bryson, N. (1982) *Vision and Painting: The Logic of the Gaze*. London: Methuen.

Chia, R. (1996) *Organizational Analysis as Deconstructive Practice*. Berlin: de Gruyter.

——(1998) "Exploring the expanded realm of technology, organization and modernity," in R. Chia (ed.) *Organized Worlds*, pp. 1–19. London: Routledge.

Cooper, R. (1998) "Assemblage notes," in R. Chia (ed.) *Organized Worlds*, pp. 108–30. London: Routledge.

Descartes, R. (1637/1968) *Discourse on Method and the Meditations*. London: Penguin.

Diringer, D. (1962) *Writing*. London: Thames & Hudson.

Durkheim, E. (1912/1965) *The Elementary Forms of Religious Life*. New York: Free Press.

Elsner, J., and Cardinal, R. (1994) *The Cultures of Collecting*. London: Reaktion Books.

Gelb, I. J. (1952) *A Study of Writing*. Chicago and London: University of Chicago Press.

Gergen, K. J., and Thatchenkery, T. J. (1998) "Organizational science in a postmodern context," in R. Chia (ed.) *In the Realm of Organization*, pp. 15–42. London: Routledge.

Goody, J. (1986) *The Logic of Writing and the Organization of Society*. Cambridge: Cambridge University Press.

Green, M. (1981) "The construction and implementation of the cuneiform writing system," *Visible Language* 15: 345–72.

Havelock, E. (1982) *The Literate Revolution in Greece and its Cultural Consequences*, Princeton, NJ: Princeton University Press.

Ingold, T. (1986) *Evolution and Social Life*. Cambridge: Cambridge University Press.

James, W. (1909/1996) *A Pluralistic Universe*. Lincoln, NB, and London: University of Nebraska Press.

——(1911/1996) *Some Problems of Philosophy*. Lincoln, NB, and London: University of Nebraska Press.

Kenner, H. (1987) *The Mechanical Muse*. New York: Oxford University Press.

King, W. L. (1982) "Foreword," in K. Nishitani, *Religion and Nothingness*, trans. J. van Bragt, Berkeley, CA: University of California Press.

Mansley Robinson, J. (1968) *An Introduction to Early Greek Philosophy*. Boston, MA: Houghton Mifflin.

McArthur, T. (1986) *Worlds of Reference*. Cambridge: Cambridge University Press.

McLuhan, M. (1967) *The Gutenberg Galaxy*. Toronto: University of Toronto Press.

McLuhan, M., and McLuhan, E. (1988) *Laws of Media*. Toronto: University of Toronto Press.

Needham, J. (1962) *Science and Civilisation in China* II. Cambridge: Cambridge University Press.

Ong, W. J. (1967) *The Presence of the Word*. New Haven, CT, and London: Yale University Press.

——(1977) *Interfaces of the Word*. Ithaca, NY, and London: Cornell University Press.

——(1982) *Orality and Literacy: The Technologizing of the Word*. London and New York: Methuen.

Pfeffer, J. (1993) "Barriers to the advance of organizational science: paradigm development as a dependent variable," *Academy of Management Review*, 18 (4): 499–520.

Prigogine, I. (1996) *The End of Certainty*. New York and London: Free Press.

Rescher, N. (1996) *Process Metaphysics*. New York: State University of New York Press.

Rorty, R. (1980) *Philosophy and the Mirror of Nature*. Oxford: Blackwell.

Sahlins, M. D. (1960) "Evolution: specific and general," in M. D. Sahlins and E. R. Service (eds) *Evolution and Culture*. Ann Arbor, MI: Michigan University Press.

Sandelands, L., and R. Drazin (1989) "On the language of organization theory," *Organization Studies*, 10 (4): 457–78.

Saussure, F. de (1966) *Course in General Linguistics*. New York: McGraw-Hill.

Schoenwald, R. (1973) "Training urban man," in H. J. Dyos and M. Wolff (eds) *The Victorian City: Images and Realities* II. London: Routledge.

Shimizu, H. (1987) "A general approach to complex systems in bioholonics," in R. Graham and A. Wunderlin (eds) *Lasers and Synergetics*. Berlin: Springer.

Treddenick, H. (1933) *The Metaphysics*. 2 vols. Loeb Classical Library, Cambridge, MA: Harvard University Press.

Whitehead, A. N. (1926/1985) *Science and the Modern World*. London: Free Association Books.

——(1929) *Process and Reality*. New York: Free Press.

——(1933) *Adventures of Ideas*. Harmondsworth: Penguin.

4

Epistemology

Donaldson argues for positivism as the best approach for organizational analysis and allows a minor role for social constructionism as descriptive of microsociological processes. He begins with a brief history of positivism (omitting mention of its initial development by Saint-Simon as a technocratic religious belief system) which has its central focus on Durkheim's stress on social facts as things. A contemporary social fact might be global competition, for example, where an organization loses business to a cheaper or more efficient competitor. It happens irrespective of its managers' preferences and they may not even perceive the identity of a foreign competitor, but, nonetheless, their organization has to either adapt or die.

Contemporary positivism differs from both logical positivism and behaviorism, with which it was once allied. Whilst the epistemology of positivism is empirical, it is, however, not inductive, as Donaldson explains. Moreover, positivism does not rest upon, or imply, logical positivism, as Donaldson is at pains to point out: thus Donaldson distinguishes positivism from behaviorism. Positivism is prepared to admit that what Donaldson refers to as mental causes may play a role, although its preference is for external causes conceived on the model of social facts.

While positivism's ontology is realist it is not necessary for its epistemology to be so. Epistemologically it can be nominalist or instrumentalist: theories are useful fictions that allow patterns to be discerned in data and provide explanation and prediction without having to presume that the theoretically postulated entities really exist. Theories are socially constructed conjectures, which theorists attempt to validate through empirical research. Progress in science is said to occur through building theories and then systematically seeking to refute them by empirically invalidating them and replacing them with theories that seem to fit the empirical observations better.

Positivism seeks to explain human action and social structure as being caused by objective factors that are external constraints of the situations in which people find themselves. In the allied theory of structural functionalism, social and organizational structures are explained as being forced to fit situational contingencies (such as organizational size and strategy) if the organizations are to avoid dysfunctions (such as low organizational performance) that objectively result from misfit. Positivism aims for generalizations of broad scope. Its scientific knowledge claims include causal processes that are not known by ordinary people (i.e., nonsocial scientists), so that positivist knowledge aims to transcend common sense. Examples can be found from the canon of positivist organizational research, such as the Aston structural contingency studies of organizations in terms of concepts of size and organizational structure. An instance Donaldson gives is that positivist research has refuted the commonsense belief that organizations become more top-heavy in managers and administrators as they grow. Empirical research shows that larger organizations actually have proportionately fewer managers and administrators.

Donaldson regards radical or critical variants of social constructivist approaches as related to Marxian humanism, which takes as its central theme the maintenance of order through false consciousness: he suggests that such theories regard functional order as something maintained through unquestioning belief in the dominant ideology on the part of organization members. It is not an interpretation of social constructivist approaches that Czarniawska develops. Against what he regards as the overly cognitivist view of constructivism, Donaldson points out that there are often unanticipated consequences of social action, so that what organizations do cannot be determined by what their individual members know or think. Donaldson contrasts his version of social constructivist approaches with the version of organization theory that he endorses, which centers on structural contingencies. Finally, he offers that the contingency approach may be improved in its micro-details by some elements of constructionism, such that it may help to explain at the micro-level how organizations are acted out and changed, within the overall framework of positivist constraints.

Czarniawska also opens her chapter with a small foray into the history of social science, although in her case it is German rather than French sources that prove useful, in so far as they staked out the foundations for Berger and Luckmann's book on the "social construction of reality." She places emphasis on the importance of both the "social" and the "construction" in social constructionism, in order to allow a role for those things, such as technologies, that fall between nature and society. In being alert to the processes of social construction these intermediary forms fulfil vital roles of institutionalization and deinstitutionalization.

Chapter 4(b) is less an attack on positivism from constructionism, except in elliptical ways, when Czarniaswka draws on the resources of contemporary philosophers such as Rorty, than an account of what constructionism can do. It is a positive statement rather more than a statement against positivism, one that proposes a "modest organization theory." The modesty of the project may be measured against the desire for organization theory to make authoritative claims, as advanced by Donaldson. Against this, social constructionism studies the formation of common sense. The metaknowledge that some organization theory aspires to, she says, is not "superior" knowledge but different knowledge.

The reader may sense a lack of engagement in these chapters: while Donaldson does attempt to engage, his engagement is less with the text that Czarniaswka has written than with a version of constructionism that seems to be rooted in a reading of Berger and Pullberg's work, and hence has strong Marxist humanist overtones. Czarniaswka seems not to engage directly with Donaldson at all, although, when she does so, it is elliptically, in her remarks on the hierarchy of everyday and constructionist knowledge, for example. Clearly, these writers are less in disagreement concerning a common enterprise than engaged in uncommon enterprises apart. Note the citations – they barely overlap. Each remains citationally secure within their respective and different hermeneutic frame of reference.

4a Position Statement for Positivism

Lex Donaldson

This position statement argues for the positivist approach to organizational theory. It briefly defines the positivist approach and articulates its philosophical base in epistemological terms. Emphasis is given to the aspirations in positivism to make generalizations of wide scope, which are underlain by knowledge of causal regularities of a kind that goes well beyond what is normally available to people through their common sense. Social constructionism is then critically examined as being a countervailing program in organizational inquiry. Its limitations are identified, including the tendency to devolve to mere descriptions of historically specific creations of each organization so that theoretical generalizations are not developed. Again, social constructionist investigations only aim to capture the intentions of the people involved and so simply document the commonsense understandings already known by those people. Social constructionism cannot stand as *the* theoretical framework for organizational theory, and positivism should remain the master framework. Nevertheless, there may be a role for constructionism as articulating the micro-level processes whereby some of the organizational changes occur within the positivist framework.

The Historical Background of Positivism

Historically, sociological positivism has its roots in the work of Comte (1853). He sought to create a body of scientific knowledge about society, analogous to the science of nature, which would provide a valid basis for social policy. Durkheim (1938) advocated rules for the creation of sociological knowledge that discover causal processes independent of the minds of societal members. "Social facts" are causes that stand outside of people and constrain them in their actions. Thus causal explanation in sociology is to be by reference to the external situations that play the role of determinants: "The determining cause of a social fact should be sought among the social facts preceding it and not among the state of individual consciousness" (Durkheim, 1938: 110). The program of explanation in sociology by facticities, that is, objective social causes, was, and is, antipathetic to psychological explanations by the inner mental states of social actors.

Positivism is sometimes confused with logical positivism, but positivism does not rest upon the philosophical doctrine of logical positivism. Logical positivism draws a strong distinction between valid knowledge, which is to say, knowledge of the scientific type, and metaphysics, which is to say, statements that are not of the scientific type (Ayer, 1959). According to logical positivism, scientific knowledge is composed of statements whose meaning is verifiable. Metaphysical statements are unverifiable and are therefore deemed to be meaningless. Religion and superstition typify metaphysical assertions, whereas science is built by expunging all such meaningless statements. This program was applied also to social science, leading to behaviorism, which studied only objective, observable and hence verifiable behavior, as well as to other tendencies.

Logical positivism, however, has subsequently been refuted by philosophy. Many theoretical statements in the natural sciences are not directly verifiable, so would be classified as meaningless by a strict application of logical positivism, thus contradicting the intent of logical positivism to build upon science. These natural science theoretical statements are meaningful, despite their not being directly verifiable. Moreover, they can be verified indirectly by examining the truth or falsity of the hypotheses derived from these theoretical statements (Popper, 1968). The hypotheses are couched in terms of observables, that is, statements about states of the world that can be observed. Therefore comparison of empirical observations with each hypothesis confirms, or refutes, that hypothesis, and thus verifies, or not, the theory from which that hypothesis was deduced. In science, a theoretical system is composed of high-level abstract theoretical propositions about unobservable concepts, like atoms, from which are deduced lower-level hypotheses about specific observable states, such as the pattern of bubbles in a bubble chamber (which is interpreted theoretically as being caused by the path of a subatomic particle). Thus there is no problem in scientific statements being unverifiable directly if they can be verified indirectly. Therefore the assertion of logical positivism that unverifiable propositions are meaningless and not scientific must be rejected, so that logical positivism must be rejected.

Thus modern-day positivism in social science can proceed without resting upon the discredited philosophy of logical positivism. Therefore there is no necessity for positivism to reject a priori concepts that refer to unobservables, such as inner mental states. Hence positivism does not have to embrace behaviorism. The focus on external causes is a theoretical preference, not the result of philosophical doctrine. Many modern positivists do not subscribe to logical positivism as their philosophical base. Popper (1968) contributed an influential refutation of positivism and many modern positivists adhere more to his line.

In summary, positivism is not based on the philosophical position of logical positivism, nor is positivism to be classified with behaviorism. Both logical positivism and behaviorism now have few adherents. Modern social scientific positivism is based upon recognition that theoretical concepts can be unobservable and that verification of theories involves testing the hypotheses deduced from them. The legacy from which modern positivism draws in social

science is that of seeking to build a science of social affairs of a broadly similar type to natural science. The success of the natural sciences provides an inspiration and role model for positivist social science. Positivist social science aims for theoretical generalizations of broad scope that explain social affairs as being determined by causes of an objective kind that lie in the situation rather than in the minds of people. These causes stand external to people and constrain them. In building up such a body of valid causal theory, the aim is to provide a knowledge base from which to make sound social policies.

The Durkheimian injunction to seek causality in the external situation rather than inside the human mind provides a salutary signpost to attend to the way that the environment molds human behavior. However, to say that the human mind should not figure in causal explanation is somewhat extreme. Moreover, Durkheim's (1964) other work embraced the mental component and so did not always strictly follow his rules. While external factors strongly influence human behavior their effects may be mediated by mental processes. Moreover, mental processes, such as thinking and feeling, are of some interest as phenomena in their own right. Therefore, positivism is best seen as a program that seeks to obtain the maximum explanatory power from external causes, without also holding that mental phenomena should never be studied. The strategy is to try to build as much knowledge as possible by studying the effects of external causes. This may facilitate, and be complemented by, nonpositivist analyses that include mental phenomena as dependent variables, or as mediating processes. Of course, some analysts may seek to show the role of mental phenomena as independent variables, that is, as causes, thus offering explanations that are alternative to positivism. These explanations, however, will be rivals to positivism, which will seek to show such non-positivist causes to be weak relative to external factors, or to be effects of external causes. The positivist position holds that reliable, scientific knowledge about social affairs will be built most rapidly by following the positivist approach (Donaldson, 1997).

Positivism in Organizational Theory

Positivism in social science centrally asserts that it is desirable to build a science of social affairs. This science is inspired by, and loosely modeled upon, the natural sciences. A key idea is that systematic inquiry, through theory construction and methodologically rigorous empirical research, can yield knowledge that is superior to common sense. In this way human beings can attain better understanding of the social world.

Positivism in its modern form has been applied to organizations in an attempt to better understand organizations and the people inside them (e.g., Blau and Schoenherr, 1971; Hannan and Freeman, 1989). A key idea of positivism in organizational studies is that there are causal regularities. Organizations, and the behavior of people within them, exhibit regularities, that is, patterns that recur across time, organizations, and individuals. Underlying these patterns are cause-and-effect relationships, whereby a cause reliably produces a specific effect. Thus both generalization and determinism are core components of positivist organizational theory (Burrell and Morgan, 1979).

The behavior of organizations and their members is molded by material factors that force compliance, even where organizational members might prefer to act in other ways. These material factors include some that are in the environment of the organization, such as the size of the population of competitors (Hannan and Freeman, 1989). Also, there are material factors within the organization, such as its size (that is, the number of organizational members to be organized) (Blau and Schoenherr, 1971). Another material factor is the organizational task, that is, the actual work that must be done by organizational members such as transforming inputs into outputs (e.g., components into a completed automobile) (Thompson, 1967).

While positivism sees material factors as important, it sees other, nonmaterial factors as causes and so as also determining organizations and the behavior of their members, e.g., pressure from government. Thus causal regularities arise from situational constraints posed by both material and nonmaterial factors.

These causes are social facts, in that they stand external to individuals and constrain them. They are not things in the sense that a physical object, such as a table, is a thing. However, these causes are like things in that they are external to the individuals and have an objective existence. Their existence does not depend on an individual wishing them to exist or necessarily perceiving them. The social fact impacts on the individual regardless of the preference of that individual or even the recognition of that social fact. For example, a garment manufacturer in America could be bankrupted by low-price imports from a firm in China. This effect of the social fact of the competitor on the firm would exist despite the American managers not wishing it and even if they remained unaware of the identity of the firm in China. In this way, social facts can be said to have an objective existence, so that they exist even if they contradict the subjective experience of some individuals.

Similarly, competition forces many organizations to adopt efficient practices, even if their managers might otherwise favor other practices, so that objective pressures limit the feasible options. Organizations and managers that give preference to less efficient practices tend not to survive, so that evolutionary processes underlie the objective requirements (Friedman, 1953). Hence such extant managers tend to seek out more efficient practices, so that they conform to the dictates of the situation, and hence their mental states do not mediate the effect of the external causes on organization.

Blau (1972: 13n), for example, is explicit that his analysis of the effect of size on administrative intensity is positivist in the tradition of Durkheim's rules of sociological method:

Another assumption is implied here: the prevailing characteristics of organizations, as distinguished from those in particular organizations, can be explained in terms of the influence of antecedent conditions in organizations (or their environment) without reference to the psychological preferences or decisions of individual managers, because these social conditions greatly restrict the options of managers who pursue an interest in efficient operations. This principle derives from Durkheim (1938: 110): "The determining cause of a social fact should be sought among the social facts preceding it and not among the state of individual consciousness."

The Scope of Generalizations

The positivist program in organizational studies seeks to build knowledge of general causal laws. How far this program can go and how successful it will be is difficult to stipulate *a priori*. Therefore its approach is to pursue the program and see how successful it can be. This is essentially an empirical approach about the ultimate success and limits of positivism. Specifically, the range of organizational phenomena amenable to positivism and the extensiveness of its generalizations in time and space are not known.

Nevertheless positivists take encouragement from the success of natural science in discovering valid general theories of the inanimate world and of human biology. From the point of view of materialist philosophy, human beings are part of nature and so must ultimately be subject to its laws. This means that social and organizational life is rooted in biology and so must be amenable to scientific laws.

Moreover, there may be a constructive role for metaphysics. Early natural scientists were inspired to search for causal regularities in nature by the Neoplatonic idea that everything in the world reflected an underlying order (often mathematical) (Moore, 1973). Analogously, some modern social scientific positivists are inspired by the conviction that there is an underlying causal order in the social, including organizational, world.

The Epistemological Base of Positivism

Positivism has connections with empiricism, but it should not be labeled as an empiricist epistemology. Positivism believes that there is a real world that exists independently of the mind of the observers. In that sense it subscribes to a realist ontology. However, it does not necessarily subscribe to a realist epistemology, which holds that theoretical entities are real. Positivism is compatible with nominalism, or instrumentalism, which holds that theories are merely fictions that are useful in that they yield predictions (Chalmers, 1999). Moreover, there is no direct access to the real world, so reality is always perceived through the lens of a theory. Hence understanding of reality is increased by comparison between theories and

then selecting the better theory and refining it. Thus knowledge is a human creation by conscious human beings. However, an important means of selecting between, and refining, theories is by empirical testing. Therefore, observations play an important role as sense data about the world. Inductivist epistemology holds that repeated, similar observations lead to generalizations whose validity is assured by the generalization having been inferred from those observations. However, there are many problems with induction, so that probably few modern positivists adhere to it and positivism does not presume an inductivist epistemology.

The causal generalizations that make up a theory are abstract statements, so that there is a gap between an observation statement and the conceptual language of a theory. Observations are specific whereas concepts are abstract. Many people repeatedly observe a phenomenon without inferring a scientific explanation for it. Moreover, repeated, similar observations are finite in number and so do not prove a general statement, because generalization implies an infinite number of observations and an as-yet-unmade observation may differ from the observations made to date (Popper, 1968). Therefore, logically, induction is not a sound basis for establishing the validity of a generalization.

Instead, Popper (1969) argued, a scientific theory is a conjecture, stated in abstract language from which are deduced hypotheses. The hypotheses are then tested by comparing them with observations, i.e., the hypothetico-deductive method. Where the hypothesis is disconfirmed the theory is falsified. Where it is supported the theory is to a degree confirmed, in that it has not been falsified on that occasion. Yet such confirmation is always tentative and temporary, because further observations of hypotheses may contradict the theory. Thus a theory is never proven or established as the truth, but rather is a fallible human conjecture that constitutes valid scientific knowledge until it is in turn falsified and replaced by a new conjecture that is better able to resist falsification. No theory is absolutely true, but rather is truer than the theories that preceded it. In this way progress in science consists of refuting untruths and replacing them with theories that are less untrue.

This sort of philosophy of science roughly characterizes the epistemological position of many positivists. It explains why positivist definitions of rigorous methodology frequently take the form of testing hypotheses. It also explains why purists insist that evidence for a theory is the rejection of the null hypothesis (i.e., nil effect) rather than affirmation of the theoretical hypotheses.

On this view, scientific inquiry is inherently a public and critical process (Popper, 1945). The scientific body of knowledge is composed of theories that have been carefully articulated and publicly recorded, which facilitates searching criticisms by other scholars. Some of the criticism pertains to the consistency and logical adequacy of the theories. However, the theories are also tested empirically against data. Methodological rules are followed to improve the validity of the data (e.g., reliable measures, large samples, etc.) and of the inferences therefrom (e.g., controlling for extraneous causes). The theoretical discussions and empirical tests are all recorded in an archival literature so that the critical process is ongoing and investigations cumulate into a body of scientific knowledge.

The original falsificationist insistence upon falsifying theories should be understood as a criterion for validly justifying a theory (i.e., by showing it has resisted falsification to date) (Popper, 1968). Science requires the construction of theories, which are works of the imagination, and there is a strong role for bold conjectures in theory construction (Popper, 1968). Therefore the psychology of science features creativity and other constructive processes, so that scientific work is much more than simply destroying existing theories.

The philosophy of science subsequent to Popper has emphasized that, historically, science involves perseverance with theories as paradigms (Kuhn, 1970) or programs (Lakatos, 1974). Apparent refutations may be resolved by further work and the development of auxiliary sciences, such as other theories or better methods, which reveal the truth of a theory (Feyerabend, 1975). There is clearly a role for belief and scientists form mutually reinforcing social groups that prosecute their theory despite criticism from antagonists (Kuhn, 1970;

Lakatos, 1974). Sociological processes of bonding and networking operate within science. Overall, this sort of philosophy and sociology of science informs modern-day positivism (Donaldson, 1985).

Beyond Common Sense

A cornerstone of the scientific world view is that science often shows that phenomena occur because of processes that are not apparent to the nonscientist. Some of these processes are invisible and involve unseen entities, such as vapor, molecules, or atomic charges. Scientific theories postulate that the structure of the natural world is not what is seen by the lay person. The Sun does not rotate around the Earth, instead the Earth rotates around the Sun. Seemingly solid objects, such as a table, are in fact composed mainly of empty space with atoms dispersed within it. Therefore scientific knowledge is esoteric (Lammers, 1981). It reveals that the world is not how lay people think it is. In this way science frequently contradicts, and advances beyond, common sense. This is why science enables humans to predict and control the world more than they can without science.

Similarly, positivism in organizational studies strives to attain knowledge that is superior to that contained in common sense. The knowledge is superior by being more valid than lay beliefs. It is superior because it uses positivist theories and methods. The validated scientific laws of organizations differ from common sense because of the operation of causal processes of which lay persons are unaware. There are constraints on organizations, such as those arising from material factors, which impel organizations and members to behave in patterned ways, even despite the preferences of organizational members. These patterns of causation may not always be visible to ordinary people, including to the members of the organizations subject to these causal regularities. Organizational members and lay observers may misperceive phenomena for many reasons, including the lack of adequate abstract concepts, or adherence to lay beliefs of an erroneous kind. Lay people may also hold erroneous views about organizations and organizational behavior because of errors introduced by their cognitive processes, e.g., ego defense mechanism or fallacies in causal attribution. Moreover, for positivists, valid causal inference requires the conscious application of methodological techniques; thus unaided lay inference from the messy data of everyday life will tend towards error.

For example, there is a widespread belief in the community that as organizations grow larger they become top-heavy, with managers and administrators proliferating, so that organizations become less efficient and effective. Positivist research examines this common sense assumption by investigation the ratio of managers and administrators in an organization to its total employees, which is called the degree of administrative intensity of the organization. The hypothesis deduced from the commonsense belief is that administrative intensity increases with size (i.e., total employees). However, the finding of most positivist research is that intensity *decreases* with size, so that the weight of evidence contradicts the lay theory (Blau, 1972; Donaldson, 1996). This is surprising for many people, because common sense says that, as organizations grow larger, their hierarchies grow taller as more and more layers of managers and administrators are added. The inference is therefore that the ratio of people at upper levels to people at lower levels – that is, the ratio of managers and administrators to operational level personnel (e.g., workers) – must rise.

This seductive logic implicitly assumes, however, that the span of control (i.e., the number of persons who report directly to a manager) remains constant. However, empirical research shows that it does not. In fact, the span of control increases more than enough to offset the increase in administrative intensity that comes from the increase in hierarchical levels as size increases (Blau, 1972). Therefore administrative intensity decreases as size increases. The increase in the span of control as size increases comes from the increasing homogeneity of the work group reporting to each manager and the programming of decision making into rules, both of which increase with size and lead to fewer managers being needed (Blau, 1972). Hence positivist organizational theory research explains how, as organizations grow, far from becoming increasingly top-heavy they

have increasing economies of scale in administration, contradicting common sense and providing superior knowledge about an important practical question.

Positivism and Organizational Structural Functionalism

Causal regularities in organizations can arise through many mechanisms. An important class of causation in organizational studies is that dealt with by sociological structural functionalism (Merton, 1949). An organization is a structure of people. Its construction typically requires considerable effort. The costs of organizing are embraced because the benefits that an organization can produce are unattainable from disorganized individuals. Organizational structures differ in their outputs, some being more functional than others. Therefore, over time, organizations become structured so as to provide effective functioning. The functions needed from an organization and the structure that will most effectively produce that function are affected in part by causal factors, that is to say, contingencies (Lawrence and Lorsch, 1967). An organization whose structure fits its contingencies will perform effectively (Pennings, 1987). Conversely, an organization whose structure misfits its contingencies will perform ineffectively (Drazin and Van de Ven, 1985). Therefore organizations become molded by these contingency factors (Donaldson, 2001). The contingencies of an organization constrain its choices, because of the ineffectiveness that results from choosing a structure that misfits those contingencies.

Hence organizational structures can be analyzed by positivist theories that postulate general regularities created by contingencies as causes. These regularities can be established through positivist methods, such as comparing organizations on quantitative variables, or qualitative codings, and making statistical analyses. The research shows that increasing size (i.e., number of organizational members) leads to greater bureaucratization of organizational structure, consistent with Weber (1968; Pugh et al., 1969). This relationship has been shown to generalize across many different kinds of organizations and sixteen nations (Pugh and

Hickson, 1976; Miller, 1987; Donaldson, 1996), including Egypt (Badran and Hinings, 1981), India (Shenoy, 1981), and Iran (Conaty et al., 1983). Similarly, research shows that diversification by firms leads to divisionalization, in order to avoid the performance loss of retaining a misfitting structure (Chandler, 1962; Donaldson, 1987). The relationship between diversification and divisionalization holds both for manufacturing (e.g., Channon, 1973) and service firms (Channon, 1978) and across many nations: Australia, France, Germany, Italy, New Zealand, Japan, the United Kingdom and the United States (Chenhall, 1979; Dyas and Thanheiser, 1976; Pavan, 1976; Hamilton and Shergill, 1992; Suzuki, 1980; Channon, 1973; Rumelt, 1974, respectively). Research finds that this pattern cannot be explained in institutional theory terms by processes of conformity (Whittington et al., 1999). These two relationships between material causes (size and diversification) and organizational structures are illustrative of the success of the positivist approach to organizational studies. The success of positivism to date provides a rational ground for holding that it may succeed in other areas of organizational analysis. The only way in which the full fruitfulness or otherwise of positivism can be established in organizational theory is to continue to fully prosecute it in future.

Social Constructionism

Social constructionism takes a different stance from positivism. It argues that people create society (Berger and Luckmann, 1967) and its constituent structures, such as organizations. In particular, an organization does not exist as any kind of supra-individual entity. An organization comes into any kind of existence only when its members play their roles, such as recognizing that one is an employee of General Motors and therefore allowing someone who is acting in the role of a manager of General Motors to give one an order (Silverman, 1970). The entity General Motors exists only as long as people play out these roles. When a person accepts the role being played out by another person and plays out the role that interlocks with it, then the role taking of that other person is validated, reinforced, and sustained.

Thus "the organization" is constructed through social interaction between people and is thus socially constructed. In that sense, the organization depends upon ongoing collusion and some agreement among members, albeit often tacit.

Over time, however, the organization becomes objectified, in that it becomes more and more a thing with a life of its own – seemingly independent of people (Berger and Pullberg, 1966). The abstraction, the organization, which originally existed only in the scripts of the role players, now has become reified. People may continue to play their roles that sustain the organization even if the organization harms the interests of those people. This process is facilitated because people see the organization as a thing with legitimacy and potent powers. The people playing their roles have lost sight of the human origins of the organization, that is, that it was created by human beings. They cannot see that the organization is sustained only because of their own personal, ongoing complicity. Thus the people that make up the organization develop a deluded consciousness that allows the organization to continue and also their oppression by it.

This kind of critical social constructionism is, of course, highly indebted to Marxian theory. In that theory, workers who accept their lot under capitalism are in a state of false consciousness that helps to sustain capitalism and their own exploitation (Marx, 1973). Thus a mission of social constructionism, in its more critical or activist variants, is to rediscover the origins of the organizations, and of organizational forms, in order to de-reify the organization (Burrell and Morgan, 1979). This shows that what is now taken as a natural thing was actually created historically, for certain purposes and to serve the interests of particular people or social groups. This opens the way for a questioning of the organizational *status quo* and the imagining of alternative organizational forms that will provide the individual with more liberty and greater benefits. Organizational members may then resist contemporary organizational forms and join the critical movement to supplant them with new forms that better serve their interests or values.

A positivist can accept many of the points of the constructionists. An organization exists only if its members play out a set of interlocking scripts that enact that organization. However, this does not mean that all organizations rest simply on the complicity or consensus of their members based on shared thoughtways or taken-for-granted beliefs about the naturalness of their organization. Some complicity by members arises calculatively, because they see benefits from membership and this motivates them to play out their roles, despite awareness of alternatives (e.g., other economic options) (Etzioni, 1975). Some compliance with organizational role requirements in other organizations rests on coercion, e.g., in prisons (Etzioni, 1975). Thus role compliance is not simply based on adherence to ideology, socialization, normative persuasion, or taken-for-grantedness. Therefore simple awareness by organizational members that the organization depends upon their continuing role performance, that the organization was historically created by concrete individuals, and that alternative organizations are possible or imaginable, does not necessarily lead to their refusing to comply and to the dissolution of the organization.

Similarly, once an organization exists, it can have systemic properties that go beyond its individual members and which may change their behaviors, even contrary to their intentions and preferences. For example, the existence of an organizational structure channels communications, affecting who talks to whom and about what, so that an organizational member may fail to learn of some information about which they would wish to know. Again, the structure has consequences for organizational performance, as we have seen, so that a structure that misfits its contingencies reduces its effectiveness (Keller, 1994). Thus the systems-level causal processes connecting organizational-level characteristics, such as structure and performance, need to be analyzed to fully understand organizations.

Moreover, the causal processes at the level of the organizational system affect the individuals who construct the organization. For instance, for a firm, the misfit of structure to contingency reduces its sales growth and profitability (Donaldson, 1987; Hamilton and Shergill, 1992), which, in turn, affects the dividends of its owners, the careers of its managers, and the wages of its workers. These change the organizational behaviors of those individuals, such as their propensity to remain with the organization, to expend effort, and to collaborate with each other (March and Simon, 1958) – that is, whether, and in what ways, they seek to construct the organization in future. In contrast, simply analyzing the processes of social construction of the organization by individuals misses organizational-level systemic processes and their effects on the individuals that constitute the organization.

Again, those organizational theories that analyze how organizations are affected by interactions between individuals who each pursue their interests according to their perceptions tend to miss events that are unintended consequences of human action (March and Simon, 1958). While human intentions are important contributors to organizational events, these events themselves have consequences (Merton, 1949) and may feed back on their perpetrators in ways that they did not expect. For example, management may set up specialized organizational subunits, intending to increase competence, but these units may then compete in ways that are dysfunctional and were not intended by management (Selznick, 1957). This is part of the way in which the organization can be said to be an objective fact and not simply the enactment of the individuals who constitute the organization.

Potential Integration of Social Constructionism with Positivism

Thus positivism sees social constructionism as having some genuine insights about some micro-level processes but as being too focused on the individual level to be adequate as a complete framework for organizational theory, which must incorporate also the supra-individual processes to which positivism attends. Moreover, there is also a difference in that social constructionism challenges the notion of strong situational constraints, preferring to view organizations as open to radical change if their members once attain the consciousness that allows them to see through the reification of organizations. In that sense constructionism is, or can easily become, a voluntaristic theory of organizations, whereas positivism emphasizes determinism and constraints on individuals.

A sounder overall organizational theory would be to hold that social construction is part of the way in which an organization is created, sustained and changed at the micro-level. However, these micro-level processes occur within the envelope of the organization as a system being shaped by causal factors, as positivism holds. Thus the organization as a system is molded by the need to adapt itself to changing contingencies in order to avoid loss of effective functioning (Parsons, 1961). The micro-level processes of organizational creation, maintenance, and change, however, include those of a social constructionist type, i.e., organizational members taking interlocking sets of roles that thereby constitute the organization. This formulation, of course, accommodates social constructionism within an overall positivist, functionalist type of framework. This is logical for positivism, but liable to be resisted as absorption or domination from the viewpoint of social constructionists, especially of the critical, radical, or pure type.

There is an additional point of confluence between social constructionism and positivism. Positivist research shows that crisis induced by low performance is required to trigger adaptive organizational change (Chandler, 1962; Ezzamel and Hilton, 1980; Hill and Pickering, 1986; Donaldson, 1987; Cibin and Grant, 1996; see Donaldson, 2001: 14–16). Thus the functionalist process of adaptation by the organization to its changing situation is controlled by the fact of whether the material condition, such as, for a firm, its financial performance, is low enough to provide an external jolt to the management system of the organization (Donaldson, 1999). Social constructionism holds that crises lead to dereification and make the origins of present organizational arrangements transparent, opening the door to choosing an alternative organizational form (Berger and Pullberg, 1966). In this way social constructionism may, again, throw light on the micro-level processes whereby organizational members behave and bring about the organizational changes found in positivist analyses.

More specifically, the crisis of low organizational performance causes management to focus on the structure and its misfit to the changed contingencies as the explanation for the low performance (Chandler, 1962). This investigation could lead to questioning of why the existing structure was adopted, and by whom, for what reasons, e.g., because it fitted the then existing contingencies and resolved the low performance that resulted from an earlier misfit. With this understanding in place, management can then see that the existing structure is in no sense a natural one, preordained for their organization. It is no longer taken for granted as being "the way we do things around here." This undermines the legitimacy of the present structure and opens the door to the consideration of alternative organizational forms, from which is selected the one that fits the new contingencies. In this way social constructionism can help articulate the organizational change process that connects misfit with adaptation and the resulting restored organizational performance.

Critique of the Constructionist Counterpoint Position

Some of the difficulties and limitations of the constructionist position are seen in the position taken here by the proponent of constructionism. At the close of her piece, the author asserts an extremely modest role for social analysts as being cleaners who reveal how something was constructed. This role is too modest given the possibilities of discovering general causal laws that allow prediction – a possibility the piece eschews. Moreover, it seems a rather fruitless exercise for organizational researchers, because, as the paper argues, people are capable of becoming conscious of the origins of their institutions, especially at times of crisis. If that is so, why do we need research to discover what the actors can know without research? If the actors themselves can answer the most important questions, what is the superior knowledge possessed by analysts?

The organizational research program proposed for social construction seems to be no more than documenting who created the organization and for what reasons, which is purely to describe the actions of certain people and their motives. Given that the people who constructed the organizations knew who they were and their reasons, the analysis is descriptive. It just records the understandings of themselves possessed by those people. In this way organizational analysis is nothing more than describing the world in terms of the common sense of its inhabitants. This fails to accord to the aspiration of science to create explanations that are superior to common sense by containing insights that are unavailable to common sense. Surely there must be some kind of meta-level understanding that the analyst can attain which the actors cannot, or normally would not, otherwise research achieves nothing and makes no social contribution.

Further, the research program advocated by social constructionism seems to lack generalization. The program seems to be that for each organization the analyst seeks to discover when and how it was founded and by whom. This involves historical analysis and the results would be specific to the time in history when each organization was founded. Illuminating as this may be about each organization, no general statement would follow. While some organizational analysts favor research findings that are strongly historically specific, nevertheless the positivist tradition in organizational studies and social science is to search for generalizations. These can offer insight to many people about wide sets of organizations and organizational behaviors. Since the program of searching for generalizations has been successful in organizational studies (Donaldson, 1996) and organizational behavior (Locke, 2000) it would be retrogressive to abandon this and just accept the severely limited program of documenting historically specific origins that this constructionist proposes.

Almost all organizational scholars are interested in generalizations and in making general statements. In particular, constructionists argue that all organizations are socially constructed – which is a highly general assertion. It is, of course, impossible to advocate a theoretical position and not believe in generalization, because any theory is an abstract general statement about the world. The constructionist herein is actually asserting a highly general theory about organizations being social constructions that have become reified, with the

transparency of their origins being revealed in crises. A positivist would suggest that this general theory should be studied. Indeed it should be put to the test and compared empirically against competing micro-level theories such as those that emphasize the role of inducements or coercion. To do this would be to move beyond the presumption of the chapter that organizations are in all decisive ways socially constructed. It treats the assumptions of social constructionism as a set of theoretical hypotheses to be tested with the possibility that it might be shown to be false. This brings in science as a critical method. Social constructionists should be prepared to question their own taken-for-granted assumptions about how the world works.

In a way, the problem of the banal and limited nature of the constructionist research program (as argued here) arises because constructionism as an intellectual position gains energy from Marxian notions of false consciousness. Yet that is now something of a dirty word, which few critical theorists would embrace. The concept of false consciousness holds that there is some other, more objective, view of the world that is truer than the subjective perception of the individual. Those wishing to argue for the subjective nature of organizational life tend to wish to eschew such concepts of objectivity. But if there is no objective knowledge possible about organizational arrangements different from the *status quo*, then there is no rational basis for organizational members to move to any alternative organizational arrangement. Therefore what is to be gained by organizational members de-reifying their organization? Without some notion of a superior, more objective view that the analysts can help actors attain through de-reification, constructionism collapses into a program of descriptive historical research that in the end attains only the common sense of people at a specific time about their organization.

References

Ayer, A. J., ed. (1959) *Logical Positivism*. New York: Free Press.

Badran, M., and Hinings, C. R. (1981) "Strategies of administrative control and contextual

constraints in a less developed country: the
case of Egyptian public enterprise," in D. J.
Hickson and C. J. McMillan (eds) *Organization and Nation: The Aston Programme* IV. Farnborough: Gower.

Berger, Peter L., and Luckmann, T. (1967) *The
Social Construction of Reality: A Treatise in
the Sociology of Knowledge*. Garden City, NY:
Doubleday.

Berger, Peter L., and Pullberg, S. (1966)
"Reification and the sociological critique of consciousness," *New Left Review*, 35: 56–71.

Blau, Peter M. (1972) "Interdependence and
hierarchy in organizations," *Social Science
Research*, 1: 1–24.

Blau, Peter M., and Schoenherr, P. A. (1971)
The Structure of Organizations. New York:
Basic Books.

Burrell, Gibson, and Morgan, Gareth (1979)
*Sociological Paradigms and Organizational
Analysis: Elements of the Sociology of Corporate
Life*. London: Heinemann.

Chalmers, A. F. (1999) *What is this Thing
called Science? An Assessment of the Nature
and Status of Science and its Methods*, third
edition. Brisbane: University of Queensland
Press.

Chandler, Alfred D., Jr (1962) *Strategy and Structure: Chapters in the History of the Industrial
Enterprise*. Cambridge, MA: MIT Press.

Channon, Derek F. (1973) *The Strategy and Structure of British Enterprise*. London: Macmillan.

——(1978). *The Service Industries: Strategy,
Structure and Financial Performance*. London:
Macmillan.

Chenhall, Robert H. (1979) "Some elements of
organizational control in Australian divisionalized firms," *Australian Journal of Management*,
4 (1), supplement: 1–36.

Cibin, R., and Grant, R. M. (1996) "Restructuring among the world's leading oil companies,
1980–92," *British Journal of Management*, 7:
283–307.

Comte, Auguste (1853) *The Positivist Philosophy*
I, trans. H. Martineau. London: Chapman.

Conaty, J., Mahmoudi, H., and Miller, G. A.
(1983) "Social structure and bureaucracy: a
comparison of organizations in the United
States and prerevolutionary Iran," *Organization
Studies*, 4 (2): 105–28.

Donaldson, Lex (1985) *In Defence of Organization
Theory: A Reply to the Critics*. Cambridge: Cambridge University Press.

——(1987) "Strategy and structural adjustment
to regain fit and performance: in defence of
contingency theory," *Journal of Management
Studies*, 24 (1): 1–24.

——(1996) *For Positivist Organization Theory:
Proving the Hard Core*. London: Sage.

——(1997) "A positivist alternative to the
structure–action approach," *Organization Studies*, 18 (1): 77–92.

——(1999) *Performance-driven Organizational
Change: The Organizational Portfolio*. Thousand
Oaks, CA: Sage.

——(2001) *The Contingency Theory of Organizations*. Thousand Oaks, CA: Sage.

Drazin, Robert, and Van de Ven, Andrew H.
(1985) "Alternative forms of fit in contingency
theory," *Administrative Science Quarterly*, 30:
514–39.

Durkheim, Emile (1938) *The Rules of Sociological
Method*. Glencoe, IL: Free Press.

——(1964) *The Division of Labor in Society*. New
York: Free Press.

Dyas, Gareth P., and Thanheiser, Heinz T. (1976)
*The Emerging European Enterprise: Strategy
and Structure in French and German Industry*.
London: Macmillan.

Etzioni, Amitai (1975) *A Comparative Analysis of
Complex Organizations: on Power, Involvement
and their Correlates*, revised edition. New York:
Free Press.

Ezzamel, M. A., and Hilton, K. (1980) "Divi-
sionalisation in British industry: a preliminary
study," *Accounting and Business Research*, 10:
197–214.

Feyerabend, P. K. (1975) *Against Method: Outline
of an Anarchistic Theory of Knowledge*. London:
New Left Books.

Friedman, Milton (1953) "The methodology
of positive economics," in *Essays in Positive
Economics*. Chicago: University of Chicago
Press.

Hamilton, R. T., and Shergill, G. S. (1992) "The
relationship between strategy–structure fit and
financial performance in New Zealand: evidence
of generality and validity with enhanced controls," *Journal of Management Studies*, 29 (1):
95–113.

Hannan, Michael T., and Freeman, John (1989) *Organizational Ecology*. Cambridge, MA: Harvard University Press.

Hill, Charles W. L., and Pickering, J. F. (1986) "Divisionalization, decentralization and performance of large UK companies," *Journal of Management Studies*, 23: 26–50.

Keller, Robert T. (1994) "Technology–information processing fit and the performance of R&D project groups: a test of contingency theory," *Academy of Management Journal*, 37: 167–79.

Kuhn, Thomas S. (1970 *The Structure of Scientific Revolutions*, second edition. Chicago: University of Chicago Press.

Lakatos, I. (1974) "Falsification and the methodology of scientific research programmes," in I. Lakaos and A. Musgrave (eds) *Criticism and the Growth of Knowledge*, pp. 91–196. Cambridge: Cambridge University Press.

Lammers, Cornelis J. (1981) "Contributions of organizational sociology" I, "Contributions to sociology: a liberal view," *Organization Studies*, 2 (3): 267–86.

Lawrence, Paul R., and Lorsch, Jay W. (1967) *Organization and Environment: Managing Differentiation and Integration*. Boston, MA: Division of Research, Graduate School of Business Administration, Harvard University.

Locke, Edwin A. (2000) *The Blackwell Handbook of Principles of Organizational Behavior*. Oxford: Blackwell.

March, J. G., and Simon, H. A. (1958) *Organizations*. New York: Wiley.

Marx, K. (1973) *Economic and Philosophical Manuscripts of 1844*, ed. Dirk J. Struik, trans. M. Milligan. London: Lawrence & Wishart.

Merton, R. K. (1949) *Social Theory and Social Structure*. Chicago, IL: Free Press.

Miller, George A. (1987) "Meta-analysis and the culture-free hypothesis," *Organization Studies*, 8 (4): 309–26.

Moore, Patrick (1973) *Watchers of the Stars*. London: Michael Joseph.

Parsons, Talcott (1961) "Suggestions for a sociological approach to the theory of organizations," in Amitai Etzioni (ed.) *Complex Organizations: A Sociological Reader*. New York: Holt Rinehart & Winston.

Pavan, Robert J. (1976) "Strategy and structure: the Italian experience," *Journal of Economics and Business*, 28 (3): 254–60.

Pennings, J. M. (1987) "Structural contingency theory: a multivariate test," *Organization Studies*, 8 (3): 223–40.

Popper, K. R. (1945) *The Open Society and its Enemies* II, *The High Tide of Prophecy: Hegel, Marx and the Aftermath*. London: Routledge.

——(1968) *The Logic of Scientific Discovery*. London: Hutchinson.

——(1969) *Conjectures and Refutations: The Growth of Scientific Knowledge*. London: Routledge.

Pugh, D. S., and Hickson, D. J. (1976) *Organizational Structure in its Context: The Aston Programme* I. Farnborough: Saxon House.

Pugh, D. S., Hickson, D. J., Hinings, C. R., and Turner, C. (1969) "The context of organization structures," *Administrative Science Quarterly*, 14 (1): 91–114.

Rumelt, Richard P. (1974) *Strategy, Structure and Economic Performance*. Boston, MA: Division of Research, Graduate School of Business Administration, Harvard University.

Selznick, P. (1957) *Leadership in Administration*. New York: Harper & Row.

Shenoy, S. (1981) "Organization structure and context: a replication of the Aston study in India," in D. J. Hickson and C. J. McMillan (eds) *Organization and Nation: The Aston Programme* IV, Farnborough: Gower.

Silverman, David (1970) *The Theory of Organizations*. London: Heinemann.

Suzuki, Y. (1980) "The strategy and structure of top 100 Japanese industrial enterprises, 1950–70," *Strategic Management Journal*, 1 (3), 265–91.

Thompson, James D. (1967) *Organizations in Action*. New York: McGraw-Hill.

Weber, Max (1968) *Economy and Society: An Outline of Interpretive Sociology*, ed. Guenther Roth and Claus Wittich. New York: Bedminster Press.

Whittington, Richard, Mayer, Michael, and Curto, Francesco (1999) "Chandlerism in post-war Europe: strategic and structural change in France, Germany and the UK, 1950–93," *Industrial and Corporate Change*, 8: 519–550.

4b Social Constructionism and Organization Studies

Barbara Czarniawska

Varieties of Constructionism

Is "constructed" "unnatural"?

Not long ago the Swedish Prime Minister, Göran Persson, engaged in a heated debate with Jacques Santer, then Chairman of the European Commission. Reacting to a letter from Santer, Persson told the Swedish press that it was a "total construction."

Had Göran Persson been a fellow constructionist I would have taken this remark as the highest complement. A total construction is, probably, a construction that covers everything, or a construction so well built that no flaws can be detected, or a construction all of one piece. But this is, of course, not what Göran Persson intended to say. He accused Santer of fabricating a lie.

Nor was he wrong. The Swedish Academy List of Words defines "constructed" as "something which is not built in a natural way and gives a forced impression." One could say, however, that the everyday use of the word does not have to coincide with the meaning attributed to it in the social sciences, which may use the same word metaphorically, or ironically, or innovatively. Alas, most of the uses of the expression in the social sciences coincide with that of Göran Persson. One of the typical contexts where the adjective is used concerns gender, as Hacking noticed (1999). When we hear "social gender is socially constructed," what is usually meant is that it is "invented," "not true," "easily influenceable," "possible to change at will" – as opposed to "biological," which is given, real, resistant, and impossible to change. How far from actual social practices such an opinion is can be seen in Deirdre McCloskey's autobiography *Crossing* (1999) that shows in painstaking detail how insignificant is the physical change of gender compared with the everyday work of constructing and maintaining it.

This does not mean, however, that social scientists – other than myself – have "misunderstood" constructionism. The usc to which I allude above has a solid basis in the history of sciences. It should most likely be related to the political move made by Wilhelm Dilthey (1833–1911) in defense against the then all-powerful natural sciences. Trying to defend his own area, history, he suggested a "division of labor," according to which the sciences would be divided into *Naturwissenschaften* and *Geistewissenschaften*. The former would take care, with their own set of methods, of "nature" and of what is "natural," leaving to the latter history, or culture, or society – all that is "constructed."

It would not be the first or the last time that a successful political move from one era became an encumbrance for another. While present day economics still evokes Darwin as the patron saint of evolutionary theory and his theory as legitimizing the "naturalization" of economy, Darwin probably borrowed his ideas from Malthus and certainly from Spencer, after much hesitation (Gould, 1995; Lewontin, 1995). That is, he borrowed from economics and philosophy because at that time they had more legitimacy than biology. The traces of previous "socialization" of natural sciences have been erased to make room for a new move. This is why the history of science, which reminds us of such uncomfortable memories, is so important, and this is why the construction of our own field should be scrutinized more often and with a longer time horizon than the usual decade or two.

Berger and Luckmann's masterpiece *The Social Construction of Reality* (1966) is still, and rightly so, the main manual of the constructionists-to-be. Interestingly enough, they do not spend much time or attention explaining their sources of inspiration. It is probably right to see their social constructivism as a product of an encounter between European phenomenology, as personified by Alfred Schütz, and American pragmatism. These are the sources given by Burkhart Holzner, whose book *Reality Construction in Society* came out in 1968, with a foreword explaining that he did not know about the other book's existence until his own was in the form of galley proofs. In this sense, social constructivism is a close cousin of symbolic interactionism and ethnomethodology. The name may come from mathematics, or from the Russian art movement called *konstruktivizm*, attributed to Vladimir Tatlin, articulated in the 1920s in the "Realist Manifesto" by Antoine Pevsner and Naum Gabo, and carried into the 1930s by El Lissitzky and László Moholy-Nagy.

Berger and Luckmann do not take up the Diltheyan division in any explicit way, but accept it somewhat by default, giving examples only from what is considered to be a "social" realm. Therefore it is legitimate to formulate a question not intended to be critical of their stance: does the dichotomy hold? Does it still make sense to insist on the two realms, the natural and the social, and the two sets of methods? Has "nature" no history, or, as Bruno Latour (1999) puts it, could Rameses II die of tuberculosis before the instrumentarium necessary to diagnose such illness and its concept existed?[1] Is "society" unnatural? After all, we are all biological creatures – how can we define ourselves as standing beyond biology? Has symbolic action no physiological basis? As Rorty (1980) points out, it is in principle possible to establish the physiological components of any kind of action, including the creation of meaning, but in practice it seems neither probable nor desirable. It is possible to describe the world fairly completely and convincingly from any given perspective: as atoms, as thoughts, as movements of fluids. What is problematic is the idea of either dividing the world into several parts according to academic disciplines or trying to make all of them commensurable at the same time. The first is the political hubris of academia, the second the impossible dream of the perfect language (Eco, 1995). In Rorty's (1991: 110) opinion, the sooner we get rid of the idea of "different methods appropriate to the natures of different objects" the better. The pragmatic questions should prevail: which vocabulary suits the purpose of my inquiry best? What is the purpose of my inquiry? The answers should be given in an "ethico-political" and not a "methodologico-ontological" key. In what follows I want to argue for a certain type of a constructionist vocabulary – and not against any other. Following Rorty's advice, I believe that one should argue for the attractiveness of one's position and not against the positions of others. Some further differentiation of vocabularies is nevertheless necessary.

Can one count "constructions"?

An additional problem in the Swedish language is that the result of the process of construction is also a construction. There is no noun "construct," as in English, so useful in individual or cognitive constructionism. But even in English "construction" denotes both the process and its result, although it would be probably less misleading to speak about the result as a "structure," following the etymological cue from Latin. In consequence, there are at least two very distinct ways of understanding the word "construction" in the social sciences in general and in organization studies in particular. One, for which I opt, understands *construction as a process where something is being built out of the existing material* (in opposition to both "creation" and "discovery"). The other, perhaps more common way, defines "construction" as an object (often an immaterial, or so-called "social object") made by people, with attributes that can be described and even measured. The use of the plural often signals the difference: "the social constructions behind the process of change." In most cases, the organization scholars who study "social constructions" start from an assumption that people construct their points of view, opinions, representations, etc., in interactions, and usually in conversation with other people. There can hardly be an objection to such an assumption, but it would be more informative to talk of "social representations" in this context, not least to be just to the enormously interesting work done around this concept by Serge Moscovici (Farr and Moscovici, 1984; Farr, 1987). This kind of research, interesting as it is, does not automatically lead to an understanding of *how* these social representations are produced, a question that I conceive as central to a constructionist approach. But, in so far as the social representations are objectified, inscribed in texts, on things, repeated in formal speeches, they mark the trail of construction, and are one of its products, Thus they are important to collect and consider.

How "social" must constructionism be?

Another problematic issue concerns the adjective "social." It is usually understood as "concerning people only" or, in an even more narrow, nominalist way, as "concerning language" (as something that only human beings use). This is again a heritage of the division of labor between natural and "spiritual" sciences, which makes authors like Bruno Latour and Karin Knorr Cetina, who are perceived as radical constructionists but are very fond of non-humans, rebel against its use. But the use of the adjective "social" can do much good, and, as I will try to show, there are no etymological traces that should tie it to "humans only."

Its use is especially important in psychology (Harré, 1986; Gergen, 1999), where there was a strong tradition of individual (cognitive) constructionism, one which goes back to Jean Piaget. Piaget's ideas can probably be linked with constructionism in mathematics, and certainly with the use of the noun "construct" to denote mental constructs. Children learn to represent the world in their heads, as it were, as a series of constructs that become richer and more sophisticated with age and experience. Harré's and Gergen's thrust is against the idea of worlds in individual heads, and aims at highlighting the collective production of the world, in relations, as Gergen repeats with emphasis (1994). Kaspar Hauser, the famous nineteenth-century "savage child," might have been an example of an individual construction, if he had ever become so skilful in social construction as to be able to share with others the world that he experienced before coming into contact with other people.

Thus the adjective "social" should be revindicated and rescued from its too narrow use, rather than thrown away. Etymologically it comes from *socius*, an ally, a companion, which can be another person but also a dog or a computer. It indicates, without detracting from, the "power of associations" so central to Latour's thought (1986). In this way the insight, known also from institutionalism but powerfully formulated by Gergen (1994), that relations create individuals and not vice versa could be resuscitated.

Another important reason to keep the adjective "social" (considering that "collective" is more or less appropriated by the political sciences) is the need to incorporate Foucault's insights about the social production and distribution of knowledge. This ambition can be seen in Burkhart Holzner's "epistemic communities" (1968), Mary Douglas's "thought worlds" (1986), Edwin Hutchins's "cultural cognition" (1995), and Karin Knorr Cetina's "epistemic cultures" (1999). People neither invent, store, nor distribute knowledge individually, but in a collective effort. This insight is of special importance to organization studies, where the notion of collective or social knowledge, usually considered in relation to organizational learning, was represented by an image of a group of individuals each of whom puts their "individual knowledge and skills" or "competences" into a common "pot."

Constructionism under Frontal Attack

That was a short review of variations of social constructionism, intended to delimit a strain that I intend to propagate – and defend – here. But there are at least three standard criticisms of a constructionist stance in general. One is its assumed proximity to the idealist philosophy, its antirealism. While the other two contravene each other, they both concern constructionism's lax morals. In one version, usually related to critical theory, constructionism is apologetic: it shows how things are done without expressing an opinion on whether it is good or bad, and without offering a suggestion of how they should be better constructed. The other version claims that constructionism offers too easy a promise of change, of constructing genders, identities, and social structures at will. There is actually a fourth criticism, concerning the ruinous effect of constructionism on the status of science, but as this point has been addressed only too thoroughly in the Sokal-Brickman debate I will not bring it up here.

Allegation of antirealism

In his introduction to the edited volume on the matters of representation, George Levine tells an anecdote that, in my reading, summarizes the antirealist argument very well. At various parties he runs into a distinguished astrophysicist who never fails to ask him whether a deconstructionist (a subspecies of constructionists) would survive a fall from a high tower using deconstruction. To which Levine supposedly replies that, to his knowledge, every deconstructionist he knows would steer away from high towers and that he fails to see what the question has in common with the literary practice of deconstruction. The "high tower" is but a variation on what Ashmore et al. called "the bottom line" argument (1994), which they divided into two lines, "Furniture" and "Death," the high-tower argument obviously belonging to the latter, while "rocks" and "middle-sized dry goods" are somewhat liberally assigned to the former. The Death argument includes two subarguments: one of undeniability, which actually belongs together with furniture, and another, of constructionism's moral irresponsibility, which I will address later.

The Furniture argument is so called because it is usually, as Ashmore et al. point out, a no-argument argument consisting of banging the table (or shoving a rock through the window) to prove that there does exist a "real" world. It is interesting because of its rhetorical properties. Its speed (bang!) helps to hide the rhetorical devices needed to exhibit the "reality," allegedly in no need of such help, and the institutional background necessarily evoked in its aid. It assumes an audience familiar with the Western tradition of eighteenth-century natural science (Schaffer, 1993) which takes demonstration as a method superior to argumentation, and which is fond of nonverbal, circuslike effects, of banging, lights, and the unexpected. Ashmore et al. accuse the "objectivists" of stealing the constructionist props and hiding them:

The idea of Furniture as things *per se* fails to resist scrutiny. There is no "*per se*." Objectivists therefore need a device for introducing reality, and having it stand as a *per se* refutation of relativism. They need to render the acts of construction, of categorization, and of rhetoric invisible. They need to put those things in place and then, quickly and invisibly, snatch away the representational props and supports while distracting our attention. (Ashmore et al., 1994: 5)

Ashmore at al. use the word "objectivists" and not "realists." Although there are explicitly idealist strains within constructionism, the latter usually does not protest realism, but *essentialism*, the "things *per se*," the world that does not need the work to exist in order to be real. As Rorty pointed out many a time, "we need to make a distinction between the claim that the world is out there and the claim that truth is out there" (1989: 5). In a similar pragmatist vein, McCloskey (personal communication) pointed out that it would be as absurd to refuse to stop at a red light because traffic signals are "only" socially constructed as to refuse to discuss them at a symbolist conference because they real. And even Goodman, who is perceived as an idealist constructivist, points out that common sense tells us that there is a world created by nonhuman forces, although we can never know for certain (Goodman, 1978). The scrutiny of that common sense, the inquiry into how it became common, need not lead to its refutation, if we cease to understand the adjective "constructed" as negative.

Thus, in response to the accusation of antirealism, a constructionist may answer, with Rorty's words, that:

her position has nothing in common with idealism save the acknowledgment that inquiry does not consist in confrontation between beliefs and objects, but rather in the quest for a coherent set of beliefs. . . . For she believes, as strongly as does any realist, that there are objects which are *causally* independent of human beliefs and desires. (1991: 101)

As Berger and Luckmann (1966) put it, reality is something that you cannot wish away.

This belief does not necessitate a return to Diltheyan duality. It can accommodate the commonsense intuition about the difference between "objects which cause you to have beliefs about them by fairly direct causal means and other objects" (Rorty, 1991: 106) – between "middle-sized dry goods" and such things as happiness and neutrinos – without attributing to them any different ontological status. Rather, as Rorty's example shows, it reshuffles the Diltheyan division that would have kept neutrinos together with dry goods and separated them from happiness. There are a great many differences between objects, but none that can justify one universal and a *priori* division of all of them into two classes. There could be many such useful and temporary divisions. For example, one might accommodate the insights of sociologists of science by elucidating the difference between those beliefs that are a matter of controversy and debate and "those beliefs which are not at the moment being challenged, because they present no problems and no one has bothered to think of alternatives to them" (Rorty, 1982: 13).

This observation of Rorty's is very pertinent to organization studies, as every time a specific construction process is subjected to scrutiny many others must be left omitted, indeed "kept constant." This does not mean giving them a "*per se*" existence or the right to an essence. It simply means lack of attention. The things I do not study are no more solid than those I do study; it is just that their turn for scrutiny did not come. The difference is like that between the figure and the ground: the ground is no more solid than the figure, it is just an optical illusion.

The antirealist accusation is not one that provokes many heated debates. As Sismondo concluded after his thorough examination of a great variety of constructivist thought, "constructivism is often fully compatible with either empiricism or realism, and thus . . . needs no special defense in a field where these are its competitors" (1993: 516). In fact, social constructionism could be placed close to critical realism, if not for the other criticism, that of its moral laxness.

Allegation of amorality

While most constructionists cheerfully admit agnosticism as their starting point, the critics extend it to a moral relativism, where the refusal to take an *a priori* stance is equated with acceptance (or at least noncondemnation) of such phenomena as the Holocaust ("after all, it is only constructed"), war, and suffering. Here the Furniture and the Death arguments meet, as Ashmore et al. point out, beginning with undeniability and ending with the need for moral indignation. They quote Langdon Winner's review of McKenzie's "Inventing Accuracy: A Historical Sociology of Nuclear Missile Guidance," presented at the SST/EASST conference in Gothenburg in August

1992: "As the bombs were going off and as the flesh was being ripped from the bone, I found it hard to stomach this kind of cool dispassionate sociological analysis of missile systems . . . Constructivism refuses to take a stand" (Ashmore et al., 1994: 7).

Sitting in the audience, I shared Winner's feelings and admired his rhetoric. Nevertheless, it was clear to me that his stance, if taken literally, would, for instance, prevent the pathologists from doing their job. The stance of moral indignation, humane and perfectly understandable, prevents studying what caused the suffering in the first place. For personal reasons I could never undertake a study of hospitals, which does not lead me to ignore the fact that I count on my colleagues to do it. In many cases, moral indignation is the reason to undertake constructivist research rather than avoid it on the grounds that its only result would be more moral indignation.

This is, however, another facet of the amorality accusation: that constructivist studies do not conclude in moral indignation. Especially in organization studies, constructivist research, including the constructivist version of institutionalism, is seen as apologetic. "Things are as they are because they were constructed as they were," to paraphrase a saying maliciously attributed to Finnish philosophers. This accusation would hold, though, only if constructionism accepted determinism, which it refuses, together with voluntarism. Showing how things are constructed reveals that practically at any moment they could have been constructed differently – within the institutionally accessible repertoire, which is always vast. McCloskey is right when she pleads for more counterfactual studies (1990) that could make this point clearer. How would the world look if Pouchet, and not Pasteur, won the battle over microbes, to use Latour's (1988) famous example? The essentialists would claim that Pouchet could not have won, as he was wrong, but, as the history of science amply shows, famous theories are constantly proved wrong. The only thing that is peculiar about it is the unwillingness of (some of) the sciences to remember this. It reminds me of the memoir of a daughter of one of the Cheka bosses, whose father never believed that he could be executed, although it had happened to the previous heads of that organization at two-year intervals. He was.

The idea that a construction process could go in many different ways lands me, however, in another quandary – that of an irresponsible promise that people can reconstruct their worlds at will. First, this would require espousing voluntarism, which, as I said before, is as unwelcome as determinism. Second, it would require an extraordinary simplification of the social, limiting it to something like "an organized group with a common purpose."

But are not work organizations exactly that, groups of people with a common purpose? If they were, they would need no management, no control, and no conflict resolution skills. This question resembles the standard criticism used by politicians against the people who choose not to vote: "What if everybody refused to vote?" The moment everybody did the same thing there would be no need for politics.

It all amounts to noticing that although there is plenty of intentional action, individual and collective, nobody gets things just as they want them, which does not amount to saying that there are hidden forces that steer the course of events. And that moral indignation, necessary and important as it is, must not prevent research into the construction of circumstances that lead to the phenomena causing moral indignation.

Ian Hacking suggests that there are "grades of commitment" in constructionism (1999: 19). "The least demanding grade of constructionism" is historical, after which follows ironic, then reformist and unmasking on the same level of commitment, then rebellious, and finally the revolutionary. While gratefully accepting the scale, I would nevertheless want to question the judgment hidden in the phrase "the least demanding." In the social sciences, full of (palace) revolutionaries, and, up to a certain age, overflowing with rebels, historical and ironic constructionism should earn higher grades. Irony may be the weapon of the weak, but is it not the weak that need to be defended – by themselves, rather than by the righteous?[2]

A Constructionist Program for Organization Studies

Not an ontology, but a study of ontologies

Stated bluntly, constructionism as an ontological imperative, as a mission to convince everybody that the world is constructed rather than given, does not seem to have much appeal. It most certainly falls outside the organization researchers' domain, as it lies outside that of the sociologists: "The philosopher is driven to . . . differentiate between valid and invalid assertions about the world. This the sociologist cannot possibly do" (Berger and Luckmann, 1966: 14). Ever since Knorr Cetina's (1981) and Latour and Woolgar's (1979) studies of work in a laboratory – two excellent if unintended organization studies – the constructionists recommend a purposeful epistemological fallacy, as Sismondo (1993) calls it, a conflation of ontology and epistemology, expressed in an attempt to study how people construct their varying ontologies. In a BBC documentary film on the Angel subway station in London (1990) a lift operator asks the passengers whether they think the earth is round or flat. He himself came to the conclusion that the earth is flat, because otherwise the lift could not function. How is it possible? How do people construct and defend their beliefs when collaborating with others who have equally strong but opposite ontologies?

Worse still, but also more interesting from the research point of view, people do not hold to their ontologies. As a project team proceed in their work, be they creating a car or a program for reform, their ontology oscillates, stabilizes for periods of time, becomes fragmented and individual, and then unifies again. It will not be possible to describe the work of such a team applying the researcher's own ontology as a standard to which all the others must be compared. (Besides, what interest has the researcher's ontology for anybody else?) What is more, objects themselves, says Latour (1999), tend to have variable ontologies: they emerge, but they also vanish; they have solid essence, then they vacillate feebly. What makes them so?

Here is one point on which contemporary research can go beyond Berger and Luckmann, for whom reification is still something that just happens. Reification requires work, and that work needs to be described. Naturalization and socialization, with their multiple meanings, are important skills in every construction. Human Resource Management requires strong naturalization and objectification of people, whereas "human capital" tries to reverse this process and socialize the "human parts" into a culture again. None of these moves should be judged *a priori*, either on validity or on moral grounds. Holzner (1978: 298) spoke of "degrees of objectness and subjectness," and Latour (1999) points out that the circulating quasi-objects carry offers of objectivity and of subjectivity.[3] People are willing to be made into objects when they believe it brings them just treatment; and objects can take up the offers of subjectivity, like Idoru, the virtual woman in William Gibson's book of the same title, or Ananova, a virtual news presenter created by PA News Media. Deciding ontological status *a priori* once and for all – and, worse still, distributing it according to a researcher's preferences – terminates the research process even before it has begun.

Ian Hacking says that the constructionist approach should be judged on the grounds of how unexpected it is, hence the title of his book *The Social Construction of What?* (1999). According to him, showing that institutions are socially constructed has no novelty to it, but showing that a rock can be constructed is another matter. Granted, surprise always increases the value of a scientific product, but work on institutions can be as astonishing as that on rocks, provided the question is not *what* but *how*. For instance, work that describes what happened when, after seventy years of apparently solid existence, the Soviet Union crumbled, revealing the sediments of the world left in 1917, and does it without feeding on such a staple diet as "deep structures" or "true nature," will be of great interest to many readers. Burawoy and Verdery (1999) collected ethnographies of organizations in former Soviet bloc countries, asking such questions as what kind of construction was "real socialism" and how did the present inhabitants of Russia and other East European countries recreate institutions supposedly long dead, with what memory traces, etc. My own work on reframing city management in Warsaw (2000) showed that, contrary to what was officially claimed, the main burden weighing down contemporary managers was not "socialist habits" but their images of "capitalist management" inspired by the strongly stylized collective memory of Warsaw in the 1930s.

One obvious gain from applying constructionism to organization studies is precisely the possibility of understanding how institutions emerge or vanish. This cannot be done as a purposeful prospective study of institutionalization, because institutions require much more than human intentions and the researcher will rarely know whether what he or she studied has become institutionalized or not. As Sismondo (1993) points out, in Berger and Luckmann's imagery, institutions grow by accretion rather then by acts of instituting anything. This is a very apt metaphor but, like all metaphors, it highlights only one aspect of the process. The ghost of the dichotomy of voluntarism–determinism is never put to rest, although the volume of studies on organizational change should by now convincingly demonstrate that the intentional action never leads to the intended results, simply because there is always a lot of intentional action directed at different aims in each time and place. Institutionalization, like power, is a *post factum* description of the resultant of all those efforts combined with the random events that accompanied them.

Thus there are actions aiming at institutionalization, and there is institutionalization, or deinstitutionalization of – something – going on in every process we study. We know much about institutionalization from retrospective studies of aggregate events. They need to be complemented with studies of institutionalization *in situ*, and this is a possibility that constructionism can offer. Will "human capital" become an institution, or just a fad that will soon vanish, to be replaced by another? Nobody can answer this question in advance, but everybody can study the trajectory of the new invention, the way it is being circulated, translated, anchored, globalized, localized, and so on. The answer will be constructed together with the construction of human capital itself.

On the other hand, there are things that look solid, that seem to have an essence. These can be depicted as extraordinarily well constructed, and therefore worth studying. How is it possible that, while almost every concept in organization theory is turned upside down, the concept of "uncertainty" continues to be taken for granted and is used as a final explanation where no other explanation can be found? Yehouda Shenhav (2000) cared enough to ask this question, which led him many years back into the beginnings of management science inside US engineering. The more work put into construction, and the more allies enrolled and mobilized, as Callon (1986) calls it, the better the chances of producing a thing with a solid ontology.

"Primitive classifications"

Both Mary Douglas (1986) and Karin Knorr Cetina (1994) encourage us to return to some neglected parts of Durkheim's work, especially that dedicated to "primitive classifications" (Durkheim and Mauss, 1903/1963). In a nominalist spirit, the premoderns believed that by giving names to objects, people, or phenomena they created new existences. This practice, as the adjective "primitive" indicates, supposedly has no place in modernity, except as an anachronism. The moderns give names to things as a matter of social convention, or aided by *a priori* knowledge about the object's "nature." Giving a newly discovered organism the name of its discoverer, or a newly constructed business school the name of its founder, is an institutional way of honoring individual contributions and cannot possibly have an influence on the object itself. Choosing a proper name for an illness or an organizational problem is part of a scientific procedure of diagnosis and results from the nature of the phenomenon rather than influencing its development, as the premoderns would believe.

And yet, claim both Douglas and Knorr Cetina, the power of primitive classification still holds. Calling expenditure a cost or an investment, Karl Weick (1985) noticed, prescribes

two different programs of action, which follow automatically from the diagnosis. The constructionist approach changes the relative weight of the two actions and shifts attention earlier in time. Once we have decided whether it was a cost or an investment, we know what to do about it. But how has that been decided? The process of classification, of negotiating categories, inventing labels, is one that needs researchers' attention.[4] As I have pointed out elsewhere (Czarniawska, 1997) the state or city budget, after it has been formulated and accepted, becomes just a dead letter, a basis for the preparation of the following year's budget. It is in the process of budgeting that control takes place, that plans are made and adjusted, that negotiations about priorities take place. And yet what is the process of budgeting if not a not-so-primitive classification, where things and events are ascribed names and numbers?

Projects, reforms and managerial technologies as trajectories of quasi-objects

Organization studies were always interested in change processes, mostly based on the ideological belief that change equals betterment, that it is informed by a drive to supply problems with solutions. Growing methodological reflection in recent years has made us aware that there may be another reason. Namely, processes of change deserve study because, in the course of change, the actors themselves question what was previously taken for granted, and therefore can understand it better when prompted and aided by the researchers. This is a valid methodological insight, and should be consciously exploited.

Change studies used to follow one template, which, however, seems to have exhausted its utility. It consisted of comparing the intentions of the change agent, to use the term very broadly, with the achieved results. This scheme has immediately produced a standard research result, namely that reforms, projects, the introduction of new technology, never go as planned. So the scheme was complemented, early on in the history of organization studies, with an interest in unintended consequences, and then by growing interest in the process of change as such. The constructionist approach, with its agnostic attitude, allows one to cast the net much wider. Projects, reforms, the introduction of new technology can be conceived of as ideas which, transformed into objects or, as Latour (1999) calls them, quasi-objects, circulate in and between organizations, from one place to another, from one time to another. In their wake, they contribute to the construction of many other things: new structures and new emotions, new services and new institutions, new products and new identities. Following their trajectory, the researchers can try to capture all this production, not worrying about what was intended and what was not, and to describe all the work that goes into the translation of ideas into objects, objects into other kind of objects, objects into identities and relations.

Without deciding in advance what should or ought to be constructed, the researcher is free to notice the unexpected and unintended, to record both positive and negative reactions, and to chronicle the changes in the idea or the object itself. Is quality assurance at Uppsala University the same as at Gothenburg University? Is a new Volvo car the same at the beginning as at the end of the development project? While in studies of symbolic classifications the time and attention frame was reversed, here the constructionist approach reverses what is expected. Far from expecting the results to match the intentions, it assumes a transformation, and is interested in what shapes it takes and what work is put into achieving it.

Institutions as fact-producing machines

Here I borrow from Karin Knorr Cetina (1994), who points out that economic organizations, just like laboratories, produce not only artifacts, or goods and services, but also, or maybe primarily, facts. There is no doubt that the media are powerful coproducers of facts and that they should be costudied. But an interesting facet of this fact production in economic organizations is that facts are no longer manually produced. There exist enormous fact-producing machines that we call institutions. Ian Hacking is right in saying that everybody knows that institutions have been constructed by humans, but Mary Douglas is right in showing how much they have been "naturalized" in past centuries. Accounting is a human invention, but it is only recently that accountants became interested in what happened to accounting in the time between Luca Pacioli and Robert Kaplan. Is the Church as an institution dying or going through one of its many revitalizations? It is rendering this process open that has the power to perplex, not the pseudo-discovery of its constructed origins.

I call institutions "machines," which can evoke protests. Since Morgan's brilliant work on metaphors, the representation of organizations as machines has become a reprehensible rhetorical operation. This is partly due to a misinterpretation of Taylor's idea: his analogy was not between people as cogs in the machine but between a system of functions or processes that is found in both. But such is the fate of metaphors: when put to use in analogical thinking, they may reveal a strain of analogies that were never intended by whoever coined the metaphor (metaphors being just another example of quasi-objects). By calling institutions machines I intend a straight, if limited, analogy encouraged by Mary Douglas's example. While machines were supposed to relieve people of physical work, institutions were supposed to relieve them of mental work. There is no criticism or irony in this statement: little though people would like to have to cut their lawns with a scythe (although this is already a simple machine) they would not want to have to rethink the whole development of modern hygiene each morning in order to decide whether to brush their teeth.

While we remember only too well that a lawnmower is a machine, we tend to forget that quality assurance is a technology, too. People kick their lawnmowers, throw them away, and buy new ones that refuse to cut grass, then take the manufacturer to court. The same people may treat quality assurance as an inevitable result of the *Zeitgeist* that allows no protest. Constructionists do not have to start revolutions: it is up to the actors to decide whether they are pleased with their lawnmowers and their quality assurance. Redescription of the emergence of lawnmowers and quality assurance in constructionist terms might help them to decide.

A Break with one Tradition, Continuity with Another

The vocation of social constructionism is still what it was for both Alfred Schütz (1953/1973) and Harald Garfinkel (1967): to reveal how the-taken-for-granted becomes taken for granted. The difference between various attempts to realize this are less important then the similarity of their intention. All living vocabularies are themselves under ongoing construction, which is the proof of their vitality. The specificity of social constructionism in organization studies is that they take up the process of construction that keeps people busy for the greater part of their lives. Earlier, when, as in Hollywood movies, "everyday life" included everything but work in a formal organization, especially of an economic nature, that was neglected. Although already Benita Luckmann (1978/285) postulated the inclusion of the "work world" among the three "omphalic small worlds" of modern people (the other two being family and ecological community) the lifeworld–system contrast introduced by the Frankfurt school turned out to be more appealing.

Thus, within the sociological tradition, constructionist organization studies mean mostly the extension of the objects studied. Within the tradition of management studies, they require a shift of focus – in time and place. What happens before organizations appear as obvious, solid, and equipped with boundaries? What is the content of black boxes that are not to be opened until a crisis? What is the content of everyday objects that are circulated as mere aids to everyday routines? What is produced, apart from the main product, in every production process? What is sold, apart from the main commodity, at every sale?

Constructionism in organization studies needs neither to be paranoid nor apologetic. It is certainly "unmasking," not in the sense of revealing nasty plots, but rather in the sense of revealing what has been forgotten or not paid attention to. Studies of construction processes may reveal heroes as well as villains, misdemeanors as well as noble deeds, or may be as prosaic as showing people that their supposedly mislaid spectacles are sitting on their nose. This has, however, nothing to do with

unmasking a "false consciousness" or "enlightening" those remaining in the dark. Social constructionism wishes to steer clear of the hubris of both critical thought and the positivist ambition of setting the world to rights according to what the researchers see as "right." The analogy is more like that between musicians and critics, or between playwrights, actors, and directors and theatre and film critics. The latter are an invaluable help to the former (not excluding occasional irritation on both sides) but there is no question of "superiority" or "competition" between the two activities; it is a pragmatic division of labor, evolved historically.

Why does not social constructionism attempt to formulate laws and predictions, why does not it attempt to generalize? Social constructionism has learned from hermeneutics (Gadamer, 1975) that meaning is, and can only be, historical. Predictions are projections of historical meaning in the future, with the hope that the world will stand still for a while, and are successful only in so far as it does. In this, social constructionism does not differ from positivism; the difference lies in stylistic preferences, as it were. "Laws," be they laws of causality, or the more modest laws of succession that Comte propagated, are rhetorical devices intended to persuade the reader. Readers who appreciate the opportunity of forming their own judgment are not fond of authors who dictate laws and formulate generalizations, as that should obviously be, and always is, the reader's prerogative.

Are these not modest ambitions? Indeed they are, in tune with what John Law (1994) called a "modest sociology" and what in the present case should be called a "modest organization theory." It is based on the conviction that there is no reason for superiority on the researchers' side, as everyone is a researcher, as Alfred Schütz pointed out long ago (1953/1973). The difference between social constructionism and common sense is that the former studies the formation of the latter. After all, metaknowledge is not a "superior" knowledge but a knowledge that comes from a different place. And as cultural studies show that there is no common sense superior to others, only more or less suitable in a given time and place, there is no reason to believe that there is a research perspective superior to others. Much as I am fond of the social constructionist perspective and grateful for the understanding of life and the world that it has allowed me to acquire, a world in which social constructionism was the only perspective would be as gray and drab as any other totalitarian world.

Notes

1 Ian Hacking (1999) would say here that one must not confound the concept with the phenomenon, but how to distinguish phenomena for which there are no concepts? The development of the illness tuberculosis in a body is a separate phenomenon from the differing uses of the concept, but the latter is a part of the history of tuberculosis (see also Knorr Cetina, 1993).
2 For further arguments in favor of irony I recommend a reading of *Irony's Edge* by Linda Hutcheon (1994).
3 While Holzner, faithful to the phenomenological tradition, is still weighed down by the issue of "consciousness," Latour avoids it altogether, which makes his research program more feasible.
4 A brilliant example of such work is Geoffrey C. Bowker and Susan Leigh Star's *Sorting Things Out* (1999).

References

Ashmore, Malcolm, Edwards, Derek, and Potter, Jonathan (1994) "The bottom line: the rhetoric of reality demonstrations," *Configurations*, 1: 1–14.

BBC (1990) *Heart of the Angel*. London: Allegra Films.

Berger, Peter, and Luckmann, Thomas (1966) *The Social Construction of Reality*. New York: Doubleday.

Blumer, Howard (1969) *Symbolic Interactionism: Perspective and Methods*. Englewood Cliffs, NJ: Prentice Hall.

Bowker, Geoffrey C., and Star, Susan Leigh (1999) *Sorting Things Out: Classification and its Consequences*. Cambridge, MA: MIT Press (paperback edition 2000).

Burawoy, Michael, and Verdery, Katherine, eds (1999) *Uncertain Transition: Ethnographies of Change in the Postsocialist World*. Lanham, MD: Rowman & Littlefield.

Callon, Michel (1986) "Some elements of a sociology of translation: domestication of the scallops and the fishermen of St Brieuc's Bay," in John Law (ed.) *Power, Action and Belief*, pp. 196–229. London: Routledge.

Czarniawska, Barbara (1997) *Narrating the Organization: Dramas of Institutional Identity*. Chicago: University of Chicago Press.

——(2000) *A City Reframed: Managing Warsaw in the 1990s*. Reading, MA: Harwood.

Douglas, Mary (1986). *How Institutions Think*. London: Routledge.

Durkheim, Émile, and Mauss, Marcel (1903/ 1963). *Primitive Classifications*. London: Cohen & West.

Eco, U. (1995) *The Search for the Perfect Language*. Oxford: Blackwell.

Farr, Rob (1987) *Social Representations*, special issue of *Journal for the Theory of Social Behavior*, 17 (4).

Farr, Rob, and Moscovici, Serge, eds (1984) *Social Representations*. Cambridge: Cambridge University Press.

Gadamer, Hans-Georg (1975) *Truth and Method*. New York: Continuum.

Garfinkel, Harold (1967) *Studies in Ethnomethodology*. Englewood Cliffs, NJ: Prentice Hall.

Gergen, Kenneth J. (1994) *Realities and Relationships: Soundings in Social Construction*. Cambridge, MA: Harvard University Press.

——(1999) *An Invitation to Social Construction*. Thousand Oaks, CA: Sage.

Goodman, Nelson (1978) *Ways of Worldmaking*. Indianapolis, IN: Hackett.

Gould, Stephen Jay (1995) "Ladders and cones: constraining evolution by canonical icons," in Robert B. Silvers (ed.) *Hidden Histories of Science*, pp. 37–68. New York: NYREV.

Hacking, Ian (1999) *The Social Construction of What?* Harvard, MA: Harvard University Press.

Harré, Rom, ed. (1986) *The Social Construction of Emotions*. Oxford: Blackwell.

Holzner, Burkhart (1968) *Reality Construction in Society*. Cambridge, MA: Schenkman.

——(1978) The construction of social actors: an essay on social identities," in Thomas

Luckmann (ed.) *Phenomenology and Sociology*, pp. 291–310. Harmondsworth: Penguin.

Hutcheon, Linda (1994) *Irony's Edge: The Theory and the Politics of Irony*. New York: Routledge.

Hutchins, Edwin (1995) *Cognition in the Wild*. Cambridge, MA: MIT Press.

Knorr Cetina, Karin (1981) *The Manufacture of Knowledge: An Essay on the Constructivist and Contextual Nature of Science*. Oxford: Pergamon Press.

——(1993) "Strong constructivism – from a sociologist's point of view: a personal addendum to Sismondo's paper," *Social Studies of Science*, 23: 555–63.

——(1994) "Primitive classifications and postmodernity: toward a sociological notion of fiction," *Theory, Culture and Society*, 11: 1–22.

——(1999) *Epistemic Cultures: How the Sciences make Knowledge*. Cambridge, MA: Harvard University Press.

Latour, Bruno (1986) "The powers of association," in John Law (ed.) *Power, Action and Belief*, pp. 261–77. London: Routledge.

——(1988) *The Pasteurization of France*. Cambridge, MA: Harvard University Press.

——(1999) *Pandora's Hope*. Cambridge, MA: Harvard University Press.

Latour, Bruno, and Woolgar, Steve (1979/1986) *Laboratory Life: The Construction of Scientific Facts*. Princeton, NJ: Princeton University Press.

Law, John (1994) *Organizing Modernity*. Oxford: Blackwell.

Levine, George (1993) Looking for the real: epistemology in science and culture," in George Levine (ed.) *Realism and Representation*, pp. 3–26. Madison, WI: University of Wisconsin Press.

Lewontin, Richard C. (1995) "Genes, environment, and organisms," in Robert B Silvers (ed.) *Hidden Histories of Science*, pp. 115–40. New York: NYREV.

Luckmann, Benita (1978) "The small life-worlds of modern man," in Thomas Luckmann (ed.) *Phenomenology and Sociology*, pp. 275–290. Harmondsworth: Penguin.

McCloskey, D. N. (1990) *If you're so Smart: The Narrative of Economic Expertise*. Chicago: University of Chicago Press.

——(1997) *Crossing: A Memoir*. Chicago: University of Chicago Press.

Rorty, Richard (1980) *Philosophy and the Mirror of Nature*. Oxford: Blackwell.

——(1982) *Consequences of Pragmatism*. Minneapolis, MN: University of Minnesota Press.

——(1989) *Contingency, Irony and Solidarity*. Cambridge: Cambridge University Press.

——(1991) *Objectivity, Relativism and Truth*. Cambridge: Cambridge University Press.

Schaffer, Simon (1993) "Augustan realities: Nature's representatives and their cultural resources in the early eighteenth century," in George Levine (ed.) *Realism and Representation*, pp. 279–320. Madison, WI: University of Wisconsin Press.

Schütz, Alfred (1953/1973) "Commonsense and scientific interpretation of human action," in *Collected Papers* I, *The Problem of Social Reality*. The Hague: Nijhoff.

Shenhav, Yehouda (2000) *Manufacturing Rationality: The Engineering Foundations of the Managerial Revolution*. Oxford: Oxford University Press.

Sismondo, Sergio (1993) "Some social constructions," *Social Studies of Science*, 23: 515–53.

Weick, Karl E. (1985) "Sources of order in underorganized systems: themes in recent organization theory," in Yvonne S. Lincoln (ed.) *Organizational Theory and Inquiry*. Beverly Hills, CA: Sage.

5

Methodology

Case is one of a number of contributors who expressed a disquiet at the debating format adopted in this book. He signals this at a number of points in the contribution. Firstly by the ironic deployment of the "Persuasive Writing Frame," a tool purportedly used to teach children to construct sound arguments, as a device with which to frame his discussion. He also treats the editorial process with irony by constructing a fictitious dialogue with the editors as a way of dealing with editorial comments on earlier drafts. Finally he constructs the whole piece with an internal autodebate with himself. The editors were suitably chastened. He is also more interested in exploring or even dissolving the boundaries between supposedly oppositional positions. Case opens sections of "debate" aphoristically, and then proceeds to unpick the aphorism – circling the reader around with the author back into the issues. There is a kind of irony too in McKinley's appropriation of "constructivism" for the purposes of pursuing a realist ontological argument.

McKinley's concerns are similar to McKelvey's (chapter 2a) in bemoaning the lack of development and advancement in the OS field. For McKinley one of the chief impediments is the lack of adequate constructs that have consensus and objectivity. The issue of objectivity becomes the centerpiece of his argument. Eschewing any naive, absolute objectivity, he engages in a rhetorical sleight of hand by which he develops the notion of a socially constructed objectivity claiming to make use of social constructivist perspectives. What he actually means by this is that the abstract constructs researchers and theorists make use of emerge through a process of consensus building. In practice this entails convergence on a definition of the construct that all can then adopt and deploy. The consensus and the convergence *are* what constitute objectivity – they are the criterion for establishing the objectivity of a construct. The existence of an agreed upon construct can then drive the measurement of the construct, and as measures converge around the construct its objectivity is reinforced. He even goes so far as to advocate a "construct dictionary" that can stand as the "definitive" guideline for what a construct means and how it should be used and measured. This is anathema to Case, who early in his piece declares himself to be unashamedly a celebrant of transitoriness, fluidity, and the movement of meaning. He would see McKinley's attempt to definitionally pin and fix construct meanings as asphyxiating and inimical to healthy development in the field.

Case is a champion of the plurivocality and undecidability of texts, and his contribution is an exemplar of that. He begins playfully with a deconstructive reversal of fact–fiction and objectivity–subjectivity. This unsettles the known universe of orthodox neopositivist ontology – at least in the sense of a perturbation caused by a tickle. He makes aphoristic claims for constructivism and for a methodology that reflects the fictive and socially constructed nature of organizations. This aphorism is immediately challenged by the more authentic view that methodology cannot be discussed in the abstract and must be linked to the specificities of particular research questions, contexts, and indexically to the paradigm which frames the question in the first place. He might have ended his piece there, but he goes on.

Case resists McKinley's attempt to place the field in a construct and hence methodo-logical straitjacket and is more of an advocate of Mao's "letting a thousand flowers bloom." But, perhaps with an eye to Maoist consequences, he is concerned that moral hazard that way lies. Methodology is seduction – it is an ideologically informed language game in which discourses of persuasion are produced: with real consequences. At the "root" of methodo-logical debates (sorry, arguments) are questions of knowledge/power and how the world is represented, by whom, and to what end. Neopositivists seek to seduce with a rhetoric of rationality, objectivity, and factuality. We do not get a clear explication of the seductive devices of constructionists, but we do get the admonishment (albeit uncomfortably given) that a methodological choice is a moral choice. Research, and its various representations, are not value-free, impersonal, apolitical, de-gendered, or ahistorical. Case further treats ironic-ally the vacuity of research that assumes the opposite by reference to a computer-aided novel analyzer that counts the words used and presents that as a summary of the novel – akin, he implies, to a statistical table as a representation of complex, dynamic, lived social phenomena. The more authentic "method" is to acknowledge the inevitable subjectivity and ideological-rhetorical incursions into any research practice, to surface that, and reflexively deal with it. Make your "moral" choices, declare them, submit them to critical scrutiny, and do not pretend otherwise.

McKinley is concerned with the "scattered" state of the field and the fact that there is a proliferation of constructs, their meanings, and the methods deployed to pursue them empirically. He might well have argued that if you let a thousand flowers bloom the garden becomes simply an unruly and indeterminate mess. The field of OS, he maintains, has too many constructs that have low consensus. A pragmatic consequence is that the field has proven to be able to offer the practitioner little of value. This is in part because of the failure to secure consensus on constructs and move forward with research and theory, but also in part because organization scholars are divorced from the practical realities of practitioners. He argues that managers are "intuitive realists" and that OS theorists are out of touch with the ontology and epistemology of their prime constituents. The notion that the ontological perspective of the researched should take precedence over the ontological assumptions of the researcher is contentious and radical – albeit not new. It is only an assumption that man-agers have a realist ontology and that there is uniformity of orientation. It is also a moot point as to whether a strict managerialist line is the most valid for OS.

McKinley's main thesis is that objectivity is achieved through a process of the social construction of consensus over the critical constructs. Apart from the dictionary, he also argues that researchers should be provided with incentives to converge on agreed-upon construct definitions. He politicizes the process of research practice and takes us into politics of research the dynamics of which remain very murky. One consequence of his advocacy of construct consensus is the diminution of operational creativity. He is prepared to sacrifice creativity in favor of a more policed field. McKinley sees the proliferation of constructs as destructive to the field, whereas Case sees the attempt to impose closure on meaning not only as damaging to intellectual inquiry but as morally reprehensible. Case sees the epistemology and methods of neopositivism in OS as a misguided importation of paradigms from the natural sciences into a field of inquiry where they are not warranted and where they introduce a stasis that the phenomenon under investigation neither exhibit nor are explained by.

5a From Subjectivity to Objectivity: A Constructivist Account of Objectivity in Organization Theory

William McKinley

Throughout the history of social science, objectivity has been a valued characteristic (Hunt, 1993, 1994) that has been subject to multiple interpretations (Megill, 1991). Megill (1991) identified four "senses" of objectivity, including absolute objectivity, disciplinary objectivity, dialectical objectivity, and procedural objectivity. Daston (1992) also discussed different interpretations of "objectivity," distinguishing in particular between ontological objectivity (equivalent to Megill's absolute objectivity) and aperspectival objectivity. Ontological or absolute objectivity "pursues the ultimate structure of reality," while aperspectival objectivity "is about eliminating individual (or occasionally group, as in the case of national styles or anthropomorphism) idiosyncrasies" (Daston, 1992: 599).

Daston (1992) concluded that aperspectival objectivity – the search for an impersonal "view from nowhere" – has come to dominate other senses of objectivity that have been evident during the history of the term. An example of the importance of aperspectival objectivity can be found in the US Supreme Court's ruling on the issue of whether to permit hand counts of "undervotes" (those ballots rejected by vote-counting machines) in the 2000 presidential election in Florida. The Court's ruling suggested that the Court was less concerned with divining the "true" intent of the Florida

voters (ontological objectivity) than with establishing vote-counting standards that would be applied in the same way across all Florida counties (aperspectival objectivity). Since the Court concluded that such standards would be elusive or impossible to implement (Espo and Fournier, 2000), it ruled against a recount of the undervotes, in effect handing the election to George W. Bush.

Since the aperspectival sense of objectivity has become dominant in the modern era (Daston, 1992), I will adopt that interpretation of objectivity in this chapter. If one combines that aperspectival sense of objectivity with the realist ontology that typifies much of organization science (see Hunt, 1990, and Godfrey and Hill, 1995, for discussions of realism), objectivity becomes a question of aperspectival *representation*. The issue is to devise representations that mirror an empirical phenomenon "out there" that a researcher wishes to compare with a theory. Representations, or measures, are said to be "objective" if they eliminate local idiosyncrasy in that mirroring process and converge on the same score when applied to the same phenomenon by different individuals. The notion of convergence across individuals – the squeezing out of individual perspective – is thus critical for the attainment of objectivity in representation. Criteria for judging this aperspectival convergence are well institution-alized in organization science, and have been formalized by methodologists (e.g., Bagozzi and Phillips, 1982; Campbell and Fiske, 1959; Scandura and Williams, 2000) and embodied in criteria such as inter-rater reliability (Perreault and Leigh, 1989). For example, in coding docu-mentary sources of data such as letters to share-holders, inter-rater reliability is assessed by noting the convergence between ratings of the same attribute by two or more independent coders. An objective measurement process maximizes this convergence by reducing the effect of in-dividual coder perspective on the coding task.

It is possible, however, to take another view of objectivity, a view that is founded on a constructivist perspective rather than a realist perspective. Here I am using the word "con-structivist" in the sense of modern historians and sociologists of science (e.g., Golinski, 1998; Latour and Woolgar, 1986; Pickering, 1984), who emphasize the social processes involved in the isolation and stabilization of phenomena by scientists. From a constructivist perspect-ive, the problem of objectivity is not so much a problem of representation as a problem of objectification. If one takes seriously the argu-ment that the abstract phenomena studied by scientists are socially constructed, at least in part, by the scholars who study the phenom-ena (Astley, 1985; Babbie, 1995; Golinski, 1998; Latour and Woolgar, 1986), objectivity becomes a function of how well that construction pro-cess takes place. I will argue in this chapter that the quality of the construction process in organization theory depends critically on how much users of organizational constructs converge on a standard definition for a given construct. In other words, organization scient-ists' ability to go from subjectivity to objectivity, to stabilize and sustain the abstract organiza-tional phenomena that they do research on, is a function of definitional consensus among the scholars. Without taking sides in the debate between realism and constructivism (see Hacking, 1999; Hunt, 1990), I simply want to explore the potential of a constructivist conceptualization of objectivity. In the position argued in this chapter, objectivity remains a valued characteristic and adheres to the aperspectival connotation that Daston (1992)

emphasized, but it is transformed from a static assessment of measurement quality to a dynamic evaluation of how well construction of organization theory phenomena by organ-izational scholars takes place.

I begin with Babbie's (1995: 116–17) argu-ment that constructs are employed to simplify reality and to capture a common element shared by a set of diverse observations. Thus con-structs have a base in reality but they do not incorporate it literally: they are abstractions from it. Subsequently, Babbie (1995) points out, there is a tendency for construct users to reify or objectify the construct, so that it attains a quality of externality that identifies it as a phenomenon separate from the user's mind. Going beyond Babbie (1995) and comment-ators such as Astley (1985), I suggest that, in organization theory, constructs vary in their degree of objectification, depending on whether a consensus exists among construct users about the definition of the construct. The definition of a construct specifies the empirical domain that the construct covers, so when different users of the same construct share a common definition for it, its empirical domain moves beyond individual perspective and achieves objective status. That objective status leads to the perception that the construct is external, a thing outside any individual user's mind. Because of the definitional convergence, meas-ures of the construct deployed by different users tend to overlap; and since measures or instruments help "carry" the phenomenon they measure (Golinski, 1998), this convergence has an effect that further solidifies the construct's demarcated, externalized status.

By contrast, I will argue that when a single definition of a construct is not widely shared among construct users, as is often the case in organization theory (Shenhav et al., 1994; Hirsch and Levin, 1999), objectification of the construct is more fragile. The construct has a less secure status as an entity outside the mind, because the definition of the construct and the empirical domain specified by that definition are more perspectival – they vary more from user to user. This interferes with the establish-ment of intersubjectivity and the construction of an abstract phenomenon that is sensed as external to the user's consciousness. In fact, from a constructivist perspective, one is dealing with a partially constructed organizational phenomenon. In that case, cross-user definitional diversity not only renders the externality of the construct problematical, but also reduces cross-study convergence in construct measures. The low measurement convergence blurs the objectified status of the construct, since nonconvergent measures seem to carry different phenomena. Often lack of cross-user measurement convergence is accounted for by invoking different "dimensions" of a construct (e.g., dimensions of organizational culture: Detert et al., 2000; dimensions of "power": Finkelstein, 1992). While low definitional convergence among construct users reduces construct objectification, it does encourage high operational creativity. Different empirical researchers can offer a variety of empirical measures as valid indicators of the construct, investing their indicators and data sets with the legitimacy and publication potential that stem from a linkage to topical "umbrella" constructs (Hirsch and Levin, 1999; McKinley et al., 1999).

After developing this constructivist argument, I will explore its implications for the objectivity–subjectivity debate that underlies this chapter. I will first briefly summarize the position taken by my counterpart in the debate. Based on that summary and my constructivist perspective, I will then specify implications and respond to some of the points made. I will argue that the low construct objectification that presently characterizes many organization theory constructs is a problem, and therefore we should strive for greater construct objectification in our field. Greater construct objectification is important because it provides abstract constructs that adequately reduce the complexity of empirical reality and can be treated as credible, clearly delineated phenomena to study. In philosophical terms, construct objectification is the way constructivism can support the "leap of faith" (Godfrey and Hill, 1995) that is necessary for studies of unobservable constructs to be reasonable. Construct objectification is also important because, I believe, the level of objectification attained in organization theory frequently lags the level routinely practised by organizational participants in their daily activities. In other

words, at the current stage of evolution of organization theory, organizational managers and employees are often more willing to objectify constructs like "organizational structure," "hierarchy of authority," "power," and the like than organizational scholars are. While any commentator might view that as a positive feature of organization theory, it may also mean that we are prevented from generating objective, believable knowledge that is utilizable (Beyer and Trice, 1982) by managers. I will argue that we need to increase construct objectification at least to the level routinely practised by organizational participants, while not losing sight of the constructed nature of the abstractions we are naming and investigating. Finally, construct objectification is critical because the definitional consensus that underlies it and is stimulated by it will enhance organization theory's capacity to reduce incommensurability between incompatible organizational schools of thought (McKinley and Mone, 1998; Scherer and Dowling, 1995).

Before proceeding to flesh out the agenda outlined above, some caveats are in order. The first caveat is that the primary foci in this chapter are the constructs that have emerged in organization theory from social science roots or have been imported by organization theorists from the world of practice. Constructs can come from many sources, of course, and these two do not exhaust all the possible origins of organization theory constructs. Nevertheless, the two sources probably account for the majority of constructs in current use in our field. Constructs like "downsizing," "shareholder value," and "profit" are good examples of constructs that have originated in the world of practice and been imported by organizational researchers into organization theory. On the other hand, the constructs that form the foundations of contemporary schools of thought in organization theory – constructs such as "institution" (DiMaggio and Powell, 1991; Meyer and Rowan, 1977), "selection" (Hannan and Freeman, 1977), "transaction" (Williamson, 1981), and "resource" (Salancik and Pfeffer, 1974; Barney, 1991) – have originated primarily from social science scholarship. Knowing some of the sources of constructs in use in contemporary organization theory may help the reader understand the construct objectification process better.

A second caveat is that this chapter takes an explicitly prescriptive stance, in contrast to the descriptive work undertaken by the same author on similar topics (e.g., McKinley et al., 1999; Mone and McKinley, 1993). I feel it is important to specify this clearly for the reader, because prescriptive ("should") statements and descriptive ("is") statements are often confounded in organization theory writing. This chapter makes statements not just about what *is* the case in contemporary organization theory, but about what *should* be the case. When I move from descriptive to prescriptive mode, as I do at the end of the chapter, I will try to make that as explicit as possible for the reader. Since I adhere to Simon's position that prescriptive statements cannot be logically derived from purely descriptive ones – no amount of information about what "is" can tell the scholar what "should be" (Donaldson and Dunfee, 1994; Simon, 1997: 68–9) – I think such signaling is critical.

A Constructivist View of Objectivity

Let us turn now to a more detailed look at Babbie's (1995: 116–17) description of the process of construct evolution (or "conceptual entrapment," as Babbie puts it). Babbie argues that a construct (or concept) is used to simplify the complexity of unmediated reality by extracting from it a common element that characterizes a number of diverse observations. For example, a number of observations of interactions between organizations and their environment might suggest that those interactions have a common element that relates to exchange of goods or services across an organizational boundary. Thus the construct "transaction" might be coined or adopted to express that common cross-boundary exchange element.

Although a construct is actually a mental representation adopted for convenience, Babbie (1995) suggests that the use of that representation by investigators typically initiates an objectification process. In that process, users begin to see the construct as an objective reality external to their minds. The objective status of the construct then prompts a search

for indicators that constitute valid measures of the construct (Babbie, 1995). This is ironic, as Babbie emphasizes, because the very observations whose common element was extracted as the basis for the mental construct are now seen as indicators of the thing that the construct has become. Continuing the example of the construct "transaction," during use of this construct by social scientists, a "transaction" becomes objectified as an external reality, and the observable interactions between organizations and their environments that gave rise to the construct become seen as indicators of that external reality.

While Babbie (1995) has rendered an unusually clear explanation of construct objectification, a central thesis of my section of this chapter is that the objectification process is not as automatic as he implies. From a constructivist standpoint, I maintain that construct objectification depends fundamentally on the degree to which a common construct definition is shared among construct users. Since the definition of a construct specifies the empirical domain covered by the construct, sharing of a common construct definition means that different users associate the construct with the same empirical domain. That in turn means that the empirical domain is outside the mind of any single user. Since being outside the mind suggests being external or an object, a common construct definition objectifies the construct with which it is associated. Put another way, a construct definition that is shared among users elevates the empirical domain of the construct to intersubjective status, and a domain shared intersubjectively seems to indicate an external object. According to this argument, an unobservable construct such as those frequently employed in organization theory research (Godfrey and Hill, 1995) will not become fully objectified unless it is based on a standard construct definition that is adopted by the investigators working with the construct. The intersubjective status of a shared construct definition links the process of construct objectification back to Daston's (1992) notion of aperspectival objectivity: objectification becomes understandable as the result of aperspectivity in construct definition and usage. In the "transaction" example, if different users of the construct "transaction" attach a common definition to the construct, the construct is objectified and elevated to the status of "phenomenon" outside the mind.

The concept of objectification being used here is similar to Berger and Luckmann's (1966) notion of "objectivation" and Tolbert and Zucker's (1996) concept of "sedimentation." Both these terms capture the quality of exteriority that is represented here by the term "construct objectification." While Berger and Luckmann (1966) and Tolbert and Zucker (1996) were concerned primarily with externalization of routinized human activity in the form of institutions, rather than the externalization of scholarly constructs, the implication of my position is that construct use by scholars can result in the same kind of objectification as frequently occurs with patterns of routinized behavior. That the latter type of objectification is also dependent on consensus is suggested by Tolbert and Zucker's (1996: 181) definition of objectification: "the development of general, shared social meanings attached to these behaviors, a development that is necessary for the transplantation of actions to contexts beyond their point of origination."

In the realm of scholarly constructs, when a standard definition of a construct is widely shared and the construct is correspondingly objectified, both the definitional standardization and the objectified status stemming from it establish constraints on the variety of construct measures that can be deployed, so operational measures of the construct will tend to be similar from study to study. Given that measures are often the markers or the carriers of constructed phenomena (Golinski, 1998), convergence in measurement across different investigations reinforces the impression of a single, coherent phenomenon. Standardization in construct measurement therefore contributes independently to the objectification of the construct that is also undergirded by definitional consistency. Convergence of measures across studies means that there is relatively little leeway for operational creativity, however, and thus there tends to be a tradeoff between construct objectification and operational creativity. When construct objectification and standardization of measurement are high, there is

little room to advance a wide range of different measures as valid indicators of a construct, and empirical researchers lose the possibility of linking diverse data sets to a "hot" construct as a way of investing their research with legitimacy (McKinley et al., 1999).

At the other extreme, when a single definition of a given organizational construct is not widely shared among construct users, the empirical domain of the construct is more a function of individual perspective. The construct therefore does not have the objective, aperspectival status that contributes to perception of the construct as a thing outside the mind. When definitions of a given construct vary widely across users, scholars see other scholars referring to diverse empirical domains when invoking the construct, and externalization and objectification of a coherent, demarcated entity is rendered difficult. In Latour and Woolgar's (1986) terminology, one could say that the "inversion" that occurs at the moment of object stabilization is partial, and it is not altogether clear whether there is any objective external phenomenon at all. In Chia's (1998: 365) words, it is difficult to make the "cuts" that enable us "to produce self-identical social objects with a stable location in a singular position, in space-time, and as possessing an enduring form with clearly bounded outlines."

Measures of such a partially constructed entity tend to vary across different empirical studies, all of which state that they are investigating the same thing. This divergence of measures reinforces the subjective ontological status of the construct, further inhibiting its stabilization as a demarcated object outside the individual mind. While objectification is low in this situation, operational creativity tends to be high, because of the freedom that definitional diversity and partial construction of the phenomenon afford to the empirical researcher. Partial construction of an organizational phenomenon blurs or eliminates its boundaries, so that many different measures of the "phenomenon" are potentially valid. This opens up space for researchers to link their data sets to the "phenomenon" in question, and an array of measures accumulates that often impresses the organization theory discipline with the fecundity of the research stream. The accumulation of different measures, while positive in some ways, does not necessarily entail an accumulation of objective knowledge, and the ultimate meaning of a body of empirical studies can become obscure. As Hirsch and Levin (1999) have remarked for the case of "organizational effectiveness," the outcome of low measurement convergence is sometimes the abandonment of a construct (and any objectified status it may have been struggling toward) and its replacement with a set of variables that originally constituted "dimensions" of the construct.

Figure 5.1 shows the underlying continua implicit in the discussion above, with the central continuum ranging from high construct objectification to low construct objectification. The top of figure 5.1 represents the situation where interscholar convergence on a single construct definition leads to clear, aperspectival objectification of the construct. In that case, high construct objectification entails low operational creativity. The bottom of the figure represents the opposite extreme, where interscholar divergence in definition of a given construct reduces construct objectification. Here we speak of partially constructed or even unconstructed organizational phenomena that are difficult to measure with aperspectival objectivity. However, the partial construction (or lack of construction) creates an opportunity for operational creativity, which may have reputational advantages for researchers seeking theoretical mileage for their data sets and empirical measures. This assumes that empirical studies are easier to publish if they offer operationalizations of

constructs that are of theoretical interest to a field at a given point in time.

Arguably, many constructs in organization theory today fall near the bottom of figure 5.1. Constructs like "transaction," "institution," "power," "institutional field," "organizational learning," "strategy," "culture," and so on each admit of a variety of different definitions (Astley and Zammuto, 1992; Hirsch and Levin, 1999). This perspectival diversity in definition is represented in the literature that has developed around each of the constructs. (See, for example, Barney and Hesterly, 1996, and Godfrey and Hill, 1995, for summaries of the transaction costs literature; Mizruchi and Fein, 1999, and Tolbert and Zucker, 1996, for discussions of the institutional theory literature; Hardy and Clegg, 1996, for a recent analysis of the literature on power; and Hirsch and Levin, 1999, for discussion of the constructs "learning," "strategy," and "culture.") The low definitional convergence that is typical of these constructs may be a function of their relative novelty – some of them have not been on the organization theory scene for more than a decade or two. Nevertheless, to the extent that my argument is correct, and definitional diversity deconstructs the phenomenon to which a construct refers, the central phenomena of many organization theory schools of thought would seem to have a deconstructed or partially constructed character. The perspectivity with which such phenomena are conceptualized and defined in the organization theory literature permits operational creativity but does not

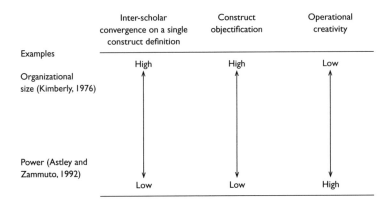

Examples	Inter-scholar convergence on a single construct definition	Construct objectification	Operational creativity
	High	High	Low
Organizational size (Kimberly, 1976)	↑	↑	↑
Power (Astley and Zammuto, 1992)	↓	↓	↓
	Low	Low	High

Figure 5.1 Construct objectification in organization theory

enhance the objectification of the constructs into demarcated external entities.

On the other hand, a few organization theory constructs seem to enjoy greater standardization in the way they are defined, pulling the construct away from perspectivity, rendering it more objective, and locating it near the top of figure 5.1. An example might be organizational size, which has been measured (and therefore defined, at least implicitly) as the "number of employees" in most of the empirical studies that have used the construct (see Kimberly, 1976). Another example might be the construct "organizational decline," whose definition has gradually become standardized around the "decrease in an organization's resource base" interpretation that Cameron et al. (1987: 224) attached to it. Note that organizational decline research is very specialized, and this may facilitate integration and standardization of construct definitions across the relatively few scholars who pursue research in that area. Nevertheless, if scholars do share a standard definition for a construct they are using, that tends to externalize the construct as an objective entity beyond the realm of individual perspective. I do not mean to imply by this that objectified constructs are "good" while less objectified ones are "bad." But I do think construct objectification has certain advantages for organization theory, some of which will be spelled out after I summarize my counterpart's position in the objectivity–subjectivity debate that anchors this chapter.

The Debate: My Counterpart's Position

Against my constructivist view of objectivity, the counterpoint's position emphasizes subjective authenticity in organizational inquiry. I believe that this "subjective authenticity" approach has three main themes, a discussion of which may be useful in summarizing his contribution. Of course, the reader should also look ahead and peruse the next section in full to assess the validity (and degree of aperspectivity) of my summary.

The first theme that underlies chapter 5(b) is the idea that subjectivity and perspectivity are to be celebrated in organizational research, because this is a more valid ("authentic") representation of life inside organizations. Organizations are portrayed, both implicitly and explicitly, as "momentary accomplishments" that are in continual flux. Thus any attempt by the scholar to fix their processes in objective, stable constructs is doomed to distortion or, worse, irrelevance. While I will reserve comment on the ontological and epistemological issue of the character of organizations until the next section, I note in passing that it is striking how much this perspective resembles the contemporary rhetoric of management consultants. Is the metaphor of fluidity a common denominator in the representations of such scholars and the models that consultants use to characterize modern corporations and sell services to their executives?

A second theme in the counterpoint section is the notion that objective knowledge occupies a privileged position over subjective knowledge in modern Western society. This is a problem, because he believes that objective knowledge underrepresents the complexity of organizations as well as supporting unwarranted attempts at control. It is necessary, according to counterpoint, to resist the dominance of objective knowledge whenever possible, and critically deconstruct the objectifications to which "positivist" organization theory gives rise. The thesis of the underprivileging of subjectivity takes on a moral overtone, with the reader enjoined to pursue subjective authenticity as the ethical choice in organizational research epistemologies.

Third, the contra argument is strongly underpinned by a recurrent theme of individualism. For the opponent, scholarly knowledge is invariably colored by the individual ideologies and intellectual pedigrees of the scholars producing that knowledge. Therefore honest scholarship must continually acknowledge and reveal the scholar's individuality; and honest scholars must continually deconstruct and critique their own knowledge claims in light of their personal histories. The celebration of individuality that is so salient in this contribution is consistent with Bauerlein's (2001) description of the rejection of objectivity by some humanities scholars. Bauerlein (2001: B14) notes that "Humanists can't be objective. Their individualism won't let them." For

Bauerlein (himself an English professor), the central role of individualism in humanities scholarship leads to a rejection of the communitarian norms that support objectivity in natural science. The contrary position eschews the view that communitarian norms in such matters as definition of organizational constructs should be a point of pride for organizational scholars.

The Debate: Implications

This is an abbreviated summary, and again I urge the reader to inspect the contrary narrative to get a fuller picture of the story it tells. I now turn to some implications of my position and the contrary position for the objectivity–subjectivity debate. These implications concern: (1) the ontological status of the debate; (2) the desirability of objectivity in construct status; (3) the need for organization theory to match the level of objectification routinely practised by participants in "real world" organizations; and (4) the need to carefully choose the level of analysis that is the locus for construct objectification attempts.

The ontological status of the debate

The first implication is that the objectivity–subjectivity debate changes character when one takes a constructivist perspective such as the one I espouse or a relativist/individualist perspective such as that advocated next. To put the matter as succinctly as possible, both our approaches convert the objectivity–subjectivity debate from a debate about methodology to a debate about ontology and epistemology. While this stretches the boundaries imposed on this chapter by the editors, and makes the chapter a less distinct "object" relative to chapters 3 and 4, the boundary stretching may nevertheless lead to significant insights. Assuming my reading of my counterpart's contribution is correct, neither of us is talking about objectivity and subjectivity in the context of measurement, representation, or other topics that are typically the province of methodology. Rather, we are using the objectivity–subjectivity dimension as the basis for a discussion about the ontological and epistemological qualities of the abstracted organizational phenomena that are captured by organization theory constructs.

The position I have taken is that many organizational phenomena are unstable and less than fully constructed because of the lack of convergence around standard construct definitions that is typical in organization studies. As noted previously, the contrary view also sees instability in organizational phenomena, but in his view it stems from a different source: organizational participants themselves. This leads to the argument that organizations are "active, collective, and momentary accomplishments of agents." I question this assessment of the primary source of instability in organizational phenomena, suspecting that the constructions of organizational participants are in many cases more stable than the constructions of organizational scholars. Of course, this claim should properly be subjected to empirical testing, and such testing would be a productive source of insight about the objectification processes in the life world and in the world of scholarship. At least we seem to agree on the general assertion that organizational phenomena are socially constructed, both by participants and by the scholars who try to abstract from and make sense of what the participants do. This basic point of agreement also seems to extend to the recognition that the constructions of participants and those of scholars are not always the same, and the constructions of participants are often more localized than those of scholars (Astley and Zammuto, 1992). We therefore converge in our focus on objectification as a reality-building process rather than as a methodological criterion; we diverge in our analysis of the source of the subjectivity that intrudes to disrupt that objectification.

The desirability of objectivity in construct status

The prescriptive view that is implicit in my perspective on objectivity is that construct objectification is an advantageous and even necessary step in building a viable organization theory, because it supplies the phenomena that organization studies scholars theorize about and do research on. The abstracted entities denoted by such terms as "power," "institution, "strategy," "culture," and so on are not totally disconnected from the empirical plane, but they are not direct representations of unmediated reality either. In fact, they would lose their reductive value if they were. Thus their object-like status is dependent on a socially driven objectification process that, I maintain, relies on cross-scholar consensus in construct definitions.

But why is it important for organization theory to have objects to investigate, constructed or not? Because, without a clear sense that we are investigating objects rather than just subjective mental images, I think there is a real danger that organization theory could eventually collapse into a tangled web of fleeting, transitory thoughts and "texts" about "idiosyncratic microstates" (McKelvey, 1997). Put another way, without some standardization of construct definitions and resulting intersubjectivity in the status of the empirical domains to which the constructs refer, the discipline could potentially deconstruct into a state where individual subjectivity is the only entity left to investigate. This would not only make for an overwhelmingly complex subject matter, it would also put the discipline on an equal footing with the arts and humanities. While I intend no disrespect to those fields, and I realize that some organization theorists (e.g., Zald, 1993, 1996), as well as the counterpart, are moving toward a closer rapprochement with them, an unanswered question is what distinctive competence a completely subjectivized organization theory would have relative to its better-established disciplinary brethren in the humanities. If "there is often greater insight into human organization to be had from studying works of literature than from the unadventurous and tedious textual rubble found in most journals that proffer the standard fare of 'organizational science'," can organization theory be successful if it simply tries to turn the "rubble" into stories (Calas and Smircich, 1999)? I fear that established novelists and poets are better purveyors of subjective fiction than we would ever be. So in my view the solution is not to become like the novelists and poets, but to investigate coherent, albeit constructed, organizational phenomena that are outside the confines of single scholarly minds. This is consistent with McKelvey's (1997: 364) statement that "organization scientists need to find ways to distance themselves

from idiosyncratic phenomena, not get even closer to them as the postmodernists would have it."

My opponent would disagree with the position articulated in the preceding paragraph, since he suggests that objectification is "responsible for the multitude of socially constructed monsters whose tails we grasp only to have our hand bitten off in return; or, to mix metaphors, apparitions we conjure the better to scare ourselves into believing that we exist." He also warns us against "easy acceptance and compliance with such reification" and cites Berger and Luckmann (1966) to justify his skeptical position toward reification. I do not agree with him either about Berger and Luckmann's (1966) standpoint on reification or about the potentially destructive effects of the reifications employed by organizational scholars as part of their "language game" (Astley and Zammuto, 1992). On the first point, my reading of Berger and Luckmann (1966) does not detect the critical view of reification that is attributed to those scholars. In my view Berger and Luckmann were simply trying to describe – rather than evaluate – the processes of reification and objectification. On the second point, since I believe organizational scholars are relatively isolated from the "real world," I am not overly concerned about the unanticipated destructive effects their construct objectifications might have on that world. And meanwhile, back on their home turf, I think the organizational scholars need their locally nurtured objectifications to structure their phenomenological worlds and provide a sense of coherence and motivation to their efforts to understand. After all, if one is not studying some coherent phenomenon, where can one find the focus and energy required to continue the whole organization theory enterprise? Is just publishing articles and winning reputation and status games really enough?

For those who might protest that the phenomena I am talking about are "just" socially constructed, and worry that that knowledge would disrupt one's ability to pursue a "reasonable realism" (McKinley, 1995), I would respond that I do not necessarily see constructivism as incompatible with realism. I believe one can take a constructivist position on the genesis of organization theory constructs but adopt a realist approach to studying those constructs. To put it even more simply, constructivism and realism can be reasonable bedfellows. Among some commentators, particularly those of a postmodern persuasion (see Calas and Smircich, 1999, for a recent review of this literature), there appears to be an assumption that, once we admit that the abstract phenomena we study are social constructs, the only logical response is deconstruction of them. I disagree, and I believe that scholars should be free to adopt the objectified constructs created by consensus among their colleagues, study them as phenomena, and participate in a process of accumulating knowledge about them. The ontological and epistemological balancing act I am recommending is actually consistent with the current position of scientific realists (e.g., Hunt, 1990; Godfrey and Hill, 1995), who suggest that we should treat organizational phenomena as real even though they may be unobservable and we may not be able to establish their existence with infallible certainty. My position also fits nicely with McKelvey's (1997) recommendation that organization scientists should pursue idealized models, at least until the discipline attains some maturity.

Matching the level of objectification in the "real" world

Though organizational scholars may be relatively isolated from the real world, they are not totally detached from it. In particular, they tend to be importers of constructs from that world (e.g., Barley et al., 1988). When it comes to that set of imported constructs, I think the case for maintaining and promoting construct objectification is even more compelling. Why? Because a strong argument can be made that managers and employees are pragmatic realists – they act as though the constructed phenomena of "profits," "organization structure," "hierarchy of authority," "market," and so on are real entities that have objective status and unequivocal consequences for their behavior and their daily lives. To provide a scholarly treatment of these phenomena as objective, while maintaining an awareness of their historically constructed nature, is to appropriately privilege the ontological status accorded to the phenomena by those who are directly involved in their daily sensing and reproduction. In fact, a case can be made that "subjective authenticity", as recommended by my counterpart would be confusing to organizational members, and would represent an unwarranted elevation of subjectivity over their objectivist predilections. This, of course, raises the thorny question of whose ontological perspective should dominate in determining the status of the phenomena being studied by organizational scholars: that of the scholars, or that of the "natives" whose world is the object of scrutiny by the scholars? If it is the latter, I think that maintenance of construct objectification is the only way to achieve authenticity.

In many cases, matching the level of construct objectification routinely practised by organizational employees and managers may require that organizational scholars cooperate more closely in developing and diffusing standard definitions of the constructs they use. McKinley and Mone (1998) have offered a practical method for establishing this kind of consensus in construct definition: the creation of a democratically produced construct dictionary modeled on the procedures used by the Financial Accounting Standards Board to formulate new accounting rules. The construct dictionary advocated by McKinley and Mone (1998) would not only assist scholars in achieving the level of objectification routinely exhibited in the real world, but could also function as a depository for preserving the *meanings* that real-world constructs have for their real-world users. This would necessitate research among organizational managers and employees to discover what those meanings are, and I believe such research would contribute greatly to the objective authenticity of our scholarly endeavors.

Such a project would not do much to protect the "impossibility of permanent meaning closure" celebrated by my opponent. In fact the goal of a construct dictionary would be to squeeze out such "impossibilities of permanent meaning closure." It is not clear to me that managers and employees are either practitioners or fans of this type of impossibility – their motives seem more closely aligned with the achievement of cognitive order and reduction of uncertainty (McKinley and Scherer, 2000; Thompson, 1967), both of which are inconsistent with the "impossibility of permanent meaning closure" idea. Nor do managers and employees necessarily benefit from the lack of closure inherent in refusing definitional consensus and embracing subjectivity. At any rate, according to the subjectivist perspective, it has to be admitted that the "impossibility of permanent meaning closure" is no more an objective truth than any other statement that would be countenanced by a subjectivist perspective. Therefore there is nothing to prevent organization theorists from deconstructing the "impossibility of permanent meaning closure" and constructing meaning closure – for example, through a democratically built construct dictionary.

Choosing the level of analysis

Assuming one buys the argument that construct objectification in organization theory is important, that it is necessary to match the level of objectification routinely accomplished by organizational employees and managers, and that there are methods for achieving the definitional consensus that would be required to support such objectification, a critical question still remains unanswered. What level of analysis should be the locus for objectification attempts in organization theory? Should one seek to objectify constructs that are positioned at the individual level of analysis, abstracting from the traits and behavior of individual human beings in organizations? In that case organization theory would become a more micro discipline than it is today, and the field would be concerned with explaining abstracted and objectified individual-level phenomena. Or should one try to objectify constructs at the organizational level, abstracting attributes that are common to diverse patterns of social interaction at that level? This would reinforce the importance of traditional organization theory constructs like "organization structure," "hierarchy of authority," and so on, and one could seek to establish definitional consensus about these constructs so they emerge as well articulated, externalized entities. Or, alternatively, should one prioritize the supraorganizational level of analysis, attempting to objectify constructs that encapsulate and abstract from the behavior of multiple organizations in demarcated environmental contexts?

Examples of the latter constructs might be entities like "niche," "institutional field," and so on. This would move organization theory in a more macro direction, a path that has been the location of much of the conceptual "action" in recent organization theory schools of thought (e.g., population ecology and neoinstitutional theory; see Davis and Powell, 1992). In those schools there have been efforts to construct new entities for scholars to study at the environmental level of analysis, creating new intellectual domains for investigators to explore.

The constructivist argument I articulated earlier suggests that any of these levels of analysis are possible targets for construct objectification efforts; but the argument itself does not indicate which level to prioritize. The question is clearly important, both from a conceptual and from a political point of view, not least because intellectual resources are limited and require concentration to generate a reasonable return. At the very least, the answer would influence which organization theory schools of thought flourish in the future. My own bias is to concentrate our construct development and objectification efforts at the organizational level of analysis, because that is the domain with which organization theory began and it remains the arena in which I believe the discipline can still add unique value. Thus I recommend a focus on constructs that capture common elements in repetitive patterns of social behavior that occur at the organizational level of analysis, with an emphasis on abstracting those elements and solidifying their objective status. The discipline of organization theory should seek to define organization-level constructs like organization structure and its dimensions (Pugh et al., 1968) as consensually as possible, whether the definitions are based on meanings supplied by managers and employees or meanings supplied by scholars. Incentives should be provided for organizational scholars to converge on a standard definition for each construct. This standardization would stimulate the externalization of constructs as entities outside the subjectivity of the individual mind, reducing the role of perspectivity and enhancing the role of aperspectival objectivity (Daston, 1992) in construct development. Thus the constructs could be dealt with as real, albeit often unobservable, phenomena, but the history of their constructed status could also be preserved, at least for the record.

Under this mandate, the job of the organizational scholar would be to develop theories to explain variance in the organization-level phenomena captured by the constructs, using as explanatory variables other constructs (e.g., organizational technology, organizational strategy, or even environmental-level constructs) whose values vary across organizations. The constructs functioning as independent and dependent variables would serve to simplify a much more complex set of observable phenomena, thus evading idiosyncratic microstates (McKelvey, 1997) and rendering the sense-making task of the theorist manageable. Theories would be tested by using observable measures as indicators of the abstract, objectified constructs (Babbie, 1995), but theorists and researchers would hopefully be more sensitive than they currently are to the reflexive nature of those indicators. That is, as noted above, the "indicators" are both the sources of the constructs and the way the constructs, having experienced objectification, are measured.

I suspect the counterpoint would disagree with this agenda, particularly given the harsh treatment he doles out to Donaldson's (1996) "normal science of structural contingency theory." However, my guess is that this concern would be less with the particular level of analysis that I advocate than with the idea of objectifying constructs at any level of analysis. My response to his anticipated critique is that the alternative to objectification is subjectification, which would mean that the phenomena being analyzed in organization theory would vary from thinker to thinker and also from momentary mental state to momentary mental state within individual thinkers. In my view, that would be to replace organization theory with a kind of stream of consciousness, and to invite a level of complexity that cannot be handled authentically by any social science discourse. It is indeed true, as my opponent points out, that concepts mutilate that to which they are applied (Burrell, 1996). But is the collapse into subjectivity any less a mutilation, especially when it is so inconsistent with the routine objectification that goes on every day

in the organizational life world? To make the point on a more personal level, is it more of a mutilation to believe that the socially defined entities with which we are surrounded – our "universities," our "students," our "colleagues," our "families" – are phenomena, or that they are just pictures in our minds?

Conclusion

I began with the charge given me by the editors – to make a vigorous case for objectivity in organization theory. But I expanded that charge beyond the domain that was the initial arena for the editors' mandate – methodology – and used the charge as a platform to develop ideas about the ontology of organizational constructs. I argued, from a constructivist standpoint, that construct objectification – the degree to which constructs become externally demarcated and perceived as distinct phenomena outside the mind – is a function of consensus in a construct's definition. Having a standard, widely shared construct definition removes the empirical domain of the construct from the idiosyncrasy and subjectivity of the single mind, and accords the construct an intersubjective, objectified status.

The process of objectification is important because it is the means by which organizational scholars stabilize the complexities with which they deal and handle them as objects. In other words, it is the way we get to the realism advocated for organizational constructs, even if they are unobservable (Godfrey and Hill, 1995; Hunt, 1990). I spelled out the implications of my constructivist approach for the objectivity–subjectivity debate that underpins this chapter, pointing out similarities and differences between my position and the position of "subjective authenticity" espoused by my counterpart in the debate. I argued that greater construct objectification would provide a needed ontological structure for the discipline of organization theory. I also claimed that construct objectification would offer a higher level of authenticity than the opponent's subjective authenticity, because objectification is closer to the routine social construction processes that organizational participants engage in daily. Furthermore, I suggested that a constructivist awareness of the genesis and objectification of organizational constructs does not necessarily exclude a realist approach to the day-to-day investigation of those constructs. Finally, I tried to engage with the level of analysis issue, arguing that construct development and objectification efforts in organization theory should privilege the organizational level of analysis rather than the individual level or the environmental level. While this would not necessarily eliminate all construct development at the latter two levels, it would establish priorities for the allocation of our limited intellectual resources. Given that we cannot do everything, and that theorizing in organization studies has probably been too fragmented in recent decades (Pfeffer, 1993), some allocation priorities of this type appear reasonable.

Perhaps the most important message of chapter 5(a) is that we need to take seriously Pfeffer's (1997) concern that organization theory does not have a strong base in phenomena. In my view, many of the abstract phenomena that organization theory purports to be studying are only partially constructed, or have become partially deconstructed, because of inadequate consensus in construct definition. This state of affairs has a superficial appeal because it gives empirical researchers considerable freedom to be creative in construct operationalization. But it also poses a fundamental dilemma that has not been explicitly recognized in philosophy of organization science discussions to date: is this freedom and creativity worth while if it is bought at the price of indistinct phenomena and the possibility that many of our constructs may fade away before we can cumulate knowledge about them (Hirsch and Levin, 1999)? Ultimately the answer to this question goes to the heart of what organization theorists want their field to be, and specifically whether they want it to evolve in the direction of the humanities or the natural sciences. That issue cannot be resolved here, but if this chapter has focused attention on the issue it will have attained the most important of its objectives.

Acknowledgment

The author would like to thank the editors for their comments on earlier versions of this chapter.

References

Astley, W. G. (1985) "Administrative science as socially constructed truth," *Administrative Science Quarterly*, 30: 497–513.

Astley, W. G., and Zammuto, R. F. (1992) "Organization science, managers, and language games," *Organization Science*, 3: 443–60.

Babbie, E. (1995) *The Practice of Social Research*, seventh edition. Belmont, CA: Wadsworth.

Bagozzi, R. P., and Phillips, L. W. (1982) "Representing and testing organizational theories: a holistic construal," *Administrative Science Quarterly*, 27: 459–89.

Barley, S. R., Meyer, G. W., and Gash, D. C. (1988) "Cultures of culture: academics, practitioners, and the pragmatics of normative control," *Administrative Science Quarterly*, 33: 24–60.

Barney, J. B. (1991) "Firm resources and sustained competitive advantage," *Journal of Management*, 17: 99–120.

Barney, J. B., and Hesterly, W. (1996) "Organizational economics: understanding the relationship between organizations and economic analysis," in S. R. Clegg, C. Hardy, and W. R. Nord (eds) *Handbook of Organization Studies*, pp. 115–47. London: Sage.

Bauerlein, M. (2001) "The two cultures again: tilting against objectivity," *Chronicle of Higher Education*, November 16: B14.

Berger, P. L., and Luckmann, T. (1966) *The Social Construction of Reality: A Treatise in the Sociology of Knowledge*. New York: Doubleday.

Beyer, J. M., and Trice, H. M. (1982) "The utilization process: a conceptual framework and synthesis of empirical findings," *Administrative Science Quarterly*, 27: 591–622.

Burrell, G. (1996) "Normal science, paradigms, metaphors, discourses and genealogies of analysis," in S. R. Clegg, C. Hardy, and W. R. Nord (eds) *Handbook of Organization Studies*, pp. 642–58. London: Sage.

Calas, M. B., and Smircich, L. (1999) "Past postmodernism? Reflections and tentative directions," *Academy of Management Review*, 24: 649–71.

Cameron, K. S., Kim, M. U., and Whetten, D. A. (1987) "Organizational effects of decline and turbulence," *Administrative Science Quarterly*, 32: 222–40.

Campbell, D. T., and Fiske, D. W. (1959) "Convergent and discriminant validation by the multitrait–multimethod matrix," *Psychological Bulletin*, 56: 81–105.

Chia, R. (1998) "From complexity science to complex thinking: organization as simple location," *Organization*, 5: 341–69.

Daston, L. (1992) "Objectivity and the escape from perspective," *Social Studies of Science*, 22: 597–618.

Davis, G. F., and Powell, W. W. (1992) "Organization–environment relations," in M. Dunnette and L. M. Hough (eds) *Handbook of Industrial and Organizational Psychology*, second edition, pp. 315–75. Palo Alto, CA: Consulting Psychologists Press.

Detert, J. R., Schroeder, R. G., and Mauriel, J. J. (2000) "A framework for linking culture and improvement initiatives in organizations," *Academy of Management Review*, 25: 850–63.

DiMaggio, P. J., and Powell, W. W. (1991) Introduction, in W. W. Powell and P. J. DiMaggio (eds) *The New Institutionalism in Organizational Analysis*, pp. 1–38. Chicago: University of Chicago Press.

Donaldson, L. (1996) "The normal science of structural contingency theory," in S. R. Clegg, C. Hardy, and W. R. Nord (eds) *Handbook of Organization Studies*, pp. 57–76. London: Sage.

Donaldson, T., and Dunfee, T. W. (1994) "Toward a unified conception of business ethics: integrative social contracts theory," *Academy of Management Review*, 19: 252–84.

Espo, D., and Fournier, R. (2000) "Gore decides to concede election," *Associated Press*, December 13.

Finkelstein, S. (1992) "Power in top management teams: dimensions, measurement, and validation," *Academy of Management Journal*, 35: 505–38.

Godfrey, P. C., and Hill, C. W. L. (1995) "The problem of unobservables in strategic management research," *Strategic Management Journal*, 16: 519–33.

Golinski, J. (1998) *Making Natural Knowledge: Constructivism and the History of Science*. Cambridge: Cambridge University Press.

Hacking, I. (1999) *The Social Construction of What?* Cambridge, MA: Harvard University Press.

Hannan, M. T., and Freeman, J. (1977) "The population ecology of organizations," *American Journal of Sociology*, 82: 929–64.

Hardy, C., and Clegg, S. R. (1996) "Some dare call it power," in S. R. Clegg, C. Hardy, and W. R. Nord (eds) *Handbook of Organization Studies*, pp. 622–41. London: Sage.

Hirsch, P. M., and Levin, D. Z. (1999) "Umbrella advocates versus validity police: a life-cycle model," *Organization Science*, 10: 199–212.

Hunt, S. D. (1990) "Truth in marketing theory and research," *Journal of Marketing*, 54 (July): 1–15.

——(1993) "Objectivity in marketing theory and research," *Journal of Marketing*, 57 (April): 76–91.

——(1994) "A realist theory of empirical testing: resolving the theory-ladenness/objectivity debate," *Philosophy of the Social Sciences*, 24: 133–58.

Kimberly, J. R. (1976) "Organizational size and the structuralist perspective: a review, critique, and proposal," *Administrative Science Quarterly*, 21: 571–97.

Latour, B., and Woolgar, S. (1986) *Laboratory Life: The Construction of Scientific Facts*. Princeton, NJ: Princeton University Press.

McKelvey, B. (1997) "Quasi-natural organization science," *Organization Science*, 8: 352–80.

McKinley, W. (1995) "Commentary: 'Towards a reconciliation of the theory – pluralism in strategic management: incommensurability and the constructivist approach of the Erlangen school'," in P. Shrivastava and C. Stubbart (eds) *Advances in Strategic Management: Challenges from outside the Mainstream*, pp. 249–60. Greenwich, CT: JAI Press.

McKinley, W., and Mone, M. A. (1998) "The re-construction of organization studies: wrestling with incommensurability," *Organization*, 5: 169–89.

McKinley, W., and Scherer, A. G. (2000) "Some unanticipated consequences of organizational restructuring," *Academy of Management Review*, 25: 735–52.

McKinley, W., Mone, M. A., and Moon, G. (1999) "Determinants and development of schools in organization theory," *Academy of Management Review*, 24: 634–48.

Megill, A. (1991) "Four senses of objectivity," *Annals of Scholarship*, 8: 301–20.

Meyer, J. W., and Rowan, B. (1977) "Institutionalized organizations: formal structure as myth and ceremony," *American Journal of Sociology*, 83: 340–63.

Mizruchi, M. S., and Fein, L. C. (1999) "The social construction of organizational knowledge: a study of the uses of coercive, mimetic, and normative isomorphism," *Administrative Science Quarterly*, 44: 653–83.

Mone, M. A., and McKinley, W. (1993) "The uniqueness value and its consequences for organization studies," *Journal of Management Inquiry*, 2: 284–96.

Perreault, W. D., Jr, and Leigh, L. E. (1989) "Reliability of nominal data based on qualitative judgments," *Journal of Marketing Research*, 26: 135–48.

Pfeffer, J. (1993) "Barriers to the advance of organizational science: paradigm development as a dependent variable," *Academy of Management Review*, 18: 599–620.

——(1997) *New Directions for Organization Theory: Problems and Prospects*. New York: Oxford University Press.

Pickering, A. (1984) *Constructing Quarks: A Sociological History of Particle Physics*. Chicago: University of Chicago Press.

Pugh, D. S., Hickson, D. J., Hinings, C. R., and Turner, C. (1968) "Dimensions of organization structure." *Administrative Science Quarterly*, 13: 65–105.

Salancik, G. R., and Pfeffer, J. (1974) "The bases and use of power in organizational decision making: the case of a university," *Administrative Science Quarterly*, 19: 453–73.

Scandura, T. A., and Williams, E. A. (2000) "Research methodology in management: current practices, trends, and implications for future research," *Academy of Management Journal*, 43: 1248–64.

Scherer, A. G., and Dowling, M. J. (1995) "Towards a reconciliation of the theory – pluralism in strategic management: incommensurability and the constructivist approach of the Erlangen school," in P. Shrivastava and C. Stubbart (eds) *Advances in Strategic Management: Challenges from outside the Mainstream*, pp. 195–247. Greenwich, CT: JAI Press.

Shenhav, Y., Shrum, W., and Alon, S. (1994) "'Goodness' concepts in the study of organizations: a longitudinal survey of four leading journals," *Organization Studies*, 15: 753–76.

Simon, H. A. (1997) *Administrative Behavior: A Study of Decision-making Processes in Administrative Organizations*, fourth edition. New York: Free Press.

Thompson, J. D. (1967) *Organizations in Action: Social Science Bases of Administrative Theory*. New York: McGraw-Hill.

Tolbert, P. S., and Zucker, L. G. (1996) "The institutionalization of institutional theory," in S. R. Clegg, C. Hardy, and W. R. Nord (eds) *Handbook of Organization Studies*, pp. 175–90. London: Sage.

Williamson, O. E. (1981) "The economics of organization: the transaction cost approach," *American Journal of Sociology*, 87: 548–77.

Zald, M. N. (1993) "Organization studies as a scientific and humanistic enterprise: toward a reconceptualization of the foundations of the field," *Organization Science*, 4: 513–28.

——(1996) "More fragmentation? Unfinished business in linking the social sciences and the humanities," *Administrative Science Quarterly*, 41: 251–61.

5b From Objectivity to Subjectivity: Pursuing *Subjective Authenticity* in Organizational Research

Peter Case

Just another Case of the Techies versus the Fuzzies?

Every discipline, I suppose, is, as Nietzsche saw most clearly, constituted by what it *forbids* its practitioners to do. (Hayden White, 1978: 126, original emphasis)

In a recent appreciation of Hans-Georg Gadamer's contribution to Western thought, Richard Rorty puts a decidedly Californian spin on C. P. Snow's famous characterization of "the two cultures." Rorty (2000) suggests that the intellectual quarrel over science vs religion, or science vs the humanities might be better rendered in contemporary parlance as a dispute between "techies" and "fuzzies." I am bound to note that a methodological debate that takes as its core issue the differences between "objectivity" and "subjectivity" looks like being drawn into laboring a similar kind of divide. The editors' purposes in lining up protagonists and antagonists is understandable – it promises to make for stimulating copy – but I have to admit to feeling a little uneasy about this structural arrangement. Accordingly, in chapter 5(b) I rehearse and critically appraise some of the central features of the dualistic debates – positivist–constructivist, realist–nominalist, determinist–voluntarist, and, most particularly, objectivist–subjectivist – that presently mark the contours of methodological discourse both in organizational research and more generally in the social sciences. By sometimes describing, sometimes walking, and sometimes trying to dissolve the line that both separates and conjoins this techie–fuzzy dichotomy, author and reader in the process "discover" that the writer is a variety of fuzzy who wantonly celebrates transience, lack of fixity and the impossibility of permanent meaning closure within social scientific discourse. Through this deconstructionist–reconstructionist endeavor I seek to induce some implications concerning the methodological attitude of organizational researchers. What follows is intended as a self-exemplifying case for the pursuit of what I call *subjective authenticity* in the study of organization.

The first point I would like to make is that it is almost impossible to say something meaningful about method in the abstract, a fact that makes of this present enterprise a very difficult matter indeed. Some readers may note that this first move borrows directly from Wittgenstein's thoughts concerning the pragmatic nature of language and its context-dependent use. "Different 'interpretations' must correspond to different applications," he reminds us. In view of this initial claim I feel compelled, post-haste, to have recourse to a method suitable to the purposes of "stating a position." But what method to adopt? As ever, at times of difficulty, my wife has come to my aid with a perfect solution. She is a primary

school teacher and, among other projects, is offering government-funded remedial teaching in literacy to ten-year-olds. One device she routinely uses is called a "Persuasive Writing Frame." It is designed to help children (year six, UK; fifth grade, US) construct arguments and consists in a series of prompts which pupils are encouraged to respond to in writing. The method runs as follows: (1) "I think that . . . , because . . ." (2) "Other people may feel otherwise, that . . ." (state opposing view and reason), (3) "However, I think they are wrong, because . . ." (4) "A further point I would like to make is . . ." (5) "Finally, I think that . . . because . . . (summing up)." Wonderfully Aristotelian as it is, what method could be more apt for a contributor to a polemical book called *Debating Organisation*?

Confession of a Countermodernist

1 "I think that . . ."

Borrowing from the nomenclature outlined in chapter 3 on ontology, *I think that organizations are more fiction than fact.*

In a preliminary statement of position prior to publication of this chapter I engaged in the worryingly Freudian maneuver of reversing these two terms, so that the sentence as subconsciously rendered appeared in my chapter proposal as "I think that organizations are more fact than fiction." One obvious reading of this slip would be that I harbor a yearning to sign up to the kind of illusory certainties promised by positivist discourses that subscribe to the self-evident nature of objective facts; that a descent into the unnecessarily tortured complexities of poststructural textuality and subject positioning, not to mention insistence on the priority of nonrational embodied passions over cognitive processes, merely betrays a deeper and more profound commitment to objective reasoning. It is a possibility that demands consideration, not least by virtue of my own espousals concerning the importance of nonrationality in apprehending human and organizational motives (Case, 1996, 1999a). Viewed in an alternative light, however, the interchange of fact and fiction may not be quite so hypocritical or self-contradictory a slip as it first appears. For we learn from the *Oxford*

English Dictionary that the word "fact" derives from the Latin *facere*, meaning "to do," and that in sixteenth-century parlance it was still used to refer to actions or deeds, particularly those relating to crimes, a meaning that is reflected, for instance, in the contemporary legal phrase "after the fact." *Facere* also forms the basis of other contemporary words like "manufacture" and "factory," both implying the active, voluntary, and, in these cases, collective *doing* of agents. Daston (1994: 45) notes, moreover, that the emergence of "fact" as "a datum of experience, as distinguished from the conclusions that may be based on it" occurs around the time of, and may be attributed to, the writings of the seventeenth-century natural philosopher Francis Bacon. In short, facts as we now conceive of them had to be *invented*.

So I am quite happy that we treat these terms "fact" and "fiction" as interchangeable, provided we stick with the arcane usage of fact to refer to "action" as opposed to the more recent semantic accretion of "a thing that is known to have occurred, to exist, or to be true." In view of Foucault's ground-shifting historical study of institutional life in *Discipline and Punish* (1977), moreover, with its suggestion that all modern organizations be apprehended as forms of prison, we might also see some renewed felicity in the sixteenth-century correspondence between "facts" and criminal acts. Organizations most definitely are *factual*. They are the active, collective, and momentary accomplishments of agents, but they most definitely are *not* "things" – in an ontological sense – that enjoy some form of independent existence and about which ultimate or singular truths can be established. Such truth claims can and frequently are made. But they are no more than historically contingent and conditioned constructions of "reality."

As to *my* claim that organizations are "fictions," I mean this in the sense that the *Oxford English Dictionary* would have it for contemporary usage: "an invented idea or statement or narrative; an imaginary thing." Organizations as represented in linguistic, pictorial, and conceptual form and as rendered in our memories, imaginations, and reports of experience are *collective inventions*. They are mental constructs forged out of publicly shared languages and enjoy no existence independent of this fictional endeavor. To present them thus is not to trivialize or make light of the issue. Mind and imagination are extremely potent forces in the universe and are responsible for the multitude of socially constructed monsters whose tails we grasp only to have our hand bitten off in return; or, to mix metaphors, apparitions we conjure the better to scare ourselves into believing that we exist. The reification of organizations is perhaps an inevitable consequence of inhabiting a conceptually creative consciousness, but my point, by means of this playful exploration of fact and fiction, *facere* and *fictio*, is to warn the organizational researcher away from easy acceptance of and compliance with such reification.[1] Just to underline this point, a consideration of the etymology of fiction, and particularly acknowledgement of its Latin origins in *fictio* and *fictionis*, indicate a direct connotative relationship with the word "fictile," meaning "made of earth or clay." So the paradoxical outcome of our short philological diversion is the discovery that, in an historical sense, the factual is actually the invented and the fictitious is actually the existent thing. The sedimented conceptual and perceptual worlds we inhabit are not necessarily what they at first seem: as with fact and fiction, the elements of those worlds might carry converse meanings to those we take for granted. Now where does that leave my Freudian slip, or my opening assertion for that matter?

To reiterate, I think that organizations are more fiction than fact.

I also think that "constructivism" is a more persuasive philosophy of social science than its "neopositivist" counterpart (taking these terms as characterized by the editors in chapter 1 and the debate in chapter 4).

Following from these assertions, *I think that students of organization should seek out anthropocentric methods that reflect the fictive, momentary, and socially constructed character of organizational accomplishments.*

Now, by applying the method offered in the "Persuasive Writing Frame," you already find that you are contradicting yourself and producing something that is less than authentic. What you have just written, particularly the italicized script, reads like some kind of formal *tractatus* or canonical creed. This isn't at all what you intended – and while it may reflect some aspect of rational consciousness that is invoked when prompted by circumstances – for example, giving a research methodology seminar, justifying a methodological position, and so forth – it is not "what you think." You actually think that it is impossible to talk about method and methodology in the abstract; that it is always bounded by a specific research context, and that if we are to have a meaningful discussion it has to relate to a particular research question. But that will not do, either, because the very notion of a "research question" is indexical and dependent on the tradition or paradigm within which it is posed. Perhaps you had better start again.

I "I think that..."

I think that a discussion of research method and methodology should take place only in relation to the research question being posed, notwithstanding the fact that what constitutes (a) a meaningful research question and (b) an adequate form of explanation depends on, and is disciplined by, the research tradition within which it is framed.

This is a bit legislative in tone. You don't really like the "should" in the preceding sentence, but you'll live with it for the sake of argument. Also it implicitly proscribes the comparison of methods across disciplines and subdisciplines and suggests that any method is as good as any other, provided it makes sense within the structure of explanation of an established research paradigm. (See the debate in chapter 2.) Is that what you think? Well, in one sense, yes, and in another, no. On the one hand you want to endorse the kind of well established views about the structure of explanation voiced by Aaron Cicourel and Gunnar Myrdal in the 1950s and 1960s and which helped form part of the backdrop to later poststructural critiques of positivist and objectivist assumptions in social science. Consider, for example, Cicourel's (1964: 24) notion of the cultural "filtering" imposed by training in the traditions and tools of research of a given paradigm:

[W]e cannot afford to ignore the three media – language, cultural meanings, and properties of measurement systems – through which we formulate theoretically derived or *ad hoc* categories and link them with observable properties of objects and events . . . Each of the three media acts as a "grid" for defining and letting certain forms of "data" through to the observer. Each "grid" becomes a "filter" for what we come to perceive and interpret as its referent, its significance, and its logical status as a datum. Each "grid" or medium shapes or influences our perception and interpretation of our commonsense and scientific experiences. (Original emphases)

In Cicourel's vision of research there are no pre-existing objective data which may be apprehended as things in themselves. "Data" – or perhaps we might more properly speak of *capta* – are manufactured by the language, concepts, and tools of investigation through which a given research community apprehends the phenomenal world. Myrdal (1958: 153) makes a related and more general subjectivist point concerning the nature of scientific investigation:

Scientific facts do not exist *per se*, waiting to be discovered by scientists. A scientific fact is a construction abstracted from a complex and interwoven reality by means of arbitrary definitions and classifications. The processes of selecting a problem and a basic hypothesis, of limiting the scope of the study, and of defining and classifying data relevant to such a setting of the problem involve a choice on the part of the investigator. The choice is made from an indefinite number of possibilities.

This kind of argument fed into the nominalism and methodological anarchy associated with philosophers like Feyerabend (1975) and Rorty (1980). As with Cicourel and Myrdal in the preceding extracts, these thinkers contend that there are no objective facts accessible to dispassionate scientific methods; instead there are many ways of generating valid knowledge, of which empiricism is merely one. According to Feyerabend, moreover, innovative scientific knowledge derives not from conformity with theory or consensus agreement over method but from mistakes, disagreements, and ruptures in which the nonrational momentarily takes precedence over the rational. This state of affairs is not in need of remedy. Instead we should celebrate diversity and cultivate research environments in which may bloom a thousand methodological flowers, as it were.

So, on the one hand, yes, you do go along with methodological anarchy in so far as it prompts radical reflection, reassessment, and perpetual transition but, on the other, there is a danger that, taken to an extreme, this philosophy could promote an amoral, and potentially quite conservative, negative consensus. We all agree that anything goes. We all do our own thing, and that's okay. Such views you would want to contest. You actually think and feel quite strongly that the consequences of deploying some methods are less damaging and promote more good than others; that there is a political and moral dimension to the choices made by social scientific researchers. In producing discursive critiques of texts – social scientific or any other textual practice – one is asking searching questions about the ideology on which a given claim about the-way-things-are is based. The arguments over methodology in social science are arguments about discursive practice, about language. And language is never neutral. It is always and inescapably concerned with the attempt to seduce the reader into one possible interpretation of a situation over an infinite set of alternative possibilities. The methodological debate therefore turns on a fulcrum of power/knowledge (*pouvoir/savoir*), to use Foucault's (1980) expression. It is about who or what discourse and associated power/knowledge regime will prevail and hence what kind of reality will be collectively manufactured. Social scientific and everyday discourses that explicitly appeal to "objectivity," "factuality," "rationality," "reasonableness," and other such rhetorical devices deserve special attention from constructivist social scientists (Potter, 1996), since they invariably smack of powermongering and the peddling of a reality that suits their privileged purveyors. Is it not therefore appropriate that the textual strategies of the objectivists be subjected to critical exposure? What do you think?

Okay, let me try this one more time. Here goes . . .

I "I think that . . ."

I think that social scientific researchers (including organizational researchers) are moral beings who *reflect their morality in the choice and deployment of a given research methodology.*

I think that the privileging of objective knowledge over subjective knowledge is a misplaced value of modern society and should properly be the focus of critical deconstruction within a politically sensitized social scientific discourse. (There you go, moralizing again – you just can't help yourself.)

So far so good. You even feel confident enough to venture to the next element of your adopted "Persuasive Writing Frame."

. . . because . . .

Hmm. And it seemed to be going so well! With respect to the first thought you feel a distinct tautology coming on. You assume that we live in and help cocreate a moral universe. You also take it that moral choice (reflected in the role of language – particularly negation, "no," and its moral equivalent "thou shalt not") and the dualism to which it gives rise are one of the defining characteristics of human consciousness. As a corollary of this we collaborate and compete in the mutual construction, transformation, and destruction of social organizations. As to the second thought and assertion, it's time for another philological excursion . . .

How does it come about that the philosophy of social science and methodological research traditions are so often positioned in relation to one or other pole of an objectivity–subjectivity divide, and why are views concerning subject–object duality so hotly disputed? Methodology texts seldom dwell on the historical origins of this debate, preferring, instead, to caricature the respective differences in outlook. Rather than go down this route unthinkingly, let me indicate how the debate has been prefigured.

According to Bell (1994), Kant was the first philosopher to use the objective–subjective distinction in its modern sense of that which is "the object of perception or thought, as distinct from the perceiving or thinking subject," or that which "is, or has the character of being, a 'thing' [object] external to the mind [subject]" (*O.E.D.*, p. 643). It was in the late eighteenth and early nineteenth centuries that Kant's *Critique of Pure Reason* (first published in German in 1781) and other critical philosophy were translated into English and hence that the new meanings began to take root, although at this time they were less than stable. Datson (1994: 37) notes, for example, that, despite Coleridge making use of the Kantian objective–subjective distinction, his rendering was somewhat loose and used to connote a difference between the "material world," as narrowly understood, and "intelligence." During the early decades of the nineteenth century, she suggests, there was a tussle between the French term *positive* and the German *objektiv* and, for a time, it was unclear which would eventually lay claim over the semantic territory we now accept as "objective" or reflecting "objectivity." As it happened, the German won out and hence the modern subject–object, subjectivity–objectivity distinctions are English renderings of *objektiv–subjektiv* and *Objektivität–Subjektivität* respectively. It was not until the mid nineteenth century that the modern distinctions between these terms had become relatively sedimented.[2] Prior to Kant and the linguistic innovation that we have briefly mapped out, the ideas associated with the terms "objective" and "subjective" actually carried meanings *converse* to those of today. On this matter Bell (1994: 312) remarks:

[I]n the writings of the scholastics, Descartes, Spinoza, Berkeley and others – the contrast between objectivity and subjectivity had a quite different sense . . . In the pre-Kantian sense, for something to be objective, or for it to exist, objectively, was for it to comprise an idea, a mental representation, a content of consciousness. Conversely the adjective "subjective" was reserved, in Descartes's words, for "the reality that philosphers call actual or formal."

Interestingly, the phenomenological school of philosophy which grew up around Franz Brentano and, later, his student Edmund Husserl in the early twentieth century tended to use "objectivity" in this more arcane sense of referring to intrinsic properties of mental acts. They concerned themselves, among other things, with the intentionality inherent in ideas, that is, the knower's relationship to a mental object and volitions associated with it. This prompts Bell (1994: 312) to conclude that phenomenology "owes more to medieval scholasticism than to Kant's critical philosophy," which revelation carries important implications for the arguments being presented here.

In attempting to provide a philosophical justification for treating knowledge acquired through engagement with artistic and literary works, the feminist Lorraine Code (1987) effectively "rediscovers" the medieval inversion of the subjective–objective duality. She argues forcefully that works of literary fiction expose readers to a form of "knowledge by second-hand acquaintance" that immerses the reader in the world portrayed and facilitates *vicarious experience* of what it would be like to be exposed to a given set of circumstances in a particular historical era, or what it would be like to be a certain character encountering others in a particular milieu. Literature constructs a knowledge of human motives and lived emotion that is explicitly proscribed by the norms of scientific reportage and therefore offers an invaluable complement to rational discourse. "Knowledge thus achieved," she asserts, "is *objective* knowledge in a special sense that involves up-ending the traditional subjective–objective dichotomy. In this up-ended sense, scientific interest in a phenomenon is properly called 'subjective'. It is an investigation of use-value for the knower, who seeks to know the general, universal, standardized meaning phenomena [*sic*]. Art and literature, by contrast, seek to understand and express individuality and particularity. In this sense, they treat their object *objectively*, in and for itself" (1987: 207, original emphases). We find Code thus reinventing the subject–object world of the medieval scholastics and using it as a means of reasserting the value of *knowledge* deriving from art and literature – knowledge that is so often viewed as being less valid in a world where scientific empiricism enjoys such epistemological privilege.[3]

As with our earlier consideration of "fact" and "fiction," a little genealogical probing into the meaning of "objectivity" and "subjectivity" reveals these concepts in a different, not to say obverse, light. Understood in terms of their philosophical history, the two terms may be interchanged and used to refer to the other's contemporary semantic field – "subjective" substituting for "objective" and vice versa – while on phenomenological and pragmatic grounds, to follow Code's reasoning, a similar inversion of meaning also suggests itself. Now where does that leave my prescriptive assertion concerning the critique of objective knowledge? To remind you: "*I think that the privileging of objective knowledge over subjective knowledge is a misplaced value of modern society and should properly be the focus of critical deconstruction within a politically sensitized social scientific discourse."*

It no longer looks as safe as it did when first penned. Maybe you should not linger too long on this paradox: the confusion could be damaging to the flow of your argument. Better to keep moving on. After all, straw opponents presented in terms of taken-for-granted epistemological categories are more easily dealt with. You return to your "Persuasive Writing Frame" in order to get yourself back on intellectual track and fend off any impending uncertainty.

2 Other people may feel otherwise, that . . . (state opposing view and reason)

You do not have to look far to uncover scholars who adopt a quite different view, indeed, a directly contrary view to yours. There are people who: (a) think that organizations are more fact than fiction; (b) think that neopositivism is a more persuasive philosophy of social science than its constructivist counterpart; (c) think that students of organization should apply instrumental methods of measurement in their research, as they more fittingly reflect the objective facticity and tangible nature of organizational actions writ large; (d) think that any methodological debate need be confined merely to the technicalities of improving the instruments of statistical measurement and interpretation available within the ongoing consensus of a "normal science" research community; (e) believe in value-neutral, depersonalized, gender-neutral, apolitical, ahistorical research; and (f) assert the primacy and unassailability of objective scientific knowledge over any other epistemological possibility.

Yes, I have to admit that this is a caricature – a straw opponent conjured for the convenience of my argument – and that even the most flagrant card-carrying objectivist would want to detract from or qualify some of the assertions just paraded. Or would they? Reading the views in chapter 5(a), it would appear that a strident objectivism remains central to certain organization theory agendas. And my counterpart is not alone in adopting this line of

reasoning. In a self-declaratory chapter entitled "The normal science of structural contingency theory," for example, Donaldson (1999) sets out an assertive and confident case for an objectivist theory and science of organizations. I do not wish to explicate that case in detail here – Donaldson does so perfectly well in this and in many other publications.[4] My purpose is simply to indicate how his characterization of contingency theory conforms to a marked extent to the extreme objectivist position to which I allude. Some years ago Burrell and Morgan (1979) produced a helpful dualistic scheme for contrasting subjectivist and objectivist approaches to social science, as in table 5.1. In terms of these conceptual criteria, Donaldson espouses a realist, positivist, determinist position that favors the application of nomothetic methods. His work, along with that of the contingency theorists he represents, may be located exclusively on the right-hand side of the table, a claim that is consistent with statements made about the "normal science of structural contingency theory." For example, the appropriate unit of analysis, Donaldson informs us, is the organization considered as a reified, discrete entity capable of action in its own right and independent of the individuals who comprise "it." In setting out a theoretical model for structural contingency research he states:

[T]he analysis is depersonalized and at the level of the organization as a collective entity pursuing its objectives. (1999: 58)

The theory and empirical evidence deployed in the structural contingency theory paradigm are positivist. (Ibid.: 57)

The theory is sociological functionalism (Burrell and Morgan, 1979). Just as biological functionalism explains the way the organs of the human body are

Table 5.1   The subjective–objective dimension

The subjectivist approach		*The objectivist approach*
Nominalism	Ontology	Realism
Antipositivism	Epistemology	Positivism
Voluntarism	Human nature	Determinism
Ideographic	Methodology	Nomothetic

structured so as to contribute to human well-being, so sociological functionalism explains social structures by their functions, that is, their contributions to the well-being of society. (Ibid.: 56)

Within this theory of organizations, the behavior of organizational entities is determined and involuntaristic. There is a tacit adoption of the Aristotelian concept of efficient causation applied to *social* facts, whereby variations in reified and discrete factors or "contingencies," such as "organizational size," "technology," and "strategy," are treated as independent variables that *cause* changes in a dependent variable, namely organizational structure:

The organization is seen as being forced to adjust its structure to material factors such as size and technology. (Ibid.: 57)

Within this research community, the role of conceptual theorizing and creativity is deliberately attenuated in order that a normal science consensus may be formed around a narrower set of causal factors (cf. the views of my counterpart). This permits the construction of "depersonalized" laws that govern the relationship between the dependent and independent variables. It would seem that the occlusion of agency and subjectivity from the structural contingency framework, far from detracting from the credibility of the account it offers of organizational behavior, is something to be coveted. To quote Donaldson again:

Ideas and values do not figure [as] prominently as causes. Moreover, little scope is seen for choice or human volition. There is little information in most contingency analyses about who exactly makes the structural decisions or what their motives are or how the structures are implemented (Pugh et al., 1969; Blau and Schoenherr, 1971) . . . There is thus the absence of an analysis at the level of the human actors. (Ibid.: 57)

Nomothetic methods are employed to investigate the causal relationships between the dependent and independent variables. Here, for illustrative purposes, is part of Donaldson's description of a simple empirical research design following the work of Woodward (1965):

A comparative study is made across a number of different organizations . . . Each contingency and structural factor is measured, either as a quantitative

scale or as a series of ordered categories. Each organization is allotted a score on each contingency and structural factor. The cross-distribution of scores of the organizations on a pair of contingency and structural factors is then examined to see whether there is an association; this is done by cross-tabulation or correlation. The theory that associations between contingency and structure reflect an underlying fit is then tested. Organizations conforming to the association are contrasted with those that deviate. If the conforming organizations outperform the deviant organizations then this signifies that the association is a fit between contingency and structure. (Ibid.: 57)

He goes on to describe more sophisticated designs that nonetheless conform to a positivist hypothetico-deductive framework and which are consistent with the overall theoretical outlook represented in this extract. My point is that we see in the work of Donaldson and fellow positivists a set of views intended to define what is to count as orthodox research in contemporary organizational studies. As my counterpart acknowledges, it is a *prescriptive* (and therefore morally normative) bid to discipline the field.

3 However, I think they are wrong because . . .

I asked Lotaria if she has already read some books of mine that I lent her. She said no, because here she doesn't have a computer at her disposal.

She explained to me that a suitably programmed computer can read a novel in a few minutes and record the list of all the words contained in the text, in order of frequency. "That way I can have an already completed reading at hand," Lotaria says, "with an incalculable saving of time. What is the reading of a text, in fact, except the recording of certain thematic recurrences, certain insistences of forms and meanings? An electronic reading supplies me with a list of the frequencies, which I have only to glance at to form an idea of the problems the book suggests to my critical study. Naturally, at the highest frequencies the list records countless articles, pronouns, particles, but I don't pay them any attention. I head straight for the words richest in meaning; they can give me a fairly precise notion of the book.

Lotaria brought me some novels electronically transcribed, in the form of words listed in the order of their frequency. "In a novel of fifty to a hundred thousand words," she said to me, "I advise you to observe immediately the words that are repeated about twenty times. Look here. Words that appear nineteen times: blood, cartridge belt, commander, do, have, immediately, it, life, seen, sentry, shots, spider, teeth, together, your . . . Words that appear eighteen times: boys, cap, come, dead, eat, enough, evening, French, go handsome, new, passes, period, potatoes, those, until . . .

Perhaps instead of a book I could write lists of words, in alphabetical order, an avalanche of isolated words which expresses that truth I still do not know, and from which the computer, reversing its program, could construct the book, my book. (Calvino, 1998: 186–9)

Perhaps instead of an account of organizational conduct I could produce a matrix of numbers, an avalanche of isolated figures (figure 5.2) which express that truth I still do not know ("trust" for "construct 3" is – 0.02), and from which the computer, reversing its program, could construct the organization; the *human* organization of my studies.

Lotaria shows me another series of lists. "This is an entirely different genre," she says, "it's immediately obvious. Just look at the list of words that recur about twenty times: analysis, data, explanation, structural, correlation (twenty), method, organization (nineteen), analyze, contingency, functional, models, multidivisional, statistical, structure (eighteen), administration, effectiveness, fit, strategy, theory (seventeen) . . . and words that appear less frequently: analyzing, cause, computing, general, objective, regression, survey (nine), analysis, decision, effects, measures, methodology, response, social, scientists, significance, valid (eight), multiple, questionnaires, varies, variance (seven) . . . down to those that make only two or three appearances: bias, generalised, linear, random, reliability, sampling, series, time, validity (3), mapping, parametric, test, testing (two), anova, cluster, clusters, loglinear, multivariate (one).

You see? Isn't it revealing? No need for any complex hermeneutic interrogation. This system cuts directly to the chase, yielding only the purest reductive precipitate. It takes you to the essence of a particular author's *métier* without any of the distracting theoretical overlay. Away with Coleridge. Away with Richards, with Leavis, with Lévi-Strauss, Barthes, Derrida, Said and the rest. Let's compute the critique. Let's get down to the calculative, essential, objective truth.[5]

4 A further point I would like to make is . . .

(You make more than one – You never were any good at sticking strictly to a prescribed "method.")

Nowadays to be intelligible is to be found out. (Oscar Wilde, 1892/1973: 9)

The reporting of objectivist research is invariably a *literary accomplishment* that relies on denying, mystifying, or masking its dependence on communicative acts in the construction of what it wants to pass off as revealed truths or facts that transcend sheer textual performance. Thomas Nagel (1986) coined a phrase to describe this characteristic feature of objectivist science and social science when he talked of the attempt to construct nonperspectival accounts of reality. The resulting "view from nowhere" is achieved by scrupulous and exclusive adherence to the use of the third-person voice in the reporting of methods and findings. By eliminating the first-person singular and plural a given objectivist discourse creates the *impression* of being an ideologically neutral, dispassionate, and nonsubjective account of actuality. The reporting is manufactured in such a way that it appears representative of consensus views shared by a *community* of researchers. To use Donaldson's (1999) text as a representative anecdote once again, he uses third-person textual moves like "Strategic choice theory argues that . . ." (p. 62), instead of "I argue that . . . ," or "the data were analysed . . . (p. 60) in favor of "I analyzed the data," and so on. This grammatical choice prevents "contamination" of the text with personal, partial, and potentially passionate perspectives that speak against the transcendental, objective, non-ideological relating of-the-way-things-are. Westwood (1999) refers to this rhetorical sleight of hand from a Foucauldian perspective as "the disguise of discourse." As he construes it:

Discourses are assertively definitive, declaring their truth-value and authority. But they rest on incorrigible propositions, and ontological and epistemic assumptions. They rely on an ideological-rhetorical practice which functions to present the claims of the discourse as self-evident, "natural," non-arbitrary representations of reality. This masks the will to power in discourse, which is the appropriation of the undecidable, the inscription of a bounded and ordered topography, and a closure of meaning. (1999: 221)

I am not making a blanket prescription to the effect that all third-person reporting should be eschewed. It is a perfectly useful grammatical

Table 2 Descriptive Statistics and Correlations Among Constructs

Construct	Mean	S.D.	1	2	3	4	5	6	7	8	9	10	11	12	13	14
Strategic Flexibility																
1. Modification	4.24	1.66														
2. Exit	4.37	1.97	0.20													
Transaction Cost Economics																
3. Asset Specificity-Intangible	36.41	25.14	-0.37	-0.63												
4. Asset Specificity-Tangible	29.25	22.36	-0.33	-0.31	0.19											
5. Balanced Asset Specificity – Intangible	28.78	13.31	0.42	0.13	0.18	0.24										
6. Balanced Asset Specificity – Tangible	32.24	22.11	0.14	0.19	0.19	0.21	0.26									
7. Hostages	0.84	0.37	0.55	0.11	0.22	0.17	0.12	0.08								
Social Exchange Theory																
8. Trust	4.09	1.44	0.69	0.47	-0.02	0.11	0.33	0.29	0.46							
9. Influence	3.88	1.42	0.40	0.06	-0.13	-0.14	-0.08	0.09	0.07	0.40						
10. Alternatives	3.19	2.04	0.13	0.32	0.07	0.18	0.13	0.19	-0.01	0.15	0.08					
11. Importance	4.32	1.84	0.07	0.45	0.02	0.08	0.09	0.13	-0.24	0.11	0.10	0.12				
12. Previous Relations	5.12	3.31	0.11	-0.27	0.06	0.10	-0.01	0.21	0.27	0.17	0.11	-0.13	-0.28			
13. Attachment	52.46	36.20	0.34	-0.44	-0.01	0.05	0.03	-0.06	0.09	0.04	-0.01	-0.07	0.05	-0.22		
14. Communication	4.79	1.50	0.60	0.51	-0.14	0.04	-0.23	-0.16	0.35	0.79	0.18	0.04	-0.17	0.17	0.09	
15. Shared Values	4.82	1.53	0.71	0.42	-0.16	0.21	0.02	0.17	0.51	0.77	0.28	0.08	-0.15	0.21	-0.04	0.46

Figure 5.2 An example of organization science. Source Young-Ybarra and Wiersema (1999: 452)

device, used judiciously. I merely want to point out that all accounts of research are "ideological-rhetorical," as Westwood would have it, and should be acknowledged as such. It is the implicit deceit entailed in rigid adherence to a convention of third-person reporting that I am objecting to and which I think should be discounted in favor of a more honest textual strategy; one that reflexively acknowledges its dependence on literary maneuvers and, where appropriate, lays bare its subjective origins.

Another literary concomitant of the choice to buy into an objectivist "view from nowhere" is the need to develop what might be called the *style of nonstyle*. In order to communicate a sense of no-nonsense solidity and certainty in respect of the factual knowledge being related, objectivist texts are obliged, in the main, to be stylistically unambitious, prosaic, and functional. Practitioners of this rhetorical art are required to avoid colorful imagery, poetic allusion, or the conscious deployment of literary tropes (with the possible exception of the occasional explanatory metaphor). Jo Gusfield (1976: 20–1) in his seminal article on the rhetoric of positivist social science characterized the style as follows:

[T]he language must be emptied of feeling and emotion. The tone must be clinical, detached, depersonalized. [The author's] language must not be "interesting," his (*sic*) descriptions colorful or his words a clue to any emotion which might be aroused in the audience . . . The language is deliberate, nonevocative, meticulous and limited in imagery. It informs the reader that the persuasion is to come from an external reality, not from the author or his use of language . . . We, the audience, are to think and not to feel.

The result is a stream of social scientific literature that would have to be judged at best "dull" by any self-respecting literary critic (witness, for example, most contributions to the *Academy of Management Review*). This seems to me to be a very great pity and lost opportunity. Social science, after all, supposedly deals with collective *human conduct* and motives (although, as we have seen, the claims of structural contingency theorists together with the prescriptions concerning "levels of analysis" advocated by my counterpart seem to challenge even this rudimentary assumption).

Organizational life is vital, contentious, artistic, poetic, and uncertain. Sometimes comic, sometimes tragic, on occasions compelling, on others less so, it is constant testimony to the creative and destructive genius of humankind. Should not the discourse of social science therefore mirror that vitality and textural variability in its multifarious accounts of organizational life?

The objectivist says nay to this proposition. S/he makes a more or less conscious decision to go the route of deathly analysis. "Concepts kill," as Burrell (1998, 1999) reminds us. "Analysis of almost any kind," he asserts, "requires the death or at least the mutilation of that which is analysed" (1999: 391).[6] While endorsing this observation, I would want to add an important qualification: concepts *can* kill, analysis *may* mutilate. There is a profound difference, I contend, between the scientistic reduction and reification of reality characteristic of positivist social science and the poetic *representation* engaged in by its constructivist counterpart. The former is concerned explicitly with what Weber (1948/1970: 139) described as the "disenchantment of the world," or with the phallocentric domination of nature, to invoke a more contemporary idiom (Burrell, 1998), whereas, at its best, the latter takes as its remit the critical interrogation of collective idiocy, misadventure, injustice, or (less often, admittedly) the celebration of achievements and ideals.

The choice of neopositivist ontology, epistemology, and method – in so far as one can meaningfully generalize about the associated structure of explanation – is morally dubious, in my opinion. I think this because it almost invariably entails a reductive and instrumental translation of human acts and interaction into quantitative form for the purposes of calculation and manipulation (Porter, 1997). In short, following the kinds of arguments mobilized by Winch (1970) and Giddens (1976), I consider it morally undesirable to apply natural scientific methods to social scientific and organizational phenomena. And, for the sake of further provocation, let me suggest that there is even a *neurotic* quality to the positivist insistence that organization phenomena be made to dance to the instrumental tune of its technocalculative devices. For the objectivist is seeking closure and fixity in a social world whose inherent transience and fluctuation simply frustrate this ambition at every turn. To persist in the pursuit of stability in the face of relentless instability is neurotic (and by this token we are almost *all* neurotic, present voice included). This egocentric urge to impose one's infantile desire for certainty on the world is picked up by Kenneth Gergen in his political and moral critique of objectivism. Gergen (1994: 283) considers the instrumentality of objectivist discourse to be a reflection of a wider cultural pattern of possessive individualism:

Not only does the discourse of objectivity generate and sustain unwarranted hierarchies of privilege – along with an accompanying array of prejudices, hostilities and conflicts – but many voices are thereby excluded from full participation in the culture's constructions of the good and the real. The conceptual underpinnings of objective language also give it a hegemonic thrust: it fails to reveal the problematics of its own origins, and wages war on all non-objective languages. The rich and varied array of alternative linguistic forms – pragmatic resources garnered from the culture's history – are thus placed under threat. They are to be replaced with a language that celebrates the sedimented common sense of *status quo* reality, and which favors forms of social isolation and self-seeking. In effect, the discourse of objectivity is yet another prop in the much-criticized ideology of possessive individualism.

I admit that all science is reductive, even the kind of social science and social-science-fiction that I am advocating. My concern is over the nature of those reductive acts and the implications they carry, both for those *re*presented and those doing the representation. My own preference, for example, is for seeing all acts – including methodological ones – in rhetorical and narrative terms. As soon as we move from the realm of sheer phenomenological sensation – "heat," "cold," "visual form and color," "sound," "sweetness," etc. – into that of representation – "I feel hot," "This honey tastes sweet," and so on – we are dealing with narratives, we are into the realm of storytelling (Gabriel, 2000; Czarniawska, 1997a, b, 1999). Storytelling implies perspective, and perspective implies relativity. Relativity implies the absence of objectivity which, in turn, implies the possibility of contention, conflict, and

agonistic[7] debate (of the sort we have in this book). Where there are multiple perspectives, there are persuasive attempts on the part of one to convince another or others of the wrongness of their ways and the rightness of her own. In short, we can, for practical purposes, reduce all acts of representation to acts of *rhetoric* with associated moral value and impetus. Commenting on C. Wright Mills's critique of "abstracted empiricism," for example, the American literary critic and social theorist Kenneth Burke observes:

There has always been somewhat of a sociology along that line, whatever it may be called, whenever there have been administrators – and if this age were not so pervasively characterized by a technological psychosis, much that is now called by its advocates or practitioners a "science" of "human engineering" (with its ideals of "prediction" and "control") might be viewed as an extension of classical rhetoric's observations on the "art" of persuasion. (1984: 407–8)

Adopting a rhetorical outlook of this sort carries the advantage of enabling the social scientist who subscribes to a broadly constructivist structure of explanation to analyze moves being made in a particular discourse or narrative and consider its espoused intentions, impact, and possible ramifications *from a critical perspective*.

In a positivist world of technocalculative translation and reduction, critique is reduced to "yes" or "no" – "accept" or "reject." It is either additional and valid factual knowledge or it is not. This epistemological attitude has a lengthy heritage, owing much to Aristotelian logic and the law of excluded middle. Consider, for example, Aristotle's definitions of falsity and truth in the *Metaphysics* (Book IV, chapter 7): "To say of what is that it is not, or of what is not that it is, is false, while to say of what is that it is, and of what is not that it is not, is true."[8] This attitude sets in train an empiricist program that is bent on establishing means by which the middle may be excluded and "what is" and "what is not" may be established with supposed certainty. Yet this process of excluding the middle marks more than a simple intellectual device, for it also gives the lie to more broadly discriminatory *social* practices. The "either"/"or" logical form is isomorphic with the social discrimination entailed in identity work.[9] By excluding the uncertainty of a middle ground we are able to establish who we are: nominalist or realist, constructivist or positivist, subjectivist or objectivist, fuzzy or techie. If we are not one, then we have by definition to be the other.[10] Moreover, the positivist's "is" or "is not" has a corresponding constructivist equivalent in the form of the moral imperative of "ought" or "ought not." Along with each identity comes a set of social obligations that prescribe how we should conduct ourselves; for instance, what to do in order to pass as a competent "objectivist" and how to pull off being a good "subjectivist" organizational researcher. Our Greco-Roman inheritance results in our playing rigged language games as far as both logical possibilities and identity work are concerned (and hence the many vocal resistances and detractions of those writing in poststructural and postmodern idioms).[11]

(Once you view the law of excluded middle in this light you see better how it prefigures modern intellectual debate, including the dualistic structures of your adopted "Persuasive Writing Frame" and those more generally of the current volume, with their emphasis on contested points of view and provocative juxtaposition. Although you may have attempted to wobble the framework a little its momentum is far too great for anything of serious consequence to derive from your philological and epistemological gymnastics. The duality is here to stay, and you find yourself inexorably drawn back into playing the very language game that you have struggled to discredit.)

In certain constructivist traditions there is much greater scope and license for the researcher to engage in a *reflexive* questioning and reporting of his or her own choices of method and their implications. The researcher's hands are not tied to an idealistic (and fantastic) post of value-free objectivity and hence s/he is not saddled with what I infer to be an incumbent sense of "inauthenticity." (I refer to the positivist researcher *qua* subject, knowing at some level – albeit perhaps quite deeply repressed – that s/he is by virtue of her humanity "contaminating" both the design and the results through acts of choice. It is a direct intuitive apprehension of the hypocrisy of

trying to sustain "the view from nowhere.") Whereas methodological issues for the positivist entail technical choices of *means* within a rubric of "normal science," certain constructivist discourses permit the researcher to engage in a form of critical metamethodology. The latter may legitimately scrutinize their own motivational calculus and examine how – through autobiographical interrogation, for example – it has influenced their methodological choices (although, of course, these acts are no less subject to disciplinary norms and the need for indexical positioning than those who suppose themselves to be conducting normal science in a positivist paradigm. Only the *criteria* of judgment employed by the research community differ. The boundaries are being policed just the same.) This is how Hardy and Clegg (1999: 383) construe the reflexive obligations of constructivist researchers:

> We must also acknowledge the researcher's arrival within the circle, not as a neutral observer, but as an implicated participant. This requires a greater awareness of who the researcher is and where he or she comes from. Researchers must make clear how they access and interpret "subjectivities" and outline methodological protocols . . . We must expose both our analysis and interpretations and our theoretical assumptions to the same kind of analysis.

Furthermore, the constructivist is at liberty to deploy (*intentionally*) in her interpretative endeavors the entire scope of natural language, with all the dramatic possibilities that brings. There is no bar to the use of comic irony, tragedy, pathos, satire, burlesque, grotesque, or any other genre that serves her interpretative purposes. In short, the subtlety, complexity, and artful sophistication of the organizational world may be more appropriately mirrored using the linguistic tools at the disposal of the constructivist than in the impaired (in representational terms) and attenuated language of positivist discourse. It is a matter of favoring *poetic* representation over *scientistic* reduction and creating a social scientific genre in which the only limitations are the sensibility, creativity, and narrative skill of the researcher. The implication of this is, of course, that the exploration of collective human motives – which is how I would characterize "organizational studies" in the last analysis – may usefully borrow and be judged by the methods of research and critique employed in areas of the arts and humanities not normally associated with social scientific inquiry. There is often greater insight into human organization to be had from studying works of literature than from the unadventurous and tedious textual rubble found in most journals that proffer the standard fare of "organizational science." When it comes to deriving insight into human organization give me works by Joyce, Borges, Lessing, Mamet, or Calvino over any number of articles published in the *Academy of Management Journal* or *Management Science*. I am being deliberately provocative, but my point is that we might usefully bring the tools of literary and cultural criticism to the assessment of research and reporting the world of organizational studies (Case, 1999b).

6

(You mean 5. Numeracy was never a strength of yours.)

5 Finally, I think that . . .

All in all constructivists are, in principle, better placed to maintain *authentic* relationships within their inner and outer life-world (*Lebenswelt*). They don't have to pretend they are doing something – offering a "view form nowhere" – that they patently are not. They have greater license to come clean; admit to the inherent subjectivity of acts of interpretation and engage in the task of persuasion in a conscious and openly critical manner. My sense is that the majority of researchers subscribing to positivist traditions of various forms do not want and/or are not permitted such subjective transparency.

. . . because . . . (summing up)

These are the conclusions to which my own biography, disposition, and research training has led me.[12]

One *cannot* speak the truth – if one has not yet conquered oneself. One *cannot* speak it – but not because one is still not clever enough. (Wittgenstein, in Von Wright, 1994: 46, original emphases)

Here Wittgenstein alludes, with a typically mind-bending twist, to the Socratic dictum "Know thyself." I warrant that few, if any, of us will ever be able to "speak the truth" according to this exacting standard. But I presume that most researchers, including the organizational variety, do what they do because they have an interest in "truth," "understanding," "wisdom," however they might interpret the possibilities connoted by such terms. I think that the traditions contributing to positivist organizational studies certainly afford the opportunity of making one "clever" but, by their very construction and intention, are less likely to promote anything beyond superficial insight and knowledge. To quote Wittgenstein again, "The truth can be spoken only by someone who is already *at home* in it; not by someone who still lives in untruthfulness, and does no more than reach out towards it from within untruthfulness" (Von Wright, 1994: 41, original emphasis). Reflexive constructivists at least enjoy the opportunity of reaching out from a position of *subjective authenticity*. (This is what I interpret Wittgenstein as meaning by being at home with the truth.) In other words, they are able in principle to be as truthful to themselves and as transparent about their research motives and methods *as is possible at the time they commit themselves to writing*.[13] They are at least on the starting blocks as far as the pursuit of truths is concerned.

Lotaria hands you one final list generated by her computer. Both gesture and result are transparent. You can see right through the author in question: constructivism, constructivist, epistemology, objectivity, research, science, social (twenty-one), epistemological, fact, knowledge, organization, organizational, positivist (twenty), collective, conscious, counter, critical, fiction, interpretative, method, methodology, organizations, structure, subjective, subjectivity, view (nineteen) . . . critique, discourse, Donaldson, dualism, dualistic, literary, logic, means, narrative, nominalist, nowhere, object, point, power, truth, universe, Wittgenstein (five) . . . achieved, adopt, agency, authentic, authenticity, Calvino, closure, Code, confession, deconstruction, Derrida, determinist, facticity, Foucault, persuasive, phenomenological, politics, reflexive, Rorty (two), anthropocentric, Californian, canonical, counterpoint, creed, deconstructionist, determinist, feminist, fictive, Gadamer, Hans-Georg, hermeneutic, ideographic,

Lex, Morgan, neurotic, nomothetic, persuasion, politics, psychosis, reflexivity, reportage, Richard, Snow's, tractatus (one).

Interview with a Countermodernist

Editor. Well, first of all, may I say thanks for sharing your thoughts on the issue of objectivity versus subjectivity in organization studies research and thanks also for agreeing to be interviewed about the chapter you've written.

Peter Case. The pleasure's all mine. You're most welcome.

Editor. Let me start by saying that I enjoyed reading through your text – I liked the attention you paid to the style of prose, I thought your choice of structure was amusing yet effective in conveying the points you wanted to make. Personally, I found myself in sympathy with the main thrust of your argument and found the notion of subjective authenticity intuitively appealing. The play on the etymology of fact and fiction was really engaging, for *me*, and I think there's real mileage in substituting –

Case. Well, it's kind of you to –

Editor. – the notion of *capta* for *data* in epistemological and methodological debate.

Case. – to say such kind things about my work. I can feel my face becoming quite flushed with embarrassment. But my guess is that –

Editor. Yeah. There were some parts of the chapter that I thought were a bit obscure and would benefit from further elaboration and clarification. I *do* want, therefore, to quiz you on some aspects of what you've written.

Case. Fine. Fine. I quite understand. Fire away.

Editor. Okay. So, first off, it struck me that you've devoted much more time and space to a critique of objectivism and positivism and done less to explicitly make the case for your own subjectivist–fictive position. It seems to me that the balance was slightly wrong here and that you could have done more to spell out your substantive points.

Case. Hm. Yes, I agree it's a shame if that's how the work came over. That wasn't my intention. I'd hoped to produce an account that balanced point and counterpoint, despite my own reservations about this structure. But to pick up explicitly on the notion of "substantive points" that you raise, I guess one of the main claims I'm trying to make or, more properly, *establish* is that there are no "substantive points" in the realm of discourse. What I attempted to do in this chapter was produce a narrative that *demonstrated* its case for subjective authenticity rather than *stated* it *per se*. There is an important difference between the two, in my view. I wanted to map, as closely as I could without potentially boring the reader, the kind of phenomenological struggle I went through in writing about the subjectivity–objectivity dialectic and to reflect the doubts and detractions that came up in my own mind as I worked through the problem. If you like, it's the textual equivalent of showing your working when solving a maths problem or deriving a statistical proof. I wanted to *show* how I arrived at the position. Now, of course, I did this by deploying a comic–ironic device. I came out with a series of bald statements, using a rudimentary writing frame in order then to ponder and, in places, deconstruct the claims being made. But, hey, I don't want anyone to go away disappointed having read my work. So if you'd like to nail me down to a decidable position then why not just treat the propositions I came out with at face value? (*Reads from his own text.*)

I think that organizations are more fiction than fact. I think that constructivism is a more persuasive philosophy of social science than its neopositivist counterpart. I think that students of organization should seek out anthropocentric methods that reflect the fictive, momentary, and socially constructed character of organizational accomplishments. I think that a discussion of research method and methodology should take place only in relation to the research question being posed. I think that social scientific researchers (including organizational researchers) are moral beings who reflect their morality in the choice and deployment of a given research methodology. I think that the privileging of objective knowledge over subjective knowledge is a misplaced value of modern society and should properly be the focus of critical deconstruction within a politically sensitized social scientific discourse.

I find it hard to imagine a more affirmative statement of position. In fact, summarized like this it sounds like some form of hideous credo and conjures in one's imagination hordes of organizational research students in institutions across the globe engaged in a collective morning recital of the canon before they set out to do their fieldwork or venture into the library for the day. If you want decidability, well, here it is. If, however, you want the grown-up version I'm afraid you'll have to live with the qualifications, uncertainties, and self-doubts of the chapter in full. The chapter *represents* my process rather than my "position" . . . I'm not sure whether I've answered –

Editor. Yes. Yes, I think you have . . .

Case. – your question?

Editor. You have. But I'm not convinced entirely . . . You say you're uneasy about the debate structure. You're not the only one. Steve Linstead has written a closing chapter, "Against debate," that, not entirely surprisingly, given the working title, engages in a critical deconstruction of the notion of debate and argues that debate is more about the construction and reconstruction of the self than mutual exchange and understanding . . .

Case. Yes. I've spoken with Steve Linstead about this project and there are, perhaps understandably, quite a few resonances between his critique and my own concerns. Although, having said that, Steve is deploying a slightly different set of theoretical tools – Derrida's discussion of the Pharmakon and Plato's *Phaedrus*, Baudrillard's views on identity formation drawn from *Cool Memories*, and so on – different tools than I use in my chapter.

Editor. Yes. Okay. Different tools, but I was hoping *you* might want to say just briefly why *you're* uneasy with the debate structure.

Case. Okay . . . Let me think . . . I suppose my problem, like Steve's, is basically philosophical. It has to do with the way in which the cultural expectations of debate and the rhetorical strategies associated with it are rigged in such a way that there's rarely a genuine meeting of hearts and minds for the interlocutors concerned. The outcome of debate is much more likely to be the entrenchment of antagonist and mutually incompatible views than a reassessment and reappraisal of one's ideas brought about by the other's argument. In other words, mutual incomprehension is a more likely outcome of the conventional academic debating process than is shared understanding. I think that's the danger of what's happening

here, in this very chapter. There, I've been brief. Is that brief enough?

Editor (laughs). Concisely put. Thanks. Okay. Another thing I want to pick you up on is your statement that we cannot really talk about methodology in the abstract. I feel this needs a bit more elaboration . . .

Case. Well, to do so would be to be seduced into the very thing I'm trying to resist, namely talking about methodology in the abstract. But I've a feeling you're not going to let me off the hook that lightly . . .

Editor. Nope.

Case. Okay. My point is this, basically: the specific kind of method that one employs is going to be dictated by the form of question being posed. In other words – and here I'm improvising on Wittgenstein's remarks concerning the nature of philosophical problems – in other words, the structure of explanation is going to follow logically from the framing of the problematic, both of which are dictated by the cultural codes of the language community within which the questions are posed and explanations rendered. That's a clumsy way of saying that I think the debate over *method* cannot take place without having already established the *question*. The form of the question will inform the method of inquiry and hence the *capta* that result. Incidentally, that's why I conjured up an expedient method – the persuasive writing frame – in my chapter just so that I could talk about objectivity and subjectivity within a self-reflexive – and in this case *ironic* – framework . . .

[*Much later in the dialogue* . . .]

Editor. Fairly early on in your chapter you talk about moral choice embodying a dualism. The meaning of that is not immediately apparent to me. Could you elaborate?

Case. Of course. I'm just taking it as axiomatic that morality is dualistic. For me, morality is intimately bound up with representation and the operation of certain forms of language. Moral choice is a defining characteristic of human consciousness, facilitated, propagated, and perpetuated by shared languages. Morality seems – in my admittedly limited knowledge and experience – to be a universal feature of social systems, and this is linked, I would contend, with universal features of language.

Our social awareness of morality is shaped by our social understanding of language. So for every "thou shalt" that we can consciously give form to there are corresponding "thou shalt nots" of which we are equally conscious. Correspondingly there is a duality between conforming to the expectations of a given language community –

Editor. But – But –

Case. – and not conforming to those expectations . . .

Editor. But aren't you resurrecting a rather outmoded humanist notion of self in saying that we have moral choices.

Case. Yes. I accept that I am and acknowledge that there is an enormously complex set of past and present supporting conditions that are brought to bear in any moment of choice – perhaps even unspeakably complex. But, that said, if we are talking about a dualistic world in which humans exist – and I fully recognize that many contemporary discourses want to blur the line between the human and the nonhuman – but in *this* dialogue I am talking about a world in which organizational studies researchers make methodological choices . . . in that world we are obliged to imbue actors with dualistic moral agency. We can choose *this* method over *that* method. Whether or not we can ethically justify that choice is, of course, another matter, and what I'm supplying in this chapter is a contribution to a vocabulary within which choices can be explained and justified – or not, of course, if you chose to reject what I'm offering!

Editor. Yes. I can't say I'm entirely convinced by your explanation of the need to reassert moral agency. It seems a bit simpleminded . . .

Case. Well I'm a simple soul, you know. I'll take being called simpleminded as a compliment. [*Both laugh.*]

Editor. . . . but there we are . . . There was another section of your chapter I wanted to pick up on: the Lotaria story and accompanying table. It remains a little obscure to me. Could you illuminate the point of this a tad further?

Case. The intention was certainly not to be deliberately obscurantist, neither was it meant to be a "harsh" commentary on Donaldson,

as I think my counterpart saw it. Quite the contrary. Writing this chapter happened to coincide with my discovery of the literary works of Italo Calvino, about which I could eulogize endlessly, but perhaps that's for another time. Lotaria is one of the characters in his book *If on a Winter's Night a Traveller* – a student of literature who comes up with a madcap scheme to conduct literary criticism using a computer. In Calvino's hands, this attempt seems deeply comical and absurd. I've juxtaposed the extract from his book with a table taken pretty arbitrarily from the journal *Organization Science*, for two reasons. Firstly, my hope was that in this particular setting "Table 2" could be viewed for its purely esthetic qualities – as a piece of conceptual art, if you will, that transcends any value it might have as an ostensible contribution to scientist knowledge. And, secondly, to suggest that the task of understanding organizational conduct by using the kinds of technocalculative methods employed by Young-Ybarra and Wiersema in their article is as absurd as trying to do literary criticism by having a computer count words in a book. Understanding human action is an artful interpretative enterprise and requires skills and practices akin to those of a trained literary critic. To repeat, I have no personal or particular gripe with Young-Ybarra and Wiersema. Any one of a thousand or more tables published last year alone would have served my purpose. What *is* at issue is their *generic* choice of means and the lack of reflexivity exhibited.

Editor. Okay. I have a much clearer picture of what you were trying to achieve there, but as you've raised the question of reflexivity I want to develop this theme a bit.

Case. Fine.

Editor. The Hardy and Clegg quote about reflexivity you cite [towards the end of the chapter] . . .

Case. Yes?

Editor. This is a repeatedly argued bit of nonpositivist rhetoric, but in reality I know of very few cases where this is fully and successfully accomplished with respect to a piece of research. I mean, I agree with the sentiment but am tired of seeing it expressed and not actioned. Can you point to some exemplars that you know of?

Case. I take your point and, no, there aren't many studies in our field that really try to take the reflexive prescriptions seriously. One would have to look, say, to the sociology of scientific knowledge and the work of Malcolm Ashmore and others,[14] or to certain forms of contemporary social psychology and the work of Beryl C. Curt[15] for such exemplars.

Having said that, reflexivity is certainly something I've tried personally to take on board, for example, in my Ph.D. thesis and in at least one article that came out of it – the one in *Studies of Organizations, Cultures and Societies* mentioned in the reference list. It's also a prescription that has informed both my chapter here and *this* present dialogue. So, if it's not overly arch of me to do so, perhaps I could say, *quod erat demonstrandum?*

Editor. "Which was the thing to be demonstrated." [*Inaudible.*]

Case. Yes. I guess we'll have to leave it to the reader to decide whether or not it has been.

Editor. Okay. Maybe we should leave it there. One thing I would ask by way of conclusion is that you have a look at the counterpoint chapter and make some kind of brief response to his work.

Case. Okay, I'll do that.

Editor. Thanks.

Case. No problem . . . Does that mean we're history?

Editor. We're history. Yes.

Brief Response to Chapter 5a

The problematic that my counterpart articulates in his account of objectivity in organization theory centers on what he takes to be scholarly divergences in the operationalization of constructs invented and deployed in the field of organizational studies. His chapter concerns itself with an exploration of *how* such divergences occur and, correspondingly, how the situation may be remedied. My counterpart takes it as axiomatic that different interpretations or, more precisely in his terms, divergent means of operationalization of the "same" construct – "downsizing," "transaction," "profit," "institution," and so on – will be damaging or even destructive to the ultimate end of organizational studies, which is to produce a stable body of objective knowledge. Daft's contrast between "lean" and "rich" channels of construct diffusion is invoked to help explain why certain domains of research are characterized by greater levels of agreement over the meaning of a construct than others. Lean channels are those means of dissemination that require little social interaction between members of a given scholastic community. They would include the publication of collections of contributions (such as this one) and journal articles that enjoy a relatively narrow readership and where the contributors do not engage beyond, at best, a superficial exchange of *ideas*. Rich channels, by contrast, are those that entail high levels of face-to-face interaction, such as in close-knit research teams. Under the latter conditions there is a much greater chance that genuine consensus can be reached over the means to investigate a given construct empirically, and hence the objective knowledge resulting from investigations will be more valid. It would seem important from my counterpart's perspective that creativity in respect of construct development is attenuated until such time as agreement has been reached over the choice and meaning of objectified constructs to be deployed in empirical investigations. My counterpart bases his entire position on a version of "constructivism" that simultaneously accepts that knowledge about organizations is socially constructed yet maintains that organizations exist as entities independent of the minds of researchers.

Being of a generally conciliatory nature, I have racked my brains in an effort to find some point of consensus between the contructivist–objectivist account of organizational research offered by my counterpart and my own subjectivist–fictive version. Regrettably, in this instance, I can find few points of mutual agreement and concord. Whether this is a result of the "lean" nature of the channel of communication being employed for our exchange or whether it results from a far more fundamental and potentially incommensurable difference in philosophical persuasion and values will be for the reader to decide. There is a neat mathematical symmetry to my counterpart's argument that I find intriguing. His problematic is framed in terms of a series of structural

dichotomies and corresponding moral judgments: rich diffusion is good, lean diffusion is
bad; interscholar convergence is good, interscholar divergence is bad; construct stability is
good, construct instability is bad, and so forth.
His narrative strikes me as being somewhat
naive to the extent that it oversimplifies a complex and textured pattern of interaction and
organizational accomplishments. To my mind
such naivety is a natural concomitant of the
technicist mind set typically associated with
the objectivist project and is precisely why
I think it is to be eschewed in favor of
more rounded and detailed accounts of the
social and political realities of organizational
conduct.

I would agree with my counterpart that face-
to-face scholarly engagement and interaction
are important[16] but not exclusively for the
purposes of arriving at consensus agreement.
People may resolve differences by discussion;
they may come to mutual understanding; they
may agree, but, equally, they may not. The
reality of interpersonal politics, which is often
particularly acute in close-knit research teams,
seems far from the ideal conjured by "rich"
channels of construct diffusion. My counterpart's *theoretical* problematic could, however,
be easily modified to become a potentially interesting empirical question about the manner
in which concepts are exchanged and disseminated in organizational studies. For example,
a researcher might usefully spend a significant
period of time doing participant observation
fieldwork with two contrasting groups of
organizational studies scholars in order to
understand how constructs are deployed and
developed. This would facilitate a comparative
analysis of, say, the similarities and differences
between a team of structural contingency theorists, on the one hand, and population ecologists on the other.

Concerning my counterpart's desire to promote agreement over the meaning of constructs,
I note that he has in mind a process of interpretative attenuation that owes much to the
widely discredited philosophy of logical positivism. He draws on the work of McKinley
and Mone (1998), for example, to support a
case for equating the meaning of constructs
with their means of operationalization. Ensuring

that the meaning of a given term is defined
entirely by its means of verification paves
the way to the creation of a falsifiable body of
objective knowledge. Whilst my counterpart
contends that he has signed up to a qualified
version of constructivism,[17] it would appear
to be a rather strange interpretation of that
approach, and one wonders whether he is actually a positivist (or at least a neopositivist)
wolf dressed up in constructivist sheep's clothing. Certainly, the concern to limit construct
meaning resonates deeply with various versions
of the positivist project. One is reminded, for
instance, of the "weak" verificationism expressed in Ayer and Carnap's "principle of confirmation" (Ayer, 1959/1978) or, perhaps most
directly, of Bridgman's (1927/1980) opera-
tionalism, which dictates that concepts must
be defined in terms of the operations employed
in applying them.

Leaving aside the not inconsiderable practical problem of operationalizing commonly used
constructs like "strategy," "policy," "culture,"
and so forth under the terms prescribed by my
counterpart, applied to the field of organizational conduct I think his general approach
unlikely to yield much in the way of *understanding*. Yes, a group of individuals can form
a community that agrees upon constructs
following the principles outlined by my counterpart. They can objectify the world of
organizations and their environments in the
fragmentary entity-like fashion that he advocates and the result will indeed be *a form of
knowledge*. But knowledge derived for what
particular ends and with what consequences?
As I have tried to argue in chapter 5(b), I think
that the objectivist project produces knowledge that is not only politically and ideologically circumscribed but also fantastic. In
bureaucratizing the imagination its proponents
contribute to a kind of collective and unreflexive
delusion that loses sight of its own fictive and
ideological nature. Hence the case I made for a
subjective authenticity that deals in a realistic
fashion with the uncertainties, complexities
and vicissitudes of conducting organizational
research.

With particular respect to my counterpart's
work, viewed from the perspective I am proposing, one would be interested in exploring

the social psychological motives expressed in his text. Like any other, it is the product of particular sociohistorical circumstances and reflects the interests and preoccupations of a specific social milieu. The individualism, consumerism, and materialism that are all-pervasive in contemporary American society are directly mirrored in my counterpart's preference for the fragmented language of object-ification and a corresponding ontology of organizational entities and discrete, decidable constructs.[18] His is a concern for "things" or "resources" that can be measured, that have market exchange value, whether commercial or intellectual. Is it any wonder, therefore, that my counterpart equates organizational studies exclusively with the study of "business organ-ization," rather than with the study, say, of *social* organization under differing sets of supporting conditions? Reading McKinley and Mone (1998), an article my counterpart draws on to substantiate his argument in several places, we are drawn into a world of Social Darwinism, wherein only the fittest academic ideas can expect to survive by achieving "competitive advantage" and wherein matters of intellectual politics can best be accommodated through a process of bureaucratic expediency and electoral democracy. This is the ideology of neoliberalism and *laissez-faire* economics writ small. There are no free lunches here. You have to earn your academic grub by competitively demonstrating "added value" to a legitimate (as bureaucratically and "democratically" defined) body of knowledge. And if you don't you have only yourself to blame and can quite reasonably expect to find yourself out in the cold. It is a vision of intellectual exchange and value as relatively red in tooth and claw as the culture that has spawned it.

I hope my counterpart will understand, therefore, if I personally decline the invitation to live in his universe of tightly circumscribed and prescribed "organizational theory." My own intellectual lineage compels me to promote a more fluid and discursive version of organizational studies, one which values human *understanding* and *compassion* over expedient scientistic knowledge, and one that neither embodies nor expresses a desire to reach the end of its history.

Acknowledgments

I should like to thank the editors as well as Ken Selvester, Steve Linstead, and Kjersti Bjørkeng for their helpful and supportive comments on drafts of this chapter. Thanks also to the doctoral students who attended the "Writing for Research Purposes" workshop organized by the European Institute for Advanced Studies in Management at Venice International University (July 2001). Their thought-provoking reception of themes developed in this chapter was appreciated.

Notes

1 In certain forms of objectivist social science the work of Berger and Luckmann (1966), differentiating as it does between subjective and objective reality, is misappropriated to *justify* the consensual reification of concepts. It is, therefore, important to bear in mind the inimical light in which Berger and Luckmann viewed acts of reification. In their words, "Reification is the apprehension of human phenomena as if they were things, that is, in non-human or possibly supra-human terms. Another way of saying this is that reification is the apprehension of the products of human activity *as if* they were something other than human products – such as facts of nature, results of cosmic laws, or manifestations of divine will. Reification implies that man is capable of forgetting his own authorship of the human world, and, further, that the dialectic between man, the producer, and his products is lost to consciousness. The reified world is, by definition, a dehumanized world. It is experienced by man as a strange facticity, an *opus alienum* over which he has no control rather than as the *opus proprium* of his own productive activity" (1966: 106, original emphases).

2 In 1856 Thomas De Quincey felt sufficiently empowered to remark of the word "object-ive" that, from being "so nearly unintellig-ible in 1821, so scholastic . . . yet, on the other hand, so indispensable to accurate thinking, and to wide thinking, [it] has since 1821 become too common to need any apology" (*O.E.D*, p. 643). As an aside, the military use of the word objective, as in reaching an

"objective point" in a military campaign, which is the conceptual ancestor of its contemporary usage in corporate life, did not appear until the latter part of the nineteenth century.

3 In a more recent work Code (1994: 180) is even more vociferous on this point. Reverting to the more common distinction between subjectivity and objectivity, she states, "It is by now a feminist commonplace that the epistemologies of modernity, in their principled neutrality and detachment, generate an ideology of objectivity that dissociates itself from emotions and values, while granting no epistemological significance to its own cognitive location . . . When human subjects become *objects* of knowledge, the paradigm assimilates their subjectivity – their specificities – to a neutral observational model. With more elaborated knowledge claims . . . these paradigms create a presumption in favor of an apolitical epistemology that is at best deceptive, at worst dangerous."

4 See, for example, Donaldson (1985, 1995, 1996).

5 With apologies to Italo Calvino.

6 Burrell (1999: 391) offers a poignant illustration of the destructive aspect of an insensitive objectivist stance: "There is the terrible example of a 4,900 year old bristlecone pine tree in Wyoming being cut down by an impatient researcher because his tree corer would not work."

7 From the ancient Greek αγωνεζ (*agones*), a noun referring to "court cases," "contests," or "sporting matches" (in which the contestants either win or lose).

8 This structure of propositions is peculiarly Western, and results from the "rediscovery" of Greek and Arabic learning by Renaissance scholars. By contrast, Oriental philosophy such as that of Hinduism, Jainism, and Buddhism can accommodate quite different logical structures. To take one example, Buddhist logic permits propositions of the form: p, not-p, both p *and* not-p, neither p *nor* not-p. These logical relations reflect more fully, one might argue, the range of ordinary language use that sometimes does (p or not-p) and sometimes does not exclude the "middle" (both p and not-p) and also facilitates talk

about metaphysical possibilities (neither p nor not-p). See Bodhi (1978).

9 A point of clarification for the benefit of logicians reading this text: I am using the terms "either"/"or" here in an ordinary language sense, that is, one that corresponds in a strictly logical sense to the "exclusive or" of the form "A XOR B" – where the outcome is true if and only if A or B is true but not if both are true. Thanks to Kjersti Bjørkeng for pointing out the possible ambiguity.

10 For a rather insistent application of this principle see Cunningham (1973).

11 See Parker (2000: 92–4) for an informative linguistic perspective on the nature of dualistic thinking in theorizing about organizations.

12 Kjersti Bjørkeng helpfully directed me to a passage in Aristotle's *Metaphysics* (Book II, chapter 3) in which he points to the force of habit and familiarity in dictating matters of intellectual preference. It would seem that there is nothing new in the "two cultures" or "techie–fuzzy" debate: "The effect which lectures produce on a hearer depends on his habits; for we demand the language we are accustomed to, and that which is different from this seems not in keeping but somewhat unintelligible and foreign because of its unwontedness. For it is the customary that is intelligible . . . Thus some people do not listen to a speaker unless he speaks mathematically, others unless he gives instances, while others expect him to cite a poet as witness. And some want to have everything done accurately, while others are annoyed by accuracy, either because they cannot follow the connexion of thought or because they regard it as pettifoggery."

13 As all writing is history the words of an historian (Jenkins, 1991: 68) on contemporary historical method might further help underscore the reflexive thesis of this chapter and my invitation to engage in subjectively authentic research: "To work in this way is to adopt a method which deconstructs and historicises all those interpretations that have certaintist pretensions and which fail to call into question the conditions of their own making; which forget to indicate their

subservience to unrevealed interests, which mask those epistemological, methodological and ideological presuppositions that . . . everywhere and every time mediate the past into history."

14 See Ashmore (1989), Mulkay (1979) and contributors to the debate in Woolgar (1988).

15 See Curt (1994). Beryl C. Curt is a pseudonym under which Chris Eccleston, Kate Gleeson, Nick Lee, Rex Stainton Rogers, Wendy Stainton Rogers, Paul Stenner, and Marcia Worrell collectively write.

16 I refer in particular to the values expressed by Habermas (1991) in his notion of the Ideal Speech Situation.

17 It seems to me that the version of constructivism arrived at by my counterpart has, conveniently from his point of view, dropped the critical dimension that was so central to Berger and Luckmann's (1966) conception of objectification. My counterpart is thus prone to the criticism of constructivist–objectivists that I mount in note 1 above. Would this liberal interpretation of "constructivism" amount to an example of just the kind of "creative construct divergence" that he seems so keen to proscribe? In other words, is it a case of "Physician, heal thyself"?

18 By suggesting that scholastic constructs in the field of organization studies should reflect the functional objectivism of lay language communities, my counterpart demonstrates the very point I make here about the sociology of objectivist knowledge. In fact I am all for close empirical study of language practices in organizations but would want to bring a degree of historical, political, and cultural relativism to their interpretation that I suspect my counterpart would find anathema. Objectivism for lay practitioners is simply one form of language game among many others. Organizational studies should, according to the position I espouse, embrace and explore the heterogeneity of language use, be it material, emotional, intellectual, or spiritual.

References

Aristotle (1998) *The Metaphysics*. London: Penguin.

Ashmore, M. (1989) *The Reflexive Thesis*. Chicago: University of Chicago Press.

Ayer, A. J., ed. (1959/1978) *Logical Positivism*. Westport, CT: Greenwood Press.

Bell, D. (1994) "Objectivity," in J. Dancy and E. Sosa (eds) *A Companion to Epistemology*, pp. 310–12. Oxford: Blackwell.

Beger, P. L., and Luckmann, T. (1966) *The Social Construction of Reality*. Harmondsworth: Penguin.

Blau, P. M., and Schoenherr, P. A. (1971) *The Structure of Organizations*. New York: Basic Books.

Bodhi, B. (1978) *The Discourse on the All-embracing Net of Views*. Kandy, Sri Lanka: Buddhist Publication Society.

Bridgman, P. (1927/1980) *The Logic of Modern Physics*. London: Macmillan.

Burke, K. (1984) *Attitudes toward History*. London: University of California Press.

Burrell, G. (1998) *Pandemonium: Toward a Retro-organization Theory*. London: Sage.

——(1999) "Normal science, paradigms, metaphors, discourses and genealogies of analysis," in S. Clegg and C. Hardy (eds) *Studying Organization: Theory and Method*, pp. 388–404. London: Sage.

Burrell, G., and Morgan, G. (1979) *Sociological Paradigms and Organizational Analysis*. London: Heinemann.

Calvino, I. (1998) *If on a Winter's Night a Traveller*. London: Vintage.

Case, P. (1996) "Information happenings: performing reflexive organizational research," *Studies in Cultures, Organizations and Societies*, 2 (1): 45–65.

——(1999a) "Remember reengineering: the rhetorical appeal of a managerial salvation device," *Journal of Management Studies*, 36 (4): 419–41.

——(1999b.) "Organizational studies in space: Stanislav Lem and the writing of social science fiction," *Organization*, 6 (4): 649–71.

Cicourel, A. V. (1964) *Method and Measurement in Sociology*. London: Collier-Macmillan.

Code, L. (1987) *Epistemic Responsibility*. London: University of New England Press.

——(1994) "Who cares? The poverty of objectivism for a moral epistemology," in A. Megill (ed.) *Rethinking Objectivity*, pp. 179–95. London: Duke University Press.

Cunningham, F. (1973) *Objectivity in Social Science.* Toronto: University of Toronto Press.

Curt, B. C. (1994) *Textuality and Tectonics: Troubling Social and Psychological Science.* Buckingham: Open University Press.

Czarniawska, Barbara (1997a) *A Narrative Approach to Organization Studies.* London: Sage.

——(1997b) *Narrating the Organization: Dramas of Institutional Identity.* Chicago: University of Chicago Press.

——(1999) *Writing Organization.* Oxford: Oxford University Press.

Daston, L. (1994) "Baconian facts, academic civility, and the prehistory of objectivity," in A. Megill (ed.) *Rethinking Objectivity*, pp. 37–63. London: Duke University Press.

Donaldson, L. (1987) "Strategy and structural adjustment to regain fit and performance: in defence of contingency theory," *Journal of Management Studies*, 24 (1): 1–24.

——(1985) *In Defence of Organization Theory: A Reply to the Critics.* Cambridge: Cambridge University Press.

——(1995) *Contingency Theory*, Vol. IX of D. S. Pugh (ed.) *History of Management Thought.* Aldershot: Dartmouth Press.

——(1996) *For Positivist Organization Theory: Proving the Hard Core.* London: Sage.

——(1999) "The normal science of structural contingency theory," in S. R. Clegg and C. Hardy (eds) *Studying Organization: Theory and Method*, pp. 51–70. London: Sage.

Feyerabend, P. (1975) *Against Method: Outline of an Anarchistic Theory of Knowledge.* London: New Left Books.

Foucault, M. (1977) *Discipline and Punish: The Birth of the Prison.* London: Allen Lane.

——(1980) *Power/Knowledge.* Brighton: Harvester.

Gabriel, Y. (2000) *Storytelling in Organizations.* Oxford: Oxford University Press.

Gergen, Kenneth (1994) "The mechanical self and the rhetoric of objectivity," in A. Megill (ed.) *Rethinking Objectivity*, pp. 265–87. London: Duke University Press.

Giddens, A. (1976) *The New Rules of Sociological Method.* London: Hutchinson.

Gusfield, J. (1976) "The literary rhetoric of science: comedy and pathos in drinking driver research," *American Sociological Review*, 41 (1): 16–34.

Habermas, J. (1991) *Communication and the Evolution of Society.* Cambridge: Polity Press.

Hardy, C., and Clegg, S. (1999) "Some dare call it power," in S. Clegg and C. Hardy (eds) *Studying Organization: Theory and Method*, pp. 368–87. London: Sage.

Jenkins, K. (1991) *Re-thinking History.* London: Routledge.

Kant, I. (1781/1973) *Critique of Pure Reason.* London: Macmillan.

McKinley, W., and Mone, M. (1998) "The reconstruction of organization studies: wrestling with incommensurability," *Organization*, 5 (2): 169–89.

Mulkay, M. (1979) *Science and the Sociology of Knowledge.* London: Allen & Unwin.

Myrdal, G. (1958) *Value in Social Theory.* London: Routledge.

Nagel, T. (1986) *The View from Nowhere.* Oxford: Oxford University Press.

Oxford English Dictionary. Oxford: Clarendon Press.

Parker, M. (2000) *Organizational Culture and Identity.* London: Sage.

Porter, T. (1997) *Trust in Numbers: The Pursuit of Objectivity in Science and Public Life.* Princeton, NJ: Princeton University Press.

Potter, J. (1996) *Representing Reality: Discourse, Rhetoric and Social Construction.* London: Sage.

Pugh, D. S., Hickson, D. J., Hinings, C. R., and Turner, C. (1969) "The context of organization structures," *Administrative Science Quarterly*, 14 (1): 91–114.

Rorty, R. (1980) *Philosophy and the Mirror of Nature.* Oxford: Blackwell.

——(2000) "Being that can be understood by language," *London Review of Books*, March 16.

Von Wright, G. H., ed. (1994) *Ludwig Wittgenstein: Culture and Value.* Oxford: Blackwell.

Weber, M. (1948/1970) *From Max Weber: Essays in Sociology*, trans. Hans Gerth and C. Wright Mills. London: Routledge.

Westwood, R. (1999) "A 'sampled' account of ~~organization~~: being a de-authored, reflexive parody of ~~organization~~/writing," *Studies in Cultures, Organizations and Societies*, 5: 195–233.

White, H. (1978) *Tropics of Discourse.* London: Johns Hopkins University Press.

Wilde, O. (1892/1973) *Lady Windermere's Fan.* London: Methuen.

Winch, P. (1970) *The Idea of Social Science and its Relation to Philosophy.* London: Routledge.

Woodward, J. (1965) *Industrial Organization: Theory and Practice.* Oxford: Oxford University Press.

Woolgar, S., ed. (1988) *Knowledge and Reflexivity: New Frontiers in the Sociology of Knowledge.* London: Sage.

Young-Ybarra, C., and Wiersema, M. (1999) "Strategic flexibility in information technology alliances: the influence of transaction cost economics and social exchange theory," *Organization Science*, 10 (4): 439–59.

PART II

Frames

6

Organization – Environment

Karl Weick offers that rare thing in organization studies: a recognizable voice coupled with a point of view. Put pithily, enactment "may begin as an expectation embedded in a reification, [which] often has material consequences." Such a view of enactment, he suggests, should be distinguished in its terms from any view of organizing or sense making. Organizing refers to the modified evolutionary process of ecological change–enactment–selection–retention, while sense making "implies that key organizational events happen long before people even suspect that there may be some kind of decision they have to make." Thus it stands as an antirationalist concept, a legacy of its ontogenesis, as Weick explains. It is opposed to determinism from contingencies, environments, and technologies because the discretion and strategic choice that some people exercise and implement at work can and do change the organizational conditions in which that work is managed and done. People enact organizationally; they use organizational resources to enact and make sense. What they do makes a difference. What they think they know informs what they think they do, but they could be mistaken, and often are. People are not the passive instruments of forces working behind their backs, beyond their ken (although sometimes they may be active instruments).

Weick's organizations have become a whole lot more ethnomethodological in chapter 6(a) – a return to the roots of his thought, as it were. When conversation is treated as the textual site of organizational emergence, the surface from which objects, agents, attitudes, and intentions are read, then the ways in which there is a reciprocal enactment of organization and environment become much clearer. Through conversation, we can know how to know, how to think, how to see, and how to say – the basics of the Weickian view of enacting peopling in enacting organizations enacting environments within which enacting enacts back.

Jennings and Greenwood take issue with Weick's characterization of institutionalism as a theory – rather it is a perspective with a fair degree of roominess on its own count. However, the focus of chapter 6(b) is to consider the role and relative weight of institutional theory versus enactment in organization research and theory. They seem to mean weight literally, using the results of comparative citations to suggest that the enactment program has not been anywhere near as successful in its wider adoption as has institutionalism, and then providing a wide-ranging survey of institutional publications. The point of doing this is to use the documentary evidence as a way of taking exception to some of Weick's claims, especially those that suggest that institutional theory is static, reificatory, too macro, and without hermeneutic appreciation. All of these points are repudiated by Jennings and Greenwood. Having dispatched some of the targets trained on by Weick, they nominate some additional ones that he should/could have focused on but did not. We will leave the reader to discover these. What is of more than passing interest is the way that they recognize that institutional theory is a set of diffuse practices embedded in a social network linking academics across the world at a small number of centers for research.

Comparing institutional and enactment theory, Jennings and Greenwood see some differences. First there is level of analysis – they regard enactment theory as principally intra-organizational, being addressed to intersubjectivity, and enactment theory as principally interorganizational and intrasubjective. Institutional theory has long-term feedback loops and lags while enactment theory is much more short-cycle. Enactment theory contains its primary mechanisms within its notion of process, while institutional theory relies on underlying mechanisms. They are near enough to be creatively combined, suggest Jennings and Greenwood, having the same "almost but not quite postmodernist" flavor. (We are not sure what that tastes like.) What institutional theory is said to add is a rich consideration of context, agency, structure, and mediated causality

In some ways, Jennings and Greenwood reach a conclusion not too dissimilar to that of Donaldson, when the latter held out the possibility of a positivist rapprochement with social constructionism. Such a rapprochement would allow processes of social construction to be seen to occur within the framework of positivist causation, constituting some of its micro-processes. Similarly, they suggest that enactment theory appears to provide a more complete explanation of the internal worlds and cognitive understandings of the intraorganizational members of interorganizational systems. Rich ethnography can thus be the appropriate if restricted role for enactment theory. Overall, the reader is well served by the two chapters in terms of an understanding of the specificity and discreteness of both institutional and enactment theory, as well as their points of connection.

6a Enacting an Environment: The Infrastructure of Organizing

Karl E. Weick

The idea of an enacted environment is a roomy framework in which it is easy to get tripped up by nouns. For the sake of a point–counterpoint format I want to describe not so much an "official" version of what enactment might mean, but rather a depiction of what themes it stands for, how it serves to remedy blind spots in organizational theory, and how it creates its own blind spots. The idea of enactment seems to be useful shorthand, which theorists ignore at their own peril. That claim is the sense in which the following discussion has a debative quality. But there is more than enough ignorance to go around, and to act as if any one formulation has the truth is to drown in hubris.

Chapter 6(a) unfolds in the following manner. First, I will present a roomy initial version of what enactment is about, using Nigel Nicholson's description as the point of departure. Second, I discuss briefly the context within which the idea of an enacted environment evolved in order to illustrate that, historically, it synthesized several salient themes of the 1960s and 1970s. Third, I ground the concept and history of enactment with a handful of examples. Fourth, I discuss several aspects of the idea that seem to have staying power because they correct blind spots in theories currently treated as mainstream. And I conclude by discussing shortcomings in the idea of enactment.

A Conceptual Delimiting of Enactment

Nigel Nicholson's (1995) informative entry on enactment in the *Encyclopedic Dictionary of Organizational Behavior* provides a solid base from which to begin. He describes enactment as a concept developed:

to connote an organism's adjustment to its environment by directly acting upon the environment to change it. Enactment thus has the capacity to create ecological change to which the organism may have subsequently to adjust . . . [The enactment process is discussed] in the context of active sense making by the individual manager or employee . . . Enactment is thus often a species of self-fulfilling prophecy . . . [Enactment is also about] the reification of experience and environment through action . . . [The idea] has found most use in strategic management to capture the dynamics of relations between organization and environment . . . One can expect enactment processes to be most visible in large and powerful organizations which have market-making capacity, but they are no less relevant to the way smaller enterprises conceive their contexts and make choices about how they will act in relation to them. (p. 155)

Having touched on most of the key properties of enactment, Nicholson concludes:

As an operational concept, enactment lacks precision and therefore cannot be expected to be much further elaborated in organizational analysis. However, it embodies an important recognition of how agency and constructive cognitive processes are essential elements in our understanding of the behavior of individuals and organizations. (pp. 155–6)

Nicholson catches a number of nuances that are often missed. Enactment is about both direct and indirect adjustment. Adjustment occurs directly through changing that which is confronted, and indirectly through changing oneself. Enactment is about direct action on an environment. Enactment occurs in the context of both organizing (it is action that induces and is shaped by ecological change) and active sense making, and in both instances resembles the mechanism associated with self-fulfilling prophecies. It is the resemblance to self-fulfilling prophecies that explains why enactment, which may begin as an expectation embedded in a reification, often has material consequences. The concept seems best suited for strategic management as expressed in large-scale initiatives deployed by powerful actors. Nevertheless, the idea remains useful to describe activities on a smaller scale as well. Enactment makes it legitimate to talk about issues of agency and construction in organizational theory, but apparently at an individual level analysis, as suggested by Nicholson's reference to enactment by "an organism," "the organism," and "the individual manager and employee."

Nicholson's judgment that the concept lacks the precision that would make for further elaboration is partially weakened by his own evidence that several different properties of organizing are encoded as a configuration by the word "enactment." "Precision" may be less tightly coupled with "susceptibility to elaboration" than is suggested.

But there is an important sense in which Nicholson is right. Some of the "lack of precision" that concerns him is attributable to the fact that there is an unclear figure–ground relationship among at least the terms "organizing," "sense making," and "enactment." We see this in Jennings and Greenwood, who, like others, tend to use these words interchangeably but with some hesitance. I separate these three terms and treat "organizing" as the modified evolutionary process of ecological change–enactment–selection–retention. These amendments to evolution are spelled out abstractly in 1969 and more organizationally in 1979. Sense making, as described in 1995, is not unrelated to organizing, but it makes a very different point. The seven properties of sense making align with the processes of organizing in a straightforward fashion: ecological change and enactment in organizing = ongoing updating and enactment in sense making; selection = retrospect, extracted cues; retention = identity, plausibility; feedback from retention to subsequent enactment and selection = feedback of identity and plausibility to subsequent enactment and selection. And all of these organizing and sense-making events are presumed to be social. The concept of sense making differs, however, from organizing in the sense that it is intended to break the stranglehold that decision making and rational models have had on organizational theory. Sense making implies that key organizational events happen long before people even suspect that there may be some kind of decision they have to make. Decision making is incidental, sense making is paramount. To focus on decisions is to miss most of what it means to reduce uncertainty and most of the ways emergent organizing attempts this reduction. Finally, the third concept, "enactment," is the "glue" that joins organizing with sense making. Enactment is the stubborn insistence that people act in order to develop a sense of what they should do next. Enactment is about two questions: What's the story? Now what? When people act in order to answer these questions, their acting typically codetermines the answer. Thus action alters what people face. It enacts part of their world, even if all that amounts to is an alteration of themselves. Enactment, at a minimum, changes the actor from inactive to active and, in doing so, deepens the actor's stake in what is being done and in its outcome. These are collective, social phenomena between people, not isolated individual phenomena inside a single head.

Complicated as all of this may appear, it boils down to a straightforward theme: *people* are in a complex *reciprocal* relationship with *their environments*. The italicized words emphasize that the referent is collective rather than individual, that causality is mutual rather than unilateral, and that the circumstances people confront are malleable and multiple, rather than monolithic and singular.

A Historical Delimiting of Enactment

A deeper understanding of what enactment means may be possible if the idea is situated in the *Zeitgeist* of the late 1960s, when it was first articulated. The juxtaposition of the first book-length statement of ethnomethodology (Garfinkel, 1967), an attempt to synthesize social psychological research on consistency among attitudes and behavior (e.g. Abelson et al., 1968), a surge of interest in existentialism (e.g., MacIntyre, 1967), and disenchantment with the passive actor in stimulus–response psychology, all converged on common themes such as action defines cognition, existence precedes essence, attitudes are draped supportively around prior actions that are tough to undo. Those themes were heretical in the context of organizational theories that presumed that top management personified rationality with their enlightened decision making, flawless forecasting, and omniscient planning.

The convergence in social science around the idea that cognition lies in the path of the action was not just heretical. It was also prophetic. These ideas coincided with a growing societal realization that administrators in Washington were trying to justify committing more resources to a war in Vietnam that the United States was clearly losing. One could not escape the feeling that rationality had a demonstrable retrospective core, that people looked forward with anxiety and put the best face on it after the fact, and that the vaunted prospective skills of McNamara's "whiz kids" in the Pentagon were a chimera. It was easy to put words to this mess. People create their own fate. Organizations enact their own environments. The point seemed obvious. What wasn't so obvious was the complications this picture created. People resonated to the idea that they were in control and could have an effect on the world. What they resisted was the further suggestion that, having changed the world, they had then become the authors of their own problems. Blaming came full circle, and people now confronted perils of their own making.

Enactment made sense in and of the 1960s and 1970s when it first appeared. The debating point is, does enactment still make sense in the circumstances of the new millennium?

I think it does, because the basics of organizing, as well as the realities of pervasive uncertainty, unknowable and unpredictable futures, learning by trial and error, and the inevitable lag of sensing behind motor actions (I see only what I've already done) haven't changed that much. The content is different. But the forms through which the content flows remain pretty much the same.

An Illustrative Delimiting of Enactment

To ground these initial descriptions of enactment, I want to describe some examples. These examples provide a feel for the phenomenon, suggest scenarios that are tough for mainstream positions to explain, and serve as templates to spot enactment in other settings. Iatrogenics, physician-induced disease, occurs when diagnostic tests, lines of questioning, or faulty procedures create sickness that was not present when the patient first consulted with a physician. The physician enacts a sicker and more complicated environment than first confronted him or her. Efforts to lessen the severity of wildland fires through preventative controlled burns usually (but not always) enact a safer wilderness for both firefighters and visitors by removing flammable underbrush that can produce hotter, taller, more explosive fires. An air traffic controller creates a holding pattern by stacking several aircraft in a small area of air space near a busy airport and, in doing so, enacts a cluttered display on the radarscope that is more difficult to monitor. Rumors that a stock trader has an unusually high hit rate often draw attention to that person's trading, which leads others to duplicate the trader's pattern of buying, which increases the action around a stock, which often raises its value, which seems to confirm that the trader is "hot," which attracts more buyers and purchases and temporary upticks. The fact that a bandwagon effect drove up the share price, and not the quality of the stock, suggests a powerful pathway for enactment in the investment community. Abolafia and Kilduff's (1988) fascinating reconstruction of attempts to corner the silver market show in detail the ways in which enactment in financial markets can build on itself. NASA enacts a lean, mean environment in which overworked employees fail to convert metric units into the same units of measurement used in the rest of the project. As a result, an entire mission fails in public view, credibility is questioned, and whatever "savings" were gained through lean operation are lost in irretrievable hardware and the addition of time-consuming damage control. When Mercedes-Benz merges with Chrysler, and Travelers merges with Citibank, these so-called "mergers of equals" administered by co-CEOs enact an acquisition of unequals in which the stronger CEO consolidates his (all four CEOs were male) initial advantage and soon ends on top. Hospitals refuse to report medical mistakes for fear of losing business and in their refusals enact new suspicions that keep away the very people they feared they would lose by disclosure. Proctor & Gamble initiate merger talks that enact shareholder flight from the stock, which drives down both share price and P&G's attractiveness as a merger partner. Organizations that encourage closeness to the client enact a permissive world that encourages outrageous customer demands that can be remedied only by firing the client they tried so hard to recruit. An arrogant management team from the Union Pacific Railroad fires personnel from the newly acquired Southern Pacific Railroad and in doing so loses expertise needed to run the tricky railyard in Houston, manage to gridlock not only the yard but the southwest region, paralyze infuriated shippers, and create a lingering suspicion of the entire railroad industry. Campaign contributions enact a more selective administration of regulative environments. Successful lobbying of Congress to start daylight saving time earlier in the year increases hours of daylight in the spring and sales of garden supplies climb, but sales of candy at Hallowe'en plummet because people are unwilling to go trick-or-treating in the dark.

So what do physicians, firefighters, air traffic controllers, traders, aerospace engineers, CEOs, hospital administrators, and lobbyists demonstrate? They show that discretion and strategic choice, implemented in ongoing work, can change the conditions of that work. They show that individual work can enact conditions that other people and other systems have to cope with. For example, iatrogenic disease does not stop at the physician's door as the newly troubled patient walks out. Instead, the altered patient walks into the medical care system, where the consequences of the initial treatment spread and where the patient's problems with the physician become other people's problems as well. Enactment creates contingencies as well as events. The initiating conditions seem small in comparison to macro events only because these examples articulate the local turning point, the point of bifurcation, the moment of initiation. These triggering moments often serve to implant small but uncontained outcomes in larger systems. These embedded, uncontained outcomes continue to grow undetected until they spawn unanticipated consequences that threaten legitimacy, competence, and control. In each of the examples it is also important to note that the actors are not passive. They do not simply scan or notice or detect or perceive or sense the environment. Instead, they probe the circumstances into which they have been thrown. These probes are not blind, since experience, socialization, job descriptions, and culture influence them. These influences are relative, however, in the sense that they still leave considerable latitude. People still act with discretion, often with only a vague idea of what they are doing and what effect it will have. Their discretionary acting is intertwined with what they sense, although it is rare for busy actors to sort out the relative contributions. But whether actors reflect on their creations or not, analysts need to be mindful that organizational environments are not just an occasion for selective perception. They are also an occasion for selective intervention and shaping. Thus to change an organization is not simply to change what people notice, but *how* they notice. Active noticing leaves traces. Those enacted traces are drawn up into systems as problems for others. Thus any attempt to increase effectiveness will fail if all it tries to affect is what people notice, and not what they do as well.

Presumptions of an Enactment Perspective

But what does an enactment perspective enable people to see and say about organizations that

they miss when they invoke the modern trinity of transaction costs, institutional theory, and population ecology (TIP)? One thing enactment does is that it buys conceptual flexibility. (One man's "imprecision" is another man's "roominess.") All three of the current mainstream positions make sense only so long as we presume that stasis rather than dynamics are what we need to explain, that reification of an invisible hand is a legitimate conceptual move, that everyday interacting and conversing are inconsequential, that there is an ontological difference between macro and micro levels of analysis, that people tell the truth when they fill out survey instruments or make entries in archival records, and that people are not distracted, preoccupied, or careless when they evaluate their options, try to follow precedent, or get thrown into the middle of someone else's mess.

Enactment helps people see constructive activity as well as maintenance and routine, because it is about verbs. Enactment is about operants, acts that operate on the world. It is about a set of words such as efferent, impose, project, shape, proact, control, manage, and establish, all of which imply agency or acting one's intentions into the world. Enacting is visible in emerging organizational structures, redesign, and reorganizing. The conversation analyst Deirdre Boden (1994) illustrates this emphasis nicely in her description of the foundational nature of turn taking as a structure in organizing. For her, the organization becomes a real and practical place:

only as the consequence of a recurrently generated ongoing conversation, multiply laminated, a world of telephone calls, meetings, planning sessions, sales talks and corridor conversations by means of which people inform, amuse, update, gossip, review, reassess, reason, instruct, revise, argue, debate, contest and actually *constitute* the moments, myths and through time, the very *structuring* of the organization . . . [T]he structuring properties of turn-taking provide the fine, flexible interactional system out of which institutional relations and institutions themselves are conjured turn by turn . . . The business of talk in the technical sense, is thereby transformed into business that gets done *through* talk. (Excerpted from Taylor and Van Every, 2000: 220)

To enact a conversational environment, close in, is to breach or bend the orderliness of turn taking. To enact opportunities and constraints into organizing is to interrupt a partner who is talking, to stay silent, to ignore, to affirm without warning, to attend, to mitigate, to reconcile, to cancel, or to close. Acts like these transform social circumstances into novel conversational texts, and these texts then provide an enacted platform for further action.

Enactment helps people see the environment as something other than resources, institutional precedents, promises, uninterpreted information, niches, models to mimic, markets, liabilities, and costs. The "something other" is that all of those preceding features are names, punctuations, and interpretations imposed in the interest of meaning. If one is puzzled, then "finding" an organization to mimic, an institutional guideline to follow, a resource to be hoarded, a market to be saturated, or a liability to be skirted are ways to make sense and allocate effort. What makes any one of these quite diverse punctuations plausible is that they are imposed on circumstances that amount to a pun. People in organizations notice circumstances precisely because something unexpected occurs or something expected fails to occur (Mandler, 1982; Heidegger, 1962; Louis and Sutton, 1991). How one acts in the face of puns influences what will have been seen and done. For example, the bridge crew on a ship running at night, who are unable to agree whether another ship ahead of them is moving toward them or away from them, by their own actions enact the traffic they face. By positioning their own ship based on the erroneous assumption that the ship in front is moving away from them, that they are overtaking it, and that they should pass it on its port side, they change the relationship between the two ships. This change now enacts a pun for the oncoming other ship. (That ship looks like it is passing us both on our starboard and on our port.) As the ships, which are actually coming toward each other, close faster and take "evasive" action based on opposite views of what is unfolding, they steer into one another (Perrow, 1984). What began as an equivocal pun for one party – a ship ahead with an equivocal pattern of running lights that could mean either that it is coming or going and that we should meet it by passing either right or left – becomes a pun for

the other party, and ends with the clarity of a collision. The issue is not decision making. The issue is what people thought they faced, a perception that was clarified by the actions they took, what those actions made salient, and the repertoire of interpretations available to them as a result of past experience and their current conversations.

The point here is simply that more than perception is involved. Perceptually, the crew faced an equivoque. Their actions to resolve the indeterminacy produced a more determinate environment. The fact that the determinate environment led to bad outcomes is not the only issue. Equally important is the issue of what happened on the input side. How did people develop a sense of what they faced, what prevented their updating of that initial sense, how did their own actions affect their sense of certainty, how much of the data remained outside their explanation, and what were they doing while all of this happened? Questions like these are common when the world is treated as an indeterminate place that people make more sensible by acting their way into it. An indeterminate world is not a random world. Instead, it is loosely coupled, amenable to multiple interpretations, malleable to action, and contingent. Indeterminacy means differentially determinant, an "obvious" partition being that technology and other material artifacts are more determinant than are social resources. I put quotation marks around "obvious" because the world does not often sort itself neatly into those two categories. Latour (1988) has made this clear in his insistence that the pairing of tools with people does not create an aggregate. Instead, it creates a fused hybrid that is unified through action, a hybrid similar to what Heidegger seems to have in mind when he describes ready-to-hand being.

The discussion up to this point is noteworthy in the sense that it illustrates a third way in which enactment captures what the big three miss. The typical referent in most discussions of enactment tends to be small: the dyad, the small group, the double interact, the conversation, the principal–agent relationship, the imagined other, the individual, the team, face-to-face interaction, the partner, the confidant, and the co-leader. Units of this size tend to be lumped together as a micro level of analysis and then dismissed as inconsequential in a world of large organizations, substantial power distance, tall hierarchies, top management teams, interlocking directorates, scripts and routines, outsourced work, organizational fields, alliances, webs, and cultures. Regardless of the imagery, it is common to separate the organization as entity from individuals as its components. Having done so, investigators then argue that communication occurs in the container of an organization, or that the organization is produced by communication, and therefore can stand alone once communication stops. It is less common to read that organizations emerge in communication and are shaped momentarily by the nature of the relationship and the forms in the language that are realized when organizing is talked and acted into existence.

This is a long-standing issue that keeps getting lost on people who reify large arbitrary assortments of people into acting entities. The issue is whether macro and micro are distinct entities. The answer from enactment is that there is no ontological difference between micro and macro, a position that is also articulated by Giddens and Latour (Taylor and Van Every, 2000: 141–72). Organization is realized in moments of conversation and joint action that are embedded in day-to-day interactions. Conversation is the site of organizational emergence, and the text generated during the conversation, its surface (Taylor and Van Every, 2000). Thus what an organization will have become is a property of communication and is read from the conversing. Said differently, organization is talked into existence again and again through conversations that overlap in time and space. Plausible summaries of these conversations that give conversants an identity, and their conversations some coherence, are fed back to participants by macro-actors. These moments of enunciation, which enable people to see what they have said and what it might amount to, occur when macro-actors (people who act on behalf of distributed conversations) are doing such things as writing an annual report, holding a press conference, issuing an order to employees, arguing for a position in the senior management committee, writing an internal report, talking employees into a strike,

writing a column for an influential business publication, and so on (Taylor, personal communication, May 21, 2000).

There are constraints on enactment just as there are constraints on the big three. But the constraints on enactment are lodged in quite different places. There are constraints in the grammar of the language that is used to convert interaction into text, constraints in the discipline of interaction, and constraints in the texts that are reflexively treated as evidence that shared images are being produced, accepted, and elaborated. To take the big three seriously is to translate their mechanisms into language, interaction, and shared images, and to pinpoint where and how they get talked into existence. Enactment thrives quite well without a macro/micro split. It does not waste time trying to, first, separate the organization as entity from the individual as component, and then, second, reconnect them. The economy of enactment lies in its treatment of organization as a form of social life that is:

invariably situated, circumstantial, and locally realized in a finite time and place involving real people . . . [M]anagerial interventions are not exogenous at all, but merely another locally realized, personally communicated act expressed in language (a speech act), with this special characteristic, that they are meant to be, and are treated as being, declarative [declarative = communication that causes a state of affairs to exist, e.g. a priest saying, "I declare you man and wife," marries the couple]. (Taylor and Van Every, 2000, p. 143)

Portraits of organization that posit autonomous structures, interorganizational relationships, and populations as containers filled with reactive individuals are convenient fictions behind which the containing gets worked out and changed through acting, conversing, and textualizing. Continuities in framing, in action, and in language from conversation to conversation, coupled with adjustments on the spot to the vagaries of interaction, produce distributed understanding that is more intelligent than is evident in any one conversation (Weick and Roberts, 1993). When macro-actors feed portions of this understanding back to the conversationalists, the feedback enables the conversationalists to talk organization into existence more readily and more prominently. The idea that organizations as well as environments are enacted is missing from many discussions of enactment, although not from those of Giddens and Latour. If conversation is treated as the site of organizational emergence, and if the text of the conversing is treated as the surface from which objects, agents, attitudes, and intentions are read, then reciprocal enactment of organization as a social form and an environment as the context of for this form, then this missing piece can fill out the picture.

A fourth quality that is invoked routinely in an enactment perspective, but less often in other perspectives, is what I will call a hermeneutic mind set. By hermeneutic mind set I mean the expectation that it takes two things to know one thing. While hermeneutics is typically equated with interpretation, I want to use the word to highlight the even more general themes of mutual determination, simultaneity, and joint realization. Consider two of Eco's (1999) wonderfully stimulating questions. (1) What did Marco Polo think he was seeing when he first saw a rhinoceros on Java (pp. 57–9)? (2) What did curators at the British Museum think they were looking at in 1798 when they first looked at a stuffed "water mole" (a platypus) sent by colonialists from Australia? In both cases the puzzled viewers took something specific and tried to tie it to something categorical, so that they could use the linkage to probe the specific more closely, and to refine the categorical more sharply. Marco Polo's best guess was that he had found an ugly, smelly, dark unicorn, and the curators' best guess was that they had been duped by the same people who had sewn fishtails on to monkeys and tried to pass them off as mermaids.

Enactment is about knowing and learning, which means it is about issues of epistemology. But the form of knowing that is involved in enactment, active probing that both shapes and meets resistance, means that it is also about issues of ontology. In fact, in Barbara Czarniawska's wonderful phrase, enactment is about ontologizing one's epistemology (private communication). Enactment is about probing that determines the nature and reality of what is probed.

There are numerous relationships in which two elements are linked and, by successive approximations, specify one another more clearly, reduce uncertainty, and heighten understanding. Some of the more obvious pairings include the reciprocal specification that occurs when parts are linked with wholes, particulars with types, sentences with narratives, objects with schemas, situations with accounts, maps with territories, and specifics with generics. All of these pairings involve enactment. In each case there is an active placement of something specific into a more general context, which clarifies both the specific and the context. It is crucial that the pairing not be treated simply as the linkage of a less clear element (the specific) with a clearer element (the context). There is ambiguity and clarity on both sides. The act of generalizing a particular stretches the general. And the act of particularizing the general alters the figure–ground structure of the particular. Linkage, in other words, produces mutual specification. The map suggests what is important in the territory, the territory is altered to fit the map, and the map is altered to fit the altered territory, all of which actually occurred when Britain tried to control the American colonies it had never seen (Taylor and Van Every, 2000: 278–80). Territory is not territory without a map. And there is no map apart from some territory. It is a chicken-and-egg nightmare all the way down. Which comes first? Who knows? But then, does it matter if cycles, cause loops, mutual causation, and simultaneity are treated as the basics?

Notice how quickly we move into the domain of organization theory and into some of its impasses. Enactment is faulted for positing culture-free action that unfolds with almost no constraints on what is done or what it means. Institutionalists are faulted for positing free-floating reified social facts that mysteriously constrain what people do and mean. If you look back at the paired terms in the previous paragraph, enactment = parts, particulars, sentences, objects, situations, territories, and specifics; institutions = wholes, types, narratives, schemas, accounts, maps, and generics. Each position has part of the answer. Or none of the answer! The answer is in the relating, the relations, the cycling. Action unattached to a narrative is senseless. But a narrative without a reader is equally senseless. Each without the other is nonsense. But the solution is not simply to take two elements and link them with two connections. Instead, the solution is to adopt the embedded act as a foundational structure. An embedded act is one whose very character is defined by and defining of context. The question for organizational theory is, what are the mechanisms by which social order shapes and is shaped by the hermeneutics of action? Any old starting place will do if, and only if, it is neither privileged nor treated as self-sufficient.

I think that the concept of enactment, by combining ontology and epistemology, makes people more sensitive to the hermeneutic quality of organizational life. And by hermeneutic quality I do not mean that the idea of interpretation or interpretation systems is closer to the truth than are the ideas of principal–agent contracts or differential survival within populations. I mean instead that reciprocal defining is the infrastructure of organizing, and that we see this root act more clearly in enactment than we do anywhere else. But surely the least productive way to see and say anything important about organizations is to partition the world arbitrarily into separate macro and micro domains, and then plead with so-called meso theorists to save us from the folly of our ways and reunite us.

Blind Spots in Enactment

While enactment addresses several themes that are elided in mainstream theories, it suffers from its own elisions. Remediation of these shortcomings constitutes an agenda for further elaboration.

The concept of enactment provides a suitable vocabulary to discuss agency in the sense of acting. But enactment is silent on the more organizationally crucial meaning of agency as acting for or acting on behalf of. It is the very fact of enacting *on behalf of*, or *for*, or *in the name of* that lends sufficient force to action that it is able to reshape circumstances. Pure agency, at least in organizing, may not be forceful enough to enact much of anything.

The concept of enactment, although collective in spirit, tends to be individualistic in execution. For example, frequent references to *self*-justification, *self*-fulfilling prophecies, and *identity* rather than reputation do not preclude collective referents, but they certainly do not encourage them, either. Attempts to work out behaviorally informed mechanisms for collective intelligence (e.g. Weick and Roberts, 1993; Hutchins, 1995; Klimoski and Mohammed, 1994; Klein, 1998; Taylor and Van Every, 2000) decouple the concept of enactment from its more individualistic origins and show how groups and teams act their way into shared meaning. These are moves in the right direction.

The concept of enactment is incomplete because there is almost no discussion of mediation or of chains of enactment. Instead, the standard scenario is one in which there is an actor, an action, an ecological change, and an unanticipated consequence for the actor. It is less typical to find enactment described as a series of actions, spread across time and space and conversations, that gradually transform something relatively safe into something quite dangerous (e.g. Vaughan, 1996, on the continued normalization of deviations that foreshadowed the *Challenger* disaster). This imbalance, however, seems to be undergoing a change. The increasingly influential body of work on the antecedents of organizational accidents (e.g. Perrow, 1984; Reason, 1997; Turner and Pidgen, 1997; Weick et al., 1999) has, as its signature, tales of distributed, cumulative enactment of increasingly unsafe conditions that eventually claim the reputations, if not the bodies, of the enactors. Recent analysis of latent and active systemic causes for adverse medical events (Kohn et al., 1999) seem to illustrate a serious attempt to understand mediated enactments rather than the more simplistic direct enactments that seem to be the last and most proximal and most visible actions that alter circumstances.

Many discussions of enactment have little to say about the stuff of organization, by which I mean the technology, artifacts, and other material forms that are so important to people like Latour and Czarniawska. That omission is surprising, because the notion of enactment frequently draws its inspiration from the sense-making recipe "How can I know what I think until I see what I say?" The only way one can see what one says, taken literally, is to read what one has written. Writing and editing and reading are major pastimes in organizational life that enact prominent environments. And yet they are invisible in many discussions of enactment. This omission is potentially serious. It is possible that the main reason environments seem so amenable to enactment is that they have been stripped clean of any technology that would impede it. The problem is not so much that the environment is loosely coupled. The problem is that it is empty. If the environment is empty then it is not surprising that people are able to enact the conditions that in turn enact them. What could interfere with the process? Or deflect it?

A subtle blind spot in discussions of enactment is the implication that when one person enacts an environment there are no competing enactors or enactments. Conflict is nonexistent in many treatments of enactment. This makes it tough to use the concept to make sense of politicized organizations. In a world of politics, the power to make an enactment stick is often the goal that people strive for rather than the means they employ to reach some less self-centered outcome. And in a world of politics, hybrid enactments comprised of compromise should be the rule. And compromised enactments should produce fragmented environments that produce new puzzles for sense making.

Taylor and Van Every (2000: 245), in their important communication-centered theory of organization, criticize the enactment formulation for its singular focus on the environment. They argue that "the enactment of the environment is merely incidental to the most fundamental enactment of all, that of the organization itself" (p. 245). There have been fleeting references to enacted organizations throughout this chapter and articulation of assumptions that make it easier to incorporate it (e.g. discussion of the hermeneutics of enactment, viewing discourse as agency). Nevertheless, if enactment consists of some form of seeing what one says in order to know what one thinks, then it remains focused on the thinking rather than the thinker. Seeing what one has said and is capable of saying, and inferring what one must have thought, are defining acts. They attract others or repulse them. They are easy or difficult to share. They resonate and organize or prove to be senseless and disorganize. Social life is the ground from which enactments emerge. How can we know who we are until we see what we do and what we face? Imprecise or not, that seems like an elaboration worth attempting.

Finally, while the problem is not unique to the enactment formulation, it is still tough to be precise about what is meant by "action." Part of the problem is that people are seldom in the state of not acting. This means that enactment may be more about redirection of a unit that is already acting than about getting the unit in motion in the first place. The theoretical problem then shifts to the specification of relationships, conversations, and contexts that interrupt, override, and redirect. Enactment, in this view, occurs concurrent with breaches, surprises, the unexpected, and events that interrupt routine responding (Weick, 1995: chapter 4). Enactment may force the breaching. Or it may respond to breaching. In either case enactment would be guided by goals and intentions associated with the breach. And yet most of the examples of enactment cited earlier seem to have consisted of routine actions such as diagnosing, ordering, merging, downsizing that gradually breached the system routines of others and produced unanticipated consequences that eventually interrupted the original actors and became their environment. Acts spread across time and space and teams and hierarchical levels were the rule in the examples of enactment.

At this point in time, enactment may derive its value from its stubborn nudging of theorists to be clearer about what circumstances people are thrown into and clearer about what people do when these circumstances are uncertain. People turn to one another in such conditions, which means that their intelligence lies between them in relationships and what those relationships will allow and not in individual heads. Enactment argues that people act in order to replace uncertainty with meaning. These actions in search of meaning spin off unanticipated consequences, and we are reminded yet again that such consequences are a constant in organizational life. Enactment directs attention earlier in time to the "innocent" acts of sense making that set in motion constraints that have the potential to enlarge and consume system resources and attention. Enactment serves as a reminder that detecting and managing these latent conditions, and the consequences that are flowing from them, is a recurrent task. Because the task recurs, the organization that performs the task must itself be reaccomplished. And, in the reaccomplishing, people relate in ways that are more or less effective for updating their sense of what is occurring and for spotting and managing the unexpected. Hence the centrality of organizing as a focus for organizational theory. Hence the centrality of sense making as the activity that smoothes over or singles out unexpected events. And, hence, the suspicion of formulations in organizational theory that talk mostly about permanent structures, routine responding, passive sensing, clear-cut options, focused strategies, munificent environments, and decisive action. There are better vocabularies available and they tend to be dominated by verbs. There are four verbs in the sensemaking recipe: to know, to think, to see, and to say. Organizing around those four verbs surely has at least as much impact as does the fluttering of the wings of a butterfly in the Amazon.

References

Abelson, R. P., Aronson, E., McGuire, W. J., Newcomb, T. M., Rosenberg, M. J., and Tannenbaum, P. H. (1968) *Theories of Cognitive Consistency: A Sourcebook*. Chicago: Rand McNally.

Abolafia, M. Y., and Kilduff, M. (1988) "Enacting market crisis: the social construction of a speculative bubble," *Administrative Science Quarterly*, 33: 177–93.

Boden, D. (1994) *The Business of Talk*. Cambridge: Polity Press.

Eco, U. (1999) *Kant and the Platypus: Essays on Language and Cognition*. New York: Harcourt Brace.

Garfinkel, H. (1967) *Studies in Ethnomethodology*. Englewood Cliffs, NJ: Prentice Hall.

Heidegger, M. (1962) *Being and Time*. New York: Harper & Row.

Hutchins, E. (1995) *Cognition in the Wild*. Cambridge, MA: MIT Press.

Klein, G. (1998) *Sources of Power*. Cambridge, MA: MIT Press.

Klimoski, R., and Mohammed, S. (1994) "Team mental model: construct or metaphor?" *Journal of Management*, 20: 403–37.

Kohn, L. T., Corrigan, J. M., and Donaldson, M. S., eds (1999) *To err is Human: Building a safer Health System*. Washington, DC: National Academy of Science.

Latour, B. (1988) *Science in Action*. Cambridge, MA: Harvard University Press.

Louis, M. R., and Sutton, R. I. (1991) "Switching cognitive gears: from habits of mind to active thinking," *Human Relations*, 44: 55–76.

MacIntyre, A. (1967) "Existentialism," in P. Edwards (ed.) *The Encyclopedia of Philosophy* III–IV, pp. 147–54. New York: Macmillan.

Mandler, G. (1982) "Stress and thought processes," in L. Goldenberger and S. Breznitz (eds) *Handbook of Stress*, pp. 88–104. New York: Free Press.

Nicholson, N. (1995) "Enactment," in N. Nicholson (ed.) *Blackwell Encyclopedic Dictionary of Organizational Behavior*, pp. 155–6. Cambridge, MA: Blackwell.

Perrow, C. (1984) *Normal Accidents*. New York: Basic Books.

Reason, J. (1997) *Managing the Risks of Organizational Accidents*. Aldershot: Ashgate.

Taylor, J. R., and Van Every, E. J. (2000) *The Emergent Organization: Communication as its Site and Surface*. Mahwah, NJ: Erlbaum.

Turner, B. A., and Pidgeon, N. F. (1997) *Man-made Disasters*, second edition. Oxford: Butterworth-Heinemann.

Vaughan, D. (1996) *The Challenger Launch Decision*. Chicago: University of Chicago Press.

Weick, K. E. (1995) *Sensemaking in Organizations*. Thousand Oaks, CA: Sage.

Weick, K. E., and Roberts, K. H. (1993) "Collective mind in organizations: heedful interrelating on flight decks," *Administrative Science Quarterly*, 38: 357–81.

Weick, K. E., Sutcliffe, K. M., and Obstfeld, D. (1999) "Organizing for high reliability: processes of collective mindfulness," in B. Staw and R. Sutton (eds) *Research in Organizational Behavior XXI*, pp. 81–123. Greenwich, CT: JAI Press.

6b Constructing the Iron Cage: Institutional Theory and Enactment

P. Devereaux Jennings and Royston Greenwood

In chapter 6(a) Professor Weick has argued that enactment is a "roomy framework" that reminds people of a central fact of organizational life: "people often produce part of the environment they face" (Pondy and Mitroff, 1979: 17). He goes on to say that enactment:

suggests that there are close parallels between what legislators do and what managers do. Both groups construct reality through authoritative acts. When people enact laws, they take undefined space, time, and action and draw lines, establish categories, and coin labels that create new features of the environment that did not exist before. (Weick, 1995: 30–1)

As a perspective, enactment "allows people to see and say four things about organizations that they miss when they invoke the 'modern trinity' of transaction costs, institutional theory, and population ecology (TIP)" (Weick, p. 000 above). First, enactment offers "conceptual flexibility"; second, it "helps people see the environment as something other than resources"; third, it bridges macro and micro, because "in enactment there is no ontological difference between [them]," and, fourth, it invokes what might be called a "hermeneutic mind set," which allows more to be said about learning and understanding.

We argue that institutional theory is not a "roomy framework" – but neither is it a "noun" or even a single theory, as Professor Weick claims. It is a perspective. Currently this perspective draws its energy from a large, diverse group of social thinkers who have been trying to modify early explanations of how institutions form and change (Parsons, 1951; Selznick, 1948; Weber, 1911, 1920). While many variants of the new wing of institutional theory – "new institutionalism" – exist (Scott, 1995, 2001), all are distinguished by this shift to a stress on human agency from an older, more structurally inert institutionalism (Powell and DiMaggio, 1991; Hirsch and Lounsbury, 1997, 1998). Older institutionalism has been a compelling perspective because it says rationalization and bureaucratization appear inexorable

in the modern world (Gerth and Mills, 1946) and because it says that normative (moral), cognitive, and regulative (authority-based) forces push actors towards rationality and cognitive complexity (Parsons, 1951). But older institutionalism also says that to understand the construction of the iron cage of bureaucracy, a theorist must assess its creation in context, a context that includes power, interest, and conflict over alternative modes of organizing and ways of understanding the world (Selznick, 1948). Newer institutionalism is even more compelling because it points to fields and networks of actors (especially organizations) as the locus of action (Meyer and Scott, 1983). New institutionalism connects these fields both with the long-term macro-development of culture, forms, and archetypes, *and* with more micro, short-term interactions among actors in the fields, especially as they seek to make sense of these fields (Scott and Meyer, 1994; Powell and DiMaggio, 1991; Scott, 1995).

Enactment is compelling in its own right, as Professor Weick has amply demonstrated. It helps "open up" and incorporate the actor as part of the action by offering the dynamic process of action, selection, retention, and adjustment over time as a means of understanding the actor and his/her behavior in the social system. As such, enactment offers an important mechanism of change, one that we will elaborate in this chapter and connect to institutional processes. Still, as a mid-range theory, enactment offers a limited repertoire for understanding stability and change; even if, as a grand theory or perspective, enactment does offer, as Weick says, "a shorthand" that should not be ignored. Also, like all shorthand, enactment oversimplifies what we know about human action and behavior in social systems. It seem unlikely, for instance, that ontological claims (knowledge) about humans and society are the same as epistemological ones (methods for generating knowledge), that these processes apply the same to all levels of analysis (e.g. individual or nation state), or that the specific context (the "stuff" that people enact) does not matter.

So what role and relative weight might organizational thinkers want to give institutional theory versus enactment when theorizing about and researching organizations? We will spend the remainder of this chapter addressing this question. We begin with a brief overview of old and new institutionalism. But, because others have reviewed these in depth, we will focus on their main arguments and research approaches, highlighting some drawbacks in the theory and research. The nature of enactment, organizing, and sense making – Weick's trinity of processes – is then reviewed, but from the perspective of institutional theory. At the end of the chapter we examine important elements of institutionalism and enactment that could be combined in models of organizational change.

The Case for Old and New Institutionalism

For institutionalists the organization and the organizing process are a specific instance of a generic process of innovation, objectification, diffusion, and legitimation (Berger and Luckmann, 1967; Clegg, 1981; Greenwood et al., 2001; Powell and DiMaggio, 1991; Zucker, 1987). Diagrams, such as figure 6.1, are frequently used to capture this stage-like process (Lawrence et al., 2001). Human beings are innovators; they generate new ideas, schemas, logics, routines,

strategies, and tools on a regular, nonrandom basis. What is created does not always become part of the conscious world of the innovator(s) – only if the innovation is ensconced in action and thought and language is it objectified, a point Professor Weick would certainly agree with. But objectification itself is insufficient: there must be some diffusion and legitimation of the objectified item within a set of relevant actors – a society or an organizational field – in order for the item to be institutionalized.

Institutionalists argue that this sharing process is critical. The process seems to have a natural direction of its own; that is, dissemination seems predisposed. But the rates and reasons for dissemination are not so clear, and require specification. Also the stability or durability of the adopted item, once it has been legitimated, is also unclear. Either sedimentation (Baron et al., 1986; Clegg, 1981) or deinstitutionalization (Oliver, 1992; Powell and DiMaggio, 1991) may occur. Professor Weick has characterized institutional theory as an approach that argues for equilibrium and stasis. This has truth only in so far as equilibrium means partial, local equilibrium and stasis means homeostasis in a complex system.

This general pattern has been studied and supported by a host of researchers. Max Weber is the best known early proponent of institutionalization. Using several comparative historical studies, Weber (1911/1952, 1920/ 1968) demonstrated how premodern societies

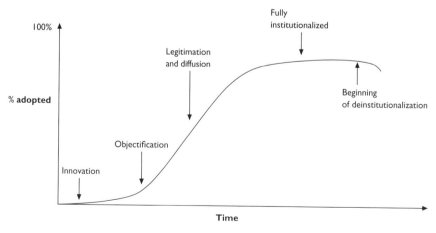

Figure 6.1　The institutionalization curve

become more modern, and in doing so adopt rational, science-based values, rational decision making, and rational means of organizing. Bureaucracy has a central place in modern society, and in the "iron cage" of bureaucracy "personal, irrational, and emotional elements which escape calculation are eliminated" (Gerth and Mills, 1946: 216). Emile Durkheim (1933) and Georg Simmel (1923/1955) were making similar comments at the beginning of the twentieth century, against a backdrop of Marxist theory which laid out this same inexorable change in society – but which attributed it to changes in the forces of production rather than changes in values, culture, and the distribution of authority.

In the middle of the century, thinkers began to focus their attention more explicitly on what we now think of as the relationship between the "organization and its environment." The evolution of intraorganizational structure and processes was examined and then connected to local community life and politics (Parsons, 1951; Selznick, 1948; Gouldner, 1954). An important argument made by these early institutionalists is that organizations develop normative systems based on the values and leadership exhibited within them, but that these systems are then jointly shaped by interaction with community members, especially by the interests and power of the different players. Selznick's *TVA and the Grass Roots*, for example, documented how the formation of the Tennessee Valley Authority (TVA) as a complex, federally run bureaucracy was the result of interaction between members of the TVA, government committees, the leadership of the TVA, and the local community. The TVA's mission and means were forged out of the values and interests of these various parties and were subsequently legitimated, in retrospective fashion, as a rational means of organizing rather than as a normative/political compromise (also see Colignon, 1997).

New institutionalists accept this argument, but, as noted by DiMaggio and Powell (1991) and Hirsch and Lounsbury (1997), new institutionalists have: (1) reframed the concepts and language of old institutionalism in less literal form, (2) specified the mechanisms of change in organizations more precisely, (3) connected

organization-level processes to processes at more macro and more micro levels, and (4) considered the possibilities of sedimentation and deinstitutionalization. Professor Weick commented in chapter 6(a) on the 1960s and 1970s move to drop the language and framework of rational thought and action. Old institutionalists had already challenged the notion of perfect markets (Chandler, 1963) and intended outcomes (Crozier, 1964). New institutionalists picked up on work in sociology and anthropology from Geertz (1973), Goffman (1956), Lévi-Strauss (1966), and Searle-Barnes (1969) that highlighted the role of prescribed, semiconscious patterns or scripts that underlie and govern much of what is viewed as rational action (see Meyer and Rowan, 1977; Zucker, 1987). Instead of talking about "activities," they discussed "routines," "rules," and "scripts"; instead of "people," "actors" and "agents"; instead of "values," "culture," "understandings," and "logics"; and instead of "interests," "regimes," "domination," and "negotiated positions" (also see Clegg, 1975).

The mechanisms of change for new institutionalists revolve around three types of pressure: coercive, mimetic, or normative (DiMaggio and Powell, 1983; Meyer and Scott, 1984; Powell and DiMaggio, 1991). More recently these pressures have been thought of not so much as mechanisms, or forces of change, but rather as "pillars" on which institutions are built and which should be examined both independently and jointly by researchers who wish to understand institutionalization (Scott, 1995). A significant research base has demonstrated the importance of these three mechanisms or pillars in the institutionalization process. Mizruchi and Fein's (1999) ten-year review of six major journals found twenty-six empirical studies that examined the working of the three different pressures for isomorphism (although the focus was selective in emphasizing mimetic pressures). DiMaggio and Powell (1983) alone were cited 566 times in these same six journals over the same time period. The research included analysis of the M-form's adoption over an eighty-year period (Davis et al., 1995; Fligstein, 1985, 1990; Palmer et al., 1993) and the adoption of personnel practices since World War II (Sutton et al., 1994). The research ranged from studies of accounting practices (Mezias, 1990), poison pills (Davis, 1991), and philanthropy (Galaskiewicz and Burt, 1991) to mergers and acquisitions (Haveman, 1993; Haunschild, 1994) and wholesale changes in the banking industry (Mizruchi and Stearns, 1988). In comparison, when one considers the same time period and journals, the number of studies of enactment, sense making, or organizing is considerably less. Our investigation on ABI/ Inform revealed only a handful of studies (six or seven, depending on how one counts), most conducted by Professor Weick or some of his close circle of colleagues.

Many studies connect organizational mechanisms to macro and micro processes. On the one hand, a large and diverse group of researchers have been examining the role in institutionalization processes of the world polity, the nation state, and regulatory agents (Scott and Meyer, 1994; Meyer and Scott, 1983; Scott and Christensen, 1995). In a focused three-country study of the railroad industry's development, Dobbin (1994) found that patterns of railroad development favored by the French, British and US governments were subsequently used for other important industries, such as utilities. Dobbin's study traced the roots of each state's approach to the time periods when that state first began intervening in industry. In France, the mercantile intervention and the creation of industrial agents in the government, along with the rapid development of Paris as the center of government and the economy, had a centralizing effect on French policy, making it strongly federalist and centrally driven. In contrast, the more *laissez-faire* and opportunistic approach to commerce of the British government fostered the rapid development of many new railroad companies and lines. Nevertheless, the British government, though historically slow to mobilize, did eventually step in to buy, organize, and consolidate some of the most critical routes in the name of public welfare. In the United States, some of the British and French patterns were apparent, but a unique pattern eventually appeared. The pro-big business and expansionist attitudes of the US government around the US civil war period led to a belief in open and *laissez-faire* market regulation, so long as competition was not unfair in the specifically

"American" definitions of the term – i.e., not monopolistic in an obvious way, and not relying on a set of practices that hurt the consumer. These three policy patterns were articulated in the national governments' approaches to their countries' industrial sectors and legitimated in national legislation over the late 1800s and early 1900s – and they continue to affect the pattern of industrial development in each nation today. In other words, Dobbin shows that patterns of industrial development are not a product of inexorable laws of the market, but, rather, are expressions of institutionalized patterns of thought.

New institutionalists have worked hard at understanding how individual actors create the social worlds that shape action through legitimated rules (Elsbach, 1994; Garud and Ahlstrom, 1997; Porac et al., 1989). Porac and Thomas's definitive study of Scottish knitwear shows how micro interactions among the industry participants structure competition and strategy – and in the long run help the industry survive. By talking to participants, observing their actions, and studying their companies over time, Porac and Thomas were able to document how strategy is jointly, though often indirectly, negotiated by participants. Rather than undercutting each other, participants decided jointly to stay in a high-value, high-end niche ("Scottish knitwear") and to set standards in order to block the entry of outside competitors, although the definition of inside and outside had to be negotiated in the process. An interesting aspect of the study is that, like the Dobbin study, it demonstrates how stability can be generated even in the face of consistent, enduring pressures for change.

However, new institutionalists have been very much aware of the main criticism leveled against institutionalism: namely, that it doesn't explain deviation and change, but only increasing conformity and isomorphism (Powell and DiMaggio, 1991). For several years, different groups of institutional theorists have been incorporating change and change dynamics in their models in different ways. Whereas some view the source of change as primarily exogenous and often random (Greenwood and Hinings, 1996; Oliver, 1991, 1992), others have discussed endogenous forces that lead to breakdown, including variability (Zucker, 1987), internal competition, and need for performance (Palmer et al., 1987), and the natural replacement of cognitive schemes by more regulative and then normative schemes (Hoffman, 1997, 199; Scott, 1995). Power and various forms of agency have often been viewed as important sources of change (Lawrence et al., 2001; Perrow, 1985; Palmer et al., 1987, 1993; Tolbert and Zucker, 1983). Power can operate both externally or internally to the organization (Pfeffer, 1981), and different forms of power appear to lead to different rates of institutionalization (Clegg, 1989; Lawrence et al., 2001).

Several important studies of deinstitutionalization have been completed. Davis et al. (1994) examined the demise during the 1980s and early 1990s of the conglomerate, and the M-form in particular, in the *Fortune* 500. They showed that the decision to drop the M-form in favor of, in most cases, related diversification was jointly determined by mimetic processes (firms copying high-performing organizations in industries with which the firms had networks ties), power (the leverage of the organizations to which the focal firm was tied), and time. Many authors discussed the importance of "sticking to the knitting" in the 1980s (e.g., Peters, 1988a, b; Mintzberg and Quinn, 1991), but the social causes that led firms to drop the conglomerate form in favor of more focused organizational strategies and forms had not been tested alongside performance-related criteria, particularly not in a systematic fashion for the *Fortune* 500. Davis et al. (1995) do not suggest that the dynamic processes of deinstitutionalization mirror exactly those that occur on the upside slope of diffusion and legitimation, but they do suggest that many of the same generic institutional pressures for legitimacy (coercive, mimetic, normative) are at work in deinstitutionalization, which extends the domain of institutional theory to deinstitutionalizing phenomena in an interesting way.

Drawbacks. We think that old and new institutionalism, taken together, provide credible accounts of the nature of innovation, objectification, diffusion, and legitimation – and even destruction – of social "facts." These social facts range from hearing devices (cochlear

implants) to forms of government. Institutional theorists have done a persuasive job of backing up these accounts with multiple studies from different angles. Still, drawbacks exist. Professor Weick cites four of them explicitly and two more by way of discussion. As we understand it, he says that institutional theory: (1) "presumes stasis rather than dynamics", (2) reifies the "invisible hand," albeit in a different way than classical economics, (3) remains primarily a macro theory, and (4) lacks hermeneutic nature.

We demur. By now the reader should see that institutional theory is inherently dynamic: it is about "institutionalizing" in just the same way that enactment is about "enacting." Most readers should also see that the majority of institutionalists explicitly wrestle with notions of agency and power, thereby making the invisible hand more visible. Is institutional theory primarily macro? It is macro in the sense that all theories derived from sociology and social psychology are macro, just as enactment is micro in the sense that all theories derived from psychology are micro. But institutional theory clearly contains elaborate mechanisms for connecting micro and macro activity to the meso level represented by organizations. Finally, to say that institutional theory is not very hermeneutic is to ignore the origins of institutional theory and the premise of new institutionalism. One of Weber's most important mentors was Wilhelm Dilthey, a pioneer of the German hermeneutics movement and the notion of *verstehen* (understanding the meaning for a social actor by getting inside the actor). Weber himself incorporated *verstehen* into his sociology by elaborating the notions of value, culture, archetypes, and value-based rationality. As Clegg (1995) has argued, Weber's approach to organizations saw them as essentially cultural phenomena. New institutionalists have returned to these roots by emphasizing the importance of social worlds and the construction of meaning by actors in the institutionalization process (Meyer and Rowan, 1977). Much of the work of the Scandanavian school of new institutionalists (eg., see Czarniawska and Sevon, 1997) is about understanding meaning and the social construction process.

But new institutionalists are also concerned with several drawbacks in institutional theory that have not been elaborated by Professor Weick. They are concerned with whether or not new and old institutionalism can be meaningfully and insightfully combined into a newer form of institutional theory (Hirsch and Lounsbury, 1997; Powell and DiMaggio, 1991). They recognize certain tensions within the theory. For example, the notion of actors, interests, and power is not easily reconciled with the notion of undirected agency, regimes, domination, and discipline. Also, the nature of values and moral leadership is not easily combined with the notion of normative systems and logics of action at the level of the world polity. For instance, recent changes in the legal and accounting fields in North America have been due to the interest-based action of entrepreneurial professionals running these firms, but have also been constrained by the normative, professional regimes of accounting and law in which these entrepreneurs participate. In addition, some entrepreneurs have drawn on market logics and the ethics of utility to justify their changes, but the state and its regulatory agencies (particularly the SEC) have channeled and curtailed change, even prohibiting some types of mergers of professional services (Greenwood et al., 2002; Suddaby, 2001). Because of these inherent conflicts among the fundamental constructs of old and new institutionalism, some institutionalists feel that real synthesis is neither possible nor necessary (Scott and Meyer, 1994; Scott and Christensen, 1995; but see Lawrence et al., 2001).

A related concern is the boundary of institutional theory. Scott (1995) has included most new and old institutionalists in a sweeping review of institutionalism. Among them are James March, whose decision-making and learning theories at the individual and organizational level (March and Simon, 1958; Cyert and March, 1963; March and Olson, 1975; March et al., 2000), are not, or so many would argue, institutional in the same way that Scott's work on organizational decision processes has been (e.g., Meyer and Scott, 1983). The work of Karl Weick is also cited at length by Scott as representing the interpretive wing of institutionalism, particularly those researching

the "cognitive pillar." Given the scope of the theory and the inherent conflict, the question arises, as with all major social changes – can the center hold? Currently the center is built around a loose affiliation of different subgroups associated with different US campuses – Berkeley, Cornell, Northwestern, Princeton, Stanford, and UCLA, as well as campuses outside the United States, such as Alberta, Copenhagen, and Oslo. The robustness of this network is questionable.

A primary concern for us is the direction that further articulation of institutional theory should take. Theories, as Professor Weick has noted elsewhere, approximate and blend rigor, relevance, and richness in unique ways. Institutional theory has been very rich in its historical detail; it has tried to be relevant to organizational, political, and societal concerns, through its selection of topics and revisionist messages. However, institutional theory is less rigorous than many organization theories. (An editor of a major management journal once said in conversation that "institutional theory isn't really a 'theory'," by which he meant that it wasn't like a well specified theory from psychology.) The potential of NIT has been played out by different generations of institutionalists, who have explored theoretical avenues from micro to macro and related institutional theory to a host of different topics. Can the theory approximate rigor? Some researchers are moving in this direction, with more exact studies of diffusion in first and second-order levels (Westphal, forthcoming). Other institutionalists favor more in-depth study of particular sectors (Scott, 2000; Hoffman and Ventresca, 2001), while still others have respecified the mechanisms of institutionalization as products of fashion (Abrahamson, 1991, 1996; Abrahamson and Fairchild, 1999), outcomes of power (Lawrence, Winn, and Ventresca, 2001; Mizruchi and Davis, 1999), or rule replacement (Schultz, 1998; March et al., 2000). Yet another set of researchers favors careful study of the role of language and meaning in institutionalization and change (Czarniawska and Sevon, 1997; Golden-Biddle and Locke, 2001).

Institutional theory, then, is a broad perspective: it moves from macro to micro, and combines elements of each; it is structuralist and interpretive; it contains multiple mechanisms for change, from coercive to mimetic to normative pressure, from the visible hand of power to the invisible hand of domination; and it relies more on richness and relevance than rigor. It is a mature theory, with a long lineage, but contains groups of new institutionalists who are extending its theoretical boundaries.

Enactment Theory

Thus far we have spent most of our time discussing the nature of institutional theory and in particular those elements Professor Weick may have mischaracterized or omitted. We have said little so far about enactment theory, which we are commissioned to counterpoint. Because we value enactment theory, it is not really a commission we relish. Moreover, how can anyone really discuss the merits and demerits of enactment theory any better than the person who enacted it, Professor Weick? Rather than trying to do so, we present our imperfect understanding of the theory's contribution and potential. Fortunately, Professor Weick has already provided a brilliant overview of enactment theory, so we shall not have to repent our faults at too great length.

Professor Weick cites Nicholson's short definition to capture the essence of enactment: "*enactment* is a concept developed 'to connote an organism's adjustment to its environment by directly acting upon the environment to change it'" (p. 185 above). Linking sense making to enactment, Weick says:

ecological change and enactment in organizing = ongoing updating and enactment in sense making; selection = retrospect, extracted cues; retention = identity, plausibility; feedback from retention to subsequent enactment and selection = feedback of identity and plausibility to subsequent enactment and selection. (p. 186 above)

One useful way to understand this organizing process, according to Weick, is to link it to the notion of ecological change as variation, selection, and retention, which is Weick's early formulation of the theory (1979: 132). We agree. Figure 6.2, adapted from Professor Weick's work and the sense making quotation above,

shows the key steps in enactment and how they relate to sense making in organizations.

In the enactment process, an increase in the volume of ecological change (the positive arrow from ecological change to enactment) stimulates the focal actor to make sense of that change. Partly, the response is a moment of enactment which feeds back immediately to the environment as an additional, new source of variation induced by the enacting actor. Nevertheless, enactment is essentially preconscious and instantaneous, and, thus, to be useful as a guide to action in the future requires some conscious sorting and selection. Sorting and selection enable the actor to subsequently recognize and act upon cues in any future perception or action. During the selection process, the equivocality of the information is reduced by iteratively cycling through a few assembly rules many times. The actor makes sense of stimuli by simplifying them. Finally, based on past experience and notions of self-identity, there is some retention of framed ecological cue. As in the selection process, the equivocality of the pattern is reduced by applying heuristic rules and repeatedly cycling through them. Retention, in turn, loops back to future rounds of selection and enactment.

Those feedback loops can be positively or negatively reinforcing, depending on the trust an actor places in his or her past pattern of dealing with such a stimulus or event. If an actor trusts his or her experience, the volume and within-pattern elaboration of the perceived stimulus will be increased; if the actor distrusts it, the volume and within-pattern elaboration are decreased, and new patterns will be sought to deal with the ambiguity. A key point of Weick's thesis is that the retention and conscious portion is always based on the earlier preconscious enactment and thus has a lagged effect on the enactment of the next moment of ecological change.

Sense making underscores the interpretive, less rational, nature of decision making. But even more than earlier enactment ideas, sense making focuses on the role of the individual. In particular, it introduces material on identity and gaps in sense making. *Someone* must make sense and enact the environment. This actor has preconceptions, values, mental maps, and

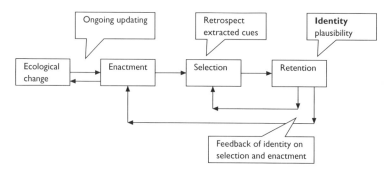

Figure 6.2 Weick's view of the relationship among enactment, organizing, and sense making.
Source Adapted from Weick (1979: 132)

emotions – sufficient to create some variation from the prevailing patterns. The actor often enacts environments (acts and understands) in ways that reinforce understanding. This implies that self is a strong component and begins to proximate "identity." Identity is self-preserving and normally seeks articulation and development. The inclusion of identity makes enactment truly "social" and "ongoing" (Weick, 1995).

A Comparison of Institutional Theory and Enactment

So how might an institutionalist reflect upon enactment in the context of institutional theory? A comparison of figure 6.1, which contains the institutionalization curve, and figure 6.2, which contains the enactment cycle, raises several observations. First, the former is inherently interorganizational, about dissemination, and intersubjective, whereas the latter is inherently intraorganizational, about inception, and intrasubjective. Second, both are nonlinear and dynamic. But institutionalization is nonlinear as a function of time and institutionalizing pressures, and implies threshold effects that change the slope of institutionalization. Feedback effects are presumed to occur in institutional theory, but only over long periods of time and adjustment. Enactment is nonlinear because it has immediate feedback loops and implies that some internal loops affect the major loop and may include discrete states or choice points.

Third, the enactment cycle contains most of its major theoretical elements explicitly as part of the process (shock/action, recognition, selection, retention, adjustment), whereas the institutionalizing curve relies on underlying mechanisms (the three forces of isomorphism, culture, values, exogenous shocks) to create the institutionalizing process. However, the cycle of enactment relies on some shock or event or action to initiate its curve, just as institutional theory relies on a creative act or exogenous force or crisis to generate new waves of institutional change. In addition, the enactment cycle implies that someone or something is selecting and retaining, but the nature of this actor is quite unclear, as is the case in institutional theory.

The comparison of the two curves and the more complex theoretical processes to which they refer makes it obvious that institutional theory and enactment complement each other to some degree, overlap in particular areas, and have the same "almost but not quite post-modernist" flavor. This leads us to consider possible combinations of the two theories, rather than seeing them as in competition. For instance, suppose we consider the Mann Gulch disaster studied by Professor Weick. In that disaster, as Professor Weick's account informs us, several firefighters lost their lives because they could not use their past knowledge, experience, and training to make sense of the fire's pattern. As a result, most fled down the wrong path in the woods and perished. A few other firefighters survived by trying novel behaviors, such as daring to wait while the brush fire passed over their partially fireproof (but not heatproof) emergency shells. The study shows, in terms of enactment theory, the breakdown of sense making and the creation of new sense. Nevertheless, the study can only be understood in light of the legitimated selection and training procedures for the firefighters and the organizational framework that allows such events to occur. Organization theorists will immediately recognize that the Forest Service was not dismantled because of the disaster, nor was the use of local crews successfully challenged. Instead, experts (such as Professor Weick) and the firefighters themselves were brought in to modify the tactics. That is partly sense making, but also relegitimation of the organization by relevant professionals. Similarly, the description of nonnormal accidents in Professor Weick's more recent work on mindfulness takes place against the backdrop of normal accidents (Weick et al., 1999). It appears that whenever enactment and sense making need a rich consideration of context, agency, structure, and mediated causality, institutional theory can help.

Institutional studies can also be deepened by the use of enactment. For instance, Professor Weick applauds the work of Porac et al. (1989) on Scottish knitwear firms because it provides a convincing account of how strategies in an industry are enacted, even among competing firms. Challenging the contention in the strategy literature that strategy is created to cope with uncertainty and pursue opportunity, Porac and Thomas show that strategies in the knitwear industry were enacted after the participants cognitively set up the competitive structure of the industry and decide that too much competition could curtail each firm's opportunity. The enacted strategy was not the product of one or two powerful actors who imposed their cognitive frames on others but negotiated across relatively equal networked members of the industry. Whenever institutional theory needs a more in-depth consideration of cognitive complexity and the nature of logics, and whenever there seems to be a strong *Weltanschauung* or "world view" guiding the behavior of members, enactment can help.

In addition, we have argued elsewhere that institutional theory needs more understanding of the mechanisms for change (Greenwood and Hinings, 1996; Jennings et al., 2001; Lawrence et al., 2001). Enactment can assist. The cycle of enactment, as described above, can lead to the amplification of deviation. Amplification of deviation refers to the selection, retention, and enactment of cues that do not fully fit the currently enacted environment, leading to breach and new enactment. This is possible because the selection, retention, and feedback patterns for each individual are unique (perhaps because of a person's identity or emotions). New institutionalists need such mechanisms which combine cognitive capacity, emotion, and value, if they are to discuss change across types of systems (cognitive, normative, and regulative). They also need such mechanisms if they are to tackle the notion of "thresholds" that are implicit in their institutionalization curves – as rates change there are saturation points at which the item is considered "legitimate." Amplification of deviation could help explain changes in the tails of the institutionalization curve (figure 6.1): either the moment of innovation or the start of deinstitutionalization.

Of course, enactment and new institutional theory can never be completely combined, and any combination of them will, in our view, be a bit lopsided. Professor Weick has acknowledged that enactment has yet to develop a sophisticated grammar, while new institutional theory has its own set of structural terms for framing and constituting enactment (power, negotiation, network interaction, diffusion). Enactment is also mute about the nature of "action." Action and emotion can be shocks in a system, but what qualifies as "action"? Somehow, thought and action are different in the model, but thought as enactment might qualify as a type of action. That means that the only real difference between thought and action is time: action is that which occurs before enactment. But if enactment is ongoing, when would that be, exactly? It also seems that different types of action are possible, from direct, individual action on an object to indirect, social interaction among the subjects themselves. The former type of action – walking, talking, laughing, or fighting – is easily recognized as discrete; the latter type seems more complex and continuous. Enactment may also have a fundamentally different view as to what constitutes events: the events in enactment are usually the equivoque or breaches or junctures. These are typically discrete, encapsulated moments that occur in a stream. They imply not just a discrete shift of value from 0 to 1 but that a whole new function is at work. In contrast, institutionalists see events as discrete, albeit within a larger system of events that is pushing for diffusion and convergence across relevant units affected by the events. The shift is from 0 to 1; but within the same rate function. That *is* a problem for actually doing empirical research using both perspectives fully and completely.

Our Opening Question

We began by raising the question: what role and relative weight should be given to enactment and institutional theory when theorizing about and researching organizations? If "completeness" is the criterion, institutional theory appears to be a fuller explanation for long-term evolution in social structure, networks, and groups. Enactment theory appears to be a more complete explanation of the internal worlds and cognitive understandings of the members of those systems as the systems evolve. If "appropriateness" is the criterion, institutional theory is more apt for interorganizational explanations and enactment theory for intraorganizational ones. If "richness" is the criterion, institutional theory both underscores the richness of context and articulates how actors build their gilded cages, whereas enactment theory better captures the richness of ambiguity. If "relevance" is the criterion, institutional research, to date, has studied more sweeping and relevant organizational phenomena than has enactment theory. If "rigor" is the criterion, the diversity of camps and the constant respecification of mechanisms make institutional theory appear less rigorous than enactment theory. If "empirical support" is the criterion, the diversity, accumulation, and multiple methods used in institutional studies over the twentieth century do make institutional theory seem, if only in this sense, what Weick refers to as

"one of the big three" (transaction costs, population ecology, and institutional theory). But if "theoretical sexiness" is the criterion, focusing on how the iron cage is gradually constructed and slowly dismantled is not nearly as sexy as thinking about how our mental worlds are destroyed in a flash, only to be raised instantly from the ashes. The reader will have to decide whether postmodern society, as it globalizes and fragments, is better described by ever higher orders of institutionalization or by ever greater ambiguity and confusion.

Acknowledgment

We would like to thank Jennifer Cliff and David Patient for their comments on drafts of this manuscript – and Professor Weick for playing with us.

References

Abrahamson, E. (1996a) "Management fashion," *Academy of Management Review*, 21 (1): 254–85.

——(1996b) "Management fashion, academic-fashion, and enduring truths," *Academy of Management Review*, 21 (3): 616–18.

Abrahamson, E., and Fairchild, G. (1999) "Management fashion: life cycles, triggers, and collective learning processes," *Administrative Science Quarterly*, 44: 708–40.

Baron, James, Dobbin, Frank, and Jennings, Devereaux (1986) "War and peace: the evolution of modern personnel administration in US industry," *American Journal of Sociology*, 92 (2): 350–83.

Berger, P. L., and Luckmann, T. (1967) *The Social Construction of Reality*. New York: Doubleday.

Chandler, A. D., Jr (1963) *Strategy and Structure: Chapters in the History of American Industrial Enterprise*. Cambridge, MA: MIT Press.

Clegg, S. R. (1975) *Power, Rule and Domination*. London: Routledge.

——(1981) "Organization and control," *Administrative Science Quarterly*, 26: 545–62.

——(1989) *Frameworks of Power*. London: Sage.

——(1995) "Of values and occasional irony: Max Weber," in S. B. Bachrach, P. Gagliardi, and B. Mundel (eds) *Research in the Sociology of Organizations: Studies of Organizations in the*

European Tradition, pp. 1–46. Greenwich, CT: JAI Press.

Colignon, R. A. (1997) *Power Plays: Critical Events in the Institutionalization of the Tennessee Valley Authority*. Albany, NY: State University of New York Press.

Crozier, Michel. (1964) *The Bureaucratic Phenomenon*. Chicago: University of Chicago Press.

Cyert, R. M., and March, J. G., eds (1963) *A Behavioral Theory of the Firm*. Englewood Cliffs, NJ: Prentice Hall.

Czarniawska, B., and Sevon, G., eds (1997) *Translating Organizational Change*. Berlin: de Gruyter.

Davis, G. F. (1991) "Agents without principle? The spread of the poison pill through the intercorporate network," *Administrative Science Quarterly*, 36: 583–613.

Davis, G. F., and Mizruchi, M. S. (1999) "The money center cannot hold: commercial banks in the US system of corporate governance," *Administrative Science Quarterly*, 44: 215–39.

Davis, G. F., Dickman, K. A., and Tinsley, C. H. (1994) "The decline and fall of the conglomerate firm in the 1980s: the deinstitutionalization of an organizational form," *American Sociological Review*, 49: 547–70.

DiMaggio, P. J., and Powell, W. W. (1983) "The iron cage revisited: institutional isomorphism and collective rationality in institutional fields," *American Sociological Review*, 48: 147–60.

——(1991) "Introduction," in W. W. Powell and P. J. DiMaggio (eds) *The New Institutionalism in Organizational Analysis*, pp. 1–40. Chicago: University of Chicago Press.

Dobbin, F. (1994) *Forging Industrial Policy: The United States, Britain, and France in the Railway Age*. New York, NY: Cambridge University Press.

Dobbin, F., and Dowd, T. J. (1997) "How policy shapes competition: early railroad foundings in Massachusetts," *Administrative Science Quarterly*, 42: 501–29.

Durkheim, E. (1933) *The Division of Labor in Society*. New York: Macmillan.

Elsbach, K. D. (1994) "Managing organizational legitimacy in the California cattle industry," *Administrative Science Quarterly*, 39: 57–88.

Fligstein, N. (1985) "The spread of the multidivisional firm, 1919–79," *American Sociological Review*, 50: 377–91.

——(1990) *The Transformation of Corporate Control*. Cambridge, MA: Harvard University Press.

Galaskiewicz, J., and Burt, R. S. (1991) "Interorganization contagion in corporate philanthropy," *Administrative Science Quarterly*, 36: 88–105.

Garud, R., and Ahlstrom, D. (1997) "Researchers' roles in negotiating the institutional fabric of technologies," *American Behavioral Scientist*, 40 (4): 523–38.

Geertz, C. (1973). *The Interpretation of Cultures*. New York: Basic Books.

Gerth, H. H., and Mills, C. Wright (1946) *From Max Weber: Essays in Sociology*. New York: Oxford University Press.

Giddens, A. (1984) *The Constitution of Society: Outline of a Theory of Structuration*. Cambridge: Polity Press.

Goffman, E. (1956) *The Presentation of Self in Everyday Life*. New York: Doubleday.

Golden-Biddle, K., and Locke, A. (2001) "Establishing Knowledge in Organizational Studies," unpublished, Edmonton: University of Alberta.

Gouldner, A. W. (1954) *Patterns of Industrial Bureaucracy*. Glencoe, IL: Free Press.

Greenwood, R., and Hinings, C. R. (1996) "Understanding radical organizational change: bringing together the old and the new institutionalism," *Academy of Management Review*, 21: 1022–54.

Greenwood, R., Suddaby, R., and Hinings, C. R. (2002) "Theorizing change: the role of professional associations in the transformation of institutional fields," *Academy of Management Journal*, 45 (1): 58–80.

Haunschild, P. R. (1994) "How much is that company worth? Interorganizational relationships, uncertainty, and acquisition premiums," *Administrative Science Quarterly*, 39: 391–411.

Haveman, H. A. (1993) "Follow the leader: mimetic isomorphism and entry into new markets," *Administrative Science Quarterly*, 38: 564–92.

Hirsch, P. M., and Lounsbury, M. (1997) "Ending the family quarrel: towards a reconciliation of 'old' and 'new' institutionalism," *American Behavioral Scientist*, 40 (4): 406–18.

Hoffman, Andrew J. (1997) *From Heresy to Dogma: An Institutional History of Corporate*

Environmentalism. San Francisco: New Lexington Press.

Hoffman, A. J. (1999) "Institutional evolution and change: environmentalism and the US chemical industry," *Academy of Management Journal*, 42: 351–71.

Hoffman, A. J., and Ventresca, M., eds (2001) *Organizations, Policy and the Natural Environment: Institutional and Strategic Perspectives.* Stanford, CA: Stanford University Press.

Jennings, P. D., Greenwood, R., and Patient, D. L. (2001) "Enactment as an Institutional Change Mechanism," working paper, Vancouver: University of British Columbia.

Jennings, P. D., Zandbergen, P. A., and Martens, M. L. (2002) "Complications in compliance: variation in environmental enforcement in British Columbia's lower Fraser basin, 1985–86," in A. J. Hoffman and M. Vantresca (eds) *Organizations, Policy and the Natural Environment: Institutional and Strategic Perspectives.* Stanford, CA: Stanford University Press.

Laumann, E., and Knocke, D. (1987) *The Organizational State: Social Choice in National Policy Domains.* Madison, WI: University of Wisconsin Press.

Lawrence, T. B., Winn, M. I., and Jennings, P. D. (2001) "The temporal dynamics of institutionalization," *Academy of Management Review*, 26 (4): 624–44.

Lévi-Strauss, C. (1966) *The Savage Mind.* London: Weidenfeld & Nicolson.

March, J. G., and Olson, J. P., eds (1975) *Ambiguity and Choice in Organizations.* Bergen: Universitetsforlaget.

——(1984) *The New Institutionalism: Organizational Basis of Politics.* New York: Free Press.

March, J. G., and Simon, H. (1958) *Oganizations.* New York: Wiley.

March, J. G., Schulz, M., and Zhou, X. (2000) *The Dynamics of Rules: Changes in Written Organizational Codes.* Stanford, CA: Stanford University Press.

Meyer, J. W., and Rowan, B. (1977) "Institutionalized organizations: formal structure as myth and ceremony," *American Journal of Sociology*, 83: 340–63.

Meyer, J. W., and Scott, W. R. (1983) *Organizational Environments: Ritual and Rationalty.* Beverly Hills, CA: Sage.

Mezias, S. J. (1990) "An institutional model of organizational practice: financial reporting at the *Fortune 200*," *Administrative Science Quarterly*, 35: 431–57.

Mintzberg, H., and Quinn, J. B. (1991) *The Strategy Process: Concepts, Contexts, and Cases.* New York: Prentice Hall.

Mizruchi, M., and Davis, G. F. (1999) "The money center cannot hold: commercial banks in the US system of corporate governance," *Administrative Science Quarterly*, 44 (2): 215–40.

Mizruchi, M. S., and Fein, L. C. (1999) "The social construction of organizational knowledge: a study of the uses of coercive, mimetic, and normative isomorphism," *Administrative Science Quarterly*, 44: 653–83.

Mizruchi, M. S., and Stearns, L. B. (1988) "A longitudinal study of the formation of interlocking directorates," *Administrative Science Quarterly*, 33: 194–210.

Oliver, C. (1991) "Strategic responses to institutional processes," *Academy of Management Review*, 16: 145–79.

——(1992) "The antecedents of deinstitutionalization," *Organization Studies*, 13 (4): 563–88.

Palmer, D. A., Jennings, P. D., and Zhou, X. (1993) "Late adoption of the multidivisional form by large US corporations: institutional, political, and economic accounts," *Administrative Science Quarterly*, 38: 100–31.

Palmer, D. A., Friedland, R., Jennings, P. D., and Powers, M. E. (1987) "The economics and politics of structure: the multidivisional form and the large US corporation," *Administrative Science Quarterly*, 32 (1): 25–49.

Parsons, T. (1951) *The Social System.* Glencoe, IL: Free Press.

Perrow, C. (1985) "Review essay: overboard with myths and symbols," *American Journal of Sociology*, 91: 151–5.

Peters, T. (1988a) "Facing up to the need for a management revolution," *California Management Review*, 30: 7–38.

——(1988b) "Restoring American competitiveness: looking for new models," *Academy of Management Executive*, 2: 103–9.

Pfeffer, J. (1981) *Power in Organizations.* Marshfield, MA: Pitman.

Pondy, L. R., and Mitroff, I. I. (1979) "Beyond open systems models of organization," in

B. M. Staw (ed.), *Research in Organizational Behavior* I, pp. 3–39. Greenwich, CT: JAI Press.

Porac, J. F., Thomas, H., and Baden-Fuller, C. (1989) "Competitive groups as cognitive communities: the case of Scottish knitwear manufacturers," *Journal of Management Studies*, 26: 397–416.

Powell, W. W., and DiMaggio, P. (1991) *The New Institutionalism in Organizational Analysis*. Chicago: University of Chicago Press.

Schulz, M. (1998) "Limits to bureaucratic growth: the density dependence of organizational rule births," *Administrative Science Quarterly*, 43 (4): 845–77.

Scott, W. R. (1995) *Institutions and Organizations*. Thousand Oaks, CA: Sage.

——(2000) *Institutional Change and Health Care Organizations: From Professional Dominance to Managed Care*. Chicago: University of Chicago Press.

Scott, W. R., and Christensen, S., eds (1995) *The Institutional Construction of Organizations: International Longitudinal Studies*. Thousand Oaks, CA: Sage.

Scott, W. R., and Meyer, J. W. (1994) *Institutional Environments and Organizations: Structural Complexity and Individualism*. Thousand Oaks, CA: Sage.

Searle-Barnes, R. G. (1969) *Pay and Productivity Bargaining: A Study of the Effect of National Wage Agreements in the Nottinghamshire Coalfield*. Manchester: Manchester University Press.

Selznick, P. (1948) "Foundations of the theory of organizations," *American Sociological Review*, 13: 25–35.

——(1966) *TVA and the Grass Roots: A Study in the Sociology of Formal Organization*. New York: Harper & Row.

Simmel, Georg (1923/1953) *Conflict and the Web of Group Affiliations*, trans. Reinhard Bendix. Glencoe, IL: Free Press.

Suddaby, R. (2001) "Field Level Governance and the Emergence of New Organizational Forms: The Case of Multidisciplinary Practices in Law," unpublished doctoral dissertation, Edmonton: University of Alberta.

Sutton, J. R., Dobbin, F., Meyer, J. W., and Scott, W. R. (1994) "The legalization of the workplace," *American Journal of Sociology*, 99: 944–71.

Tolbert, P. S., and Zucker, L. G. (1983) "Institutional sources of change in the formal structure of organizations: the diffusion of civil service reform, 1880–1935," *Administrative Science Quarterly*, 28: 22–39.

Weber, M. (1911/1952) *The Protestant Ethic and the Spirit of Capitalism*. New York: Scribner.

——(1920/1968) *Economy and Society: An Outline of Interpretive Sociology*. New York: Bedminster.

Weick, K. E. (1969) *The Social Psychology of Organizing*. Reading, MA: Addison-Wesley.

——(1979) *The Social Psychology of Organizing*, second edition. New York: McGraw-Hill.

——(1995) *Sensemaking in Organizations*. Thousand Oaks, CA: Sage.

Weick, K. E., Sutcliffe, K. M., and Obstfeld, D. (1999) "Organizing for high reliability: processes of collective mindfulness," *Research in Organizational Behavior*, 21: 81–123.

Westphal, J. (forthcoming) "Second-order imitation: uncovering latent effects of board network ties," *Administrative Science Quarterly*.

Zucker, L. G. (1987) "Institutional theories of organization," *Annual Review of Sociology*, 13: 443–64.

——(1991) "The role of institutionalization in cultural persistence," in W. W. Powell and P. J. DiMaggio (eds) *The New Institutionalism in Organizational Analysis*, pp. 83–107. Chicago: University of Chicago Press.

7

Power and Institutions

COMMENTARY: THE DYNAMICS OF INSTITUTIONS

This chapter provides an exemplar vindicating the aspirations of the book. The counterparts present an instance of very productive engagement wherein there is mutual recognition of the value of the work of the other, and at least some intimations of the grounds for points of rapprochement. At stake are the issues of power and language in the processes of institutionalization.

Institutional theory has proven to be a particularly fecund perspective on organization theorizing in recent times. It has also shown itself to be a dynamic approach capable of expansion and modification. Lounsbury provides a concise and cogent overview of developments in institutional theory over the past couple of decades, with emphasis on what has come to be called the "new institutionalism." Institutional theory has moved on considerably from the earlier analysis of processes of isomorphism and symbolic legitimation. As Lounsbury notes, the approach has responded to criticisms that it has perpetuated a static view of organizations and underplayed issues of both human agency and power. The charge, by Phillips and others, that institutional theory has failed to tackle these issues is countered by the claim it *has*, given recent developments within new institutionalism, been concerned with process and with change, and perforce therefore with issues of power. The attacks are seen as being directed at a straw person.

At the root of the debate here is one that Reed (1999) cited as being pervasive and perennial in organization studies, that of the relative significance of structure and human agency. As Lounsbury sees things, the critical discourse perspective proposed by Phillips is concerned with the agency of individuals and groups in their capacity to inscribe order on an ineluctably disorganized world through the construction of interactions, texts, and discourses. New institutional theory, on the other hand, works an analysis based on the view that individuals are embedded in a durable, historically connected set of social structures, and whilst these may not be totally deterministic, they are inescapable aspects of the social context in which people must act. The historical interpretation is important for Lounsbury, since institutions are "drenched in the societal interactions and discourses of the past." This historicized context means that the institutional frame contains factors that transcend the specific, localized, and intentional actions of individual agents.

Phillips would argue that institutions are socially constructed and that to propose anything else is to reify and objectify in an unwarranted manner. Institutions are instantiated through the interactional engagements of intending agents. People construct texts (broadly conceived) as they interact and pragmatically and symbolically engage, and it is these texts that constitute an institution. Phillips maintains that sets of text somehow aggregate or coalesce into a discourse. However, a discourse is not only a set of interrelated texts but also a set of related practices of "production, dissemination, and repetition that brings objects into being." The relationship between text and discourse remains somewhat vague, and it is not entirely clear how texts form into discourses, or how discourses and texts actually come to instantiate an institution. Perhaps the given task of presenting a position paper precludes that level of depth and detail. Phillips argues that critical discourse theory is concerned with the "how" of socially constructed ideas and entities, with the process. In the context of this chapter a clear picture of the processes involved is not presented. It is, however, clear that power relations are central to these processes, since the construction of a text, let alone a discourse or an institution, involves a process of inclusion and exclusion. That is, a text is constructed and promulgated in relation to other texts – with different interpretations and meanings – that either are also produced or potentially could be. For a text to come to the fore, to be seen as the more meaningful or as containing the more viable interpretation, it must somehow carve out a position of intelligibility with respect to some language community and come to have perceived veracity, legitimacy, or pragmatic efficacy.

Phillips acknowledges that text and discourse construction occurs within a wider social context. It is this inclusion of context – the focus on power, knowledge, and ideology – that Phillips claims distinguishes critical discourse analysis from other forms of discourse analysis. Thus it shares with institutional theory a concern with context, but complains that institutional theory conceptualizes context only as a determining and constraining factor in relation to human agency. For Lounsbury, the concept of "field" provides an analytic device for incorporating the wider social and cultural context into the analysis of institutional processes. However, he argues that a field is itself shaped by extant structures that have a clear ontological status existing beyond the socially constructing efforts of interacting individuals. Specific and local organizational practices emerge in interaction with a field, but the field is already preconfigured by an already constituted set of structures. It is here that the ontological positions of the counterparts diverge. Lounsbury accepts that an analysis of discourse might contribute to an understanding of some of the microprocesses of institution, but still maintains that discourse takes place within the context of durable structures and power relations. Furthermore, he argues that individual agents are constituted and constrained by social structural arrangements.

Critical discourse analysis gives itself the label "critical" because it claims to focus on the processes by which certain discourses attain positions of privilege and dominance, whilst others are silenced or marginalized. There is an expressed concern to reveal these silencing and marginalizing processes, presumably with some prospect of creating conditions under which resistance and transformation can be formulated. Since discourses also constitute persons (or, rather, subject positions), there is concern for the liberatory potential of the analysis. It is the notion of subject positions that reinstates individual agency, since people occupying certain subject positions have a legitimized capacity to invoke certain discourses and to produce certain types of texts in certain types of ways. Agency is also re-enacted, since discourses are too incomplete and multiple to be totally determining: there are gaps and intersections where human agency can be interpolated and find room to "play." Lounsbury maintains that a focus on the disenfranchised may be morally important but has no compelling claim on institutional theory's agenda. However, he does acknowledge that institutional theory might benefit from resurrecting notions of stratification, particularly occupational ones. He notes that there has been a tendency within institutional theory to focus on elites and that other strata within the social structure have been neglected. In the end, for Lounsbury, although he gives value to the pursuits of critical discourse analysis and is prepared to consider some variables and issues that it trades in, the basic ontological issues and core problematics are too disparate to allow any real convergence.

Reference

Reed, M. (1999) "Organization theorising: a historically contested terrain," in S. R. Clegg and C. Hardy (eds) *Studying Organization: Theory and Method*, pp. 25–50. London: Sage.

7a The Problem of Order Revisited: Towards a more Critical Institutional Perspective

Michael Lounsbury

The new institutionalism is a key perspective in organizational theory, one that shifts analytical attention away from reductionist accounts that valorize efficiency or narrow self-interest as primary causal mechanisms (Schneiberg and Clemens, forthcoming). It views organizational action as fundamentally shaped by broader social and cultural processes (Scott, 2001). As is typical of theories that become central in a field, there have been an increasing number of efforts by scholars from a diverse array of perspectives to find points of connection to this stream of research. This has provided opportunities to expand the scope of institutional analysis as well as helped to make the new institutionalism one of the most vibrant theoretical streams in organizational research.

One exciting intellectual movement that has the potential to contribute to the ongoing development of institutional theory is that of critical organization studies (e.g., Calás and Smircich, 1991; Clegg, 1990; Clegg et al., 1996; Kaghan and Phillips, 1998). Drawing on postmodern sensibilities, critical organization scholars aim to highlight the multitude of voices

that inhabit social systems. In order to reveal hidden voices and the multiplicity of actors that contribute to institutional processes, critical discourse analysis, an interpretive approach to the study of society, is one important technique that has been employed. Critical discourse analysts are particularly attentive to active forms of resistance by those who are disenfranchised. While new institutionalists have tended to avoid issues having to do with societal stratification (Lounsbury and Ventresca, 2002), critical theorists have concentrated a good deal of energy on discourses of oppression and the possibilities of emancipation.

By focusing so intently on emancipatory possibilities, however, critical discourse analysts risk overemphasizing agency in relation to social structure. I argue that one of the main limitations to the integration of critical discourse analysis and the new institutionalism as well as the establishment of a more constructive dialogue between institutionalists and critical scholars has to do with philosophical assumptions embedded in their divergent orientations towards the analysis of social systems. I first provide a brief review of the new institutionalism and discuss the theoretical barriers that may inhibit the use of critical discourse analysis by new institutionalists. I then focus attention on new directions in institutional research, highlighting how field analytic approaches and relational methods are helping to shed light on new kinds of questions about how institutions change. I close with a comment on the possibilities for the development of a more critical institutional perspective.

Institutional Analysis and the Problem of Order: the Challenge of Critical Discourse Analysis

Following Durkheim, who highlighted the deep interpenetration of social relations and cultural beliefs (e.g., Durkheim, 1912/1995; Durkheim and Mauss, 1903/1963), contemporary institutional analysts in sociology conceptualize institutions as relatively durable structures that consequently shape the practices and behaviors of actors in a given social system. Through the 1980s and into the 1990s institutionalists mainly focused their attention on how new institutions take shape (e.g., Meyer and Scott, 1983; Powell and DiMaggio, 1991). Primarily through case studies of how particular kinds of practices become standardized and diffuse throughout organizational populations, institutionalists have demonstrated, across a wide variety of contexts, how the behaviors and structures of organizations become similar as a result of isomorphic processes (see Strang and Soule, 1998, for a review). The emphasis on processes of isomorphism in the 1980s, however, led to a number of critiques that claimed that institutional analysts had defocalized actors and under analyzed political process (e.g., DiMaggio, 1988; Hirsch and Lounsbury, 1997; Perrow, 1986).

While some critiques, such as those that claimed that institutional analysts viewed institutions as static structures, often overstated the case, since institutional analysis is inherently process-oriented, it is true that there was a restricted range of questions being asked (Powell, 1991). Unfortunately, though, a stylized view of institutional arguments as somehow lacking attention to agency and change became pervasive. In fact, institutionalists have

been very concerned with approaching the study of social change in ways that take seriously the idea that structure and agency are profoundly interrelated and need to be studied dialectically. Hence any critiques or serious arguments about how to extend or broaden institutional analysis must move beyond straw caricature and deal with the full complexity of its theoretical architecture.

Even though critical discourse analysis has much to offer by highlighting how the daily lives and experiences of actors are filled with creative engagements with the world, the direct applicability of such critical perspectives to institutional analysis is less certain. Critical discourse analysis is not a value-neutral method (Collins, 1984) but is informed by ontological assumptions that fundamentally differ from those employed by institutionalists. Therefore, in order to explore the potential contribution of critical discourse analysis to the new institutionalism, it is important to consider the different kinds of orienting questions that animate institutional and critical organization analysts (Burrell, 1996).

For critical organizational researchers, discourse analysis is heavily influenced by Foucauldian genealogical approaches that provide an imagery of institutions as comprised of continuously shifting and inherently unstable relations of power (Clegg, 1998; Hardy and Clegg, 1996). While Foucault's work sought to avoid a philosophical problematic of the subject (Foucault, 1977), critical organizational approaches have adapted Foucauldian ideas in a way that is more actor-oriented, focusing attention on power and how the fragmentation of institutions enables challengers to successfully confront elites in both direct and indirect ways (Alvesson and Wilmott, 1992; Smart, 1985; Wilmott, 1993). As Clegg (1998: 31) remarks, Foucault's conception of power is similar to "Machiavelli's strategic concerns or Gramsci's notion of hegemony as a 'war of maneuver,' in which points of resistance and fissure are at the forefront." Thus critical organizational approaches, including critical discourse analysis, are part of a more explicit political enterprise that aims to foreground actors with little institutionalized power and concomitantly draw attention to the problem of order.

The problem of order, the focus of long-standing debates in philosophy around the writings of Aristotle and Hobbes, raises important questions about why humans maintain regular social interactions rather than live in relative isolation and conflict (Wrong, 1994). Hobbes's invocation of the "war of all against all" is exemplary of the problem of how society and social order can exist in a world comprised of self-interested individuals seeking to further their own interests or act upon their passions without regard to the public good. The problem of order, however, has not been an important element driving institutional research. New institutionalists have subverted the Hobbesian problem of order by rejecting the idea that individual action deserves primacy in social analysis.

For institutionalists to adopt and employ critical methods, they would have to agree that assumptions rooted in the idea of social disorder provide a useful starting point for analysis. This is difficult given the deep commitment to a more historically rooted notion of institutions as drenched in the social interactions and discourses of the past (Marx, 1852/1994; Stinchcombe, 1978). One of the main limitations, therefore, of employing critical discourse analysis as a way to extend institutional analysis has to do with the fact that institutional and critical organization researchers are guided by quite different problematics and imageries of social systems. Critical theorists aim to highlight agency and action within a disorderly world, while institutionalists alternatively theorize actors as embedded in durable, historically embedded social structures.

I believe that there is scope for a dialogue among institutional and critical theorists, but that any serious dialogue must be situated in a broader conceptual understanding of the different problematics and commitments that drive these research streams. Further, such a dialogue must also be attuned to cutting-edge developments in both traditions. In the next section I review recent developments in the institutional analysis of fields that show how the scope of institutional analysis has been expanded since critiques about the defocalization of actors began in the late 1980s. I then argue that, while the usefulness of critical discourse

analysis for extending institutional analysis will be limited, critical organizational approaches have the potential to contribute importantly to institutional analysis by focusing attention on issues related to societal stratification.

New Directions in Institutional Analysis: the Concept of Field and the Mapping of Culture and Structure

Institutional analysts spent a considerable amount of time detailing processes of isomorphism in the 1980s, which provided important cumulative knowledge about how the local practices of organizations were profoundly shaped by broader cultural rules or logics (Dobbin et al., 1993; Friedland and Alford, 1991; Strang and Meyer, 1993). Nonetheless, in an effort to shift attention away from questions that led to views of institutions as constraining and institutionalization as a binary outcome variable (Tolbert and Zucker, 1996), some researchers have begun to focus more explicitly on issues of heterogeneity and change (e.g. Greenwood and Hinings, 1996; Lounsbury, 2001; Ruef and Scott, 1998; Thornton and Ocasio, 1999). Increasingly, institutionalists began to draw on the concept of field, the constellation of actors and practices that comprise a recognized area of institutional life, to guide empirical analysis (Hoffman, 1999; Ruef, 2000; Scott, 1994). Field approaches direct attention towards the broader social context that shapes the actions of similarly situated organizations. More important, they aim to uncover the heterogeneity of actors and their practices as well as the multilevel processes by which fields retain coherence and become transformed (DiMaggio, 1983; DiMaggio and Powell, 1983; Powell, 1991; Scott et al., 2000).

Some researchers have used field approaches as a way to concentrate attention on the relation between broader societal shifts and organizational forms. For example, Haveman and Rao (1997) highlighted the co-evolutionary connection between societal level logics and organizational forms by showing how the rise of Progressivism around the turn of the nineteenth and twentieth centuries facilitated the rise of new kinds of thrift organizations. Similarly, in a study of the field of Finnish newspapers,

Dacin (1997) focused attention on how societal norms systematically shaped the kinds of newspapers that were created. Specifically, she showed how the strength of nationalist fervor in Finland limited the spread of Swedish-language newspapers, even in Finnish cities that were predominantly Swedish-speaking.

Shifting attention to how specific organizational practices change in tandem with shifts in logics, Thornton and Ocasio (1999) showed how a change from an editorial to market logic in higher education publishing led to lower-level organizational changes in how executive succession occurred in publishing houses. Somewhat differently, Leblebici et al. (1991) argued that changes in practices in the radio broadcasting field occurred as a result of innovations at the periphery of the field, which migrated to the core after they had been shown to be effective. Among other important things, that study highlighted how nonroutine action was systematically shaped by the social structure of a field. Focusing on how broader field-level processes and actors shape variation in organizational practices, Lounsbury (2001) showed how an environmental social movement organization helped to instantiate ecologically committed recycling activists in bureaucratic educational organizations.

While a standard approach to field analyses has yet to emerge, Scott et al. (forthcoming) propose that the objective should be to identify how the structures and processes operating at the field level mediate between wider societal structures such as state systems and professional associations and lower-level organizational practices. For instance, by tracking the dynamics of institutional actors, logics, and governance systems in the health care field since the 1940s, they show how field-level changes were driven not only by the claims of actors but also by shifting belief systems and regulatory structures that took shape at the field level. The approach of this study differs somewhat from previous studies because the field provides an important analytical unit in its own right. All of the studies discussed, however, draw attention to how lower-level organizational practices are shaped by broader field and societal dynamics, highlighting how analytical foci have shifted away from the study of

isomorphism and towards problematics having to do with institutional variation, change and transformation.

Even though field analyses are still a nascent development within the new institutionalism, the embrace of field approaches has occurred simultaneously with a broadening out of institutional research circles to include sociologists and other scholars who have been focused more on issues and debates in cultural and political analysis. In fact, one of the most exciting developments in institutional analysis has to do with efforts to employ concepts and methods that enable culture and discourse to be systematically mapped (Ventresca and Mohr, 2002). Of course, the study of discourse is nothing new to institutionalists. Hirsch's (1986) analysis of how a shift in framing facilitated the legitimation and diffusion of hostile takeovers focused attention on the importance of language in structural transformation. Content analytic techniques have also become increasingly popular as institutionalists have become more interested in detailing processes of legitimation and other cultural dynamics (Hybels, 1994; Zelizer, 1979).

Influenced by the emergence of theories that maintain that the study of culture cannot be separated from the study of more material dimensions of analysis (Bourdieu, 1977; Geertz, 1973; Giddens, 1984; Ortner, 1994), new relational approaches to the study culture and discourse have developed. These promise to usefully extend field analytic approaches by providing a systematic means for uncovering the dimensions of similarity and difference that structure relationships in a field. Analytically, institutional and cultural sociologists have begun to draw on a wide variety of relational methods such as multidimensional scaling, cluster analysis, network analysis and correspondence analysis to study how cultural beliefs and social relations provide distinct yet overlapping dimensions that structure practices in fields (Mohr, 1998). For instance, Mohr and Guerra-Pearson (forthcoming) show how meaning-making activities that defined the status categories of welfare relief recipients facilitated the replacement of settlement houses with social work bureaucracies as the key organizational solution in the emerging field of community social welfare services around the end of the nineteenth century. Drawing on the technique of multidimensional scaling, their analysis centers on discursive status categories. Categories were constructed to organize relief recipients, such as men, women, boys, girls, the classes of social problems encountered, such as criminality, delinquency, disability, etc., and technologies of organizational action, such as general relief, employment assistance, character building, etc.

In a similar vein, Ruef (1999) tracked how discourse on organizational forms in the US health care field of organizations such as hospitals, health maintenance organizations, and nursing homes, was transformed after the passage of Medicare and Medicaid Acts in 1965. Logics of accessibility and quality gave way to an emphasis on clinical and functional efficiency. Discursive data came from a systematic content analysis of over 32,000 texts from medical journals extracted from Medline. Drawing on map analysis (Carley, 1993) and multidimensional scaling techniques, Ruef was able to demonstrate how broad changes in discourse at the field level provided an opportunity for the social space of organizational forms and the status order of field participants to be transformed.

Relational methods have also been used to document more fine-grained dynamics that unfold over shorter time periods. For example, Mische and Pattison's (2000) analysis of the cultural and organizational dynamics underpinning the 1992 Brazilian impeachment of President Fernando Collor de Melo on corruption charges highlights how pro- or anti-impeachment organizational coalitions formed as a result of discursive positioning in the field of Brazilian politics. They drew on discursive data from a systematic analysis of public relations materials, pamphlets, resolutions, and other organizational documents. Using these, they showed how a wide variety of organizational forms and the interconnections and alliances between them, and their discursive claims about the particular kinds of projects in which they were engaged, shaped the impeachment dynamic. Professional, religious, labor, nongovernmental, peak business, youth, political party, and state organizations were all implicated.

Methodologically, galois lattice techniques (Duquenne, 1991; Freeman and White, 1993) were employed to analyze the social and cultural dynamics of the impeachment movement.

These new kinds of analytical approaches not only provide methodological rigor to the study of culture but, importantly, also foster deeper connections between the theory of practice and the ideas guiding institutional analysis (Bourdieu, 1977). Contemporary practice theorists reject "older" structuralist lines of investigation rooted in the work of Lévi-Strauss (1963) and Foucault (1977) which suggest that discourse can be studied as a cultural phenomenon that is discrete and separate from social interaction. Practice theorists believe that cultural systems are "structured as an embodiment of the range of activities, social conflicts, and moral dilemmas that individuals are compelled to engage with as they go about negotiating the sorts of everyday events that confront them in their lives" (Mohr, 1998: 353).

Similar to social constructivist and related interpretive approaches to social analysis (e.g., Berger and Luckmann, 1967; Burrell and Morgan, 1979), practice theorists focus attention on ontological problems having to do with how conceptions of reality are rooted in broader social and historical processes that operate beyond the direct consciousness of actors but are visibly instantiated in daily activities (Meyer et al., 1987). In exploring the deeper cultural categories and meanings that inform practices in fields, institutional analysts are moving towards a more direct examination of social ontologies that aim to "uncover the rules that bound the objects populating our natural and social worlds" (Ruef, 1999: 1405). Field-level analyses employing practice theories and methods, therefore, expand the scope of institutional analysis by redirecting attention to temporal and spatial variations in meaning and the ways in which actors, enmeshed in relatively durable power relations, engage in continual struggles for positional advantage.

Unlike most theoretical approaches in the social sciences, however, practice theorists and institutionalists do not assume that actors have any *real* essence, but instead regard them as constituted by the broader-scale arrangements within which they are embedded. The concept of field helps to provide a systematic approach to the employment of these theoretical commitments. As Pierre Bourdieu has argued:

The notion of field reminds us that the true object of social science is not the individual, even though one cannot construct a field if not through individuals, since the information necessary for statistical analysis is generally attached to individuals or institutions. It is the field which is primary and must be the focus of the research operations. This does not imply that individuals are mere "illusions," that they do not exist: they exist as *agents* – and not as biological individuals, actors, or subjects – who are socially constituted as active and acting in the field under consideration by the fact that they possess the necessary properties to be effective, to produce effects, in this field. And it is knowledge of the field itself in which they evolve that allows us best to grasp the roots of their singularity, their *point of view* or position (in a field) from which their particular vision of the world (and of the field itself) is constructed. (Bourdieu and Wacquant, 1992: 107)

While field-level analyses of discourse and organizations have not become standard fare for all institutionalists, they highlight important new directions in the analysis of institutional processes. Attention to field-level dynamics highlights how institutions are never fixed, but vary in their degree of coherence and durability as various kinds of actors make claims about the nature of reality, social structure, and resources (Clemens and Cook, 1999). From an institutionalist perspective, discourse cannot be adequately studied purely as a local claims-making process, as urged by some critical scholars. The study of culture must be tied to analyses of the broader social structures and relationships that shape discursive dynamics (DiMaggio, 1986). These efforts to develop the concept of field and employ associated relational methods provide an important advance in the study of institutions by enabling more systematic approaches to the study of social change and organizations.

Towards a more critical Institutional Analysis

While field analyses are still nascent in institutional analysis, they do provide a fresh direction for research that usefully moves us beyond a stylized understanding of institutional analysis

as the study of diffusion processes. Further, field analyses offer a distinctive approach to the study of power, agency, and discourse that draws on relational imageries and methods from cultural sociology and social theory. Field approaches focus on how broader cultural beliefs and discourses constitute actors and identities, rejecting more realist approaches to social analysis that privilege the individual. Even though the emphasis on disorder and hidden voices advanced by critical discourse analysts has the potential to extend the range of institutional analysis, it is unclear how such insights can be pragmatically integrated into the institutionalist toolkit.

By highlighting the role of disenfranchised actors, however, critical theorists do draw attention to issues having to do with social stratification that remain relatively neglected by institutional analysts (Lounsbury and Ventresca, 2002; Perrow, 2002; Stinchcombe, 1965). One of the reasons is that a good deal of institutional empirical research has focused primarily on the role of elite actors in standardizing practices and structuring fields. This is not only because many organizational theorists, including institutional analysts, are located in business schools (Stern and Barley, 1996), but also because powerful actors are mainly responsible for creating and reinforcing rules (Fligstein, 1996). It seems that a more complete, and somewhat different, institutional analysis would result if marginalized or less privileged actors were given an equal amount of attention.

In order to bring issues of inequality back to the fore, new kinds of questions need to be asked. One obvious and important way to make stratification issues more central would be to reconnect the study of organizations and occupations (Barley and Tolbert, 1991). While organizations and occupations used to be studied simultaneously (e.g., Zald, 1971), they have become increasingly separate intellectual realms since mid century, with organizational sociologists employing structural approaches to the analysis of rational bureaucracies while sociologists of work mainly engage in interpretive studies of workers inside single organizations (Hirsch, 1985). If institutionalists began to focus attention on the dynamics of occupations and organizations in fields, extant theories of institutional process could be usefully extended to account for conflict over authority and jurisdiction (Abbott, 1988). A central analytical focus could be on how status competition among different kinds of organizations and specialized occupations open up opportunities for upward and downward mobility as new actors emerge, others die, and as boundaries structuring the organization of work get refashioned (Lounsbury, 2002; Lounsbury and Kaghan, 2001).

Another line of inquiry that is gaining attention focuses on the role of social activism and movements in transforming institutions and organizations (Clemens, 1997; Creed and Scully, 2000; Davis and Thompson, 1994; Davis and McAdam, 2000; Moore, 1996; Rao et al., 2000; Zald and Berger, 1978). How do broader societal mobilization processes transform organizational fields and enable the rise of new kinds of practices or economic institutions such as industries? How do social movement-like activities within fields reshape institutionalized practices? An explicit focus on social movements focuses attention on the role of conflict and how grievances enable identity and resource mobilization processes in an effort to change extant rules and beliefs (Lounsbury et al., forthcoming). Since analyses of institutions and social movements have natural complementarities, this provides a sensible new direction that could usefully extend the domain of organizational analysis by fostering re-engagement with the study of the politics of social organization (e.g. Becker, 1963; Espeland, 1998; Gouldner, 1954; Gusfield, 1963; Selznick, 1949; Stinchcombe, 1965).

Critical organizational scholars can importantly contribute to this refashioning of institutional analysis by demanding that attention be paid to such issues. While institutionalists do not ignore considerations of power, they have tended to abstract away from the study of winners and losers (Hirsch and Lounsbury, 1997). Institutional analysis, however, will not, nor should it, come to resemble critical analysis. As I have argued, the kinds of problems and analytical approaches of interest to critical theorists will not be easily translatable into the repertoire of institutional analysis. Different

approaches to the problem of order as well as conflicting social imageries of the relationship between culture and power lead institutional and critical analysts of organizations to ask different kinds of questions. This is not to say that critical organizational analysis is fruitless. By highlighting points of instability in institutions, critical approaches to organizations certainly provide an important corrective to approaches that view institutions as objective constraints (Brinton and Nee, 1998). Further, the development of a constructive dialogue among institutionalists and critical theorists could usefully encourage the investigation of new kinds of problems that focus on issues having to do with conflict and inequality. Such a dialogue just might lead to a more critical institutional perspective.

References

Abbott, A. (1988) *The System of Professions.* Chicago: University of Chicago Press.

Alvesson, M., and Wilmott, H. (1992) "On the idea of emancipation in management and organization studies," *Academy of Management Review*, 17: 432–64.

Barley, S. R., and Tolbert, P. S. (1991) "At the intersection of organizations and occupations," *Research in the Sociology of Organizations*, 8: 1–13.

Becker, H. S. (1963) *Outsiders: Studies in the Sociology of Deviance.* New York: Free Press.

Berger, P. L., and Luckmann, T. (1967) *The Social Construction of Reality.* New York: Doubleday.

Bourdieu, P. (1977) *Outline of a Theory of Practice.* Cambridge: Cambridge University Press.

Bourdieu, P., and Wacquant, L. J. D. (1992) *An Invitation to Reflexive Sociology.* Chicago: University of Chicago Press.

Brinton, Mary C., and Nee, Victor, eds (1998) *The New Institutionalism in Sociology.* New York: Russell Sage Foundation.

Burrell, G. (1996) "Normal science, paradigms, metaphors, discourses and genealogies of analysis," in S. R. Clegg, C. Hardy, and W. R. Nord (eds) *Handbook of Organization Studies,* pp. 624–58. Thousand Oaks, CA: Sage.

Burrell, G., and Morgan, G. (1979) *Sociological Paradigms and Organizational Analysis.* London: Heinemann.

Calás, M. B., and Smircich, L. (1991) "Voicing seduction to silence leadership," *Organization Studies*, 12: 567–602.

Carley, K. (1993) "Coding choices for textual analysis: a comparison of content analysis and map analysis," *Sociological Methodology*, 23: 75–126.

Clegg, S. R. (1990) *Modern Organizations*. Newbury Park, CA: Sage.

——(1998) "Foucault, power and organizations," in A. McKinlay and K. Starkey (eds) *Foucault, Management and Organization Theory*, pp. 29–48. Thousand Oaks, CA: Sage.

Clegg, S. R., Hardy, C., and Nord, W. R., eds (1996) *Handbook of Organization Studies*. Thousand Oaks, CA: Sage.

Clemens, E. S. (1997) *The People's Lobby: Organizational Innovation and the Rise of Interest Group Politics in the United States, 1890–1925*. Chicago: University of Chicago Press.

Clemens, E. S., and Cook, J. M. (1999) "Politics and institutionalism: explaining durability and change," *Annual Review of Sociology*, 25: 441–66.

Collins, R. (1984) "Statistics versus words," in *Sociological Theory*, pp. 329–62. San Francisco: Jossey-Bass.

Creed, W. E. D., and Scully, M. (2000) "Songs of ourselves: employees' deployment of social identity in workplace encounters," *Journal of Management Inquiry*, 9: 391–412.

Dacin, M. T. (1997) "Isomorphism in context: the power and prescription of institutional norms," *Academy of Management Journal*, 40: 46–81.

Davis, G. F., and McAdam, D. (2000) "Corporations, classes, and social movements after managerialism," *Research in Organizational Behavior*, 22: 195–238.

Davis, G., and Thompson, T. (1994) "A social movement perspective on corporate control," *Administrative Science Quarterly*, 39: 141–73.

DiMaggio, P. J. (1983) "State expansion and organizational fields," in R. H. Hall and R. E. Quinn (eds) *Organizational Theory and Public Policy*, pp. 147–61. Beverly Hills, CA: Sage.

——(1986) "Structural analysis of organizational fields: a blockmodel approach," in B. Staw and L. Cummings (eds) *Research in Organizational Behavior*, pp. 335–70. Greenwich, CT: JAI Press.

——(1988) "Interest and agency in institutional theory," in L. Zucker (ed.) *Institutional Patterns and Organizations*, pp. 3–22. Cambridge, MA: Ballinger.

DiMaggio, P. J., and Powell, W. W. (1983) "The iron cage revisited: institutional isomorphism and collective rationality in organizational fields," *American Sociological Review*, 48: 147–60.

Dobbin, F., Sutton, J. R., Meyer, J. W., and Scott, R. W. (1993) "Equal opportunity law and the construction of internal labor markets," *American Journal of Sociology*, 99: 396–427.

Duquenne, V. (1991) "On the core of finite lattices," *Discrete Mathematics*, 88: 133–47.

Durkheim, E. (1912/1995) *The Elementary Forms of Religious Life*. New York: Free Press.

Durkheim, E., and Mauss, M. (1903/1963) *Primitive Classification*. Chicago: University of Chicago Press.

Espeland, W. N. (1998) *The Struggle for Water: Politics, Rationality, and Identity in the American Southwest*. Chicago: University of Chicago Press.

Fligstein, N. (1996) "Markets as politics: a political-cultural approach to market institutions," *American Sociological Review*, 61: 656–73.

Foucault, Michel (1977) *Discipline and Punish: The Birth of the Prison*. Harmondsworth: Penguin.

Freeman, L. C., and White, D. R. (1993) "Using Galois lattices to represent network data," *Sociological Methodology*, 23: 127–45.

Friedland, R., and Alford, R. (1991) "Bringing society back in: symbols, practices, and institutional contradictions," in W. Powell and P. DiMaggio (eds) *The New Institutionalism in Organizational Analysis*, pp. 232–63. Chicago: University of Chicago Press.

Geertz, C. (1973) *The Interpretation of Cultures*. New York: Basic Books.

Giddens, A. (1984) *The Constitution of Society: Outline of a Theory of Structuration*. Cambridge: Polity Press.

Gouldner, A. (1954) *Wildcat Strike*. Yellow Springs, OH: Antioch Press.

Greenwood, R., and Hinings C. R. (1996) "Understanding radical organizational change: bringing together the old and the new institutionalism," *Academy of Management Review*, 21: 1022–54.

Gusfield, J. (1963) *Symbolic Crusade: Status Politics and the American Temperance Movement.* Urbana, IL: University of Illinois Press.

Hardy, C., and Clegg, S. (1996) "Some dare call it power," in S. Clegg, C. Hardy, and W. R. Nord (eds) *Handbook of Organization Studies*, pp. 622–41. Thousand Oaks, CA: Sage.

Haveman, H. A., and Rao, H. (1997) "Structuring a theory of moral sentiments: institutional and organizational coevolution in the early thrift industry," *American Journal of Sociology*, 102: 1606–51.

Hirsch, P. M. (1985) "The study of industries," *Research in the Sociology of Organizations*, 4: 271–309.

——(1986) "From ambushes to golden parachutes: corporate takeovers as an instance of cultural framing and institutional integration," *American Journal of Sociology*, 91: 800–37.

Hirsch, P. M., and Lounsbury, M. (1997) "Ending the family quarrel: toward a reconciliation of 'old' and 'new' institutionalisms," *American Behavioral Scientist*, 40: 406–18.

Hoffman, Andrew J. (1999) "Institutional evolution and change: environmentalism and the US chemical industry," *Academy of Management Journal*, 42: 351–71.

Hybels, R. C. (1994) "Legitimation, Population Density, and Founding Rates: The Institutionalization of Commercial Biotechnology in the United States, 1971–89," Ph.D. dissertation. Ithaca, NY: Johnson Graduate School of Management, Cornell University.

Kaghan, William N., and Phillips, Nelson (1998) "Building the Tower of Babel: communities of practice and paradigmatic pluralism in organization studies," *Organization*, 5: 191–215.

Leblebici, Huseyin, et al. (1991) "Institutional change and the transformation of interorganizational fields: an organizational history of the US radio broadcasting industry," *Administrative Science Quarterly*, 36: 333–63.

Lévi-Strauss, C. (1963) *Structural Anthropology.* New York: Basic Books.

Lounsbury, M. (2001) "Institutional sources of practice variation: staffing college and university recycling programs," *Administrative Science Quarterly*, 46: 29–56.

——(2002) "Institutional transformation and status mobility: the professionalization of the field of finance," *Academy of Management Journal*, 45: 255–66.

Lounsbury, M., and Kaghan, W. N. (2001) "Organizations, occupations and the structuration of work," *Research in the Sociology of Work*, 10: 25–50.

Lounsbury, M., and Ventresca, M. J., eds (2002) *Social Structure and Organizations Revisited*, Research in the Sociology of Organizations 19. New York: JAI Press/Elsevier.

Lounsbury, M., Ventresca, M. J., and Hirsch, P. M. (forthcoming) "Social movements, field frames and industry emergence: a cultural-political perspective on US recycling," *Socioeconomic Review*.

Marx, K. (1852/1994) *The 18th Brumaire of Louis Bonaparte.* New York: International Publishers.

Meyer, J. W., and Scott, W. R., eds (1983) *Organizational Environments: Ritual and Rationality.* Beverly Hills, CA: Sage.

Meyer, J. W., Boli, J., and Thomas, G. M. (1987) "Ontology and rationalization in the Western cultural account," in G. M. Thomas et al. (eds) *Institutional Structure: Constituting State, Society, and the Individual*, pp. 12–37. Thousand Oaks, CA: Sage.

Mische, A., and Pattison, P. (2000) "Composing a civic arena: publics, projects, and social settings," *Poetics*, 27: 163–94.

Mohr, J. W. (1998) "Measuring meaning structures," *Annual Review of Sociology*, 24: 345–70.

Mohr, J. W., and Guerra-Pearson, F. (forthcoming) "The differentiation of institutional space: organizational forms in the New York social welfare sector, 1888–1917," in W. W. Powell and D. Jones (eds) *Bending the Bars of the Iron Cage.* Chicago: University of Chicago Press.

Moore, K. (1996) Organizing integrity: American science and the creation of public interest organizations, 1955–75," *American Journal of Sociology*, 101: 1592–627.

Ortner, S. B. (1994) "Theory on anthropology since the 1960s," in N. B. Dirks, G. Eley, and S. B. Ortner (eds) *Culture/Power/History: A Reader in Contemporary Social Theory*, pp. 372–411. Princeton, NJ: Princeton University Press.

Perrow, C. (1986) *Complex Organizations: A Critical Essay*, third edition. New York: McGraw-Hill.

——(2002) *Organizing America: Wealth, Power, and the Origins of Corporate Capitalism.* Princeton, NJ: Princeton University Press.

Powell, Walter W. (1991) "Expanding the scope of institutional analysis," in W. W. Powell and P. J. DiMaggio (eds) *The New Institutionalism in Organizational Analysis*, pp. 183–203. Chicago: University of Chicago Press.

Powell, W. W., and DiMaggio, P. J., eds (1991) *The New Institutionalism in Organizational Analysis*. Chicago: University of Chicago Press.

Rao, H., Morrill, C., and Zald, M. N. (2000) "Power plays: social movements, collective action and new organizational forms," *Research in Organizational Behavior*, 22: 237–82.

Ruef, M. (1999) "Social ontology and the dynamics of organizational forms: creating market actors in the health care field, 1966–94," *Social Forces*, 77: 1405–34.

——(2000) "The emergence of organizational forms: a community ecology approach," *American Journal of Sociology*, 106: 658–714.

Ruef, M., and Scott, W. R. (1998) "A multidimensional model of organizational legitimacy: hospital survival in changing institutional environments," *Administrative Science Quarterly*, 43: 877–904.

Schneiberg, M., and Clemens, E. S. (forthcoming) "The typical tools for the job: research strategies in institutional analysis," in W. W. Powell and D. Jones (eds) *Bending the Bars of the Iron Cage*. Chicago: University of Chicago Press.

Scott, W. R. (1994) "Conceptualizing organizational fields," in Hans-Ulrich Derlien, Uta Gerhardt, and Fritz W. Scharpf (eds) *Systemrationalität und Partialinteresse*, pp. 203–21. Baden Baden: Nomos.

——(2001) *Institutions and Organizations*, second edition. Newbury Park, CA.: Sage.

Scott, W. R., Mendel, P., and Pollack, S. (forthcoming) "Environments and fields: studying the evolution of a field of medical care organizations," in W. W. Powell and D. Jones (eds) *Bending the Bars of the Iron Cage*. Chicago: University of Chicago Press.

Scott, W. R., Ruef, M., Mendel, P., and Caronna, C. (2000) *Institutional Change and Health Care Organizations: From Professional Dominance to Managed Care*. Chicago: University of Chicago Press.

Selznick, P. (1949) *TVA and the Grass Roots.* Berkeley, CA: University of California Press.

Smart, B. (1985) *Michel Foucault*. London: Tavistock.

Stern, R. N., and Barley, S. R. (1996) "Organizations and social systems: organization theory's neglected mandate," *Administrative Science Quarterly*, 41: 146–62.

Stinchcombe, Arthur L. (1965) "Social structure and organizations," in James G. March (ed.) *Handbook of Organizations*, pp. 142–93. Chicago: Rand McNally.

——(1978) *Theoretical Methods in Social History*. New York: Academic Press.

Strang, David, and Meyer, J. W. (1993) "Institutional conditions for diffusion," *Theory and Society*, 22: 487–512.

Strang, D., and Soule, S. A. (1998) "Diffusion in organizations and social movements: from hybrid corn to poison pills," *Annual Review of Sociology*, 24: 265–90.

Thornton, P. H., and Ocasio, W. (1999) "Institutional logics and the historical contingency of power in organizations: executive succession in the higher education publishing industry, 1958–90," *American Journal of Sociology*, 105: 801–43.

Tolbert, P. S., and Zucker, L. G. (1996) "The institutionalization of institutional theory," in S. Clegg, C. Hardy, and W. Nord (eds) *Handbook of Organization Studies*, pp. 175–90. Thousand Oaks, CA: Sage.

Ventresca, M. J., and Mohr, J. W. (2002) "Archival research methods," in J. A. C. Baum (ed.) *Companion to Organizations*, pp. 805–28. Oxford: Blackwell.

Wilmott, H. (1993) "Strength is ignorance: slavery is freedom: managing culture in modern organizations," *Journal of Management Studies*, 30: 515–52.

Wrong, Dennis H. (1994) *The Problem of Order*. New York: Free Press.

Zald, M. N. (1971) *Occupations and Organizations in American Society*. Chicago: Markham.

Zald, M. N., and Berger, M. A. (1978) "Social movements in organizations: *coups d'état*, insurgency, and mass movements," *American Journal of Sociology*, 83: 823–61.

Zelizer, V. A. (1979) *Morals and Markets: The Development of Life Insurance in the United States*. New York: Columbia University Press.

7b Discourse or Institution? Institutional Theory and the Challenge of Critical Discourse Analysis

Nelson Phillips

In chapter 7(b) I argue that discourse analysis provides a significant challenge to existing work in institutional theory. In particular, I argue that discourse analysis provides a broader, more developed explanation for the nature of institutions, the process of institutionalization, and the role of agency and power in institutional dynamics. In other words, discourse analysis provides a much more nuanced view of institutional processes than institutional theory! While the roots of new institutionalism lie in the social constructionism of Berger and Luckmann, in its current form it provides little explanation of the processes of social construction that underlie institutions, no explanation of the role of self-interested action, and no theory of power. At the same time, the new institutionalism has developed an interesting and useful perspective on the constraining aspects of institutions and has contributed the useful idea of an institutional field. Furthermore, the development of neo-institutional theory as an alternative to the new institutionalism is beginning to provide a more satisfactory view of institutions and institutional dynamics while retaining much of the contribution of the new institutionalism. In fact, in the latter part of the chapter, I argue that the neo-institutional perspective may be productively combined with ideas from discourse analysis to provide a much more balanced and nuanced alternative to the new institutionalism.

There is an important theoretical affinity between discourse analysis and institutional theory: where institutional theory is concerned with the effects of institutions as they appear and propagate across institutional fields, discourse analysis is intimately concerned with the processes of social construction that underlie institutions. But the exact nature of this affinity has gone largely unexplored, perhaps in part because of the difficulty of dealing with the range of approaches to discourse analysis and institutional theory that exist in their respective literatures, and in part because of the relative newness of relevant approaches to discourse analysis. In this chapter I will explore the link between institutional theory and discourse analysis and argue that one form of discourse analysis, critical discourse analysis (e.g., Fairclough, 1992, 1995; Fairclough and Wodak, 1997; Mumby and Clair, 1997), has the most potential for constructively critiquing existing forms of institutional theory and for supporting the development of an alternative and more robust theory of institutions.

Critical discourse analysis stands as a strong critique of several weaknesses of institutionalism in general, and of the new institutionalism (e.g., Powell and DiMaggio, 1991) in particular. First, critical discourse analysis highlights the failure of the new institutionalism to deal with power and agency, the most serious theoretical challenge to further work in this area. Interestingly, new institutionalists have for some time noted that they have failed to deal with these issues and have even coined the term "institutional entrepreneur" (DiMaggio, 1988: 14) to describe an actor who works to manage his or her institutional environment. At the same time, little has actually been done to re-inject a concern for purposeful action undertaken to manage an actor's institutional context. Critical discourse analysis challenges new institutional theory to take their self-critiques seriously and to work much harder to develop a theory of institutional processes that includes the earlier focus of the old institutionalism on power and agency and the new institutionalists' interest in isomorphism and broad social processes. While neo-institutional theorists (e.g., Greenwood and Hinings, 1996; Martin de Holan and Phillips, forthcoming) have begun this process, the critiques of critical discourse analysis highlight how much more work remains and point in some potentially fruitful directions.

Second, institutional theory has failed spectacularly in dealing with the issue of social construction. While the roots of the new institutionalism lie in social constructionism

(Berger and Luckmann, 1967; Meyer and Rowan, 1977), there has been an almost complete failure to develop an understanding of how institutions are actually constructed. While the occasional nod is given towards structuration (e.g., DiMaggio, 1988; Phillips et al., 2000; Ranson et al., 1980; Barley and Tolbert, 1997), no real attempt has been made to include a strong constructionist epistemology or to integrate recent developments in social constructionism (e.g., Gergen, 1999, 2001) into institutional theory. Instead, new and neo-institutionalism have concentrated on the effects of institutions while not exploring their constitution in social practice. Discourse analysis is specifically concerned with processes of social construction and, in particular, in the constitution of the institutions that populate social reality. Discourse analysis therefore provides a critique of institutionalism but also a potentially productive synergy of concern and contribution.

Critical discourse analysis and the new institutionalism therefore exist in a precarious position. While sharing obvious empirical interests and theoretical forebears, they are also at odds in terms of theoretical focus and practical emphasis. While institutionalists technically accept the role of institutions in constraining and enabling action, their actual theoretical and empirical work focuses almost exclusively on the constraining aspect. Institutions are seen as acting "behind people's backs" to shape their behavior and limit choice. The availability of institutions as resources for powerful agents is largely missing from new institutionalism. Furthermore, the ability of agents to act purposely to shape institutions in ways that advantage them is largely absent from the institutional theory literature. Where critical discourse analysis points to the central role of purposeful action in the shaping of institutional contexts, mainstream institutional theory views institutions as coming in to being and disappearing through an institutional logic that proceeds outside of the world of everyday actors. Institutions affect actors, appear, change, and disappear, following an internal logic of their own that is inaccessible to actors in the domain and that is largely taken for granted in institutional theory.

But this version of institutional theory is showing serious wear and tear, for several reasons. First, this idea of institutional processes can be sustained only by focusing on the most macro levels of organizational behavior. As institutional theorists begin to abandon the very long time frames and large populations of organizations that made up the early focus of research in this area, the active role of the institutional entrepreneur becomes evident. When time frames are shorter and the focus is redirected to individual organizations, it is clear that actors are highly involved in the processes of structuration that underlie institutionalization. They act strategically to shape the institutional context through a range of strategies aimed at changing the mimetic, coercive, or normative pressures experienced by other actors in their domain. Second, institutions embody relations of power that advantage and disadvantage actors, and this system of advantage provides the motivation for actors to act as institutional entrepreneurs. Understanding the connection between institutions and power is therefore not just about understanding how agents use power to shape institutions, but also about understanding the dynamics of institutions as a backdrop for interorganizational activity. While this system of advantage and disadvantage is obvious to participants in institutional fields, it remains outside of conventional discussions of institutional theory. Third, institutions depend on sets of texts that bring them into being, that maintain them, and that may, at times, lead them to disappear. It is not the practices themselves that disseminate across fields but stories, reports, descriptions, and a variety of other texts describing the practice. It is at this level of social construction that agents work to affect processes of institutionalization in ways that fit with their interests. The relation between textual production and institutions is therefore a critical topic for institutional theorists as they attempt to integrate a concern with power and agency into institutional theory.

In exploring the challenge and potential of the connection between critical discourse analysis and institutional theory, I will proceed in three steps. First, I will present a general overview of discourse analysis, focusing in particular on critical discourse analysis and its usefulness in understanding the production of social reality. Critical discourse analysis is particularly helpful in developing a more balanced view of institutions, given its sensitivity to power and agency. Second, I will discuss the development of institutional theory and some of the current ideas regarding institutions, institutionalization, and institutional fields that are common in the literature. Finally, I will draw together the institutional and critical discourse strands of my argument. I will argue that critical discourse analysis provides important arguments for a view of institutional theory that fits closely with recent arguments for neo-institutional theory, but that includes a much more developed idea of the processes of social construction that underlie institutions and of the role of power in institutional dynamics.

Understanding Discourse Analysis

Like many concepts in social science, the term "discourse analysis" has been defined and used in many ways. But this diversity, and the complex arguments that go along with it, have little to add to the discussion of institutional theory and discourse analysis that I am presenting here. (See van Dijk, 1997, for a detailed discussion.) Instead, what we need is a general and inclusive idea of what is meant by terms like "discourse" and "discourse analysis" in order to proceed with our discussion. In this section I will therefore define discourse and several related terms in a way that is most useful for us here and provide an overview of the broad diversity of approaches to discourse analysis that exist in the literature. I will then focus on the form of discourse analysis that I believe is the most useful in considering institutionalization and institutions.

Discourse, text, and context

Discourse analysis shares the concern of all qualitative approaches with the meaningfulness of social life (Winch, 1958). But, unlike more traditional qualitative methods, it adopts a strong social constructivist epistemology (Oswick et al., 2000). It does not assume a social world and then seek to understand the meaning of that world for participants. Instead,

it tries to explore the ways in which the socially produced ideas and objects that populate the world are created and maintained. This is the most important contribution of discourse analysis. Where other qualitative methodologies work to understand or interpret social reality as it exists, discourse analysis endeavors to uncover the way it is produced. It examines how language constructs phenomena, not how it reflects and reveals it. In other words, discourse analysis views discourse *as* constitutive of the social world, not a route to it, and assumes the world cannot be known separately from discourse.

[Discourse analysis] is not only about method; it is also a perspective on the nature of language and its relationship to the central issues of the social sciences. More specifically, we see discourse analysis as a related collection of approaches to discourse, approaches that entail not only practices of data collection and analysis, but also a set of metatheoretical and theoretical assumptions and a body of research claims and studies. (Wood and Kroger, 2000: x)

Within the discourse analysis literature, a discourse is commonly understood as an interrelated set of texts, and the related practices of production, dissemination, and reception, that bring an object into being (Hardy and Phillips, 1999; Parker, 1992). For example, the collection of texts of various kinds, and the related discursive practices, that make up the discourse of psychiatry brought the idea of an unconscious into existence in the mid nineteenth century (Foucault, 1965). Prior to the appearance of this discourse, there was no concept of the "unconscious" that could be used to understand and explain human mental processes. Since the appearance of this discourse, it is widely taken for granted (in Western countries, at least) that humans have something called an unconscious and our idea of how the human mind functions has therefore fundamentally changed. The discourse of psychiatry constituted a particular social object, the unconscious, and made it available as a resource for social action.

Discourses are embodied and enacted in a variety of texts, but exist beyond the individual texts that compose them (Chalaby, 1996). Texts are thus both the building blocks of discourse and a material manifestation of it.

Texts are the sites of the emergence of complexes of social meanings, produced in the particular history of the situation of production, that record in partial ways the histories of both the participants in the production of the text and of the institutions that are "invoked" or brought into play, indeed a partial history of the language and the social system, a partiality due to the structurings of relations of power of the participants. (Kress, 1995: 122)

Texts may take a variety of forms, including written texts, spoken words, pictures, symbols, artefacts, etc. (Grant et al., 1998). What is interesting from a discourse analysis perspective is how they are made meaningful – how they draw on other texts and other discourses, how and to whom they are disseminated, and the ways in which they are produced, received, and consumed (Phillips and Brown, 1993) – and what effect collections of texts have on the social context in which they occur.

Discourse analysis, therefore, is the structured and systematic study of collections of interrelated texts and the processes of their production, dissemination, and consumption. But this is not a simple task. Discursive activity does not occur in a vacuum, and discourses do not "possess" meaning that can be mechanistically measured. Instead, the meanings of texts and discourses are complex and shifting, emanating out of interactions between social actors and occurring within the complex societal structures in which the discourse is embedded. Thus, to understand discourses and their effects, we must also understand the social context in which they arise (Sherzer, 1987; van Dijk, 1997).

Discourse is not produced without context and cannot be understood without taking context into

consideration . . . Discourses are always connected to other discourses which were produced earlier, as well as those which are produced synchronically and subsequently. (Fairclough and Wodak, 1997: 277)

The study of discourse is therefore "three-dimensional" (Fairclough, 1992) in the sense that it (1) focuses on texts (2) located in a discourse (3) that is inextricably linked to a social context which produces it and which it, in part, constitutes. It is this connection between discourse and society that makes discourse analysis interesting to social scientists and where discourse analysis and institutional theory come together. From a discourse perspective, institutions are constituted in discourse.

Approaches to Discourse Analysis

While the above definition of discourse analysis provides a clear understanding of discourse analysis, it is intentionally broad. It is not surprising, then, that there are many different approaches that fit this definition, and anyone interested in discourse analysis faces the challenge of making sense of the diversity of the field. In analyzing a series of empirical studies of discourse analysis Phillips and Ravasi (1998) found that they could be categorized along two key theoretical dimensions. The first dimension concerns the relative importance of text versus context in the research. The second dimension concerns the degree to which the researcher focuses on the relationship between discourse and power. Figure 7.1 combines these two dimensions to identify four main perspectives in discourse analysis (Phillips and Ravasi, 1998; Phillips and Hardy, 2002).

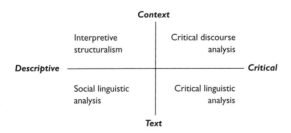

Figure 7.1 Different approaches to discourse analysis

The vertical axis shows the continuum between *text* and *context*. This continuum may seem surprising, given the last section, where I emphasized the importance of seeing discourse as being constituted by multiple texts in a particular social and historical context. The need for three-dimensional approaches to research means that researchers should include text *and* context in their studies, and consider discourse "as a constitutive part of its local and global, social and cultural contexts" (Fairclough, 1995: 29). While this represents an important theoretical ideal, conducting empirical research is another matter, since researchers are forced to make choices about the data they select – no researcher can study everything. Consequently, empirical studies tend to focus more closely on either the broad social context or on a particular piece of text (Burman and Parker, 1993; Keenoy et al., 1997; Alvesson and Karreman, 2000). Some studies will focus on the microanalysis of particular texts; others will conduct a broader sweep of the discursive elements of particular contexts; and, since this is a continuum not a dichotomy, some studies combine some elements of both.

The horizontal axis reflects the choice between *critical* approaches, which include an explicit interest in the dynamics of power, knowledge, and ideology, and *descriptive* approaches that simply explore the way in which a particular social reality has been constructed. Critical studies are relatively common in discourse analysis, owing to the early influence of Foucault's work. In addition, the role of discourse theory in reinvigorating critical research agendas has led to a substantial body of critically informed empirical work.

Not all work is so explicitly interested in power, however, and many studies explore the constructive effects of discourse without explicitly considering the political dynamics. Important bodies of work in disciplines such as sociology (Gergen, 1991) or psychology (e.g., Harré, 1995; Parker, 1992; Potter and Wetherell, 1987) have produced empirical work that is more focused on descriptions of constructive processes than power and politics *per se*. Rather than exploring who benefits or is disadvantaged by a socially constructed "reality," these researchers are more interested in

understanding the way in which discourses ensure that certain phenomena are created, reified and taken for granted and come to constitute that "reality" (e.g., Hirsch, 1986; Dunford and Jones, 2000).

By combining the two axes we can identify four major perspectives that are adopted in empirical studies (Phillips and Ravasi, 1998). They are social linguistic analysis, interpretive structuralism, critical discourse analysis, and critical linguistic analysis. (For other categorizations see Putnam and Fairhurst, 2000.) It is important to keep in mind that the dimensions of this framework are continua, not simple categories or dichotomies. The end points of the axis of the framework represent ideal types in the Weberian sense: not all research will necessarily fall neatly into a particular category. However, these four categories do allow us to identify quite different styles of empirical research.

But while all of the approaches to discourse analysis provide important insights into processes of social construction, the above typology makes it clear why some kinds of discourse analysis are more useful and interesting for critiquing and contributing to institutional theory. First, institutional theory focuses squarely on context. Institutional theory is interested in the role of institutions in shaping social action and on the emergence and development of institutional fields. Therefore, discourse analytic perspectives that focus more on context will more directly connect to the concerns of institutional theory. Second, more critical perspectives provide the tools to include power in considerations of institutional processes. While more descriptive forms of discourse analysis may fit more comfortably with existing approaches to institutional theory, it is the more critical forms that have the most to contribute to the development of new, more powerful forms of institutional theory.

Critical discourse analysis and institution theory

Critical discourse analysis focuses on the role of discursive activity in constituting and sustaining power relations:

Discourse as a political practice establishes, sustains and changes power relations, and the collective entities (classes, blocs, communities, groups) between which power relations obtain. Discourse as an ideological practice constitutes, naturalizes, sustains and changes significations of the world from diverse positions in power relations. (Fairclough, 1992: 67)

Researchers engaged in critical discourse analysis attempt to analyze "dialogical struggle (or struggles) as reflected in the privileging of a particular discourse and the marginalization of others" (Keenoy et al., 1997: 150; Mumby and Stohl, 1991). Often drawing on the work of Fairclough (1992), this perspective focuses on how discursive activity structures the social space within which actors act – how it privileges some actors at the expense of others, and how broad general changes in the discourse result in different constellations of advantage and disadvantage. For example, Phillips and Hardy's (1997) study of the discourse surrounding refugees showed how certain groups in the refugee system had the right to speak while others were silenced, and how different groups attempted to draw on discourses that gave them a greater right to speak.

From this perspective, discourses constitute three kinds of social entities: concepts, objects, and subject positions (Fairclough, 1992; Hardy and Phillips, 1999). These broad categories provide an important typology for understanding the sorts of things constituted in discourse and will provide the basis for understanding types of institutions in the next section.

But what differentiates concepts, objects, and subject positions? While all three kinds of social constructions have similar ontological status, they are differentiable in important ways. Concepts are the "ideas, categories, relationships, and theories through which we understand the world and relate to one another" (Hardy and Phillips, 1999: 3). They are more or less contested social constructions residing only in the realm of the ideal that form the culturally and historically situated frame for understanding social reality. They are often the site of struggles as actors with different interests contest particular understandings as they work to shape the social world to their advantage. More specifically, they are ideas like sustainable development or Total Quality Management that have effects in the material world through their influence on behavior but that

themselves are purely ideal. They exist in structured collections of texts of various kinds – discourses – and are critically important for their role in structuring the social world and providing us with the meaningfulness that underlies social action and interaction.

Objects, on the other hand, are part of the practical realm. They are partially ideal but have a material aspect. When a concept is used to make some aspect of material reality meaningful, an object has been constituted. This is not to say that discourse "reveals" some pre-existing reality but rather that it makes some part of an essentially meaningless and undifferentiable material world meaningful and differentiable. For example, in their study of refugee determination, Hardy and Phillips (1999) differentiated between the concept of a refugee which existed only in the ideal and the individuals who were constituted as refugees through the discursive practices associated with the refugee determination process. These individuals were not refugees in some essential sense whose refugee status simply needed to be revealed by the determination process. Rather, the discourse of refugee determination provided a set of discursive practices and the concept of a refugee that allowed refugees to be constituted. And, just as the definition of a concept is often highly contested, this process of constituting objects is often highly contested, as it may have significant ramifications for those involved.

Subject positions differ fundamentally from objects and concepts in that they are locations in social space from which certain carefully delimited agents can produce certain kinds of texts in certain ways. As Hardy and Phillips (1999: 4) explain:

These different subject positions have different rights to speak. In other words, some individuals, by virtue of their position in the discourse, will warrant a louder voice than others, while others may warrant no voice at all.

For example, the discourse of psychiatry includes the subject position of psychiatrist, who has the right to produce texts that determine the sanity of individuals. This ability to produce texts is important for two reasons. First, being able to inhabit a subject position allows the agent to have particular effects on how objects are constituted. Second, many of the texts that make up the discourse are produced from certain socially constructed positions that can be inhabited by certain kinds of agents. Being able to inhabit one of these positions allows the agent to have particular effects on the discourse. However, at the same time, the kinds of texts that can be produced are highly constrained. Producing texts that "break the rules" often results in the agent losing the legitimate right to take up the subject position. Obviously, the nature of these positions and the discursive privileges associated with them are often the focus of intense struggle as different agents with different interests come into conflict.

The analytic framework of critical discourse analysis that I have presented up to this point focuses our attention on the role of discourse, the importance of power, and the existence of struggle. What is missing is a sense of agency. It is critical to temper the tendency to view discourses as deterministic by two observations. First, discourses are never completely cohesive, without internal tensions, and therefore able to determine social reality. They are always partial, often cross-cut by inconsistencies and contradiction, and almost always contested to some degree. Second, agents are commonly embedded in multiple discourses. The tension between these discourses produces discursive space in which the agent can play one discourse against another, draw on multiple discourses to work to create new forms of interdiscursivity, and otherwise move between and across multiple discourses. The result of these limits of discourse is a substantial space within which agents can act self-interestedly and work towards discursive change that privileges their interests and goals.

The idea of a more or less well bounded and cohesive discourse producing concepts, objects, and subject positions provides a very useful framework for examining processes of institutionalization and the production of institutional fields. From this perspective, institutions are social constructions produced by discourses. Discourse shapes the actions of agents, but agents also act to shape discourse and hence the institutional field in which they act.

Discourse and Institutions

In this section I will begin with a brief overview of institutional theory as a prelude to discussing institutionalism from a critical discourse perspective. My summary of institutional theory is intentionally brief and rather schematic, as my primary interest in this section is the ramifications of discourse analysis for institutional theory. I intend my discussion to be thought-provoking and preparatory. I will simply outline some initial thoughts on the challenge and potential contribution of discourse analysis to a reinvigorated and grander version of institutional theory.

Institutionalism

The relation between change and stability is a point of some contention within institutional theory and provides a useful departure point for understanding the different perspectives that exist within institutional theory. On the one hand, much of recent institutional theory – the new institutionalism (e.g., DiMaggio and Powell, 1983; Meyer and Rowan, 1977; Powell and DiMaggio, 1991) – has focused on the role of institutions in reducing variety, limiting choice, and stabilizing the practices, technologies, and rules that characterize a particular institutional field (Leblebici et al., 1991). From this perspective, institutional forces work to reduce choice and produce similarity in organizational characteristics of various kinds. At the same time, early forms of institutional theory (e.g. Selznick, 1948, 1949, 1957), as well as some more recent work (Dougherty, 1994; Lawrence, 1999; Oliver, 1991), have pointed to the role of institutional processes in producing change: in particular to the fact that individuals or coalitions may act as institutional entrepreneurs and purposely produce change in institutions of various kinds in ways that help them reach their goals (Lawrence et al., forthcoming; Lawrence, 1999; Oliver, 1991). From this perspective, influence, coalitions, and values are the keys to understanding the institutions that grow out of the interaction among actors in a complex institutional field.

But this split between old and new forms of institutionalism is becoming less clear, and it would appear that some form of "neo-institutionalism" is appearing that "involves all of the elements of the old and new institutional theory" (Greenwood and Hinings, 1996: 1023). This new form of institutionalism combines ideas of legitimation and isomorphism, and their limitations on behavior, with ideas of agency and institutional entrepreneurship that recognize institutional processes as a legitimate arena for purposeful action. The result is a more nuanced theory that argues that these are not opposing perspectives at all, but rather describe different aspects of the same phenomenon that appear more or less clearly in particular cases depending on the nature of the processes at work. Sometimes institutional forces stabilize, sometimes they create strong pressure for change; sometimes institutional entrepreneurs may act to create change, sometimes to buttress existing arrangements. The challenge, then, is to understand when the dynamics of institutional processes will result in which sort of pressure.

This new variant of institutional theory, however, remains undeveloped. While neo-institutionalism provides a framework for understanding the complex institutional pressures for and against change (and, in particular, helps in analyzing the events that precipitate organizational change), it provides little guidance in understanding the process of institutional management and the resulting dynamics of institutional change. Researchers have made significant progress in identifying the kinds of institutional phenomena that are important, but it is still unclear how they develop and interact. As Greenwood and Hinings (1996: 1023) argue:

Institutional theory is not usually regarded as a theory of organizational change, but as an explanation of the similarity ("isomorphism") and stability of organizational arrangements in a given population or field of organizations. Here we present the opposite view, agreeing with Dougherty that the theory contains an "excellent basis" for an account of change . . . As formulated, however, neo-institutional theory is weak in analyzing the internal dynamics of organizational change. As a consequence, the theory is silent on why some organizations adopt radical change while others do not, despite experiencing the same institutional pressures. Nevertheless, neo-institutional theory contains insights and suggestions that, when elaborated, provide a model of change

that links organizational context and interorganizational dynamics.

My arguments in this chapter are therefore primarily directed at critiquing the intentionally onesided view of new institutionalism and supporting the development of a more balanced view of institutions and their dynamics. The value of focusing on the constraining aspect of institutional processes that characterized new institutionalism in its early forms has been replaced by an "institutionalized" myopia regarding change and agency. Something more like neo-institutional theory combined with a strong constructivist epistemology is needed that will push for a much greater sensitivity to change, agency, and power.

A discursive theory of institutional processes

Critical discourse analysis therefore stands as a critique of the new institutionalism and a strong supporter of neo institutionalism. It offers an epistemology and a method that support the general interests of institutional theory while providing an important critique of the increasing narrowness of new institutionalism. In this section I will discuss several key concepts in institutional theory from a critical discourse perspective.

The core concept in institutional theory is, of course, institutionalization. How institutions come into being is the fundamental process in a world constituted by institutions. But this is not a concept that is well defined in the institutional theory literature. In fact, it is seldom defined at all. There is a general consensus in the institutional theory literature that the production of institutions is a process of social construction (Powell and DiMaggio, 1991; Meyer and Rowan, 1977), and there has been some discussion of how institutions come into being through a process of structuration (e.g., Barley and Tolbert, 1997; Powell and DiMaggio, 1991; Ranson et al., 1984), but the resulting understanding fails to provide a sufficient framework for theoretical discussion and empirical research. For example, consider the following definition of institutionalization:

the social process by which individuals come to accept a shared definition of social reality – a conception whose validity is seen as independent of the actor's own views or actions but is taken for granted as defining the "way things are" and/or the "way things are to be done." (Hannan, 1997: 196)

While this is a cogent and convincing description of the effects of institutionalization, it says very little about the underlying mechanism or social process at work. What makes things "taken for granted as defining the way things are"? Critical discourse analysis provides the beginnings of an answer by focusing the attention of institutionalists back on the underlying processes of social construction. When a sufficient number of texts have been produced by actors who can make those texts stick, then an institution comes into being. The greater the number of texts and the more well structured the discourse, the more "institutionalized" the institution becomes. In other words, where there is an institution there must be a discourse, and where we find well delimited discourses we would expect highly institutionalized practices and understandings. Understanding the process of discursive production is therefore the basis for understanding the process of institutionalization and for broadening institutional theory to include a concern with institutional production, as well as with how institutions disseminate and their resulting effects.

Conversely, discourse analysis also provides an explanation for the process of deinstitutionalization: institutions become deinstitutionalized when the discourse that supports them becomes eroded and fragmented. As contrary texts are produced, either purposely or accidentally, or as the discourse is no longer reproduced, the discourse upon which the institution depends weakens and the institution becomes less institutionalized. This can occur through the activities of institutional entrepreneurs within the field or owing to changes in the broader societal framework on which the discourses that characterize a particular field depend. In any case, the result is a loss of coherence and structure within the discourse and a resulting loss in the "taken-for-grantedness" of the institution.

One very important point here is that it is not the practices or understandings themselves that propagate, but descriptions of the practice or understanding. For example, TQM did not become institutionalized in particular institutional fields because the practice itself was somehow disseminated, but because of a range of texts that were produced describing and detailing the practices and experiences of organizations. It was these texts that disseminated throughout the field and led to the insitutionalization of TQM as a practice. These texts collected into a discourse of TQM that constituted a set of concepts that other organizations could adopt. The concept of TQM was used within particular organizations to constitute an object, which was the particular TQM program in a particular company.

The production of an institutional field can be similarly explained by critical discourse analysis. An institutional field is a social space encompassing a set of organizations that "constitute a recognized area of institutional life" (DiMaggio and Powell, 1983: 148) and that is characterized by "a particular distribution of institutionalized rules and resources, cultural and structural equivalence, and network interconnections" (Hardy and Phillips, 1999: 5). When a set of discourses come to dominate the interorganizational context of a set of organizations a field will be constituted. Each of the institutions that characterize the field will depend on a more or less developed discourse and we can say that the field itself is constituted by this set of discourses.

In both the cases, texts are produced by actors of various kinds with varying degrees of access to channels of communication and varying skills at text production. More powerful actors will generally be able to affect this process more directly by being able to create more convincing texts that draw more creatively on other texts and discourses and distribute them more widely. In other words, institutional entrepreneurs will produce texts in an effort to shape the discourse, and hence the institutional field, in ways that fit with their interests. How exactly this happens in the sorts of institutional fields that management researchers are interested in is an empirical question that a discourse analytic framework and methods will allow institutional theorists to explore.

While I can only begin to explore the potential synergies between institutional theory and discourse analysis in this section, it is clear that critical discourse analysis provides a useful foundation for building a much more powerful version of institutional theory that includes a sensitivity to power and agency along with an appreciation for the constraining effect of institutions. Institutions constrain, but they are not all-powerful, and the activities of agents shape institutions over time; agents work to shape the institutional field in which they act but are limited in their ability to act by the institutional field they are in and by the way the existing institutions shape their interests. How this dynamic plays out is an empirical question that requires much more research. However, the nature of this relation is invisible from the perspective of new institutionalism, and only by adopting a strong constructivist epistemology and a critical perspective can it be unraveled.

Conclusion

Institutional theory and discourse analysis sit in an uneasy relation. On the one hand, discourse analysis can be seen as a strong critique of institutional theory, or perhaps even as an alternative that describes the same phenomena but without some of the limitations and blind spots that are associated with the new institutionalism. On the other hand, discourse analysis can be seen as an ally of institutional theory, sharing its interest in institutions and its strong social constructionist foundations. From this perspective the two theoretical frames come from the same epistemological roots, and the constructive tension between the two has important potential to contribute to the development of a broader and more powerful version of institutional theory that avoids some of the excesses of the new institutionalism, that includes a focus on the processes of social construction that underlie institutions, and that includes an explicit concern with power and agency.

I am obviously a strong supporter of the latter view. While it is clear that some approaches to institutional theory have lost touch with their roots in social constructionism, much of the most interesting work in institutional theory remains complementary to the epistemology and methodology of discourse analysis. In fact, discourse analytic methods will help challenge a tendency in the new institutionalism to lose touch with the fact that institutional processes are highly social. The early formulations of Meyer and Rowan (1977) and DiMaggio and Powell (1983) included an important concern with meaning, interpretation, and legitimacy that can too easily be lost in the enthusiasm to apply statistical methods and mathematical models. A loss that strikes at the heart of institutionalism and threatens to lose touch with what has made institution theory arguably the dominant paradigm in organization theory.

In conclusion, the meeting point between discourse analysis and institutional theory is a very interesting and potentially productive place. In this chapter I have just begun to scratch the surface of the complex relationship between the two frameworks and to point to some of the potential contributions of discourse analysis to a new, reinvigorated institutional theory constructed along the lines argued by neo-institutionalists. In fact, I would argue that discourse analysis as a method and a methodology provides just the theoretical framework and empirical tools for neo-institutionalists to begin to show how much more institutional theory can contribute to our understanding of organizational and interorganizational dynamics!

Acknowledgment

In writing chapter 7(b) I have drawn heavily on ideas and frameworks that have grown out of my ongoing research collaboration with Cynthia Hardy and Thomas Lawrence. Without their intellectual contribution the chapter would not have been possible.

References

Alvesson, M., and Karreman, D. (2000) "Varieties of discourse: on the study of organizations through discourse analysis," *Human Relations*, 53 (9): 1125–49.

Barley, S. R., and Tolbert, P. S. (1997) "Institutionalization and structuration: studying the links between action and institution," *Organization Studies*, 18 (1): 93–117.

Berger, P. L., and Luckmann, T. (1967) *The Social Construction of Reality: A Treatise on the Sociology of Knowledge.* Garden City, NY: Anchor Books.

Burman, E., and Parker, I. (1993) "Against discursive imperialism, empiricism and constructionism: thirty-two problems with discourse analysis," in E. Burman and I. Parker (eds) *Discourse Analytic Research: Repertoires and Readings of Texts in Action,* pp. 155–72. London: Routledge.

Chalaby, J. K. (1996) "Beyond the prison-house of language: discourse as a sociological concept," *British Journal of Sociology,* 47 (4): 684–98.

DiMaggio, P. J. (1988) "Interest and agency in institutional theory," in L. G. Zucker (ed.) *Institutional Patterns and Organizations: Culture and Environment,* pp. 3–22. Cambridge, MA: Ballinger.

DiMaggio, P. J., and Powell, W. W. (1983) "The iron cage revisited: institutional isomorphism and collective rationality in organizational fields," *American Sociological Review,* 48: 147–60.

Dougherty, D. (1994) "Commentary," in P. Shrivastava, A. Huff, and J. Dutton (eds) *Advances in Strategic Management* X, pp. 107–12. Greenwich, CT: JAI Press.

Dunford, R., and Jones, D. (2000) "Narrative in strategic change," *Human Relations,* 53 (9): 1207–26.

Fairclough, N. (1992) *Discourse and Social Change.* Cambridge: Polity Press.

——(1995) *Critical Discourse Analysis: The Critical Study of Language.* London: Longman.

Fairclough, N., and Wodak R. (1997) "Critical discourse analysis," in T. A. van Dijk (ed.) *Discourse as Social Interaction* I. London: Sage.

Foucault, M. (1965) *Madness and Civilization: A History of Insanity in the Age of Reason.* New York: Vintage Books.

Gergen, K. (1991) *The Saturated Self.* Thousand Oaks, CA: Sage.

——(1999) *An Invitation to Social Construction.* London: Sage.

——(2001) *Social Construction in Context.* London: Sage.

Grant, D., Keenoy, T., and Oswick, C. (1998) "Organizational discourse: of diversity, dichotomy and multi-disciplinarity," in D. Grant, T. Keenoy, and C. Oswick (eds) *Discourse and Organization,* pp. 1–14. London: Sage.

Greenwood, R., and Hinings, C. R. (1996) "Understanding radical organizational change: bringing together the old and new institutionalism," *Academy of Management Review,* 21: 1033–54.

Hannan, M. T. (1997) "Inertia, density and the structure of organizational populations: entries in European automobile industries, 1886–1981," *Organization Studies,* 18 (2): 193–229.

Hardy, C., and Phillips, N. (1999) "No joking matter: discursive struggle in the Canadian refugee system," *Organization Studies,* 20 (1): 1–24.

Harré, R. (1995) "Discursive psychology," in J. A. Smith, R. Harré, and L. van Langenhove (eds), *Rethinking Psychology,* pp. 143–59. Thousand Oaks, CA: Sage.

Hirsch, P. M. (1986) "From ambushes to golden parachutes: corporate takeovers as an instance of cultural framing and institutional integration," *American Journal of Sociology,* 91: 800–37.

Keenoy, T., Oswick, C., and Grant, D. (1997) "Organizational discourses: text and context," *Organization,* 2: 147–58.

Kress, G. 1995. "The social production of language: history and structures of domination," in P. Fries and M. Gregory (eds), *Discourse in Society: Systemic Functional Perspectives,* pp. 169–91. Norwood, NJ: Ablex.

Lawrence, T. B. (1999) "Institutional strategy," *Journal of Management,* 25: 161–87.

Lawrence, T., Hardy, C., and Phillips, N. (forthcoming) "The institutional effects of interorganizational collaboration: the case of Mère et enfant (*Palestine*)," *Academy of Management Journal.*

Leblebici, H., Salancik, G. R., Copay, A., and King, T. (1991) "Institutional change and the transformation of interorganizational fields: an organizational history of the US radio broadcasting industry," *Administrative Science Quarterly,* 36: 333–63.

Martin de Holan, P., and Phillips, N. (forthcoming) "Managing in transition: a case study of institutional management and organizational change in Cuba," *Journal of Management Inquiry.*

Meyer, J. W., and Rowan, B. (1977) "Institutionalized organizations: formal structure as myth and ceremony," *American Journal of Sociology*, 83: 340–63.

Mumby, D., and Clair, R. P. (1997) "Organizational discourse," in T. A. van Dijk (ed.) *Discourse as Social Interaction*, pp. 181–205. London: Sage.

Mumby, D., and Stohl, C. (1991) "Power and discourse in organization studies: absence and the dialectic of control," *Discourse and Society*, 2: 313–22.

Oliver, C. (1991) "Strategic responses to institutional processes," *Academy of Management Review*, 16: 145–79.

Oswick, C., Keenoy, T., Grant, D., and Marshak, B. (2000) "Discourse, organization and epistemology," *Organization*, 7 (3): 511–12.

Parker, I. (1992) *Discourse Dynamics*. London: Routledge.

Phillips, N., and Brown, J. (1993) "Analyzing communication in and around organizations: a critical hermeneutic approach," *Academy of Management Journal*, 36 (6): 1547–76.

Phillips, N., and Hardy, C. (1997) "Managing multiple identities: discourse, legitimacy and resources in the UK refugee system," *Organization*, 4 (2): 159–86.

——(2002) *Discourse Analysis*, Thousand Oaks, CA: Sage.

Phillips, N., and Ravasi, D. (1998) "Analyzing Social Construction in Organizations: Discourse Analysis as a Research Method in Organization and Management Theory," presented at the third International Conference on Organizational Discourse: Pretexts, Subtexts and Contexts, London.

Phillips, N., Lawrence, T., and Hardy, C. (2000) "Interorganizational collaboration and the dynamics of institutional fields," *Journal of Management Studies*, 37 (2): 23–43.

Potter, J., and Wetherell, M. (1987) *Discourse and Social Psychology: Beyond Attitudes and Behaviour*. London: Sage.

Powell, W., and DiMaggio, P. (1991) *The New Institutionalism in Organizational Analysis*. Chicago: University of Chicago Press.

——(1991) *The New Institutionalism in Organizational Analysis*. Chicago: University of Chicago Press.

Putnam, L. L., and Fairhurst, G. (2000) "Discourse analysis in organizations: issues and concerns," in F. M. Jablin and L. L. Putnam (eds) *The New Handbook of Organizational Communication: Advances in Theory, Research and Methods*, pp. 235–68. Newbury Park, CA: Sage.

Ranson, S., Hinings, B., and Greenwood, R. (1980) "The Structuring of organization structures," *Administrative Science Quarterly*, 25 (1): 1–14.

Selznick, P. (1948) "Foundations of the theory of organizations," *American Sociological Review*, 13: 25–35.

——(1949) *TVA and the Grass Roots*. Berkeley, CA: University of California Press.

——(1957) *Leadership in Administration: A Sociological Interpretation*. New York: Harper & Row.

Sherzer, J. (1987) "A discourse-centered approach to language and culture," *American Anthropologist*, 89: 295–309.

van Dijk, T. A. (1997) *Discourse as Structure and Process* I. London: Sage.

Winch, P. (1958) *The Idea of a Social Science*. London: Routledge.

Wood, L. A., and Kroger, R. O. (2000) *Doing Discourse Analysis: Methods for Studying Action in Talk and Text*. Thousand Oaks, CA: Sage.

8

Globalization

COMMENTARY: THE POLITICS OF INCLUSION AND EXCLUSION IN GLOBALIZATION

The nature and impact of globalization have been one of the most hotly debated issues over the last couple of decades. It is of significance not only to organizational theorists in terms of organizational design and behavior, but also because of its social, cultural, political, and economic ramifications. Indeed, it is this very complexity and embeddedness that both make the issue an imperative for organizational theorists to come to grips with and a major source of difficulty in constructing any model or explanation. Both contributors seek, in their different ways, to do justice to the complexity and breadth of globalization as a phenomenon of great moment.

In chapter 8(b) Jones historically contextualizes globalization, tracing a trajectory from Fordism and the machinations of organized capitalism to the amorphous post-Fordist era of advanced liberal capitalism. He sees a disarticulation of the structures of capitalism at the national level with a re-articulation at the global level. The changes are broad and multi-faceted, from redesigns of work flows and divisions of labor to significant time/space compressions and industrial restructuring, to shifts in state policies and the politico-legal framework for the mechanics of trade and capital. This lengthy discursus on the development and transitions of capital and the economic order is a useful prelude to a consideration of the contemporary structure, dynamics, and consequences of globalization. Jones's real contribution, however, is in his analysis of advanced capitalism into two segments: the techno-economy and the "grunge" economy. The latter is the domain of the increasingly disenfranchised, marginalized, and impoverished occupants of unskilled and semiskilled positions whose position is highly contingent and insecure. The techno-economy is the main game and the grunge economy is an appendage – necessary, but increasingly lacking centrality and power. Furthermore, it is only the techno-economy that is really globalized, whilst the grunge economy remains as a local attachment to the global structures of that economy, thereby consolidating the exclusionary structuring.

For both authors there is explicit engagement with the ethics of globalization. Indeed, the critical core of the globalization debate is about an assessment of the impact of globalization. Parker is unwilling to see the arguments in black-and-white terms. She acknowledges that there are discernible negative effects arising from the globalization process and the activities of transnational corporations, but there are also positivities derived from integrative consequences. Indeed, she defines globalization in terms of a set of integrative processes. This is the essence of Parker's position, that whilst globalization has the disjunctive and exclusionary effects so starkly outlined by Jones, it also has integrative and inclusionary consequences. Not only are the effects mixed and somewhat uncertain, the process itself is messy, nonlinear, and contradictory. This makes for a troublesome phenomenon, not only for those involved with the pragmatics of globalization, but also for the organizational researcher seeking understanding and explanation. The complexity and interrelatedness that Parker points to, pose difficulties for research and theory, in part because the issues traverse traditional disciplinary boundaries and academic endeavor is still hampered by its own parochialism.

The role of transnational corporations (TNCs) in the globalization process is an essential feature of the debate both here and more widely. Parker argues that, whilst TNCs are an essential component of the globalization process, they are clearly not the only one of importance and relevance. She argues that a narrow focus on a limited number of highly visible TNCs has tended to distort the picture of globalization. The central point she makes is that TNCs become involved in a complex set not only of vertical relationships, but also of horizontal relationships with local small to medium-size enterprises, nongovernmental organizations, government and quasigovernmental agencies, other businesses, and communities. Not all of these relationships are detrimental to local organizations and communities in areas where TNCs engage. Indeed, Parker argues that this set of relationships and networks is part of a positive process of integration and that there are developmental spinoffs. Jones also sees the emergence of complex networks formed around TNCs, but he is far less sanguine about their impact. He sees them as essentially hierarchical in nature, with TNCs at the top and progressively weaker and more disempowered entities and groups lower down. There is a kind of replication of his techno-grunge economy structure, to which he adds the presence of an expanding informal economy. Parker also argues that the evidence for the damaging effects of industry consolidation under globalization is actually mixed, whereas Jones sees it as underestimated. These are not naive arguments. Parker recognizes the negative instances and effects of globalizing processes, but is arguing against a simplistic demonizing set of arguments – a nuanced analysis of all the complexities and contradictions is required. Jones would maintain that on balance the effects are exclusionary and exploitative.

Both authors also address the homogenizing and "steamrolling" effects of globalization on indigenous cultures and social systems. Jones perceives a complex dialectic here. He argues that the notion of innocent and pure indigenous culture is already rather passé under colonialist and international trade influences at earlier periods. There is implicit acknowledgement of the hybridization processes that the postcolonial literature has explicated in recent times. In other words, the invasion of a local culture by a colonial or other form of dominant culture does not necessarily involve a process of cultural imposition. The local culture may appropriate, incorporate aspects of the invasive culture, and turn to confront the dominant culture with this hybrid. The interaction between the two cultures is thereby transformed and contains new and complex dynamics. The key process for Jones is at the level of consumer capitalism, where he does see some imperialistic and homogenizing effects. The effects are potentially beyond the common adoption of consumption habits with respect to goods and services; the more transformative effect is in terms of identities and lifestyles. He does, however, recognize some options for resistance – one of which is through the dynamics of hybridity. Parker pays rather less attention to these aspects of the globalization process, but does argue that there are instances wherein globalization actually serves to strengthen local cultural and social traditions.

The contributors do a sterling job in surfacing the issues surrounding globalization and do justice to the complexity and nuances involved. The differences in position are matters of interpretation and emphasis. Deciding which interpretation is more valid and what emphasis should be given more weight depends on one's ideological and political orienta- tion, what evidence one is attuned to, and very much upon the perspective from which the dynamics are viewed. Perhaps the issue less well attended to by the contributors is not so much the nature of globalization, and an account of the mechanics and dynamics, as the question of who participates in, directs, and controls the processes. On balance, the evidence would seem to suggest that the politics of exclusion are more in evidence than the politics of inclusion.

8a The Disorganization of Inclusion: Globalization as Process

Barbara Parker

Globalization is a process that includes organ- izations of every size and type operating throughout the world. Accordingly, and as sug- gested by the partner section of this chapter, "organizational studies should be at the fore- front of efforts to comprehend the meaning(s) of globalization." However, as the comments below indicate, I believe that globalization represents more than organization of exclu- sion. Rather, the process of globalization has inclusive as well as exclusive elements, and a simultaneous look at both yields a more nearly representative picture of globalization and its meaning for organizations. Further, I argue that, while major transnational businesses (TNCs) are near the core of globalization, they are not the only organizational actors in the vicinity. Finally, it is useful to note that the internal vertical networks of major TNCs are complemented by other networks, including external ones that develop horizontally. To- gether these vertical and horizontal networks alter organizational boundaries and in turn they may reshape distributional effects of global pro- duction and labor as well as the discourse on globalization.

The arguments made above and others like them found in this chapter, clearly promote what Held et al. (1999) call the "transformationalist thesis" of globalization. This view holds that globalization is a histor- ically unprecedented process that is rapidly reshaping the context of virtually all human activity. The many contradictions embedded in this largely disorganized process are reflected in new patterns of inclusion and exclusion that are not always linear. These points are later demonstrated with separate looks at con- tradictory conclusions associated with industry consolidation among TNCs, views of them as stateless entities, and the myriad influences they have over trade, wages, and global values development.

Few deny the fact of globalization – defined here as worldwide integration in virtually every sphere. Globalization is almost everywhere apparent, and because it is visibly manifested by global brands and services as well as other business activities there is a tendency to think of globalization as primarily relating to business and therefore principally or solely an economic phenomenon. The latter view has elsewhere been described as a "hyperglobalization" thesis where "economic globalization is constructing new forms of social organization that are supplanting, or will eventually supplant, traditional nation-states as the primary economic and political units of world society" (Held et al., 1999: 3). Although hyperglobalizers come from different ideological frameworks, Held and his colleagues assert that the bond among them is the shared conviction that globalization is primarily an economic phenomenon. My argument here and elsewhere is that the globalization process occurs in political, cultural, economic, technological, business, environmental, and related spheres (Parker, 1996). Activities in these global spheres also interact, sometimes leading to new and unexpected outcomes and sometimes reinforcing tradition.

Global political entities like the World Trade Organization or APEC regularize business on a global scale, but at the same time they yield unexpected interdependences between and among nation states and foster global affinity groups that exist in virtual space as well as in geographic clusters. The latter groups can serve society or, as in the case of global terrorism, they aim to destroy some part of it. Improved travel facilitates the global spread of diseases like hepatitis or acquired human immune syndrome even as transport improvements enhance responses to disasters worldwide or facilitate global production and distribution. Global technologies – particularly those that involve telecommunications – facilitate a 24/7 world for trade but they also make it possible for nongovernmental organizations (NGOs)[1] to share strategies and rapidly disseminate information worldwide. More particular to the topic at hand, information abundance creates new challenges for scholarship and practice. Alternative explanations for the same events challenge decision making when they force managers to put their faith in one source or a differing one when both are credible. Similarly, scholars confront a vast array of findings that often contradict. A look at some of those contradictory findings in the pages to follow demonstrates how the inclusion of contradiction increases complexity. It also shows how this inclusion reflects the complex and messy realities of the globalization process.

The questions raised by what has been an ever-increasing pace of global change are expressed in languages that differ worldwide, and the intensity of interest varies, but most wonder where globalization will take us. Questions abound, but one seems central to this discussion: is globalization a good thing or a bad thing? Many answers to the good–bad question posed by globalization revolve around the activities and intentions of transnational corporations (TNCs), and extend the question also to ask: is business a force for good or a force for evil? Globalization as exclusion may view TNCs as strictly self-interested entities whose activities disrupt the possibility of integrating narratives on progress and lead to disenfranchisement for many. Others similarly argue that TNC self-interest is destructive (see Sklair, 1995) and these concerns are reflected in titles such as *When Corporations rule the World* (Korten, 1995) and *The Case against the Global Economy* (Mander and Goldsmith, 1996).

This chapter argues that TNCs are one among many sets of actors and activities in the global sphere. That is, although the roots of globalization often are traced to businesses, events occurring in and initiated by other types of organizations in the political, cultural, economic, technological, and natural spheres also promote worldwide integration (Amin, 1996; Lodge, 1995). The following overview of perspectives on globalization sets the stage for looking at the various roles businesses – particularly transnational corporations – play relative to other global actors and activities.

The Fallacy of Primary Drivers

The topic of globalization has been noted by many commentators with little agreement as to its cause and effects. Among academics and practitioners alike there has been a tendency to view globalization through disciplinary filters that shape the definition of globalization, views on it, and appropriate responses to it. However, it seems valuable to note that, at this point in the globalization process, perspectives on it differ between disciplines and even within them. For example, Pieterse (1995) observes that there are almost as many conceptualizations of globalization as there are disciplines in the social sciences. Streeten (2001) illustrates this point more graphically with an appendix that lists thirty-five different definitions of globalization. These differences of opinion about globalization give rise to different views on what causes globalization, and often result in what I call "primary driver" assertions that trace globalization to a single or finite set of sources that lead to known or knowable consequences. The primary driver perspective first emerged in the popular press, but is taken up by scholars as well. According to some, technology is the driving force powering globalization (*Economist*, 2000d; Naisbitt, 1994; Ostry and Nelson, 1995). Others believe globalization is powered by economics (Govindarajan and Gupta, 2000; Ohmae, 1995; van Bergeijk and Mensink, 1997), business (Bannock et al., 1998; Harris, 1993; O'Neill, 1997; Reich, 1991), cultural factors (Barber, 1992; Huntington, 1993), or communications and transport innovations (ODI, 2000; Mandle and Ferleger, 2000).

In failing to acknowledge simultaneously occurring events emanating from other global spheres, the primary driver approach limits analysis of globalization. Further, singular approaches to thinking about the sources of globalization imply that there is "one best way" to organize it. In conforming to a (mostly Western) tradition that relies on linear thinking and scientific rationality, the primary driver approaches simply do not admit all the data. A primary driver approach to globalization also may invite a simplistic approach to thinking about challenges that are inherently complex not only because they take place on a global stage but also because activities taking place in any one sphere of activity are necessarily related to activities occurring in other spheres as well. For example, the middle-class phenomenon of global teens who share interests, fashions, and musical tastes emerges only in relationship with a global infrastructure for telecommunications, global businesses able to create and/or satisfy demand, a global politic that facilitates trade, and so on. In other words, a main problem with a primary driver approach to globalization is that it simply does not include enough information. Recent scholarship demonstrates a growing tendency to combine two or more global "drivers,"

particularly technological shifts and business shifts (Mandel and Ferleger, 2000). However, as others note, there are many more than two or three drivers for globalization and it is important also to look at their interrelationships (Clough, 1996; Lodge, 1995). Admitting many drivers and their interrelationships opens the door for greater complexity than does the primary driver approach. Further, the latter approach may prematurely narrow the parameters of debate about any aspect of globalization, e.g., its causes, current outcomes, future scenarios.

Not surprisingly, those who favor the primary driver approach to globalization also tend to be grounded within the discipline and perspective promoted, and the resulting analysis quite naturally employs the tools, theories, and language of that discipline. A possible result may be premature paradigm development within disciplines when what may be needed is cross-disciplinary fertilization leading to a more complex paradigm that integrates theories and accommodates diverse voices and perspectives. A third problem is that an emphasis on a primary driver approach to globalization may encourage decision makers to themselves adopt a primary driver approach to thinking about and acting on globalization. As was noted earlier, this approach may oversimplify when we view globalization as a problem that requires a solution. For example, pressure on TNCs to curtail child labor could lead to the desired result, but also could force working children to take jobs in dangerous industries or work as prostitutes or drug runners (*Economist*, 1995a). The primary driver approach to thinking about sources of globalization represents a tendency also to think about globalization as "prefiguring a singular condition or end-state" (Held et al., 1999: 11) – a view that is inconsistent with a transformationalist perspective.

Although there has been a tendency to adopt primary driver approaches to understanding globalization, the practice is not universal. Several believe that globalization is a complex interrelationship among multiple global forces (Held et al., 1999; Robertson, 1992; Scholte, 1996). Held et al. (1999), for example, suggest that "globalization might be better conceived as a highly differentiated process which finds expression in all the key domains of social activity" (p. 12). The argument here is that inclusion and exploration of complex global interrelationships enriches understanding of sources and possible outcomes from the globalization process.

Transnational Corporations

Business activities are understood to stimulate some part of the globalization process, but there is little agreement as to how, why, or to what effect. As noted earlier, the focal point for global business activities has been transnational corporations, but there is as yet no shared definition of what constitutes a TNC. Bartlett and Ghoshal (1989) described the TNC as an integrated network that balances efficiency against local responsiveness to encourage both global competitiveness and flexibility. They concluded that the transnational's dedication to organizational learning and innovation would help it operate most successfully in a complex world. In other quarters, however, TNCs are viewed as "'synonymous with multinational enterprises" (Daniels and Radebaugh, 1992: G-21), "a firm which has the power to coordinate and control operations in more than one country, even if it does not own them" (Dicken, 1998), as a firm that sees the world as a single market (Ohmae, 1995), or as one among many firms worldwide whose activities are monitored by the UN Center on Transnational Corporations (UNCTAD). This centre uses the term "transnational" as an umbrella term that could fit any of the four definitions proposed by Bartlett and Ghoshal, i.e., international, multinational, global, or transnational.

UNCTAD concludes there were about 60,000 transnational businesses operating worldwide in the year 2000 (UNCTAD, 2001). Many are headquartered in advanced economies, but the role of large TNCs from developing and transitional economies also has increased in recent decades. For example, the share of developing economies in outward foreign direct investment (FDI) rose from about 3 percent in the early 1980s to 9 percent by 2000 (ibid., 2001). The direct control these firms have over hundreds of thousands of subsidiaries worldwide and the trillions their combined assets represent make them important to economic growth and development around the world. This list includes both publicly and privately held TNCs like Sony, Sanro, Nestlé, Coca-Cola, and Benetton, as well as many more TNCs that manufacture products or provide services that are less well known globally, e.g., Cemex, Barilla. Most public and academic interest focuses on the relatively narrow group of major TNCs that produce highly visible branded goods or services. These and other major TNCs appear on lists such as the UNCTAD's Top 100, *Fortune*'s Global 500, and *Business Week's* Global 1000, making the latter visible and accessible on a global basis. This access is available to all rather than a few and it provides a mechanism for social controls. For example, in the case of Nike, NGOs used the scope of the Internet to highlight supplier labor problems, the discovery of which led to Nike's uneven efforts to advocate fair-trade employment standards. In this case the interaction between business activities, NGO monitoring, and telecommunications brought changes in organizational behavior.

Among other things, critics perceive these major TNCs concentrate power via industry consolidation, encourage trade liberalization to enhance their own wealth and position, create wage inequalities, and hasten cultural homogeneity. Some assert that the combined power of global branding and information dissemination from the Western world helps both service companies and manufacturers to spread consumerism, and further consolidate and enhance their own position (Barnet and Cavanagh, 1994; Klein, 2000; Korten, 1995). "Globalization from above," manifested by the activities of economically and politically strong nations and organizations at the world's apex, is said to benefit them and them alone (Falk, 1993) while others belief that "stateless corporations are effectively transforming nation-states to suit their interests" (Clark, 1996: 299). This perspective on TNC activities implies that globalization is leading to an end point where TNCs will be winners and governments, civil society, the already marginalized, etc., will be losers. This perspective often leads to a catalog of examples demonstrating how economic actors serve their own interests. While this approach appropriately identifies bad TNC behavior, it tends to minimize or remain silent on the good that TCNs do. For example, foreign firms pay their workers more than the national average, spend more on R&D in countries where they invest than their domestic counterparts, and tend to export more than domestic ones. According to the OECD study upon which these conclusions are based, the effects of business activities like these are bigger in poorer economies than in richer ones (*Economist*, 2000a). In addition, a focus on TCNs may overlook bad behavior on the part of domestic businesses or bad results that occur even when intentions are good. For example, First World donations of used clothing have all but destroyed the textile industry in developing economies like Zambia. A look at the broad array of businesses and other organizations operating globally provides a more comprehensive view of both the benefits and the dangers of a more global world, could enhance understanding of global business and its interrelationships with other aspects of the global integration process, and might lead to a more critical theory of globalization (Scholte, 1996).

Offsetting claims that TNCs dominate world business is the fact that in 1990 they accounted only for about 7 percent of world output, a percentage less than that found at the beginning of the 1980s (Lipsey et al., 2000). Since the relative volume of world business generated by TNCs has declined, it follows that many organizations other than TNCs engage in global business as well. For example, late-mover businesses from developing economies have carved out global business space (Bartlett and Ghoshal, 2000), as have global startups (Hordes et al., 1995) and medium-size firms (Simon, 1996). In 1999 smaller firms accounted for over 90 percent of companies in the European Union and many were export-oriented (Demick and O'Reilly, 2000). Some of the former are family-owned firms accounting for "66 percent of Germany's GDP and 75 percent of its work force; and around 50 percent of Britain's work force" (*Economist*, 1996). There are about 50,000 private family-owned German companies with sales between

$13 million and $250 million, and, according to the French Association of Medium-size Family-owned Companies, family-owned businesses in France account for 80 percent of companies with sales of £7 million to $290 million (Raghavan and Steinmetz, 2000). In the United States almost half of GDP is generated by family-owned or closely held businesses, but some 95 percent of US exporters are small businesses (usually defined as employing fewer than 500 people and earning less than $20 million in annual revenues). This suggests that a look at family firms also is warranted.

Additionally, intergovernmental organizations (INGOs) and nongovernmental organizations (NGOs) such as the Worldwide Fund for Nature and Amnesty International operate within nations and worldwide. About 30,000 NGOs are global or international in scope, up from 6,000 in 1990 (*Economist*, 1999b). Among their principal interests are environmental sustainability, humanitarian aid, trade issues, and economic justice. Jubilee 2000, for example, seeks debt relief for developing economies. Others function to encourage or force businesses to serve social goals. Still others are trade groups that represent business interests, e.g., associations of sugar growers. Both INGOs and NGOs benefit from interacting with businesses, they increasingly support their own activities with income-generating activities, and they play roles that aid business development and enhance business opportunities. For example, many NGOs in developing countries, e.g., Bangladesh, India, some parts of Central and Latin America, the Philippines, provide seed money to establish microenterprise businesses. In doing so, these NGOs assume traditional governmental roles in stimulating development and allocating resources, and they also play roles more frequently played by banks and other lending institutions. Possible effects are changes in assumptions about sectoral work, and enterprise practices that merge business and social service habits and norms, including decisions about who is creditworthy, or how profits can be generated. Finally, criminal and terrorist organizations that operate outside legitimate sectors also shape globalization.

These various organizations all populate the global landscape of business. In the following section the relationship between TNCs and SMEs is examined to show that the latter's global participation and power relative to that of TNCs is increasing rather than decreasing, suggesting that we might find similar surprises were we to look at TNC relations with other organizations.

Small and Medium-size Enterprises as Transnationals

The global enterprise develops a network of interrelated businesses to support its activities (Wilkins, 1994). These global production and distribution systems depend not only on ownership and control but also on cooperative activities between different organizations (Borrus and Zysman, 1998), including supply chain linkages with SMEs found throughout the world. These networks are operated by SMEs as well as by TNCs, suggesting that traditional multinational dominance of global production and distribution systems is eroding (Held et al., 1999: 237). Communication and transport infrastructures admit SMEs to global production processes, and while some may be suppliers captured by TNC production networks; others use this infrastructure to decrease dependence on TNCs. For example, SMEs use communication technologies to network with each other, through which they establish cooperative ventures that enhance collective bargaining power or create niche markets (Castells, 1996). Thus the network of global manufacturing established by TNCs can disperse rather than consolidate traditional TNC positions as SMEs. The growing ability of SMEs to operate outside spheres of TNC influence is facilitated by the former's ability to leverage the same information and transport infrastructures that benefit large TNCs. Small and medium-size TNCs, especially those in Japan, are increasingly investing in developing countries (Fujita, 1995), suggesting they may be more attracted to opportunities large TCNs reject. Most assume that smaller firms operate in different ways than larger firms, but this has yet to be explored in the literature on SME internationalization (Coviello and McAuley, 1999). In summary, market participation of SMEs on a global scale shows they participate

in internal networks of TNCs and also create their own such networks, perhaps reducing the distributional dominance of existing TNCs. The presence of global SMEs increases the diversity of organizations in the global market place. Diversity also has grown because TNCs from developing economies participate in the global market place (Gereffi, 1994).

Industry Consolidation

The phenomenal rate of proposed and completed global mergers and acquisitions suggests industry consolidation is a powerful force. The $1.2 trillion posted in worldwide 1997 mergers and acquisitions reached $2.489 trillion in 1998 and $3.4 trillion in 1999 before declining in 2000. The 2001 total of mergers and acquisitions was $1.9 trillion. Major industries subject to these mergers include advertising, aerospace, airlines, pharmaceuticals, energy, telecommunications, and many others. Whether motivated by costs, efforts to establish technological leadership, fear of industry shakeout, or other factors, consolidation seems to presage a single business world unbounded by national borders, time, space, and other boundaries. The evidence for industry consolidation is decidedly mixed.

Based on their study of twenty industries over forty years, Ghemawat and Ghadar (2000) concluded that industry consolidation is not resulting from these global mergers. Their argument is that concentration in globalizing industries has decreased since 1945. A KPMG report indicates half of these mergers have destroyed value and many have had no measurable effect on the parent's success (*Economist*, 2000c). An alternative explanation to that of industry consolidation as a trend is that it was a fad that has already run its course, much as occurred following conglomeration activity in the 1980s. A look at US TNCs from 1984 to 1997 showed that equity value of them relative to assets was 9–17 percent lower than similar domestic companies, suggesting that globalization is far from a sure shot at profits (Click and Harrison, 2000). Data like these challenge assertions that industry consolidation is occurring or that it leads to TNC wealth and dominance.

TNCs as Stateless Entities

Despite assertions to the contrary (Vidal, 1997), there is not much evidence to show that businesses are ungoverned actors on the global stage. Most forces of globalization remain under the control of political machinations in home countries (Gilpin, 2000), and businesses from them largely remain responsive to the political, economic, and cultural constraints of their home nations (Doremus et al., 1998). For most firms operating on a global scale, the bulk of their assets and employees are found in the home countries where ownership is located and to which the companies turn for political or diplomatic protection (Hu, 1992). Others point to the fact that most investment flows primarily between or to advanced economies as evidence that multinationals are primarily located within national or regional geographies (Ruigrok and Van Tulder, 1996; Thompson and Allen, 1997). These and similar findings suggest that neither TNCs nor MNCs are rootless monoliths but are instead grounded in national cultures or regions that guide their opportunities and temper their self-interest.

Benefits and Costs of Trade

Beginning in the 1960s, the activities of all global businesses, including TNCs, were facilitated by significant reductions in trade barriers. The answer to the question "Who benefits?" depends on which data one chooses to present as well as on author perspective (Levy, 1999) and the interrelationships noted. As indicated earlier, some believe businesses stimulate these activities in order to be the only beneficiaries of them (Korten, 1995; Anderson and Cavanagh, 1997). Part of the logic of this argument is that trade helps the rich get richer and it keeps the poor poor. Political action groups, lobbying activities, and face-to-face meetings are among many ways that TNCs and other businesses protect their interests in the political agenda. At the same time, global businesses also have been advocates of a vast array of global standards meant to "even the playing field" and harmonize business practices. In the absence of global standards, markets often are chaotic, and this affects

businesses no less than consumers, governments, and NGOs. Although it follows that businesses set standards in order to benefit from them, this does not preclude benefits for others. For example, competitors benefit from greater access, consumers from higher standards and greater transparency, governments from established rules that they can enforce, and so on.

According to almost every World Bank and UN measure, the world is better off than it was twenty-five years ago: fewer people live below the poverty line; food production is rising faster than population growth; educational levels are rising; life spans are longer; and infant mortality has decreased substantially (United Nations, 2000; World Bank, 2000/1). Between 1987 and 1999 the share of the population in developing and transitional economies living on $1 a day fell from 28 percent to 24 percent (World Bank, 2000/1). Poverty has come to be defined not only as material deprivation but also as low achievement in education and health. This richer, multidimensional measurement of poverty makes it more difficult to compare achievements in the overall assessment of poverty. For example, health could improve even as real income worsens. As a percentage of GNP, world expenditure on education increased from 3.9 percent to 4.8 percent between 1980 and 1997 (World Bank, 2000/1).

Data like these reinforce belief that all boats rise with improved economic activity and might lead one to conclude that economic activity leads to good results. Others cite growing worldwide income disparities to suggest that only the yachts of the rich are rising on global business tides. For example, a reduction in the number of people who live on $1 per day does not reflect the relatively uneven nature of this decline even within regions. East Asia dramatically reduced its population of those living on $1 a day; South Asia saw an increase. Variations in poverty within nations also are not reflected by aggregated data.

Some part of anticorporate sentiment in the Western world springs from the notion that developing economies would be better off without Western influence (Easterbrook, 2000). But this too may reflect Western perspectives and standards (Steingard and Fitzgibbons, 1996) of what is right or good for the world. In the developing economies many want to be part of the global economy because they believe economic development is their only chance of a sound future (Mitra, 1999). Similarly, while human rights and/or environmental concerns carry considerable weight in advanced economies, developing economies may view them as yet another way for Western economies to shut the door against them.

Trade also increased through 2000, and developing economies have been shown to participate in and benefit from the global economy, but there is little agreement as to whether this helps or hurts developing economies. The latter point is illustrated by Sachs (1998), who notes that enthusiasts for globalization will see the inclusion of developing economies in world trade as evidence of increased gains from trade and faster growth for both sides of the worldwide income divide. For skeptics, the integration of rich and poor nations promises increasing inequality in the former and greater dislocation in the latter (Sachs, 1998). Even as we see that GDP in developing economies grew by more than 3 percent from 1987 to 1996, the number of people living on less than $2 a day increased from 2.5 billion to 2.7 billion (World Bank, 2000). Data like these are used to argue that this new tide of wealth is concentrated in only a few hands, leading to growing disparity between "haves" and "have nots" (Green and Ruhleder, 1996). Shocking pay disparities between some CEOs and US workers often are used to bolster this argument.

These contradictions present a more complex picture of the globalization process and they pose thornier problems for it. That is, the picture that emerges when we also look at trade interdependences over time, global political action, technological change, and demographic shifts within and across nations, e.g., worldwide growth of the middle class, environmental effects of increased business activities, and labor rights, as well as TCN activities, we see two things: messiness and reduced ability to pin blame on single actors. Despite these difficulties, including more data points could at the same time provide new insights. For example, demographic change in the United States

resulted in fewer persons per household formed, and this is quite a different explanation for lower median household income than the income gap argument. The change in the size of households is itself a second order occurrence following on cultural and political shifts that allow female access to professional jobs, postpone marriages, cheapen imports that free resources to pay for single housing, and the like.

Additionally, a re-examination of such data admits new knowledge that enriches understanding of them. For example, while wage gaps have grown in the United States, aggregate reports of them obscure the fact that women and people of color have made more income gains than white men (US Census Bureau, 2000). Additionally, they do not show the full picture, which is that income disparities vary widely by region (Ford and Barta, 2000). As Dollar and Kraay (2000) note, we know little about what causes changes in income distribution, but having analyzed income in eighty countries over a four-decade period they find little change in the poverty growth relationship in recent years. Trade patterns doubtless affect labor in advanced economies, but others suggest trade is not the only driver of these patterns. Trade accounts for a positive yet relatively small share of rising wage and income distribution in inequalities in advanced economies (Slaughter 1998). Trade may be an equal contributor to wage changes for unskilled workers in advanced economies to that of technological innovation (Minford et al., 1997). For example, the computer revolution may have contributed to wage inequalities because organizations favored skilled workers over unskilled ones (Sachs, 1998). Minford et al. (1997) also suggest that openness to foreign trade benefits the poor to the same extent that it benefits the economy as a whole.

Further, as businesses expand their global reach, they also participate in and are subject to constraints emerging from their own and other sectors. Increased access to media and growing activism among NGOs creates one incentive for businesses to weigh self-interest against the public interest, and this has in turn led most large TNCs to develop global standards for health, safety, and the environment

(*Economist*, 2000b) and for industries. For example, the CERES Principles include over eighty business signatories that pledge to reduce negative environmental impacts and regulate their own performance. The Fair Labor Association is a US-based organization that monitors compliance with the Apparel Industry Partnership's Workplace Code of Conduct. In the Netherlands, industry participants shape their own standards and monitor each other to see that agreements are kept. Finally, transnational NGOs and other representatives of civil society set norms that have the capacity to reconfigure power relations between businesses and global society (Newell, 2000). For example, in the face of pressure from environmental protection NGOs, multinational businesses have implemented codes of conduct, production guidelines, and monitoring standards covering their own activities as well as those of suppliers (Gereffi et al., 2001). This motivates MNCs to ensure compliance among suppliers, and illustrates that horizontal and vertical networks can improve business practices.

Businesses with economic power also may use it to stimulate social synergies, and they demonstrate how to link economic self-interest to more broadly defined interests of the global community. For example, businesses such as the Body Shop, Canon, Sara Lee, Du Pont, Hitachi, BP, Ford, Royal Dutch Shell, and others have responded positively to pressure for social responsibility, e.g. protecting child workers, preserving the natural environment, developing indigenous people, and some have themselves created pressure for social change. Further, their activities demonstrate that the win–lose assumptions of the good–bad business debate are neither the only approaches to nor the only potential results of globalization when businesses act as global community members (Brown, 1992). As the regulatory authority of nation states shifts to the private sector, civil society increasingly demands greater accountability from businesses (Murphy and Coleman, 2000), suggesting that the vacuum of power left by nation states is being filled by civil society as well as by TNCs in the globalization process.

Finally, while much economic growth in the last quarter of the twentieth century was generated by businesses, such activity would not have been possible without global political agreements like GATT and its successor the WTO, technological improvements that make it possible to distribute goods and services broadly, and many demographic shifts. These activities have distributed sufficient riches to create a growing middle class in many countries, particularly East Asian and Latin American countries; distributed more jobs globally, and generated opportunities worldwide that never existed before. For example, according to ILO statistics, between 1985 and 1991, in thirty-nine of forty-one countries surveyed, women's opportunities had increased to include a greater number in managerial jobs with higher pay and status, and more authority over decisions making. The latter alterations doubtless result from many activities, but the important point is that businesses as well as other organizations contribute to them.

Wage Inequities

The 60,000 transnational corporations tracked by UNCTAD and their affiliates abroad employed about 40.5 million people in 1999, an increase from 23.6 million in 1990 (UNCTAD, 2000). This represents less than 2 percent of the world's 2.5 billion workers. Yet TNCs are at the center of labor debates. This occurs for many reasons: they are identifiable; they added many jobs in the 1990s to developing economies; and they are viewed as much more potent forces for change than are domestic forces. For example, the addition of paid TNC jobs in the formal sector is meaningful in developing economies where work remains concentrated in the informal sector. In developing economies low-skill labor has contributed to increased exports, while in advanced economies there is greater reliance on goods produced by higher-skill workers. In both cases this has produced international convergence of wages for workers in similar skill groups (Wood, 1994). In the longer run, and without trade barriers, some believe worldwide wages may equalize for similar work (Larudee, 1994). Debate concentrates on whether wage equalization is a "race to the bottom" (Korten, 1995) especially for low-skill workers, or a "race to the top" (Larsson, 2001) for knowledge workers. Those who believe that TNCs will be the deciding factor in determining wages (Kurzer, 1993) also should consider the role of factors outside the business sphere. For example, worker productivity plays a role in wages and it appears that low wage economies are those where labor productivity also is low (Rodrik, 1997). Additionally, many nations invest in education as a way to improve the skill set of their workers.

Returns to education command a premium in developing economies (United Nations, 1995). For women, returns to education have increased around the world, but the second-order effect is that women are perceived as more valuable members of social groups when they earn income. In Bangladesh, for example, the status of women has increased along with their role as wage earners. When governments perceive that businesses are the linchpin in the trade-paved path to national prosperity they are further motivated to improve educational levels to attract business. Innovative collaborative arrangements among development agencies, governments, NGOs, and businesses have helped to improve educational standards upon which many domestic economies rest (Waddell, 1999), and they further serve to integrate business, government, and civil society.

Because they create many of the jobs upon which domestic economies are based, some believe, businesses are the only entity with sufficient clout to make changes (Hawken, 1993). Others think it is government's job to improve the labor force via education or by creating sociopolitical and economic conditions that favor economic development. (Simai, 1994) and still others think change will come only when business, government, and society move in tandem on labor concerns and labor rights (Annan, 2000). Clearly it will take more than single actors to establish worldwide labor standards and employment rights. Paradoxically, even as advanced-economy workers benefit from the reduced prices they enjoy, thanks to lower tariff barriers, they campaign against job exports and/ or labor immigration and pressure national and global political entities to create labor barriers. Also forgotten is that work that moves from the informal to the formal sector is subject to better, more regulated labor standards.

Networks of Influence

Internal networks

Many organizational theories believe TNCs increasingly employ interorganizational networks to access markets, utilize assets, and acquire resources (Dunning, 1993). Sometimes these networks are composed of parent companies linked to specialized subsidiaries throughout the world (Ghoshal and Bartlett, 1990; Gupta and Govindarajan, 1991) in the form of interfirm trade. In other instances networks are composed of TNCs and SME suppliers (Held et al., 1999). For the most part, these types of networks are vertically configured networks that are managed via internal mechanisms.

External networks within the business sector

Dicken (1998) notes that TNCs also participate in complex networks of externalized relationships between independent and quasi-independent firms. The latter networks are brought about in part by global infrastructural changes that make it desirable for TNCs to operate beyond the parameters of their own internal boundaries (Held et al., 1999: 257). One way they reach beyond internal boundaries is with loose or formal alliances among competitors in the same or different industries (Hull et al., 1988). In joining competitors, the latter networks create horizontal links for businesses to manage. Businesses also develop horizontal linkages with INGOs and NGOs operating in other sectors.

External cross-sector networks

The same global pressures faced by businesses also challenge organizations in other sectors. The specific example here is nongovernmental organizations that (like businesses) also fill the gap governments leave as they shrink and privatize (Weisbrod, 1997). NGO influence has been shown to be increasing in the twenty-two developed and developing economies studied by Salamon et al. (1998), accounting for 5 percent of jobs and 23 percent of job growth in nine countries. NGO growth also has occurred in response to demand for specialization in an increasingly diverse population. The growing number of nongovernmental organizations worldwide creates competition among them for charitable funds and charitable activities. In Nicaragua, for example, the number of micro-lenders far exceeds the number of borrowers. Having experienced success with market-based activities (or witnessed its success for other NGOs), some are adopting business tools and techniques, and others are shifting their activities away from charity and wealth transfer toward more systemic and sustained solutions to social problems (Bornstein, 1999). As they move into revenue-producing ventures NGOs also become more "businesslike" in the way they conduct their activities (Dees, 1998). For example, when Greenpeace suffered from low internal morale, leaders successfully restructured, downsized, and outsourced, just as many businesses have done (*Economist*, 1995b).

Businesses also are subject to social pressures that push them toward interaction with INGOs and NGOs. For example, a study of 100 top leaders of global organizations found growing emphasis among them on social and community responsibility (McFarland et al., 1993). Among other reasons, businesses adopt socially responsible roles because the public perceives them to be the only entities with the collective clout to resolve global social problems (Hawken, 1993; see Waddock and Smith, 1999, for a broader discussion of global businesses as social change agents) and their expanding global role has made them more central to social development issues (Lawrence and Hardy, 1999). Further, global businesses face growing costs from not being socially involved and have experienced bottom-line improvements from social involvement. For example, according to the Dow Jones and Sustainable Asset Management Index (*Economist*, 1999a), companies with an eye on the triple bottom line of economic, environmental, and social sustainability outperform their peers, particularly in technology and energy. Growing pressures among businesses to be more socially responsive and for NGOs to be more "business-like" have resulted in horizontal cross-sector relations that include corporate volunteerism, resource swapping and trading, cause-based marketing activities, and project partnerships organized around common interests.

As Austin (2000) notes, some NGO/business relationships are transactional in nature and others foster collective action and organizational integration. Examples of the latter include the Marco Polo project partnership between MCI Worldcom, National Geographic, the Kennedy Center ArtLinks and US teachers which helps to reduce the digital divide for low-income children. Another example is Starbucks–Conservation International partnership efforts to promote fair-trade coffee grown in Chiapas, Mexico. These partnerships can involve many partners or two, combine organizations of different sizes and scope, are initiated by outside influences, organizational leaders, grass-roots efforts among employees, or they are effectively forced by NGO actions. They also can be face-to-face or virtual (the variety of NGO–business partnerships organized around environmental issues are well explored in Bendell, 2000). Whether they come about by chance, design, or are forced, these kinds of partnerships create external and horizontal networks that each partner must manage. Further, they link businesses with NGOs in horizontal networks.

Other kinds of horizontal external networks have emerged to coordinate business responses to social challenges. For example, in the wake of an anthrax outbreak in the United States in 2001, pharmaceutical companies reorganized their R&D functions better to serve governmental needs. In Africa, major pharmaceutical businesses partnered with national governments and each other to improve the distribution of low-cost AIDs vaccines. These two examples of external and horizontal networks demonstrate that the same organization may emphasize distribution in one network and R&D in another. These horizontal networks link businesses with other sectors and in doing so they reduce business options for entirely self-interested behavior.

Global Values

In the twentieth century, cultural groupings were based primarily on nation-state influences, but in the twenty-first it has become easier to transcend geographic and other boundaries to speak or write English as a global business language or otherwise adopt global habits, norms, behaviors, and values. Technological breakthroughs of the Internet also create opportunities to connect with and even develop affinity groups, and in facilitating these and other activities the Internet enhances knowledge and understanding and creates awareness of options that did not previously exist. Travel facilitates broader cultural exposure, as do films and television.

Some believe that the result of greater exposure to other cultures is that they will merge. They conclude that cultural exposure is a form of neo-imperialism capable of eliminating cultural variety (Tomlinson, 1991), leading to destructive forms of conflict between civilizations (Huntington, 1993) or groups (Appadurai, 1990). Barber's (1992) view that McWorld or Jihad is the likely outcome of cultural merging is indicative of this line of thinking, which is that globalization of culture reduces cultural variation and choice. The concept of "McWorld" describes Western technology, popular culture, and integrated markets as a force against which the retribalization of Jihad must react.

Others suggest that the cultural borrowing associated with "creolization," "mestizaje," "orientalization," and the like enhance, but do not redefine, culture (Pieterse, 1995). "Glocalization," or loose connections between what is local and what is global, may instead be forged (Robertson, 1995), leading to the multiplication of cultural differences through globalization rather than their reduction (Kahn, 1995). Instead of globalization of a predominantly Westernized culture, where business language, values, and behaviors are standardized and homogenized on a worldwide basis, Robertson (1995) argues, cultural influences *from* East *to* West have been seriously underestimated. There are growing pressures for homogeneity within cultures, but travel of persons and information has increased heterogeneity. As time and space compression bring us to a realization of one world, they also expose us to the infinite variety and diversity of the world. These tensions create opportunities and they exact costs for nations, organizations, and

individuals, chief of which is the need to balance pressures to be both homogeneous and heterogeneous. But just as people now find it possible to live within the same nation and subscribe to different cultural rules of family, religion, or ethnic group, so too should it be technically possible for people also to live comfortably with global business culture and national culture.

Among the benefits of cultural exposure is that learning can result. For example, the collapse of the Soviet Union undermined authoritarian regimes and led to the realization that there are many forms of capitalism (Clegg and Redding, 1990; Hampden-Turner and Trompenaars, 1993; Sharp, 1992). Political and economic pressures to reduce trade barriers admit new players in formerly controlled markets. This reduces the monopoly power of crony capitalists, who are forced to improve the quality of their products or to lower prices to compete, and it helps the consumer by offering a wider range of choices at competitive prices. Thus, while some might consider competition a problem, others believe it provides opportunities. Among businesses, we see convergence toward best practices that advance progress and human development, even as we believe other forms of convergence constitute a threat.

A final point to be made about cultural exposure highlights interrelations between self-interested individuals and businesses. Just as TNCs are urged to be more socially responsive, they are at the same time encouraged to improve short-term gains. This tension is the basis of the Rhine/Anglo-Saxon debate, where the Rhine model balances profits with social good and the Anglo-Saxon model emphasizes stockholder benefits (Albert et al., 1993). In the short term the Anglo-Saxon model appeared to be ascendant, its progress hastened by powerful pension funds charged with preserving the fiduciary interests of individuals. In the wake of business failures and scandals that began with Enron's demise the self-interest trajectory may be diverted. Further, any shift to the Anglo-Saxon model reflects a paradox for self-interest: we want higher returns and we want more socially responsive organizations.

A Global World for Businesses

An international world was one defined according to national interests, and built around assumptions of national sovereignty. Established by colonialism, this world relied on and has been defined by competition where haves and have-nots are divided along North–South lines. A more global world is one where self-interest is defined less in terms of each nation on each issue and more in terms of how joint activities serve more of the world more of the time. On the world scene, an example of the tensions between international and global interests is found in WTO activities. The organization's charter is for member nations to reach consensus on a common set of worldwide trading standards by which all member organizations abide. Although many implementation problems remain, the consensus approach and dispute resolution mechanisms of the WTO offer leverage to smaller, less economically developed countries than was ever possible in a more international world.

There are benefits and costs in a more global world, just as there were for a more international world. Markets are opened that have not been open in an international world, creating new businesses opportunities through trade and cross-national synergies. But the same market is open to new firms and organizations that may drive profits down, and it is open to global gangs and global terrorists. Consumers have new choices that come from around the world and they may see an increase in quality, but local producers who cannot match price or quality may die. Any move toward global standards admits new players, but a common set of rules brings about revision of local rules and concomitant changes in the cultural rationale that brought them about. On the "down" side is that, even in a global world, markets do not deal with externalities, and thus there is growing need for global forms of governance emerging from businesses and other social actors. According to the authors of the UN *Human Development Report* for 1994, "the concept of one world and one planet simply cannot emerge from an unequal world. . . . Global sustainability without global justice will always remain an elusive goal." Thus it is critical to avoid marginalization of those who live in less developed economies, particularly sub-Saharan Africa, and while this is or can be the function of intergovernmental organizations like the WTO or the ILO, the latter may not be well equipped to play such a role.

Effects of Globalization on Organizational Form, Design, and Governance

Having incorporated features of the international, multinational, and global organizations that Bartlett and Ghoshal (1989) describe, their transnational organization becomes a far more complex entity than its predecessors and it faces management challenges that also are complex. Held et al. (1999), for example, suggest that information technology and other global factors have increased modes for organizing international production from internal MNC hierarchies to less hierarchical forms of management that encourage two-way communication between parent and subsidiary, and allow greater autonomy for the latter. Maintaining global presence also might mean transcending internal vertical boundaries between levels and ranks of employees or horizontal boundaries between functions and disciplines (Ashkenas et al., 1995) and transcending external boundaries between sectors and among organizations located in the same industry. The language of business remains profit-centered, but the vocabulary also reflects growing need for dialogue, negotiation, and collaboration in addition to rather than as a substitute for tradition.

The traditional Western ideal for businesses is based on the assumption of undisputed organizational and even national autonomy. Today transnational enterprises (and in turn domestic organizations) answer to many more in the global community than were at the table as part of an international world organized around nation-state interests alone. This process creates organizational challenges that affect stakeholder relations and internal form and design. There is greater pressure for transparency in corporate governance, and the trend among TNCs is to create organizational hybrids able to integrate profit with social objectives.

A shift toward cooperative forms of activity does not eliminate competitive thinking, but suggests competition and collaboration operate simultaneously in the same organization. Thus mobile phone producer Ericsson can partner with the United Nations to provide mobile and satellite telephones for relief workers in disaster areas, and sell telephones at a profit. Starbucks can profit from the double tall latte, but also collaborate with Conservancy International and the Songbird Foundation to produce more shade-grown coffee. And Fuji and Kodak, among others, can collaborate in R&D and then compete against each other on the basis of marketing and distribution. Increasingly, businesses experience pressure to achieve economic efficiencies via integration with broader social issues such as labor rights, environmentalism, and justice. Responsibility for realizing the promise of integrating social and business initiatives is as much on individuals as on corporations and may mean changes in our own lives that we are reluctant to initiate.

Conclusion

The review of global business activities above identifies only some of the many contradictions that confound understanding of the globalization process. In the case of major transnational corporations, these contradictions make it difficult to reach clear conclusions about the intent and effects of industry consolidation among them or the roles they play and benefits received from trade development, wage inequalities, and global value shifts. Similar contradictions would doubtless have emerged had we looked at other organizational actors or other spheres of global influence. In face of these contradictions, questions like "Is globalization a good thing or a bad thing?" or "Are businesses a force for good or evil?" might well be answered by "It depends," but that is not a satisfactory answer. It raises too many subsequent questions, and it impedes our ability to act. The contradictions raised and the uncertainties they create illustrate a flaw associated with an inclusionary approach to thinking about the globalization process. In as much as it is an ongoing process, there will always be more data to include, more voices, certainly more contradictions.

The alternative conclusion to be reached from these contractions is that the globalization process is uneven and has resulted in both gains and losses. Businesses, including TNCs from around the world, SMEs, and organizations in other sectors contribute to those gains and losses, and as a group they are all unequal agents of both positive and negative outcomes. Slotting organizations and events into good/bad categories may not adequately describe the more complex roles available in a global world, nor does it reflect the variety of global activities in which organizations increasingly engage. Organizing the good–evil debate around businesses has been shown to obscure some part of objective reality, and it may make it less possible to understand the process of globalization. Thus organizational studies may be enriched by examining the many activities, many interactions, and many outcomes in which diverse organizations are globally engaged.

This chapter demonstrates the benefits of inclusion, and similarly illustrates its limitations for scholarship. The nonlinear nature of the globalization process makes the path of globalization uneven, discontinuous, ambiguous, complex, and unclear. The pattern of dots that emerges from looking at contradictions defies the predictions that can be more readily made from observing a clean regression line. Unclear outputs are one challenge, but as this chapter shows, there also are a broad array of inputs from which to choose when building a case around globalization.

The inclusive and interdisciplinary approach to globalization endorsed here is subject to constraints imposed by our own disciplinary training. The latter process exposes would-be scholars to the traditions of any given field, and the publication process tends to reinforce them when networks of scholars enforce tradition. These practices can exclude alternative voices. The conventions of scientific discovery that characterize much organizational research also can be exclusionary. For example, interesting questions may be driven out by less interesting ones that better lend themselves to measurement. Interesting findings may be discounted unless they are grounded in the known. Almost by definition, the inclusionary approach endorsed here creates a risk for scholars because it is probably impossible to speak authoritatively from all the disciplines where globalization is relevant. Inclusive scholarship also might mean incorporating qualitative as well as quantitative evidence, but that is not to say that we will be able to assemble that information correctly. For example, *post hoc* analysis of terrorist attacks in September 2001 shows there were sufficient quantitative and qualitative data to explain the attack but not to predict it. Economic downturns that emerged in 2000 have yet to run their course, making it difficult to predict their global effects as well. The transformationist view reflected throughout this chapter does not assume that globalization "must simply evolve in a single direction" (Held et al., 1999: 11). Together, the disorganization of inclusion and the organization of exclusion outline different alternatives associated with global activities, and together they enrich our understanding of it and of the role organizations play in the globalization process.

Note

1 In chapter 8a the term "nongovernmental organization" and its acronym NGO are used interchangeably with "nonprofit organization."

References

Albert, Michel, Haviland, Paul, and Rohatyn, Felix G. (1993) *Capitalism vs Capitalism: How America's Obsession with Individual Achievement and Short-term Profit has led it to the Brink of Collapse*. New York: Four Walls Eight Windows.

Amin, Samir (1996) *The Challenge of Globalization: Review of International Political Economy*. New York: Routledge.

Anderson, Sarah, and Cavanagh, John (1997) *The Top 200: The Rise of Global Corporate Power*. Washington, DC: Institute for Policy Studies.

Annan, Kofi (2000) *We the Peoples: Millennium Report of the Secretary General of the United Nations*. New York: United Nations.

Appadurai, Arjun (1990) "Disjunctures and difference in the global cultural economy," in Mike Featherstone (ed.) *Global Culture*, pp. 295–310. Newbury Park, CA: Sage.

Ashkenas, Ron, Ulrich, Dave, Jick, Todd, and Kerr, Steve (1995) *The Boundaryless Organization*. San Francisco: Jossey-Bass.

Austin, James E. (2000) *The Collaboration Challenge: How Nonprofits and Businesses succeed through Strategic Alliances*. San Francisco: Jossey-Bass.

Bannock, Graham, Baxter, R. E., and Davis, Evan (1998) *Dictionary of Economics*. New York: Wiley.

Barber, Benjamin (1992) "Jihad vs McWorld," *Atlantic Monthly*, 269 (3): 53–61. Published in book form 1995.

Barnet, R. J., and Cavanagh, John (1994) *Global Dreams*. New York: Simon & Schuster.

Bartlett, Christopher A., and Ghoshal, Sumantra (1989) *Managing across Borders: The Transnational Solution*. Boston, MA: Harvard Business School Press.

——(2000) "Going global: lessons from late movers," *Harvard Business Review*, 78 (2): 132–42.

Bendell, Jem, ed. (2000) *Terms for Endearment*. Sheffield: Greenleaf.

Bornstein, David (1999) "Reshaping society through people power," *New York Times* on the Web, July 10, http://nytimes.org.

Borrus, Michael, and Zysman, John (1998) "Globalization with borders: the rise of Wintelism as the future of industrial competition," in John Zysman and Andrew Schwartz (eds) *Enlarging Europe: The Industrial Foundations of a new Political Reality*, pp. 27–63. Berkeley, CA: International and Area Studies, University of California.

Brown, Juanita (1992) "Corporation as community: a new image for a new era," in John Rensch (ed.) *New Traditions in Business*, pp. 123–39. San Francisco, CA: Berrett-Koehler.

Castells, Manuel (1996) *The Rise of the Network Society*. Oxford: Blackwell.

Clark, Tom (1996) "Mechanisms of corporate rule," in Jerry Mander and Edward Goldsmith (eds) *The Case against the Global Economy*, pp. 297–308. San Francisco, CA: Sierra Books.

Clegg, Stewart R., and Redding, S. Gordon, eds (1990) *Capitalism in Contrasting Cultures*. Berlin: de Gruyter.

Click, Reid W., and Harrison, Paul (2000) *Does Multinationality Matter? Evidence of Value Destruction in US Multinational Corporations*. Washington, DC: US Federal Reserve Board.

Clough, Michael (1996) *Shaping American Foreign Relations: The Critical Role of the*

Southeast. Muscatine, IA: Stanley Foundation New American Dialogue.

Conference Board (2000) *Perspectives on a Global Economy*. New York: Conference Board.

Coviello, Nicole E., and McAuley, Andrew (1999) "Internationalisation and the smaller firm: a review of contemporary empirical research" I, *Management International Review*, 39 (3): 223–56.

Daniels, John D., and Radebaugh, Lee H. (1992) *International Business*, sixth edition. Reading, MA: Addison-Wesley.

Dees, J. Gregory (1998) "Enterprising nonprofits," *Harvard Business Review*, January–February, pp. 5–15.

Demick, David H., and O'Reilly, Aidan J. (2000) "Supporting SME internationalisation: a collaborative project for accelerated export development," *Irish Marketing Review*, 13 (1): 34–45.

Dicken, Peter (1998) *Global Shift*, third edition. New York and London: Guilford.

Dollar, David, and Kraay, Aart (2000) *Growth is Good for the Poor*. Washington, DC: World Bank Development Research Group.

Doremus, Paul N., Keller, William W., Pauly, Louis W., and Reich, Simon (1998) *The Myth of the Global Corporation*. Princeton, NJ: Princeton University Press.

Dunning, John (1993) *The Globalization of Business*. New York and London: Routledge.

Easterbrook, Gregg (2000) "Who's afraid of globalization?" *Wall Street Journal*, April 14, p. A18.

Economist (1995a) "Human rights," *Economist*, June 3, pp. 58–9.

——(1995b) "Greenpeace means business," *Economist*, August 19, pp. 59–60.

——(1996) "The family connection," *Economist*, October 5, p. 62.

——(1999a) Dow Jones Index and Sustainable Investment Index, *Economist*, September 11.

——(1999b) "The non-governmental order," *Economist*, December 11, pp. 20–1

——(2000a) "Foreign friends," *Economist*, January 8, pp. 71–4.

——(2000b) "Doing well by doing good," *Economist*, April 22, pp. 65–7.

——(2000c) "How mergers go wrong," *Economist*, July 22, pp. 19–20.

——(2000d) "The case for globalization," *Economist*, September 23, pp. 19–20.

Falk, Richard (1993) "The making of global citizenship," in Jeremy Brecher, John Brown Childs, and Jill Cutler (eds), *Global Visions*, pp. 39–50. Boston, MA: South End Press.

Ford, Constance Mitchell, and Barta, Patrick (2000) "Income gap broadens amid boom," *Wall Street Journal*, January 18, pp. A2, A16.

Fujita, Masataka (1995) "Small and medium-sized transnational corporations: trends and patterns of foreign direct investment," *Small Business Economics*, 7 (3): 183–204.

Gereffi, Gary (1994) "The organization of buyer-driven global commodity chains," in Gary Gereffi and M Korzeniewicz. (eds) *Commodity Chains and Global Capitalism*. Westport, CT: Praeger.

Gereffi, Gary, Garcia-Johnson, Ronie, and Sasser, Erika (2001) "The NGO–industrial complex," *Foreign Policy*, 125: 56–65.

Ghemawat, Pankaj, and Ghadar, Fariborz (2000) "The dubious logic of global megamergers," *Harvard Business Review*, July–August, pp. 65–72.

Ghoshal, Sumantra, and Bartlett, Christopher (1990) "The multinational corporation as an interorganizational network," *Academy of Management Review*, 15 (4): 603–25.

Gilpin, Robert (2000) The *Challenge of Global Capitalism: The World Economy in the Twenty-first Century*. Princeton, NJ: Princeton University Press.

Govindarajan, Vijay, and Gupta, Anil (2000) "Analysis of the emerging global arena," *European Management Journal*, 18 (3): 274–84.

Green, Carolyn, and Ruhleder, Karen (1996) "Globalization, borderless worlds, and the Tower of Babel," *Journal of Organizational Change*, 8 (4): 55–68.

Gupta, Anil, and Govindarajan, Vijay (1991) "Knowledge flows and the structure of control within multinational corporations," *Academy of Management Review*, 16 (4): 768–92.

Hampden-Turner, Charles, and Trompenaars, Alfons (1993) *The Seven Cultures of Capitalism*. New York: Doubleday.

Harris, Richard G. (1993) "Globalization, trade, and income," *Canadian Journal of Economics*, 26 (4): 755–76.

Hawken, Paul (1993) *The Ecology of Commerce*. New York: Harper.

Held, David, McGrew, Anthony, Goldblatt, David, and Perraton, Jonathon (1999) *Global Transformations*. Stanford, CA: Stanford University Press.

Hordes, Mark W., Clancy, J. Anthony, and Baddaley, Julie (1995) "How global companies win out," *Academy of Management Executive*, 9 (2): 7–11.

Hu, Yao-Su (1992) "Global or stateless corporations are national firms with international operations," *California Management Review*, 34 (2): 107–26.

Hull, Frank, Slowinski, Gene, Wharton, Robert, and Azumi, Koya (1988) "Strategic partnerships between technological entrepreneurs in the United States and large corporations in Japan and the United States," in Farok J. Contractor and Peter Lorange (eds) *Cooperative Strategies in International Business*, pp. 445–6. Lexington, MA: Heath.

Huntington, Samuel (1993) "The clash of civilizations," *Foreign Affairs*, 72 (3): 22–49.

Kahn, Joel S. (1995) *Culture, Multiculture, and Postculture*. Beverly Hills, CA: Sage.

Klein, Naomi (2000) *No Logo*. New York: St Martin's Press.

Korten, David C. (1995) *When Corporations rule the World*. San Francisco: Berrett-Koehler.

Kurzer, Paulete (1993) *Business and Banking: Political Change and Economic Integration in Western Europe*. Ithaca, NY: Cornell University Press.

Larsson, Tomas (2001) *The Race to the Top*. Washington, DC: Cato Institute.

Larudee, Metrene (1994) "Who gains from trade?" *Dollars and Sense*, September–October, p. 29.

Lawrence, Thomas, and Hardy, Cynthia (1999) "Building bridges for refugees: toward a typology of bridging organizations," *Journal of Applied Behavioral Science*, 35 (1): 48–70.

Levy, Frank (1999) "Rhetoric and reality: making sense of the income gap debate," *Harvard Business Review*, September–October, pp. 3–7.

Lipsey, Robert E., Blomstrom, Magnus, and Ramstetter, Eric D. (2000) "Internationalized Production in World Output," working paper. Washington, DC: National Bureau of Economic Research.

Lodge, George C. (1995) *Managing Globalization in the Age of Interdependence*. San Francisco, CA: Jossey-Bass

Mandel, Jay R., and Ferleger, Louis (2000) Preface, *The Annals of the American Academy of Political and Social Science*, 570. Thousand Oaks, CA: Sage.

Mander, Jerry, and Goldsmith, Edward. (1996) *The Case against the Global Economy*. San Francisco, CA: Sierra Books.

McFarland, Lynne, Senn, Larry, and Childress, John (1993) *Twenty-first Century Leadership*. New York: Leadership Press.

Minford, Patrick, Riley, Jonathan, and Nowell, Eric (1997) "Trade, technology, and labor markets in the world economy," *Journal of Development Studies*, 34 (2): 1–35.

Mitra, Barun S. (1999) "WTO protestors vs the poor," *Wall Street Journal*, December 9, p. A26.

Murphy, David E., and Coleman, Gill (2000) "Thinking partners: business, NGOs and the partnership concept," in Jem Bendell (ed.) *Terms for Endearment: Business, NGOs and Sustainable Development*, pp. 207–15. Sheffield: Greenleaf.

Naisbitt, John (1994) *Global Paradox*. New York: Morrow.

Newell, Peter (2000) "Globalization and the new politics of sustainable development," in Jem Bendell (ed.) *Terms for Endearment: Business, NGOs and Sustainable Development*, pp. 31–9. Sheffield: Greenleaf.

O'Neill, Helen (1997) "Globalization, competitiveness and human security: challenges for development policy and institutional change," in Cristobal Kay (ed.) *Globalization, Competitiveness and Human Security*, pp. 20–1. London: Frank Cass.

ODI (2000) "Can there be a Global Standard for Social Policy? The "Social Policy Principles" as a Test Case," briefing paper, Overseas Development Institute, www.odi.org.uk/briefing/2_00.html, May 2.

Ohmae, Kenichi (1995) *The End of the Nation State*. Cambridge, MA: Free Press.

Ostry, Sylvia, and Nelson, Richard R. (1995) *Techno-nationalism and Techno-globalism: Conflict and Cooperation*. Washington, DC: Brookings Institution Press.

Parker, Barbara (1996) "Evolution and revolution: from international business to globalization," in Cynthia Hardy and Stewart Clegg (eds) *Handbook of Organizations*. London: Sage.

——(1998) *Globalization and Business Practices: Managing across Boundaries*. London: Sage.

Pieterse, Jan N. (1995) "Globalization as hybridization," in Mike Featherstone, Scott Lash, and Roland Robertson (eds) *Global Modernities*, pp. 45–68. London: Sage.

Raghavan, Anita, and Steinmetz, Greg (2000) "Europe's family firms become a dying breed amid succession woes," *Wall Street Journal*, March 31, pp. A1, A10.

Reich, Robert (1991) *The Work of Nations: Preparing ourselves for Twenty-first Century Capitalism*. New York: Knopf.

Robertson, Roland (1995) "Glocalization: time–space and homogeneity–heterogeneity," in Mike Featherstone, Scott Lash, and Roland Robertson (eds) *Global Modernities*, pp. 25–44. London: Sage.

Rodrik, Dani. (1997) "Sense and nonsense in the globalization debate," *Foreign Policy*, 107: 19–38.

Ruigrok, Winfried, and Van Tulder, Rob (1996) *The Logic of International Restructuring*. New York: Routledge.

Sachs, Jeffrey (1999) "Helping the world's poorest," *Economist*, August 14, pp. 17–20.

——(1998) "International economics: unlocking the mysteries of globalization," *Foreign Policy*, 110: 97–112.

Salamon, Lester, Anheier, Helmut, and associates (1998) *The Emerging Sector Revisited*. Baltimore, MD: Johns Hopkins University Institute for Policy Studies.

Scholte, Jan Aart (1996) "Beyond the buzzword: toward a critical theory of globalization," in Elenore Hoffman and Gillian Youngs (eds) *Globalization: Theory and Practice*, pp. 43–57. London: Pinter.

Sharp, Margaret (1992) "Tides of change: the world economy and Europe in the 1990s," *International Affairs*, 68 (1): 17–35.

Simai, Mihaly (1994) *The Future of Global Governance*. Washington, DC: US Institute of Peace.

Simon, Hermann (1996) *Hidden Champions: Lessons from 500 of the World's best Unknown Companies*. Boston, MA: Harvard Business School Press.

Sklair, Leslie (1995) *Sociology of the Global System*. Baltimore, MD: Johns Hopkins University Press.

Slaughter, Matthew (1998) "International trade and labour-market outcomes: results, questions, and policy options," *Economic Journal*, 108 (450): 1452–62.

Steingard, David S., and Fitzgibbons, Dale E. (1996) "Challenging the juggernaut of globalization: a manifesto for academic praxis," *Journal of Organizational Change Management*, 8 (4): 30–54.

Streeten, Paul (2001) *Globalization: Threat or Opportunity?* Copenhagen: Copenhagen Business School Press.

Thompson, Graham, and Allen, John (1997) "Think global, then think again: economic globalization in context," *Area*, 29 (3): 213–28.

Tomlinson, John (1991) *Cultural Imperialism*. Baltimore, MD: Johns Hopkins University Press.

UNCTAD (2000) *World Development Report, 2000*. New York: United Nations.

——(2001) *Promoting Linkages*, World Investment Report. Geneva: UNCTAD.

United Nations (1995) *By How Much does Education raise Wages?* Human Development Report, New York: Oxford University Press.

US Census Bureau (2000) *Current Population Survey, 2000*. Washington, DC: Bureau of the Census (analysis from the Center on Budget and Policy Priorities).

van Bergeijk, Peter A. G., and Mensink, Nico W. (1997) "Measuring globalization," *Journal of World Trade*, 31 (3): 159–68.

Vidal, I. (1997) "Industry terrified at the outbreak of ethics," *Guardian* Ecosoundings, p. 263.

Waddell, Steve (1999) "Business–Government–Nonprofit Collaborations as Agents for Social Innovation and Learning," paper presented at the Academy of Management, Chicago, August.

Waddock, Sandra A., and Smith, Neil (1999) "Relationships: The real Challenge of Corporate Global Citizenship," working paper, Boston, MA: Boston College.

Weisbrod, Burton A. (1997) "The future of the nonprofit sector: its entwining with private enterprise and government," *Journal of Policy Analysis and Management*, 16 (4): 541–55.

——(1998) "Conclusions and public-policy issues: commercialism and the road ahead," in Burton A. Weisbrod (ed.) *To Profit or not to Profit*, pp. 287–305. Cambridge: Cambridge University Press.

Wilkins, Mira (1994) "Comparative hosts," *Business History*, 36 (1): 1–18.

Wood, A. (1994) *North–South Trade, Employment and Inequality: Changing Fortunes in a Skill-driven World*. Oxford: Oxford University Press.

World Bank (1995) "Twice the workers – and twice the productivity," *World Bank Policy Research Bulletin*, 6 (4): 1–6.

8b Globalization and the Organization(s) of Exclusion in Advanced Capitalism

Marc T. Jones

At the end of the second millennium political, economic, and social configurations are characterized by contradictions and juxtapositions sharper than at any time during the twentieth century. This is particularly true in the advanced (post)industrial countries, where social formations are fragmenting at a rapid rate to an unheard-of degree. For some groups the bonds of place, nation, and embedded identity have been superseded by a transnational cosmopolitanism directly linked to particular roles in an unfolding global economic system. For others, beyond the gravitational pull of global forces due to a lack of education, skills, or simply being in the wrong place at the wrong time, local factors are becoming an increasingly important source of identity and security – a psychosocial shelter from the global storm.

The forces behind these developments are associated with the term "globalization," which I define as a product of two linked processes. The first is constituted by the spatial expansion of the forces and relations of capitalism, represented most clearly by the continuing (although uneven) integration of financial, product, and labor markets across national boundaries. The second manifests as the compression of space, time, culture, and government policy, which reduces the transaction costs of international business activity (see Jones, 1998a). I date the beginning of the globalization era with two events; the fall of the Berlin Wall in 1989 and the publication of Francis Fukuyama's *The End of History and the Last Man* in the same year. The former signaled the end of the Cold War as well as the material competition between capitalism and socialism/communism; the latter, perhaps even more important, registered the ideological victory of liberal capitalism over

its challengers, including not only hardline socialism/communism but also (as would become increasingly apparent over the next decade) the distributive or developmental variants of capitalism present in most of Western Europe, Scandinavia, and East Asia (see Weiss, 1998).

Globalization and advanced capitalism are involved in a complex dance in which there is no clear leader; that is, they are internally distinct but inextricably intertwined phenomena. Nor is it clear that the empirical content of globalization corresponds to its discursive power to shape the understanding and influence the actions of key stakeholder groups. What is clear, however, is that organizations and organizational dynamics – specifically, transnational corporations and cascading networks – are at the core of both globalization and advanced capitalism. Therefore, organizational studies should be at the forefront of efforts to comprehend the meaning(s) of globalization, particularly its distributional implications.

From post-Fordism to . . . what?

A basic understanding of the transition from Fordism to post-Fordism is necessary to contextualize the current analysis. It is within the dynamic and fragmented environment characteristic of post-Fordism that the genesis of advanced capitalism can be detected. This section briefly outlines the distinguishing characteristics of Fordism and post-Fordism. I then derive from the latter three key sets of drivers which provide the foundations for the emergence of advanced capitalism.

Fordism was the dominant institutional order for the three decades following World

War II (Armstrong et al., 1984). It was manifest in the articulation of the Keynesian welfare state and mass-production technology in most advanced capitalist countries. Fordism involved a (formal or *de facto*) corporatist configuration in which mass production and consumption activities, articulated where necessary by state intervention, constituted the foundation of national economic systems. It has thus been referred to as "organized capitalism" (Lasch and Urry, 1987). Fordist social formations were essentially closed systems in which stable oligopolies dominated core industrial sectors. The interface with the international economy was largely limited to exports of surplus production and imports of raw materials and specialty products not produced domestically. These transactions occurred within an international financial system of fixed exchange rates organized by the Bretton Woods institutions. During the Fordist era the global economy was thus basically an aggregation of relatively autonomous national economies. This manifested in terms of nationally based industries operating in relative isolation from each other, usually behind significant protectionist barriers. For a variety of reasons, Fordism as a viable institutional order unraveled in the 1970s (see Harvey, 1989; Piore and Sabel, 1984).

In the 1980s post-Fordism became a ubiquitous (and contentious) term employed to denote a new set of institutional arrangements (Bagguley, 1991; Hall and Jacques, 1989). In post-Fordism the role of the state shifted from the active maintenance of corporatist arrangements and Keynesian demand management to a very different form of interventionism supporting privatization, deregulation, labor intensification, and monetary management. Economic relations between states occurred within an environment of floating exchange rates as the Bretton Woods system was superseded by increasing capital mobility (see Eichengreen, 1996). Formally protected domestic industrial markets were subjected to internationalizing pressures, with resulting increases in competitive intensity and instability. At the organizational level, post-Fordism was associated with downsizing, spatial deconcentration, an increased use of subcontracting (outsourc-

ing), and a proliferation of temporary and part-time employment. Flexible technologies able to exploit economies of scope took precedence over Fordist technologies oriented to achieving economies of scale. The labor–management relationship was recast in terms of a cooperative association between a core segment of skilled workers and management, usually without union participation. Some observers of post-Fordism also linked its transformation of material structures and processes to a contemporaneous shift in discursive formations and cultural systems from a modern to a post-modern inflection (see Jameson, 1991; Lasch and Urry, 1987).

Yet it is incorrect to refer to post-Fordism as a coherent institutional order in the manner of Fordism – that is, as an actually existing socioeconomic paradigm. In fact there was never any widespread consensus as to what exactly constituted post-Fordism (see Amin, 1994). Post-Fordism is thus more accurately understood as the piecemeal negation of Fordism rather than as its empirical successor as a total system. Nevertheless, each of the major institutional elements which have been associated with post-Fordism represents a substantial break with the economic, political, social, and cultural assumptions and organizing principles upon which Fordism was constructed and sustained. There was therefore general agreement that national business systems, industries, and firms in the core countries had passed from reasonably coherent Fordist arrangements to something else since the late 1970s. "Post-Fordism" constituted an appropriate term for the new arrangements to the extent that "post" simply signified "after" rather than indicating a new and coherent institutional configuration.

In an overall sense, then, it is fair to note that the rise of post-Fordism was widely understood as the end of organized capitalism for those observers whose focus was primarily at the national level. However, others pointed out that, while business systems were becoming disarticulated at the national level, a parallel process was occurring at the transnational level in which capitalism was becoming ever more tightly organized through escalating financial market integration, geographical mobility, and flexible responses in labor and consumer markets (see Smart, 1992). From this perspective, the increasing disorganization observable at the national level was thus understood as an effect of the globalization process, particularly as the latter diminished the ability of governments to autonomously manage their national economies (Jones, 1996). The level of order essentially shifted from the national to the global, the latter being constituted by a matrix linking major cities, regional economies, and far-flung production and consumption enclaves in developing and underdeveloped countries.

Emerging from the post-Fordist environment were three key sets of drivers which together constituted the foundational conditions necessary for the genesis of advanced capitalism. The first set arose from the massive industrial restructuring of the past two decades, itself generated by an historically unprecedented level of technologically induced "time–space compression" (Harvey, 1997) as well as changes in government policies. New technologies have driven the convergence of formally discrete industries such communications, information processing, and news and entertainment, creating a huge multimedia sector operating partly in "electronic space" (Castells, 1996). Meanwhile, changes in government regulations have fostered the intersection of banking, insurance, and financial services within and across national markets (Dicken, 1998). Product life cycles have continued to shorten as advertising has intensified and consumers tastes for constant novelty appear insatiable (e.g., the Apple iMac computer, which comes in several vivid colors totally divorced from any functional consideration). Profitability has become concentrated in particular high-technology sectors to an extent not previously seen, with major implications not only for investment flows but also for employment patterns, occupational structures, and income and wealth distribution (see Sassen, 1998).

Relatedly, and perhaps most important, in these core superprofit sectors the generation of goods and services has become decoupled from employment. That is, the relative number of "good" jobs that the contemporary economy generates is far less than in the old Fordist manufacturing-based economy. These trends

were recognized with respect to the manufacturing sector during the 1980s (see Harrison and Bluestone, 1988), but they have become much more pronounced in recent years as the duality of service sector employment has become more evident. Luttwak (1999) offers as an example of this trend the case of Microsoft versus General Motors, noting that the market value (and market power) of the former considerably exceeds the latter. Yet Microsoft has approximately 20,000 employees worldwide whereas GM still directly employs over 200,000 people. His basic point is that this single anecdote extended into a system property creates a highly exclusionary and skewed economy with a huge potential for social fragmentation and even violent upheaval. Rifkin (1997) offers a similar treatment of these developments, referring dramatically to "the end of work." Yet, as Castells (1996) suggests, a more appropriate phrase would be "the end of good work for the average worker." I would add that "good work" is increasingly being replaced by "shit work" – some combination of unsatisfying, insecure, and poorly paying employment, usually in the service sector, often performed by female and/or immigrant labor (Waring, 1998).

The second set of drivers refers to changing state polices usually associated with "New Right" ideology. These struck Great Britain and the United States in the late 1970s, diffused to the other Anglo-Saxon countries (Canada, Australia, New Zealand) in the 1980s, and penetrated many Western European nations in the 1990s (see Gray, 1998). With the relative autonomy of core states (from capital) decreasing as capital mobility increased over this period, most states adopted programs which supported regressive measures to lower wages and production costs – and, even more fundamentally, middle and working-class expectations (regarding future living standards, income levels, state funded retirement, etc.) (see Krugman, 1990). A typical policy mix incorporated the internationalizing of national economies through the lowering of barriers to foreign trade and investment; the deregulation and privatization of most sectors which had formally been state-controlled or owned; a shift away from Keynesian macroeconomic management to a focus on controlling inflation through monetary policy, leaving the articulation of supply and demand to market forces; changes to industrial relations systems which marginalized unions and individuated employment contracts; contraction of welfare programs and the lowering of the social wage; and a shift in tax policy towards lowering taxes on corporate profits, capital gains, and high incomes and increasing (regressive) taxes on property and consumption, as well as raising fees for basic services (through the "user pays" approach). Kelsey's (1996) account of the "New Zealand experiment" constitutes one of the most trenchant analyses of the totalistic implementation – and social effects – of such a program.

In the aggregate, such measures served to shift socioeconomic patterns of income, wealth, and life chances from a diamond shape (with a bulge at the middle signifying a large middle class) to an hourglass shape (representing growing segments of haves and have-nots and a shrinking middle class) (Galbraith, 1998). Sassen (1998) observes that these developments have directly impacted consumption patterns, contributing to the fragmentation of Fordist mass markets and the growth of two modal market segments. The first incorporates very well off (and generally urban) "yuppies" who demand customized products and services oriented to particular "lifestyle models." (The irony here is that the satisfaction of these demands depends on the existence of a large pool of cheap labor to keep entertainment prices down, gentrify inner-city housing for yuppie occupation, etc. – thus casting a predatory light on the privileged classes whose "quality of life" increasingly relies on the low wages of other groups.) The other dominant market segment consists of highly price-sensitive consumers who shop at discount stores, factory outlets, and similar sites to maximize their purchasing power. These consumers continue to be served by standardized products and services (e.g., "generic" or "house brands").

The third set of drivers concerns the strategic choices made by business firms – most importantly by transnational corporations (TNCs) – as they dominate the high-profit segments of major global industries (Dicken,

1998). These firms have adopted new strategies to improve their cost and/or revenue structures in accordance with the opportunities and threats that the globalization of their industries has generated. On the demand side, the shortening of product life cycles has forced accelerated new product development. As a result, economies of scope have come to take precedence over those of scale as firms struggle to keep abreast of changing patterns of consumer demand. The rise of the newly industrializing countries (NICs) and global media have simultaneously fostered increasing levels of convergence in consumer preferences from country to country (particularly with respect to middle and high-income consumers). This has allowed TNCs to horizontally link particular market segments from country to country, thus enabling the pursuit of scale-based focus strategies (Porter, 1985) on a transnational basis and preventing overreliance on particular national markets.

On the supply side, the end of the Cold War, the continuing progress of the NICs, and technological developments which enhance command and control capabilities have vastly expanded the population of potential sites for TNCs to locate particular value-chain activities. These firms are now able to pursue absolute advantage by articulating their specific resources and capabilities with country-specific locational factors. As a result, the entry barriers to core segments of key industries have considerably increased in recent years, despite the rising prominence of the small business sector as a site of innovation and employment (see Harrison, 1997). Contemporary megamergers occurring within (and at the intersection) of key industries further the concentration of ownership and control. These developments – while partly a reaction to other events outlined above – have substantially changed the bargaining position (or leverage) between TNCs and other major stakeholders (primarily states and workers) in favor of the former, as well as directly impacting industry structures, employment patterns, and government policies (Jones, 1999). This last point is significant: that the three sets of drivers discussed above all interact with each other through feedback loops in political, economic, technological and sociocultural processes, leading to cumulative causation (Sassen, 1998).

Advanced Capitalism: Structure and Dynamics

Following Jones (1998b), advanced capitalism is a dualistic structure composed of two key segments, the "techno-economy" and the "grunge economy." The techno-economy is characterized by capital intensity (although the capital is increasingly in the form of knowledge rather than traditional industrial plant and equipment), high-technology, work processes based around automation and flexible systems, the deployment of advanced information and communications systems, multiskilled and educated "symbolic analysts" (Reich, 1991), and cutting-edge management approaches based on principles of "strategic human resource management" and "fourth blueprint systems" (Limerick et al., 1998), all of which combine to generate very high levels of value added and profitability.

The techno-economy is concentrated in the core value-adding segments of leading industries such as telecommunications, multimedia, computing, information technology, pharmaceuticals, banking and financial services, commercial aviation, defense systems, consumer electronics, and motor vehicles. The primary activities that are undertaken in the techno-economy include research and development, product design, marketing, branding, distribution, after-market service, and specialized business services (e.g., consulting, executive recruitment), as well as the overall coordination of these activities. Spatially, the techno-economy is dominated by transnational corporations based in the so-called "triad" regions of North America, Western Europe, and East Asia (Ohmae, 1985) and headquartered in "global cities" (Sassen, 1991) such as New York, London, and Tokyo, although its reach extends far beyond such cities and regions.

The second element of advanced capitalism is a grunge economy made up of generally downgraded labor (Sassen, 1984). This grunge economy is itself bifurcated, firstly into a segment composed of semiskilled workers employed on an "at will" basis, largely in small

firms acting as subcontractors to much larger corporates in the techno-economy. This contingent segment amounted to 25 percent of the American labor force in 1992 and was projected to increase to 35 percent by the year 2000 (Castells, 1996). Its tremendous growth is due to the shift away from Fordist arrangements and the consequent changes in organizational structures (e.g., downsizing, networks), employment patterns (casualization), and industrial relations regimes (see Moody, 1997).

The contingent segment represents the source of "just in time" employees for the corporate sector in the techno-economy. This labor can be accessed when demand warrants and shed in a frictionless manner which minimizes transaction costs for the firm, thus enhancing flexibility and treating this category of labor as a variable cost to which management has no long-term liability (financial or otherwise). This segment is characterized by labor-intensive but low value-adding activities (e.g., component assembly, payroll processing, custodial work), the presence of deskilling technologies, casual employment contracts and minimal unionization, high proportions of female and female immigrant labor, and bureaucratic (rule-based) and technical management systems (Edwards, 1979). While these activities can and still do occur within the organizational boundaries of large firms, they have been the focus since the 1980s of massive downsizing and outsourcing efforts by these firms, resulting in the explosive growth of the business services sector (Sassen, 1998). This sector caters not only to tertiary industries like banking and finance, but also to manufacturing industries whose firms have outsourced peripheral or support activities.

The second element of the grunge economy is the informal segment, composed of an underclass of unskilled and/or redundant labor working sporadically under extreme conditions outside of the formally regulated and taxed economy. This segment is characterized by the multiplicity of labor processes in evidence, including the revival of domestic, familial, and paternalistic labor systems based on labor-intensive, low-technology, and low value-added work, as well as a very high rate of participation by (young) female and/or immigrant groups. The dominant management approach in this segment is that of simple control (Edwards, 1979) based on direct supervision of the labor process, or output controls (e.g., piece-rate systems) where production occurs in "cottage industry" locations. The emergence and growth of thriving enclaves of unskilled, labor-intensive activities performed by women and new immigrants within the most advanced metropolises of core economies is evidence of the systematic expansion of this segment (see Ross, 1997). The continuing existence – much less the systematic growth – of these activities is totally unexpected in so-called "advanced industrial economies" (Sassen, 1998). Significantly, it is the new production, information, and communications technologies and forms of organization in the techno-economy which have permitted or driven these developments in the informal economy.

Castells and Portes (1989) observe that informal activity in the United States has grown significantly since the early 1970s, while Redcliff and Mingione (1985) note similar tendencies in Western Europe. Research sponsored by the European Commission estimated that informal sector activity amounts to 40 percent of the "official" Greek economy, 30 percent of the Belgian and Italian economies, 16 percent of the French, 14 percent of the German, and 8–10 percent of the British economy (Deloitte and Touche, 1998).

In general, the informal economy tends to develop with the tolerance, if not under the auspices of, government authorities (Castells and Portes, 1989). If the necessary linkage between the techno and grunge economies exists, state polices oriented to the containment of the informal sector would be expected to have loosened up over the past two decades or so. Minimally, this would take the form of increased tolerance of informal activities from both police and tax authorities. In some cases, however, it might extend to the encouragement of such activities, conceived of as "organic entrepreneurialism," through the provision of training programs, credit facilities, marketing assistance, and similar policies which directly or indirectly underwrite entrepreneurial initiatives. For example, Sassen (1998) argues for government programs designed to promote entrepreneurial activity in the informal sector

as a means of fostering social integration and insulating decaying urban regions from more damaging criminal undertakings (e.g., the drug economy). Both of these types of approach have been increasingly apparent in many countries, both developed and developing, since the early 1970s (see Castells, 1996; Portes et al., 1989).

Importantly, the state itself needs to be understood as a fragmented actor in its oversight capacity, in terms of both potential contradictions in informal-sector policies and enforcement across governmental levels (federal, state, local) as well as across bureaucracies (e.g., police, tax, social services) with different vested interests (see Alford and Friedland, 1985). Were it acting to preserve the functional integrity of the overall social formation (i.e., in the interests of capital as a whole rather than on behalf of specific capitalists), the state would likely respond to the growth of informal economic activity either passively or supportively. However, if the state is a site of conflict (whether between capitalist and/or state elites or on a broader basis), it is more likely that the informal economy will be criminalized and subjected to increased surveillance in order to recover tax revenues from these activities as a partial offset to decreasing corporate tax revenues from the techno-economy (see Vernon, 1998). While this remains an open empirical question, the majority of theoretical and empirical research on the state would suggest that the second scenario is far more likely to eventuate.

The linkages between the techno and grunge economies come in two primary forms. They can occur within a given firm's value chain (Porter, 1985) – the total set of functions, activities, and processes that occurs within a firm's administrative boundaries. For example, most companies incorporate dual internal labor markets, one constituted by managers, analysts, and technically skilled workers ("core employees"), the other by less skilled staff performing routine administrative or support tasks ("noncore employees"). Core and noncore employees experience very different work environments and employment conditions, and their loyalties tend to be with those of similar backgrounds rather than extending to each other (see Gorz, 1989).

A more significant source of linkages between the techno and grunge economies, though, increasingly spans the value chains of multiple firms which are linked through networking or subcontracting relationships – the basic difference between these being the extent to which a core firm (or prime contractor) manages its sourcing as an integrated system (network) or as a series of bilateral relationships (subcontracting). As major TNCs have restructured their operations in recent years they have focused on core activities and outsourced noncore functions to external providers. This practice has been the focus of a substantial amount of research over the past decade, the most significant of which is Harrison's (1997). He critically examines popular accounts of the rising importance of the small business sector in many advanced economies, finding that the corporate sector, though restructured to be "lean and mean," continues to be the primary site of market power and innovation in most major industries. Smaller firms are increasingly part of these production complexes through their membership in network systems, but these are dominated by core firms and are subject to powerful centralizing tendencies which can lead to extreme pressure on marginal network members – sometimes driving them into the informal economy.

Proceeding to the dynamic properties of advanced capitalism, the most salient point is that the expansion of the techno-economy leaves more and more people out of its value and employment-generating processes, widening the gap between haves and have-nots and increasing social fragmentation. This is because the techno-economy is far more efficient than its Fordist-Keynesian predecessor in containing positive externalities and directing its benefits to vested stakeholder groups – primarily owners, the professional–managerial classes, technically skilled labor, and moneyed consumers. Other groups – most particularly the semiskilled industrial working class which was effectively integrated into the mass-production/mass consumption calculus of Fordism-Keynesianism – are excluded from the techno-economy. This insight marks the most significant point of differentiation between the current analysis and other, more sanguine

accounts of the "new economy" (cf. *Business Week*, 1998).

A substantial amount of existing empirical research can be cited in support of the preceding observations. Castells (1996), Harvey (1989), Galbraith (1998), and Rifkin (1995) each provide extensive accounts of the massive changes in labor markets, occupational structures, employment patterns, and income and wealth distributions in various advanced industrialized countries since the 1970s. They agree that most of these countries are characterized by increasingly polarized social structures, where the top and bottom segments have increased their representational shares at the expense of the middle. This exclusionary dynamic is the most important feature of advanced capitalism, as its effects flow from the realm of the economy to the political and cultural spheres, reshaping the contours of society as it does so.

It follows, then, that the expansion of the grunge economy is a necessary corollary to the continued growth of the techno-economy. Necessary firstly for firms based in the techno-economy to improve their cost structures (owing to increasing competitive pressures) by accessing cheaper inputs in the contingent and/or informal segments of the grunge economy. Necessary secondly for those firms which supply specialized goods and services to the high and low-end segments which have replaced Fordist mass markets, given the generally labor-intensive nature of their core processes. Necessary thirdly for those groups who are somehow excluded from the circuit of high value creation in the techno-economy and need primary or supplemental means to obtain the resources necessary for social reproduction. Necessary finally in order to prevent total social fragmentation and the ensuing violence which would disrupt wealth generation in the core techno-economy by securing at least a minimal amount of legitimation to the social order and the role of the state (see Standing, 1989).

Expansion of the grunge economy is directly beneficial to corporate capital (in the techno-economy) in two ways. Firstly, there are direct linkages (generally through networking arrangements) between corporate capital and the contingent segment of the grunge economy, and from the latter to the informal sector through cascading networks (see below). These arrangements drastically lower production costs and increase flexibility for corporate capital. Secondly, the expansion of the informal sector facilities a lower tax liability for corporate capital with respect to expenses for social welfare and similar redistributionary measures, since labor reproduction need be secured only partially through paid wages and official government assistance (see Offe, 1985).

This analysis differs from that of traditional (mainstream and Marxist) development theories, which expected the informal economy to contract as modernization proceeded and labor was absorbed into the formal economy (cf. McMichael, 1996). It also is distinguished from contemporary theories of the informal economy, which identify the association between economic restructuring and the growth of the informal sector in many advanced countries, but fall considerably short of positing the necessary relationship I assert here (cf. Castells and Portes, 1989). Only Sassen (1998) makes this connection in an explicit manner. However, her analysis devotes considerably less attention to the role of TNCs, nor does she address the practice of cascading networks in depth.

The Globalization of Advanced Capitalism

Capitalism is increasingly integrated and centralized on a global basis. Yet there are major differences between nationally organized (Fordist) capitalism and a globalized form of advanced capitalism. The term "organized capitalism" at the national level denotes the administrative articulation of production and consumption, the regulation of competition to promote stable oligopoly market structures in the industrial economy, and the support and maintenance of corporatist structures by a relatively autonomous state. This institutional structure is therefore both fairly integrative in its incorporation of societal stakeholders (particularly organized labor) and democratic in terms of its vulnerability to public pressure exerted through representative political systems (Lasch and Urry, 1987).

Conversely, the globalization of advanced capitalism suggests a loosely knit and largely privatized system whose institutional parameters are defined primarily by the conditions necessary to secure capital accumulation. The only necessary institutions here are those to facilitate the exchange process, enforce contracts, and protect property rights. Conspicuously absent from this ensemble is a central administrative apparatus tasked with the articulation of production and consumption. The lack of such a political-administrative center necessarily makes advanced capitalism considerably less stable than nationally organized capitalism – particularly from the perspective of individual states which struggle to support their home-based capital in an increasingly turbulent international environment. Capitalism is thus becoming globally organized but not globally regulated, a situation which fosters various types of market failure such as chronic overinvestment, particularly in state-targeted sectors (see Brahm, 1995). The absence of a political center or institutional mechanisms to support public participation also effectively marginalizes the ability of noncapitalist stakeholders to affect the international capital accumulation process. The mass protests at WTO meetings in Seattle and elsewhere highlight the frustration of groups such as labor unions, environmentalists, and developing countries which feel alienated from the benefits of globalization.

The configuration of a globalized advanced capitalism is as follows: banking and financial services, corporate command and control functions, and research-based activities are concentrated in global cities located in core countries (e.g., New York, London, Tokyo); operational centers are distributed among a wider group of second-tier (although still prominent) cities in both core and newly industrializing countries; manufacturing-type activities are more widely dispersed still according to country and region-specific locational factors (see Dunning, 1993). The articulation of advanced capitalism thus takes the form of an amalgam of local grunge economies linked by transnational institutions in the techno–economy facilitating the movement of capital, products, and people. The global matrix touches down in "real" spaces such as global cities, markets, and production enclaves, in addition to occupying electronic spaces largely beyond state or interstate regulation. Only the techno-economy is truly global in scope. It overlooks a domain of diverse grunge economies which are fundamentally local in character, and increasingly so as nation states fragment and states lose power to both multilateral and regional/local institutions. Yet the local character of the numerous grunge economies is fundamentally conditioned by the nature and extent of their relation to the global techno-economy. According to Castells (1996: 102–3):

the new global economic system is highly exclusionary.... While the dominant segments of all national economies are linked into the global web, segments of countries, regions, economic sectors, and local societies are disconnected from the processes of accumulation and consumption ... most people in the planet do not work for or buy from the ... global economy. Yet all economic and social processes do relate to the structurally dominant logic of such an economy.

The zones unconnected to the techno-economy in some manner have no value as markets, production platforms, or sources of raw materials. They are thus irrelevant to the key agents of advanced capitalism, TNCs, and will be bypassed. As Castells (1996: 113) observes, "some rural regions of China, India, and Latin America, entire countries around the world, and large segments of the population everywhere are becoming irrelevant (from the perspective of dominant economic interests) in the new pattern of international division of labor." He refers to these sociospatial areas as constituting the "Fourth World" (Castells, 1998), and argues that their condition will be one of structural irrelevance, which he believes to be worse than dependence. The so-called "information revolution" exacerbates this exclusionary process, as recent comparative research on the Internet has confirmed (Elliot, 1999; US Dept of Commerce, 1999). Interestingly, even the World Bank has begun to explicitly use the term "two-tier global economy" to describe current patterns of economic development (Aslam, 1998). In terms of its distributional properties, advanced capitalism constitutes a rejection of normative notions of universal material progress and human development. It can therefore be understood as constituting a postmodern formation.

This last point merits elaboration. Previously I noted that post-Fordism has been widely associated with a postmodern sensibility in areas such as literature, aesthetics, and architecture (see Docherty, 1993). Following Harvey (1989), however, I suggest a more materially grounded notion of post-modernism, understood as the cultural response to the new economic conditions which arose after the end of the post-World War II boom. These conditions are characterized by widespread exclusion from the fruits of economic development, diminished expectations for the masses, and horizontal/transnational over vertical/national identifications. From this perspective, it would be fair to say that advanced capitalism is post-modern owing to the distributional effects associated with its dualistic structure; the consequent need for the development of a sociocultural order (probably to some extent directed or catalyzed by state policies) which normalizes the dualistic structure of economic development, including the notion that "progress" no longer is associated with increasing social integration; and the necessary and parallel growth of the techno and grunge economies, including the informal sector – this last attribute a defining structural characteristic of advanced capitalism, differentiating it from all previous "modern" capitalist social formations in which informal economic activity was supplanted by waged and salaried employment in the formal economy.

Advanced capitalism thus evidences post-modern attributes in its material characteristics and symbolic forms. I use the term "post-modern" rather than "postmodern" because modernist narratives organized around concepts such as modernization, universal progress, emancipation, social integration, political citizenship, and democracy seem to be in the process of being left behind – or contorted beyond recognition – as advanced capitalism articulates (see Lasch, 1995). From this perspective a country such as South Korea, embroiled as it is in the throes of industrialization and democratization struggles, rates as more modern than the United States, which epitomizes most of the post-modern characteristics outlined above.

I close this section with two architectural examples which effectively convey the nature of advanced capitalism's material and semiotic landscape. The first relates to the demolition of numerous large-scale public housing developments in the United States and Great Britain since the early 1980s, the second to the physical and semiotic attributes of the Bonaventure Hotel in Los Angeles (see Jameson, 1991). The housing project as an architectural form represented high modernism and the welfare state's desire to transform the social and spatial landscape, to integrate disenfranchised groups into the whole (albeit on a hierarchical basis). Some observers have interpreted the demolition of many of these developments as an institutional acknowledgment of the failure of the overall project of modernity (Harvey, 1989): a relegation to the grunge economy of entire segments of the population. Conversely, the Bonaventure Hotel represents a postmodern artifice, part of the techno-economy. This is due to several features: the fact that it is a private space; the designed-in difficulty of entry and overall inaccessibility to those lacking the cultural codes (Bourdieu, 1986) with which to navigate its landscape, its internally self-contained environment which produces an overall experience for its occupants totally divorced from the immediate external surroundings, and the fact that it is intended for use by members of the transnational elite – international business travelers and tourists. Its fundamentally exclusivist nature epitomizes advanced capitalism's distributional properties.

Advanced Capitalism and Global–Local Dialectics

The relationship between the global and the local in advanced capitalism is extremely complex. Conceptualizations of a global–local dialectic are particularly useful as they create a theoretical space for reconciling culturalist analyses (emphasizing the specificity of the local) with international business or political economy approaches (stressing the universality of the global) by cutting a middle ground between the two. For example, Appadurai (1997) argues against the notion of pure, unadulterated (primordial) indigenous culture as epistemologically suspect and empirically untenable in all but the rarest of cases. Instead

he posits the fundamentally dialectical association between global and local, which he frames as the tension between cultural homogenization and cultural heterogenization (see also Dirlak, 1996; Featherstone, 1996). Barber (1996) also argues that globalism and localism are locked in an inescapable dialectical relationship. Globalism, most particularly in the form of consumer capitalism, dissolves the social and economic barriers between nations, weaving the world's diverse populations into a series of relatively uniform global markets. Simultaneously, formally nationally based political landscapes are being fragmented into smaller local units owing to ethnic, religious, and racial conflicts springing from the undermining of nationally constituted cultural systems by globalization. He writes (p. 215):

If [globalism] in its most elemental negative form is a kind of animal greed – one that is achieved by an aggressive and irresistible energy, [localism] in its most elemental negative form is a kind of animal fear propelled by anxiety in the face of uncertainty and relieved by self-sacrificing zealotry – an escape out of history.

Barber feels these developments serve most importantly to undermine democracy and the nation state.

A timely example of global–local conflict relates to the backlash against that aspect of globalization associated with cultural imperialism (sometimes also referred to as "Americanization"). The constant barrage of foreign images through electronic media undermines notions of national identity (and the link between nation and state), substituting an intense but shallow pastiche of signs which have no coherent meaning in local contexts. Observers such as Barber (1996) and Castells (1996) suggest that the shock of this inundation by global media causes some groups to revert to primary identity sources tied to very local affiliations with place, ethnicity, and religion – which combine to forge coherent, meaning-laden, deep identity structures – as substitutes for undermined national identity. Relevant recent examples in this regard include the fragmentation of Yugoslavia and the rise of the Taliban in Afghanistan.

Many contemporary observers of globalization, both advocates and critics, hold that it necessarily entails a swamping of indigenous (local) cultural systems (cf. Wilson and Dissanayake, 1996). I would disagree. An amusing irony is that contemporary business gurus like Theodore Leavitt and Kenichi Ohmae have a great deal in common with Karl Marx's analysis of the cultural impact of a globalizing capitalism. Marx argued that the progressive articulation of the forces and relations of capitalism would spread among the more advanced nations and ultimately, through the mechanism of imperialism, throughout the world (Marx, 1967). The key dynamic here was the expansionary logic of the capital accumulation process, represented by the 'M–C–M' formulation. While Marx clearly recognized the brutalizing aspects of this process, he nonetheless thought capitalism an historically progressive force to the extent that its articulation would culminate in the transition to socialism (Lorrain, 1989).

Marx's position is apparent in his famous observation that, in capitalism, "all that is solid melts into air." By this he meant that the ongoing tensions between the forces and social relations of capitalism fostered a dynamic and spatially expansive modernizing process which continually destabilized traditional sociocultural institutions, practices, and roles (see Berman, 1988). This globally aspiring modernization process was directly hostile to local cultures in the sense that the local was suppressed or marginalized in various ideologies of modernity which identified civilization and progress with political, social, and cultural homogenization through the application of scientific–technical rationality, justifying the suppression of the local in the name of the general and the universal (Dirlak, 1996). The generic Marxist understanding of globalization, commodification, and culture thus falls into what Appadurai (1997: 32) terms the "cultural homogenization argument" which "subspeciates into either an argument about Americanization or an argument about [commodification], and very often these arguments are closely linked."

Max Weber's work is also relevant to the present discussion. He maintained that the proliferation of bureaucratic rationality in the business and state sectors would ultimately lead to the total organization of social life and the consequent marginalization of spirituality.

Society would become increasingly organized and efficient, with increasing organization and efficiency as dominant social goals in themselves (Weber, 1946, 1978). Weber foresaw the ensuing backlash against this metaphysical vacuum in the form of the rise of various kinds of fundamentalisms which rejected commodification, rationalization, and the overall project of modernity. This is illustrated in the following passage (Weber, 1978: 506):

As intellectualism suppresses belief in magic, the world's processes become disenchanted, lose their magical significance, and henceforth simply "are" and "happen" but no longer signify anything. As a consequence, there is a growing demand that the world and the total pattern of life be subject to an order that is significant and meaningful.

This disenchantment-generating aspect of modernization, and its "irrational" offspring, are ubiquitous features of the landscape of the contemporary world (see Castells, 1998) – even in the United States, supposedly the most technologically advanced and "modern" society on the planet. Extending Weber's analysis, Waters (1995) argues that contemporary fundamentalisms are not only antimodern but also antipostmodern: "Resistance to contemporary globalization [is] opposition not merely to the world as one, homogenized system but also . . . to the conception of the world as a series of culturally equal, relativized entities or ways of life" (p. 102).

Weber outlined a straightforward action–reaction model of modernization–disenchantment–rejection–remystification. Yet there are more theoretically interesting and empirically significant possibilities fostered by the interaction of global and local forces. For example, Featherstone (1996) observes that various forms of hybridization emerge in which the meanings of foreign goods, information, and images are reworked and blended with existing cultural traditions and forms of life. In a similar vein, Castells (1998: 333) argues that "it is by inhabiting the space of media flows that traditional cultures and popular interests assert their power. So doing, they survive, but they transform themselves at the same time." An example of this point is proffered by Shohat and Stam (1996: 151), who studied the use of electronic media by the Kayapo people of central Brazil. The Kayapo use video:

to record their own traditional ceremonies, demonstrations, and encounters with whites (so as to have the equivalent of a legal transcript). They have documented their traditional knowledge of the forest environment and plan to record the transmission of myths and oral history . . . The Kayapo not only sent a delegation to the Brazilian Constitutional Convention to lobby delegates debating indigenous rights, but also videotaped themselves in the process, winning international attention to their cause . . . this site-specific activism becomes translocal when representatives of the Kayapo go to Canada and meet the Cree Indians . . . and make common cause on the basis of a pan-indigenous valorization of ancestral land . . . their video work concentrates not on the retrieval of an idealized precontact past but on the processes of identity construction in the present.

Similarly, Miyoshi (1996: 81) notes that "colonized space cannot reclaim autonomy and seclusion; once dragged out of their precolonial state, the indigenes of peripheries have to deal with the knowledge of the outside world, irrespective of their own wishes and inclination." Such cultures must necessarily be informed by the modernity that they reject (Dirlak, 1996). They will necessarily be hybrid products composed of authentic historical developments, imagined histories, and dialectical encounters with the global. Thus we come to the "tricky" version of the local which operates within the global, largely subject to the latter's logic (Wilson and Dissanayake, 1996).

Therefore both "globalists" and "localists" are right (and wrong). Globalists are correct in their assertion that institutional structures are converging and thereby lowering the transaction costs of conducting business across national borders. They are wrong in arguing that deep and homogenizing cultural transformations must necessarily accompany the adoption of "modern" capitalist institutions in the economic sphere. Localists are correct in stressing the continuing salience of substantial cultural differences both across and within national territories. However, they go too far when they deny either that local cultures have been profoundly impacted by their encounters with the global or that key sectors of local economies

have articulated irrevocably with transnational economic institutions.

Hence it can be argued that advanced capitalism should be less of a threat to indigenous or local cultures than either Fordist capitalism or state socialism, assuming that these cultures will be widely excluded from participation in the techno-economy. Fordism was a model of economic and political development which explicitly strove to foster a large middle class and an industrial working class which were integrated by consumption, unifying national symbols, and cultural homogenization, all woven into the master narrative of "modernization" (McMichael, 1996). State socialism followed a generally similar program, although with a different mix of economic and political integration mechanisms. Both systems were nationally based and vertically oriented (in terms of integrating people across the social hierarchy).

In advanced capitalism, however, there is much less effort to integrate societies through master narratives and nationalistic symbolism. Instead, transcultural unification is achieved through the promulgation of consumer lifestyle models; the orientation is thus horizontal (transnational) rather than vertical. The focus of intensive social integration is confined to the capitalist managerial classes who own, fund, and/or administer the overall system, as well as moneyed consumers (see Castells, 1996). Among these groups, there is evident a convergence of lifestyle, habitus, and demeanor in the deterritorialized cultures in global cities such as New York, London, and Tokyo (Featherstone, 1996).

An important aspect of these deterritorialized cultures is a new conceptualization of citizenship based on economic rather than political principles. Following Held (1995; see also Christopherson, 1994), this new citizenship is constituted by several primary features. First, people attain citizenship status through their ability to purchase goods and services; citizenship is therefore a matter of economic status rather than political capacity or spatial locatedness. Second is the presumption that access to a wide diversity of consumer goods, services, and cultural products will be provided by the "system." Third, the right to cross national boundaries at will as tourists (or, more limitedly, as guest workers) is seen increasingly as a human right. The economistic reorientation of the citizenship discourse is consistent with the exclusivist trajectory of advanced capitalism's material and discursive development.

The Transnational Corporation and Cascading Networks

Turning to the transnational corporation, I begin by noting that this institution occupies a special position with respect to the articulation of advanced capitalism. It diffuses institutional structures and practices from the core countries, furthering the processes of rationalization and normative integration (Sklair, 1995). It centralizes the administration of global economic activity in a relative handful of private organizations in the techno-economy, located in various global cities and linked by a common discursive and normative orientation. Its pursuit of transnational sourcing arrangements serves to articulate a new international division of labor through the spatial restructuring of value chains from primarily national to regional or global configurations. Finally, its adoption of vertical network arrangements in place of vertical integration is directly formative of the dualistic structure of advanced capitalism.

The complex global–local character of advanced capitalism is directly reflected in the changing strategies and structures of TNCs over the past two decades. The increasing integration associated with globalization has resulted in TNCs shifting from international and multinational to global and transnational strategies (Bartlett and Ghoshal, 1995). Briefly, multinational strategies are market-oriented approaches which involve firms reproducing their value chains in each national market in which they participate. International strategies are product-oriented, innovation-based approaches in which a firm enters international markets based on the novelty or superiority of the goods or services it provides in its home market. Global strategies are production-driven approaches based on achieving maximum economies of scale and taking advantage of essentially homogeneous consumer demand across countries. Transnational strategies involve a combination of aspects of the three

previous strategies in that product innovation, market sensitivity, and efficient production are all necessary to obtain competitive advantage in certain industries. For example, Sony Corporation describes its operational strategy in the consumer electronics industry as one of "global localization" (Lasch and Urry, 1994). This is a competitive approach based on providing consumers with products tailored to meet their unique needs in the most efficient manner possible through the design of common platforms which can be customized at low cost – an approach also epitomized by the term "mass customization."

Each of the major TNC strategies has different implications for a firm's approach to its host markets and their cultural integrity. Both international and global strategies are insensitive to host cultures, expecting foreign markets to desire (through demonstration effects) the high-quality products designed for affluent consumers in core countries. Global strategies, in particular, assume a significant degree of homogenization of consumer preferences, and are themselves active agents in fostering that homogenization by forcing foreign products on to markets, oftentimes edging out domestically produced goods. The backlash to cultural imperialism (as manifested in international or global strategies) can subvert transnational business, but it need not. It can also create market opportunities for firms sufficiently culturally sensitive and creative to provide goods and services tailored to local preferences – that is, firms following either multinational or transnational strategies.

Both multinational and transnational strategies are predicated on significant continuing differences in consumer demand, government regulations, and the like across countries. While of course they both rely on the existence of consumer societies, they also benefit from the perpetuation of differences between such societies. In fact, as catering to national (or even subnational) differences in consumer preferences would constitute a basis of competitive advantage for TNCs following such strategies, these firms would have an intrinsic interest in maintaining the (at least partial) integrity of cultural systems which perpetuated such differences in preferences. TNCs can thus, under particular conditions, be allies of tradition as well as engines of modernization. For example, customized ethnic and/or nostalgia-oriented products could be targeted to alienated groups, whose consumption of such goods would both reinforce their primary identity structures and (in a somewhat convoluted manner) increase their integration into the global economy. This is consistent with Lasch and Urry's (1994: 100) observation that:

consumerist global capitalism . . . is wrapped into the increasingly thematized particular–universal relationship in terms of the connection between globewide, universalistic supply and particular demand . . . The contemporary capitalist creation of consumers frequently involves the tailoring of products to increasingly specialized regional, societal, ethnic, class and gender markets – so-called "micro-marketing."

An interesting example of micro-marketing can be found in New Zealand. Lion Nathan, a transnational brewing company, produces a wide range of beers. Several of Lion's brands are targeted to specific localities and marketed to articulate with the embedded cultural identity of consumers in regionally defined markets. These brands are marketed in terms of their local and nostalgia-invoking aspects, thus fostering a powerful semiotic response from consumers longing for an imagined past (see Appadurai, 1997). Obviously we are dealing here with commodities, and also with a sizable TNC, but that is not the entire story – for these beers, resonating as they do with very local identity formations, serve to reinforce the local against the global (defined in this case by Lion's major competitor, which sells nationally branded products). This case is interesting because it manifests some of the contradictions of globalization: the site of production has gone from small, locally owned breweries to a TNC owned largely by foreign (Japanese) interests; consumption of these products transfers income from local environments to international investors; consumption increases the buyer's integration into consumer society (versus home brewing, a relatively popular pursuit in New Zealand); yet consumption also enhances the consumer's identification with his local habitus as a source of identity. In this case the local effect is a result of commercial decisions taken at the global level, but that does not diminish

the fact that the products (although inauthentic) take their place among constellations of local signifiers, adding their semiotic power to those constellations and fueling a factually false but experientially "real" component of identity.

The TNC itself needs to be understood as an evolving institutional form within multiple and dynamic economic, political, technological, and sociocultural fields. A particularly significant development has been the adoption of new sourcing arrangements, as noted earlier. These arrangements are typically constituted by the national dis-integration of a given firm's value chain and the relocation of its nodal segments to multiple host countries. In the new production structure, intermediate products are transferred from one nodal point to another for further processing as they move along the value-chain. These developments are reflected in the steady rise of intrafirm trade over the past two decades (see Dicken, 1998).

A related development of much significance has been the growing tendency for TNCs to replace hierarchically governed, vertically integrated production systems with network systems – groups of interdependent, vertically linked suppliers and/or distributors coordinated by focal TNCs to produce goods or services in a manner which maximizes flexibility and minimizes risk for TNCs. The hierarchical network form of organization allows TNCs to reduce their transaction costs and increase their flexibility by delegating nonessential activities to subcontractors which bear most of the risks associated with uncertain market conditions (Harrison, 1997; Jones, 1996). These subcontractors are locked in TNC-centered value chains in which they have little power and in which the intermediate goods they produce have little trading value outside of the chain in which they are located. TNCs can then focus on high value-added activities based upon proprietary knowledge, technological intensity, and scalar economies. These firms are thus able to have their cake and eat it too by enjoying the benefits of control without the liabilities of ownership. Moreover, they are able to do so precisely because of their structural power over their network affiliates.

It follows from the increased use of networking arrangements that the traditional definition of the firm (based on ownership) is in need of revision. This definition, founded as it is on an assumed identity between ownership and control, is largely obsolete in light of contemporary organizational arrangements. Increasingly, control extends widely beyond the boundaries of ownership as vertically integrated forms give way to nominally independent production networks organized around focal firms (in which ownership and control are disarticulated). Given these developments, it seems that a broadened definition of the firm based on effective strategic control rather than ownership is needed (Cowling and Sugden, 1987). Such a conceptualization of the TNC is central to understanding advanced capitalism, as it leads directly to the linkages between the techno and grunge economies, and the essential subordination of the latter to the needs of the former.

An important related point is that official data on industrial concentration rates seriously underestimate the increasing level of strategic control TNCs exert in the international economy. This needs to be considered together with other developments such as the unprecedented level of merger and acquisition activity occurring in industries such as automobiles, commercial aviation, and banking and finance over the 1990s, as well as the proliferation of (anticompetitive) strategic alliances in technology intensive, scale-sensitive industries (see Brahm, 1995). These trends toward market consolidation raise serious concerns for long-term consumer welfare and democratic accountability (Strange, 1998).

Another development of great significance is that the network model has been widely adopted by TNC affiliates for essentially the same reasons as for TNCs themselves. This means that TNC vertical networks are actually constituted by networks of networks, a form of organization which is driven by a practice I refer to as cascading networking. Cascading networking represents the key organizational practice (spanning multiple firm boundaries) which links the three segments of advanced capitalism's economy. It is largely an outgrowth of the new generation of TNC strategies and structures discussed above. These developments have been driven by increasingly

intense competition between TNCs as globalization has unfolded, and by ensuing efforts by TNCs as collective institutional actors to restructure their value chains to maximize their leverage against stakeholders which lay claim to their income streams (employees, states) as well as alternative forms of economic organization (local firms, exporters) (see Jones, 1999). Castells (1996) and Harrison (1997) discuss several examples of such restructured production arrangements in a range of industries, concluding that they generally result in a bipolar labor force composed of highly skilled designers and telecommunicating sales managers, on the one hand, and low-skill, low-paid manufacturing workers, located either offshore or in American domestic workshops/sweatshops, on the other.

A striking example of the collision between advanced technology and precapitalist labor processes can be found in Silicon Valley, where employees of high-tech firms do "homework" after hours – manually assembling electronic components and subsystems such as circuit boards and cables according to piece-rate systems (*South China Morning Post*, 1999). In such cases the firms and employees involved participate in both the techno and the informal economies. The firms, by encouraging their employees to engage in after-hours work which is outside the direct control of those firms, as well as beyond the reach of government workplace regulations. The employees, by undertaking this informal-sector activity as a means to supplement inadequate compensation from their waged work. Vitally, these examples are not limited to "low-tech" industries but extend to technologically advanced sectors such as machine tools and consumer electronics (Dicken, 1998; Sassen, 1998).

The case of Nike offers another useful example of a situation which links the techno and grunge economies, while simultaneously representing a case which tests the limits of TNC strategic control, and of the network form itself. Nike, a techno-economy firm, made the strategic choice to restrict itself to key value-adding activities such as product development, marketing, and distribution. The firm constructed a vertical network of suppliers organized into several tiers according to how close (and exclusively) they were involved with Nike (see Dicken, 1998). The top-tier suppliers were originally Taiwanese, but since the 1980s these firms have shifted their factories to countries such as Indonesia and mainland China, primarily owing to changes in comparative labor costs (Bartlett and Ghoshal, 1995). All of these parties were part of the formal economy: Nike the techno segment and the prime subcontractors the contingent segment (owing to their relatively low-technology and labor-intensive operations). However, the prime subcontractors also developed their own networks (hence the term "cascading networks"), and these on occasion extended into the realm of household labor undertaken by young women and children – thus crossing into the informal segment of the grunge economy through multiple sets of cascading networks.

In recent years Nike has come under criticism for exploitative labor practices occurring in some of its network affiliates – and their network affiliates, this latter group having nothing directly to do with Nike at all. Nevertheless it is Nike which has the global profile and is thus the subject of consumer boycotts and widespread media coverage (see Klein, 2000). This and similar cases may in the future force core firms to recalculate the transaction costs of forming and maintaining network systems as an alternative to vertical integration, as the practice of cascading networks increases auditing costs and changes the overall economics of the network form. This will be particularly true of firms with a high public profile – mainly branded consumer goods companies as well as large industrial firms (e.g., Exxon, Union Carbide) – which may be held to higher standards of behavior in countries where corporate legitimacy is a stakeholder-based concept rather than simply a matter of shareholder imperatives and *caveat emptor* attitudes.

Implications and Conclusion

Advanced capitalism exhibits several major tensions and contradictions as it develops. It is driven by a high-technology core which is the site of superprofit generation, yet this sector is increasingly reliant on direct and indirect linkages to far less advanced – in many cases even premodern – forms of capital accumulation. Its spatial dynamic links cities and regions widely separated by physical distance yet divorces these same areas from their immediate surroundings. It links people in the transnational professional classes with their counterparts in different countries while distancing them from their fellow citizens a few miles (or even doorways) away. It excludes increasing numbers of people from its wealth-creating activities as production becomes increasingly divorced from employment. It erects vertical barriers to social mobility while removing horizontal barriers to the migration of very high and low-skilled people. Finally, it generates the material changes that drive a cultural shift to post-modernism, which primarily means the abandonment (in fact if not in political rhetoric) of notions of universal progress, social integration, and democracy.

The key insights generated by this analysis include the necessary linkages between the techno and grunge economies in which the expansion of the former is conditioned on the growth of the latter; the dominance of the contingent segment of the grunge economy as the modal site of employment for the bulk of the population; the increasing importance of the informal economy (driven by both competitive imperatives in the small business sector as well as by inadequate and unstable access to wages in the contingent segment); and the focus on the transnational corporation as the primary institutional form – and on cascading networks as the primary organizational practice – which link the techno and grunge economies.

The articulation of advanced capitalism raises several important research questions. The most significant stems from its exclusionary properties and concerns its implications for societal development. Two development paths and their associated stakeholder effects for key groups can readily be envisaged. These paths differ on the question of whether a (formal or *de facto*) alliance of the capitalist, professional managerial, and technically skilled working classes will pursue a strategy of spatial and institutional containment of the underclass and/or one of self-containment within fortified communities, workplaces, etc. Aspects of both of these scenarios are already clearly visible in cities such as Los Angeles, where members of the techno-economy live within gated communities patrolled by private armed security, while the most downgraded members of the grunge economy are subjected to social and spatial "dividing practices" (Foucault, 1979) through which they are contained in ethnic ghettoes defined by the configuration of housing prices, transport corridors, infrastructural provision (or the lack thereof), and police surveillance patterns. The spaces between these groups are occupied by members of the contingent segment of the grunge economy (see Blakely, 1999; Davis, 1990).

A linked question concerns what the reactions will be to increasing exclusion and disenfranchisement among those groups so affected? Important considerations here include the extent of systemic consciousness and understanding of these developments, the nature of class, racial, gender, and other forms of identity and solidarity, and the existence of alternative narratives around which to organize for effective political action. Given the current state of affairs in most advanced nations, the prospects for the formation of an effective political bloc of "New Social Movements" would seem remote; the continuation and intensification of (necessarily fragmenting) interest-based politics are rather more likely. An individuation of the effects of increasing social exclusion – and of the reactions to it in the form of violent and criminal activity (see Castells, 1998) – also seems probable. This is particularly true in the United States, where Luttwak (1999) notes that 2.8 percent of the adult population (5.5 million people) are criminalized (in detention or on parole). Overall, we may expect the "Brazilianization" (Barnett and Muller, 1974) of advanced societies as massive and increasing social disparities and other attributes of chronically segmented social formations become normalized aspects of the cognitive, cultural, and material landscapes.

Note that the pessimistic picture painted above does not preclude the possibility that excluded groups might generate – from the bottom-up – new forms of social and economic organization which point the way towards a more equitable and sustainable future. As

I have suggested, globalization as an empirical phenomenon may be considerably less of a force than many observers believe it to be. If the global techno-economy effectively restricts its participants to those with the money and skills it requires, most of humanity will be left behind to fend for itself in expanding grunge economies. Whilst such a development would represent many material hardships for very many people, from a culturalist perspective it might actually support the integrity of indigenous cultures, along with the revival of many compromised cultures as the intrusive benefits of modernization recede from the horizon.

A final set of questions concerns the role of the state in advanced capitalism. As noted earlier, states have certainly lost some of their power of economic management to both supra- and subnational bodies. Relatedly, Sassen (1998) notes that, within states, bureaucracies concerned with social equity have lost influence to those which are financially oriented and promote globalization (with the support of powerful interests in the business sector). Yet states retain an essential monopoly over military force and the means of direct control over persons within their territories. Further, most (all?) advanced states have in recent years substantially increased the information they collect on individuals (stat[e]istics), expanded police powers, and rescinded various civil liberties and protections afforded to citizens and employees (see Jessop, 1994; Smart, 1992). An argument can be made that "the state" is evolving in a postdemocratic direction, or possibly devolving around an early modern set of functions focusing on maintaining social order through force (and the ritual display of force) as described by Foucault (1979). Perhaps we are in the midst of a transformation in which the state is becoming the primary disciplinary mechanism for global capital, while its other (social equity) functions are either shifted to alternative institutions or terminated altogether? Only time will tell.

References

Alford, R. and Friedland, R. (1985) *Powers of Theory*. Cambridge: Cambridge University Press.

Amin, A., ed. (1994) *Post-Fordism*. Oxford: Blackwell.

Appadurai, A. (1997) *Modernity at Large*. Minneapolis, MN: University of Minnesota Press.

Armstrong, M., Glyn, A., and Harrison, J. (1984) *Capitalism since World War II*. London: Routledge.

Aslam, A. (1998) "World Bank looks at two-tiered global economy," *InterPress Third World News Agency*.

Bagguley, P. (1991) "Post-Fordism and enterprise culture," in R. Keat and N. Abercrombie (eds), *Enterprise Culture*. London: Routledge.

Barber, B. (1996) *Jihad vs. McWorld*. New York: Ballantine.

Barnett, R., and Muller, R. (1974) *Global Reach*. New York: Simon & Schuster.

Bartlett, C., and Ghoshal, S. (1995) *Transnational Management*. Chicago: Irwin.

Berman, M. (1988) *All that is Solid melts into Air*. New York: Basic Books.

Blakely, E. (1999) *Fortress America*. Washington DC: Brookings Institution.

Bourdieu, P. (1986) "The forms of capital," in J. Richardson (ed.), *Handbook of Theory and Research for the Sociology of Education*. New York: Greenwood Press.

Brahm, R. (1995) "The theory of excessive competition," *Strategic Management Journal*, 19 (2): 71–91.

Business Week (1998) "The twenty-first century economy," August 24–31.

Castells, M. (1996) *The Rise of the Network Society*. Oxford: Blackwell.

——(1998) *End of Millenium*. Oxford: Blackwell.

Castells, M., and Portes, A. (1989) "World underneath," in M. Portes, M. Castells, and L. Benton (eds) *The Informal Economy*, pp. 11–37. Baltimore, MD: Johns Hopkins University Press.

Christopherson, S. (1994) "The fortress city: privatized spaces, consumer citizenship," in A. Amin (ed.) *Post-Fordism*. London: Blackwell.

Cowling, K., and Sugden, R. (1987) *Transnational Monopoly Capitalism*. Brighton: Wheatsheaf.

Davis, M. (1990) *City of Quartz*. London: Verso.

Deloitte & Touche (1998) *Informal Economic Activities in the EU*. Brussels: European Commission.

Dicken, P. (1998) *Global Shift*. London: Paul Chapman.

Dirlak, A. (1996) "The global in the local," in R. Wilson and W. Dissanayake (eds) *Global/Local*. Durham, NC: Duke University Press.

Docherty, T. (1993) *Postmodernism*. New York: Columbia University Press.

Dunning, J. (1993) *Multinational Enterprises and the Global Economy*. Reading, MA: Addison-Wesley.

Edwards, R. (1979) *Contested Terrain*. New York: Basic Books.

Eichengreen, B. (1996) *Globalizing Capital*. Princeton, NJ: Princeton University Press.

Elliot, L. (1999) "A New World Disorder," *Sydney Morning Herald*, September 4.

Enderwick, P. (1985) *Multinational Business and Labour*. London: Croom Helm.

Featherstone, M. (1996) "Localism, globalism, and cultural identity," in R. Wilson and W. Dissanayake (eds) *Global/Local*, pp. 46–77. Durham, NC: Duke University Press.

Foucault, M. (1979) *Discipline and Punish*. New York: Pantheon.

Galbraith, S. (1998) *Created Unequal*. New York: Free Press.

Gorz, A. (1989) *Critique of Economic Reason*. London: Verso.

Gray, J. (1998) *False Dawn*. London: Granta.

Hall, S., and Jacques, M. (1989) *New Times*. London: Lawrence & Wishart.

Harrison, B. (1997) *Lean and Mean*. New York: Basic Books.

Harrison, B., and Bluestone, B. (1988) *The Great U-turn*. New York: Basic Books.

Harvey, D. (1989) *The Condition of Postmodernity*. Oxford: Blackwell.

——(1997) *Justice, Nature and the Geography of Difference*. Oxford: Blackwell.

Held, D. (1995) *Cosmopolitan Democracy*. Cambridge: Polity Press.

Internal Revenue Service (1994) *The Impact of Informal Economic Activities*. Washington, DC: GPO.

Jameson, F. (1991) *Postmodernism*. Durham, NC: Duke University Press.

Jessop, B. (1994) "Post-Fordism and the state," in A. Amin (ed.), *Post-Fordism*, pp. 251–79. Oxford: Blackwell.

Jones, M. (1996) "Institutions of Global Restructuring," unpublished .

——(1998a) "Globalization: a user's guide," *New Zealand Strategic Management*, 3 (3): 14–24.

——(1998b) "Blade Runner capitalism, the transnational corporation, and commodification: implications for cultural integrity," *Cultural Dynamics*, 10 (3): 287–306.

——(forthcoming) "The competitive advantage of the transnational corporation as an institutional form: a reassessment," *International Journal of Social Economics*.

Kelsey, J. (1996) *The New Zealand Experiment*. Auckland: University of Auckland Press.

Klein, N. (2000) *No Logo*. London: Verso.

Krugman, P. (1990) *The Age of Diminished Expectations*. Cambridge, MA: MIT Press.

Lasch, C. (1995) *The Revolt of the Elites*. New York: Norton.

Lasch, S., and Urry, J. (1987) *The End of Organized Capitalism*. Cambridge: Polity Press.

——(1994) *Economies of Sign and Space*. London: Sage.

Limerick, D., Cunnington, B., and Crowther, F. (1998) *Managing the New Organization*. Sydney: Business & Professional.

Lorrain, J. (1989) *Theories of Development*. Oxford: Blackwell.

Luttwak, E. (1999) *Turbo-capitalism*. New York: HarperCollins.

Marx, K. (1967) *Capital* I. New York: International Publishers.

McMichael, P. (1996) *Development and Social Change*. London: Pine Forge Press.

Miyoshi, M. (1996) "A Borderless World? From Colonialism to Transnationalism and the Decline of the Nation State," in R. Wilson and W. Dissanayake (eds) *Global/Local*, pp. 78–106. Durham, NC: Duke University Press.

Moody, K. (1997) *Workers in a Lean World*. New York: Verso.

Offe, C. (1985) *Disorganized Capitalism*. Cambridge, MA: MIT Press.

Ohmae, K. (1985) *Triad Power*. New York: Free Press.

Piore, M., and Sabel, C. (1984) *The Second Industrial Divide*. New York: Basic Books.

Porter, M. (1985) *Competitive Advantage*. New York: Free Press.

Portes, M., Castells, M., and Benton, L., eds (1989) *The Informal Economy*. Baltimore, MD: Johns Hopkins University Press.

Redclift, N., and Mingione, E. (1985) *Beyond Employment*. Oxford: Oxford University Press.

Reich, R. (1991) *The Work of Nations*. New York: Vintage.

Resnick, S., and Wolff, R. (1987) *Knowledge and Class*. Chicago: University of Chicago Press.

Rifkin, J. (1995) *The End of Work*. New York: Putnam.

Ross, R. (1997) *No Sweat*. New York: Verso.

Sassen, S. (1984) "Growth and informalization at the core," in *The Urban Informal Sector*, pp. 492–518. Baltimore, MD: Department of Sociology, Johns Hopkins University.

——(1991) *The Global City*. Princeton, NJ: Princeton University Press.

——(1998) *Globalization and its Discontents*. New York: New Press.

Shohat, E., and Stam, R. (1996) "From the Imperial Family to the Transnational Imaginary," in R. Wilson and W. Dissanayake (eds) *Global/Local*. Durham, NC: Duke University Press.

Sklair, L. (1995) Sociology of the Global System, Baltimore, MD: Johns Hopkins University Press.

Smart, B. (1992) *Modern Conditions, Postmodern Controversies*. London: Routledge.

South China Morning Post (1999) "High-tech firms turn to hidden labour in search for profit," July 6.

Standing, G. (1989) "The British experiment," in M. Portes, M. Castells, and L. Benton (eds) *The Informal Economy*, pp. 279–97. Baltimore, MD: Johns Hopkins University Press.

Strange, S. (1998) *The Retreat of the State*. Cambridge: Cambridge University Press.

US Department of Commerce (1999) *The Great Divide*. Washington, DC: GPO.

Vernon, R. (1998) *In the Hurricane's Eye*. Cambridge, MA: Harvard University Press.

Waring, W. (1998) "Shit Work," public lecture, Auckland: University of Auckland.

Waters, M. (1995) *Globalisation: The Reader*. London: Routledge.

Weber, M. (1946) *From Max Weber*, trans. and ed. H. Gerth and C. W. Mills. New York: Oxford University Press.

——(1978) *Economy and Society*, trans. and ed. G. Roth and C. Wittich. Berkeley, CA: University of California Press.

Weiss, L. (1998) *The Myth of the Powerless State*. London: Routledge.

Wilson, R., and Dissanayake, W., eds (1996) *Global/Local*. Durham, NC: Duke University Press.

PART III

Structure and Culture

9

Structure

Bob Hinings has been a central player in at least two of the major attempts to study organizational structures over the past forty years. Initially, there was the Aston school, whose studies into structural contingency for many researchers epitomized the strength of a scientific project for organization studies. More recently, he has been involved in a twenty-year project into professional service firms, their structures, strategies, and trajectories of change. In chapter 9(a) he reflects on the centrality of structure to organization studies.

Weber announced the theme, with his concern for the fifteen attributes that contributed to his typology of bureaucracy in a rational–legal mode. Subsequently, these attributes, as well as others implied in a broader literature, were to be of the utmost significance for the Aston school as they sought to operationalize the dimensions of organization structure. Consequently, understanding organization structure has become central to organization studies, with a key impetus of its development being to understand effective and efficient organizing, through structural design. More recently, other approaches to organization structure issues have developed apart from structural contingency theory, which Hinings considers. In typological and taxonomic approaches the focus has been on a "holistic" structure, especially in Mintzberg's well known work.

Outside of the structural contingency approach, a rather different perspective on organizational structure is found in two of the most prolific schools of US organization theory, namely population ecology and institutional theory. Neither of these schools sees structure as mandated by efficiency concerns. In the former, structure is regarded as something imprinted at birth. Population ecology has produced a theoretically and methodologically complex structure of concepts, causal systems and operationalizations in understanding organizational births and deaths and the evolution of organizational forms. In institutional theory, rather than address the variation in organization forms that is a central question for population ecology, the central focus is quite the obverse: given that there are so many organizations in the world, how come there is so little variability between them in structural forms? The answer goes back to Weber, but not the Weber that structural contingency theory constructs. Rather, it is a more sociological Weber, a Weber concerned with issues of legitimacy above all. (Incidentally, despite what the structural contingency school maintains, there is precious little textual evidence to suggest that efficiency was a key concern of Weber's.) Legitimacy concerns translate into practices of isomorphism on the part of organizations unsure what their structure should be: sometimes the isomorphism is coercively mandated, by external actors; other times it is normatively mandated, but of particular interest are the many cases where it is mimetic. In these, organizations consciously choose to mimic what appears as a highly valued form of social capital associated with structural design. Choosing something associated with prestigious social capital factors, such as designs operated by very visible, successful, or influential organizations would be the basis for these structure choices.

More recently, design and structure issues have entered the popular lexicon, with the growth of "downsizing," continuous improvement, lean production, business process re-engineering and economic value-added operations, all of which, to the extent that they are part of the discourse of management, frame organizations in structural terms. To the extent that these ideas find implementation then they will have structural implications. Structure has been vital for organization discourse in the past and it is likely to remain so in the future, suggests Hinings.

By contrast, Munro suggests that it is not organization structure so much as "disorganization" that is all the rage. Moreover, in consequence, organization structure is no longer as hegemonic a concern as it used to be. Munro reminds us of the "turn" to organization culture that has seen structure's displacement from center stage for many researchers and practitioners. Thus, to equate formal organization with structure, and structure alone, he suggests, is already both a notable forgetting and a noteworthy conflation: a forgetting of much recent history and a conflation of one concern to the central concern. "The question," suggests Munro, for those who would organize, "is *which order?*" are they going to address. Today, he suggests, our institutional realities are such that to speak of a single source of order as that which is authoritatively designed as such is to miss the situated complexity with which any such order will be enacted. Of particular note is the impact of politics – through the introduction of markets into previously hierarchical forms – on these forms. In a nice turn of phrase, Munro notes that for "those on the New Right, the point of stripping down managerialist structures is exactly to do away with 'buffers' to market information and, thus, create a rarefied atmosphere of price information in which only *homo econimus* survives." An unanticipated elective affinity between the new institutionalism and the New Right reveals itself. As structures are challenged, and markets dismantle, identities change and steer new routes between hierarchies and markets, and through networks. The consequence is, Munro suggests, that:

> The days of reading organizations in terms of a single valued logic, or dominant coalition, seem numbered. For managers to be able to switch direction, there also has to be available – on demand – *social* processes which can bring into play the new agenda. When every agenda is to be encouraged, for instance, Child's (1973) proposition of there being a single, dominant coalition within each organization no longer holds. Dominance is a now a partial and provisional phenomenon. Even if viewed as "a political process in which constraints and opportunities are functions of the power exercised by decision-makers in the light of ideological values" (Child, 1972: 16), executive actions are invariably caught up inside the identity work of their own power struggles in the race to keep up with "outside" events.

Munro ends on a grim note: he sees a labor of division having been turned inwards on to the self, internalizing neurotic self-surveillance and anxiety as the new norm of work in organizations, creating wretches who work only to work more. It is a very different tone from that of Hinings. The two contributions barely connect, directly. Hinings offers a straightforward account of the central role of structure in organization analysis, while Munro mounts a critique of not only the analysis of organizations associated with structural contingency but also of the very real changes that many people in organizations have been experiencing in recent decades. Whereas Munro captures some of the pain of organizations changing gear, Hinings reflects smooth machinery, still well oiled, needing only some tinkering by organization analysts to make it function more efficiently.

9a Organization

Bob Hinings

Organizations and their Structures

The concept of organization structure is at the very heart of organizational studies, historically and contemporaneously. The central, informing question, initially given to the field, analytically, by Max Weber and carried through by the likes of Selznick, Blau, Scott, Woodward, Burns, Lawrence and Lorsch, and the Aston group is "How are people brought together in an organized, structured way?" Indeed, for a time the concept of organization was almost synonymous with that of structure. This was similarly historically bolstered by the managerial concerns of, *inter alia*, Fayol, Taylor, Sloan, Barnard, and Drucker. And the centrality of the concept of organization structure can be seen in the way in which the question of "How do we organize?" has produced the "flip side" question of "What prevents effective organizing?" The taken-for-granted position is that understanding organization structure is central and the thrust of the discipline of organization theory is to understand effective and efficient organizing, through structural design. As Pfeffer (1997: 198) has put it, "issues of design have much to recommend them as important ways of analyzing and understanding organizations."

Historically, the principal approach to understanding organization has been through the concept of structure. And this is rightly so, because a major way in which organizational members think about their organizations is as structural entities. One of the results of this is that activities such as reorganizing, planning, decision making, communicating, etc., are structurally led. That is, the roles, relationships, and authority underlying each activity are examined and worked out as a way of understanding processes. Whenever such activities are being changed, they are "re-organized" through the specification of roles, and the detailing of relationships. It is through structures that activities are shaped and it is through structures that emergent activities are given legitimacy. Even when the starting point for change is a process, e.g., the introduction of a new management information system, it is structurally enshrined, with the system being expressed and often understood in terms of the structural position of those with authority for it and the relationships that flow from that.

The concern with organizational structure is now completely embedded in organization theory, and properly so. Indeed, it still provides a richness of approach that is mined in a variety of ways. The primary way is in structural contingency theory, with its concern for establishing the relationships between structural aspects of organization and such factors as size, technology, task uncertainty, strategy, and ideology. Organizational efficiency and effectiveness are a function of the fit between structure and these contingencies. Organizations adapt to these contingent conditions in order to remain effective. Contingency theory continues to be an important, parsimonious, and empirically tested approach to understanding organization.

A secondary way in which studies of organizational structure contributes to a vibrant study of organization is through a concern with typologies and taxonomies. Rather than examining structural elements as individual variables these approaches are more concerned with a "holistic" structure, again reaching back to the typological concerns of Weber. Such approaches are seen in the work of Mintzberg (1979), Miller and Friesen (1984), Doty et al. (1993), Meyer et al. (1993), Hinings and Greenwood (1988), and Greenwood and Hinings (1993) and others. The emphasis in much of this work is on the coherence of organization, the ways in which elements of structure combine into a limited set of organizational forms and how such coherence and combination produce efficiency and effectiveness.

Overall, then, the study of organization structure is one that has and does dominate many approaches to understanding organization, and rightly so. It continues to be represented in population ecology and institutional theory, the two dominant North American schools for studying organizations. It is at the heart of both analytical and managerial concerns that fit with issues of restructuring, re-engineering, and new organizational forms. Indeed, the study of structure has much to say in the current debates over the emergence of new forms such as team-based organizations, the differentiated network form, and even the so-called learning organization. The description of such forms always has a strong structural component. The rest of chapter 9(a) will outline these particular approaches to structure and their place and promise in organization theory.

As Weber (1947) pointed out, central to notions of organization is the idea of authority. Authority in its various legitimate forms is the "glue" that binds an organization together. It is a key structural component. The issue of authority arises from the functional nature of organizations. In order to carry out the tasks that are at the heart of what we mean by an organization, some form of division of labor, or specialization, is introduced. Much of the discussion about organization, academic and managerial, is about appropriate levels of specialization, both horizontally and vertically. From this arises the issue of "imperative coordination," of how the various functional and decision-making specialisms are integrated. Again, there are structural answers through authority (centralization/decentralization), policies and procedures (standardization and formalization), and other structural devices such as teams, task forces, and committees. It is in relation to these organizational "dilemmas" that Weber (1947) discussed bureaucracy (and his other forms of imperative coordination), Burns and Stalker (1961) wrote about mechanistic and organic forms, the Aston group (Pugh et al., 1968; Pugh et al., 1969) developed their dimensions and taxonomies, Lawrence and Lorsch (1967) produced their ideas of differentiation and integration, and Blau and Schoenherr (1971) extended work on hierarchy and differentiation.

Thus, much of the historical basis of organization theory and the sociology of organizations was rooted in the work of Weber and his concern with systems of imperative coordination, i.e., the nature of organization. It was the issues of how organizations are structured to carry out their tasks and provide their services that gave the study of organizations a foundation and an impetus that have carried through to today in so many different theories and issues.

Stating that the study of organization structure is an important and vital element of understanding organizations is not meant to imply that "there is no other way." There have been many important critiques of the approaches being outlined in this chapter. There are other ways of understanding organizations, even through the idea of "dis-organization." Of course, the idea of disorganization is a counterpoint to its root of "organization." It can be understood only as a state of not being organized. One of the points of this chapter is to argue that a regular and understandable response to disorganization is to re-organize. So the aim is to examine one set of approaches, extant in the field, which represent *organization theory*, not *disorganization theory*.

Contingency Theory

Structural contingency theory continues to be an important, parsimonious, and empirically tested approach to understanding organizations. It grew out of parallel attempts to understand and explain diversity in organization structure. Parallel attempts because, on the one hand, there were scholars exploring the Weberian issue of bureaucracy, suggesting that there were variants within and outside that construct (Pugh et al., 1968; 1969) and, on the other, those examining issues of differentiation and integration between organizations (Lawrence and Lorsch, 1967). Given the empirical variation, attempts began to explain these phenomena by examining the context of organizations, leading to the triumvirate of explanations through size, technology, and environmental uncertainty. Out of this grew the notion of "fit" (Van de Ven and Drazin, 1985), suggesting that to be both effective and efficient, i.e. to achieve optimal performance, the structure of an organization had to be appropriately adapted to its context. Thus contingency theory has four general conceptual areas:

1 Structure.
2 Context, which explains structure.
3 Performance, which is the outcome of
4 The fit between structure and context.

Contingency theory dominated organization theory of the 1960s and 1970s, becoming more and more refined in its conceptual, methodological, and empirical content. Indeed, it is possible to argue that the emergence of organization theory as a subject separate from the sociology of organizations can be traced to contingency theory, especially because of its move away from a concern with structures of authority to a concern with efficiency and effectiveness. The study of organization structure established modern organization theory, something that gives it a certain historical importance. But, of course, historical significance is for the history books, the "classics" of organization theory. However, it goes beyond that, because the study of organizations through structural contingency theory continues to be a vibrant approach.

The main proponent of a renewed approach to contingency theory has been Lex Donaldson (1986, 1985, 1996, 2001). Indeed, in his four, interrelated, books Donaldson has argued that contingency theory can embrace all of the critiques that have been made of it, such as strategic choice, social action, and critical theory (Donaldson, 1985); that it is relevant to the concerns of practitioners, unlike many currently fashionable theories (Donaldson, 1995); and that it is the only really empirically established and testable theory in the study of organizations (Donaldson, 1996, 2001). What this argument does is, rightly, put structural contingency theory at the heart of positivist approaches to understanding organizations (Clark et al., 1997). As Üsdiken and Pasadeos (1995) have shown, positivist approaches are central to the work of North American organizational theorists, and contingency theory is alive and well in their writings. Essentially it is flourishing in a positivist environment where explanations of structure and performance are important, and carried out in ways that can be adapted to managerial concerns.

Typologies and Taxonomies

We also see the continuing importance of the study of structure in the discussion and use of typologies and taxonomies of organizations. Meyer et al. (1993) argued that notions of configuration continue to be important in the study of organizations and have, indeed, had something of a revival in the 1980s and 1990s both theoretically and methodologically. These ideas of configuration arise from a long-standing concern with typologies and taxonomies in organization theory that have had concepts of structure as an important part of their theoretical system (Miller, 1987). Again, there is a strand here back to the historical concern with organization theory in the typological concerns of Weber. Rather than examining structural elements as individual variables these approaches are more concerned with a "holistic" structure. The emphasis in this work is on the coherence of organization, i.e., the ways in which the various elements of structure combine into a limited set of organizational forms and, as with contingency theory, how such coherence produces efficiency and effectiveness. Examples of these approaches are the work of Pugh et al. (1969),

Hall et al. (1963), Mintzberg (1979), Miller and Friesen (1984), and Doty et al. (1993).

An example of how to put all of this together as a way of defining the essential character of organizational study is found in the work of McKelvey (1982). For McKelvey the critical issue in the study of organizations is to produce a "biological equivalence" (my term), by establishing the ultimate taxonomy of genus and species, without which, according to him, systematic study is impossible. McKelvey criticized previous attempts at taxonomies as being too limited both in the elements used and in the samples from which data were gathered. He also suggested that it was necessary for organization theorists to use advanced methods of numerical taxonomy to properly establish basic species of organization. The point is that the starting point for such efforts is the existence of structural taxonomies that have fascinated and exercised organization theorists for nearly fifty years.

Taxonomizing and typologizing have another similarity to structural contingency theory with the idea of coherence. This idea is that elements of structure such as specialization, standardization, centralization, formalization are related to each other in patterned ways to produce a coherent management structure. Child (1972), for example suggested that organizations that have a high degree of functional specialization have to decentralize authority to those specialists but then utilize formal policies and standard practices to produce coherent control. The point is that the coherence between these organizational elements will then establish a stable organization that will be more efficient and effective. These issues were taken further both by Ouchi (1980) and Williamson (1970), for both of whom structural issues were important.

Mintzberg (1979) has produced possibly the most influential typology in organization theory with his distinctions between the Machine Bureaucracy, Professional Bureaucracy, Divisionalized Form, Adhocracy and Simple Structure. (He did later also write of the missionary form.) Structure is very important to these distinctions, even though there is more to them than this. While this typology is attractive because it has the promise of species that McKelvey has asked for, Doty et al. (1993)

found it impossible to empirically establish these types, that is, to use them as a taxonomy. Pugh et al. (1969), in their work elaborating and testing Weber's concept of bureaucracy, produced an empirical taxonomy of the Full Bureaucracy, the Personnel Bureaucracy, the Workflow Bureaucracy and the Implicitly Structured Organization.

At the heart of attempts to typologize and taxonomize organizations through their structural elements (and other aspects) are two central issues of understanding organizations. The first is to understand the range of organizational variation. We are faced with a wide array of organizations, operating in myriad industries and sectors; one only has to look at any Standard Industrial Classification to understand that. Studying structure has been and remains an excellent way to get a handle on this variation. Second, we need to go beyond understanding variation, *per se*, to some form of classification that enables us to reduce variation to manageable and graspable proportions so that we can perform the task of theory, to describe and understand, parsimoniously.

Population Ecology and Institutional Theory

A further, rather different take on organizational structure is found in the two most prolific schools of North American organization theory, namely population ecology and institutional theory, which demonstrate the continued importance of studying structure. Üsdiken and Pasadeos (1995) have documented their centrality in the development of organizational research. Of course, they are not concerned with structure in the same way. It is not my intention here to give a comprehensive overview of either theory – that has already been well done elsewhere (e.g., Donaldson, 1995; Scott, 2001; Aldrich, 2000) – but to show, briefly, how each deals with organizational structure, keeping a concern with structure at the forefront of organizational theorizing.

Population ecology

Population ecology is centered on explaining why there is so much variation in organizations and the consequential patterns of births and deaths. In doing that it has organizational form as a central concept, and this is primarily structurally defined. As with McKelvey (1982) there are notions of species and forms, e.g., generalist/ specialist. While the idea of form has been strongly developed in both contingency and institutional theory, it is only weakly developed here. However, because of the focus on organizational variety and the evolution of organizational forms through variation and selective retention, a critical issue is the identification of distinct organizational forms. For example, bureaucracies are seen as a distinct class of organizations which have evolved through a process of rationalization and mastery through calculation.

Of course, population ecology has produced a theoretically and methodologically complex structure of concepts, causal systems, and operationalizations (Aldrich, 2000). The point here is that at its heart is a concern with structure; with the assumption that, in understanding organizational births and deaths and the evolution of organizational forms, the concept of structure is critical. The study of structure is alive and well and living in population ecology.

Institutional theory

Institutional theory tackles the opposite question to population ecology, that is, instead of asking why there is so much variation it asks why organizations come to look alike. And its answers are to be found in concepts of isomorphic processes and legitimacy within organizational fields. For us the interesting point is that, once again, much of the analysis is of elements of organizational structure. What is it in organizations that becomes similar across a field? It is elements of organization structure. A central idea is that organizations adopt structures and systems, not for efficiency reasons in a direct contingency sense, but in order to gain legitimacy. This concern with structure as an element in legitimacy is found in the seminal writing of Meyer and Rowan (1977) and DiMaggio and Powell (1983).

It is also found in the work of Tolbert and Zucker (1983), who suggest that contingencies may produce the initial structural responses but institutional forces then take over. Similar ideas are found in the way in which institutional theory has developed in the 1990s (Scott, 2001). While there is a concern with practices and systems as well as structure, the historical weight of explanation has been on mimetic processes, in particular (Mizruchi and Fein, 1999), that lead to similarity in organizational structures. This "structural substitution" has been seen to be key for organizations where the measurement of performance is problematic.

As with population ecology, institutional theory has developed a relatively complex set of concepts and methodological approaches to deal with its concerns (DiMaggio and Powell, 1991; Scott, 2001; Mizruchi and Fein, 1999). Again, the important point for my argument is that one of its major concerns is to analyze and explain organizational structure because of its importance to understanding organizations. Both population ecology and institutional theory suggest that the study of organization structure is critical for our understanding of organization and the activities and processes that underlie structure.

Structure and New Organizational Forms

Since the mid 1980s a literature, both analytical and normative, has appeared which has two interrelated themes. One theme is that of reorganization, reorientation, and transformation (Nadler and Tushman, 1989, 1990; Hinings and Greenwood, 1988; Miller, 1990; Greenwood and Hinings, 1996), that organizations have been increasingly facing radical changes in their organizational forms (Greenwood and Hinings, 1993). This theme is found more normatively in the concern of these same years with such management innovations (fads and fashions?) as downsizing, continuous improvement, lean production, business process re-engineering, and economic value-added operations (cf. Grant et al., 1994; Choi and Behling, 1997; Cascio, 1993; McKinley et al., 1995). A second theme is that of the development of new organizational forms such as team-based organizations, the differentiated network form, and even the so-called learning organization (Senge, 1990; Nohria and Ghoshal, 1997). The description of such forms always has a strong structural component.

There is an important principle about both of these themes in the analysis and management of organizations. The starting point, unlike most of contingency theory and taxonomizing, is *not* structure but is more to do with processes. So approaches such as Total Quality Management (continuous improvement) and Business Process Re-engineering are initially geared to changing the nature of activity systems in organization. But, from an analytical standpoint, these processes and activities are actually embedded in new roles, relationships, and authority, the stuff of structure. Also, from a managerialist perspective, there has been criticism of the implementation of these ideas as being far too structural; that is, the "natural" bent of many managers is to redesign structures as a way of dealing with new processes. Downsizing, instead of being about strategy and positioning, becomes about removing levels in the hierarchy, merging functional departments and outsourcing activities, all structural. Continuous improvement becomes about formalizing and standardizing quality processes and setting up quality departments, a frequent criticism of ISO standards.

Similarly, discussions of new organizational forms become heavily "contaminated" with structural discussions. Although the starting point is, for example, learning, or networks, they have to be concerned with structure, and structural descriptions are central to their nature. Key structural concepts in the notion of a learning organization are to "challenge specialization," which actually means building different kinds of specialization in teams rather than functional departments. But a team is a structural device. There is much talk about "removing bureaucracy" through increased decentralization and "empowered" teams, in other words, to change the structure of authority, not to get rid of it. Also, there is an emphasis on networking. A network is, of course, a structure of relationships, formed differently from hierarchical relationships in a bureaucratic organization. It is an inherently structural concept and device.

Similarly, in dealing with the differentiated network organization when describing new organizational forms for multinational enterprises, Nohria and Ghoshal (1997) state:

that the *structure* [my emphasis] of the MNC can be understood as a differentiated network composed of distributed resources linked through different types of relations: (1) the "local" linkages within each national subsidiary, (2) the linkages between headquarters and the subsidiaries, and (3) the linkages between subsidiaries themselves. (Nohria and Ghoshal, 1997: 4)

A main starting point for them is *structure*. In the differentiated network organization, assets and resources are widely distributed, highly specialized, and integrated. Subsidiaries are assigned different roles and responsibilities within the worldwide organization based on a variety of factors. The nature of control between the headquarters and the various subsidiaries is different, depending on the nature of the dependence headquarters has with subsidiaries and subsidiaries have with one another (Rose and Hinings, 1999). The point is, of course, less to do with the actual analytic description than to note its placing in structural concepts.

Again, as with the other sections of chapter 9(a), the argument being made is that once again we see the importance of structure – indeed, the impossibility of talking about any new organizational form or even process without analyzing how those forms and processes are embedded in a structure. It is not possible to hold a meaningful conversation about an organization without talking about its structure (or to meaningfully write anything).

Conclusion

There are a number of strands to the argument about the importance of structure being put forward here. They are that:

1 Structure has been historically central to the development of what we know as organization theory.

2 Structure continues to be of importance through the way in which it is dealt with in contingency theory, typologies and taxonomies, population ecology theory, institutional theory, and the discussion of new organizational forms.

3 Structure also needs to be a prime analytical construct for organizational theorists because it is central to the thinking of managers.

To this point, the primary aim of the chapter has been to demonstrate the first two strands by showing the historical and current status of studies of structure. Interwoven to a lesser extent has been the third strand, especially when dealing with new organizational forms. Structure has been historically central and continues as such because it is a very comprehensible way for thinking about organizational design and how to change such designs. And not only is this true for practitioners but also for students and academics; structure seems to be tangible and easy to grasp.

This can be seen in the way in which change processes in organizations often work out. As I suggested with regard to management ideas such as TQM or BPRE, even though they emphasize process in their basic thinking they often are implemented as structures. So a reasonably typical change path would be to start with a structural change, e.g., the introduction of Quality Circles or the redesign of the distribution of functions between senior executives. This is an easily understood starting point and a "taken for granted" way of thinking. However, it will almost inevitably lead to a need to redesign organizational activities; indeed, the activities are subsumed under the new structural elements, but their working out in practice is not assured. And, if the change is really a major one, the structure, activity (system) steps will then be followed by the need to re-examine cultural (ideological) assumptions and political patterns. Over time, a radical organizational change requires attention both analytically and managerially to a wide range of organizational features (Greenwood and Hinings, 1996; Nadler and Tushman, 1990), but the starting point so often is structural redesign.

Thus structure is vitally important to any comprehensive understanding of organizations. It is one of the basic building blocks of organization. Weber, together with the early management theorists such as Sloan, Urwick, Fayol, Follett, and Barnard, recognized the importance of seeing organizations as structures. And the reason was not that structure is everything; it is not. It is not that there are no other ways of analyzing and understanding organizations; there are. It is that the activities, the processes, the operations, the products and the services

which in many ways are at the heart of organizational design are enshrined and embedded in structures. The necessity, therefore, is to include the analysis and study of structure as one of the key conceptual areas of organization theory. This does not mean that it is an exclusive domain that deals with all that there is to know about organization. It does mean that a key departure point for understanding organization is the study of structure. We only have to examine our historical giants, contemporary analysis, and the day-to-day concerns of managers to know that this is so.

References

Aldrich, H. (2000) *Organizations Evolving*. London: Sage.

Blau, P., and Schoenherr, R. (1971) *The Structure of Organizations*. New York: Basic Books.

Burns, T., and Stalker, G. M. (1961) *The Management of Innovation*. London: Tavistock Press.

Cascio, W. F. (1993) "Downsizing: what do we know? What have we learned?" *Academy of Management Executive*, 7: 95–104.

Child, J. (1972) "Organization structure, environment, and performance: the role of strategic choice," *Sociology*, 6: 1–22.

Choi, T. Y., and Behling, O. C. (1997) "Top managers and TQM success: one more look after all these years," *Academy of Management Executive*, 11: 37–47.

Clark, T., Ebster-Grosz, D., and Mallory, G. (1997) "From a universalist to a polycentric approach in organizational research," in T. Clark (ed.) *Advancement in Organizational Behaviour: Essays in Honor of Derek S. Pugh*. Brookfield, VT: Ashgate.

DiMaggio, P., and Powell, W. (1983) "The iron cage revisited: institutional isomorphism and collective rationality in organizational fields," *American Sociological Review*, 48: 147–60.

——eds (1991) *The New Institutionalism in Organizational Analysis*. Chicago: Ballinger.

Donaldson, L. (1985) *In Defence of Organization Theory: A Reply to the Critics*. Cambridge: Cambridge University Press.

——(1995) *American Anti-management Theories of Organization: A Critique of Paradigm Proliferation*. Cambridge: Cambridge University Press.

——(1996) *For Positivist Organization Theory*. London: Sage.

——(2001) *The Contingency Theory of Organizations*. Thousand Oaks: Sage.

Doty, D. H., Glick, W. H., and Huber, G. P. (1993) "Fit, equifinality, and organizational effectiveness: a test of two configurational theories," *Academy of Management Journal*, 36: 1196–250.

Grant, R. M., Shani, R., and Krishnan, R. (1994) "TQM's challenge to management theory and practice," *Sloan Management Review*, 35: 25–34.

Greenwood, R., and Hinings, C. R. (1993) "Understanding strategic change: the contribution of archetypes," *Academy of Management Journal*, 36: 1052–81.

——(1996) "Understanding radical organizational change: bringing together the old and new institutionalism," *Academy of Management Review*, 21: 1022–55.

Hall, R. H., Haas, J. E., and Johnson, N. J. (1963) "An examination of the Blau–Scott and Etzioni typologies," *Administrative Science Quarterly*, 12: 118–39.

Hinings, C. R., and Greenwood, R. (1988) *The Dynamics of Strategic Change*. Oxford: Blackwell.

Lawrence, P., and Lorsch, J. (1967) *Organization and Environment*. Boston, MA: Graduate School of Business Administration, Harvard University.

McKelvey, W. (1982) *Organizational Systematics*. Berkeley, CA: University of California Press.

McKinley, W., Sanchez, C. M., and Schick, A. G. (1995) "Organizational downsizing: constraining, cloning, learning," *Academy of Management Executive*, 9 (2): 32–44.

Meyer, A., Tsui, A., and Hinings, C. R. (1993) "Configurational approaches to organizational analysis," *Academy of Management Journal*, 36: 1175–95.

Meyer, J., and Rowan, B. (1977) "Institutionalized organizations: formal structure as myth and ceremony," *American Journal of Sociology*, 83: 340–63.

Miller, D., and Friesen, P. (1984) *Organizations: A Quantum View*. Englewood Cliffs, NJ: Prentice Hall.

Miller, D. (1987) "The genesis of configuration," *Academy of Management Review*, 12: 686–701.

——(1990) *The Icarus Paradox*. New York: Harper.

Mintzberg, H. (1979) *The Structuring of Organizations*. Englewood Cliffs, NJ: Prentice Hall.

Mizruchi, M., and Fein, L. (1999) "The social construction of organizational knowledge: a study of the uses of coercive, mimetic, and normative isomorphism," *Administrative Science Quarterly*, 44: 653–83.

Nadler, D. A., and Tushman, M. L. (1989) "Organizational frame bending: principles for managing reorientation," *Academy of Management Executive*, 3: 194–204.

——(1990) "Beyond the charismatic leader: leadership and organizational change," *California Management Review*, 32: 77–97.

Nohria, N., and Ghoshal, S. (1997) *The Differentiated Network*. San Francisco: Jossey-Bass.

Ouchi, W. (1980) "Markets, bureaucracies and clans," *Administrative Science Quarterly*, 25: 129–41.

Pfeffer, J. (1997) *New Directions for Organization Theory: Problems and Prospects*. New York: Oxford University Press.

Pugh, D. S., Hickson, D. J., and Hinings, C. R. (1969) "An empirical taxonomy of structures of work organizations," *Administrative Science Quarterly*, 14: 115–26.

Pugh, D. S., Hickson, D. J., Hinings, C. R., and Turner, C. (1968) "Dimensions of organization structure," *Administrative Science Quarterly*, 13: 65–105.

——(1969) The context of organization structures, *Administrative Science Quarterly*, 14: 91–114.

Rose, T., and Hinings, C. R. (1999) "Global client management systems," in D. Brock, M. Powell, and C.R. Hinings (eds) *Restructuring the Professional Organization: Accounting, Health Care and Law*. London: Routledge.

Scott, W. R. (2001) *Institutions and Organizations*, second edition. Thousand Oaks, CA: Sage.

Senge, P. (1990) *The Fifth Discipline*. New York: Doubleday/Currency.

Tolbert, P., and Zucker, L. (1983) "Institutional sources of change in the formal structure of organization: the diffusion of civil service reform, 1880–1935," *Administrative Science Quarterly*, 28: 22–39.

Üsdiken, B., and Pasadeos, Y. (1995) "Organizational analysis in North America and Europe: a comparison of co-citation networks," *Organization Studies*, 16: 503–26.

Van de Ven, A., and Drazin, R. (1985) "The concept of fit in contingency theory," in B. M. Staw and L. L. Cummings (eds) *Research in Organizational Behaviour* VII, pp. 333–65. Greenwich, CT: JAI Press.

Weber, M. (1947) *The Theory of Social and Economic Organization*. New York: Oxford University Press.

Williamson, O. (1970) *Corporate Control and Business Behavior: An Inquiry into the Effects of Organizational Form on Enterprise Behavior*. Englewood Cliffs, NJ: Prentice Hall.

9b Disorganization

Rolland Munro

Thick descriptions . . . of organization may well be disorganized because that's the way organizations are. (Karl Weick, *The Social Psychology of Organizing*, 1979)

Opening Statement

Disorganization seems all the rage. According to their own testimony, many managers find themselves "bothered and bewildered" (Knights and McCabe, 1999) with endless changes in structure. And, across diverse public and private institutions, they also express concern over a current *lack* of organization. Time and again, in addition to the familiar refrain "There's too much change!" I hear middle managers ask, "Where are the decisions?" Much as they are oppressed by a never-ending series of change agendas, they are also deeply frustrated with waiting for direction from senior colleagues (see also Watson, 1994).

It is this story of "undoing" structure that I unravel in chapter 9(b). To find leading academics like Cooper (1986/1990) anticipating the debate about disorganization is less surprising than to find managers themselves deeply implicated in a process of disordering. For example, devices once seen as rational, such as tall hierarchies and the time-honored division between line and staff, are now fingered as part of the problem. In their place is a raft of dismantling logics, including customerization, empowerment, flexibility, lean production, and outsourcing. These change agendas leave nothing as sacred. In the white water of globalization, the hype is that only the fittest

will survive. As ever, Darwin is abroad, breathing selection into markets, with the Lamarckian visors of corporate planning and prediction now relegated to hindsight.

All this beguiles a contemporary mood of reversal in the once obligatory diktat: *organize!* But we should hesitate before attributing the sea change to radical critique, as others have (e.g., Hassard and Parker, 1993).[1] Using market rhetoric to excite discourses of corporate culture, a new breed of consultants has been urging managers to embrace complexity and "thrive on chaos" (Peters, 1989). Indeed, changing culture is a theme enjoined by many senior managers. For example, Jack Welch, the much praised CEO of General Electric during the 1990s, argues:

Changing the culture starts with an attitude. I hope you won't think I'm being melodramatic if I say that the institution ought to stretch itself, ought to be able to reach the point where it almost becomes unglued. (Tichy and Sherman, 1996: 7)

The counterpoint to organization theory's fix on structure, with its overtones of planning and prediction, is *disorganization*. This motif covers many themes, including deconstruction, unintended consequences, remote control, cellular networks, and terrorism, only some aspects of which are touched upon below. The present chapter focuses on ways management has been *withdrawing* itself from classical modes of organization. The post-bureaucracy argument, for example, is that organization structure – in its managerial and administrative conceptions of information and decision making – has all but been abandoned in favor of a thousand mutations. What I hope to show, by way of contrast, is how managers are recomposing their projects around a "performativity" (Lyotard, 1984) of identities.

Disorganization or De(con)struction?

The kinds of readings which go by the name of deconstruction are often concerned to reveal a "violent hierarchy" (Derrida, 1981: 41), in which one term of a pairing is privileged over and above another term on which it is operating interdependently. This second term is called the *supplement*, and deconstructive readings often expose a systematic effacement of supplementary terms. Thus, for example, a privileging of male over female creates a form of history as "*his* story," in which the work and achievement of women are constantly either erased or degraded.

As a continuation of the "paradigm wars" bears testament, this kind of privileging of one side of a story is highly prevalent in organization studies. In chapter 9(a), for example, the case for contingency theory is presented as if the "turn" to organization culture had never occurred. Even organization theory's debt to social interactionism – long the pre-eminent alternative to a dalliance with "systems" approaches – is all but erased. On the way to jettisoning earlier links with the sociology of organization, the author of the previous chapter reinterprets the formative question of "social order" as "How are people brought together in an organized, structured way?" Of course, such a formulation already decides the debate about formal and informal (Dalton, 1959; Gouldner, 1954) in favor of formal organization.

In its conflation of formal organization with structure, chapter 9(a) also silences a major debate over *social* underpinnings. For example, Selznick (1949) and Gouldner (1954) were "attentive to fundamental similarities between formal organizations and other social institutions" (Willmott, 1990: 45). This remains an important sociological tradition, as indicated in contemporary research like Grieco's (1996), which presses economic analysis in terms of repeated social exchange. More pressingly, in

chapter 9(a) there is an erasure of the evidence that "organization" is the production of its members (Bittner, 1965; Garfinkel, 1967). To appreciate institutional insights in sociology, it is vital to distinguish organization as a "social accomplishment" of members from arrangements that appear merely informal.[2]

Ironically, contingency theory has more or less imploded within its own inversion. As chapter 9(a) delineates, interest in the rationale of organizational structure is now almost incidental to a privileging of *markets* as determining efficiency and effectiveness. Attention is devoted to normative texts, all preaching the new religions of "fit" and "adaptation" through the rubric of performance management and learning organizations (Hinings, chapter 9a). More, then, is at stake than a dismissal of the concept of formal organization, or a defacement of its monuments: administrative centralization, standardization, central planning, and the division of labor. So much so that none of these will ever again be "innocently understood as the rational expedients of modern administration" (Cooper, 1990: 195–6).

The Rational Limits of Rationality

Writing about organization/disorganization, Cooper (1990: 196–7) remarks that "the statements of that discourse we call 'organization theory' are supplementary, for they represent the 'organization of organization'." This should remind us that an ontological debate about the social underpinnings of everyday practice is not the only issue: epistemological concerns are also paramount. As Cooper adds, texts on organization – both theories and statements about practice – are themselves "organized" according to certain normalized criteria – often called scientific and/or academic – so that "it becomes impossible to disentangle the content of organization studies from the theory of methodology that frames it" (Cooper, 1990: 197).

When statements "produce" what each denotes, and orders are ordered, the matter of "organization" no longer appears straightforwardly rational. In assessing claims about the organization of organization, therefore, we often need to ask the critical question *Who benefits?*

There are, after all, alternatives. For example, against the classical approach, which Simmel defines as a "closed system [which] aims to unite all truths, in their most general concepts, into a structure of higher and lower elements" (quoted by Cooper, 1990: 185), Simmel (1980) argues that "form, although necessary as a categorizing device, is partial, temporary and cannot exhaust (i.e., fully comprehend) the infinite nature of the raw material of life."

The question, then, for those who would organize, is *Which order?* In selecting among different sets of orders, however, formal logic is of little assistance. All logical deduction can help decide is whether a particular order is coherent or not. In this sense, formal logic remains permissive rather than mandatory. Logic helps someone avoid making self-contradictory statements, but cannot of itself establish whether an order is itself a true, original, best, or natural order. As Haraway (1985) points out, there is no God's eye view from which everything appears in place. Inclusion under one schema, insist feminists and cultural or critical theorists, results in the exclusion of something, or someone, else. So that a process of ordering, simultaneously and inevitably, is also a process of disordering. Order and disorder have to be taken together.

Adding order is particularly vexatious whenever the aim of a new "order" seems to be to efface, or even erase, the different kinds of orders already in place. To contest such erasure is of course to be concerned with the issue of history, or rather "theirstory," and, in particular, the law of sedimentation to which institutional theory adheres. But that is not all. Contrary to classical notions of rationality that demand a single dominant order, we find instead a *multiplicity* of orders with which the world is already layered and sewn.[3] This is not only to address vexed matters of culture, tradition, and custom. As is discussed later, technology also plays its part. Well before managerial structures assert direction, knowledge has already been distributed and sedimented into machines through the spread of automation on the one hand and through conduct being affected by "the making up" (Hacking, 1990) of governable persons on the other.

Undoing the Organization

Wherefore *dis*organize? There is an oddity about managers making injunctions to "unglue," or "get messy." Common experience suggests an inviolate asymmetry to organizing. Left to themselves, surely things just do become disorganized? They hardly need any help. As Geoffrey Bateson once pointed out, his daughter's question is about why she is always being asked to tidy; she wonders why no one gets asked to mess things up (see Cooper, 1981). A systems theorist as well as a noted anthropologist, Bateson assumed the answer to his daughter's question lay in the laws of entropy, the universal tendency for disorder to increase. In this view, order is always something being added.

Managerial structure, for much of the twentieth century, was presumed to be a "supplement" necessary to control operational parts of the organization. Order had to be added. But from where? From inside or from outside? For, in Derrida's view, the purity of the object's "inside" can be attained only if the "outside" is branded as a supplement that is "not necessary in itself" (Cooper, 1990: 196). Thus, for structure to avoid being seen as supplementary ("not necessary in itself"), structure had to be brought *inside* the organization – in the form of clear lines of authority and short spans of control. Structure (although increasingly recognized as influenced by context) could not be contemplated as something extra, to be imposed by those left outside.

With the advent of market rhetoric, a reverse argument holds sway. Formal structure, with its connotations of rigidity and regulation, becomes the unwanted supplement. In programs such as "delayering" and "flattening the hierarchy" the tendency for formal structures to be insular and self-serving is vilified and their (partial) dismantling becomes the ambition. It is the "outside" – in the form of markets – which is to be brought inside. To those on the New Right, the point of stripping down managerialist structures is exactly to do away with "buffers" to market information and, thus, create a rarefied atmosphere of price information in which only *homo economicus* survives. Where this emphasis on *outputs* creates a more full exposure to the "deep structure" of capitalism, disorganization offers a back-to-reality agenda in which organization culture is to be de(con)structed as fast as organizational structure can be disentangled.

Locked into a program of perpetual change, it seems that the corporate landscape – always more heterogeneous than theory might ever suppose – is being emptied of some of its more familiar landmarks. For example, many markers of position and status have been effaced. While remaining skeptical of talk of "flattening the hierarchy" (see also Munro, 1997a, 1998), it is undeniable that offices have become open-plan, that the more ubiquitous sandwich has replaced elaborate tiers of dining rooms, and that e-mail with personal computers has taken over much secretarial support. The general tone, if not the reality, is captured by Cleveland (1990: 331):

nowadays in many offices orders that used to be routinely accepted are now resisted or refused. In the modern American office, if you want a cup of coffee, you don't take that co-worker, your secretary, off her (or his) own work to get it for you.

Where before managers reproduced their symbols of authority, public and private corporations alike are now characterized more by an effacement of displays of status.

The new object of desire is the market; it is *this* "outside" that is to be added back to complete and compensate what was once thought complete. In systems theory terms, the rationale is to move institutions from a "closed" bureaucracy to an "open" market-based system. However, much more is at stake, since it is systems theory itself which is suspect. For example, attempts to reduce organization theory to matters of structure and context exactly sequester analysis in systems theory terms. Within contingency theory there is not only a privileging of structure as "inside" material over context as "outside" matters. This privileging reaches its apotheosis whenever organization is theorized as separate from "its" environment.

The "Functions" of Disorganization

The urge to tidy is much to the point of the study of the social and the dramatic shift away from reducing organization to the abstractions of "input–output systems." In particular, adherents of a social action framing (Berger and Luckmann, 1967; Silverman, 1970) and ethnomethodologists (Bittner, 1965; Garfinkel, 1967) pressed the case that social interaction is *already* organized by members in their production and reproduction of social reality. While recognizing a prevalence of specialization, standardization, hierarchy, and centralization, these were seen as "features," which social actors accomplish and reproduce through the routines and repetition of their everyday activities. As such, the component features of formal organization are repositioned as *effects*, rather than causes, and within institutional theory need no longer be accorded any rational status with regard to necessity or efficiency.

Within a history of everyone actively making things tidy, it follows therefore that there may be little need for managers to organize others. In Meyer and Rowan's (1977) view, for example, formal structures are mainly "legitimating" devices, while organizations continue to be ruled by their sedimentation of the routines and repetition of social interaction. Unfortunately, once in the hands of the New Right, such insights about "decoupling" can be turned about – illustrating an often overlooked symmetry in unintended consequences. The original institutionalist point that (social) order is brought about by (social) interaction is "forgotten." Instead, the loss of structure – if "decoupled" – is recognized to be no loss at all. Indeed, formal structure starts to look more like ideology, a self-sealing logic that is actually, it is claimed, protecting the sedimented and introverted forces of custom and tradition.

A further argument for dismantling stems from Foucault (1979). His insights into disciplining effects of discourse make much supervision and surveillance of employees look redundant. Indeed, much of the "bewitchment" of logics like customerization, quality, and empowerment can be traced to the seduction of subjects stepping into the place of the king and consuming the sovereignty of "expert" ways of seeing (Munro, 1994). Nor do the disciplining effects of discourse run only one way. Employees have long been instructing each other over the importance of resisting Little Hitlers, and much discursive attention has been given to the dysfunctional relations excited by the exercise of authority. For example, there is much common discourse in circulation which instructs people to resist "authoritarian" regimes, encapsulated, say, by the "Victorian Dad" cartoons in the magazine *Viz*, or in everyday conversation about "control freaks."

So, too, in a story of conflict, management is viewed as a supplement, and frequently an intrusive and unnecessary one. As Gouldner (1954: 47–8) noted in his study of a gypsum plant:

Workers seemed to distinguish, and react differently to, two types of discipline. One of these refers to disciplinary efforts having some evident connection with the work process, and which workers feel are intended to gain efficiency. There were few complaints about such disciplinary efforts. Sometimes, however, workers felt that discipline was being imposed upon them for its own sake, or merely as a way of proclaiming the superiority of those who wielded it. This second, perhaps "authoritarian," pattern of discipline was considered improper and usually aroused resentment.

The message from the shop floor is to leave the local to sort itself out and, for the most part, experienced managers soon learn to resist engaging in local disputes: never knowing who they may need to make alliances with next, they feel they take sides at their peril.

In addition to this emphasis on local knowledge, self-organization becomes the name of the game. Considerable advice, for example, is circulated in more general discourse about the dangers of perpetuating a "nanny" state. This populist advice, which has adversely affected the plight of the homeless and refugees, also penetrates back to reverse basic ideas of child care. Today parents may get warned not to retrieve toys from prams in case they are training the baby to throw them out. As parents, for example, we were told to leave our new child to scream in the night; not only might he be waking up because he thought we wanted him to, but by feeding him we were rewarding him!

Other "unintended" consequences of wielding authority are also now widely acknowledged among managers themselves. For example, it is much put about in managerial "chat" that junior managers use the artifacts of organizational structure to reduce uncertainty and evade responsibility for making their own decisions. As one senior manager put it to me, all his managers were after in contacting him was "comfort" (cf. Munro, 1995a). In such circumstances, what senior managers think they need to do is disrupt the very structure which is creating "the culture of dependence" and organize instead the "wake-up calls."

Again this view supports and advances the cause of perpetual change and further encourages management to become even more inaccessible and recessive within the everyday. The mistake, as always, is to underestimate a potential symmetry in unintended consequences. For example, many schemes for democratization of the workplace actually tighten domination structures (cf. Barker, 1993). Elsewhere I have argued that hierarchy is often made recessive under the doctrines of delegation and empowerment: that is, power may increasingly work through the social, but it does so in ways which restitute hierarchy rather than destroy it (Munro, 1997a, 1998). Power, as Giddens (1968) remarked, is at its best running silently.

The Hollowing out of Structure

When legitimate authority is read as no more than a facade, the way forward (if the phrase is not too ironic) is a program of disorganization: a process willing to peel back structures and expose routines and customs fully to market elements. Of course, in the view of institutional theory, such a pure conversion from structure to markets is impossible. Most likely, all that is achievable, if Foucault is right, is that, as individuals, managers step momentarily from one truth regime into another. If so, managers might be better understood as poised "in between" two polarized opposites, one moment assuming administrative legitimacy, by exercising line authority and command forms of communication, and the next moment talking up a discourse of markets, in which these structures are assumed to have been more or less dismantled.

As it happens, these two "moods" of management uncannily match two phases of withdrawal. The first phase culminates in the consumption of a strategy discourse (Knights and Morgan, 1991). In their initial withdrawal from everyday organization, the supervision of operations, managers retreated to what Cooper (1990: 170) calls "the all-important function" of the *frame*. In systems theory terms, this is to place themselves in between the "system" and its "environment." "At its most fundamental, the frame is what differentiates between the inside and the outside and thus must be understood as a structure which produces two mutually defining points of view." In their ability to intervene over what is to kept inside and what is to be kept outside, managers have thus positioned themselves as intermediaries, regulating both the system *and* the environment, a point implicitly accepted in Weick's (1979) idea of managers "enacting" their environment.

As long as they continued to "frame" both system and environment, managers added structure to organization, by specifying roles and by detailing relationships. For reasons to be discussed next, however, managers seem to have withdrawn even from these more indirect functions. Using accounting numbers, many senior managers act primarily as "spokespersons" for the market (Munro, 1995b). At first blush, speaking for markets seems appropriate to New Right conceptions of a framing role. But not all is what it seems. Since new markets take time to become visible, and downturns are to be traced only with hindsight, often months after the fact, the putative market framing can fail to materialize from want of knowledge.

In the resulting vacuum of instruction, priorities are often left unstated, winners left uncertain, and normal permissions withheld. Pragmatism militates a vagueness and ambiguity in any reading of "markets," exemplified by the waffle of most mission statements and the majority of policy documents. As Weick (1979) notes, "Organizations deal with equivocality routinely, but their ways of dealing are often themselves equivocal and subject to many interpretations." At most, managers create, momentarily, warmer and colder microclimates in which specific permissions can be adduced. But since effects are complex, and contested, it makes little sense to treat an ecosystem as a "variable," as population ecologists do (cf. chapter 9a). In circumstances of self-induced uncertainty, divisions over direction perpetuate themselves; resolution is unlikely to be made explicit or

stable long enough to become the "neglected variable" that must be identified and measured to attain "greater predictive certainty" about the contingent relation between context and structure (cf. Willmott, 1990: 46).

Overall, disorganization is as much an effect of the new managerialism's withdrawal from instruction as it is a consequence of any dismantling logics. To be sure, political coalitions are at work, but the volatility of "events" militates against a conspiracy of communication, in which one group of managers have continued access to secret agendas and others do not. Alongside singing hymn sheets of well rehearsed rhetorics of strategy and policy, other directions and alternative values are always being nurtured and harbored. Agreement, at least the appearance of it, is more usually hosted through a "family" of compromise, favors and fudge.

From Instructions to Identities

Often more concerned with confirming theories than with investigating practice, critical attack can overestimate the dominance of managerialism, with its bland portrayals of a unidirectional nature to control systems. Prone to cast conflict into black-and-white dualisms, pitting workers against managers and the market against the state, critique exhibits a tendency to marginalize the extent to which struggle and appropriation interpenetrate social action at its most minute and mundane (Knights and Willmott, 1985; Alvesson and Willmott, 1996).

As Munro (1995a, 1999a) found in his ethnography of a market leader in financial services, there is an "archeology" of control technologies sedimented into any organization. In contrast to presumptions about managers organizing themselves into a hegemony of control, his argument is that managers, wittingly and unwittingly, *activate* different control technologies as and when they find occasion so to do. In line with the thesis that management has withdrawn itself from organization, the argument of "Managing by ambiguity" is that managers have *decoupled* themselves from being associated with any one single control technology. When each new technology is put in place, it tends to be *added* to the armory of control (see also Munro, 2001c). In the glare of initial management attention, this process of accretion often leaves the artifacts of previous control technologies displaced, but seldom discarded or removed altogether. Subsequently, in the shifts and turns of management agendas, it is around these "shelves" of artifacts that much day-to-day conflict within organizations takes place.

The key ingredients of this decoupling of managers from systems aspects of structure are not hard to specify. First, what is generally acknowledged to be distinctive about the new managerialism is its abandonment of command and control conceptions in favor of *performativity* – a shift in the setting of targets from inputs to outputs. However, the social implications, mostly ignored by managerial texts on performance, are profound. On the one hand, for example, this emphasis on performativity creates a great variety of new *lines of sight* in which "visibility" is accomplished by the delivery of different sets of auditable numbers. On the other, in line with talk of empowerment, managers try to take for granted the delivery of the routine and the repetitious. Hence managerial demands are always future-oriented; past performance, and past loyalty, are always so much water under the bridge.

Second, rather than issue instructions – in ways that could also sediment complacency in operations – managers now intervene more indirectly by consuming each other through *identities*. This is what circulates: "She delivers," referring, say, to an ability to complete a project on time. Or "He's just a glorified supervisor," referring to a manager's proclivity to hands-on management. And so on. Since this kind of identity is fickle to changing agendas (Munro, 1997a, 1999a), managers can no longer be said to "frame" the organization in any single, or constant, manner. In line with the pleas of middle managers at the start of this present chapter, managers find they need to conform with *multiple* sets of instructions. In conditions of equivocality, and faced by the threat of being made invisible by changes in agendas, the propensity of people to be drawn into action to please superiors is instensified, often bypassing the requisite instructions of hierarchy (Munro, 1993). A hint from the right quarters is often enough to incite someone to take up an agenda in order to make themselves "visible" and "available" (Munro, 1999a).

Third, senior managers preoccupy themselves in finding new questions to ask and novel areas with which to magnify themselves and so highlight their agendas. By asking questions – as and when these seem pertinent – they initiate a process of connection/disconnection (Munro, 1997a) in which different kinds of control artifacts are mobilized together and brought into presence *intermittently*, either in answer or in resistance. Thus staff and less senior managers are encouraged, or held back, in their actions in ways that create *passages* through which new agendas can circulate. While dinosaurs grind their teeth in frustration over a lack of resources, putative winners feel empowered to lead the way with fresh initiatives.

Once targets for outputs are in train, emphasis on performativity helps create a "culture of enhancement" (Strathern, 1995, 1997; Munro, 2000a) in which calls for improvement take on the "logic of excess" (Botting and Wilson, 2000). So much so that the desire for market information can be drowned in the clamor for "More!" More quality, more output, more profit, more liquidity, more security, more incentives, more responsiveness, more flexibility, more strength, more simplicity. This is an individuated world of measurement and benchmarking in which the successful in meeting targets find their rewards deferred and "losers" are punished by expulsion from "fields" of visibility. The exact nature of this "expulsion" needs some further elaboration.

Steering Identities between Hierarchy and Markets

The shift from organizing persons to managing identities has a venerable history, much connected with the interpenetration of organization theory by systems thinking. For example, Foucault's (1979: 10–11) analysis of the emergence of government contrasts sociotechnical models of a ship, and its cybernetic metaphors of "steering," with a traditional paternalism modeled on "the head of a family over his household and goods." In drawing attention to these different ways of framing organization, Cooper (1992: 264) notes that members of a family have to be *cared for*, but the ship has to be *managed*. In other words, it does matter to the family exactly who each specific member is and what happens to them.

The key point is that as people get "represented" they are also *re*presented as a "hand" or a "resource." Or they become identified in the form of a number or a statistic. Representation, according to Cooper (1992), is really a *reversal*, in which a disadvantage is turned into an advantage. In Scarry's (1985) simple examples of human technology, a glove represents the hand and a chair represents the folds in a human skeleton, each "re-placing" these parts of the body in its dealing with the world. For instance, where the natural hand is frail, easily burnt, the industrial glove is robust and refractory.

Here is a material way of understanding why changing metaphors matter. Within the "caring" metaphor of the family, members are seen as "frail, easily burnt", as in need of support. Within the framing of the ship or the factory floor, however, it does not really matter who exactly succeeds in what they set out to do: any "hand" will do. The concerns of the ship look outward to the reefs, or the storm, and take priority over persons. Trying to care for persons, other than, say, providing the requisite technology like gloves, is perceived to inculcate so-called dependence cultures, harbors where "wasters" can hide and "losers" stay on board. Indeed, in a meritocracy, or in the "bidding system" of government, to care about *which* person actually succeeds is to be guilty of cronyism, if not nepotism.

In the culture of enhancement it does not matter precisely which kind of institutional structure is being nurtured.[4] Such structures may be more of the partnership or network variety. The demand is only that the means to accomplish an agenda are ready to hand, waiting to be valorized by someone in authority as a "ship" that we have to "get on board before it is too late." Provided existing processes are delivering what has already been "ordered" (cf. Heidegger, 1977) through the targets, the necessary "passages" mentioned above can be excited and constructed, albeit temporarily, by a new change agenda. The issue of "networks" is now discussed.

Networks as Mutable Structures

In a later essay on "Formal organization as representation" Cooper (1992) might seem to offer a different analysis from his earlier theme of disorganization. Against managers' pleas of there being no structure, his focus on remote control might suggest that the control function of middle (and even senior) management has simply been bypassed. Drawing on Latour's (1987) idea of a *center of calculation*, for example, Robson (1992) has theorized the use of accounting numbers to create a panopticon effect and permit the possibility of managing "at a distance."

In Cooper's reading, Latour's (1983, 1988) discussion of Pasteur as a center of calculation in his development of an antidote to the anthrax bacillus has a very different rationale. In direct contrast to the kind of "remote" surveillance attributed to Foucault, Pasteur's displacements back and forth between laboratory and farm demonstrate that the "inside and the outside world can reverse into one another very easily" (Latour, 1983: 154). As Cooper (1992: 262) points out, when farm becomes laboratory and laboratory becomes farm there is an "artificiality in thinking in terms of discrete terms such as laboratory and farm, organization and environment," since "they also displace the traditional static distinction between 'inside' and 'outside'."

As a consequence of the wave of dismantling logics which institutions have undergone in recent years, organization is now networked through and through by a *multiplicity* of centers of calculation, from budgets to the statistical processes of quality control. In these circumstances, organization is continuously being re-enacted through a variable set of movable boundaries:

Organizing thus becomes a network of mobile and non-localizable associations instead of a static distinction between organization and its environment. Organizing . . . is the transformation of boundary relationships which are themselves continually shifting. (Cooper, 1992: 260)

The danger of the static emphasis on managerial structures, as with a narrow understanding of the organization chart (Munro, 1998b), is that these specify hierarchical relations as paramount, rather than stress the importance of noticing key shifts in boundary relations.

In place of the showpiece of organization structure, the division of labor – with its specification of roles and detailing of relationships – increasing reliance seems to be being placed on the social processes of what we have termed elsewhere a *labor of division* (Munro, 1997b; Cooper, 1997). In the absence of fixed "boundaries," imagined by systems theory, boundaries become mutable and manifold by virtue of their being embodied within the relations of persons. Inclusion and exclusion are conducted, as always, through the identity work of persons, but are no longer mutually exclusive. It is my contention that the shaping and timing of boundaries is made more complex by an expansion of "thresholds," time–space passages within which agendas, people, and materials are kept waiting, being neither "in" nor "out."

Instead of helping "organize out" strange events, people, or materials as disruptive, as the maintenance of bureaucracy insists, diverse interpretations of shifts in the "outside" can be rerepresented within a whole range of pending agendas. In these circumstances, persons are no longer to be rendered in terms of "cultural dopes." As the metaphor of "unglueing" indicates, people are invited to take their chance and "define" their own destiny. Under the mantra of "Be who you wanna be," you are expected to exercise your choice of role – role is no longer specified for you. So too, in an age of networks, you are to choose your own relations. Since relationships are no longer detailed by organization charts, these are seen to be framed by your will to succeed. In the absence of a command-and-control economy the net of potential relationships is now much wider, including the customer, or the supplier, or a team member, or indeed anyone with relevant expertise or information to pass on (Munro, 2001b).

The overall effect is to excite a *decentering* of structural "agents" and effects. Facing a future that is hard to read, the trick of survival is to clamber aboard each agenda without fully embracing the values of whatever aspect of corporate culture is currently being talked up. In terms related to Goffman's insight of "role distance" (cf. Kunda, 1992), the ethos of membership may be no more than keeping a wary eye on which flags are flying and making a "display" of a relevant artifact (Munro, 1999a). This allows one to hang fire and keep one's options open, recognizing that no one group can fully direct events. Thus, rather than just remain sedimented into the routines of repeated social exchange – the delivery of which is mandatory – people are also expected to find their own level, and then advertise themselves as "available" accordingly.

A Dissemination of Comparison?

Within its teleology of efficiency, the kind of rationality Weber saw as culturally inevitable seeks to excise redundancy from its system. As discussed earlier, however, rationality and efficiency are not the same.[5] Western conceptions of rationality seek to eliminate *difference*, not similarity. In contrast, by denigrating the routines and repetition of institutional practice as irrational, Euro-American managers appear to conflate the elimination of redundancy with rationality. It is of course unsurprising that a process of accretion and sedimentation appears irrational to the modern eye. For example, thinking of practices like the confessional perpetuated in the Roman Catholic Church, Clegg (1994: 74) suggests, "Things, forms and practices may be valued for and in themselves, irrespective of their contribution to the efficiency of the organization."

As Strathern (1997) explicates, embedded within their own "deep structure" of *comparison*, Euro-Americans remain intolerant of mere division, differentiation, and want to valorize one side over another. And this tendency has been very true of managers and employees alike (cf. Parker, 2000), at least until recently. Perversely, perhaps as a consequence of the sedimentation of the "cultural cleansing" programs unleashed during the last quarter of the twentieth century, more diversity has now begun to be called for, albeit serially or severally, and in ways that simultaneously deny the compatibility of these diverse parts. Operating as a "public secret" (Taussig, 1999), the postmodern turn for managers is one of dismantling the main structure that *prevents* diversity – *their* own privileging of a single dominant order (see also Munro, 2001c). Not only may the deviant, the dirty, and even the difficult turn out to be useful, as US President George W. Bush is finding out in his "war" on terrorism; trying to eliminate this kind of waste becomes seen itself as a wasteful expenditure of a manager's time. Instead, in order to order their orders, managers seem happy to pull through what they want, when they want.

Western civilization, I am arguing, appears to be moving towards a point where it constantly wants to dismantle structure – without noticing how, simultaneously and continually, it also "calls" *for* structure; for example through its espousal of common values. In particular, as a consequence of their reliance on target setting and bidding processes, senior managers learn to find ways of making choices *after the fact*. Consequently, they may help settle the scale of targets, but are no longer in full control of who succeeds. Where they retain discretion is over the *timing* of sanctions (Munro, 1999b). Managers still enjoy a limited ability to call "time" on the delivery of others and count, or discount, the score; and they can also bias the dice by allocating more resources or better locations to favorites. But even here their discretion is limited, since they too are caught within the fold of numbers. If they are not in the game of picking winners, they too may end up as a loser, not so much excluded as "relegated" to the bottom of the heap.

So, in one sense, the proponent for organization structure is right. Despite the pandemonium of change, and the recent emphasis on process, structure is always being found, and this chapter is no exception. In addressing processes of disorganization, while simultaneously answering the eternal call for structure, managers could be discovering the benefits of dismantling the very kind of structures that hold in place the Euro-American mode of comparison. Or, at least, dismantling those "deep" structures holding in place a single, dominant mode of comparison?

What remains of organizational structure are managerial processes for accumulating credit and divesting blame. No one should suppose contemporary injunctions around the motif of disorganization implies that "anything goes." To the contrary, as has been discussed, the injunctions of the new managerialism help to *restitute* hierarchy rather than eliminate it. So, too, the shrill voices that excited companies to get lean and mean, to cut the fat and go with the flow, excite a deepening of both kinds of macho management: the silence of the tough wait-it-out deferral of instruction and the helter-skelter of quick-fix seat-of-the-pants spin doctoring. Here the carrier of today's can of worms remains the employee. In as much as firms use accounting numbers to lay workers off, people still enter organizations on demand and are forced to exit when no longer needed.

Drawing the "Excess" from Difference

Briefly, what is at stake in social theory are different ways people make themselves consumable (see also Latimer, 2001). In demonstrating "fitness for purpose," all of us have to *punctualize* our identities (Munro, 2000b), timing their availability and making each "visible" sequentially to a range of target audiences that include colleagues and strangers across a wide variety of organizational fora. In terms of our being different, we work through a more or less carefully circumscribed *labor of division* – in which each of us is expected, more and more, to refine what it is we specifically have to offer. And, in terms of being the same, we are expected to "post" the more interpretative aspects of our conduct along *circuits of information* that align ourselves with corporate agendas in one gesture, or advertise ourselves as team players in the next.

Against Weber's emphasis on efficiency, Simmel's idea of "play," more fully explored by Cooper (1990), seems relevant today in permitting diversity and protecting the possibility of social responsiveness. This emphasis on play and diversity should not, however, be mistaken as a plea for *requisite variety* (Ashby, 1956), an idea where parts are matched between system and environment. Once markets are "inside" organizations as much as organizations are "outside" markets, people can no longer be thought of as making themselves available as "functionaries" by adopting well specified roles or by becoming expert in particular skills. This is not just to claim operational processes are subject to centers of calculations which are transorganizational, such as stock exchanges, credit rating agencies, and consumer protection bodies. Or that supervisory procedures are increasingly "re-engineered" to ensure work is pulled through quasi-automatic processes in which managerial direction becomes virtually zero. Or even that tasks are to be completed less because people are being told what to do than because they need those numbers for their performance statistics.

For the moment, Simmel's emphasis on play can be given only limited credence. In a *dissemination* of targets and league tables out to all the provinces – to the school, to the hospital and to the prison, or to each plant, or each cell, or each job or body part – we are still to be entertained by comparison. All eyes are turned to the moments in which the goals are scored. This is what restitutes and extends the mode of comparison into the capillaries. In its ability to divide and rule, comparison remains the dominant mode of ordering: it is no longer just to be reckoned with as one big playing field, in which a single career path might be figured; nor even, to stretch the metaphor, a topography of playing fields, each rhizome having its own winners and losers. In a multitude of "sideshows" the league tables are to be endless.

That said, it is likely that my analysis of disorganization will be found wanting. How else to deal with my failure to engage fully in comparison – valorizing, say, the ethos of bureaucracy (du Gay, 2000) over an enterprise culture? Almost certainly my narrative of an *excess* of parts, brought about by managers inciting the "inside" of organization to resemble its "outside," will be dismissed as fanciful by contingency theorists, particularly those, we are told in chapter 9(a), who have turned from prediction to "parsimony." But which, other readers may ask, are the most important features? The "excess" offered up by the taken-for-granted routines of social interaction or the "excess" generated by the occasional slick "pass" from one manager to another, or by the inspired guess of a few employees about their manager's intentions?

What is problematic about the play of making oneself "visible" and "available" today, either *as* different or *as* the same, is that possible audiences are themselves moving targets. For example, a manager can be a friend or mentor one minute and a superior the next (Munro, 2001a). Or a colleague can be in a Quality Circle one moment and in another moment become "the market," indifferent to who gains the next contract (Munro, 1998). Over these more recessive kinds of inclusions and exclusions, time-honored distinctions – such as staff and line, work and play, formal and informal, manager and employee, and even market and organization – become part of the resources of a culture of enhancement and are no longer analytically sharp or helpful.

Conclusion

In drawing up this counterpoint of "disorganization" I have argued that the rationale for endless change – even when made up unwittingly or on the hoof – seems to be going far beyond the earlier emphasis on processes becoming flexible to markets (Atkinson, 1984; Procter et al., 1994), and even beyond thinking in terms of a shift from closed to open systems (Cooper, 1990: 170). Or even a decentering of structure, with the World Wide Web as its paradigm example. It is the very process of "technological normalization" that seems up for question. What was once dismissed as redundant, failing the all-important economic test of efficiency, can now be understood in terms of accumulating a diversity of "standing reserves" (Heidegger, 1977).

The days of reading organizations in terms of a single-valued logic, or dominant coalition, seem numbered. For managers to be able to switch direction, there also has to be available – on demand – *social* processes which can bring into play the new agenda. When every agenda is to be encouraged, for instance, Child's (1973) proposition of there being a single dominant coalition within each organization no longer holds. Dominance is a now a partial and provisional phenomenon. Even if viewed as "a political process in which constraints and opportunities are functions of the power exercised by decision makers in the light of ideological values" (Child, 1972: 16), executive actions are invariably caught up inside the identity work of their own power struggles in the race to keep up with "outside" events.

To be sure, hegemony is likely being decentered, not abandoned altogether. For the moment, we are far from even recognizing, far less celebrating, the current diversity within the world of organization. There is as yet no "exuberant irrationality" for difference at the core; instead there is a steely determination on the part of those charged with delivery to take routine production for granted and affirm the presence of excess by "ordering" it only when needed for purposes of recording "enhancement." As befits Darwinian theory (cf. Popper, 1981), the random nature of mutations incited by change agendas can easily be exaggerated. Ignited by the occasional "poem" (Botting and Wilson, 2000), and spurred on by endless replay and expert discussion to facilitate comparison, there is almost complete effacement over the extent to which the clock of habit still turns the great wheels of production.

Disorganization is not chaos, and I have suggested how a "deep structure" of comparison – endemic to the West – can help instill the mode of production. In my analysis, comparison works its double dealing – as it always has – through approval and appropriation on the one hand and by denigration and denial on the other. What is different today is the way Euro-Americans have effectively turned a labor of division inwards on to self, settling accounts on the coat tails of the occasional nod of approval from superiors and by equating silence over the extra effort we are giving with our own denigration of routines and repetition. We know that no one in authority wants to know anything about the grueling stints on the factory floor, the thrall of mundane teaching, or hours spent home at night compiling those reports. Supposedly already paid for these tasks, we have no warrant to ask for more.

Notes

1   In retrospect, Burrell and Morgan's (1979) distinction between the sociology of regulation and the sociology of radical change was hardly cast into the bronze of a dualism before the radical agenda had been seized by the New Right. In the same year Margaret Thatcher was voted into government on an agenda of reforming the United Kingdom's previously revered public institutions. In what might cynically be called the sociology of relegation, nearly all corporations – public and private alike – have been putting in place programs of audit and accountability and reshaped their apparatus of command and control around the introduction of "bidding" systems.

2   Possibly the expectation is that social theory would have its say in this present reply. However, while some self-proclaimed postmodern writing may laud de(con)struction as undermining functionalism (and even capitalism), serious critique is hallmarked more by "hesitation". A particular danger for deconstruction is that of simply making an "inversion" in the abstractions of analysis: putting up what was down and putting down what was up. As Strathern (1997) illustrates over gender, the problem of critique is one of unwittingly reproducing the Western "structure" of *comparison*, so that the previously degraded term becomes valorized and the privileged term is reduced to supplement.

3   What is particularly challenging to classical notions of rationality is to learn that formal logic itself has no quarrel with multiplicity, only with claims that reduce multiple matters to a single form. It is not diverse materials themselves which are prohibited; it is their *representation* – as if each type of material were of one single common kind – which is placed under scrutiny in Canguilhem's (1978) "will to cleanse." And this is where things become more clear. For it turns out conceptions of rationality addressed by Weber (being also a mode of organization) are particularly suspect. In privileging single modalities of ordering, bureaucracy both implicates single-value logics *as* rational and restitutes itself *as* organization.

4   In discussing the topic of disorganization I am also widening this analysis from people to include structures themselves. As Barry Schofield, a doctoral student at Keele, is finding in his research, there is a *structured indifference* to the framing and funding of contemporary institutions. Everyone has his

favorite structure, but no one can predict safely the particular set of networks which will emerge to provide "joined up" government; consequently, no one knows any longer which particular set of "providers" can deliver. Public or private, the source of delivery to the recipient just doesn't matter.

5 "Excess" may yet turn out to be a more significant cultural value than efficiency (and one closer to Weber's own interpretative position of *verstehen*). In any case, the rationality of formal logic is not incompatible with the idea of redundancy, as is so often assumed. To the contrary, in its reliance on noncontradiction, formal logic harbors redundancy. For example, to make statements of equivalence, as indicated in the first step in many mathematical proofs "Let $a = a$," is one certain way to avoid self-contradiction.

References

Alvesson M., and Willmott, H. (1996) *Making Sense of Management*. London: Sage.

Ashby, W. R. (1956) *Introduction to Cybernetics*. London: Chapman & Hall.

Atkinson, J. (1984) "Manpower strategies for flexible organizations," *Personnel Management*, August, pp. 28–31.

Barker, J. (1993) "Tightening the iron cage: concertive control in self-managing teams," *Administrative Science Quarterly*, 38: 408–37.

Berger, P. L., and Luckmann, T. (1967) *The Social Construction of Reality*. Harmondsworth: Penguin.

Bittner, E. (1965) "On the concept of organization," *Social Research*, 32: 239–55.

——(1967) "The police on Skid Row: a study of peace keeping," *American Sociological Review*, 32 (5): 699–715.

Botting, F., and Wilson, S. (2000) "Homo econopoesis" I, paper presented at the ESRC Complexity Seminar, CSTT, Keele, May.

Burrell, G., and Morgan, G. (1979) *Sociological Paradigms and Organizational Analysis*. London: Heinemann.

Canguilhem, G. (1978) *On the Normal and the Pathological*. Dordecht: Reidel.

Child, J. (1972) "Organization structure, environment and performance: the role of strategic choice," *Sociology*, 6: 1–22.

——(1973) "Strategies of control and organization behaviour," *Administrative Science Quarterly*, 18: 1–17.

Clegg, S. R. (1994) "Max Weber and contemporary sociology of organizations," in L. J. Ray and M. Reed (eds) *Organizing Modernity: New Weberian Perspectives on Work, Organization and Society*, pp. 46–80. London: Routledge.

Cleveland, H. (1990) "The twilight of hierarchy," in S. Corman et al. (eds) *Foundations of Organizational Communication: a Reader*, pp. 327–41. New York: Longman. Reprinted from *Public Administration Review*, 1985.

Cooper, D. (1981) "A social and organizational view of management accounting," in M. Bromwich and A. G. Hopwood (eds) *Essays in British Accounting Research*. London: Pitman.

Cooper, R. (1986/1990) "Organization/disorganization," in J. Hassard and D. Pym (eds) *The Theory and Philosophy of Organizations*, pp. 167–97. London: Routledge. Reprinted from *Social Science Information*, 25 (2): 299–335.

——(1992) "Formal organization and representation: remote control, displacement, abbreviation," in M. Reed and M. Hughes (eds) *New Directions in Organization Theory*, pp. 254–72. London: Sage.

——(1997) "The visibility of social systems," in R. Munro and K. Hetherington (eds) *Ideas of Difference: Social Spaces and the Labour of Division*, Sociological Review Monograph, pp. 32–41. Oxford: Blackwell.

Dalton, M. (1959) *Men who Manage*. New York: Wiley.

Derrida, J. (1978) *Writing and Difference*, trans. A. Bass. London: Routledge.

——(1981) *Positions*. Chicago: University of Chicago Press.

du Gay, P. (2000) *In Praise of Bureaucracy: Weber, Organization, Ethics*. London: Sage.

Foucault, M. (1970) *The Order of Things: An Archaeology of the Human Sciences*. London: Tavistock Press.

——(1979) *Discipline and Punish: The Birth of the Prison*. Harmondsworth: Penguin.

Garfinkel, H. (1967) *Studies in Ethnomethodology*. Englewood Cliffs, NJ: Prentice Hall.

Giddens, A. (1968) "Power in the recent writings of Talcott Parsons," *Sociology*, 2: 257–72.

——(1984) *The Constitution of Society*. Cambridge: Polity Press.

Goffman, E. (1958) *The Presentation of Self in Everyday Life*. New York: Doubleday.

Gouldner, A. (1954) *Patterns of Industrial Bureaucracy*. New York: Collier-Macmillan.

Grieco, M. (1996) *Worker's Dilemma: Recruitment, Reliability and Repeated Exchange*. London: Routledge.

Hacking, I. (1990) *The Taming of Chance*. Cambridge: Cambridge University Press.

Haraway, D. (1985) "A manifesto for cyborgs: science, technology and socialist feminism in the 1980s," *Socialist Review*, 80: 65–107.

Hassard, J., and Parker, M., eds (1993) *Postmodernism and Organizations*. London: Sage.

Heidegger, M. (1977) *The Question concerning Technology, and other Essays*, trans. W. Lovitt. New York: Harper & Row.

Knights, D., and McCabe, D. (1999) "Bewitched, bothered and bewildered: the meaning and experience of team working for employees in an automobile company," *Human Relations*, 53 (11): 1481–517.

Knights, D., and Morgan, G. (1991) "Strategic discourse and subjectivity: towards a critical analysis of corporate strategy in organizations," *Organization Studies*, 12 (2): 251–74.

Knights, D., and Willmott, H. (1985) "Power and identity in theory and practice," *Sociological Review*, 33 (1): 22–46.

Kunda, G. (1992) *Engineering Culture: Control and Commitment in a High-tech Corporation*. Philadelphia: Temple University Press.

Latimer, J. (2001) "All-consuming passions: materials and subjectivity in the age of enhancement," in N. Lee and R. Munro (eds) *The Consumption of Mass*, pp. 158–173. Sociological Review Monograph. Oxford: Blackwell.

Latour, B. (1987) *Science in Action: How to follow Scientists and Engineers through Society*. Milton Keynes: Open University Press.

——(1983) "Give me a laboratory and I will raise the world," in K. Knorr-Cetina and M. Mulkay (eds) *Science Observed: Perspectives in the Social Study of Science*. London: Sage.

——(1988) *The Pasteurization of France*. Cambridge, MA: Harvard University Press.

Lyotard, J-F. (1984) *The Postmodern Condition: A Report on Knowledge*, trans. G. Bennington and B. Massumi. Manchester: Manchester University Press.

Meyer, J. W., and Rowan, B. (1977) "Institutionalized organizations: formal structure as myth and ceremony," *American Journal of Sociology*, 83: 340–63.

Munro, R. (1993) "Power and Ethos: Organizational Knowledge in Perpetually Disintegrating Volumes," Midlands Organization Behaviour Group, Keele University, December.

——(1994) "Worlds Apart: Writing Management in the Space of Disciplines disciplining the Disciplines," unpublished.

——(1995a) "Managing by ambiguity: an archaeology of the social in the absence of management accounting," *Critical Perspectives on Accounting*, 6: 433–82.

——(1995b) "Governing the new province of quality: autonomy, accounting and the dissemination of accountability," in H. Willmott and A. Wilkinson (eds) *Making Quality Critical*, pp. 127–55. London: Routledge.

——(1996) "Complexity and Poststructualism," CSTT Seminar on Complexity, Keele University, November.

——(1997a) "Connection/disconnection: theory and practice in organization control," *British Journal of Management*, 8: 43–63.

——(1997b) "Ideas of difference: stability, social spaces and the labour of division," in K. Hetherington and R. Munro, *Ideas of Difference: Social Spaces and the Labour of Division*, pp. 1–22. Sociological Review Monograph, Oxford: Blackwell.

——(1998) "Belonging on the move: market rhetoric and the future as obligatory passage," *Sociological Review*, 46 (2): 208–43.

——(1999a) "The cultural performance of control," *Organization Studies*, 20 (4): 619–39.

——(1999b) "Power and discretion: membership work in the time of technology," *Organization*, 6 (3): 429–50.

——(2000a) "The culture of enhancement: performance measurement and the new managerialism," in A. Neely (ed.) *Performance Measurement: Past, Present and Future*, pp. 395–402. Cranfield: Cranfield University.

——(2000b) "Punctualising Identity: Time and the Demanding Relationship," paper presented at the British Sociological Association, York.

——(2001a) "Calling for accounts: numbers, monsters and membership," *Sociological Review*, 49 (4): 473–93.

——(2001b) "After knowledge: the language of information," in R. Westwood and S. Linstead (eds) *The Language of Organization*. London: Sage.

——(2001c) "Unmanaging/disorganization," *Ephemera: Critical Dialogues on Organization*, 1 (4): 395–403.

Parker, M. (2000) *Organizational Culture and Identity*. London: Sage.

Peters, T. J. (1989) *Thriving on Chaos*. London: Macmillan.

Popper, K. (1981) "The rationality of scientific revolutions," in I. Hacking (ed.) *Scientific Revolutions*, pp. 80–106. Oxford: Oxford University Press.

Procter, S. J., Rowlinson, M., Mcardle, L., Hassard, J., and Forrester, P. (1994) "Flexibility, politics and strategy: in defence of the model of the flexible firm," *Work, Employment and Society*, 8 (2): 221–42.

Robson, K. (1992) "Accounting numbers as 'inscription': action at a distance and the development of accounting," *Accounting, Organization and Society*, 17: 685–708.

Scarry, E. (1985) *The Body in Pain: The Making and Unmaking of the World*. New York: Oxford University Press.

Selznick, P. (1949) *TVA and the Grass Roots*. Berkeley, CA: University of California Press.

Silverman, D. (1970) *Theory of Organizations*. London: Heinemann.

Simmel, G. (1980) *Essays on Interpretation in Social Science*. Manchester: Manchester University Press.

Strathern, M. (1995) *The Relation: Issues in Complexity and Scale*, Cambridge: Prickly Pear Pamphlet No. 6.

——(1997a) "From Improvement to Enhancement: An Anthropological Comment on the Audit Culture," Founder's Memorial Lecture, Girton College, University of Cambridge.

——(1997b) "Gender: division or comparison?" in R. Munro and K. Hetherington (eds) *Ideas of Difference: Social Spaces and the Labour of Division*, pp. 42–63. Sociological Review Monograph, Oxford: Blackwell.

Taussig, M. (1999) *Defacement: Public Secrecy and the Labour of the Negative*. Stanford, CA: Stanford University Press.

Tichy, N., and Sherman, S. (1996) *Control your own Destiny or Someone else Will: How General Electric is revolutionizing the Art of Management*. London: HarperCollins.

Watson, T. J. (1994) *In Search of Management: Culture, Chaos and Control in Managerial Work*. London: Routledge.

Weick, K. (1979) *The Social Psychology of Organizing*. Reading, MA: Addison-Wesley.

Willmott, H. (1990) "Beyond paradigmatic closure in organizational enquiry," in J. Hassard and D. Pym (eds) *The Theory and Philosophy of Organizations*, pp. 44–60. London: Routledge.

10

Culture

As with many others in this volume, the debate here revolves around the ontological status of organizations and their cultures. Ashkanasy believes that organizational culture is a legitimate and authentic phenomenon deserving of empirical scrutiny and theoretic development. He also believes that cultures have a clear, if complex, ontological status and can be measured. Ashkanasy suggests that there are three ontological positions identifiable in the literature with respect to organizational cultures. The first, and the one he promotes, is a "structural realist" ontology, which, he argues, is consistent with Likert's conceptualization of organizational climate. Likert had argued that, even though a construct such as "climate" was not directly observable, could not be known by single subjectivities, and was not overtly produced, it can be taken as having objective (or, and here he hedges his bets, a subjective) reality and be measurable. Ashkanasy rejects the two remaining ontological positions, which he characterizes as based on social constructionism and "linguistic convenience" respectively. The latter is an odd label and one that he aligns with Gadamar's (1989) hermeneutic interpretation. He does not elaborate, but later berates a postmodern perspective for being primarily concerned with treating culture as an artifact of the rhetoric and power play of organization theorists as they seek to promote their own positions and interests. He dismisses this view of the postmodern position as "little more than a cynical oversimplification of an intrinsically interesting phenomenon." He might well be correct if that were the postmodern position. It is true that a postmodern position (if there is such a thing) draws attention to the reflexivity by which the theorist's representations and representational practices are constitutive of the phenomena under investigation. However, a postmodern position is also concerned with the discursive conditions that have produced a space in which the notion and practice of "organizational culture" have emerged and attained legitimacy. It is also concerned with the processes and practices by which organizational members instantiate a notion of "culture" and the discursive and power resources used to accomplish that. In other words, Ashkanasy presents a limited and distorted interpretation of the postmodern position, which he then seeks to summarily dispatch.

Chan's case is not particularly overtly postmodern in timbre, but he also worries at the ontological status of organizational culture. In his view the study of organizational culture is hampered and misguided by a persistent conceptualization of culture as an entity – or as a state of being or static property. He argues that it is more meaningful to consider culture as a "process" – essentially as a process of ongoing meaning construction. If culture is seen as a "property" of an organization or group there is a tendency to depict it as a unitary, unambiguous, and unchanging constituent. For Chan this is a false and misleading imposition of structure and stasis on to a phenomenon that is dynamic, emergent, ambiguous, and fluid. In contrast to Ashkanasy's three ontologies, Chan offers three processual views of culture, each with a nuanced point of ontological and epistemological differentiation. The first he refers to as akin to a negotiated order view of culture – culture as an ongoing accomplishment of the mundane interactional work of members in a plural framework. The second he represents as a kind of socially embedded view. Here organizational culture is in a continuous process of mutual interaction and influence with the wider social system and culture in which it is embedded. Organizational cultures cannot be conceived of as hermetically sealed entities. The third view he depicts as an "organic" interpretation of organizational culture. This argues against conceptualizing culture as a monolithic and uniform framework imposed by a managerial regime. It argues that organizational members interact creatively with an overt and "official culture" in an ongoing process of reactance, adaptation, refinement and resistance. The "lived" culture is produced and reproduced through these processes.

An important subtext in the debate is the consideration of the relationship between organizational climate and organizational culture. The two constructs have been entwined in the field since at least the 1950s but it has never been an easy or clearly delineated relationship. Ashkanasy prefers to see continuity and the potential for convergence – provided culture theorizing and research adopts the ontological and empirical positions pursued by the climate camp. Chan sees a fracture and argues that culture has not gone through the smooth process of construct development and consensus witnessed in the climate literature. The culture (sub)field is characterized by dissensus and paradigmatic "war games" (Martin, 2001) that show little sign of diminishing.

Here the protagonists are in agreement: "climate" has clearer construct development, delineation, and consensus; "culture," on the other hand, is in relative disarray. Ashkanasy's response to this malaise has echoes of the solution to perceived incoherence in the OS field more generally put forward by the likes of Pfeffer, Donaldson, McKelvey (chapter 2a), and Boal, Hunt, and Jaros (chapter 3a). That response is to insist on marshalling behind a realist ontology, instilling construct definitions that promote consensus, and adopting an objectivist epistemology and methodology. For Ashkanasy construct consensus is to be achieved through a "common law" approach. This seems to imply that the most commonly deployed definitions and uses of the construct should be taken as indicative of their salience and veracity and as grounds for their further adoption. This is a kind of *vox pop.* science! Since Ashkanasy argues for "phenomenological overlap" between climate and culture, he sees it as logical that culture be studied in the same manner. For him the key to culture is a set of shared value dimensions and that these are determinable and measurable. Chan disavows the coherence of climate and culture, and rejects an objectivist methodology and realist ontology. He speaks favorably of an ethnomethodological approach in which the process by which a sense of culture is accomplished by organizational members is the focus of analysis.

In the end, though, he proposes an approach informed by a Weickian notion of sense making. However, a reading of Weick's chapter 6(a) in this volume suggests that the approach to sense making pursued by Chan is with an ethnomethodological slant.

References

Gadamar, H-G. (1989) *Truth and Method*, trans. J. Weinsheimer and D. G. Marshall, second edition. New York: Crossroads.
Martin, J. (2001) *Organizational Culture: Mapping the Terrain*. London: Sage.

10a The Case for Culture

Neal M. Ashkanasy

In this "point" chapter, I argue that organizational culture is an authentic phenomenon, in the sense that it has specific effects on organizations, constituent parts of organizations, and organizational members, and that it is measurable. In line with this argument, I adopt Ashkanasy and Jackson's (2001) definition of organizational culture as a consistent set of attitudes and values held by organizational members, and the practices that result from these attitudes and values. This is in contrast to the approach taken by my counterpart in chapter 10(b), where culture is presented as a dynamic process of organizational sense making (cf. Weick, 1995). I base my case on five principal arguments. These are that organizational culture: (1) can coexist at multiple levels of organizations, (2) is intrinsically a reflection of organizations as systems of values, (3) is associated with organizational climate but nevertheless conceptually distinct from climate, (4) is something that can be measured, and (5) is associated with organizational performance, although not always in a simple fashion.

Together with its sister construct, organizational climate, organizational culture has played a prominent role in industrial and organizational psychology since Lewin (1948, 1951) and Jaques (1951). It is appropriate therefore to consider briefly its genesis in psychological and sociological literature. The construct of organizational culture first appeared more than twenty years prior to its more commonly acknowledged emergence (Pettigrew, 1973; see

Ashkanasy et al., 2000b) in the writings of Jaques (1951), and also as a derivative of Lewin's (1948, 1951) field theory. In the latter respect, Lewin et al. (1939) argued, from a *Gestalt* psychology perspective, that field theory predictions vary with organizational context. In 1939, however, means for recognizing and categorizing these contexts had yet to emerge. Consequently, Lewin and his colleagues coined the term "organizational climate" to represent the collective attitudes, feelings, and social processes of organizational members. They went on to identify three distinct climates that remain at the core of most models of climate today (see Ashkanasy et al., 2000b): *autocratic, democratic,* and *laissez-faire.*

Likert (1961) was the next link in the chain. He reconceptualized organizational climate in terms of his System 4 view of effective management. Likert's contribution in particular was to develop means of measuring organizational climate dimensions. In this instance, what Likert did was revolutionary at the time – he introduced the notion that it was both feasible and psychologically sound to measure a construct of organizational climate that, theoretically, could neither be known personally nor created artificially. Likert's legacy is most evident in the measurement scale that bears his name. For thirty years, the 1960s to the 1980s, students and practitioners of organizational climate almost invariably used surveys based on Likert scales to describe social processes within organizations. Of course, the Likert scale format has also become familiar in other disciplines as well.

By the 1970s and 1980s, nonetheless, increasing disquiet was expressed by many in the field that the climate construct, based on survey measurement, was an inadequate characterization of organizational decision-making environments (e.g., see Reichers and Schneider, 1990). As a consequence, interest shifted to the related construct of organizational culture, drawn from the field of anthropology, and introduced into the mainstream of scholarly management literature by Pettigrew (1973). The new culture researchers employed a holistic approach to understanding organizations, and spoke of systems of meaning, values, and actions. The pioneering researchers of the 1980s (e.g. Deal and Kennedy, 1982; Ouchi, 1981; Peters and Waterman, 1982; Schein, 1990, 1992) based their research and understanding on their own experience in organizations, and promulgated the idea that culture can best be described and understood through inductive intuition and ethnography.

Ashkanasy et al. (2000b), in a broad review of the anthropology literature on culture, identified three categories of culture, reflecting different ontological assumptions. The first ontology, based on the Likert climate model, but often applied to culture, is predicated on a structural realist view, where organizations exist as structures that have an identifiable and measurable climate and a culture. The second, founded in social constructionism, focuses on the regularity with which events occur in organizations based on organizational members' underlying assumptions or paradigms (see Shotter, 1993). In this view, observers select a set of related events based on their assumptions about the nature of reality, and use these to define culture. Finally, in the third view, organizations and culture are treated as linguistic conveniences, akin to Gadamer's (1989) notion of hermeneutic interpretation (see Gergen, 1996). In this chapter, however, I specifically reject this view, and propose that culture is identifiable as an objective or subjective social reality.

Definitions of climate and culture also reflect three epistemological approaches. The first of these is the deductive approach, which emphasizes broadly applicable cultural dimensions or analytic categories. Knowledge comes from constructing these dimensions, looking to see where organizations fall along them, and revising the dimensions when previously overlooked phenomena are noticed. In the second category are inductive approaches that recognize the presence of the tacit elements. These tacit elements can sometimes be made explicit, but always shape the experience of specified constructs. Finally, radical approaches view the observer as dispassionately interested not so much in accuracy as in producing constructions that acknowledge the interpolation of the researcher into the research practice.

The interplay between the different paradigms (Schultz and Hatch, 1996) has been a feature of research into organizational culture and climate and will continue to be so. Thus, while many scholars argue that an ontology, epistemology, and method appropriate for studying cultures holistically is more appropriately provided by the interpretive traditions within anthropology, others argue that the constructs can be examined within the quasi-scientific frameworks of psychology, based on the use of surveys and of a positivist epistemology (see Thatchenkery, 1996). In chapter 10(a) I review a variety of approaches from the different paradigms, with a view to enlightening readers about the ongoing controversies and flow of ideas in this exciting field.

Organizational Culture at Multiple Levels

One of the most trenchant criticisms of organizational culture as a field of study is that it is fragmented and lacks coherence. In this respect, Martin and Frost (1996) posit that there are, in fact, four different perspectives on organizational culture that vary in the extent to which culture is integrated within the organization, or otherwise differentiated or fragmented.

The first of Martin and Frost's (1996; see also Meyerson and Martin, 1991) perspectives is *integration*. In this view, organizational culture is seen to consist of an organized set of common values (cf. Schein, 1992). These values, in turn, shape the ways in which organizational members understand organizational experiences. Organizational culture in this view focuses on the consistencies of values, attitudes, and behaviors within a particular organization that distinguish it from others. The implications of this approach are that a common set of values is seen to exist within each organization. Further, proponents of this view (e.g. Peters and Waterman, 1982) would see the benefits in promoting a consistent set of values throughout the organization. This then allows organizational members to work together in a coordinated manner, based on a common set of values. To a large extent, the integration perspective is the lay conceptualization of organizational culture, where each organization is characterized by its own unique culture (e.g. as in Peters and Waterman, 1980). But, as Martin and Frost argue, this is an oversimplification of culture. The remaining three perspectives make this clear.

The second of Martin and Frost's (1996) perspectives is *differentiation*. Under this perspective, different cultures associated with different values and practices can coexist within the one organization (see Sackmann, 1991; Trice and Beyer, 1993, Turner, 1971). The intra-organizational "subculture" differences are brought about through differences in management practices and human resource policies in different parts of the organization that are occasioned by different environmental and resource contingencies, both formal and informal. Subcultures also form around the diversities inherent to the work force such as occupational grouping, functional or geographic location, and even ethnicity, gender, and culture (Trice and Beyer, 1993). Thus, for example, while all organizational units can think of themselves as a part of the collective team, the culture in the R&D department is likely to be distinct from the culture in the manufacturing department, which, in turn, will differ from that found in sales. Essentially, the different themes all center on how organization members construe meanings based on the value criteria that are relevant in their subculture. The fact that there may be different subcultures within the one organization, however, does not negate the authenticity of organizational culture. It's just that organizations in themselves can consist of suborganizations, each with a different variant of the organization's culture. When the subcultures are aligned with different goals, however, subculture conflict can become problematical.

The third perspective is *fragmentation*. In this view, culture does not exist in the sense of the previous two perspectives. Fragmentation assumes that meanings within the organization are diverse and disorganized. Management practice and human resource policies in this view lack cohesion both at organizational and at suborganizational levels. As a consequence, influence strategies are unpredictable. Culture here plays no role in shaping organizational members' views either of their organization or of their environment. While the pluralist view of organizational culture (as reflected, for example, in chapter 10b) would support this view, I maintain that the vast accumulation of contrary research evidence (e.g. see Ashkanasy et al., 2000a; Cooper et al., 2001) makes it difficult to sustain this perspective as anything more than a rare phenomenon.

The final perspective is *postmodern*. In this view, organization sense making is based on power perceptions. Here culture becomes an artifact of analysis, and meanings emerge as no more than the expression of power (see also Hardy, 1995). In a more radical sense, culture may be seen as a rhetorical device deployed by managerial elites as part of a panoply of control mechanisms. Martin and Frost (1996) advocated the postmodernist perspective as an addition to the three originally propounded in Martin (1992) and Meyerson and Martin (1991), and it represents perhaps the strongest challenge to traditional views of organizational culture. Thus, rather than culture being an authentic phenomenon in organizational science, it emerges as a product of the dynamic interplay among management scholars, where each group tries to promote its own views of culture as a means to establish its own credibility and legitimacy.

Consistent with the view expressed in my *Handbook* introduction (Ashkanasy et al., 2000b), I argue that the postmodernist perspective is little more than a cynical oversimplification of an intrinsically complex phenomenon. In particular, this view assumes that culture scholars are solely interested in achieving power through promulgating a particular stance. Thus, while some might find that they can achieve eminence in pursuing a particular ontological position, there is little evidence to suggest that this practice is anywhere near universal. Further, given the interdisciplinary nature of organizational culture scholarship, it is most unlikely that one or two scholars in particular disciplinary areas will be able to determine the directions of scholarship for more than a brief period of time.

In summary, while the fragmentation and postmodernist perspectives on organizational culture are typical of the robust debate that is so often generated in the organization sciences (e.g., as represented in Clegg et al., 1996, and by the contributions to this book), the influence of these perspectives serve paradoxically to emphasize the relevance of the culture concept in the management disciplines. Further, since Martin (1992) published her thesis that organizational cultures within organizations can take such different forms, scholars seem to have lost sight of the possibility that the different forms can coexist. Thus a company-wide organizational culture can still be maintained, even if subunits of the company manifest different cultural values, and irrespective of whether or not management scholars are pursuing their own ends in a power game. I argue that the construct of organizational culture exists in one form or another at every level of the organization, starting with individual values, and that diversity of cultural perspectives and types does not diminish the idea of culture. In the following section I develop this idea further through discussion of the role of personal value systems in shaping organizational culture.

Organizational Culture as a Value System

Although often misrepresented or misinterpreted, personal values lie at the root of attitudes and behavior (Ajzen and Fishbein, 1980). The organizational context is no exception (Becker and Connor, 1986). In this component of my case, I argue that values constitute a fundamental component of social interaction, and comprise the most basic element of organizational culture. Consequently, to deny organizational culture is, in effect, to ignore

the role within organizational settings of a fundamental dimension of human cognition: human values.

Values provide an especially cogent vehicle for linking the psychological and anthropological views of organizational culture. Ashkanasy et al. (2000b) argue that values have meaning in both disciplines. This is because values can be construed to exist at multiple levels. They can be defined in social, cognitive, or behavioral terms. Thus values at the social level embody the understandings that the members of a society have experienced in their historical development. In this case, values are primarily cognitive in nature. They therefore represent deeply held beliefs about the unfolding of the society's norms. Consequently, values are also reflected in behavior. For example, rites, rituals, and ceremonies engaged in by particular societies serve to reinforce values. At a deeper level, values underpin the way in which members of societies and organizations interact with one another in everyday exchanges. Ashkanasy et al. (2000b) note further, however, that the difficulty with values is that they are often applied differently to different concepts. Indeed, because values emerge from historical experience, the same value label can be applied to quite different phenomena at different levels of analysis (see Rousseau, 1985).

Interestingly, and perhaps counterintuitively, the values construct constitutes one area where the psychological and anthropological views intersect. Thus, while the psychological view is that values represent individual differences among an organization's members, the anthropological sense of values simply extends it to the level of community values. Hulin and Blood's (1968) work, showing that socialization into communities determine members' value preferences, would seem to support this idea. As such, values as individual differences are not just a function of heredity or of random variation. Consequently, societal values antedate individual values. From an organizational perspective, this implies also that individual members bring to the organization a set of pre-existing personal values based on their society's norms and values. A corollary of this argument is that organizations do not exist in a societal vacuum, and that ideas and concepts derived from the discipline of anthropology provide critical insights into the development of organizational culture. Within the organizational domain, however, these values are represented at the individual level – the domain of organizational psychology. In effect, organizational culture represents a critical synergistic relationship between the psychological and anthropological view, in contrast to the irreconcilable views that many detractors of organizational culture suggest is applicable.

It follows from the foregoing that the application of concepts based on values is justified in organizational climate research. Indeed, values provide the critical link for organizational culture researchers that enable them to move easily between the idea of studying cultural dimensions based on value dimensions and the more broadly defined concept of organizational culture that includes behaviors and practices. Ashkanasy et al. (2000b) emphasize in particular "values seem such a natural part of a society's cultural tradition that it is surprising that organizational culture research did not take value dimensions from some source in cultural anthropology" (p. 10). They explained that this might be because anthropologists were slow to make the transition from the study of ancient culture to modern organizations. Indeed, more than fifty years ago Kroeber and Kluckhohn (1951) emphasized the importance of values in the definition of culture.

A major impetus for bringing societal values into the organizational culture domain was provided in Hofstede's (1980) analysis of culture differences in IBM offices in forty national cultures. Hofstede and Peterson (2000) note further that the Hofstede (1980) analysis of national culture was based on a taxonomy of societal issues identified by Inkeles and Levinson (1969). While Hofstede's work has been influential, the predominant approach to values in organizational culture research has not been derived from studies of societal culture, however. Instead, two more direct approaches have been adopted, as I discuss next.

The first of the direct approaches to studying culture as values is based on the work of Rokeach (1968, 1973). Rokeach was interested in the way that individuals in society structure their values in categories he described as

instrumental and *terminal*. Although perhaps more in the climate research tradition of Rokeach, various researchers have adapted his approach to organizations (see Stackman et al., 2000; Rose et al., 2000; Sagiv and Schwartz, 2000). The second is based on the competing values model developed by Quinn and Rohrbaugh (1983). Again, this approach is akin to the early climate studies, but can be applied powerfully to describe cultural dimensions in applied contexts (see Zammuto et al., 2000).

One problem with the values model, particularly those based on Hofstede (1980), Rokeach (1973), and Quinn and Rohrbaugh (1983), is that these approaches seek in essence to identify particular value dimensions that can be used to compare across organizations. Martin and Frost (1996), among others, refute this position, and argue that culture cannot be reduced to a set of quantitatively determined dimensions. Still, the alternatives that are derived from an ostensibly anthropological position seem incapable of coming up with a consistent means to describe cultures in a manner that enables organizations to be compared systematically. The postmodern and critical approaches (e.g., Alvesson, 1983; Alvesson and Deetz, 1996) seem largely to sidestep this issue, as does the counterpoint chapter here. Whilst I acknowledge that there are difficulties in capturing the breadth and depth of something as deeply embedded in the human psyche as cultural values, I am concerned that, without the values conceptualization, scholars are not going to be able to analyze organizations or societies in a manner that will allow the kind of understanding at the *individual* levels that will advance our understanding at the *organizational* level.

Still, it is clear from the foregoing that there remains considerable controversy as to the extent that organizational culture can be captured in terms of objective and reliable measures. As I have argued earlier (e.g. Ashkanasy et al., 2000b; Ashkanasy and Jackson, 2001), and consistent with Kluckhohn and Strodtbeck (1961) and Rokeach (1968), I posit that there must be certain universal values that underpin human attitudes and behavior. Without identification of these values, it is difficult to see how our understanding of organizations can progress.

Even postmodernist theorists need to have a set of communicable labels with which to describe the behavior of individuals, organizations, and societies (Gergen, 1996). Ashkanasy et al. (2000b) argue further that, even if the issue of universal values is debatable, surely there must be a set of universally recognized issues, functions, and problems that people in societies must deal with. In today's global world, this point takes on added validity.

In this discussion of values and organizational culture, I have argued that values lie at the core of culture. In this view, values link the psychological and anthropological perspectives of culture that, on the surface at least, may be seen to be antagonistic. I thus argue that, far from being antagonistic, the psychological and anthropological perspectives on values are complementary. Values therefore reinforce the case for culture. Whilst I acknowledge that there continue to be some important unresolved issues in values research, particularly relating to levels of analysis and measurement, the thrust of my argument is that cultural value dimensions lie at the core of our understanding of organizational functioning. In particular, even if the issue of universal values were arguable, few would dispute the issue that there are universal problems that all societies, and consequently organizations, face. The values that underlie organizational culture would seem therefore to provide a workable means to compare across societies and organizations, and possibly the only viable means to understand how individuals, organizations, and societies deal with their common problems.

Organizational Culture and Organizational Climate

I have noted earlier that organizational climate historically antedates organizational culture in the literature (Reichers and Schneider, 1990), and is frequently confused with the culture construct. Indeed, while culture and climate are conceptually distinct, they are nevertheless closely related in a phenomenological sense (Denison, 1996). The point I make here is that organizational climate is already accepted as an identifiable construct in organizational studies, at least within the tradition that has flowed from Likert's (1961) work. As a consequence, and within this view, organizational culture must also be an identifiable construct if it is to be related to climate.

This issue lies at the core of why we need to study organizations as complete entities of human organization. Scholars such as Trice and Beyer (1993), for example, have been careful to provide definitions of culture that meet the aims of their discourse on the topic. In this respect, the theoretical line taken serves to shape the arguments that follow. In many ways, the theoretical view of the protagonist may be the only distinction between culture and climate, or between different definitions and descriptions within culture and climate. Ashkanasy et al. (2000b: 7) suggest that a "common law approach," or working from common usage, may be the best way to view definitions of culture and climate. They argue further that the common law approach explains why different researchers and different research ontologies have adapted Lewin's conceptualization of climate over the years, until the concepts of climate and culture seem almost entirely to have merged. In this view, both climate and culture are often defined in terms of attitudes collectively or individually held by organizational members (e.g., see Payne, 2000). Indeed, the most recent *Handbook* (Cooper et al., 2001) to assume this view. Apart from one chapter (Payne, 2001), culture and climate in the Cooper et al. *Handbook* appear to be undifferentiated, and even Payne's contribution proffers climate and culture as equal precursors of *cultural* change.

Of course, for many anthropologists and, indeed, for my counterpoint author, the idea of culture as a set of measurable attitudinal dimensions is anathema. In this respect, understanding is achievable only through a holistic approach and ethnographic research (e.g., see Schein, 1992). But this is still intrinsically a narrow perspective – as narrow as a psychologist's view that everything must be measured as a set of quasi-objective attitudinal dimensions. In this respect, the common law of climate and culture will dictate which view is most appropriate, given the ontology, epistemology, and methods that are most applicable in each circumstance.

Payne (2000) provides an exemplary illustration of the contingent use of climate as culture. Using a questionnaire measure of "cultural intensity," Payne argues that it is possible to differentiate between Martin's (1995) concepts of cultural integration, diversification, and fragmentation. Taking this argument a step further, Payne used quantitative measures of pervasiveness, intensity, and cultural context to describe unique cultures of integration and fragmentation in the organizations that he studies (Payne reiterates this approach in his 2001 article). This point is reinforced when measures of culture and climate surveys are constructed to reflect the unique features of particular organizations. In the next section I develop this idea further in a discussion of measures of culture and climate.

In summary, it is becoming increasingly difficult to draw the line between culture and climate. While purists would like to maintain the distinction, common usage is tending to blur the distinction. In this chapter, however, I reiterate the view, consistent with Denison (1996), that, while the constructs are conceptually distinct, they are nonetheless closely related phenomena.

Measurement of Organizational Culture and Climate

The point that emerges from my earlier discussion, that culture and climate need not be so sharply differentiated, is controversial and is disputed by my counterpart (10(b)), but it nevertheless represents an important foundation of the case for culture presented in chapter 10(a). This point is especially salient in respect of measurement issues. The concept of climate fits paradigmatically within the perspective of scientific realism. As such, methodology is driven by an objectivist epistemology (Lincoln and Guba, 1989). If it is indeed true that culture and climate overlap phenomenologically, then it follows that methods developed in respect of climate may well have legitimate counterparts in respect of culture. This is at the core of quantitative measures of culture, and drives the current popularity of survey culture measures in management consulting practice (e.g., see Cooke and Szumal, 2000).

A further corollary of this line of argument, identified by Smircich (1983), is that culture can be viewed in two ways: something an organization *has*, or is it something an organization *is*? Given the phenomenological overlap of culture and climate identified in earlier discussion, it follows that culture, like climate, is measurable, and therefore is appropriately viewed as something an organization *has*. This point is reinforced by Martin's (1992) position that organizational culture is best assessed using multiple models. Although an advocate of the interpretivist view of organizational culture, and clearly unlikely to advocate a survey approach to culture measurement, Martin clearly implies that culture is something that can be measured, at least in part. In this section, therefore, I discuss measurement of culture as an analog of climate, and therefore amenable to quantitative assessment through measurement.

I have already pointed out that surveys have been widely used to measure climate, beginning with Likert's (1961) pioneering work. As I have also noted, the same approach has been employed to measure dimensions of culture. Overshadowing the overlap of culture and climate as constructs, however, is that elusive nature of the dimensions that comprise these constructs. Over recent years, there has been an explosion of measures of climate and culture, with a bewildering array of different dimensional structures proffered (see Rousseau, 1990). Ashkanasy et al. (2000) classified measures of culture into two broad categories: typing and profile measures. The Organizational Culture Inventory (OCI: Cooke and Rousseau, 1988) is an example of a measure used to identify different culture "types" among organizations. These measures are in contrast to profiling measures, that are designed to "profile" organizations, based on particular dimensions of culture, such as "leadership," "communication," human relations," and so on. Ashkanasy and his associates also identified three groups of profiling surveys. The first of these are *effectiveness surveys* that are designed to focus on cultural dimensions assumed to be related to high levels of organizational performance. Effectiveness surveys (e.g. Woodcock, 1989), because of their performance focus, are relatively common. The second group of profiling surveys comprises *descriptive surveys*. These do not purport to relate directly to organizational effectiveness or performance, but instead measure a range of value dimensions that characterize particular organizations or societal groupings. These surveys are also relatively frequently encountered in the literature, perhaps the best known being Hofstede's (1980) instrument. The third group of profiling surveys comprises *fit profiles*. These measure are designed to measure the extent to which members of the organization "fit" the organization's culture, often defined in terms of the match between culture at management and shop-floor level (e.g. O'Reilly et al., 1991).

As I noted earlier, the central problem with multidimensional questionnaire measures of organizational culture is the difficulty of defining and distinguishing dimensions. Ashkanasy et al. (2000) discuss this problem in respect of development of the ten-dimensional Organizational Culture Profile (OCP). The dimensions of this measure were arrived at following an extensive literature review, but factor analysis indicated that only two dimensions, Instrumental and Expressive, were statistically discernible. Ashkanasy and his colleagues concluded that the more highly dimensional models of organizational culture have applicability for specific problem areas, while the broader dimensions are needed to meet validity and reliability criteria. A similar issue emerges in respect of Cooke and Rousseau's (1988) more widely used OCI. As I noted earlier, this is a typing instrument, based on twelve norms. In practice, however, and similar to the OCP, the OCI recognizes three broader categories, each encompassing four related norms. These categories are labeled Constructive, Passive–defensive, and Aggressive–defensive, respectively (Cooke and Szumal, 2000).

Interestingly, Cooke and Szumal (2000) note that culture, as defined by the OCI categories, can be "bypassed" under certain conditions. Thus external contingencies, especially those involving special resources, proprietary technologies, or standardized products, may demand a particular business culture which may not be consistent with organizational members' values, and may even be inimical to the longer-term success of the organization. In this instance, technology and structure determine operating systems and procedures, even if these are inconsistent with the organization's inherent culture. In the following section I take this idea further, in a discussion of the relationship between culture and organizational effectiveness.

In summary, and despite technical issues such as type versus profile and dimensionality, and the deeper issues of construct validity, questionnaire measures seem to have become widely adopted and recognized measures of culture. The worldwide commercial popularity of the OCI (see Cook and Szumal, 2000) attests to this. Cook and Szumal's identification of culture bypass, however, points to the importance of seeing cultural profiles and types in the context of organizational contingencies. In the respect, measures of culture provide only one, albeit important, window on the inner workings of organizational culture and climate.

Organizational Culture and Performance

The final argument I present in support of the organizational culture construct relates to the effect of culture on performance. Consistent with Kotter and Heskett (1992), however, I argue that the link is not necessarily direct. The issue is not so much that strong culture is associated with performance, but that performance is predicated on the fit between culture and the organization's objectives. This applies both to the *nature* and to the *strength* of the culture. Depending upon circumstance, a strong culture may enhance or inhibit organizational performance. Further, given the arguments I have presented earlier that culture is a multilevel construct, it remains a challenge to researchers to demonstrate the effects of culture on performance.

A further problem in establishing the nexus between culture and performance concerns the measurement of organizational performance. Wilderom et al. (2000) discuss this issue at some length, and conclude that uncertainty in performance measurement is more of a concern than are issues of culture measurement. Thus, while performance measures such as share price, return on investment, and sales volumes are ostensibly concrete, problems of accounting and time scale render the interpretation of overall organizational effectiveness questionable. In this respect, Ashkanasy and Jackson (2001) argue that, while there is widespread concurrence with the idea that something as abstract as organizational performance can be measured, it's odd that an impression has emerged that an equally abstract phenomenon, organizational culture, cannot be measured.

Finally, I note a different slant on this argument, advanced by Wiley and Brookes (2000). Similar to Cooke and Szumal (2000), Wiley and Brookes argue that positive culture and climate are components of what they refer to as "high-performing organizations." In their "Linkage Research Model" members' personal performance goals and achievements are an integral part of the organization's culture. In this respect, culture, climate, effectiveness, and performance merge into one overall montage of the organization.

Conclusion

In chapter 10(a) I have proffered five reasons to support the idea that culture is an authentic phenomenon. Specifically, I have argued that organizational culture coexists at multiple organizations levels, that culture is derived from organization members' value systems, that climate is linked to organizational climate, that culture can be measured, and, finally, that culture is associated with performance, although not necessarily in a straightforward fashion. Moreover, I have stressed that culture, because of its relationships with other variables, including climate, effectiveness, and performance, is intrinsically a complex and multifaceted phenomenon. In particular, one of the critical challenges facing organizational culture researchers is to identify the effects of culture at different organizational levels. If this can be accomplished, then we will have a much clearer understanding of this complex yet important phenomenon.

In effect, the uncertainty and confusion that have surrounded organizational culture since its modern emergence in 1973 reflect the developmental nature of the construct itself. To this extent, I am in agreement with the position in chapter 10(b). The ontological

confusion is further exacerbated by the murkiness of organizational systems in general. As Wiley and Brookes (2000) posit, however, culture cannot easily be separated from ostensibly equally mysterious phenomena such as climate, effectiveness, and performance. But no one seriously doubts the legitimacy of these constructs. My point is that culture is no less authentic than organizational performance or effectiveness, and equally deserving of research attention in the foreseeable future.

Acknowledgment

My thanks go to the editors for their constructive comments on drafts of this chapter.

References

Ajzen, I., and Fishbein, M. (1980) *Understanding Attitudes and Predicting Social Behavior.* Englewood Cliffs, NJ: Prentice Hall.

Alvesson, M. (1993) *Cultural Perspectives on Organizations.* Cambridge: Cambridge University Press.

Alvesson, M., and Deetz, S. (1996) "Critical theory and postmodern approaches to organizational studies," in S. R. Clegg, C. Hardy, and W. R. Nord, *Handbook of Organization Studies*, pp. 191–217. Thousand Oaks, CA: Sage.

Ashkanasy, N. M., and Jackson, C. R. A. (2001) "Organizational culture and climate," in N. Anderson, D. S. Ones, H. K. Sinangil, and C. Viswesvaran (eds) *Handbook of Work and Organizational Psychology*, pp. 398–415. Thousand Oaks, CA: Sage.

Ashkanasy, N. M., Broadfoot, L., and Falkus, S. (2000) "Questionnaire measures of organizational culture," in N. M. Ashkanasy, C. P. M. Wilderom, and M. F. Peterson, *Handbook of Organizational Culture and Climate*, pp. 131–46. Thousand Oaks, CA: Sage.

Ashkanasy, N. M., Wilderom, C. P. M., and Peterson, M. F., eds (2000a) *Handbook of Organizational Culture and Climate.* Thousand Oaks, CA: Sage.

——(2000b) "Introduction," in N. M. Ashkanasy, C. P. M. Wilderom, and M. F. Peterson, *Handbook of Organizational Culture and Climate*, pp. 1–18. Thousand Oaks, CA: Sage.

Becker, B. W., and Connor, P. E. (1986) "On the status and promise of values research," *Management Bibliographies and Reviews*, 12: 3–17.

Clegg, S. R., Hardy, C., and Nord, W. R., eds (1996) *Handbook of Organization Studies*. Thousand Oaks, CA: Sage

Cooke, R. A., and Rousseau, D. M. (1988) "Behavioral norms and expectations: a quantitative approach to the assessment of organizational culture," *Group and Organization Studies*, 13: 245–73.

Cooke, R. A., and Szumal, J. L. (2000) "Using the Organizational Culture Inventory to understand the operating cultures of organizations," in N. M. Ashkanasy, C. P. M. Wilderom, and M. F. Peterson, *Handbook of Organizational Culture and Climate*, pp. 147–62. Thousand Oaks, CA: Sage.

Cooper, C. L., Cartwright, S., and Earley, P. C. (2001) *The International Handbook of Organizational Culture and Climate*. Chichester: Wiley.

Deal, T. E., and Kennedy, A. A. (1982) *Corporate Culture: The Rites and Rituals of Corporate Life*. Reading, MA: Addison-Wesley.

de Geus, A. (1997) *The Living Company*. Boston, MA: Harvard Business School Press.

Denison, D. R. (1996) "What *is* the difference between organizational culture and organizational climate? A native's point of view on a decade of paradigm wars," *Academy of Management Review*, 21: 619–54.

——(1990) *Corporate Culture and Organizational Effectiveness*. New York: Wiley.

Gadamer, H-G. (1989) *Truth and Method*, trans. J. Weinsheimer and D. G. Marshall, second edition. New York: Crossroads.

Gergen, K. J. (1996) "Social psychology as social construction: the emerging vision," in C. McGarty and A. Haslam (eds) *The Message of Social Psychology: Perspectives on Mind in Society*, pp. 113–128. Oxford: Blackwell.

Hardy, C., ed. (1995) *Power and Politics in Organizations*. Aldershot: Dartmouth Press.

Hofstede, G. (1980) *Culture's Consequences: International Differences in Work-related Values*. Beverly Hills, CA: Sage.

Hofstede, G., and Peterson, M. F. (2000) "Culture: national values and organizational practices," in N. M. Ashkanasy, C. P. M. Wilderom, and M. F. Peterson, *Handbook of Organizational Culture and Climate*, pp. 401–16. Thousand Oaks, CA: Sage.

Hulin, C. L., and Blood, M. R. (1968) "Job enlargement, individual differences, and worker responses," *Psychological Bulletin*, 69: 41–55.

Inkeles, A., and Levinson, D. J. (1969) "National character: the study of modal personality and sociocultural systems," in G. Lindzey and E. Aronson (eds) *The Handbook of Social Psychology*, second edition, pp. 418–506. Reading, MA: Addison-Wesley.

Jaques, E. (1951) *The Changing Culture of a Factory*. London: Tavistock Institute.

Kluckhohn, C., and Strodtbeck, F. L. (1961) *Variations in Value Orientations*. Evanston, IL: Row Peterson.

Kotter, J. P., and Heskett, J. L. (1992) *Corporate Culture and Performance*. New York: Free Press.

Kroeber, A. L., and Kluckhohn, C. (1952) *Culture: A Critical Review of Concepts and Definitions*. Cambridge, MA: Harvard University Peabody Museum of American Archeology and Ethnology.

Lewin, K. (1948) *Resolving Social Conflicts*. New York: Harper.

——(1951) *Field Theory in Social Psychology*. New York: Harper.

Lewin, K., Lippitt, R., and White, R. K. (1939) "Patterns of aggressive behavior in experimentally created climates," *Journal of Social Psychology*, 10: 271–99.

Likert, R. (1961) *New Patterns of Management*. New York: McGraw-Hill.

Lincoln, Y. S., and Guba, E. G. (1989) *Naturalistic Inquiry*. Beverly Hills, CA: Sage.

Martin, J. (1992) *Culture in Organizations: Three Perspectives*. New York: Oxford University Press.

——(1995) "Organizational culture," in N. Nicholson (ed.) *Encyclopedic Dictionary of Organizational Behaviour*, pp. 376–82. Oxford: Blackwell.

Martin, J., and Frost, P. (1996) "The organizational culture war games: a struggle for intellectual dominance," in S. R. Clegg, C. Hardy, and W. R. Nord (eds) *Handbook of Organization Studies*, pp. 599–621. Thousand Oaks, CA: Sage.

Meyerson, D., and Martin, J. (1991) "Cultural change: an integration of three different views," *Journal of Management Studies*, 18: 1–26.

O'Reilly, C. A., Chatman, J. A., and Caldwell, D. (1991) "People and organizational culture: a profile comparison approach to assessing person–organization fit," *Academy of Management Journal*, 34: 487–516.

Ouchi, W. (1981) *Theory Z: How American Business can meet the Japanese Challenge*. Reading, MA: Addison-Wesley.

Payne, R. L. (2000) Climate and culture: how close can they get?" in N. M. Ashkanasy, C. P. M. Wilderom, and M. F. Peterson (eds) *Handbook of Organizational Culture and Climate*, pp. 163–76. Thousand Oaks, CA: Sage.

——(2001) "A three-dimensional framework for analyzing and assessing organizational culture/climate and its relevance to cultural change," in C. L. Cooper, S. Cartwright, and P. C. Earley (eds) *The International Handbook of Organizational Culture and Climate*, pp. 107–22. Chichester: Wiley.

Peters, T. J., and Waterman, R. H. (1982) *In Search of Excellence: Lessons from America's Best-run Companies*. New York: Harper & Row.

Pettigrew, A. M. (1973) *The Politics of Organizational Decision Making*. London: Tavistock Institute.

Quinn, R. E., and Rohrbaugh, J. (1983) "A spatial model of effectiveness criteria: toward a competing values approach to organizational analysis," *Management Science*, 29: 363–77.

Reichers, A. E., and Schneider, B. (1990) "Climate and culture: an evolution of constructs," in B. Schneider (ed.) *Organizational Climate and Culture*, pp. 5–39. San Francisco: Jossey-Bass.

Rokeach, M. (1968) *Beliefs, Attitudes and Values: A Theory of Organization and Change*. San Francisco: Jossey-Bass.

——(1973) *The Nature of Human Values*. New York: Free Press.

Rose, G. M., Kahle, L. R., and Shoham, A. (2000) "Role relaxation and organizational culture: a social values perspective," in N. M. Ashkanasy, C. P. M. Wilderom, and M. F. Peterson (eds) *Handbook of Organizational Culture and Climate*, pp. 437–46. Thousand Oaks, CA: Sage.

Rousseau, D. M. (1985) "Issues of level in organizational research: multi-level and cross-level perspectives," in L. Cummings and B. M. Staw (eds) *Research in Organizational Behavior* VII, pp. 1–37. Greenwish, CT: JAI Press.

——(1990) "Assessing organizational culture: the case for multiple methods," in B. Schneider (ed.) *Organizational Climate and Culture*, pp. 153–92. San Francisco: Jossey-Bass.

Sackmann, S. A. (1991) *Cultural Knowledge in Organizations: Exploring the Collective Mind*. Newbury Park, CA: Sage.

Sagiv, L., and Schwartz, S. H. (2000) "A new look at national culture: illustrative applications to role stress and managerial behavior," in N. M. Ashkanasy, C. P. M. Wilderom, and M. F. Peterson (eds) *Handbook of Organizational Culture and Climate*, pp. 417–36. Thousand Oaks, CA: Sage.

Schein, E. H. (1990) "Organizational culture," *American Psychologist*, 45: 109–19.

——(1992) *Organizational Culture and Leadership*, second edition. San Francisco: Jossey-Bass.

Schultz M., and Hatch, M. J. (1996) "Living with multiple paradigms: the case of paradigm interplay in organizational culture studies," *Academy of Management, Review*, 21: 529–57.

Shotter, J. (1993) *Cultural Politics of Everyday Life: Social Constructionism, Rhetoric and Knowing of the Third Kind*. Buckingham: Open University Press.

Smircich, L. (1983) "Concepts of culture and organizational analysis," *Administrative Science Quarterly*, 28: 339–58.

Stackman, R. W., Pinder, C. C., and Connor, P. E. (2000) "Values lost: redirecting research on values in the workplace," in N. M. Ashkanasy, C. P. M. Wilderom, and M. F. Peterson (eds) *Handbook of Organizational Culture and Climate*, pp. 37–54. Thousand Oaks, CA: Sage.

Thatchenkery, T. J. (1996) "Organizational learning, language games and knowledge creation," *Journal of Organizational Change Management*, 9: 4–11.

Trice, H. M., and Beyer, J. M. (1993) *The Culture of Work Organizations*. Englewood Cliffs, NJ: Prentice Hall.

Turner, B. A. (1971) *Exploring the Industrial Subculture*. London: Macmillan.

Weick, K. (1995) *Sensemaking in Organizations*. London: Sage.

Wilderom, C. P. M., Glunk, U., and Maslowski, R. (2000) "Organizational culture as a predictor of organizational performance," in N. M. Ashkanasy, C. P. M. Wilderom, and M. F. Peterson (eds) *Handbook of Organizational*

Culture and Climate, pp. 193–210. Thousand Oaks, CA: Sage.

Wiley, J. W., and Brookes, S. (2000) "The high-performance organizational climate: how workers describe top-performing units," in N. M. Ashkanasy, C. P. M. Wilderom, and M. F. Peterson, *Handbook of Organizational Culture and Climate*, pp. 177–92. Thousand Oaks, CA: Sage.

Woodcock, M. (1989) *Clarifying Organizational Values*. Aldershot: Gower.

Woods, J. A. (1997) "The six values of a quality culture," *National Productivity Review*, 16 (2): 49–55.

Zammuto, R. F., Gifford, B., and Goodman, E. (2000) "Managerial ideologies, organization culture and the outcomes of innovation: a competing values perspective," in N. M. Ashkanasy, C. P. M. Wilderom, and M. F. Peterson (eds) *Handbook of Organizational Culture and Climate*, pp. 261–78. Thousand Oaks, CA: Sage.

10b Instantiative versus Entitative Culture: The Case for Culture as Process

Andrew Chan

My interlocutor has argued in chapter 10(a) that conceptions of organization culture will consolidate and merge, in a way that will be similar to the concept of organizational climate within its indigenous discipline of organizational psychology. For organizational psychologists, culture in organizations is treated as shared meanings and as a variable, much as is organizational climate. He believes that accommodation and convergence of climate and culture studies will take place under the universal adoption of a "common law approach" in which differences in research and ontology will become entirely superseded and merged in a unified science.

It is said that such a convergence in organizational climate research has happened in organizational psychology, but not in organizational culture studies, because:

[T]here remains considerable controversy as to the extent that organizational culture can be captured in terms of objective and reliable measures ... there must be certain universal values that underpin human attitudes and behaviors. Without identifying these values, it is difficult to see how our understanding of organizations can progress. (Ashkanasy, p. 304 above).

In the twelve-year period between 1990 and 2001 three major handbooks were published: *Organizational Climate and Culture* (Schneider,

1990), *Handbook of Organizational Culture and Climate* (Ashkanasy et al., 2000), and the *International Handbook of Organizational Culture and Climate* (Cooper et al., 2001). Leading researcher of climate and editor of the first *Handbook*, Benjamin Schneider, and the more contemporary editor of the second *Handbook*, Neal Ashkanasy, believe that climate and culture are very similar concepts, a belief that is in line with closely held assumptions of their parent disciplines of industrial and organizational psychology.

Schneider contributed to the opening chapters of both the first and second *Handbooks*. In these two chapters he provided an account and an update, respectively, of the evolution of the two constructs, pointing out the elements for a concept to be invented, discovered, and borrowed successfully from another field (Reichers and Schneider, 1990; Schneider, 2000). He reviewed the state of the development of climate and culture, and he traced the "psychological life" of the two constructs over that ten-year time frame. My reading of the two lead chapters in the first and second *Handbooks*, i.e., Reichers and Schneider (1990) and Schneider (2000), respectively, actually leads me to see a very different portrait – and that the process of identification of culture as a "useful" applied concept with that of climate may be less smooth than some suggest.

First, Schneider argued that the indigenous construct of organizational climate was born within industrial and organizational psychology. Because organizational psychologists and behaviorists are comfortable in pursuing its study, climate has had little resistance in terms of what Schön called the "displacement" or borrowing process (1963, quoted in Morey and Luthan, 1985). Different camps within climate research have "substantial agreement on the appropriateness of the overall research strategy" (Reichers and Schneider, 1990: 25), something that applies only in climate and not in culture research, as we shall see in a moment.

Second, Reichers and Schneider (1990) elaborate on Schön's idea that there are three stages in the displacement process, namely (1) introduction and elaboration, (2) evaluation and augmentation, and (3) consolidation and accommodation. Organizational climate has passed through these three stages of construct development more smoothly than has organizational culture, a concept borrowed from anthropology and sociology. The situation in 1990, as Schneider described it, was that the relative dearth of empirical research and critical review required of the culture construct as a concept in stage 2 had made its advancement towards mature consolidation and accommodation less smooth than had been the case for climate.

Ten years on, Schneider (2000) admitted that culture and climate represent "two parallel, non-overlapping tracks of research that still exist at [the time of] this writing" (p. xix, my additions). Schneider intimated that organizational culture had hardly emerged from the second stage that he had in mind. He remained "perplexed by the denial of the contributions of climate research by many culture scholars" (p. xviii). "From my vantage point, it seems to me that some culture researchers protest too much about the relevance and importance of climate theory and research for their own thinking and research" (p. xviii).

Schneider admitted that climate researchers, but not culture researchers, have been more "prone to see potential overlap in the two concepts or less denial of the other's contributions" (2000: xix). So, given the preparedness of the climate stream of researchers to explore complementary ground, why is there still a

nagging divergence? There are several explanations. First, culture researchers are seen as ignoring climate as a legitimate pursuit in organizational culture studies. Schneider continues: "Trice and Beyer (1993) state that culture is not climate; Martin (1992) does not index the word climate; Schein (1992) dismisses climate and equates it with artifacts" (2000: xviii).

The contest within the culture field has been characterized as a paradigmatic "war game" (Martin and Frost, 1996; Martin, 2001), where culture researchers prefer to follow their own bent and become factional "king of the mountain" (Martin and Frost, 1996). Schneider (2000), however, believes that the warfare, compared to the cessation of hostilities in the climate camp, is because of the relative emphasis on stage 1 versus stage 2 of the displacement process. Given the passage of ten years, there is little sign of convergence, and the dissensus and war games continue.

At issue with the desire for climate and culture to converge is that in the first and second *Handbooks* Schneider continued to believe that organizational climate, "as a more specific construct," has to have a focus, a target, so that climate research has to be a climate for something. In other words climate is best in partnership with a particular referent, as in "climate for service," "climate for well-being," or "climate for safety" (Reichers and Schneider, 1990: 23; Schneider, 2000; Schneider et al., 2000: 25–6). In order for culture to be less amorphous, both climate and culture researchers need to work closely so that the two subfields converge in the third phase of the displacement process that Schneider and Schön have in mind, i.e., consolidation and accommodation. During this stage, Schneider (1990: 7) explains,

controversies wane and reviews of the literature state matter-of-factly what is and is not known. One or two definitions of the construct become generally accepted, and relatively few operationalizations or operationalization procedures dominate. The antecedents and consequences of the concept are well known, and boundary conditions are specified.

Ashkanasy and contributors to the second *Handbook* represent this effort to work towards culture's accommodation and convergence, arguing for a way to "analyze organizations in a manner that will allow *the kind of* understanding that will advance our understanding of organizations" (Ashkanasy, p. 304 above, italics added). The kind of understanding that he has in mind is propelled by the proposition that "cultural value dimensions lie at the core of our understanding of organizational functioning." The assumption is that such understanding assumes a shared universe of problems that all societies and organizations will have to face (ibid.). This notion of sharedness of understanding will be examined later.

Edgar Schein (2000), however, contributes an introductory chapter to the Ashkanasy *Handbook*. Schein entitled it "Sense and nonsense about culture and climate" and he intimated that culture still has to develop from the second stage of concept displacement, that of elaboration and augmentation. On the second phase Reichers and Schneider (1990) consider that:

Critical reviews of the concept appear, [and] address issues of faulty conceptualization, inadequate operationalization, and equivocal empirical results . . . articles appear that attempt to overcome some of the major criticisms and augment preliminary findings. Researchers present data that support the uniqueness of the concept and demonstrate its distinctiveness from other, similar concepts. Reconceptualizations of the construct appear, and it is applied to a variety of theoretical and/or practical problems. (Reichers and Schneider, 1990: 6–7)

Though Schein is not labeled by my counterpart as one of those "detractors of organizational culture" whose predominantly postmodernist perspectives protest the strongest challenge to traditional views of organizational culture, it is ironical that Schein's own approach is not in alignment with the "common law approach."

A chronic issue in conceptualizing "culture" seems to be whether we should think of culture as a "state" or static property of a given group/organization or as a human process of constructing shared meaning that goes on all the time. (Schein, 2000: xxiv)

Although Schein acknowledged the legitimacy of the "common law approach" of "building typologies of cultural 'states' and categories that freeze a given organization at a given point in time" as well as the constructionist approach of "analyzing the moment-to-moment interac-

tions in which members make sense of their experience" (2000: xxv), his "prime objection to questionnaires as research tools for the study of culture is that they force researchers to cast their theoretical nets too narrowly . . . and thereby limit the domain of inquiry" (ibid.: xxvii). I wish to point out that, earlier, Schein held both an interpretive and a positivist approach, shown when he hankered for a positivist hold on an organizational arena of slippery intangibles, arguing that culture was an object capable of standing free of its context: "We cannot build a useful concept if we cannot agree on how to define it, 'measure' it, study it, and apply it in the real world of organizations" (Schein 1991: 243).

Culture as Process

We have seen how leading authorities on organizational climate and culture have already observed that culture's association with the "unsmiling construct of climate" (Schneider, 2000: xx) does not necessarily make the two concepts more likely to converge (Reichers and Schneider, 1990; Schneider 2000). Besides methodological divergence, the psychology stream and their counterparts in anthropology place different emphasis on ontology and the "sharedness" of culture. Culture as a property of a "group" that persists over time in the sense of being unchanging, and is shared, means that there is consensus and no ambiguity. The process view of culture assumes the opposite – treating culture not as entitative structures but as instantiations that give meanings to actions and behaviors. This view suggests that material aspects of organizations are made real only by being given meaning. This meaning giving is seen as a continuous process. Specifically this view is premised on culture being constructed and instantiated in and through meaning giving and sense making (Weick, 1995, 2001).

The treatment of culture as a fixed, unitary, bounded entity has to give way to a sense of fluidity and permeability. It requires also that explanation of cultural forms be situated in a larger context and a wider arena of different forces. We get a glimpse of this aspect in the following comment about the state of research of culture of corporations by anthropologist George Marcus in *Corporate Futures* (1998):

In anthropology, the concept of culture . . . while still defining a coherent group or community, is highly mutable, flexible, open to shaping from many directions at once in its changing environments, and most importantly, a result of constructions continuously debated and contested among its highly independent, even unruly membership. The discourse about corporations as cultures now focuses on this sense of flexibility over solidity, multiplicity over standard models. (Marcus, 1998: 6)

Three further perspectives in the tradition of a process view of culture showcase the limitations of treating culture as a "real" entity. Organizational anthropologists, organization theorists, and ethnomethodologists have proposed several perspectives on understanding culture as process: that of the meaning making in a negotiated order view, an "organic" view, and, in particular, the enactment or sensemaking view. We shall examine these now.

An early study by Strauss et al. (1963) analyzed a hospital as a "negotiated order" whereby the organization was treated as a continuous process of meaning making, negotiating, and organizing. Although the hospital's workplace ethos of "turning out patients in better shape" was shared by all, there were diverse and sometimes contrasting ways of achieving this aim. People were bound by a minimal number of formal rules, and professionals and patients created and sustained a sense of order through negotiating agreements over how individual patients were cared for. These agreements formed into patterns of understanding among members of staff who worked together for periods of time but were still subject to regroup at short notice. New patterns of understandings emerged as and when mini-crises of negotiation broke out, whereby participants made formal decisions or "rules" that persisted until they were forgotten. Both formal and informal arenas were part of a daily round of negotiated order. This processual analysis situated "culture" as the activity of continuously organizing and negotiating order in the surface of everyday activities.

A second processual view questions if there is a clear distinction between "organization" and "nonorganization," and it challenges the boundaries between "organization" and the "social environment." This view posits that it is difficult to maintain a clear boundary because actors acquire their identities not just from their work organizations but also from the wider community and social settings. A static view neglects diversity and processual aspects in culture's reciprocal interaction with the larger contexts that make up the environment in which organization are inserted. In their participant observation study of slaughtermen in an English abattoir, Ackroyd and Crowdy (1990) observed that the value systems as well as the occupational identity of these high-performance slaughtermen were reinforced by and, at the same time, reciprocally challenged the *mores* of their social environment. Their attachment to a work ethos or an organizational culture was both a reflection and procreation of expressive forms that justified these cultural forms and mind sets at their workplace. Such a view regards cultures as by no means static entities but as continually evolving, taking cues from the multiple links they maintain with other cultures. Because culture change is not amenable to any single source of pressure, Ackroyd and Crowdy (1990) believe that managers and consultants who vouch for corporate culture change programs are seen only as indexing the substance of their change efforts on behalf of top-down management fiat or managerial prerogative.

Linstead and Grafton-Small (1992) suggest a third, "organic" view of organizational culture, which may be contrasted with the concepts of corporate culture devised and imposed by management fiat through rites, rituals, and values. Adherents to "strong" corporate cultures contend that shared meanings, beliefs, and values ensure uniqueness in the character of organizations that can become key success factors and sources of competition that are often impenetrable and difficult to imitate. Linstead and Grafton-Small critique this fixed ontology in an "organic view" that explains that workers are not just passive consumers of corporate culture but also engage in a creative process, producing culture from mundane details of their work through innumerable transformations of the dominant culture, adapting it to their interests. One criticism of this "organic approach" is that, nevertheless, it accepts, *a priori*, that there is a dominant culture and a dominant group of managers holding on to it.

In all three examples, the social interactions of groups and participants exploit ambiguities of cultural forms, they adopt forms more expressive of their interests, and even create new forms to answer new circumstances. The foundations of these critiques may be found in arguments related to ethnomethodology. In fact the processual perspective has its strongest foundation in ethnomethodological enquiries (e.g., Sudnow, 1965; Garfinkel, 1967; Sacks, 1972). It is argued that the major issue at stake is the ontology of culture. It is to this we turn next.

Instantiative versus Entitative Culture: the Enactment View

In his well known study of images of organization, Morgan (1986) refers to the enactment view of culture, which he traces back to Garfinkel (1967) and Sudnow (1965), and then sees its emergence in organization studies via Weick (1979). It is worth mentioning that both Garfinkel and Weick were interested in the phenomenological approaches of Alfred Schutz (Garfinkel, 1967: 68, 76, 105–6; Weick, 1989: 194) and Martin Heidegger (Weick, 1995: 43 and 90). Morgan, like Garfinkel and Weick, empathizes with phenomenology and the processual quality of culture. Morgan issues cautions that one should not view culture as a set of distinct variables, in a mechanistic, manipulative, and an instrumental mode. Rather, it is more holographic than mechanistic:

The holographic diffusion of culture means that it pervades activity in a way that is not amenable to direct control. In studies of organizational culture, enactment is seen as being a voluntary process under the direct influence of the actors involved . . . people play an important part in the construction of their realities (1986: 139–40)

Morgan refers to the ways in which ethnomethodology radicalized and deontologized culture and considered it not as a given premise but as embedded in the process of enactment through which people proactively bring their realities into being. The character of the activities and actions between actors takes shape, has its rationality, sense and understandability,

as an outcome of their "accomplishments" (Garfinkel, 1967) or interactions and *ad hoc* improvisations of meanings (e.g., Sudnow, 1965). The focus turns to the interactional processes through which actors create and "accomplish" their world (*instantiate* it) via interpretive schemes that are not necessarily elements of shared meaning systems (*entitative*). Through Sacks's (1972) well known conversational analyses and investigations of supposedly rule-based conversational sequencing, he subsequently rejected a "deterministic model of culture" and reconsidered culture as an "inference-making machine" (Sacks, 1992: 119). Sacks and his followers reject the idea of treating rules of conversational sequence as *given* by culture (Sacks, 1992: 624–32), and concentrate on behavioral and interactional dimensions rather than seeking recourse to commentators (the researchers' key informants) to interpret the "meaning" of their culture.

In Sudnow (1965) it was demonstrated that even in the highly rule-based arenas of jurisprudence administration, where human activities are supposed to be determined by clearly defined rules, the application of specific laws calls upon a series of subjective decisions and contextual knowledge. Judges, lawyers, and legal officers invoke rules as a means of making a particular activity or particular judgment sensible and meaningful to themselves and to others: parties in these processes are involved in an improvised search for and among competing definitions of the situation being considered as well as the definition of the rules that are to be applied.

The commonsensical approach to understanding social exchanges and situations is the hallmark of ethnomethodology. Garfinkel's well known "disruptive studies" (1967) radicalized the Parsonian concept of coordination of activities assumed to be brought about by the motivated compliance of the social actors and by the existence of a finite province of meaning, recognizably displayed and shared through common experience and shared knowledge. This view is close to qualitative aspects of the corporate culture concept when it states that we are able to do those things that we do in organizational life because we are predisposed to act in suitably interrelated ways. The structures of action, as systems with emergent patterns or "culture," become codifiable into a shared social system of understandings and rules that become accessible to and understood by actors of a social collective. The membership of a collectivity is determined through a shared culture, and the actors display their possession of such a common culture. In turn, this culture is itself the defining characteristic of the system as a whole.

In the Parsonian framework, the rationality of action is underpinned by the shared rules and definitions embedded in a culture. In other words, the Parsonian perspective assumes shared understanding and motivated compliance to maintain social structure, without which human interaction becomes incomprehensible and will break down. Since the presumption that mutual understanding and rationality already exist, the shared character of the rules is made implicit and invisible. To make them visible necessitates researchers finding instances in which behavior failed to conform to expectations and hence proving that rules have been violated. The social encounters that Garfinkel arranged as exercises for his students were ones in which failure was engineered to occur. They demonstrated, against Parsonian theory, that when shared understandings break down ordinary social life does not necessarily become impossible. Each of these demonstrations took a familiar setting and introduced a dimension of quite inappropriate behavior: friends were interrogated as to what they meant by remarks such as "How are you?" Students acted as boarders at home, temporarily witnessing exchanges between their family members as if "under a mild amnesia," spouses giving answers randomly, and others endlessly probing for the meaning of words such as in formulations that questioned the mundaneity of expression – "What do you mean, you had a flat tire?" (Garfinkel, 1967: 42–9). Breaking the expectations would mean that it was no longer possible to define meanings and actions as rationally understood and shared. People would not know how to treat them and the encounters would become senseless.

These famous disruptive studies took on familiar social encounters and introduced elements of quite inappropriate behavior to open up taken-for-granted mutual understanding to critical interrogation. Social order did not collapse. Although at the time things got uncomfortable and people were offended, and sometimes it seemed as if it was impossible to make sense of what was going on, no complete failure of mutual understanding occurred.

Social order, it seems, is not as fragile and precarious as Parsons would have us think: in those demonstrations things just ran their course so long the engineered failure did not appear to affect anything in a material way. Even in the face of the attempted breach of expectations and trust, the order of daily life exerted such an imperative and powerful presence that substantive effort was made in order to retain, if at all possible, the things-as-usual character of ordinary life. Whatever character activities and social encounters have, their sense and understandability (what Garfinkel calls their "accountability") must be treated as an *outcome* of their *actions*, their "accomplishment." People make sense of the rationality and understanding of actions only as a result of what people do (*instantiative*) and not as a given premise (*entitative*) of any prior shared meanings and understandings. People collectively use words and actions to construct settings and structures that have real consequences. Everyday realities have a "habit of imposing themselves on us as taken for granted, the ways things are" (Morgan, 1986: 130). The moral order of daily life forms a strong imperative, showing that it is insufficient to use a structuralist treatment of culture as a system of deep meanings "underlying" and "informing" surface interactions symbolically manifested in the rules and decisions of actors.

Morgan recognized that we make sense of the realities of our everyday world by invoking and bringing to bear prior experience and assumptions – essential templates of social behavior that constitute collectively what mainstream organizational theorists call "culture." Morgan comments succinctly:

When we observe culture, whether in an organization or in society at large, we are observing an evolved form of social practice that has been influenced by many complex interactions between people, events, situations, actions, and general circumstances. Culture is always evolving. Though at any given time it can be seen as having a discernible pattern . . . this pattern is an abstraction imposed on the culture from the outside. It is a pattern that helps the observer to make sense of history in retrospect, but it is not synonymous with experience in the culture itself. Our understanding of culture is usually much more *fragmented* and *superficial* than the reality. (1986: 139, emphases added)

Using Sudnow and Garfinkel, Morgan (1986) leads us to see that fragmentation and superficiality in culture are precisely the precarious process of reality construction that allows people to see and understand particular events, objects, actions, or situations in distinct ways. The proactive role that actors play in exchanging, shaping, structuring, and procreating realities lead to the accomplishment and achievement of rationality that takes place *in* and *through* the performance of actions themselves, hence enactment as processual culture. Morgan leads us to see that the tradition of "practical sociology" (Garfinkel, 1967; Sacks, 1972) serves to remind us of the necessity of deontologizing culture so as to consider it as embedded in the enactment of social reality (Morgan, 1986: 128–31).

To conclude, it transpires that for ethnomethodologists and those in organization theory who have learnt from them, such as Weick and Morgan, that a straitjacket evocation of a prelearned set of static rules (or presumed sharedness of understandings) to gauge and recalibrate social behavior will not suffice. We are left with the lesson that the way forward might be to suspend the assumption of a "shared culture" and with it the means–ends rationality of action. A common culture and its presumption have to be suspended and set aside. The understandability of action is not a given premise but becomes available only from the steps people take in their interpretation of the social encounters and activities in front of them. What has been taken for granted needs to be scrutinized; the character of the activities between actors only take shape, if at all, and have their rationality, sense and understandability only as a result and outcome of their actions, their "accomplishments," or *ad hoc* improvisations of meaning. Culture is therefore best seen as a process that constructs and reconstructs meaning in the light of identifiable determinants.

Weick (1995) points out that the characterization of culture should be detached from the tired association and/or equation of culture with the "social glue of shared meaning." Inspired by Weick's "sense making" and its connected comments and links with organizational culture, the direction forward that I want to discuss is to think of culture as a verb.

Thinking of Culture as a Verb

There are refreshing implications about the subtle connections between sense making and culture in Weick (1995), although culture is not the major theme of his book. After reading Weick (1995), we may usefully think of culture as an "enactment process" similar to *post hoc* sense making that, according to Weick, should be treated literally as a "making of sense" (1995: 4, 12–14). Sense making highlights "action over cognition,"and, unlike interpretation, sensemaking is:

clearly about an activity and a process, whereas interpretation can be a process but is just as likely to describe a product. Even when interpretation is treated as a process, the act of interpreting implies that something is there, waiting to be discovered and approximated. Sensemaking, however, is less about discovery than it is about invention. To engage in sensemaking is to construct, filter, frame, create facticity, and to render the subjective into something more tangible. (Ibid.: 13–14)

Sense making also differs from the "negotiated order" view where an order (e.g., an aim, a climate or a work ethic) remains an immanent outcome. Those entitative outcomes and rules of a "negotiated order" form a discernible pattern of shared understanding but they are only an abstraction superimposed on the culture from outside. Sense making highlights localized instantiation of a culture that ethnomethodologists call "evolved forms of social practice" that actors bring to bear on their mundane, everyday life skills in the "making of sense."

Weick's perspective has a distinctive take on culture. Basically, he states that people may have "shared experience" (such as, for example, an outdoor team-building exercise) but it is problematic for actors to have "shared meaning" (Weick 1995: 188). The trouble with that characterization is that, when people examine the things they did to infer what it means, those meanings are idiosyncratic because individuals have different prior experiences. Although people may not share meaning, they do share experience. Weick goes on to explain that this shared experience may be made sensible in retrospect by equivalent meanings, but seldom by similar meanings, because individual background, upbringing, and socialization are too diverse to produce similarity.

If people want to share meaning, they need to talk about their shared experience and hammer out a common way to encode and talk about it. They need to see their joint saying about the experience to learn what they think happened. . . . Novel, joint experience tends to be made meaningful with a common vocabulary. People construct meaning for a shared experience. But . . . to handle the reality of shared experience and unshared meaning, the shared experience [should be] accepted for what it is, and people evoke the same mindset as that associated with shared meaning [by simply recounting] the shared experience in detail. (Weick, 1995: 188–9, my additions)

Recounting the details of the experience is sufficient to establish a common referent. Weick goes on to comment that, for managers to produce a "culture-like effect," they just need to make common experience salient:

Once this happens then people are in a common frame of mind that is not all that different from the frame that is implied when people talk about culture as shared meaning. Culture, in this revised view, is what we have done around here, not what we do around here. (Weick, 1995: 189)

Morgan (1986) suggests treating culture as an enactment process: "culture is an on-going, proactive process of reality construction" (p. 131). Sense making takes up, in trial-and-error fashion, micro-selections and struggles in a "contest of meanings." In his earlier rendition of sense making, Weick describes sense making and its connection with fittedness: "Fittedness is one way retrospectively to make sense of earlier activities. Fitness is a judgmental label that is superimposed on data generated by enactment process after-the-fact" (1979: 185).

Patterns of *post hoc* "sensible accounts" provide a reciprocal basis of justifying one's behavior and decisions. Note that, in this line of thinking, culture is the mediator conducive to arriving at a distinctive interpretation of a situation. I consider that shared meaning is difficult to attain, unless, of course, people's citing of these meanings is sanctioned by management *fiat*. A consensual experience is what individuals may "share," and such experiences are, Weick argues, glue of a different sort from that which managers can hope to attain. So our final implication is this: if people share anything, what they share is actions, activities, moments, and joint tasks. What actors have is shared experiences which are not isomorphically mapped by meaning representations and are, thereby, extremely difficult for managers to engineer or bring into alignment. This points to important implications for managerial practice.

Weick (1979, 1995, 2001) has always believed that closer to the nature of organization is the idea that there are "*issues* to be managed rather than *problems* to be solved." Weick (1995) has pointed out tersely that in organizations people tend to deal with problems, whereas in fact they have issues to deal with. The concretization of features of organizing that is essentially about flows, change, and processes give rise to a control mentality that extends itself to managing fixed entities that are seen as fixable by people. Weick urges managers to "stamp out nouns" in their efforts to understand organizing. Problems are all nouns – fixed entities – such as "quality," "environment," "knowledge," and "organizational culture," things that people believe they can fix and, once fixed, are supposed to stay fixed. Weick observes that managers get defensive, immobilized, and angry if they see the world as filled with problems that cannot be solved once and for all. He believes that issues, though they keep recurring and never go away, are "built largely of trade-offs and dilemmas that keep being resolved due to changes in the context." Since problems are moments of interruption in a process, thinking in terms of verbs reminds people that they are dealing with activities and issues in the environment rather than resistance (Weick, 1995: 188). It is from this angle of deciphering culture that I would argue that the notion be appreciated much more fruitfully as process and as a verb, not as an entity.

Conclusion

Though there are always advantages and disadvantages in using qualitative and quantitative methods, it is argued that the process view of culture is preferable to a quantitative gauging of culture. I have suggested in this chapter the possible difficulties of the quantitative approach to the study of culture. Culture is more appropriately treated as a process of reality construction enabling people to understand and make sense of certain events, action, things, and situations in distinctive ways. Ethnomethodology or "practical sociology" is a perspective most suited to the questioning of (organizational) culture as "manifest phenomenon" because the enactment perspective shows how culture is not just "recipes," "rule-following" "shared meanings" and "value reflection."

Schein (2000) also drew attention to major disadvantages in drawing upon sociopsychological theories in designing questionnaire dimensions that try to take a measure of culture: the deliberate relinquishing of the salience of certain dimensions may be considered to be potent to the degree to which such dimensions are assumed to determine behavior. The advantage of the qualitative approach (ethnographic, ethnomethodogical, and clinical research methods), as Schein (2000: xxvii) points out, is that we can constantly train ourselves to minimize the deterministic and limiting impact of our own models and to remain open in the face of those new experiences and concepts that we may come across.

References

Ackroyd, S., and Crowdy, P. (1990) "Can culture be managed? Working with 'raw' material: the case of the English slaughtermen," *Personnel Review*, 19 (5): 3–13.

Ashkanasy, N., Wilderom, C., and Peterson, M., eds (2000) *Handbook of Organizational Culture and Climate*. Thousand Oaks, CA: Sage.

Cooper, C., Cartwright, S., and Earley, P., eds (2001) *The International Handbook of Organizational Culture and Climate*. New York: Wiley.

Garfinkel, H. (1967) *Studies in Ethnomethodology*. Englewood Cliffs, NJ: Prentice Hall.

Linstead, S., and Grafton-Small, R. (1992) "On reading organizational culture," *Organization Studies*, 13 (3): 331–55.

Marcus, G. (1998) *Corporate Futures: The Diffusion of the Culturally Sensitive Corporate Form*. Chicago: University of Chicago Press.

Martin, J. (1990) "Breaking up the mono-method monopolies in organizational research," in J. Hassard and D. Pym (eds) *The Theory and Philosophy of Organization: Critical Issues and New Perspectives*. London: Routledge.

——(1992) *Cultures in Organizations: Three Perspectives*. Oxford: Oxford University Press.

——(2001) *Organizational Culture: Mapping the Terrain*. London: Sage.

Martin, J., and Frost, P. (1996) "The organizational culture war game: a struggle for intellectual dominance," in S. Clegg et al. (eds) *Handbook of Organization Studies*. London: Sage.

Morey, N., and Luthan, F. (1985) "Redefining the displacement of culture and the use of scenes and themes in organizational studies," *Academy of Management Review*, 10 (2): 219–29.

Morgan, G. (1986) *Images of Organizations*. London: Sage.

Reichers A., and Schneider, B. (1990) "Climate and culture: an evolution of constructs," in B. Schneider (ed.) *Organizational Climate and Culture*. San Francisco: Jossey-Bass.

Sacks, H. (1972) "An initial investigation of the usability of conversational data for doing sociology," in D. Sudnow (ed.) *Studies in Social Interaction*. New York: Free Press.

——(1992) *Lectures on Conversation*, ed. G. Jefferson. Oxford: Blackwell.

Schein, E. (1991) "What is culture?" in P. Frost et al. (eds) *Reframing Organizational Culture*. Newbury Park, CA: Sage.

——(1992) *Organizational Culture and Leadership: A Dynamic View*, second edition. San Francisco: Jossey-Bass.

——(2000) "Sense and nonsense about culture and climate," in N. Ashkanasy et al. (eds) *Handbook of Organizational Culture and Climate*. London: Sage.

Schneider, B., ed. (1990) *Organizational Climate and Culture*. San Francisco: Jossey-Bass.

——(2000) "The psychological life of organizations," in N. Ashkanasy et al. (eds) *Handbook of Organizational Culture and Climate*. London: Sage.

Schneider, B., Bowen, D., Ehrhart, M., and Holcombe, K. (2000) "The climate for service: evolution of a construct," in N. Ashkanasy et al. (eds.) *Handbook of Organizational Culture and Climate*. Thousand Oaks, CA: Sage.

Schön, D. (1963) *Displacement of Concepts*. London: Tavistock.

Strauss, A., Schatzman, L., Ehrlich, D., Bucher, R., and Sabshin, M. (1963) "The hospital and its negotiated order," in E. Friedson (ed.) *The Hospital in Modern Society*. New York: Macmillan.

Sudnow, D. (1965) "Normal crimes: sociological features of the penal code in a public defender office," *Social Problems*, 12: 255–76.

Trice, H., and Beyer, J. (1993) *The Cultures of Work Organizations*. Englewood Cliffs, NJ: Prentice Hall.

Weick, K. (1979) *The Social Psychology of Organizing*, second edition. Reading, MA: Addison-Wesley.

——(1995) *Sensemaking in Organizations*. Thousand Oaks, CA: Sage.

——(2001) *Making Sense of the Organization*. Oxford: Blackwell.

PART IV

Identity and Relationships

11

Gender and Identity

The reader will note a different format to this chapter. Instead of two protagonists in a point-counterpoint structure, we have three scholars discussing issues related to gender and organization in a mutual and collaborative conversational style. Gheradi, Marshall and Mills were not the only contributors to find in the oppositional structure adopted in this book a reproduction of masculinist and/or non-productive orthodox structures and practices. This concern with the debating format is, in a way, a precursor to a collective meditation by this chapter's contributors on the problematic of knowing, talking about, and representing gender from within the prison house of male dominated structures, language and discourse. They clearly recognize, however, that escaping structures such as that deployed in this book does not provide an escape from that prison – the issues are more complex and the bars more extensive.

This position presupposes that the discourses of organizations and of organization theory are gendered and gender biased. This is a widely attested to, but not universally agreed upon, position (Calas and Smircich, 1999; Mills and Tancred, 1992). Gheradi, Marshall and Mills are particularly concerned with the limits and boundaries of ways of thinking about and theorising gender. Rather than trace various philosophical and theorising trajectories, as Calas and Smircich (1999) do in their overview of feminist approaches to organization studies, they pursue the issue more from the position of personal experience and reflection – and use the proposed format of the book and its apparent gendered reproductions as a spring board for discussion. In the sense suggested by Marshall in the chapter, they try to "show" the problems of theorising gender in the way they dialog, rather than "tell" us about the problems in a formalist manner.

Apart from reflecting on the debate format, they also reflect on the exclusionary practice of being positioned as "expert" and the presumptiveness of talking about or on behalf of others. This is particularly acute for Mills as a pro-feminist or "aspirational" feminist male. More generally they each worry about their own location and their right and capacity to "represent" those more marginalized. Mills talks about the problems of subverting dominant power structures from a position of security within those power structures as represented by the academy and its discourses. Marshall talks about writing from positions of marginality, but recognizes that accepting an invitation to write as "expert" or "leading exponent" in a book such as this runs the risk of short-circuiting that positioning. She maneuvers reflexively to suggest that having to confront that decision mirrors the types of pressures for conformity to the *malestream* that women perpetually confront. Gheradi also asserts the marginality of feminist theorising and practice (and, indeed, insists that feminism is a practice and not a theory) and addresses the problem of attempting to construct a critique from within the ineluctable confines of gendered relations, structures and language. Similar concerns of assumed expertise, representing the "other," and centre-margin relations are a critical preoccupation in the post-colonial literature, perhaps to an even more acute degree.

Gheradi proffers a number of potential "escape" routes to the problem of women's inability to "auto-signify" themselves. Subjectivities, particularly gendered subjectivities, are constructed in the dominant discourses circulating in society; a critical and resistant position is sought and necessary, but can only be mounted from within those discourses. The practice that Gheradi particularly favours is irony. Language can be turned upon itself through the subversions of irony and other devices such as (knowing) hypocrisy. An alternative pursued by some feminist organization researchers is deconstruction (e.g. Calas and Smircich, 1991; Martin, 1990) but that option is not pursued here. Deconstruction can open up a text/discourse, subvert the knowledge hierarchies present therein, and reveal the aporia that the dominant discourse and its accompanying rhetoric seeks to mask. The aspiration of irony is that it will wobble the dominant discursive structures. It could be argued, however, that irony is a "gentle" form of subversion. It may be a form that points to the lacunae, inconsistencies and inadequacies of the dominant discourse through deploying its own forms and resources, but this "pointing out" does not, of itself, alter the discourse or its structures of dominance. Marshall is alert to this and wonders if irony might not be the "comfortable retreat of the intellectual." One does indeed wonder whether the truly marginalized will appreciate the wit of irony and find it liberatory.

Seeking to know, theorize and represent gender in ways that are alternative to or avoid the male-dominant epistemologies, methodologies and modes of representation is undoubtedly a key question and worthy of being raised. An ironical practice is the only solution offered in this chapter; unless we consider a polyvocalism and a multi-positional practice, as evidenced by the format adopted by the authors, as another.

REFERENCES

Calas, M. and Smircich, L. Voicing seduction to silence leadership. *Organization Studies*, 12 (4): 567–601, 1991.

Martin, J. Deconstructing organizational taboos: The suppression of gender conflict in organizations. *Organization Science*, 1 (4): 339–59, 1990.

Mills, A. J. and Tancred, P. (eds.) *Gendering Organizational Analysis*. Newbury Park, CA: Sage. 1992.

Theorizing Gender and Organizing

Silvia Gherardi, Judi Marshall, and Albert J. Mills

This chapter offers four voices – those of the three contributors and another, shared voice of commentary (this one) providing some structure and reflective sense making. The chapter was contentious to write for all three of us, and the dilemmas we faced seemed highly gender-associated. We rebelled against the proposed point–counterpoint approach to the book. For a long time we did not write, despite helpfully intended prompts and suggestions from an editor. We each felt guilty, but did not stir. Eventually Albert suggested an image of engaging, of doing the chapter "like a discussion group," which drew Silvia and Judi in, as it reframed the potential process and therefore form. One person would start by making a comment and throwing out questions to the other two. And so we could move forward, in a "journey of discovery," building on each others' contributions rather than arguing competing positions. Albert volunteered to write the first piece if neither Silvia nor Judi objected. The next person would respond, and so on. We wanted to give "a real feel of debate" and a sense of reflective time between contributions.

Albert circulated his contribution. Silvia and Judi wrote responses, also introducing new themes. These latter two pieces overlapped in time, and Silvia's was posted in two parts, with a pause between them. Each contribution commented both on issues of getting started, theorizing these through a gender lens, and more generally on themes of gender and organizing. How we started – that is, in resistance to an offered form of speaking – influences what we have generated, what approaches of the many available we have each taken to theorizing gender and organizing. Drawing together this collected dialog of e-mails, a draft chapter was shaped by Judi. This arranged the material under three headings reflecting different aspects of our conversations. It was then reviewed by all three of us, and further revised.

The chapter's next section offers our reflections on the first topic heading of "getting started", working with gender, knowledge, and power. It elaborates our writing process. In each person's contribution there were statements which expressed their perspective, interests, and positioning. These are collected in the following section, showing where we are each coming from. A further section draws out issues about gender and organizing, viewed through our different, mutually informing, lenses. Occasionally a contributor speaks briefly alongside another person's voice, in closer commenting. These pieces were inserted during the final drafting, and so are not responded to in the text. They are in italics to show this different timing.

To show some of the background to this chapter, we quote from the editors' original framing:

Gender issues in organization studies have had a short but vigorous history. Informed originally by the pragmatics of discrimination and segmentation and the concerns of feminist critique, the issues identified have increased dramatically in complexity and sophistication. A critical point in contemporary debates centres on the very conception of gender and its place and relevance in organizations and organization theory.

The editors went on to depict some of the wide variety of ways in which the field of gender and organizing is therefore approached, and the variety in what are then considered core issues and topics. The theme of how to think about gender is central below.

Theorizing our "Slowness" in Getting Started through a Gender Lens

Albert. For all three of us this chapter should be fairly straightforward. What could be easier than engaging in a dialog on gender and organizations? Certainly it is no accident that we three have been asked to collaborate on the paper. All three of us have spent much of our adult lives writing about some aspect of the subject. Yet there has been something problematic about the process. It has taken us close to a year to begin to write. Perhaps it seemed too simple. Or perhaps too many other things overwhelmed us. But perhaps it was something else, something more personal and profound.

Judi. *Yes, and more political.*

Albert. I know that it did cross my mind that a paper on gender and organizations was doable at a later date. Yet on those occasions that I made time to think of what I was going to write I was hit with a number of emotions, reflections, and questions that weren't easy to marshal (pardon the pun) into a comprehensive semblance of order. Eventually, taking a leaf out of Judi's book (Marshall, 1984), it came to me that our emotions, reflections and questions were far more valuable as a starting point than any attempted nod at rationality and order. Perhaps in this way we can engage in a process of contributing to an understanding of gender and organizations that goes beyond any expected point and counterpoint.

My very first reflection is on the process of being asked to collaborate on this chapter. I am very flattered yet very troubled. I am flattered that someone should think me particularly knowledgeable ("an expert") on gender and organizations, but profoundly troubled that I am constantly engaged in a process that appears to disempower the voices of others. By authorizing certain actions and outcomes as "an area of study" I fear that we may be replacing one set of imposed subjectivities with another (Foucault, 1980). It is one thing to create "cultural dopes," yet another to contribute to the creation of gendered dupes, i.e., people whose gendered identities the gender expert knows "more fully" than they. It was a failure to put that concern to the forefront of my thinking that led to my arrogance in assuming that gender and organizations were an easy "subject" to write about. Of course, I am not the first to voice this concern. Jeff Hearn (1992: 65) sums up the problem well when he says that "organizational research . . . is no longer likely to be a distanced academic exercise, but one where the boundaries between the objects of research, research method, and personal life begin to break down." Nonetheless it is one thing to recognize the problem and another to avoid

it. The privileges of academic life and the requirements of research and writing impose conventions on the communication of ideas that have implications not only for how we "view" others but also for our own sense of identity in a modernist world. How do/should we deal with the problem of subverting power from within the privileged discourses of academic life? Specifically, how do we address gender inequities at work from a position that privileges some voices over others?

That brings me to the idea of "point and counterpoint" as a mode of discourse. Like you, I am used to challenging viewpoints that I perceive as encouraging discrimination. But this is different. Here are three feminist writers asked to debate the issues of gender and organization. Is it appropriate to engage in a style of debate where any disagreements could be understood in terms of the specific parameters of debate (i.e., a point followed by a counterpoint)? My personal answer is simply to bring the issue to the fore and share with each other and the reader that we see this more as a journey of discovery, a collaborative effort where we share our differences.

Silvia. I want to thank Albert, for two reasons. The first is that he took the courage to kick off the process of starting to write this chapter, that in my mind was becoming a nightmare, and the second reason is for starting by airing his emotions. It gives me a good excuse both for starting in the same way, and letting my feelings come out, and at the same time grounding my reasoning on a feminist methodological principle that continues to prove highly valuable despite the changing of the meanings of "feminism." *Let's start from our own experience* was the motto I learnt when first I came to practice feminism. Following it, I wish to share with you my reaction to the invitation made by the editors.

I have to confess that I was not flattered but annoyed by the subtitle *Point–Counterpoint*. My first thought was "My God, another boyish thing! Only men can be so excited by the idea of the war game. Either they do it with weapons or they do it with thought, but the pattern is always the same. The stage can be the monthly faculty meeting or the medieval crusade, but the music is always the same! I'm fed up with it and refuse to be continually forced to play this game and will decline the invitation with a polite letter."

Immediately after, I realized how I was using gender stereotypes, casting all men as stupid warriors, forgetting how many women like the same game, and most of all I was thinking in terms of men and women as categories of people, assuming that the game was gendered! I felt so ashamed of myself, and so unprofessional as a gender scholar, that I had to admit that oppositional thinking is so deeply ingrained in our Western culture as to deserve some reflection and elaboration with a gender approach in mind. Therefore the editors hit the point and I sent them an abstract with this title "The privilege of an ironic perspective on gender and gendering." I had in mind to start from the statement the editors made when they invited a "text constructed around dyads of point and counterpoint, thesis to antithesis, paradigm against paradigm," and wonder whether a gender subtext was implicit in their claim to knowledge. At the time I didn't know that the three of us were expected to engage in a conversation.

Judi. Firstly, I find myself working on how I approach this task, as I see each of you doing. I *was* slow to write, partly because of too many other things to do, as Albert says. But there was also something more profound, more political, about the nature of knowing and how it is shaped, often unwittingly, by forms of expression. I was very influenced by my reaction *against* the initial framework suggested for each book chapter – debate, point, and counterpoint. This shaping of the way of doing knowledge offended me, as it did Silvia. I see form and epistemology as so closely associated.

What has happened so far has, I think, mirrored, and therefore been informative about, issues in theorizing (and living) gender and organizing. For me, stance (by which I don't mean something necessarily fixed or clear) is vitally important to any work on gender, and is reflected in the form or pattern of any writing on this topic. *How* we think about gender is often more important than the "content" of what we think – the epistemology is primary,

and it informs how ideas are held, and can then be used. (Berman: "*How* things are held in the mind is infinitely more important than *what* is in the mind, including this statement itself," 1990: 312.)

Being told, however flexibly intended, how to think and how to discuss gender with each other when we were invited to join this project created resistances for each of us. Whilst I had much empathy with the original rationale for the book – the "expressly polyvocal, multipositional text," I was especially concerned about the core notion of debates, the adversarial style proposed, the potential for polarized "either/ or" thinking, the inherent notion of position taking. The original intention had been swiftly turned into a dominant, inherently suspect, form, leaving undisturbed (perhaps reinforced) some aspects of reasoning with epistemological and gender/power associations. I could not imagine speaking authentically, creatively, into such a structure, saw it as a *de facto* trap, was concerned about what we might be replicating. And I thought the notion of debate was inherently gender-biased, in a more "masculine ideal" image, with the potential to create differences in a negative way. Is there a parallel here with how difference, in gender and other terms, often has to be created through an active process, has to be made to arise from what is potentially more plurality of form? There are issues of politics, the nature of knowing and access to expression here. (Which Silvia explores below in connection with Italian feminists.)

We sought to renegotiate the contract, were understood and were granted a different format from other contributors – instead of "an oppositional point–counterpoint structure" we were to have a three person "round-table" format (editor's e-mail) – "partly in recognition of the fact that the debate format is masculinist in nature" (editor's e-mail). We were, however, encouraged still to have a "vigorous engagement" and each "to press their perspective strongly." We were being given cues about "good quality thinking" in a dominant mode. These sat uneasily for me. But I did not want to write a treatise on alternative ways of knowing (Belenky et al., 1986), valuable as these are to amplify the field: that would have been to join in the polarizing. And so still we could not get started. Having rejected one form did not mean that we effortlessly created another. The parallels to the epistemology of working with gender echo strongly here. For example, whilst we may not want to become entangled in the limited choice of either consenting to or resisting dominant, male ideal, patterns of leadership, it is not so easy to create new possibilities in unoccupied space. Too often, styles imagined as alternative sound like stereotypes of women's qualities reproduced (Calás and Smircich, 1993).

So we have resisted the suggested form of this chapter, but I now feel more than slightly hesitant about how these sharp shafts of insight and positioning appear to be directed at the editors. I do not see it as personal, and trust they will not take it in that way, given their willingness to negotiate form. They are being used as an example of a general principle – *and* (tricky, this) they are also using and reinforcing dominant power to dictate format, and therefore shape epistemology, in this project. People wanting consistency is a (sometimes unwitting) way in which plurality is under threat these days. Are we, though, into point–counterpoint in our relationship with the editors rather than among ourselves, I wonder? And so should we be a little suspicious of ourselves? And, at the same time, I do agree that acknowledging our resistance feels as if it has opened the opportunities for a different way of engaging. A simple attention to process, and to not colluding in dominant forms, seems valuable, *and* to have had action consequences.

It was an issue for me too, Albert, that the contributors would be "leading exponents in the field." This is both ego-massaging and elitist, privileging – perhaps encouraging me to take the sound of my own voice too seriously. Like you, it led me to reflect on whose voices get incorporated and whose "omitted" from "mainstream" discourse. Those who see the world other than as debate and as amenable to expression with sharp edges (a normative form) are not there, leaving the "central" field for those willing to engage on its terms – of whom there are still many, men and women. And so the dominant pattern of rhetoric is maintained.

But listening to the voices of those who choose to inhabit the margin is central to understanding gender and organizing. For example, in her writing hooks *shows* gender, race, and class intersecting, she does not just tell me that they do (e.g., hooks, 1989).

Another aspect of the invitation to be a "leading exponent" was that it invited me to self-monitor, to shape my behavior in ways which warrant/maintain this sense of implied (and will I ever believe it really?) membership in the elite of those who are invited to speak. A self-disciplining circularity here. In accepting the invitation I therefore censored my own queries about where I stand in the "field" of gender studies these days. I am *doing gender* in my scholarship, but at times it is a more interwoven, less overt, theme than it used to be. (An issue to which I return.) And so we enact here some of the processes of potential conformity which affect women, people from ethnic minorities, and others considered "different" in organizations.

Can we be part and apart, generally and in this setting? Silvia offers the possibility of irony, which delights me. Albert wonders if we can subvert power from within the privileged discourses of academic life. ("Yes!" I write in the margin. "And how can we achieve that here?") These are questions I live with, which are part of my praxis (at least, my aspirations for praxis; I would not want to claim too much), as well as my thinking. I work, for example, with notions of multiple positioning, and also with the notion of "aware and chosen marginality" (Marshall, 1995), applying this self-injunction to my positioning both in mainstream *and* in potentially alternative cultures.

Starting writing in this more person-based way grounded us in engagement together. We exchanged e-mails appreciating each others' contributions, and expressing warmth at the dialog. By finding an alternative process and form it did seem that we had created a culture of engagement which enacted mutuality, which we preferred to one of oppositions. It allowed us to be more fully ourselves and diverse, but also connected, bringing an expanding richness, and sometimes the value of agreement, to our conversation.

Overtly stating Aspects of our Perspectives

Some of our e-mail contributions were saying who we are, how we came to the approaches we have, and how we hold our ideas. These are three stories from a multiplicity of potential paths to wanting, needing, to understand gender and organizing in some of its multidimensional complexity.

Albert. Now, in my opening section I said "three feminists," and I should deal with that issue and all that it entails. It is almost certainly problematic that I should choose to label you both – you may want to approach the issue with a different voice, so my apologies. It is also problematic that I choose to encase us all in an all-inclusive yet profoundly exclusive term: we are "in," others are not "in." Here I apologize to anyone reading this who may see my use of the term "feminist," however intended, as something privileging one group of people. Profoundly, of course, we come to the question of men in feminism (cf. Jardine and Smith, 1987). To begin with, there is the question of the label itself. Can a man be a feminist? My own preference for dealing with this problem has been to characterize my approach as "aspirational feminist" (Mills, 1994): "It is aspirational in that it (i) recognizes the limitations of 'male' experience in trying to represent 'female' experience and (ii) attempts to avoid notions of (political) correctness and closure of debate by suggesting that a (male) feminist position is something to be constantly striven for." Jeff Hearn has taken this much further by focusing on men and masculinities in the making of discriminatory environments (cf. Collinson and Hearn, 1994, 1996; Hearn, 1992, 2001).

Silvia. In reading Albert's remarks [that is, material developed in the following section] I had the feeling that "organizations" are not so crucial for him, as if they are only the stage for gender relations. While what was challenging his desire to understand more or better is gender and he links gender to inequities at work and discrimination. I see his line of reasoning and can easily follow it, and trace it in the discourses which frame gender as constructed in relations of power and dominance. In understanding his position I understand better my tacit representation of gender and my intellectual journey into feminism. In mirroring myself into his reasoning I became able to see how my understanding of gender is more linked to knowledge than to power, albeit both are interdependent.

For me the mirror symbolizes how we understand and account for similarity and difference. And the image of the mirror recalled for me the feminist appropriation of the archetype of the witch. The witch in early feminism was the symbol of female knowing, of women being in relation with nature, the body, herbs, and the oral transmission of their knowledge in a matrilineal genealogy. Feminist historians studying medieval processes attributed to witches the cultural representation of a way of knowing which tried to escape the control of men, the Church and official medicine. When, in my experience, Italian feminists were on the streets striving for the legalization of abortion and were crying, "Tremate, tremate, le streghe son tornate" (Quake, quake, the witches are back!), they were giving voice to a suppressed knowledge, to a reappropriation of the body and sexuality and were also representing themselves as the living embodiment of men's fear of women. The witch is the symbol of the woman who releases herself from man's control and male culture. A counterculture was the historical answer to the question "Who, what, is a woman?" (Albert's question) in feminist theorizing on knowledge in the 1970s. The unity of the Cartesian subject was delegitimized by another subject who posed herself as "An Other Knower." Therefore in my historically situated grasping of the category of "gender" it came to represent another methodological principle, represented by the question: whose knowledge is considered legitimate and whose is heretical? Gender for me has to do primarily with the politics of knowledge and the opposition to any official truth. The reappropriation of the body represented also a bodily grounded way of knowing and the transition from an object of pleasure to a subject of pleasure (i.e. aesthetics and eroticism as modes of knowing the world).

Judi. *Silvia, your reflections offer a sense of how some feminist positions on theorizing have emerged, and what they may contribute as themes and suspicions to understanding gender and organizing. By telling this story of your development you tacitly ask anyone in this field, and the reader, "How have you come to hold the ideas you do, in the ways you do?" And this journey of development will then shape those ideas. My sense is that there are significantly different groundings for North American and European feminists from different countries.*

Judi. Albert, feminist is one of my identities, but not my only self-description these days, rather one among many. In fact I do not want one identity, or too much clarity of this kind. I want to range widely, occupying different perspectives as they seem "appropriate." If I were to choose a root, it would have to be critical action inquiry or something like that; it would have to be a process.

I like you opening with *starting from our own experience*, Silvia, which I concur with as fundamental. This relates to Albert's suggestion that we note and work with the interconnections of lives, theorizing, and inquiry. (I just want to refute any implication that life is "personal" and separate from theory or inquiry – a gender-associated polarization. What I am as an academic/practitioner/person is thoroughly integrated.) As you move into notions of giving voice to suppressed knowledge I associate with that too, and see it as a major life task I have set myself (perhaps not always consciously). This does not necessarily carry the headline "gender," because that is often less important to me than pointing to broader horizons – such as ecology, social justice, a deeper sense of generative humanity. (These are obviously highly gender-associated.) And so I work to expand, ground, develop notions of inquiry and systemic thinking (for example, in my "Living life as inquiry" article, Marshall, 1999). I see myself as willingly, willfully, working with processes which have been gender-associated and devalued, seeking to re-claim and reintegrate them – in my own living practice and in my ways of thinking.

Silvia. *I would like to stress that any "feminism" is first of all a practice – and a political*

practice – on which a theory is grounded. No "armchair theorizing" can be done on gender relations!

Judi. For me, theorizing organizational life requires an active scanning of possible approaches to sense making, combining a multiplicity of frames, a richness of possible perspectives. This includes moving between focusing in on gender – drawing on a plurality of feminist positions – and defocusing gender as more generic issues such as power, the dynamics of inclusion/exclusion, and so on, become figural. And we need to incorporate multiple frames on difference – gender, race, class, and more (Collins, 1990; hooks, 1989). This could be described as a "both/and" approach, but I balk at such a descriptor, it sounds too harmonious, balanced, easy to achieve. I have a strong, jangling imagery here, challenging, politically aware, distinctions sharp, not blurred, robust. So, in any thinking or praxis, my question is *In what ways are gender, race, aspects of difference, at issue here?*

I am seeking to work in multiple perspectives, rather than to achieve a reconciliation of supposed opposites, because I believe we need complexity of understanding to appreciate complexity of phenomena (what Bateson, 1973, calls learning level III and Ashby the law of requisite variety, Conant and Ashby, 1970). This could allow us to transcend or circumvent the polarized, either/or reasoning of much gender discussion. Invoking plurality leads me to how much I value your work, Silvia and Albert, and what each of you has contributed to my ways of working with gender. And it reminds me of some other people whose contributions could be in here – for example, the incisive unwillingness to be fooled of Marta Calás and Linda Smircich (1993), and the persistence with which Joanne Martin points to how gender is embedded, including in the theorizing and practices of organizational studies (Martin, 2000).

Using the space of this chapter to enact pluralism seems a more appreciative approach than fighting each other, but I do not advocate it to avoid critical analysis, rather as a generative, integrative, form of critical analysis. (There seems a common thread here, Silvia, with your exploration of irony, below, about whether critique is inherently suspect, or can be done differently.)

And so we move on to the third main area we addressed, which has already been fore-shadowed above, that of how to theorize gender and organizing.

Exploring Issues of Gender and Organizing

Albert. The possibility of even an aspirational feminist approach depends in large part on the way the "subject" of the debate is understood. I'm referring to the ongoing debate among "feminist organizational analysts" concerning whether the focus is on "women" *per se* or on "gender" (Calás and Smircich, 1996). What actually are we studying when we analyze the relationship between organization and gender? For some it is about identifying and address-ing those workplace processes that discrimi-nate against women. Judi's book on women managers (Marshall, 1984: back cover), for ex-ample, "looks at the assumptions that are made about women's worth and how these commonly accepted assumptions affect our judgment about whether women could, or should, become good managers."

Judi. *Interesting that you should quote that. It now feels to me a sign of its time, of sense making then unfolding, and so only part of the picture. Analyses have become more multilayered, complex, rich, and detailed. Now I would talk more about gender, also, as embedded and enacted process.*

Albert. For some it is about identifying how "organizational factors" contribute to the social construction of gendered persons and the im-plications for individuals and organizations. Rosabeth Moss Kanter's (1977) work on men and women in corporate life, for example, explores how discriminatory organizational structures inhibit both the progress of female (and some male) employees and their potential contribution to the organizational ends (e.g., growth, profitability, etc.). While Silvia's work on gender, symbolism, and organizational cultures "explores the 'symbolic order' of gender in organizations – looking at how gen-der relations are culturally and discursively

produced and reproduced, and how they might be 'done' differently" (Gherardi, 1995: back cover). Sometimes a focus on gender is com-plementary to a "women-centered" approach, where gender is seen as "culturally specific patterns of behavior that may be attached to the (biological) sexes" (Oakley, 1972). But in some gender studies discussion of "women" is viewed as essentialist (cf. Rakow, 1986).

My own concern over the years has centered on whether a focus on discrimination against women (see, for example, Mills and Murga-troyd, 1991) ultimately reinforces the notion of difference, of women as "Other." But I have had an equal concern that the deconstruction of women (and men) will undermine the political agenda of addressing gender discrim-ination at work (see, for example, Wicks and Mills, 2000). Two incidents over the years have heightened my disquiet. One involved the name change of the Women in Management to the Gender and Diversity Division of the (US) Academy of Management in the mid 1990s. The other event, also in the mid 1990s, in-volved the firing of a "transsexual" from the Vancouver Rape Relief Society. The first event, initiated on the grounds that a "women in man-agement" focus was too narrow in concept, left me, nonetheless, concerned that we may have lost a political space where women or "women" could define their "own" issues. Debatably, a focus on gender and diversity is more vague as to its political agenda and the role of "women" in that agenda. [I also, despite my own work (cf. Mills, 1998), share the concern that a focus on men and masculinities may push concern with "women" to the background.]

Judi. *Yes. I share your concern about losing political spaces, whilst I do not want only women-only spaces. The increasing use of diversity language is contributing to this loss of political space in many arenas, although offering valuable contributions of its own.*

Silvia. *My concern is different. I am more concerned with the invisible masculinity that "wo-men's studies" in a sense helps to reproduce. I feel uncomfortable with the focus on "women" or the equation "sex = gender" and "gender = women." It looks like the only persons with gender are the women. These are not only misunderstandings due to inexperience or to a linguistic operation which attenuates the social embarrassment caused by the word "sex," replacing it with a more "polite" one. They are an ideological operation which allows gender studies to continue without calling the gender relation – that is, the relation between the male and the female, men and women, masculine and feminine – into question. In this manner, maleness is made invisible, removed from critical reflection, and continues to be the prime term, the one in relation to which the other is defined by default. Gender is a relational concept, which calls into question men and women, and social practices of gender relations. Albert's example of the Rape Relief Society (below) is a good example of how gender is "done" in concrete organizational practices.*

Judi. *I very much share the concerns you both express about replicating, often unintentionally, dominant forms of power relations.*

Albert. The second event raises profound questions about gender, embodiment, and gender politics. According to a press report, "Kimberly Nixon, who has undergone surgery and has been living as a woman for about 20 years, volunteered in 1995 to be a crisis counsellor with the Vancouver Rape Relief Society." A center coordinator asked her to leave, and she renegotiate redress through the British Columbia Human Rights Tribunal. Testifying at the tribunal in December 2000, Judy Rebick, the former president of Canada's National Action Committee on the Status of Women, argued in favor of the Rape Center: "The issue at stake is whether a women's group has the right to decide who its members are" (quoted in Bailey, 2000). She went on to state that:

The challenge is, "Who is a woman"? . . . What makes this tense is, there's no question that transgendered people suffer from discrimination, they suffer a great deal. So, of course, [in] your heart as a feminist you want to be on their side in every fight but you can't because there is a conflict of rights. It goes to the very heart of what the women's movement is and what feminism is. It's a very important discussion and a difficult one. I have a reputation of always being on the side of the most oppressed women, but here the question is "Who is a woman?" It's a different kind of question" (Quoted in Bailey, 2000)

This shifts debate from "What is a woman?" (How are specific notions of women and men socially constructed?) to "Who is a woman?" (Who or what is "the subject" in gendering organizations?). For me the Vancouver case raises a number of issues about the relationship between discriminatory practices, embodiment, experience, and political action. If political action hinges on collective struggle against discrimination, what determines the basis of collective action? A shared sense of embodiment? [This would include all those labeled "women," including transgendered persons.] And/or a sense of shared experience based on the assumption of shared embodiment? [In terms of female being, this might exclude transgendered persons from some types of experience, such as menstruation, for example.] These issues are not insurmountable, but they are vexing and need careful consideration.

Finally, I want to revisit the issue of why "the organizational context" should be of interest to feminists. This is probably much more of an issue for those focused on the social construction of gender than for those scholars who are interested in women and organizational discrimination. In the latter case, a solid argument can be made for the pervasiveness of organizations in the lives of us all (Denhardt, 1981). Organizational life is not just a special case. Organizations are central to the structuring of relations in society, and their influence (e.g., economic structuring, advertising images, job status, and class) often reaches far beyond their own particular boundaries. Workplace discrimination is misnamed, because it has ramifications not only for hiring and promotion at a particular job site but also for assumptions about women's worth in society as a whole. Arguably, if too few organizations employ females at anything but the lower levels this contributes to a general sense of women's worth (cf. Abella, 1984). But the powerful impact of organizational life is not really in question: the debate is around how much weight we should place on organizations, in contrast to, say, the structuring of work (Armstrong and Armstrong, 1990), or the patriarchal family (Wolff, 1977). There are those who argue that organizations, as local "sites of sexuality" (Burrell, 1992), play a unique role in the social construction of gender. Kanter's (1977) work is a prime example. This approach does not discount broader societal influence but, rather, contends that organizational dynamics bring about unique configurations of gender construction and experience. In contrast, there are those who argue for the primacy of "pre-existing gendered relationships," contending that "organizational forms . . . are inevitably shaped by a wide variety of social forces, gender notably amonst them. Organizations are the embodiment of different forms of patriarchal power relations . . ." (Witz and Savage, 1992: 57). And then there are those feminist scholars who give more or less equal weighting to organizational and extraorganizational factors, particularly those involved in the work–family debate (Haas et al., 1999; Lewis and Lewis, 1996). As I have argued elsewhere (Mills, 1997), my own preference is to argue for the primacy of organizational dynamics, but I wanted to raise the issue to indicate some of the epistemological difficulties raised with the study of gender and organizations.

In short, far from being simple, study of the relationship between gender and organization raises profound questions about the role and identity of the researcher, the relationship between feminism and academic discourse, the subject and the field of enquiry.

Judi. Albert, your input shows how wide the boundaries of the potential field and issues we might consider are, and the difficulty of doing them justice here. I hope we have exemplified some critical issues about how to think about gender and organizing so that readers can apply their own versions to any material in this field.

I like your suggestion that we should appreciate the interconnectedness of aspects of this field, especially those of the researcher, method, and field of inquiry.

I appreciate the several ways in which political awareness appears in your section, for example, noting the possible loss of political space if we move into the language of diversity. I agree. (And diversity as a label can also have its benefits. It is sometimes more acceptable as an educational invitation – for example,

allowing me to raise issues of masculinity with MBA students, who may not quite expect it – opening up space which I might not access if labeled feminist and talking about women.) Another example of potential political erosion is the incorporation of "tame" bits of gender awareness into organizational theorizing. For example, some of the popular management literature on men, women, and communication has appeal, and could be opening up gender understanding. But it seems limited in its appreciation of power and of its own meaning making, and so could reinforce old stereotypes rather than help people understand gender as complex and processual. Tannen (1991), for example, depicts men as more often into the language of status and women into the language of relationship. She claims these as equal but different. But this ignores the likely dynamic that status language will seek precedence over other forms. So the theorizing risks reinforcing dominant value patterns, not only about the relative merits of different codes of behavior but where women and men are positioned by them.

Finally, for now, I want to explore an issue that concerns me greatly – the replication of power–gender–knowing patterning, which seems so often to occur despite attempts at creating new initiatives. (Our concerns about the book's debate format were about this too.) I will illustrate from my current work.

During the last five years much of my time and energy has been devoted to developing, tutoring, and administering the M.Sc. in Responsibility and Business Practice we initiated at the University of Bath (in partnership with the New Academy of Business) in 1997. It is a two-year, part-time, action research-based degree, inviting participants to explore the challenges of integrating concern for ecology, social justice, and ethics with more established notions of organizational purposes. The (vast) territory of the degree is riddled with issues linked to gender, and to the devaluing of some aspects of human and ecological functioning relative to others. The power of dominant economic mind sets is, for example, readily apparent in many fields.

I wonder whether in this developing territory gender–power patterns are open to revision or are being recreated. My sense is that both revision and replication are happening, and I am concerned that the latter appears extremely powerful. Much is *apparently* changing, for example, with increasing corporate attention to sustainability, social responsibility, and such issues. I think we need radical change, not just adjustments within mind sets. But how can I know *how* this might come about? Does it matter that (white) men's voices, many from the United States, already dominate this field? I would prefer to see pluralism. Does it matter that gurus – of sustainability, social justice, corporate responsibility – seem to be appearing? Is this a replication of hierarchic leadership, which I think we need to escape as a dominant pattern? What concerns me even more is the replication I see of the primacy of currently dominant forms of knowing, favoring intellectual, value-neutral knowing, seeking control. In these initiatives to live differently on the planet and in a global community we especially need to engage in multidimensional, whole-self, connected knowing – I believe. These are all gender-associated issues.

Silvia. *I am reading the near-final draft of our contribution on the balcony of my summer house near Genoa the day after the end of the G–8 meeting held here. Judi's concern about the replication of dominant forms of thinking, acting, and knowing links with the discussions of these days in the antiglobalization debate. In fact it is more and more evident that other voices, other knowledges, other practices urge to be heard and want to be heard in a nonviolent context. At the same time it is paradoxical to claim for plurality and inclusion in the place where the first death occurred in confrontation around globalization.*

Judi. My understandings of gender and organizing are nothing to me if they do not enable me to act with integrity and creativity in the space of this new degree and similar ventures, and in my everyday practice in my organizational, and other, life roles.

Silvia returned to her interest in offering irony as a choice beyond oppositional thinking. This is a major part of her contribution to the discussion, highly appropriate and playfully serious, and so it is reproduced here fully.

There are two parallel framing statements for this offering. In her original reply to the Editors' invitation, Silvia wrote:

Silvia. My intention is to show the similarities between the so-called gender trap (the impossibility of stepping out from gender, or of defining gender as "positive") and critical thinking. I want to pose the question: is a critique possible which produces new meanings, which opens and produces insights instead of new power games? In order to answer that question I'll point to one possible solution – "irony." (Another possibility is "situated knowledge.")

In the text itself, leading on from part one of her contribution, Silvia wrote:

Silvia. At this point I had to interrupt myself. A lot of time had passed since writing the previous paragraphs, I received Judi's contribution, and I could not continue writing as if nothing had happened. In reading Judi's words I was impressed by a common underlying understanding: feminism is not only a theory, but is mainly a practice. And it is a collective practice. I wish to take up Judi's phrase: "'aware and chosen marginality' (Marshall, 1995)." Even if I do not know the article Judi refers to, I would like to elaborate on producing knowledge from the margins (i.e., far from the mainstream).

Feminist theory (assuming for a moment that there is something like a unified feminism!) represents a theory of knowledge critical of any mainstream, foundational, and universal knowledge.

French and Italian feminism view the body as the symbolic rather than the physical origin of the subject "woman." This subject is unable to "auto-signify herself" because Western philosophical thought has imposed itself as male thought, devising a universal and neutral subject which defines and represents the world in its own terms. As a consequence, women have been denied access to the symbolic. A "woman" is a paradox, present and absent from language. The metaphor of the eccentric subject denotes a subject aware of constituting itself in an ever-becoming history, in an interpretation and rewriting of self based on another cognition of society and culture. This subject is eccentric with respect to the social field, to institutional devices, to the symbolic, to language itself. It is a subject that simultaneously responds to and resists the discourses that interpellate it. The eccentric subject is capable of multiple identifications and belongings, but also of disidentification and displacements. The eccentric subject is not immune or external to gender, but is distant, critical, ironic, excessive. Feminism therefore takes a reflexive stance on the constitution of subjectivities in and through language and social practices of knowledge production.

Distrust in any claim to universal knowledge, suspicion in representations which try to fix a normative subjectivity for women, everyday practices which witness the political of the personal, are mundane traits of practicing feminism.

Other images try to capture the idea of a subject which is at the very same time internal to the language which produced it and resistant to it: the semiotic and the abject (Kristeva, 1977), the divine (Irigaray, 1982), the post-colonial (Spivak, 1987), the cyborg (Haraway, 1990), the lesbian (Wittig, 1992), the nomadic subject (Braidotti, 1994). In so doing, feminist thought produced the cultural effect of delegitimizing the unity and stability of the Cartesian subject. There emerges a strengthened difference which evades hegemonic thought. The subject thus defined traces knowledge itineraries through multiple points of intersection: differences between men and women, differences among women, differences within men. The politics of knowledge that derives therefrom is, in the words of Rosi Braidotti (1994), a set of conceptual trajectories that constitute a plural and open project: a polyphonous game of multiplicity.

An ironic, nomadic, eccentric knowing subject resists integration into mainstream disciplinary knowledge, but not from a desire for isolating but for producing knowledge from the margins and retaining a reflexive theoretical stance on the practices of knowledge production both in the mainstream and at its margins. Marginal practices retain the power of undermining local stability and insinuate

suspicion in taken-for-granted *habitus*, beliefs, and meanings. Irony, transgression, hypocrisy, subversion of gender codes may be considered as marginal practices undermining the stability of gender order and introducing playfulness in gender performances.

For me the meaning of staying at the margins is not only to be critical of the mainstream, but also to be in a liminal position, in a position of transgressing the boundaries, not recognizing the legitimacy of the borders. We can also transgress by flouting transgressive models: by emphasizing our female appearance, by exploiting gender privileges, exploring gender as a game. Hypocrisy protects the explorer and the innovator by providing symbolic substitutes. Can hypocritical endorsement of gender relations create room for experimentation by people of different sexes jointly in search of solutions? Can it help them feel more at ease in their sexed bodies? If so, complicity may be a bond which reveals the contradictions between gender as we think and want it, and gender as we do it. Exposing contradictions without claiming to resolve them is the prerequisite of a Socratic attitude towards self-knowledge based on irony as its resource.

Irony, as a metacommunicative resource, as an instrument of resistance, as a post-modern attitude, has undergone a renaissance in recent years. The pragmatics of irony is the destabilization in gender arrangements that ironic discourse can produce. Irony, in fact, insinuates doubt. It suggests that the world can be described in different terms, but it does not propose these other terms as alternative, "better," "more correct," or "truer." Irony is a processual invitation; an invitation to consider how things (gender relations, for example) can be redefined; how common sense can be problematized. Irony does not offer solutions; instead, it calls the linguistic games which produce a certain vision of the world into question.

Irony thus becomes a valuable resource when gender must be positioned within discursive practices and when a description of a male-centered world is to be contrasted with a female-centered one. The awareness of gender trap and linguistic trap are intertwined. Awareness of a choice among several vocabularies, of the contingency and fragility of each of them, of the historicity of the affirmation of one rather than the other, of the nonneutrality of linguistic games, produces an ironist.

Every discourse at the same time allows some possibilities and disallows others: the ironic touch stresses the possibility of switching from one discourse to another, of casting doubt on the rules and procedures which govern a discourse and the relations between language and people. An ironist is not a good player in the "point–counterpoint" game, since her/his commitment to the game is too low!

Judi. *Silvia, I am delighting in how irony disentangles you, and me when I take this approach. And also you are stirring some of my repeated concerns as I look at some forms of current theorizing, especially those which are more deconstructive. Astute and valuable as they are, I worry that they are not enough alone. They may take us too far away from practice, and from the close alliance between theorizing and practising. I see dangers of cynicism, detachment, of an appreciation of multiple perspectives and therefore no willingness or need to take sides on issues, such as those of social and ecological justice. Can irony sometimes be the comfortable retreat of the intellectual? Is it a robust basis for praxis?*

Silvia. We are the products of a discourse while at the same time we produce discourses, but we can introduce the instability of these categories into our discourses. We can play with them, try to see the world differently by changing positions, lay bare the power relations which tie us to a discursive position. Of course, to convey an ironic message we must be self-ironic, we must also cast doubt on our own final vocabulary. That is to say, we must not take ourselves too seriously, and we must stop believing that we have direct access to the truth. This conflicts, for example, with that brand of feminism that asserts a truth principle – male domination – from which it derives a political consequence. Perhaps the political nature of irony is not as evident as a political program, but it undermines the foundations of all power based on the monopoly of absolute truth. As all totalitarian regimes (discourses) well know, it is impossible to respect a power structure which makes you laugh.

Irony as a communicative frame raises doubts over the truth and seriousness of what is asserted. Irony may therefore be employed as an offensive or a defensive maneuver in interaction. I would like to be able to develop a dialog as three ironists who have been invited to take seriously a knowing practice which they cannot take into serious consideration but do not want to offend their hosts. We are kept in a double bind, that's why we started writing by saying that we were unable to write. Ciao!

Here we closed the discussion, with many issues left open to further exploration. We had each dealt with the dilemmas and opportunities of writing in our own register of speaking, reflecting our own life processes of working with gender as both ideas and practice, and had offered these in conversation, giving some sense of a polyphony of styles, views, and lives lived. We thank the editors for bringing us together.

References

Abella, R. S. (1984) *Equity in Employment. A Royal Commission Report.* Ottawa: Ministry of Supply and Services Canada.

Armstrong, P., and Armstrong, H. (1990) *Theorizing Women's Work.* Toronto: Garamond.

Bailey, I. (2000) "Rebick defends rape center's right to reject transsexual," *National Post,* Tuesday, December 19, p. A4.

Bateson, G. (1973) *Steps to an Ecology of Mind.* London: Paladin.

Belenky, M. F., Clinchy, B. M., Goldberger, N. R., and Tarule, J. M. (1986) *Women's Ways of Knowing: The Development of Self, Voice, and Mind.* New York: Basic Books.

Berman, M. (1990) *Coming to our Senses: Body and Spirit in the Hidden History of the West.* London: Unwin.

Braidotti, Rosi (1994) *Nomadic Subjects: Embodiment and Sexual Difference in Contemporary Feminist Theory.* New York: Columbia University Press.

Burrell, G. (1992) "Sex and organizational analysis," in A. J. Mills and P. Tancred (eds) *Gendering Organizational Analysis,* pp. 71–92. Newbury Park, CA: Sage.

Calás, M. B., and Smircich, L. (1993) "Dangerous liaisons: the 'feminine-in-management' meets 'globalization'," *Business Horizons*, March–April, pp. 71–81.

——(1996) "From 'the woman's' point of view: feminist approaches to organization studies," in S. R. Clegg, C. Hardy, and W. R. Nord (eds) *Handbook of Organization Studies*, pp. 218–57. London: Sage.

Collins, P. H. (1990) *Black Feminist Thought: Knowledge, Consciousness, and the Politics of Empowerment*. Boston, MA: Unwin Hyman.

Collinson, D., and Hearn, J. (1994) "Naming men as men: implications for work, organization and management," *Gender, Work and Organization*, 1 (1): 2–22.

——eds (1996) *Men as Managers, Managers as Men*. London: Sage.

Conant, R. C., and Ashby, W. R. (1970) "Every good regulation of a system must be a good model of that system," *International Journal of Systems Science* 1 (2): 89–97.

Denhardt, R. (1981) *In the Shadow of Organization*. Lawrence, KS: Regents Press of Kansas.

Foucault, M. (1980) *Power/Knowledge*. New York: Pantheon.

Gherardi, S. (1995) *Gender, Symbolism, and Organizational Culture*. London: Sage.

Haas, L., Hwang, P. O., and Russell, G. (1999) *Organizational Change and Gender Equity: International Perspectives on Parents at the Workplace*. Thousand Oaks, CA: Sage.

Haraway, Donna (1990) "Manifesto for cyborgs," in D. Haraway, *Simians, Cyborgs, and Women*. London: Free Association Books.

Hearn, J. (1992) *Men in the Public Eye: The Construction and Deconstruction of Public Men and Public Patriarchies*. London: Routledge.

——(2001) "Men, identities and organizational cultures: alternative conceptualizations and theoretical perspectives," in I. Aaltio-Marjosola and A. J. Mills (eds) *In the Flux of Organizing and Privacy: Organizational Culture and the Making of "Women" and "Men."* London: Harwood.

Hearn, J., and Parkin, P. W. (1992) "Gender and organizations: a selective review and a critique of a neglected area," in A. J. Mills and P. Tancred (eds) *Gendering Organizational Analysis*, pp. 46–66. Newbury Park, CA: Sage.

hooks, b. (1989) *Talking Back: Thinking Feminist, Thinking Black*, Boston MA: South End Press.

Irigaray, Luce (1982), *Ethique de la différence sexuelle*. Paris: Minuit.

Jardine, A., and Smith, P., eds (1987) *Men in Feminism*. London: Methuen.

Kanter, R. M. (1977) *Men and Women of the Corporation*. New York: Basic Books.

Kristeva, Julia (1977) *Pouvoirs de l'horreur*. Paris: Seuil.

Lewis, S., and Lewis, J. (1996) *The Work–Family Challenge: Rethinking Employment*. London and Thousand Oaks, CA: Sage.

Marshall, J. (1984) *Women Managers: Travellers in a Male World*. Chichester: Wiley.

——(1995) *Women Managers Moving On: Exploring Career and Life Choices*. London: Thomson.

——(1999) "Living life as inquiry," *Systemic Practice and Action Research*, 12 (2): 155–71.

Martin, J. (2000) "Hidden gendered assumptions in mainstream organization theory and research," *Journal of Management Inquiry*, 9 (2): 207–16.

Mills, A. J. (1994) "No sex, please, we're British Airways: a model for uncovering the symbols of gender in British Airways' culture, 1919–91," paper presented at the twelfth annual conference of the Standing Conference on Organizational Symbolism (SCOS), Calgary, Alta.

——(1997) "Practice makes perfect: corporate practices, bureaucratization and the idealized gendered self," *Hallinnon Tutkimus* (*Finnish Journal of Administrative Studies*) 4: 272–88.

——(1998) "Cockpits, hangars, boys and galleys: corporate masculinities and the development of British Airways," *Gender, Work and Organization*, 5 (3): 172–88.

Mills, A. J., and Murgatroyd, S. J. (1991) *Organizational Rules: a Framework for Understanding Organizations*. Milton Keynes: Open University Press.

Oakley, A. (1972) *Sex, Gender and Society*. London: Temple Smith.

Rakow, L. F. (1986) "Rethinking gender research in communication," *Journal of Communication*, 36 (4): 11–24.

Spivak, Gayatri (1987) *In Other Worlds.* New York: Routledge.

Tannen, D. (1991) *You Just Don't Understand: Men and Women in Conversation.* London: Virago.

Wicks, D., and Mills, A. J. (2000) "Deconstructing Harry: a critical review of men, masculinity and organization," *Finnish Journal of Economics*, 3: 327–49.

Wittig, Monique (1992) *The Straight Mind.* Hemel Hemsted: Harvester Wheatsheaf.

Witz, A., and Savage, M. (1992) "The gender of organizations," in M. Savage and A. Witz (eds) *Gender and Bureaucracy*, pp. 3–62. Oxford: Blackwell.

Wolff, J. (1977) "Women in organizations," in S. Clegg and D. Dunkerley (eds) *Critical Issues in Organizations*, pp. 7–20. London: Routledge.

12

Trust

The issue of trust has long been a critical issue in organization studies, given its centrality in all manner of coordinated human interaction and exchange. Whilst explicit in the early sociological deliberations of Weber, Simmel, and Parsons, the notion of trust has remained as something of a subtext – apart, perhaps, from the work of the Oxford academic Alan Fox – until its recent re-emergence center-stage during the 1990s. It is not easy to determine the motivating spirit behind the recent flurry of literature centered on the issue of trust. One view would be that it is an expected and belated return to this core aspect of human interaction. Another view would see it as a reaction to the partial dissolution of tight structures and the emergence of the more loosely coupled, contingent, temporary, and networked structures of many contemporary organizational forms and relationships. Others would see it as a partial offshoot of corporate culture perspectives where explicit controls are traded off against more normative, tacit, and implicit systems of control and coordination. Whatever the precipitating cause, the issue of trust has grabbed the attention of the academy.

In this chapter both Kramer and Sievers note the proliferation of texts in the popularizing literature trading in trust with some alarm. Both signal their disquiet at attempts to position trust as a panacea for all types of organizational ills and as yet another of the panoply of managerial tools available to rectify problems and enhance performance. In other words, neither contributor is prepared to have the wool pulled over his eyes by a shallow treatment of trust that glibly promises the world. This is not to say that they do not accept the importance of trust – indeed, in their different ways their negative reaction to the popularization of the issue is an indication of the significance with which they view it. Both offer the reader a considered and thoughtful view of trust.

Sievers' is the bleaker view. He sees the current treatment of trust as somehow misplaced, since he envisions contemporary organizations as fundamentally psychotic, perverse, and devoid of trust. The issue for him is not how to "engineer" trust so as to enhance performance, but rather how to unravel the conditions which have led to the blindness about the impoverished state of contemporary organizational experience and the absence of trust in our organizations. In the postmodern *Zeitgeist* trust is interpolated as a substitute for the elemental lack of meaning that constitutes organizational life. Current value systems elevate material and monetary ends, but relationship values have been eroded. The interest shown in trust is an indication of an underlying, even subconscious, anxiety about the decline of relationship values, meaning, and trust. People can sense the lack: they can see breaches and violations of trust in their organizational dealings at almost every turn, from large corporations that eviscerate the environment to breaches of the psychological contract, to dysphasic and damaging manager–subordinate relationships. At a pragmatic level, it is hard to countenance a new rhetoric of trust in organizations within the same discursive (and material) space as: large and legitimized structural unemployment; layoffs; the new social contract of individual responsibility for job, skills, and career; downsizing and other human resource and organizational design strategies that signal the precariousness of people's place in organizations and the labor market. A rhetoric of trust rings hollow in a climate in which such managerial strategies are made manifest in the name of economic rationalism. But Sievers is also concerned about the poverty of theory with respect to trust. For him current approaches lack depth and operate at a rather surface or merely technical level. Current perspectives are deficient at both ends of the spectrum. They are deficient by focusing at the psychosocial level whilst neglecting a more macro analysis at the organizational and societal level. At the same time, whilst looking at trust from the level of individual psychology, current approaches lack the depth that a psychoanalytic perspective might bring.

Instead of trading in the "politics of salvation," Sievers argues, we need to face up to the double nature of trust – not just its positivity in terms of risk reduction, but also its negativity in terms of sadness, lack, despair, and meaninglessness. Trust is necessary for effective social functioning and well-being, but we do not secure a better future with simplistic quick fixes.

There is a case for the virtues of trust, according to Kramer, but they are hard won and complex. He is in accord with Sievers in dismissing the simplistic quick fix. The virtues are societal in terms of developing social capital and a civic society, and organizational in terms of reducing transaction costs and fostering appropriate corporate citizenship behaviors. Kramer is scrupulous in anchoring his arguments to the research evidence. He does this in his considered and nuanced support for the benefits of trust, and in his analysis of what can actually be done in organizations to foster trust. He admits that the theorizing is still deficient and that there are major gaps in the research evidence. The need to consider trust in a contextualized manner is another point of agreement between Kramer and Sievers. Part of the concern with organizational trust emanates from the fact that the level of impersonalism in organizations and in business precludes the type of personal knowledge upon which people would normally establish and build trust. In the absence of personal knowledge (of the other) organizations have perforce developed various "proxies" that enable "trustlike" conditions to be established. Kramer documents the evidence for the effectiveness of such proxies.

Kramer's somewhat technical analysis contrasts with Sievers' more polemical essay, but they still find quite a bit to agree upon. He does adopt a more expansive style towards the end. His is a somewhat mediated advocacy of the virtues of trust. He recognizes the many grounds for distrust and the rationality of suspicion and distrust that exist and ends with the cautionary tale of Hemingway's vindicated paranoia.

12a The Virtues of Prudent Trust

Roderick M. Kramer

When invited to contribute to this provocative and timely volume I immediately responded positively for several reasons. First, I found the challenge posed by the editors to argue an affirmative case for trust rather intriguing. The editors sealed my interest with their challenging assertion that "It is hard to countenance a new rhetoric of trust in organizations within the same discursive (and material) space as structural unemployment, layoffs, the new social contract of individual responsibility for jobs, skills, and career, downsizing and other human resource and organizational design strategies that signal the precariousness of people's place in organizations." A rhetoric of trust, they sharply suggested, "rings hollow in a climate in which such managerial strategies are made manifest in the name of economic rationalism." The editors then threw down one more gauntlet – inviting me to "take the point position and mount a rigorous case" for trust.

I found myself unable to resist this call to arms. I had recently completed an edited volume (Kramer and Tyler, 1996) and review (Kramer, 1999) that seemed to provide a reasonable defense of trust and offered arguments in favor of its affirmative role in organizational life. Thus to abandon trust to its skeptics or critics seemed premature and to retreat from its defense cowardly. Once having accepted the editors' challenge, however, I immediately experienced the author's equivalent of "buyer's remorse." As I tried to imagine myself in the role of "angel's advocate" for trust, I realized my antipathy towards such a onesided role. Like most scholars, I suspect, I am leery of unbridled enthusiasms for what often turn out to be ephemeral whims and passing fads in both the academic and the popular management literatures. The perils of arguing in favor of Panglossian pronouncements regarding the powers of trust were all too evident. Indeed, my orientation with regard to trust has been to see all along its virtues (e.g., Kramer et al., 1996) coexistent with and companion to its dark sides and limitations (Kramer, 1994, 1998,

2001). Of course, I am hardly alone in my appreciation of the problems of trust – my counterpoint author (Sievers, chapter 12b) does a thorough job of articulating some of the more suspect enthusiasms and other problems with an uncritical stance towards and acclaim for trust. Such appreciation has been long standing (e.g., Gambetta, 1988; Sitkin and Roth, 1993).

The only sensible course for any levelheaded scholar, therefore, would be to agree to walk a middle road embracing the virtues of trust while remaining mindful of its shortcomings. Consequently, as I struggled dutifully to comply with the editors' assignment of mounting a rigorous case for trust, I was torn between two minds, feeling not unlike the hilariously schizoid character of Dr Strangelove (in the film of the same name): every time I tried to speak with conviction only about the virtues of trust – trying to stay "on task" – the other voice inside me whispered, "Caveat emptor!"

Recognizing that my intellectual Id and Superego were at war when it came to taking any monistic and overly simplistic stance towards trust, the responsible Ego in me finally persuaded me to simply fulfill my half of the bargain (paint the case for trust), leaving my counterpoint author to mount a rigorous case for the opposing view. My hope was that, when both chapters were read side by side, the reader would enjoy a balanced perspective of the issues and evidence, just as, when opposing attorneys both argue well, jurors can make better decisions.

After completing a first draft, some time later, in early September 2001, when the editors asked us for revisions, I dutifully brought my draft on board a United Airlines flight heading for Boston's Logan airport, heading to begin a stint as a visiting scholar at the John F. Kennedy School of Government. Only two days after I arrived in Boston, the terrible events of September 11, 2001, played out. It was hard not to think about matters of organizational trust – how much and toward whom and under what circumstances? When can we trust the individuals of an organization on whom our safety depends? How can we know that the systems necessary to provide trustworthiness are really in place? Are we foolish to place too much trust in trust? Is a little paranoia perhaps more prudent than Panglossian trust? All of these meditations moved from the abstract to the concrete as news programs examined the reliability and trustworthiness of organizations involved in the provision of security in the air traffic system. Those events, curiously, urged me to affirm even more strongly the benefits that accrue from the right kind of trust – even if we don't yet have it, we must never shrink from its pursuit. For, as difficult and problematic as trust may be, its substitutes constitute inferior alternatives.

Arguing the Affirmative: a Brief for *Prudent* Trust

The ascension of trust as a major focus of recent organizational theory and research, I would argue first, is hardly accidental. It is not the result of organizational theorists simply having tired of other topics or having nothing better to occupy their time. Instead, the rise to prominence of the topic of trust reflects, in no small measure, two converging influences. The first influence reflects an appreciation of the substantial evidence that has accumulated regarding the varied benefits, both individual and collective, that accrue when trust is in place. The second influence reflects the appreciation that, however desirable trust might be, it tends to be elusive, fragile – and even, as my counterpart argues in chapter 12(b), fundamentally problematic in character.

Because I am charged with presenting the affirmative case, my task has been made all the more easy by the simple fact that others have recently already done much of the job for me. The foundations for an affirmative case, after all, have been boldly laid out in a variety of influential books and articles. Perhaps foremost in this regard have been Putnam's (1993) provocative findings implicating trust as a critical factor in explaining the origins of civic engagement and its role in the development of democratic regimes in Italian communities.

Fukuyama's (1995) subsequent survey of the evidence that trust plays a critical role in societal functioning added further momentum to this push. These works converge on the conclusion that trust constitutes an important source of social capital within social systems. Sztompka's (1999) and Putnam's (2000) overviews, along with other works, have added even more weight to the argument.

Although the framing of the social capital argument is new, the intellectual sentiments underlying it, of course, are not: the virtues of trust as a form of social capital in organizations have been long recognized by others, in substance if not in name (see, e.g., Gambetta, 1988; Zucker, 1986). Within organizational settings, these virtues have been discussed primarily on three levels: (1) the constructive effects of generalized trust on reducing transaction costs within organizations, (2) the role trust plays in fostering various forms of "spontaneous sociability" among organizational members, and (3) the role of trust in facilitating appropriate (i.e., adaptive) forms of deference to organizational authorities. I consider each of these important roles briefly. It has long been appreciated that, in the absence of personal knowledge about others, or without adequate grounds for conferring trust on them presumptively, trust within organizations must be either individually negotiated or adequate substitutes for trust located (Barber, 1983; Kollock, 1994; Sabel, 1993; Shapiro, 1987; Sitkin, 1995; Sitkin and Roth, 1993). Negotiated trust can be obtained from histories of dense, repeated interactions with familiar others (Lindskold, 1978). In the absence of such opportunity, substitutes for trust – such as legalistic remedies for regulating exchange – may be employed (Sitkin and Roth, 1993). Similarly, technological solutions to problems of collective trust may be employed.

Even when effective, such approaches and remedies are often inefficient and costly. Negotiated trust takes time and, as players and their power and interests change, must be renegotiated or one risks having one's trust levels "out of date" with current circumstances or conditions. Substitutes for trust work at the level of providing some degree of reassurance, but often have potent and unattractive side effects (see Kramer, 1998, 2002). Recognition of these problems has led a number of theorists to focus on the role of trust in reducing these costs (Bromiley and Cummings, 1995; Chiles and McMackin, 1996; Creed and Miles, 1996; Granovetter, 1985; Uzzi, 1997; Williamson, 1993; Zucker, 1986). From a psychological perspective, one way in which trust can function to reduce transaction costs is by operating as a "default" social decision heuristic. Social decision heuristics represent behavioral rules of thumb that social actors use when making decisions about how to respond to various kinds of social dilemma situations they encounter (Allison and Messick, 1990). The utility of such heuristics in trust dilemma situations has been documented by Uzzi, in his 1997 study of exchange relations among firms in the New York apparel industry. Uzzi found that trust in this setting operated not like the calculated risk of economic models, but more like a heuristic assumption that decision makers adopted, "a predilection to assume the best when interpreting another's motives and actions" (p. 43). As evidence of the heuristic quality of judgment and action in this setting, he noted the absence of formal monitoring or measuring devices for gauging and enforcing reciprocity. Instead, individuals spontaneously and unilaterally engaged in a variety of actions that helped solve others' problems as they arose.

In interpreting these findings Uzzi reasoned that "The heuristic character of trust permits actors to be responsive to stimuli" (p. 44). In this fashion, he noted, trust heuristics facilitate the exchange of a variety of assets that are difficult to put a price on, but that mutually enrich and benefit each organization's ability to compete and overcome unexpected problems. The security of transactions is reflected in the decreased fear of exploitation or abuse and/or enhanced perception of reciprocity from others. Such trust is manifested behaviorally in terms of willingness to engage in presumptive acts of cooperation and helping, in the expectation they will be reciprocated by others – or at the very least not exploited. Recent research on the evolution of cooperation within complex social systems provides further evidence of the substantial benefits that accrue, both at the individual and collective level, from

heuristic forms of trust behavior (Bendor et al., 1991; Kollock, 1993; Messick and Liebrand, 1995; Parks and Komorita, 1997; Kramer et al., 2001). Viewed in aggregate, the findings from these studies suggest that heuristics predicated on positive expectations or generosity with respect to giving others the "benefit of the doubt" when "noise" or uncertainty regarding their trustworthiness is present can produce substantial increases in both individual and joint payoffs – at least within the context of ecologies in which reasonable (i.e., sufficient) numbers of other trustworthy actors are present. (In ecologies in which there are not a reasonable number of such players, many of my counterpart's (chapter 12b) concerns loom large and come into play. In Kramer (2001) I offer a conceptual framework for thinking about the conditions under which such presumptive trust fails to be forthcoming. A second arena in which trust has room to operate are those situations where collective action problems can be solved by voluntary compliance or engaging in extra-role behaviors. Fukuyama (1995) argued, along these lines, that one of the most important manifestations of trust as a form of social capital is the *spontaneous sociability* such trust engenders. When operationalized in behavioral terms, spontaneous sociability refers to the myriad forms of cooperative, altruistic, and extra-role behavior that members of a social community engage in that enhance their collective well-being and further the attainment of jointly valued goals (Pew, 1996).

Within organizational contexts, such spontaneous sociability assumes many forms. Organizational members are expected, for example, to contribute their time and attention to the achievement of collective goals (Olson, 1965), they are expected to share useful information with other organizational members (Bonacich and Schneider, 1992), and they are expected to exercise responsible restraint when using valuable but limited organizational resources (Messick et al., 1983) even when so doing technically is outside their formal role or contract.

Several empirical studies document the important role this kind of trust plays in people's willingness to engage in such behaviors. Messick et al. (1983) investigated the hypothesis that trust, operationalized in terms of individuals' expectations of reciprocity (i.e., their belief that, if they cooperated, others would do so as well) would influence individuals' willingness to voluntarily reduce their consumption of a rapidly depleting common resource pool. In support of this prediction, they found that as individuals received feedback that collective resources were becoming more scarce, those who expected reciprocal restraint from others were much more likely to exercise restraint themselves. In contrast, those individuals whose expectations of reciprocity were low displayed little self-restraint. Significantly, the behavior of low and high-trust individuals did not diverge when resources were plentiful. Thus this trust is not sentimental or naive or fixed – nor an expression of purely dispositional tendencies. Rather, it was sensibly calculative and responsive to ambient environmental realities.

Subsequent studies by Brann and Foddy (1988), Parks and Hulbert (1995), and Parks et al. (1996) provide further evidence that trust enhances individuals' willingness to engage in various forms of spontaneous sociability. Moreover – and of particular importance to the point here – they suggest that often even the most minimal of social cues are sufficient to elicit trustworthy behavior from social actors and prompt presumptions of others' trustworthiness. At the same time a careful and comprehensive survey of their results reminds us also that trust works in complex and often unexpected ways (and certainly some of the peculiar and unexpected interactions obtained in these studies provide empirical grounds for my counterpart's reservations about blind or naive trust).

A third important stream of organizational research has examined the relationship between trust and various forms of voluntary deference within hierarchical relationships within organizations. Despite all the rhetoric of flat, lean, and "transformed" organizations, hierarchical relationships remain among the most prevalent and most important form of organizing. Although hierarchical relationships assume varied forms (e.g., leader–follower, manager–subordinate, employer–employee), the centrality of trust within such relationships has long been recognized (Arrow, 1974; Miller, 1992).

From the standpoint of those in positions of power and authority in such relationships, trust is crucial for a variety of reasons. First, as Tyler and Degoey (1996a) noted, if organizational authorities have to continually explain and justify their actions, their ability to effectively manage would be greatly diminished. Second, because of the costs and impracticality of monitoring performance, authorities cannot detect and punish every failure to cooperate, nor can they recognize and reward every cooperative act. As a result, efficient organizational performance depends upon individuals' willingness to comply with directives and regulations, and their willingness to voluntarily defer to organizational authorities' accounts, explanations, entreaties, pleas, exhortations, etc. In addition, when conflict arises, trust is important because it influences acceptance of dispute resolution procedures and outcomes. Research has shown that individuals are more likely to accept outcomes, even if unfavorable, when they trust an authority's motives and intentions are benevolent (Tyler, 1994).

Long recognizing its importance, researchers have investigated the conditions under which people are likely to attribute trustworthiness to those in positions of authority. Early research on this topic sought to identify specific attributes associated with perceived trustworthiness. For example, Gabarro (1978) found that such things as perceived integrity, benign motivation (e.g., caring and concern), consistency, and openness contributed to attributions of trustworthiness between vice-presidents and presidents. Along similar lines, Butler (1991) found that perceived availability, competence, consistency, fairness, integrity, loyalty, openness, overall trust, promise fulfillment, and receptivity influenced subordinates' judgments of an authority's trustworthiness.

More recent social psychological research has refined and extended our understanding of the factors that influence trustworthiness attributions. The most systematic research on this topic has been conducted by Tyler and his associates (reviewed in Tyler and Degoey, 1996b, and Tyler and Lind, 1992). This research identifies several important components of trustworthiness attributions. These include *status recognition*, which reflects the extent to which authorities recognize and validate individuals' sense of full-fledged membership in their organization, as well as *trust in benevolence*, which refers to individuals' belief that authorities with whom they deal are well intentioned and honest in their decisions. A third important factor is *neutrality*, which implies perceived fairness and impartiality in decisions. Another finding from this stream of research is that trust matters more in relationships when some sort of common bond exists between authorities and their subordinates.

Other research by Brockner and his associates has investigated the influence of procedural variables on attributions regarding authorities' trustworthiness. Brockner and Siegel (1996) noted that procedures are important because they communicate information not only about an authorities' motivation and intention to behave in a trustworthy fashion, but also their ability to do so, a factor they characterize as procedural competence. In support of their general argument, they report evidence that procedures that are perceived as structurally and interactionally fair tend to increase trust, whereas lack of perceived structural and procedural fairness tend to elicit low levels of trust.

Brockner et al. (1997) explored some of the conditions under which trust matters more or less. They argued that, all else being equal, trust matters more to individuals when outcomes are unfavorable. In explaining why, they noted that receipt of favorable outcomes does not really raise issues with respect to authorities' trustworthiness, because the outcomes themselves constitute clear evidence that the authorities can be counted on to perform behaviors desired by the trustor. Under these circumstances, consequently, "trust is neither threatened nor critical in determining support for authorities" (p. 560). In contrast, when outcomes are unfavorable, trust or, perhaps more precisely, confidence in their trustworthiness becomes more critical and authorities are unlikely to receive much support. Brockner et al. tested this general prediction in three different studies and found, consistent with it, that trust was more strongly related to support for an authority when outcomes were relatively unfavorable. Studies in this vein, when viewed in aggregate, amply demonstrate

the importance of trust in the pursuit of organizational aims.

As I noted in the introduction, the editors of this volume were careful to remind us of the conditions under which such trust might not be readily forthcoming. And certainly my counterpart (chapter 12b) has done a brilliant job of ruminating about the elusive character of the right sort of trust and the individual and collective dangers that attend the wrong sort. I have made an effort to explicate some of these as well in Kramer (1998, 2001).

Securing the Benefits of Trust: the Pragmatics of Trust Building

Even if acknowledging the benefits of trust, such benefits are of little value if they can't be secured – and this goes to the heart of my counterpart's appropriate caveats and cautions. Trust may be a useful commodity in the abstract, but it is a fragile and elusive one when one attempts to make it concrete (cf. Arrow, 1974). As the events of September 11, 2001, reminded us on so many levels, even if organizational trust in all of its forms, and on all of its levels, is hard to secure, the quest to succeed in so doing is vitally important.

To be sure, our understanding of the behavioral, social, and structural bases of trust remains far from complete. However, there already exist considerable theory and research identifying the foundations on which trust within and between organizations can be built (Creed and Miles, 1996; Lewicki and Bunker, 1995; Sheppard and Tuchinsky, 1996; Zucker, 1986). These foundations encompass the psychological, social, and organizational factors that influence individuals' expectations about others' trustworthiness and their willingness to engage in trusting behavior when interacting with them. I will begin with a very brief account of what we know about creating trust through "local actions," i.e., interpersonal strategies for proximate trust building.

Research on trust development has shown that individuals' perceptions of others' trustworthiness and their willingness to engage in trusting behavior when interacting with them are largely history-dependent processes (Boon and Holmes, 1991; Deutsch, 1958; Lindskold,

1978; Pilisuk and Skolnick, 1968; Solomon, 1960). According to such models, trust between two or more interdependent actors "thickens" or "thins" as a function of their cumulative interaction. Interactional histories give decision makers information that is useful in assessing others' dispositions, intentions, and motives. This information, in turn, provides a basis for drawing inferences regarding their trustworthiness and for making predictions about their future trust-related behavior.

Evidence of the importance of interactional histories in judgments about trust comes from a substantial body of experimental research linking specific patterns of behavioral interaction with changes in trust. For example, numerous studies have demonstrated that reciprocity in exchange relations enhances trust, while the absence or violation of reciprocity erodes it (Deutsch, 1958; Lindskold, 1978; Pilisuk et al., 1971; Pilisuk and Skolnick, 1968).

In noting the formative role that interactional histories play in the emergence of trust, these models draw attention to two psychological facets of trust judgments. First, individuals' judgments about others' trustworthiness are anchored, at least in part, on their expectations about others' behavior. Second, and relatedly, those expectations change in response to the extent to which subsequent experience either validates or discredits them. Boyle and Bonacich's (1970) analysis of trust development is representative of such arguments. Individuals' expectations about trustworthy behavior, they posit, tend to change "in the direction of experience and to a degree proportional to the difference between this experience and the initial expectations applied to it" (p. 130). According to such models, therefore, interactional histories become a basis for initially calibrating and then updating trust-related expectations. In this regard, history-based trust can be construed as an important form of knowledge-based or personalized trust in organizations (Lewicki and Bunker, 1995; Shapiro et al., 1992).

Although personal knowledge about other organizational members represents one possible foundation for trust, such knowledge is often hard to obtain. Within most organizations, it is difficult for decision makers to accumulate sufficient knowledge about all of the persons with whom they interact and/or on whom they depend. The degree of social and structural differentiation found within most large, complex organizations precludes the sort of repeated interactions and dense social relations required for the development of such personal trust. As a consequence, "proxies" or substitutes for direct personal knowledge are often sought or utilized as a basis for presumptive trust (Creed and Miles, 1996; Zucker, 1986). I consider next some examples of such effective substitutes. Recent research suggests there are several bases for this sort of presumptive trust in others.

The first is *category-based trust*, which is predicated on information regarding a trustee's membership in a given social or organizational category. Sometimes this information is linked to stereotype-based expectancies, such as beliefs about gender and trust or ethnic identities and trustworthiness (Brewer, 1981; Kramer, 1994; Orbell et al., 1994). This information, when psychologically salient in an exchange or transaction, often influences others' judgments about their trustworthiness (Kramer, 1994). As Brewer (1981) noted, there are a number of reasons why membership in a salient social category can provide a basis for presumptive trust. First, shared membership in a given category can serve as a "rule for defining the boundaries of low-risk interpersonal trust that bypasses the need for personal knowledge and the costs of negotiating reciprocity" when interacting with other members of that category (p. 356). Further, because of the cognitive consequences of categorization and ingroup bias, individuals tend to attribute positive characteristics such as honesty, cooperativeness, and trustworthiness to other ingroup members (Brewer 1996). As a consequence, individuals may confer a sort of *depersonalized trust* on other ingroup members that is predicated simply on the basis of awareness of their shared category membership.

(On the other hand, to the extent that organizations are highly differentiated, functionally heterogeneous, and socially diverse, category-based forms of depersonalized distrust at the intergroup level may trump any superordinate-level collective trust. See Kramer, 1994; Kramer et al., 1996.)

Role-based trust represents a second important source of presumptive trust found within organizations. As with category-based trust, role-based trust constitutes a form of depersonalized trust because it is predicated on knowledge that a person occupies a particular role in the organization, rather than on specific knowledge regarding the person's capabilities, dispositions, motives, and intentions.

Roles can serve as proxies for personalized knowledge about other organizational members in several ways. First, as Barber (1983) noted, strong expectations regarding technically competent role performance are typically aligned with roles in organizations, as well as expectations that role occupants will fulfill the fiduciary responsibilities and obligations associated with the roles. Thus, to the extent that people within an organization have confidence in the fact that role occupancy signals both an intent to fulfill such obligations, and the competence required for carrying them out, individuals can adopt a sort of presumptive trust based upon knowledge of role relations, even in the absence of personal knowledge about the individual in the role or absence of history of prior interaction.

Such role-based trust develops from and is sustained by people's common knowledge regarding the barriers to entry into organizational roles, their presumptions regarding the training and socialization processes that role occupants undergo, and their perceptions of various accountability mechanisms intended to ensure role compliance and due diligence in role performance. As numerous scholars (Barber, 1983; Dawes, 1994; Meyerson et al., 1996) have noted, it is not the person in the role that is trusted so much as the *system of expertise* that produces and maintains the role-appropriate behavior of role occupants. As Dawes (1994) aptly observed in this regard, "We trust engineers because we trust engineering and believe that engineers are trained to apply valid principles of engineering" (p. 24). Moreover, he goes on to note, we have evidence every day that these principles are valid when we observe airplanes flying" (p. 24).

As with other bases of presumptive trust, roles function to reduce uncertainty regarding role occupants' trust-related intentions and capabilities. They thus lessen the perceived need for and costs of negotiating trust when interacting with them. Similarly, roles facilitate unilateral acts of cooperation and coordination, even when the other psychological and social antecedents usually associated with trust are missing (Meyerson et al., 1996; Weick and Roberts, 1993). However, role-based trust also can be quite fragile and produce catastrophic failures of cooperation and coordination, especially during organizational crises or when novel situations arise which blur roles or break down role-based interaction scripts (Mishra, 1996; Webb, 1996; Weick, 1993). As the events of September 11, 2001, remind us, imprudent role-based trust may cause us to be too relaxed about the extent to which organizational systems, roles, and those who occupy them can do what they are supposed to do.

If trust within organizations is largely about individuals' diffuse expectations and depersonalized beliefs regarding other organizational members, then both explicit and tacit understandings regarding transaction norms, interactional routines, and exchange practices provide an important basis for inferring that others in the organization are likely to behave in a trustworthy fashion, even in the absence of individuating knowledge about them. Organizational rules, both formal and informal, capture much of the knowledge that members have about such collective understandings (March, 1994).

Rule-based trust, accordingly, is a form of trust that is predicated not on a conscious calculation of consequences, but rather on these shared understandings regarding the *structure* of rules regarding appropriate behavior and the extent to which they are perceived as binding. As March and Olson (1989) posited, rule-based trust is sustained within an organization "not [by] an explicit contract . . . [but] by socialization into the structure of rules" (p. 27). When reciprocal confidence in members' socialization into, and continued adherence to, a set of rules is high, mutual trust can acquire a taken-for-granted quality.

Fine and Holyfield (1996) provided a nice illustration of how explicit rules and tacit understandings function to create and sustain high levels of mutual trust within an organization. They examined the bases of trust in the

Minnesota Mycological Society, an organization that consists of amateur mushroom aficionados. This organization provided a rich setting in which to study the bases of trust for several reasons. First, the cost of misplaced trust can be quite severe: eating a mushroom that someone else in the organization has mistakenly declared safe can lead to serious illness and even, in rare instances, death. Given such risks, Fine and Holyfield noted, credibility is lost only once, unless a mistake is reasonable. Consequently, members are likely to be highly vigilant about assessing and maintaining mutual trust and trustworthiness. Second, because membership in the organization is voluntary, exit is comparatively costless. If doubts about others' trustworthiness become too great, therefore, members will take their trust elsewhere and the organization will simply die. The organization's survival depends upon its ability to successfully instill and sustain perceptions of mutual trustworthiness among its members.

Fine and Holyfield identified three important bases of trust within this organization, which they termed *awarding trust*, *managing risk*, and *transforming trust*. One way trust is created, they observed, is to award trust to others even when confidence in them may be lacking. For example, considerable social pressure is exerted on novices to consume dishes at banquets prepared by other members. As Fine and Holyfield put it, there is an insistence on trust. Even if members remain privately anxious, their public behavior connotes high levels of trust. Collectively, these behavioral displays of trust in other members constitute a potent form of social proof to members that their individual acts of trust are sensible.

This insistence on trust is adaptive, of course, only if collective trustworthiness is, in fact, actually in place or warranted. Accordingly, a second crucial element in the management of trust within this organization occurs through practices and arrangements that ensure competence and due diligence. This result is achieved partially through the meticulous socialization processes that newcomers to the organization are subjected to. Novices participate in these socialization processes with appropriate levels of commitment because it helps them manage the risks of mushroom eating

and also to secure a place in the social order of the group. In turn, more seasoned organizational members teach novices out of a sense of obligation, having themselves benefited from the instruction of those who came before them. This repaying of their own instruction constitutes an interesting temporal (transgenerational) kind of depersonalized trust.

Over time, Fine and Holyfield argued, as members acquire knowledge about the organization, the nature of trust itself is transformed. Early on, the organization is simply a "validator" of trust for new members. Over time, however, it becomes an "arena in which trusting relations are enacted and organizational interaction serves as its own reward" (p. 29). As with trust in engineers, this form of trust is not simply trust in the expertise of specific individuals but, more important, trust in a *system* of expertise.

Another way in which rules foster trust is through their effects on individuals' self-perceptions. As March (1994) observed in this regard, organizations function much like "stage managers" by providing "prompts that evoke particular identities in particular situations" (p. 72). Miller (1992) offered an excellent example of this kind of socially constructed and ultimately self-reinforcing dynamic. In discussing the underpinnings of cooperation at Hewlett-Packard, he noted that "The reality of cooperation is suggested by the open lab stock policy, which not only allows engineers access to all equipment, but encourages them to take it home for personal use" (p. 197).

From a strictly economic perspective, of course, this policy simply reduces monitoring and transaction costs. However, from the standpoint of a rule-based conception of trust-related interactions, its consequences are more subtle and far-reaching. As Miller (1992) observed, "the open door symbolizes and demonstrates management's trust in the cooperativeness of the employees" (p. 197). Because such acts are so manifestly predicated on trust in others, I would argue, they tend to breed trust in turn.

Rule-based practices of this sort can exert subtle influences not only on individuals' perceptions of their own honesty and trustworthiness, but also on their expectations and beliefs about other organizational members' honesty and trustworthiness as well. As Miller noted in this regard, by eliminating time clocks and locks on equipment room doors, Hewlett-Packard built a "shared expectation among all the players that cooperation will most likely be reciprocated," thereby creating "a shared 'common knowledge' in the ability of the players to reach cooperative outcomes" (p. 197). By institutionalizing trust through practices at the macro-organizational level, trust became internalized at the micro (individual) level. Thus rule-based trust can become a potent form of *expectational asset* (Knez and Camerer, 1994) that facilitates spontaneous coordination and cooperation among organizational members.

There is another side to the social dimension of trust building from the ground up, and it is one that brings the power of third parties to bear. Appreciating both the importance of information regarding others' trustworthiness and the difficulty in obtaining such information, Burt and Knez (1995) argued that third parties in organizations are important conduits of trust because of their ability to diffuse trust-relevant information via gossip. As they demonstrated in a study of trust among managers in a high-tech firm, gossip constitutes a valuable source of "second-hand" knowledge about others. However, the effects of gossip on trust judgments are complex and not always in the service of rational assessment of others' trustworthiness. Part of the problem, Burt and Knez theorized, is that third parties tend to make only partial disclosures about others. In particular, third parties often communicate incomplete and skewed accounts regarding the trustworthiness of a prospective trustee because people prefer to communicate information consistent with what they believe the other party wants to hear. Consequently, when a person has a strong relation to a prospective trustee, third parties tend to convey stories and information that corroborate and strengthen the tie, therefore increasing certainty about the person's trustworthiness. Thus, third parties tend to amplify such trust. (Unfortunately, but hardly surprisingly, they found that third parties also amplify *distrust* when the "news" to be spread is noteworthy but negative.)

Uzzi's (1997) study of exchange relations among firms in the New York apparel industry, mentioned earlier, provides further evidence of the crucial role third parties play in the development and diffusion of trust. He found that third parties acted as important "go-betweens" in new relationships, enabling individuals to "roll over" their expectations from well established relationships to others in which adequate knowledge or history was not yet available. In explaining how this worked, Uzzi argued that go-betweens transfer expectations and opportunities of existing embedded relationships to newly formed ones, thereby "furnishing a basis for trust and subsequent commitments to be offered and discharged" (p. 48).

Final Thoughts regarding the Virtues of Trust – and Second Thoughts about them

Like all virtues, trust has its vices – and in his adopted role of *advocatus diaboli* my counterpart amply documents why trust often feels like a rather fragile foundation on which to build anything substantial and enduring. There are many ways in which the requirements of complex organization seem to militate against any solid foundation for trust, as the editors of the volume remind us. Moreover, our aversion to such uncertainty and vulnerability may explain, at least in part, the persistent "antipathy" towards trust that people often experience (Kipnis, 1996).

The problems of trust, to be sure, are many. There can be "false consciousness" about trust and trustworthiness within organizations. Authorities can be skillful at looking trustworthy even when they don't behave in a trustworthy fashion. We live in a time when there is a powerful behavioral technology for helping project images of trust and trustworthiness, even when those images constitute nothing more than a thin veneer spread over cynical, manipulative, and self-interested actions.

It is good, therefore, not to overload the concept of trust. Too many burdens and inflated expectations can be placed on the concept. In some ways, so many popular management books on trust have the quality of exhorting us to be more trusting and trustworthy, in the same tone as popular leadership books that exhort us to be more charismatic. The imperative "Trust me!" presents the actor with a daunting paradoxical injunction, in much the same way as the plea "Be more spontaneous!" does so. Few people doubt the virtues of such imperatives – the devil is in the details of implementing them.

Some scholars have even questioned whether trust can be consciously or intentionally "built" at all (Blois, 1999). To be sure, it is true that conscious steps to trust building can be executed clumsily and can backfire. An appreciation of the many ways we can stumble on the way to trust animates my counterpoint's thoughtful critique of the trust literature. His are reasonable concerns and he is right to remind us that they prompt sensible reservations. Having noted them, however, it is useful to affirm also the undeniable progress in trust research over the past few years. Only two decades ago Luhmann (1988) was able to lament the existence of "a regrettably sparse literature with trust as its main theme" (p. 8). That regret has been lessened. Trust has rightly moved from bit player to center stage in contemporary organizational theory and research. Nor does Williamson's (1993) assessment not so many years ago that trust remains a "diffuse and disappointing" (p. 485) concept in the social sciences seem as true today as it did then. Recent theory and research have sharpened our understanding of the complexity of trust within organizations and enhanced our appreciation of the myriad and often subtle benefits such trust confers (Putnam, 2000; Sztompka, 1999).

I am not naive enough to think that we are entering a new Golden Age with respect to the emergence of "high trust" organizations, as many of the popular books on trust claim or imply. This sort of inflated expectation and hyperbole will probably, in a few years, look just as naive as do many of the books on "total quality" and "transformational leadership" from a few years back. So I do not and would not oversell the virtues of trust *per se*. However, I would argue the virtues of what I will term, for want of a better expression, *prudent trust* (which I view as a sensible stance involving appropriate

trust balanced with prudent wariness and reserve). Additionally, I would argue that even a very well developed and complete appreciation of the limits of trust, and the difficulties in securing its benefits, should not deter us from pursuing them. Many of the most cherished states and conditions to which human beings aspire and after which they earnestly quest – including happiness, love, and wisdom – share these same hard-won and fragile features. They are clearly worth pursuing. In the end, I remain optimistic about the prospects for a mature behavioral science of trust, as well as a finer-grained and appropriately bounded appreciation of the artful organizational arrangements and behaviorial practices that will help secure them.

Implicit in so much of the argument I've moved toward, however, is that the kind of trust that gets us to where we want to get is not naive or blind or indiscriminate trust. Rather, it is a kind of appropriate, bounded, and prudent trust. It is a level of trust (and, where appropriate, distrust) that is adaptive to the environment in which it operates (see Kramer et al., 2001).

There are several observations that prompt consideration of such prudent trust, thus defined. First, distrust and suspicion are not always bad or irrational. As the editors of this volume pointed out in setting up this point–counterpoint argument on trust, there is much in the contemporary organizational scene to make us cynical and wary about the prospects for simple trust. In highly competitive or intensely political organizational environments, for example, individuals often have quite legitimate causes for suspicion and concern about others' trustworthiness. In such environments, the costs of naive or misplaced trust can be quite high – and sometimes even fatal to one's career. In organizations populated by individuals who lack trustworthiness, a propensity to vigilance with respect to detecting others' lack of trustworthiness may be quite prudent and adaptive (cf. Bendor et al., 1991).

Similarly, in highly competitive interorganizational environments, it may prove fatal to underestimate one's competitors by trusting them too much or relaxing one's guard. As

Intel president and CEO Andrew Grove (1996) once asserted, in a memorable maxim, "Only the paranoid survive" (p. 3). In elaborating on what he meant by this maxim, he added:

The things I tend to be paranoid about vary. I worry about products getting screwed up, and I worry about products getting introduced prematurely. I worry about factories not performing well, and I worry about having too many factories. I worry about hiring the right people, and I worry about morale slacking off. And, of course, I worry about competitors. I worry about people figuring out how to do what we do better or cheaper, and displacing us with our customers. (p. 3)

In expounding further on the adaptive value of organizational paranoia, Grove noted:

I believe in the value of paranoia. Business success contains the seeds of its own destruction. The more successful you are, the more people want a chunk of your business and then another chunk and then another until there is nothing left. I believe that the prime responsibility of a manager is to guard against other people's attacks and to inculcate this guardian attitude in the people under his or her management. (p. 3)

Both for individuals in power and for those who feel powerless, success and even survival may be contingent on continuous, even if effortful, vigilance regarding emerging threats in the organizational landscape. A functionalist account of organizational paranoia emphasizes, therefore, the role such paranoia plays in individuals' attempts at making sense of the potentially perilous environments in which their organizational actions are embedded. Under the best of circumstances, sense making in organizations is a problematic enterprise, fraught with ambiguity and risk (Weick, 1995) – but this may be especially true when it comes to deciding who one can trust, how much, and under what conditions. As former US President Richard Nixon (1991) once mused:

We often hear that someone worries too much. But in some fields, you can't worry too much, especially if worrying means recognizing that things may go wrong and planning how to deal with these inevitable setbacks. Those blissful souls who speed so self-confidently along life's straight, smooth highway are often the ones who end up in the ditch when the road suddenly veers.

By maintaining a heightened, even if (to others) misplaced or exaggerated, sensitivity to the interpersonal dangers that surround them, individuals can maintain their alertness and focus. As Lewis and Weigert (1985) noted in this regard, distrust and suspicion help reduce complexity and uncertainty in organizational life by "dictating a course of action based on suspicion, monitoring, and activation of institutional safeguards" (p. 969). Along similar lines, former presidential aide and speechwriter Richard Goodwin (1988) once observed that a predisposition to paranoia can help individuals remain "on the alert – observing and listening – to discern the hidden intentions of others – their concealed ambitions, weaknesses, greeds, and lusts" (p. 398).

Of course, at the very heart of the sense-making predicament confronting individuals embedded in trust dilemmas of this sort is not simply *whether* to trust or distrust others, but rather *how much* trust and distrust are appropriate in a given situation. In this regard, it is interesting to view the final months in the life of the writer Ernest Hemingway as a cautionary tale. Late in his life, Hemingway began to display many of the classic symptoms of clinical paranoia. He claimed, for example, that the FBI was intercepting his mail and was tapping his phone lines:

"It's the worst hell. The god damnedest hell," he confided to friend A. E. Hotchner. "They've bugged everything. That's why we're using Duke's car. Mine's bugged. Everything's bugged. Can't use the phone. What put me on to it was that phone call with you. You remember we got disconnected? That tipped their hand . . . [even my] mail [is being] intercepted." (Hotchner, 1966: 231)

Moreover, Hemingway was convinced he was under surveillance by the FBI and was being followed by agents. Thus, much to the dismay of his wife and drinking companions, he would sometimes point out various men in dark suits who, he asserted, were FBI agents sent by J. Edgar Hoover to follow his movements and harass him. On one occasion, when friends tried to reassure him that two men sitting across the bar had indicated they were simply salesmen having a drink, Hemingway angrily retorted, "Of course [they'd say] they're salesmen. The FBI is noted for its clumsy disguises. What do you think they'd pose as – concert violinists?" (Hotchner, 1966: 232).

At the time Hemingway's claims, as well as the vehemence with which they were asserted, were viewed by psychiatrists treating him as compelling evidence of his clinical paranoia. To be sure, Hemingway was suffering from a variety of mental difficulties linked to depression, chronic alcohol abuse, painful physical ailments, and writer's block. However, several decades later, we now know that at least some of Hemingway's perceptions were veridical. Documents released under the Freedom of Information Act have revealed that, in fact, Hemingway was under FBI surveillance and that, at J. Edgar Hoover's instigation, the FBI was engaged in an intense program of surveillance. Moreover the scope of this surveillance was greater than even Hemingway himself had imagined. Hemingway's FBI file was opened on October 8, 1942 (years before Hemingway even had begun to suspect he was under surveillance), and remained open thirteen years after his death (the last entry was dated January 25, 1974). The file contained 125 pages of single-spaced entries. As it turns out, even his Mayo Clinic phone was bugged (although his physicians viewed Hemingway's "paranoia" about hearing noises on his phone lines as proof of the validity of their diagnosis). Thus the saying "Just because you're paranoid doesn't mean they aren't out to get you" may contain more than a kernel of truth.

Such ironic realizations bring us full circle back to what was from the outset an ambivalent attitude on my part towards affirming only the virtues of trust. When embedded in sensemaking conundrums of the sort Hemingway and those around him struggled with, untangling truth from error with respect to trust is an enterprise often fraught with peril. Although more self-assured organizational perceivers may be bemused – and amused – by the ease with which their paranoid counterparts are lulled into a false sense of insecurity, just as easily they themselves may underestimate the concealed dangers lurking in their organizational environment. They press nonchalantly onward, much like the smug but unknowingly imperiled character in the Brecht play who "laughed because he thought that they could not hit him

– he did not imagine they were practising how to miss him" (cited in Watzlawick et al., 1967: 167).

It is this possibility, of course, that draws attention to the other edge of the sword of suspicion. As Shapiro (1965) aptly noted, "suspicious thinking is unrealistic only in some ways . . . in others, it may be sharply perceptive . . . Suspicious people are not simply people who are apprehensive and 'imagine things.' They are, in fact, extremely keen and often penetrating observers. They not only imagine, but also *search*" (pp. 55–8). In his rich and evocative study of the Sicilian Mafia, Gambetta (1993) documented how, in such a world, *everything* must be scrutinized – even luck. For, as Gambetta noted, "there is nothing as suspicious as luck" (p. 224).

Weick's (1995) thoughtful meditation on the nature of wisdom offers a balanced perspective on how to navigate on the edge of this judgmental razor. In defining wisdom, he quotes Meacham (1983): "To be wise is not to know particular facts but to know without excessive confidence or excessive cautiousness" (p. 134). Such wisdom, according to Meacham, is best conceptualized as "an attitude taken by persons toward the beliefs, values, knowledge, information, abilities, and skills that are held, a tendency to doubt that these are necessarily true or valid and to doubt that they are an exhaustive set of those things that could be known" (p. 134). As Weick goes on to elaborate, "Extreme confidence and extreme caution both can destroy. . . . It is this sense in which wisdom avoids extremes and improves adaptability" (p. 134).

The philosopher and essayist William Thoreau long ago expressed the conviction that "we may safely trust a good deal more than we do." Certainly that is true if we operate with the *right* kind of trust. And, when defined and studied in the right way, we may also trust the concept of trust in the organizational sciences a good deal more than some might suggest to us.

References

Allison, S. T., and Messick, D. M. (1990) "Social decision heuristics in the use of shared resources," *Journal of Behavioral Decision Making*, 3: 195–204.

Arrow, K. (1974) *The Limits of Organization*. New York: Norton.

Barber, B. (1983) *The Logic and Limits of Trust*. New Brunswick, NJ: Rutgers University Press.

Bendor, J., Kramer, R. M., and Stout, S. (1991) "When in doubt: cooperation in the noisy prisoner's dilemma," *Journal of Conflict Resolution*, 35: 691–719.

Blois, K. J. (1999) "Trust in business to business relationships," *Journal of Management Studies*, 36: 197–215.

Bonacich, P., and Schneider, S. (1992) "Communication networks and collective action," in W. G. Liebrand, D. M. Messick, and H. A. M. Wilke (eds) *A Social Psychological Approach to Social Dilemmas*, pp. 131–48. Oxford: Pergamon Press.

Boon, S. D., and Holmes, J. G. (1991) "The dynamics of interpersonal trust: resolving uncertainty in the face of risk," in R. A. Hinde and J. Groebel (eds) *Cooperation and Prosocial Behavior*, pp. 87–102. New York: Cambridge University Press.

Boyle, R., and Bonacich, P. (1970) "The development of trust and mistrust in mixed-motives games," *Sociometry*, 33: 123–39.

Brann, P., and Foddy, M. (1988) "Trust and the consumption of a deteriorating resource," *Journal of Conflict Resolution*, 31: 615–30.

Brewer, M. B. (1981) "Ethnocentrism and its role in interpersonal trust," in M. B. Brewer and B. E. Collins (eds) *Scientific Inquiry and the Social Sciences*, pp. 341–63. New York: Jossey-Bass.

——(1996) "In-group favoritism: the subtle side of intergroup discrimination," in D. M. Messick and A. Tenbrunsel (eds) *Behavioral Research and Business Ethics*, pp. 79–87. New York: Russell Sage.

Brockner, J., and Siegel, P. A. (1996) "Understanding the interaction between procedural and distributive justice: the role of trust," in R. M. Kramer and T. R. Tyler (eds) *Trust in Organizations*, pp. 360–72. Thousand Oaks, CA: Sage.

Brockner, J., Siegel, P. A., Daly, J. P., and Tyler, T. (1997) "When trust matters: the moderating effects of outcome favorability," *Administrative Science Quarterly*, 43: 558–83.

Bromiley, P., and Cummings, L. L. (1995) "Transaction costs in organizations with trust," in R. Bies, R. Lewicki, and B. Sheppard (eds) *Research and Negotiations in Organizations* V, pp. 219–47. Greenwich, CT: JAI Press.

Burt, R., and Knez, M. (1995) "Kinds of third-party effects on trust," *Journal of Rationality and Sociology*, 7: 255–92.

Butler, J. (1991) "Toward understanding and measuring conditions of trust: evolution of a conditions of trust inventory," *Journal of Management*, 17: 643–63.

Chiles, T. H., and McMackin, J. F. (1996) "Integrating variable risk preferences, trust, and transaction cost economics," *Academy of Management*, 21: 73–99.

Creed, W. D., and Miles, R. E. (1996) "Trust in organizations: a conceptual framework linking organizational forms, managerial philosophies, and the opportunity costs of controls, in R. M. Kramer and T. R. Tyler, *Trust in Organizations*, pp. 13–36. Thousand Oaks, CA: Sage.

Dawes, R. M. (1994) *House of Cards: Psychology and Psychotherapy Built on Myth*. New York: Free Press.

Deutsch, M. (1958) "Trust and suspicion," *Journal of Conflict Resolution*, 2: 265–79.

Fine, G., and Holyfield, L. (1996) "Secrecy, trust, and dangerous leisure: generating group cohesion in voluntary organizations," *Social Psychology Quarterly*, 59: 22–38.

Fukuyama, F. (1995) *Trust: The Social Virtues and the Creation of Prosperity*. New York: Free Press.

Gabarro, J. J. (1978) "The development of trust and expectations," in A. G. Athos and J. J. Gabarro (eds) *Interpersonal Behavior: Communication and Understanding in Relationships*, pp. 290–303. Englewood Cliffs, NJ: Prentice Hall.

Gambetta, D. (1988) "Can we trust trust?" in D. Gambetta (ed.) *Trust: Making and Breaking Cooperative Relationships*, pp. 47–58. Oxford: Blackwell.

Goodwin, R. N. (1988) *Remembering America: A Voice from the Sixties*. New York: Harper & Row.

Granovetter, M. (1985) "Economic action and social structure: the problem of embeddedness," *American Journal of Sociology*, 91: 38–49.

Grove, A. (1996). *Only the Paranoid Survive: How to Survive the Crisis Points that Challenge every Career*. New York: Doubleday.

Hotchner, A. E. (1966) *Papa Hemingway*. New York: Scribner.

Kelley, H. H. (1980) "On the situational origins of human response tendencies," *Personality and Social Psychology Bulletin*, 9: 8–30.

Kipnis, D. (1996) "Trust and technology," in R. M. Kramer and T. Tyler (eds) *Trust in Organizations*. Thousand Oaks, CA: Sage.

Knez, M., and Camerer, C. (1994) "Creating expectational assets in the laboratory: coordination in 'weakest link' games," *Strategic Management Journal*, 15: 101–19.

Kollock, P. (1993) "An eye for an eye leaves everyone blind: cooperation and accounting systems," *American Sociology Review*, 58: 768–86.

——(1994) "The emergence of exchange structures: an experimental study of uncertainty, commitment and trust," *American Sociology Review*, 100: 313–45.

Kramer, R. M. (1994) "The sinister attribution error," *Motivation and Emotion*, 18: 199–231.

——(1998) "Paranoid cognition in social systems," *Personality and Social Psychology Review*, 2: 251–75.

——(1999) "Trust and distrust in organizations," *Annual Review of Psychology*, 50: 569–98.

——(2001) "Organizational paranoia: origins and dynamics," in B. M. Staw and R. Sutton (eds) *Research in Organizational Behavior*, pp. 1–42. Greenwich, CT: JAI Press.

Kramer, R. M., and Tyler, T. R., eds (1996) *Trust in Organizations*. Thousand Oaks, CA: Sage.

Kramer, R. M., Brewer, M. B., and Hanna, B. (1996) "Collective trust and collective action in organizations: the decision to trust as a social decision," in R. M. Kramer and T. R. Tyler (eds) *Trust in Organizations*, pp. 181–203. Thousand Oaks, CA: Sage.

Kramer, R. M., Wei, J., and Bendor, J. (2001) "Golden rules and leaden words: exploring the limitations of tit-for-tat as a social decision rule," in J. Darley, D. M. Messick, and T. Tyler (eds) *Ethics and Social Influence*, pp. 177–99. Mahwah, NJ: Erlbaum.

Kramer, R. M., Hanna, B. H., Wei, J., and Su, S. (2000) "Collective identity, collective trust, and social capital: linking group identification and group cooperation," in Marlene Turner (ed.) *Groups at Work: Advances in Theory and Practice*, pp. 173–96. Hillsdale, NJ: Erlbaum.

Lewicki, R. J., and Bunker, B. B. (1995) "Trust in relationships: a model of trust development and decline," in B. B. Bunker and J. Z. Rubin (eds) *Conflict, Cooperation, and Justice*, pp. 67–94. San Francisco: Jossey-Bass.

Lewis, J. D., and Weigert, A. (1985) "Trust as a social reality," *Social Forces*, 43: 967–85.

Lindskold, S. (1978) "Trust development, the GRIT proposal, and the effects of conciliatory acts on conflict and cooperation," *Psychology Bulletin*, 85: 772–93.

Luhmann, N. (1988) "Familiarity, confidence, trust: problems and alternatives," in D. Gambetta (ed.), *Trust: Making and Breaking Cooperative Relations*, pp. 94–108. Cambridge, MA: Oxford Press.

March, J. G. (1994) *A Primer on Decision Making*. New York: Free Press.

March, J. G., and Olsen, J. P. (1989) *Rediscovering Institutions: The Organizational Basis of Politics*. New York: Free Press.

Meacham, J. A. (1983) "Wisdom and the content of knowledge," in D. Kuhn and J. A. Meacham (eds) *On the Development of Developmental Psychology*, pp. 111–34. Basel: Karl.

Messick, D. M., and Liebrand, W. G. (1995) "Individual heuristics and the dynamics of cooperation in large groups," *Psychology Review*, 102: 131–45.

Messick, D. M., Wilke, H., Brewer, M. B., Kramer, R. M., Zemke, P. E., and Lui, L. (1983) "Individual adaptations and structural change as solutions to social dilemmas," *Journal of Personality and Social Psychology*, 44: 294–309.

Meyerson, D., Weick, K., and Kramer, R. M. (1996) "Swift trust and temporary groups," in R. M. Kramer and T. R. Tyler (eds) *Trust in Organizations: Frontiers of Theory and Research*, pp. 111–24. Thousand Oaks, CA: Sage.

Miller, G. J. (1992) *Managerial Dilemmas: The Political Economy of Hierarchies*. New York: Cambridge University Press.

Mishra, N. (1996) "Organizational responses to crisis: the centrality of trust," in R. M. Kramer and T. R. Tyler (eds) *Trust in Organizations*, pp. 47–65. Thousand Oaks, CA: Sage.

Nixon, R. M. (1991) *Leaders*. New York: Touchstone Books.

Olson, M. (1965) *The Logic of Collective Action*. New Haven, CT: Yale University Press.

Orbell, J., Dawes, R., and Schwartz-Shea, P. (1994) "Trust, social categories, and individuals: the case of gender," *Motivation and Emotion*, 18: 109–28.

Parks, C. D., and Hulbert, L. G. (1995) "High and low trusters' responses to fear in a payoff matrix," *Journal of Conflict Resolution*, 39: 718–30.

Parks, C. D., and Komorita, S. S. (1997) "Reciprocal strategies for large groups," *Personality and Social Psychology Review*, 1: 314–22.

Parks, C. D., Henager, R. F., and Scamahorn, S. D. (1996) "Trust and reactions to messages of intent in social dilemmas," *Journal of Conflict Resolution*, 40: 134–51.

Pew Research Center for the People and the Press (1996) *Trust and Citizen Engagement in Metropolitan Philadelphia: A Case Study*. Washington, DC: Pew.

Pilisuk, M., and Skolnick, P. (1968) "Inducing trust: a test of the Osgood proposal," *Journal of Personality and Social Psychology*, 8: 121–33.

Pilisuk, M., Kiritz, S., and Clampitt, S. (1971) "Undoing deadlocks of distrust: hip Berkeley students and the ROTC," *Journal of Conflict Resolution*, 15: 81–95.

Putnam, R. D. (1993) *Making Democracy Work: Civic Traditions in Modern Italy*. Princeton, NJ: Princeton University Press.

——(2000) *Bowling Alone*. New York: Simon & Schuster.

Rotter, J. B. (1980) "Interpersonal trust, trustworthiness, and gullibility," *American Psychology*, 35: 1–7.

Sabel, C. F. (1993) "Studied trust: building new forms of cooperation in a volatile economy," *Human Relations*, 46: 1133–70.

Sato, K. (1988) "Trust and group size in a social dilemma," *Japanese Psychological Research*, 30: 88–93.

Shapiro, D. (1965) *Neurotic Styles*. New York: Basic Books.

Shapiro, D. L., Sheppard, B. H., and Cheraskin, L. (1992) "Business on a handshake," *Negotiations Journal*, 8: 365–77.

Shapiro, S. (1987) "Policing trust," in C. D. Shearing and P. C Stenning (eds) *Private Policing*, pp. 57–71. Thousand Oaks, CA: Sage.

Sheppard, B. H., and Tuchinsky, M. (1996) "Micro-OB and the network organization," in R. M. Kramer and T. R. Tyler (eds) *Trust in Organizations*. Thousand Oaks, CA: Sage.

Sitkin, S. B. (1995) "On the positive effects of legalization on trust," *Research on Negotiation Organization*, 5: 185–217.

Sitkin, S. B., and Roth, N. L. (1993) "Explaining the limited effectiveness of legalistic 'remedies' for trust/distrust," *Organization Science*, 4: 367–92.

Solomon, L. (1960) "The influence of some types of power relationships and game strategies upon the development of interpersonal trust," *Journal of Abnormal Social Psychology*, 61: 223–30.

Sztompka, P. (1999) *Trust: A Sociological Theory*. Cambridge: Cambridge University Press.

Tyler, T. R. (1994) "Psychological models of the justice motive," *Journal of Personality and Social Psychology*, 57: 830–8.

Tyler, T. R., and Degoey, P. (1996a) "Collective restraint in social dilemmas: procedural justice and social identification effects on support for authorities," *Journal of Personality and Social Psychology*, 69: 482–97.

——(1996b) "Trust in organizational authorities: the influence of motive attributions on willingness to accept decisions," in R. M. Kramer and T. R. Tyler (eds) *Trust in Organizations*, pp. 351–65. Thousand Oaks, CA: Sage.

Tyler, T. R., and Lind, E. A. (1992) "A relational model of authority in groups," in M. Snyder (ed.) *Advances in Experimental Social Psychology*, 25: 115–92. New York: Academic Press.

Uzzi, B. (1997) "Social structure and competition in interfirm networks: the paradox of embeddedness," *Administrative Science Quarterly*, 42: 35–67.

Watzlawick, P., Beavin, J. H., and Jackson, D. D. (1967) *Pragmatics of Human Communication: A Study of Interactional Patterns, Pathologies, and Paradoxes*. New York: Norton.

Webb, G. (1996) "Trust and crises," in R. M. Kramer and T. R. Tyler (eds) *Trust in Organizations*, pp. 89–99. Thousand Oaks, CA: Sage.

Weick, K. E. (1979) *The Social Psychology of Organizing*. Reading, MA: Addison-Wesley.

——(1993) "The collapse of sense making in organizations: the Mann Gulch disaster," *Administrative Science Quarterly*, 38: 628–52.

——(1995) *Sensemaking in Organizations*. Thousand Oaks, CA: Sage.

Weick, K. E., and Roberts, K. (1993) "Collective mind in organizations: heedful interrelating on flight decks," *Administrative Science Quarterly*, 38: 357–81.

Williamson, O. (1993) "Calculativeness, trust, and economic organization," *Journal of Law and Economics*, 34: 453–502.

Zucker, L. G. (1986) "Production of trust: institutional sources of economic structure, 1840–1920," in B. Staw and L. Cummings (eds) *Research in Organizational Behavior*, pp. 53–111. Greenwich, CT: JAI Press.

12b "Fool'd with Hope, Men favour the Deceit," or, Can we Trust in Trust?

Burkard Sievers

Though I listen to the message, I can't believe it. (Goethe, *Faust*)

Trust is the mother of deceit. (Proverb)

The ambiguities that surround trust in collective contexts should invite a form of adaptive vigilance. (Kramer et al., 1996)

Trust is a double-edged sword. It can open opportunities of mutual productive work and, at the same time, can be a sophisticated trap, in which the partners of trust are captured. (Amitzi and Schonberg, 2000)

Why, this is strange, I trow. (Coleridge)

While the point position is anchored in *empirical* studies, mine is primarily a reflection of my own experience, both as a theoretician and as a practitioner, and what I see being propagated in the contemporary academic and applied literature on trust. My interest is in understanding the social (and political) thinking underlying the academic and nonacademic views of trust in and among organizations. Thus my enquiry is not primarily about the nature of individual relationships; my reflections and interpretations are more on a macro-level.

My counterpoint position is based on the assumption that contemporary organizations and their cultures can, to a varying extent, be understood as being characterized by psychotic and perverse dynamics. Psychotic dynamics find their expression in the increasing aggression, sadism, and destructivity exhibited by contemporary organizations. This is in reaction to the apparent threat and persecution perceived as emanating from the outer world of markets and competitors. In defending against these perceived and actual threats, the inner world of organizations is caught in a behavior and way of thinking that reflect social psychosis, as described by Bion (1957; Sievers, 1999a). The perverse state of mind (Long, 2001) is evidenced by the prevalence of narcissism, individualism, and the inherent values of self, greed, consumerism, and acquisition. The emergence of these dynamics has largely been ignored and has, in fact, generally been regarded as normal.

To the extent that the future and survival of both individuals and organizations as a whole are at risk, psychotic and perverse tendencies undermine the pursuit of trust. In order not to be misunderstood, I would like to emphasize that these dynamics are not regarded as an expression of individual psychopathology. I perceive psychotic and perverse dynamics in organizations as being socially induced. The thinking (or nonthinking) in organizations (or organizational subsystems) induces members to mobilize the psychotic and perverse rather than the nonpsychotic and nonperverse parts of their personalities. They are thus made to react in less mature ways than they would in other circumstances (cf. Lawrence, 1995).

As I read and reflected on trust in my role as *advocatus diaboli* I often experienced loneliness and felt like an outcast from the respective scientific community, its mainstream conceptualizations and theories. These reactions are certainly not a result of doubting the relevance of trust both in everyday life and in organizations and society at large. How could anyone be against trust *per se*? It is – like motherhood and apple pie – a good thing and a necessary constituent of the social fabric. Or, as Jaques (1996: 15) put it, "People do not have to love each other, or even to like each other, to work together effectively. But they do have to be able to trust each other in order to do so." My reaction stems from the fact that I just do not buy the predominant praise of the virtues of trust both in the field of study and in the prevalent management practice. Though I hesitate to join the underlying thinking that reduces social reality to an exclusively economic one (cf. Aktouf, 1996: 448–54), I do agree that trust constitutes an important source of social capital within social systems (Fukuyama, 1995; Kramer, chapter 12a). However, it appears to me that the apparent lack of trust in organizations, the inflation of its necessity and its occasional bankruptcy, is too often neglected. The absence of trust is broadly denied by the emphasis on "the substantial and varied benefits, both individual and collective, that accrue when trust is in place" (Kramer, chapter 12a). Instead of acknowledging the lack of trust as a significant reality and contemporary problem, trust is propagated as an external entity and a needed solution. All we need is more trust! As Fox (1974: 95, quoted in Hardy et al., 1998: 67) accurately states regarding the manager–subordinate relationship from the perspective of the latter, " 'We've got to trust them' means in fact 'We don't trust them but feel constrained to submit to their discretion.' This simply describes, of course, a power relationship."

For purposes of representing the counterpoint position I have not written a monograph on the present state of the literature on trust. Given the bias of this role, I could not do justice to the broad variety of perspectives, research studies, and approaches confirming the pro and counterpoint positions. Being quite aware that every way of seeing is also a way of not seeing, I hope to make my own bias somehow clearer in the further course of my argument.

My reservations about the present use of trust both as a managerial tool and as a topic of organization theory concern its fashionable character and the "lightness" (not to say "naivety") with which it is often treated both in practice and theory. "Leadership is a relationship, founded on trust and confidence. Without trust and confidence, people don't take risks. Without risks, there is no change. Without change organization movements die"

(Kouzes and Posner, 1995, quoted in Dando-Collins, 1998: 26) is an extreme example of what is widely propagated as business wisdom. Despite this tendency, I want to note that there are a number of authors in this field of study who go beyond such a naive, fashionable, and glib representation of trust.

The idea that trust is "the new social cement which will reintroduce coherence and stable order to organizations and relationships between organizations" – as suggested in the editors' original brief for the contributors to this book – reminds me of the architects and their clients some decades ago who believed in the almost unlimited possibilities of concrete for the building industry. Only much later – when bridges and other buildings showed severe damage or even collapsed – did the illusion become obvious. The price of this illusion was enormous costs in maintenance, repair, and reconstruction.

As trust is necessary for organizations – global and virtual enterprises in particular – to function, it is often assumed that it has to be enforced and engineered, despite the common experience that organizations and their (top) management are often not at all trustworthy. Enterprises and their management are often confronted with the dilemma of "enforcing" trust. This is reminiscent of the debate on the lack of organizational heroes nearly two decades ago. "Heroes are required for an enterprise in order to be successful. If you don't have them, create them!" was the almost cynical suggestion of authors like Deal and Kennedy (1982). Not unlike these "situational heroes" (ibid.: 38), much of what is taken for trust in contemporary enterprises is "situational," in the sense that it just meets the needs required to survive the next battle; it is but "hope for a season," as the poet Thomas Campbell put it. To illustrate, Mishra (1996: 282) states:

Recent discussions by both scholars and the business press suggest that trust is a central factor in organizational behavior and organizational survival for both public and private organizations, even in noncrisis contexts. Several scholars have recently proposed that trust is a central factor enhancing organizations' long-term success and survival, especially because environments have become more uncertain and competitive.

Both the increasing lack of trust in contemporary organizations and the insight "that many extant models of trust from the social sciences provide inadequate or incomplete foundations for an organizational theory of trust" (Tyler and Kramer, 1996: 129; cf. Hardy et al., 1998; Knights et al., 2001; Sydow, 1998) have led scholars to attempt to refine the definition of the concept. "Both practitioners and scholars have even proposed that a new paradigm of management and organization must be developed with trust as a core component if organizations, both profit and not-for-profit, are to survive into the twenty-first century" (Sculley, 1987: 125, quoted in Mishra, 1996: 283). This is a common view in much of the scientific literature, i.e. that trust is one of the few white spots left on the organizational map and that the improvement of work efficiency relies to a major extent upon the effectiveness with which trust will be engineered and/or exploited.

In face of "the growth of trust as a central topic in recent social science research" (Tyler and Kramer, 1996: 3; cf., e.g., Bachmann et al., 2001; Dasgupta, 1988; Gambetta, 1988b; Kramer et al., 1996; Lane and Bachmann, 1998; Sitkin et al., 1998) trust is seen as a lucrative "commodity" for improving one's scientific reputation. It appears as if trust is not only a "saleable product" (Zucker, 1986: 54) on the insurance, bank, and investment markets but also in the field of organization and management. Though trust cannot be produced in the same way as soap or metal (ibid.: 65), the ever growing "market" for trust seems to be driving the increasing amount of research and publications on the topic (cf. ibid.: 54). The literature on trust somehow has become a self-referential closed system. To get an overview – not to mention a deeper understanding of the diversity and the often contradictory approaches and research findings of the increasing number of publications on the subject of trust – would take an enormous amount of time and quite some discipline.

There can be no doubt that most people in general and in organizations in particular no longer subscribe to the slogan "In God we trust!" which was taken for granted by previous generations. Trust – to an enormous extent – has lost the certainty which faith once provided. Even if this seems somewhat romantic, the notion of trust originates from and refers to a quality of relatedness of "man" to his various "objects" – fellows, "nature," the world and God(s) alike – and may be regarded as a human "trait" as old as humankind. Both existentially and etymologically trust is related to and is an expression of reliability, fidelity, confidence, help, support, consolation; as a noun it is based on *tru-*, which is also the root of truth (Hoad, 1986: 507–8). Its Middle English version *trist* (cf. the French *triste* or the Latin *tristis*) still indicates the relatedness of trust to the feeling or expression of sorrow or sadness (Brown, 1993: 3399). Contemporary social science puts the main emphasis on risk, in the sense that the problem of trust is a problem of "risky precommitment" (*Vorleistung*) (Luhmann, 1968: 21). We may also be reminded that trust, in its "ancient" notion, was embedded in faith and was, as such, an expression of *Eros*, the will for life. Notions of truth, faith, sorrow, or even love are strikingly absent in the organizational discourse on trust. The debate on trust is certainly not complete and can find further depth by addressing these "ancient" dimensions of organizational reality – even though at first sight they may appear antiquated. Trust again has to be regarded as an indispensable dimension of "human life and its organization and not . . . [of] 'organizations and human life'" (Burrell, 1997: 25).

My interest in trust as an academic topic was first stimulated by Niklas Luhmann (1968, cf. 1979, 1988) more than three decades ago. Luhmann's emphasis on the function of trust and its conceptualization as a mechanism to reduce social complexity was a revelation to me. Together with Simmel's (1908, 1950) seminal work on the subject, more than half a century before, Luhmann's analysis inspired my decision to choose secrecy in organizations for my doctoral dissertation (Sievers, 1974). Secrecy – in general and in organizations in particular – requires a certain level of trust both in the secrecy itself and in the trustworthiness of those people in on the secret. At the same time secrecy exists when there is a conviction that others cannot be trusted. The fact that Luhmann's view of trust is still regarded as "the most extended and insightful theoretical" analysis (Lane, 1998: 12) by many scholars confirms the impression we had as his students.

My own interests have since shifted toward a psychoanalytic study of organizations, with a recent focus on psychotic intra- and inter-organizational dynamics. In the course of reading recent mainstream literature on trust I must say that I found much, if not most, of it uninspiring and at various times experienced boredom and disappointment. Of course, there were also some quite interesting contributions and a few which do not join the choir of hymns in praise of trust (e.g. Bachmann et al., 2001; Gebert and Boerner, 1999; Hardy et al., 1998; Kramer, chapter 12a), but the predominant impression I am left with is the prayer-wheel character in which trust – in the context of management and organization – is largely regarded as a *Wunderbegriff* (miracle concept) (Miettinen, 2000). Trust seems to be broadly perceived as a *Wunderwaffe* (superweapon) which will overcome the increasing conflicts characteristic of the catastrophic changes in the contemporary business world and the way work is and will be organized in the future.

Though there cannot be any doubt that both individuals and organizations would not be able to face or survive to the next day without a high amount of trust, the excessively important role given to trust in the literature on organizations is, to a major extent, not in accord with my own experience of working with people in enterprises.

In my attempt to find my counterpoint position to the predominant praise of trust, I am also reminded of my concern more than a decade ago at finding a stance in relation to the equally broadly accepted term of motivation and motivation theory in the context of management and organization (Sievers, 1986, 1994). On that earlier occasion it ultimately became "more and more evident to me that the whole notion of motivation itself has to be questioned" (Sievers, 1994: 8). I was working with the hypothesis that:

motivation only became an issue – for management and organization theories as well as for the organization of work itself – when meaning disappeared or was lost from work; that the loss of meaning of work is immediately connected with the increasing amount

of fragmentation and splitting in the way work has been and still is organized in the majority of our Western enterprises. In consequence, motivation theories have become surrogates for the search for meaning. (Ibid.: 9)

There would be some reason to develop my counterpoint position on trust from a similar line of thought, i.e. that the increasing loss of meaning of work in contemporary organizations and the concern for its presence in future working contexts – dominated by increasing globalization and virtualization – nurture the idea that trust is a substitute for meaning or even its functional equivalent. The latter would confirm the business wisdom that, in a world dominated by information and money, any question about the meaning of work or life in general is irrelevant. As one of my colleagues notes, the predominance of monetary concerns over relational ones has led to "the erosion of relation values, specifically that of trust" (Hinshelwood, 2001: 167).

The less the meaning of work and the credibility of knowledge authenticate authority, status, and orientation, the more society and organizations are forced to place hope in trust (Bolz, 2000: 130). Bolz's (ibid.: 131) statement that "questions of meaning cannot be answered by information; in order to understand, information has to be destroyed" may be equally true for information from the social sciences, as it comes to a more appropriate conceptualization and understanding of trust. Therefore, instead of repeating or extending my previous hypothesis, the following one appears more accurate in the context of the present debate.

The ongoing dominant concern for trust both in organization theory and in management practice reflects ambiguity on the part of organizational theoreticians. Whereas on the one hand they increasingly regard trust as a more accurate concept for a better understanding and management of organizational reality, they seem, on the other hand, to lack the courage to actually face and acknowledge the organizational "heart of darkness" (Joseph Conrad). Predominantly guided by "politics of salvation" (Lawrence, 2000b), organizational theoreticians tend to suggest solutions to people and organizations based on the assumption that they themselves are lacking both the competence and the authority to alter their own situation. They have lost sight of the tragic dimensions which inevitably characterize life and work in organizations as well as in our private and personal worlds in general. Theories about human nature, work, and life, which mainly underlie the image of trust in the present debate, are restricted by the emphasis on *Eros*, the will for life and survival. They do not sufficiently take into account the destructive and deadening dynamics of organizational reality, which are expressions of *Thanatos*, the "drive" for destruction, annihilation, and ultimately death. The predominant emphasis on trust and the praise of its virtues foster a perspective on work and life in organizations in which social experiences and dynamics like anger, rage, shame, contempt, denial, humiliation, suffering, or despair are either nonexistent or deliberately neglected. The debate on trust mainly produces monochromatic images of organizational reality instead of making full use of the palette of colors.

As the latest in an almost endless series of managerial panaceas, trust is often seen as the current "saving grace" of organizations. Though the present emphasis on trust may to some extent be interpreted as a kind of reverberation from the debate on organizational culture and its rhetoric (e.g. Graf, 2000), it can also be seen as a defense against the underlying anxieties experienced by management in its attempts to cope with the unavoidable chaos inside its organizations and in the respective external environment. Like whistling in a dark forest, it obscures the common contemporary experience of disorientation and the resulting fear and despair. The predominant "trust in trust" defends both social scientists and managers alike against the idea that traditional modes of organization, and the organization of work in particular, may no longer be adequate to meet the more difficult and chaotic challenges facing today's organizations. The regressive use of trust functions as a means of re-establishing "order/organization" in order to cope with "disorder/disorganization" (Cooper, 1986; cf. Knights et al., 2001). The emphasis on trust and the tendency to engineer it in familiar ways can therefore be interpreted as an expression

of a deep lack of hope for more creative and innovative developments both in the field of study and in its object. In order to elaborate my reservations about the present debate on trust in theory and practice a bit further, I would like to sketch the following four assumptions.

1. The debate on trust is broadly biased, lacking at the same time a metadebate on the assumptive framework of both trust itself and the "nature" of "people," organization, their relatedness, and the meaning of work for life. As Kramer et al., (1996: 382) indicate, "the assumptive frameworks from which we start influence not only the problems surrounding trust that we anticipate in our theorizing but also – and in very profound and consequential ways – the kinds of remedies to problems of trust we consider." The rhetoric on trust often resembles the Guinness advertisement. Like "Guinness is good for you!" trust must be, too (Nieder, 1997; Landau et al., 1998; Marshall, 1999; Newstrom and Scannell, 1998; Ryan and Oestreich, 1998; Shurtleff, 1998). Just as Guinness is predominantly driven by an increase in market share (and profit) through the consumption of its product while neglecting its impact on the fostering of alcoholism, it often seems that the propagators of more trust are not concerned with the consequences of "overconsumption" or a "watering down" of trust. The implicit assumptions of the underlying "image of man" or the assumptive frameworks of trust's relevance for the meaning of work in organizations are seldom made explicit. The debate on trust too often mirrors the wisdom found in "Heathrow organization theory" (Burrell, 1997: 27).

2. Though the role and function of trust are analyzed in various contexts – individual, dyadic, groups, intra-, inter-, network organization, and (on a few occasions) society – an integrative, systemic perspective is broadly missing. The literature on trust, in American publications in particular, is dominated by the social-psychological perspective that trust is primarily an individual, dyadic, or group phenomenon. On the other side, there is remarkable concern for trust as a collective dimension, as it is related to broader organizational contexts both in and between organizations (e.g.,

Bachmann, 2001). These different views – often referred to as the micro–macro link – are seldom interrelated or integrated (Bachmann, 1998). Whereas on the one side researchers tend to regard trust as almost exclusively a trait of the individual in relation to other individuals, others have accepted Luhmann's (1968, 1979) suggestion that trust, as an object of research for the social sciences, and for sociology in particular, is to be regarded as a mechanism of reduction of complexity in social systems. It appears that the polarization of trust as either an intersubjective or a systemic phenomenon is an expression of a more general deficit in social theory – especially the theory of social systems, which broadly lacks a common frame for relating the individual and the organization.

What is missing is the "binocular vision" perspective promulgated by Bion (1961: 8; cf. Lawrence, 1997, 2000a), the British psychoanalyst. Referring to the Oedipus myth as a metaphoric frame, he emphasized that – contrary to Freud's exclusive interest in the triadic relationship between Oedipus and his parents, Laius and Jocasta – a more adequate fulfillment of the myth requires an equally deep concern for its other part, the project of the Sphinx, which is related to the broader question of the nature of humankind and the political constituency of knowledge. As opposed to monocular vision, which views trust as either an individual or an organizational phenomenon, Bion's binocular vision provides a way of understanding how the social and psychic dynamics of trust are interrelated; it suggests that trust can be understood as socially induced by the organization. An organization's ability to provide containment for hope and trust has a major impact on whether role holders will experience and activate trust or regress into a kind of social retreat, in which they reduce their contributions to the organization to the minimal requirements demanded from them in their roles.

3. *As the main emphasis lies on the production of trust by management, broader organizational and societal issues are neglected.* Although there is repeated reference to the increasing impediments to trust in contemporary organizations in some of the literature, it seems to me that a deeper analysis and understanding of the dynamics and factors which enhance the difficulty and improbability of trust in today's organizations are missing. The extent to which these impediments are primarily indicated but not further investigated is exemplified by the suggested tools for the improvement of trust – e.g., Management by Objectives, Quality Circles, self-managing work teams, team building, and training (Newstrom and Scannell, 1998; Ryan and Oestreich, 1998; Steinle et al., 2000: 12). They are the standard repertoire of organization development and human resources management, which no long appear innovative or appropriate.

As the source of trust in organizations is mainly seen as coming from management, the main or often exclusive "social" variable taken into account is the respective "management philosophy" from which the attitudes and behaviors of managers supporting trust are derived. "In organizations . . . the predisposition to trust or distrust is embedded in managers' philosophies and has been displayed throughout time in the different organizational structures and mechanisms that their philosophies prescribe and/or accommodate" (Creed and Miles, 1996: 23). Since previous management philosophies have not prevented trust failures, which reduced efficiency and raised costs, these authors are propagating a "Human Investment Philosophy" (ibid.: 30–2) as a more appropriate management philosophy. They are convinced that the underlying concept of investment implies risk taking. Thus trust would be appropriate for those employees whose "trustworthiness" could somehow be measured and guaranteed. However, they leave the reader pondering how these changes in management thinking can be implemented at a point in time when top management, with its continual pursuit of shareholder value optimization, is increasingly dependent on investment and pension funds whose representatives they cannot trust (Sievers, 1999a, 2001). As a journalist recently noted regarding the present European business climate of corporate restructuring, "Self-conscious business leaders are mutating into henchmen of the capital markets; the shrill bustle does not even give employees and customers the time to reflect upon their feelings of insecurity" (Student, 2000: 124).

Referring to Gambetta (1988b) and Rousseau and Parks (1993), Creed and Miles (1996: 32) emphasize that "building trust depends in part on the emerging knowledge of mutual interest . . . and a genuine concern for the well-being of organizational participants." Despite their good intentions, I find myself quite skeptical, as they do not hesitate to borrow from Rousseau and Parks (1993) "good generals" as "the managerial mirror image of the employee as a good soldier" (Creed and Miles, 1996: 34). Though one may assume that the metaphor mainly refers to times of peace, it makes me question whether it does not also imply the opposite case, i.e. the times of war. From my own study of a German corporation (Sievers, 2000) I am led to assume that the notion of competition both in organization theory and in the business world may be more often than not a euphemism which hides the often underlying dynamic of destruction or even annihilation (Stein, 1995, 1997, 1999). Despite the apparent absence of bloodshed or casualties in enterprises, big corporations in particular tend to projectively ascribe their failures and losses in the markets to their competitors, who are then regarded as enemies. As a consequence they are mobilized to defeat them either by grasping bigger market share or by incorporating them through acquisition or merger. The incorporation of a former competitor often enough results in rationalizations, downsizing, and the cannibalization of unprofitable units.

To the extent that there is some truth to the assumption that competition among big corporations actually is war, and thus has a critical impact both on intercompany dynamics and on the inner world of corporations, the creation and maintenance of trust become highly problematic if not impossible. Contrary to the case described by Hardy et al. (1998: 76–8), in which management deliberately deceived its work force into believing that it could be trusted even as it was closing down a production site, the problematic character of trust in the context of war results from major unconscious dynamics. There is, for example, a high probability that war itself, inside the corporation and towards its competitors, is dealt

with as an "unthought known," a term which has been offered by the British psychoanalyst Bollas (1987, 1989). It refers to what "is known at some level but has never been thought or put into words, and so is not available for further thinking" (Lawrence, 2000a: 11–12). This knowledge cannot be grasped, because it cannot be phrased in language or metaphor. As it cannot be thought, named, or put into an idea, it is acted out primarily in situations of high anxiety and chaos, which foster the exportation of the threat of internal terror. In a paradoxical sense, it seems that the increasing use of war metaphors in the business world is primarily intended to keep the known truth unthought – that, in many corporations and major sectors of the global economy, the world is in a state of ongoing and ever intensifying war. As the apparent experience of war has to be denied, the underlying reality, that competition is war, has to be concealed and hidden.

4. The debate on trust in organizations is based on theories and methodologies that emphasize rational and behavioral dimensions of organizational reality. As a result, unconscious dimensions and dynamics of organizations and their relevance for trust are ignored. People in organizations and organizational theorists have both broadly come to accept the "rational madness" (Lawrence, 1998: 126; Sievers, 1999b) in organizations as normal. They have lost sight of the actual irrationality, madness, and suffering (Dejours, 1998) that are part of the daily experience of organizational members. If psychoanalysis as a science of culture, society, and organization is acknowledged as meaningful at all, it usually tends to be regarded as a subdiscipline of psychology or the medical sciences. Instead of being used as a means of conceptualization and further understanding, psychoanalysis is mainly perceived as offering a separate source of insights, which – at best – may be applied. The lack of psychoanalytic contributions to the exploration of trust in organization theory so far, may, at first sight, be explained by the fact that trust is a term which usually is not listed in psychoanalytic dictionaries. The only exception I found (Rycroft, 1995: 189) refers to Erikson's (1958) discrimination of trust and basic trust. This illustrates my point. "A well developed

psychoanalytic theory of trust does not yet seem to exist, although the main elements for it are quite ready . . . to use" (Amitzi and Schonberg, 2000: 5).

It would, however, be misleading to assume that psychoanalysis could not contribute further insight into trust, particularly in relation to the above stated hypothesis. Questioning the praise of trust in the face of the prevailing organizational vision shared by most top management – permanent growth, shareholder value optimization, and/or maximization of profits – a psychoanalytic perspective sees the apparent amount of mistrust, anxiety, pain, hopelessness, or even despair as a kind of undercurrent to (or dark shadow of) these megalomaniac goals. That they are commonly taken for granted may well be explained by the fact that, as members of organizations, we permanently lie to one another and pretend to believe the lies in order not to face our experience of confusion, impotence, and despair in our attempts to cope with the unrelenting pressure to meet targets derived from top management's vision. Once visions are stated, they no longer are to be questioned openly, despite apparent doubts. As a consequence, contempt (Aktouf, 1996: 506; Sievers, 1994: 74–82) for top management gradually replaces a sense of trust in its reliability and in the belief that one's job is relatively safe and that the enterprise will survive even if targets are not met.

In the contemporary business world, enterprises themselves are commodities on international (capital) markets and thus the target of takeovers and mergers; they often undergo turbulent restructuring with a focus on reduced costs, increased accountability, and decreased security for management and work force alike. Even in nonprofit organizations "financial issues outweigh human ones," and there is increasing evidence "that market mentality, which bases transactions on price and return, has entered into the fabric of organizational life" (Astrachan and Astrachan, 2000: 46). People in organizations have subsequently become commodities themselves, and can easily be fired if no longer required, or replaced if "outworn." As a consequence, they are in danger of abandoning all hope. And as they are no longer able to "calculate" the risk of trust, trust tends to

be replaced by illusions, whose self-deceiving character is hidden in order to escape the underlying despair.

The literature often emphasizes that trust not only manages risk, uncertainty, and expectations but also conveys the requirement of "one party's willingness to be vulnerable to another party" (Mishra, 1996: 265; cf. Miettinen, 2000; Rousseau et al., 1998: 395). Though the acceptance of vulnerability is "based upon positive expectations of the intentions or behavior of another" (Rousseau et al., 1998: 395), it further requires the capacity to deal with injury, humiliation, and loss, if one's trust is disappointed or ultimately fails. The greater the risk trust has to "absorb," the greater the capacity required to cope with the loss if one's trust is violated. Aside from more institutionalized forms of trust, which allow for certain legal procedures of investigation and reparation, there are at least two contrary ways in which an organization and/or its members cope with the loss caused by disappointed or failed trust: mourning and avenging. Psychoanalytically, they can be differentiated as nonpsychotic (mourning) and psychotic (avenging). The nonpsychotic reaction demands more, because it means acknowledging the loss as bereavement and undertaking the labor of mourning in order to ultimately accept it. The psychotic reaction is based on the assumption that the loss cannot be accepted; it is a wrong, which, as it has been caused by others, has to be avenged.

As the "choice" between these two reactions is mainly an expression of unconscious organizational dynamics, and not conscious ones, there usually is no further reflection or questioning. Whether organizations react to failed trust by mourning or by revenge (Bies and Tripp, 1996) is to a high degree dependent on the extent to which their internal nonpsychotic or psychotic dynamic predominates. As further elaborated on other occasions (Sievers, 1999a, 2000, 2001), there is convincing evidence that organizations and enterprises in particular – driven by greed, omnipotence, megalomania, tyranny, and contempt – tend to cope with disappointment and loss mainly in a psychotic way. This is partly due to the fact that projecting wrong on to others, who can then be sued or attacked, defends one against the acknowledgment that one's strategies and actions have failed. The psychotic dynamic nurtures control and power, because it cannot bear the inherent uncertainty, vulnerability, and risk that trust implies. In a similar way, the psychotic parts of an organization may be activated when previously reliable structures come under increasing threat (cf. Grey and Garsten, 2001; Heisig and Littek, 1995). The present ongoing economic threat, for example, to health care institutions and universities in most of the Western world is as serious in its own way as the impact of the many mergers and acquisitions in the private sphere. The merger of two major German steelworks, Krupp and Thyssen (cf. Sievers, 1999a: 599–605), is an example. Originally set about as an unfriendly takeover in the spring of 1997, the newly formed corporation Krupp-Thyssen is still caught in the psychotic dynamics characterizing the early merger initiative. At the end of 2001 there is still no proof that the venture has brought any of the results hoped for as a result of the merger.

Conclusion

As I conclude this argument I must leave it up to the reader to consider whether "psychotic organizations" and their inherently perverse states of mind are found exclusively in fairy tales and (science) fiction or in our contemporary business world as well. If my assumption is shared, then the debate on trust in organizational theory would need to be extended and reframed.

I am quite aware that the above thoughts are just a sketch. What I am arguing for, and what I would like to express with the title I have partly borrowed from the poet John Dryden, is not only that we cannot work and live in organizations without trust, but that a serious concern for trust in contemporary organizations cannot be restricted to a claim for the necessity of more trust. Instead it has to seriously take into account the reservations, difficulties, and despair which people experience again and again in their attempts to trust their organization and give the organization their trust. Instead of further managing or engineering trust "through the institution of relevant procedures (Zucker, 1986) or the display of

the appropriate symbolic representation (Lewis and Weigert 1985)" (Hardy et al., 1998: 67) we have to learn new ways of *creating* trust between partners who do not necessarily share the same goals and values. The paradoxical and tragic understanding of trust which such a venture requires is expressed in St Paul's notion of *spes contra spem* (Rom. 4, 18), i.e. any serious attempt to trust will inevitably trigger the impossibility of trust – or to trust against all reason.

Note

Owing to some technical problems and timing issues, Sievers was not in receipt of the final counterpoint chapter in time. – *Editors.*

References

Aktouf, Omar (1996) *Traditional Management and Beyond: A Matter of Renewal.* Montreal: Morin.

Amitzi, Verred, and Schonberg, André (2000) "'I don't know why, but I trust you.' Trusting the Consultants in a Paranoid Environment: A Case Study," paper presented at the 2000 Symposium of the International Society for the Psychoanalytic Study of Organizations, London. http://www.sba.oakland.edu/ispso/html/2000Symposium/schonberg2000.htm

Astrachan, Boris M., and Astrachan, Joseph H. (2000) "The changing psychological contract in the workplace," in Edward B. Klein, Faith Gabelnick, and Peter Herr (eds) *Dynamic Consultation in a Changing Workplace*, pp. 33–50. Madison, CT: Psychosocial Press,

Bachmann, Reinhard (1998) "Conclusion. Trust: conceptual aspects of a complex phenomenon," in Christel Lane and Reinhard Bachmann (eds) *Trust within and between Organizations: Conceptual Issues and Empirical Applications*, pp. 298–322. Oxford: Oxford University Press.

——(2001) "Trust, power and control in trans-organizational relations," *Organization Studies*, 22: 337–65.

Bachmann, Reinhard, Knights, David, and Sydow, Jörg, eds (2001) "Trust and Control in Organizational Relations," special issue of *Organization Studies*, 22 (2).

Bies, Robert J., and Tripp, Thomas M. (1996) "Beyond distrust: 'getting even' and the need for revenge," in Roderick M. Kramer and Tom R. Tyler (eds) *Trust in Organization: Frontiers of Theory and Research*, pp. 246–60. Thousand Oaks, CA: Sage.

Bion, Wilfred R. (1957) "Differentiation of the psychotic from the non-psychotic personalities," *International Journal of Psychoanalysis*, 38: 266–75.

——(1961) *Experiences in Groups, and other Papers*. London: Tavistock.

Bollas, Christopher (1987) *The Shadow of the Object: Psychoanalysis of the Unthought Known*. London: Free Association Books.

——(1989) *Forces of Destiny*. London: Free Association Books.

Bolz, Norbert (2000) "Wirklichkeit ohne Gewähr," *Der Spiegel*, 26: 130–1.

Brown, Lesley, ed. (1993) *The New Shorter Oxford English Dictionary on Historical Principles* II. Oxford: Clarendon Press.

Burrell, Gibson (1997) *Pandemonium: Towards a Retro-organization Theory*. London: Sage.

Cooper, Robert (1986) "Organization/disorganization," *Social Science Information*, 25: 2: 299–335.

Creed, W., Douglas, E., and Miles, Raymond E. (1996) "A conceptual framework linking organizational forms, managerial philosophies, and the opportunity costs of control," in Roderick M. Kramer and Tom R. Tyler (eds) *Trust in Organizations: Frontiers of Theory and Research*, pp. 16–38. Thousand Oaks, CA: Sage.

Dando-Collins, Stephen (1998) *The Penguin Book of Business Wisdom*. Ringwood, Vict: Penguin.

Dasgupta, Partha (1998) "Trust as commodity," in Diego Gambetta (ed.) *Trust: Making and Breaking Cooperative Relations*, pp. 49–72. New York: Blackwell.

Deal, Terrence E., and Kennedy, Allan A. (1982) *Corporate Cultures: The Rites and Rituals of Corporate Life*. Reading, MA: Addison-Wesley.

Dejours, Christophe (1998) *Souffrance en France: la banalisation de l'injustice sociale*. Paris: Seuil.

Erikson, Erik H. (1958) *Childhood and Society*. New York: Norton.

Fox, A. (1974) *Beyond Contract: Work, Power and Trust Relations*. London: Faber.

Fukuyama, F. (1995) *Trust: The Social Virtues and the Creation of Prosperity*. New York and London: Free Press.

Gambetta, Diego, ed. (1988a) *Trust: Making and Breaking Cooperative Relations*. New York: Blackwell.

——(1988b) "Can we trust Trust?" in Diego Gambetta (ed.) *Trust: Making and Breaking Cooperative Relations*, pp. 213–37. New York: Blackwell.

Gebert, Diether, and Boerner, Sabine (1999) "Krisenmanagement durch Vertrauen? Zur Problematik betrieblicher Öffnungsprozesse in ökonomisch schwerigen Situationen," in Joachim Freimuth (ed.) *Die Angst der Manager*, pp. 137–61. Göttingen: Verlag für Angewandte Psychologie.

Graf, Andrea (2000) "Vertrauen und Unternehmenskultur im Führungsprozess," *zfwu*, 1: 339–56.

Grey, Chris, and Garsten, Christina (2001) "Trust, control and post-bureaucracy," *Organization Studies*, 22: 229–50.

Hardy, Cynthia, Phillips, Nelson, and Lawrence, Tom (1998) "Distinguishing trust and power in interorganizational relations: forms and facades of trust," in Christel Lane and Reinhard Bachmann (eds) *Trust within and between Organizations: Conceptual Issues and Empirical Applications*, pp. 64–87. Oxford: Oxford University Press.

Heisig, Ulrich, and Littek, Wolfgang (1995) "Wandel von Vertrauensbeziehungen im Arbeitsprozeß," *Soziale Welt*, 46: 282–304.

Hinshelwood, Robert D. (2001) *Thinking about Institutions: Milieux and Madness*. London: Jessica Kingsley.

Hoad, T. F., ed. (1986) *The Concise Oxford Dictionary of English Etymology*. Oxford: Clarendon Press.

Jaques, Elliott (1996) *Requisite Organization: A Total System for Effective Managerial Organization and Managerial Leadership for the Twenty-first Century*. Arlington, VA: Cason Hall.

Knights, David, Noble, Faith, Vurdubakis, Theo, and Willmott, Hugh (2001) "Chasing shadows: control, virtuality and the production of trust," *Organization Studies*, 22: 311–36.

Kramer, Roderick M., and Tyler, Tom R., eds (1996) *Trust in Organizations: Frontiers of Theory and Research*. Thousand Oaks, CA: Sage.

Kramer, Roderick M., Brewer, Marilynn B., and Hanna, Benjamin A. (1996) "Collective trust and collective action: the decision to trust as a social decision," in Roderick M. Kramer and Tom R. Tyler (eds) *Trust in Organizations: Frontiers of Theory and Research*, pp. 357–89. Thousand Oaks, CA: Sage.

Kouzes, James M., and Posner, Barry Z. (1995) *The Leadership Challenge*. San Francisco: Jossey-Bass.

Landau, Robert J., Kreuger, John, and Krueger, John E. (1998) *Corporate Trust Administration and Management*. New York: Columbia University Press.

Lane, Christel (1998) "Introduction. Theories and Issues in the Study of Trust," in Christel Lane and Reinhard Bachmann (eds) *Trust within and between Organizations: Conceptual Issues and Empirical Applications*, pp. 1–30. Oxford: Oxford University Press.

Lane, Christel, and Bachmann, Reinhard, eds (1998) *Trust within and between Organizations: Conceptual Issues and Empirical Applications*. Oxford: Oxford University Press.

Lawrence, W. Gordon (1995) "The seductiveness of totalitarian states of mind," *Journal of Health Care*, Chaplancy 7: 11–22.

——(1997) "Centering of the Sphinx for the Psychoanalytic Study of Organizations," paper presented at the 1997 symposium of the International Society for the Psychoanalytic Study of Organizations, Philadelphia. http://www.sba.oakland.edu/ispso/html/ 1997Lawr.htm

——(1998) "Social dreaming as a tool of consultancy and action research," in W. G. Lawrence (ed.) *Social Dreaming at Work*, pp. 123–40. London: Karnac.

——(2000a) "Thinking refracted," in *Tongued with Fire: Groups in Experience*, pp. 1–30. London: Karnac.

——(2000b) "The politics of salvation and revelation in the practice of consultancy," in *Tongued with Fire: Groups in Experience*, pp. 165–79. London: Karnac.

Lewis, J. D., and Weigert, A. (1985) "Trust as a social reality," *Social Forces*, 43: 967–85.

Long, Susan (2001) "Organizational Destructivity and the Perverse State of Mind," paper presented at the 2001 symposium of the International Society for the Psychoanalytic Study of Organizations, Paris. http://www.sba.oakland.edu/ ISPSO/html/2001Symposium/Long.htm

Luhmann, Niklas (1968) *Vertrauen. Ein Mechanismus der Reduktion sozialer Komplexität*. Stuttgart: Enke.

——(1979) *Trust and Power*. Chichester: Wiley.

——(1988) "Familiarity, confidence, trust: problems and alternatives," in Diego Gambetta (ed.) *Trust: Making and Breaking Cooperative Relations*, pp. 94–107. New York: Blackwell.

Marshall, Edward M. (1999) *Building Trust at the Speed of Change: The Power of the Relationship-based Corporation*. New York: AMACOM.

Miettinen, Asko (2000) "Virtuality and swift trust as a management challenge," in Hans-Jobst Pleitner and Walter Weber (eds) *Die KMU im 21. Jahrhundert. Impulse, Ansichten, Konzepte*, pp. 81–9. Beiträge zu den "Rencontres de Saint-Gall." St Gallen: KMU/HSG.

Mishra, Aneil K. (1996) "Organizational responses to crisis: the centrality of trust," in Roderick M. Kramer and Tom R. Tyler (eds) *Trust in Organizations: Frontiers of Theory and Research*, pp. 261–87. Thousand Oaks, CA: Sage.

Newstrom, John, and Scannell, Edward (1998) *The Big Book of Team-building Games: Trust-building Activities, Team Spirit Exercises, and other Fun Things to Do*. New York: McGraw-Hill.

Nieder, Peter (1997) *Erfolg durch Vertrauen. Abschied vom Management des Mißtrauens*. Wiesbaden: Gabler.

Rousseau, D. M., and Parks, J. M. (1993) "The contracts of individuals and organizations," in B. M. Staw and L. L. Cummings (eds) *Research in Organizational Behavior*, pp. 1–43. Greenwich, CT: JAI Press,

Rousseau, Denise M., Sitkin, Sim B., Burt, Ronald S., and Camerer, Colin (1998) "Not so different after all: a cross-discipline view of trust," *Academy of Management Review*, 23: 93–404.

Ryan, Kathleen, and Oestreich, David K. (1998) *Driving Fear out of the Workplace: Creating the High-trust, High-performance Organization*. San Francisco: Jossey-Bass.

Rycroft, Charles (1995) *A Critical Dictionary of Psychoanalysis*. London: Penguin.

Sculley, J. (1987) *Odyssey*. New York: Harper & Row.

Shurtleff, Mary (1998) *Building Trust: A Manager's Guide for Business Success*. Menlo Park, CA: Crisp Publications.

Sievers, Burkard (1974) *Geheimnis und Geheimhaltung in sozialen Systemen*. Opladen: Westdeutscher Verlag.

——(1986) "Beyond the surrogate of motivation," *Organization Studies*, 7: 335–51.

——(1994) *Work, Death and Life Itself. Essays on Management and Organization*. Berlin: de Gruyter.

——(1999a) "Psychotic organization as a metaphoric frame for the socio-analysis of organizational and interorganizational dynamics," *Administration and Society*, 31 (5): 588–615.

——(1999b) "Accounting for the caprices of madness: narrative fiction as a means of organizational transcendence," in Richard A. Goodman (ed.) *Modern Organizations and Emerging Conundrums: Exploring the Postindustrial Subculture of the Third Millennium*, pp. 126–42. Lanham, MD: Lexington Books.

——(2000) "Competition as war: towards a socio-analysis of war in and among corporations," *Socio-analysis*, 2: 1–27.

——(2001) "Your Money or Your Life? Psychotic Implications of the Pension Fund System: Towards a Socio-analysis of the Financial Services Revolution," paper presented at the 2001 Symposium of the International Society for the Psychoanalytic Study of Organizations, Paris. http://www.sba.oakland.edu/ispso/html/2001Symposium/SymposiumProgra.htm

Simmel, Georg (1908) "Das Geheimnis und die geheime Gesellschaft," in *Soziologie. Untersuchungen über die Formen der Vergesellschaftung*, pp. 337–402. Leipzig: Duncker & Humblot.

——(1950) *The Sociology of Georg Simmel*, ed. K. H. Wolff. New York: Free Press.

Sitkin, Sim B., Rousseau, Denise M., Burt, Ronald S., and Camerer, Colin, eds (1998) *Academy of Management Review* special topic forum "Trust in and between Organizations," 23 (3).

Stein, Howard F. (1995) "Domestic wars and the militarization of american biomedicine," *Journal of Psychohistory*, 22: 406–15.

——(1997) "Euphemism in the language of managed care," *Journal of the Oklahoma State Medical Association*, 90: 243–7.

——(1999) "The Case of the Missing Author: From Parapraxis to Poetry and Insight in Organizational Studies," presentation at the 1999 symposium of the International Society of the Psychoanalytic Study of Organizations, Toronto. http://www.sba.oakland.edu/ispso/html/1999Symposium/schedule.htm

Steinle, Claus, Ahlers, Friedel, and Britta, Gradtke (2000) "Vertrauensorientiertes Management," *Zeitschrift Führung und Organization*, 4: 208–17.

Student, Dietmar (2000) "Es wogt hin, und es wogt her. Corporate restructuring," *Manager Magazin*, 8: 122–9.

Sydow, Jörg (1998) "Understanding the constitution of interorganizational trust," in Christel Lane and Reinhard Bachmann (eds) *Trust within and between Organizations: Conceptual Issues and Empirical Applications*, pp. 31–63. Oxford: Oxford University Press.

Tyler, Tom R., and Kramer, Roderick M. (1996) "Whither trust?" in Roderick M. Kramer and Tom R. Tyler (eds) *Trust in Organizations: Frontiers of Theory and Research*, pp. 1–15. Thousand Oaks, CA: Sage.

Zucker, L. G. (1986) "Production of trust: institutional sources of economic structure, 1840–1920," in B. M. Staw and L. L. Cummings (eds) *Research in Organizational Behavior*, pp. 53–111. Greenwich, CT: JAI Press.

13

Question Time: Notes on *Altercation*

Stephen Linstead

My love she speaks like silence,
Without ideals or violence,
She doesn't have to say she's faithful,
Yet she's true like ice, like fire.
People carry roses,
Make promises by the hours,
My love she laughs like the flowers,
Valentines can't buy her.

In the dime stores and bus stations,
People talk of situations,
Read books, repeat quotations,
Draw conclusions on the wall.
Some speak of the future,
My love she speaks softly,
She knows there's no success like failure
And that failure's no success at all.

The cloak and dagger dangles,
Madams light the candles.
In ceremonies of the horsemen,
Even the pawn must hold a grudge.
Statues made of matchsticks
Crumble into one another,
My love winks, she does not bother,
She knows too much to argue or to judge.

The bridge at midnight trembles,
The country doctor rambles,
Bankers' nieces seek perfection,
Expecting all the gifts that wise men bring.
The wind howls like a hammer,
The night blows cold and rainy,
My love she's like some raven
At my window with a broken wing.

(Bob Dylan, "Love minus Zero – No Limit," *Bringing it all back Home*, 1965)

Introduction: On Knowing too Much and Saying too Little

Nothing is more unfitting for an intellectual resolved on practising what was earlier called philosophy, than to wish, in discussion, and one might almost say in argumentation, to be right. The very wish to be right, down to its subtlest form of logical reflection, is an expression of that spirit of self-preservation which philosophy is precisely concerned to break down (Adorno, 1978: 70).

"She knows too much to argue or to judge." In a culture which identifies silence with ignorance, in which saying nothing means having nothing to say, Dylan's lover is adopting a strategy which makes wisdom vulnerable to the charge of idiocy or allows it to be incorporated as unconditional assent. If language is about power and knowledge, then so is silence. Silence itself may be innocently neutral, but we rarely allow it to remain so once discovered, and it cannot be so when knowingly deployed, when we *become* silent or we are *silenced*. Silence can be threatening when used by the powerful:

When I delivered the lecture on *différance*, not far from here, in Oxford, in 1967 . . . On that occasion the *silence* which followed it was obviously eloquent. Eloquently saying: "There is no arguing here and there is no prospect of arguing with this man, or with this discourse." Strawson was there – and very politely kept silent. Ryle was there – didn't say a word. It was very embarrassing for me; a very embarrassing situation. (Derrida, in Bennington, 2001: 52–3)

The silence of the powerful dismisses us; casts us to the margins, even beyond the margins; silences us. They have no questions for us because we have nothing to yield of worth. Even our secrets have no value. Silence and violence are not far apart here. But the silence of the powerless is also problematic:

A question met with silence is like a weapon rebounding from shield or armour. Silence is an extreme form of defence, whose advantages and disadvantages are almost equally balanced. It is true that a man who refuses to speak does not give himself away, but on the other hand he may appear much more dangerous than he is; his silence is taken to mean that he must have something to hide, more than he may in fact have, and this makes it seem all the more important not to let him go. Persistent silence leads to cross-examination and torture. (Canetti, 1973/1984: 333)

So silence is used to intimidate; to resist; to evade the violence of language and to occasion the use of force. It may be serene or terrible. Above all, and most relevant to the purposes of this book, it instantiates alterity in discourse, and therefore is a very important element of debate.

Debates usually end with questions. I'm going to question *debate*. I'm going to speak, with some irony, *against* debate, but I hope without saying as much. I'm going to compromise my stance by speaking *for* silence rather than trying to speak *through* silence, although I hope the silences are as much a part of the message as what I am able to articulate. Indeed, I want at least to imply, as does Dylan in the poem above, a Deleuzean position that recognizes that we must partake a little of that which we critique in order to critique it at all – that we must in a minor sense *become* the object of critique. I'm also going to talk about tyranny – the tyranny that entraps us at the very moment that it seems to offer us emancipation through debate. It happens because language, through the forms it tends to assume on such occasions, and because of its essentially abstract and necessarily inadequate relation to the world of sense and experience, hijacks an exploratory and collaborative project and inevitably turns it into an oppositional one. Even resorting to "conversation" as distinct from debate, as Richard Rorty or Gareth Morgan would have us do, either eventually slips back into genteel disagreement, lurches forward into barbaric opposition, or glides into decadent collusion, which is itself another form of tyranny. The underlying problem, of course, is, as I hinted above, that of alterity, which we either deny or exploit for our own selfish purposes, recognizing the other only as a mirror of our own past or possibilities – a rear-view mirror that stands in front of us but reflects the distance behind, in which the struggle to make sense of who we were shapes who we are becoming as these virtualities collide in the praxis of the present under the gaze of the other.

In this chapter I want particularly to examine the possibility that debate works through the silence which it explicitly dismisses and suppresses – which it silences by not being silent. As Socrates remarks, pictorial and sculptural arts manage to make meaning in silence – "even complete silence wouldn't stop them accomplishing whatever it is their expertise is for" – and the silence of their space is quite normal (Socrates, in Plato 1994a: 9; Derrida, 1981: 137). But writing more seriously denatures speech by its silence as:

it inscribes in the space of silence and in the silence of space the living time of voice . . . writing estranges itself immediately from the truth of the thing itself, from the truth of speech, from the truth that is open to speech. (Derrida, 1981: 137)

How this relates to the idea of debate, which rests on the speech of two or more animate minds together in real time, depends on whether the separation of speech and writing can meaningfully be sustained. If the flaws of writing somehow adhere to speech, then even that writing which explicitly attempts to bridge the two and capture the essence of central debates in a field – such as this book[1] – becomes not a guarantor of or even a modest guide towards truth, not even a story or narrative about truth, but a much more problematic and potentially mischievous phenomenon *which takes us in the opposite direction*. We will return to explore this below. In the process, in a world where things are not as they seem, we will entertain the idea of language as a poor solution to its own problems; consider the media temperature of debate; reflect on silence; whisper of secrecy, and puzzle over the significance of questions. For my part in this dialogue I shall try to avoid building an argument as such, but I will of course fail to a significant degree. Even if I were to succeed, in my own terms, it would not guarantee that a reader more perceptive than I might not determine the outlines and shadows of an argument where I failed. As Derrida (1988, 1989: 2, 1987a) argues, it is difficult to *avoid* speaking, even if you know that you cannot say what you need or want to say, because the important elements of understanding are the elusive ones that slip right past language (Linstead, 1999). I hope, then, that I will proceed with caution, despite my unreliability as a guide, though I can't guarantee it, and may even find merit in occasionally throwing it to the winds (Linstead and Westwood, 2001), as language is a dangerously slippery ally, both epistemologically and moral-ethically (Linstead, 1993: 104, 1994: 3–4). Still, as Eco (1986: xii) notes, sometimes you just have to say *something* even though it isn't unassailable. So here goes.

Knowing too Little and Saying too Much: Language as a poor Solution to its own Problems

Language, we may as well observe at the outset, not being isomorphic with the reality it represents, is false to its object; yet it is also false to itself and never completely conceals its tracks in creating the appearance of isomorphism – it can always be deconstructed by turning it against itself, and thus the betrayal is doubled. And yet, even given this double betrayal, language sets up another one by triggering meanings that its speakers never intended, giving them away as pure productivity. So it proves false again to its speakers, and in carrying unintended meanings must therefore betray also its hearers and interpreters who think that they know and understand through its mediations. So language quivers with a double duality. At the epistemological level there is the problem of its adequacy first in grasping the phenomenological truths of experience (representation), and then in rendering them intelligible to other perspectives and other experiences (re-presentation) – a problem of construction and reproduction. Such is the problem of poetic evocation, where a poet might capture a moment in a way which seems perfect for the writer who experienced it, but remains impenetrable to others – and all language works through some poetic elements. The second duality is the problem of how well the speaker is integrated with, and hence representative of, and worthy therefore of trust by, the listening community. Is the speaker a member or a stranger, a foreigner? The foreigner problem is an important one because even though speakers speak only for themselves, they nevertheless represent another community in their speech to the one that listens (Silverman, 1975). The speaking subject is not, we know, the phenomenological subject, the knowing and experiencing subject of which it speaks. How then can we give credit to its knowledge or consider it a technically reliable witness, let alone trust it, given the distancing operations through which language forces it? For the moment we are making the assumption that debate occurs between members of a common language community as a means of exchanging and exploring differences, and perhaps even resolving them. Even so, it rests on a language which trembles with instability.

But, this situation notwithstanding, what's so wrong with the idea of academic debate? Surely it's part of the job and comes with the territory? The *Shorter Oxford Dictionary* offers us as its first definition of the term "*strife*, dissension, *quarrelling*; a quarrel" before moving on to "contention in argument; dispute, *controversy*; discussion." It also notes that as a verb it means "to *fight*, strive, *quarrel, wrangle*" and "to *contest*, dispute; to contend for; to carry on a *fight*; to dispute about, argue, discuss; to engage in discussion especially in a public assembly." A violent business it seems, even more emphatically so when we notice the provenance of the word in the Old French *debatre*, and the Modern French *débattre*, meaning to fight, but literally constructed from *de*, "down," and *battre*, "to beat." Even the primitive Old French acceptation of the verb *argue* carried the sense of attacking, harassing, and generally giving someone a hard time (Bennington, 2001: 35). Even *discussion* shares a root with percussion and concussion – having the sense of breaking up, fragmenting (Bohm, 1996: 6). The tools of argument are used in debate to attack and harass someone with the object of doing them grievous semantic harm. One enters a debate with the intention of *beating down* one's opponent, no matter how silky one's rhetorical skills, and at the risk of coming away with significant collateral damage to one's ego, if nothing else.

But if it does get a little rough at times, isn't this all in the interests of *truth*, of establishing the better argument, of moving the dialectic along to a resolution? Isn't it the case that there's nothing personal in the argument? Emotions don't drive the fight, if there is one, just a rational seeking after truth regardless of whether it turns out to be on your side or not. Unfortunately, this can't be taken for granted either. Even Socrates himself, the original master of debate, felt it necessary to check it out and obtain agreement from his interlocutors before pursuing his argument with the self-satisfied but hapless Gorgias:

People find it difficult to agree on exactly what it is they're trying to talk about, and this makes it hard for them to learn from one another and so bring their conversations to a mutually satisfying conclusion. What happens instead, when two people are arguing about something, is that one person tells the other that he's wrong or has expressed himself obscurely, and then they get angry and each thinks that his own point of view is being maliciously misinterpreted by the other person, and *they start trying to win the argument* rather than look into the issue they set out to discuss. (*Gorgias* 457d, in Plato, 1994a: 21)

Socrates continues, having obtained the necessary agreement, to pursue his line of

"inquiry" into the nature of rhetoric. The irony is manifold here – Socrates deflates and defeats his opponents with his skillful use of the very tool whose nature they are, on the surface of it, exploring and in which Gorgias claims to be the *expert*. Having rendered the flabbergasted Gorgias more or less speechless, Socrates turns his attentions to his disciples, the verbose Polus and the aggressive and sullen Callicles, and in fact deliberately provokes them at a personal level to produce the very reaction which he condemns in the passage above. Polus is so bamboozled by Socrates that he ends up letting Socrates tell him the questions that Polus himself should be asking of Socrates – he who was so full of words that previously no one could get one in edgeways ends up having them put in his mouth by Socrates. This sort of outcome is not to be considered unusual, however, for it is Socrates' practice to "reduce others to perplexity" (*Meno* 80a, in Plato, 1981). Agathon also accuses Socrates of trying to bewitch him, of casting a spell over him (*Symposium* 194a, in Plato, 1994b). Indeed, Derrida in the middle of his discussion of the nature of writing, triggered by Plato's depiction of it as a *pharmakon* (a powerful drug that may be both remedy and cure) notes that Socrates himself is often presented as a *pharmakeus*, a master of the *pharmakon*, a master writer who does not write, a sophist powerful enough to defeat sophistry. A living paradox. Derrida argues that the portrait of Eros given in this particular dialogue is in fact one of Socrates:

neither rich, nor beautiful, nor delicate, spends his life philosophizing; he is a fearsome sorcerer, magician and sophist. A being that no "logic" can confine within a noncontradictory definition, an individual of the demonic species, neither god nor man, neither immortal nor mortal, neither living nor dead, he forms "the medium of the prophetic arts, of the priestly rites of sacrifice, initiation and incantation, of divination and of sorcery." (Derrida, 1981: 117)

Poor Gorgias and his followers were therefore outmatched from the start, which is exactly Derrida's point – or at least one of them. Speech, which is privileged explicitly throughout Plato's work, is so done through a condemnation of writing, most extensively in the *Phaedrus* (Plato, 1973) where the concept of the *pharmakon*, the mixed blessing/curse, is central. But the concept is not original – Gorgias himself used it in one of his own writings, the *Encomium of Helen*, to argue contrastingly that it is speech, not writing, that is a *pharmakon:*

Speech is a powerful lord . . . The effect of speech upon the condition of the soul is comparable to the power of drugs over the nature of bodies. For just as different drugs dispel different secretions from the body, and some bring an end to disease and others to life, so also in the case of speeches, some distress, others delight, some cause fear, others make the hearers bold, and some drug and bewitch the soul with a kind of evil persuasion. (Gorgias, in Derrida, 1981: 116; see also Kennedy, 1991: 286–7)

Socrates himself in *Phaedrus* on more than one occasion admits to having a kind of addiction to the spoken word, both his inspiration and his weakness, before beginning his condemnation of writing. Yet Plato's representation of Socrates' argument about the superiority of speech is compromised because it is presented in that very writing which he condemns and is subject to the same strictures (Derrida, 1987b). Two of the most important points of the critique are, firstly, that there is a loss of immediacy, of presence of thought (and hence truth), in writing, in that it acts as a mnemonic prosthesis and creates dependence:

Those who acquire it will cease to exercise their memory and become forgetful; they will rely on writing to bring things to their remembrance by external signs instead of on their own internal resources. What you have discovered is a receipt for recollection, not for memory. And as for wisdom, your pupils will have the reputation for it without the reality: they will receive a quantity of information without proper instruction, and in consequence be thought very knowledgeable when they are for the most part quite ignorant. And because they are filled with the conceit of wisdom instead of real wisdom they will be a burden to society. (*Phaedrus* 275, in Plato, 1973: 96–7)

Second, and consequent upon the first, writing cannot be interrogated to provide such instruction – it cannot specify the conditions of its own reception, just as Wittgenstein (1972) would later argue that a rule cannot prescribe the conditions of its own interpretation. When regarding written words:

you might suppose that they understand what they are saying, but if you ask them what they mean by

anything they simply return the same answer over and over again. Besides, once a thing is committed to writing it circulates equally among those who understand the subject and those who have no business with it; a writing cannot distinguish between suitable and unsuitable readers. And if it is ill-treated or unfairly abused it always needs its parent to come to its rescue; it is quite incapable of defending or helping itself. (*Phaedrus* 275, in Plato, 1973: 97)

So for both these reasons "writing" needs the supplement of speech to confirm and fix its meaning, to legislate for it, to protect it against misinterpretation. For Socrates, this authoritative or insightful speech is a sort of discourse "that is written on the soul of the hearer together with understanding; that knows how to defend itself, and can distinguish between those it should address and those in whose presence it should be silent." This is "the living and animate speech of a man with knowledge, of which written speech might fairly be called a kind of shadow" (*Phaedrus* 276, Plato, 1973: 98). Speech then is both prior to and a necessary supplement to writing.

But, as Derrida (1981: 149) observes, here writing as false brother or simulacrum has to envisage the legitimate brother not as absolutely different but as *another kind of writing* – speech as "an *inscription* of truth in the soul." So the opposition between writing and speech becomes a differentiation between two kinds of writing – good and bad. The good is natural, living, knowledgeable, intelligible, internal, expressed in speaking, whilst the bad is moribund, imitative, ignorant, external, mute artifice for the senses (ibid.). The first, planted like a seed carefully inside the appropriate hearer, is fertile; the second is sterile because it is scattered wastefully to all and sundry, at the risk, as Derrida puts it, of *dissemination*, or dis-semination. To condense a long and complex argument, good writing is known then through the practices of meaning which it adopts in order to render it with the necessary qualities to avoid unreserved and wasteful spending, infertile dissemination. This generalized writing is a combination of ordering, spacing, bounding, dividing, sequencing, marginalizing, deleting, and other practices that comprise, not any specific inscription, but a grammar by which such inscriptions can be made and understood.

Good writing, however, as an inscription passed on as a trace, remains only an inscription and not truth itself. Truth is not, as we might have thought, present in speech after all, but is deferred by the very speech which invokes it as a possibility. The icon, phantasm, or simulacrum's pseudotruth evokes the possibility of its being true whilst at the same time being not-true; it is immediately doubled in *différance* and raises the possibility of its truth in the possibility of its *repetition*. There would be no truth without repetition, only a singular *occurrence*; but both truth and untruth are species of repetition, and the structure of repetition is this generalized writing. On the one hand, repetition is the condition and confirmation of truth, truth being "that which can be repeated, being the same, the clear, the stable the identifiable in its equality with itself"; a repetition of life, and, by the same token, a tautology – returned to itself in the same condition as it was dispatched. On the other hand, it is also the movement, the slippage of nontruth: "the presence of what is gets lost, disperses itself, multiplies itself through mimemes, icons, phantasms, simulacra . . . through phenomena" (Derrida, 1981: 168). Yet only through this variability does it become perceptible to the senses, which detect variability, bad memory, nonideality: returned with difference, altered through *play*, through the play of the supplement.

Derrida's argument then is that, because of the workings of inscription and play, at the deepest level speech and writing are actually both varieties of writing – the underlying generalized processes of ordering that make sense of life. Because of the need for and workings of the supplement, we must read and write in a "single, but doubled gesture" (Derrida, 1981: 64). We must understand the nature of the game, the *language* game, for Lyotard and Wittgenstein, with a perhaps narrower compass, that constitutes a form of life which makes language itself intelligible. Although such autopoesis is a game, it still requires some commitment of the self – simply following rules of "methodological prudence," "norms of objectivity," and "safeguards of knowledge," as Derrida puts it, would not enable the player to read at all; whilst players who felt they could

add anything at all to the meaning game, whatever they felt like, would in fact add nothing and the game would collapse in confusion. Reading/writing requires a balance of foolishness and sterility in both the serious and the nonserious. As Derrida concludes, "The reading or writing supplement must be rigorously prescribed, but by the necessities of a *game*, by the logic of *play*, signs to which the systems of all textual powers must be accorded and attuned" (1981: 64).

To return to Socrates and his Attic interlocutors, then, Socrates is the master of the game, the master of the *pharmakon*, luring in and setting traps for those players who are, perhaps, deserving of such treatment. In the archaic sense of debate we have already encountered, they are beaten down. Whilst Socrates declares himself to be open to correction and critique, he nevertheless retains control of the board, because he establishes the discursive rules by which the game is to be played, and his opponents are left demoralized. But, because of the play of supplementarity, the fact that the supplement needed to fully complete meaning is never fully present because it is an *irreducible excess*, as Derrida and Bataille both note, means that the game is never *finally* decided. Because language, whether written or spoken, rests upon this play, it cannot resolve its own problems, and language forms such as debate cannot therefore resolve the very matters before them in debate. The appearance of a resolution is achieved through such devices as mutual rule following, but the question of *how* a rule is to be followed, as Socrates' own rule-following behavior shows, remains problematic.

Of Heat and Silence

Let us play with our own rules for a moment and step aside from the language of debate to consider the nature of debate as a medium within its context. One of the problems of trying to speak at the present time, to whatever audience, is that there is so little space left to do it. The world is overflowing with information, much of it useless. As Baudrillard (1996: 25) puts it, the only perfect crime is the crime against reality accomplished through the hyperacceleration of signification because in it the body disappears – all of our acts and events are transformed into pure information and the world is exterminated and replaced by its double. How many football supporters have never seen a live football game? How many chatliners have difficulty carrying on a real-time conversation?

At least the idea of the *spectacle*, the object of Debord and the Situationists (Debord, 1994), left room for critique and demystification, but for Baudrillard the virtual nature of counterfeit reality means that we are neither alienated nor dispossessed because we are in most respects in possession of *all* the information, and not just that which we need. We are not spectators at the spectacle, able to critique its unreality, but actors in the performance, compelled to enact its hyperreality. Whenever we open our mouth, it is filled with words that are not our own and yet which we own (Derrida, 1998: 8–11). Whenever we open our eyes, we no longer have to look in order to see, for that has all been done for us. Even our sense of wonder has been taken care of by high-technology kitsch. The medium itself has passed into life, as Baudrillard (1996: 28) argues, and we are becoming virtual:

All this digital, numeric, electronic equipment is merely incidental to the deep-seated virtualization of human beings. And if this so grips the collective imagination, that is because we are already – not in some other world, but in this life itself – in a state of socio-, photo- and videosynthesis. And if we are able today to produce a clone of a particular famous actor which will be made to act in his place, this is because, long ago, without knowing it, he became his own replica or his own clone, before he actually was cloned.

So we no longer pity the unwitting stars of the *Truman Show* or *EDTV*, because they at least had self-authenticity through unself-consciousness. All we can do is long for a few moments on Jerry Springer, or Oprah Winfrey, or *Big Brother*, in which we can simulate taking command of the space which engulfs us, claim our privacy by making it a public event. We have our fifteen minutes of fame to claim, and we are going to do it, because that is the object of an existence which has become performance, to dramatize selves which when

cloned become roles that we no longer even try to shed, because we are already High Definition. Marshall McLuhan had a sense of what was happening which influenced Baudrillard profoundly (Genosko, 1999):

The crux of hot and cool is that media which are loud, bright, clear, fixed ("hot" or "high definition") evoke less involvement from perceivers than media whose presentations are soft, shadowy, blurred and interchangeable ("cool" or low definition). The psychological logic of this distinction is that we are obliged and seduced to work harder – get more involved – to fill in the gaps with the lower profile, less complete media. (Levinson, 2001: 9)

Thus with "cool" media we are more involved, more active in reading, more likely to have a personal experience or interpretation of what is conveyed which differs from that of other readers, hearers, or viewers. But this does not necessarily mean that cool is to be automatically valued over hot.

Cool connotes a profound, effortless synchronicity with the universe as it actually is and will likely be, speaks softly of deep pools, of being in tune with the future. Hot is fast cars indeed, fast food, life in the fast lane, encounters quick, overwhelming, intense – hot buns, hot abs, hot babes and hunks, embrassez-moi, run me over and leave me senseless. (Levinson, 2001: 110)

They are just different modes of experience. One to which we abandon ourselves, which takes us over, possesses and in turn abandons us; the other which is given to us to do as we will with it, to improvise upon, add to, and make our own. But a medium is not solely a technological one – or, if it is, only in the sense that it is a representational technology. Thus writing as such a representational technology may be a medium, and different forms of writing themselves may be hotter or cooler according to how conventional they are and how well understood the roles of the interactants are. Poetry is cooler than prose, for example, but a novel is cooler than a cookery book. Hot and cool, in fact, are more meaningful when hott*er* and cool*er*. Speech, because the presence of the speaker gives us more information through tone of voice and body language to fix meaning, is hotter than the written word. Yet perhaps, because the speaker is present for us to interrogate, in a way which is not available in text, speech as dialogue may be cooler than the speech of a public lecture without questions. In principle this *could* be so, but in practice, because power inequalities are always present in talk in interaction, the ideal communicative situation does not exist and one party or the other has greater freedom to impose their rules upon, or write them into, the exchange. This makes the dialogue cooler for one and hotter for the other. Ironically, when we talk about the heat of debate, we are usually referring to those emotional occasions when rationality is overcome and rule following forgotten. However, in McLuhan's terms, debate would be a hot form of interaction – structured, positioned, regulated, systematic, purposeful, and designed to produce a specific outcome through well known means and modes of contestation.

Debate is a language game, and its proliferating forms may occur in everyday interaction as well as in formal settings. In such cases, it is almost impossible not to get drawn into them, and become positioned and placed and defined even as one attempts to escape from their clutches. It is such positioning which McLuhan would regard as hot. For Adorno (1991), it is important not to be seduced by the easy attractions of forms of argumentation – the seductions of the binary opposition, for example. Indeed, Adorno, in discussing art, argued that authentic "art" disrupts surface aesthetics and prevents the viewer from relaxing or being absorbed in the immediacy of the work, *refusing* to communicate. To paraphrase Vattimo, "In a world where consensus is produced by manipulation, authentic [experience] speaks only by lapsing into silence, and . . . arises only as the negation of all its traditional and canonical characteristics" (1988: 56).

Adorno's (1991) negative aesthetics, the self-negation of the work (Adorno's exemplar is Beckett) applied to social science makes questions like "What is the point of this work?" or "What does this *say?*" unanswerable, even perhaps unaskable. It refuses to deliver a simplified message, denies the need to express its own *poetic* or *apologia* – silence is not nothing to say but everything to say, everything remaining to be said, and everything that must remain unsaid. It refuses to be fixed. Indeed,

much meaning needs to be *unsaid* in order to become more *meaningful*. Baudrillard develops this idea from mass consumption, which was Adorno's main concern, to mass politics with his concept of the "silent majorities" whose only resistance is silence, and parallels Adorno's (1991) "death of art" with the "death of the social" (Baudrillard, 1983). Similarly, Lyotard (1988) talks of the "differend" – the incommensurable silences between accounts of the world and the world itself, and between those accounts among themselves – the quiet debate that is never resolved. Derrida goes so far as to argue that even the idea of a community of philosophers – a philosophical community – existing and communicating in the contemporary world can at best indicate "people who do indeed share this situation of absolute misunderstanding, who know that . . . They discourse in ways that cannot be translated into one another" (Derrida and Ferraris, 2001: 86).

Secrets and Questions

This untranslatability may well have deeper roots than language. In discussing the idea of radical evil – that human beings are inherently evil – Kant notes that such a thesis cannot be proved, although "from what one knows of the human being through experience he cannot judge otherwise of him, or, that one can presuppose evil to be subjectively necessary in every human being, even the best" (1996: 6–32). This inner urge toward mendacity, which Žižek (1993) considers to be the equivalent of the death drive, as it can never be proved, can never be revealed – we can never be fully exposed, even to ourselves. Thus all our expression and intercourse partakes of a "secret falsity" – not only can we not believe everything we read, we cannot believe all of anything we read, even our own conscience. Trust? As Derrida (1997a) reminds us, Kant was very fond of Aristotle's admonition "O my friends, there is no [such thing as a] friend."

If this propensity [to "secret falsity"] is presupposed in all its radicality, then falsity among friends constitutes nothing more than the later "development" of a prior disposition: the original "secret falsity" lies in the relation of the self to itself. Kant generally calls such falsity "the inner lie" . . . If it makes sense to speak of an "inner lie," then action not only has its source in secrecy but can also take place in a secret secrecy, a secrecy one hides from oneself. Concealing from itself the source of its freedom, the "I" hides from itself the responsibility for the actions it undertakes, and this hiding is itself an action for which it is responsible and from which it hides itself. . . . And so on ad infinitum . . . under this condition reason may be "naked" but can reveal nothing – neither itself nor anything else. (Fenves, 2001: 111)

For Canetti (1973/1984: 333), a secret is "something denser than the matter surrounding it, not continuous with it and kept in almost impenetrable darkness," and whatever its contents the secret is always dangerous, even if only because it has been kept secret. A secret once established as a secret can never be innocent, even after its revelation, and neither can we for having harbored it. So if we pause for a sharp intake of breath, we can see that the consequences of such thinking are that self-revelations, confessions, or any form of revelatory discourse such as the position statements in this book, are not innocent or neutral or disinterested activities and cannot operate without *secrecy*, without some sort of blind spot. Debate may at times appear to hinge on revealing the *aporia* of the other, the hidden weaknesses in their argumentation, but even this operation is another deflection of scrutiny, as it obscures the connection between self and other, especially as one of *desire*. As Baudrillard observes:

Everyone has an imperious need to put the other at their mercy, along with a heady urge to make the other last as long as possible so as to savour him . . . For desire for the other is always also the desire to put an end to the other. (Baudrillard, 1993: 159–60)

The question of the resolution of debates is always a question of power, and Plato's version of the Socratic dialectic offers several examples of Socrates putting the other at his mercy, relishing his toying with them, apparently in the interests of truth. One simple way in which Socrates exercises and enjoys his power in achieving resolution in the dialogues is through the question – indeed, this particular device gives him a stranglehold on most arguments. As Canetti notes:

In Plato's *Dialogues* Socrates appears as the supreme master of the question . . . He despised all the normal forms of power and sedulously avoided everything resembling them . . . but . . . The *Dialogues* are full of questions and most of them come from Socrates, including all the more important ones. He is shown pinning his hearers down and compelling them to make choices of every possible kind. He dominated them exclusively through questions. (Canetti, 1973/1984: 335)

Pirsig (1974: 362) discovers this in *Gorgias* but also in himself – and goes on to find that the whole Western philosophical tradition is implicated in this contradiction or duplicity. He notes first that Socrates pretends false innocence in asking Gorgias what he does – Socrates knows this very well, but by his questions he manages to turn Gorgias' answers, which are somewhat naive in pretending to be simple descriptions of what Sophists do, into something else. "Rhetoric," he argues, "has become an object, and as an object has parts. And the parts have relationships and the relationships are immutable. . . . Socrates' analytic knife hacks Gorgias' art into pieces." The pieces are to become the basis of Aristotle's rhetoric, and the modern understanding of rhetoric as a minor technical skill, but for the Sophists rhetoric was far more. It was a means of discovering the Good.

Socrates opposed the Sophists with a passion, not for their relativism, but for their humanism, which placed man at the center of things and suggested that human experience was their "measure" – our way of knowing good from evil, for example. However, Socrates believed in the Truth, an unchangeable idea that was independent of human perspectives or interests, external to us and waiting to be discovered by us through the operation of the dialectic, his question-and-answer technique. He eventually died for his commitment to this idea and his refusal to play the games of Athenian politics, so we should remember that there was potentially much at stake in these dialogues. Serious play to the point of death.

Yet despite his protestations to the contrary, as Pirsig (1974: 363) notes, Socrates is not trying to understand rhetoric through dialectic, but to destroy it. His questions are not real questions, but traps which he sets for his interlocutors to step into. Yet the irony is that, rather than rhetoric being a technical form which enhances the working of dialectic, Socrates in fact reveals dialectic itself to be entirely dependent on rhetoric for its success – a creation of rhetoric. Pirsig discovers the disturbing power of dialectic through silence, as his Professor attempts to trap him into a dialectical exchange which Phaedrus cannot win:

Phaedrus is silent and tries to work out an answer. Everyone is waiting. His thoughts move up to lightning speed, winnowing through the dialectic, playing one argumentative chess opening after another, seeing that each one loses, and moving to the next one, faster and faster – but all the class witnesses is silence . . . His mind races on and on, through the permutations of the dialectic, on and on, hitting things, finding new branches and sub-branches, exploding with anger at each new discovery of the viciousness and meanness and lowness of this "art" called dialectic . . . seeing now at last a kind of evil thing, an evil deeply entrenched in himself, which pretends to try to understand love and beauty and truth and wisdom but whose real purpose is never to understand them, whose real purpose is always to usurp them and enthrone itself. Dialectic – the usurper. (Pirsig 1974: 364)

Socrates' questions create difference. In questioning, the questioner creates otherness as the addressee finds that here is someone who does not understand them, who wishes to make them accountable, and indeed renders them *foreign* (Derrida, 1997b; Dufourmantelle and Derrida, 2000). They want to know who you are, where you are coming from, and why. They want you to make choices. But why do we respond, why fall into the traps set? Because, as Derrida again notes, *hospitality* and *hostility* have the same roots linguistically and experientially as a response to otherness (Dufourmantelle and Derrida, 2000; Derrida, 2000). We do not know whether the host's questioning is intended to help us be made more comfortable or to oppress us more effectively. Indeed, we can never be sure of this whenever we provide information, whether we are Aborigines entertaining anthropologists or surfers shopping on the internet. Desire to entertain the other may be desire to understand the other, desire for the other, or desire to incorporate and thus destroy the other. For Socrates the urge was

powerful, although it was not until Aristotle that the full process of destruction/incorporation was worked out. But because it was worked out, and perhaps because Plato's intervention in *writing* in Socrates' project perhaps made his agenda more aggressive, Socrates' dialogues seem haunted by the specter of their own interior otherness, the other which Pirsig clearly sees in himself.

Pirsig may even have captured the source of the urge to dominate the other – the need to assert sovereignty over our self. As Boldt-Irons (2001: 87) argues, coming to terms with Otherness involves not only *differentiation* (which is the province of all the analytical tools of reason) but also *recognition*. Pirsig, as Phaedrus (the name used in the book for his former self before his mental breakdown), like Socrates, seemed to have a different purpose.

I think his pursuit of the ghost of rationality occurred because he wanted to wreak *revenge* on it, because he felt he himself was so shaped by it. He wanted to free himself from his own image. He wanted to destroy it because the ghost was what *he* was and he wanted to be free from the bondage of his own identity. (Pirsig, 1974: 82)

Our own debates are still too closely linked to this idea of destruction, of asserting difference as a prelude to domination rather than recognition as a prelude to understanding. But is the aggressive project itself already a doomed one? Vattimo would think so because matters are simply too complex to be dealt with in simple oppositions, linguistic ping-pong – even in its most subtle forms. As he argues, in illustration, the oft-predicted death of art in the twentieth century never happened, because art is itself a complex system of relations – it is not so easy either to imitate, or to exterminate. Our collective inquiry, then, need not seek its revenge on rationality, the *death* of organizational science, but should seduce its *decline* through greater silence rather than "better" argument (Vattimo, 1988: 58–9). So perhaps our conversation – if there is to be one at all – needs to involve the injection of silence into our work as a refusal to draw conclusions, make definitions, and prove hypotheses, to refuse to stand up for ourselves or our ideas or those of others, remembering, with Dylan's lover, that there's no success like failure and that failure's no success at all. We will need to stop wanting to be *successful*. Additionally, we will need to appreciate those inevitable silences always already there within the work rather than attempt to cover them up – to keep them secret. This would entail a move from the positive affirmative aspect of science (and even when seeking to falsify *hypotheses* science nevertheless affirms its *self*) which is almost a *sine qua non* of debate and debating structures, to an unbounded reflexively critical one, one which opens up new avenues of contradiction, which allows possibilities without making claims on reality. Our scientific community, expressing itself in this way, would be a "crowd of eccentrics rejoicing in each other's idiosyncracies" (Rorty, 1991: 75). Because only in this way do we discover our quietly unfolding selves. "It is precisely in losing the certainty of truth and the unanimous agreement of others that man becomes an individual" (Kundera, 1986: 159).

Note

1 But including also the works of Plato, in particular, who places the issue in clearest focus – more on him later.

References

Adorno, Theodor (1978) *Minima Moralia*. London: Verso.
——(1991) *The Culture Industry*. London: Routledge.
Baudrillard, Jean (1983) *In the Shadow of the Silent Majorities*. New York: Semiotext(e).
——(1993) *The Transparency of Evil*. London: Verso.
——(1996) *The Perfect Crime*. London: Verso.
Bennington, Geoffrey (2001) "For the sake of argument," with a response from Jacques Derrida, in Simon Glendinning (ed.) *Arguing with Derrida*, pp. 32–56. Oxford: Blackwell.
Bohm, David (1996) *On Dialogue*. London: Routledge.
Boldt-Irons, Lesley Anne (2001) "Bataille and Baudrillard: from a general theory of economics to the transparency of evil," *Angelaki*, 6 (2): 79–90.
Canetti, Elias (1973/1984) *Crowds and Power*. London: Peregrine.

Debord, Guy (1994) *The Society of the Spectacle*. New York: Zone Books.
Derrida, Jacques (1981) *Dissemination*. London: Athlone.
——(1987a) "How to avoid speaking," in Sanford Budick and Wolfgang Iser (eds) *Languages of the Unsayable: The Play of Negativity in Literature and Literary Theory*. New York: Columbia University Press.
——(1987b) *The Postcard: from Socrates to Freud and Beyond*. London: University of Chicago Press.
——(1988) *The Ear of the Other*. Lincoln, NE: University of Nebraska Press.
——(1989) *Of Spirit: Heidegger and the Question*. Chicago: University of Chicago Press.
——(1997a) *The Politics of Friendship*, London: Verso.
——(1997b) *On Cosmopolitanism and Forgiveness*. London: Routledge.
——(1998) *Monolingualism of the Other, or, The Prosthesis of Origin*, trans. Patrick Mensah. London: Routledge.
——(2000) "Hostipitality," *Angelaki*, 5 (3): 3–18.
Derrida, Jacques, and Ferraris, Maurizio (2001) *A Taste for the Secret*. Cambridge: Polity Press.
Dufourmantelle, Anne, and Derrida, Jacques (2000) *Of Hospitality*. Stanford, CA: Stanford University Press.
Eco, Umberto (1986) *Faith in Fakes*. London: Secker & Warburg.
Fenves, Peter (2001) "Out of the blue: secrecy, radical evil and the crypt of faith," in Richard Rand (ed.) *Futures of Jacques Derrida*, pp. 99–129. Stanford, CA: Stanford University Press.
Genosko, Gary (1999) *McLuhan and Baudrillard*. London: Routledge.
Kant, Immanuel (1996) "Religion within the boundaries of mere reason," trans. George di Giovanni, in *Religion and Rational Theology*, ed. Allen Wood and George di Giovanni. Cambridge: Cambridge University Press.
Kennedy, George A. (1991) "Gorgias: encomium of Helen," in *Aristotle: On Rhetoric – A Theory of Civic Discourse*, trans. George A. Kennedy, pp 283–8. Oxford: Oxford University Press.
Kundera, Milan (1986) *The Art of the Novel*, trans. Linda Asher. New York: Grove Press.
Levinson, Paul (2001) *Digital McLuhan: A Guide to the Information Millennium*. London: Routledge.

Linstead, Stephen (1993) "From postmodern anthropology to deconstructive ethnography," *Human Relations*, 46 (1): 97–120.

——(1994) "Objectivity, reflexivity and fiction: humanity, inhumanity and the science of the social," *Human Relations*, 47 (11): 1321–46.

——(1999) "Ashes and madness : the play of negativity and the poetics of organization," in S. A. Linstead and H. J. Höpfl (eds) *The Aesthetics of Organisation*, pp. 61–93. London: Sage.

Linstead, Stephen, and Westwood, Robert (2001) "Meaning beyond language: monstrous openings," in R. I. Westwood and S. A. Linstead (eds) *The Language of Organization*, pp. 329–46. London: Sage.

Lyotard, Jean-François (1988) *The Differend: Phrases in Dispute*. Manchester: Manchester University Press.

Pirsig, Robert M. (1974) *Zen and the Art of Motorcycle Maintenance*. London: Corgi.

Plato (1973) *Phaedrus and Letters VII and VIII*, trans. William Hamilton. London: Penguin.

——(1981) *Five Dialogues: Euthyphro, Apology, Crito, Meno and Phaedo*, trans. G. M. A. Grube. New York: Hackett.

——(1994a) *Gorgias*, trans. Robin Waterfield. London: Penguin.

——(1994b) *Symposium*, trans. Robin Waterfield. London: Penguin.

Rorty, Richard (1991) *Essays on Heidegger and Others*, in *Philosophical Papers* II. Cambridge: Cambridge University Press.

Silverman, David (1975) *Reading Castaneda: A Prologue to the Social Sciences*. London: Routledge.

Vattimo, Gianni (1988) *The End of Modernity: Nihilism and Hermeneutics in Postmodern Culture*. Cambridge: Polity Press.

Wittgenstein, Ludwig (1972) *Philosophical Investigations*. Oxford: Blackwell.

Žižek, Slavoj (1993) *Tarrying with the Negative*. Durham, NC: Duke University Press.

Index

Note: page numbers in **bold** type indicate detailed discussion of the topic

Basis of our approach

Practice theory - ethno / A T.   (a comp.? between them)

    cultural system "structured as ~~a cultural~~
    on embodiment of the range of activities, social
    conflicts & moral dilemmas ... r219

    how conceptions of reality rooted in broader social
    & historical proms ...

{ Our interest to get things changed.
{ underpinning cntns of IT, see 220